The Future of Identity in the Information Society

Kai Rannenberg • Denis Royer
André Deuker
Editors

The Future of Identity in the Information Society

Challenges and Opportunities

Springer

Editors
Prof. Dr. Kai Rannenberg
Denis Royer
André Deuker

Goethe University Frankfurt
Institute of Business Informatics
Chair for Mobile Business and Multilateral Security
Grüneburgplatz 1
60629 Frankfurt am Main
Germany
Kai.Rannenberg@m-chair.net
Denis.Royer@m-chair.net
Andre.Deuker@m-chair.net

PUBLISHED: 24th APRIL 2009.

ISBN 978-3-540-88480-4
Springer Dordrecht Heidelberg London New York

Library of Congress Control Number: "PCN applied for"

Cover design: WMXDesign GmbH

Printed on acid-free paper

Springer is part of Springer Science+Business Media (www.springer.com)

Foreword

During the past decade the Information Society has firmly established itself in Europe and elsewhere, and ICT has deeply and irreversibly dyed the economic and social fabric of society. A stage of development has been reached that is characterised by massive amounts of personal data being generated, collected, analysed and processed, exchanged, recombined, and stored sometimes for a life-time or more. The contours of the digital age have rapidly taken shape and with this, the creation and management of individual identity has emerged as one of the central challenges in digital life. Citizens look for value in the activities they do on the Internet. Therefore they want to be able to trust the technology and services provided and the actors behind it. For that trusted electronic identity management is crucial.

On-line services can provide a lot of benefits and convenience to citizens and huge competitive advantages to European industry. Yet for such services to enjoy large-scale growth, people and organisations must have sufficient confidence that their personal dignity and legitimate business interests are properly safeguarded. It goes without saying that Europe needs an innovative and competitive ICT services sector to meet the challenges of the digital economy, to remain competitive and to foster investment, growth and jobs. This can only be successful if it is based on a privacy protecting ID management framework providing authentication mechanisms that protect human dignity, ensure protection against malicious behaviour and deceit, and allow for accountability and liability, and hence the rule of law in digital space. Europe's strong social values must be transferred to future digital life.

Trust in the use of eServices, in digital communications and applications, in eCommerce, eHealth, eGovernment, and ensuring the free movement of knowledge – the so-called "Fifth Freedom" – and open collaboration is evolving with society. There is no single 'silver bullet' solution to information identity risks. To achieve a true European culture of trust and security in digital life, decision-makers in business and government, regulators and technology developers must work together in a multi-stakeholder dialogue to find the right mix of methods, technology and regulation. In this respect, I would like to point to the Commission's policy initiative "i2010 – A European Information Society for growth and employment". i2010 identifies security, in a broad sense including trust and privacy, as one of the four main challenges posed by digital convergence, which is at the heart of the creation of the single European Information Space. Furthermore trust, identity management and privacy protection are strong elements in European supported research, organised within the broader Framework Programme for Research and Development of the European Union.

Our society calls for diversity, openness, interoperability, usability and competition as key drivers for trust and security. Diversity reduces the risk stemming from the dependence on one type of technology and introduces natural safeguards. Open standards and interoperability are key to competition and for empowering users to freely choose products and services that they find useful, and for creating business opportunities for small, medium and large companies alike.

FIDIS has put Europe on the global map as a place for high quality identity management research. It has, together with several other EU supported activities, effectively contributed to creating the conditions for a flourishing digital economy and digital life, which are key aims of the Commission's regulatory and research policy.

I would like to thank the FIDIS project and all contributors to this "FIDIS Summit Book" for the opportunity to draw attention to the European Commission's efforts in this domain, and for putting Europe on the map as a global thought leader in privacy protective digital identity management. The fact that the Summit Event takes place in Cyprus – one of the recent EU Member States – is to be seen as a tribute to the shared European values of democracy, freedom and civil liberties.

Brussels, March 2009

Viviane Reding
Member of the European Commission,
Responsible for Information Society and Media

Acknowledgements

Editing and writing a multidisciplinary book like the one at hand is not something that is possible without 'an army' of helping hands that dedicated their knowledge, expertise, and time to make the work a success. Among the countless people that worked on this FIDIS volume, we would like to give a special thanks to:

- The partners, chapter editors, and researchers in the NoE FIDIS that contributed to this book and the deliverables (cf. Annex A) this book is based on.
- The reviewers of the chapter that dedicated their time to improve and streamline the different chapters.
- The people that helped to create this book:
  - Birgit Leick and later Christian Rauscher at Springer for helping us publish this piece of work.
  - George Scott for transforming much of the Englishish in the draft versions of this book into English.
  - Markus Richter for making this book agreeable to the eye.
  - Frieder Vogelmann for all sorts of trouble-shooting.
  - Our colleagues at the Chair of Mobile Business and Multilateral Security at Goethe University Frankfurt for keeping our backs covered when producing this book.
- The European Commission for funding FIDIS, as well as its Project Officers (Dirk van Rooy, Günter Schumacher, Richard Sonnenschein, Alain Jaume) and their management (Jacques Bus, Gerald Santucci, Andrea Servida), who kept up with whatever developments and challenges such a large and lively network is putting up.
- Last but not least Stefan Figge, without whom the successful FIDIS proposal would have never come into existence.

Frankfurt am Main, February 2009

Kai Rannenberg
Denis Royer
André Deuker

Table of Contents

1 Introduction

Kai Rannenberg, Denis Royer, and André Deuker

The value of identity of course is that so often with it comes purpose.
Richard Grant

The ever increasing digitisation of information has led to an Information Society, in which more and more information is available almost anywhere and anytime. The related digitisation of personal characteristics and personal information is progressively changing our ways of identifying persons and managing our relations with them especially in virtual interactions, e.g., over the Internet. As the Internet has opened new spaces for (virtual and supplementary) lives, supplementary digital identities, so-called virtual identities are being created for reasons of security, profit, convenience or even fun (e.g., for leisure communities). What used to be a 'natural' identity, e.g., the personal appearance of an individual at a counter, is now as virtual as a user account at a web portal, an email address, or a mobile phone number. These virtual and multiple identities and the paradigms behind them are feeding back into the 'physical' world, offering a mix of physical and virtual plural identities and processes to deal with them. Both the new artefacts as well as the new processes challenge the traditional definitions of identity.

At the same time identities are subject to diverse forms of management in business, administration, and among citizens: There is almost no week, which does not see a new initiative aiming at 'better' identification of citizens, customers, consumers, or entities in general. In this context 'better' can have many different meanings, often depending from the point of view of the respective stakeholder: States and their administrations try to identify 'their' citizens, while citizens want to be able to influence the respective identification, e.g., its rationale, its degree, its process and last but not least the information flow around it, starting with the question whether or not identification is needed for a transaction or for participating in a certain element of life in society. The core question and often the source of conflict is who owns how much identity information of whom and who needs to place trust into which identity information to allow access to resources.

While this book cannot answer all questions related to identity it presents some relevant results from the EU funded research project FIDIS (Future of Identity in the Information Society). This chapter is an introduction to the book. It first raises some exemplary issues of identity and its application in a changing world, describing the role and aim of FIDIS in this situation. Following this, a short overview of the respective parts of the book (also as a look in to the engine room of FIDIS) is presented, before the chapter is concluded with the thanks and acknowledgements.

1.1 Identity in a Changing World

For a long time identity has been an issue of thought and analysis, as well as of doubt and crisis. Now also in the Information Society, identity is becoming an issue of discussion and sometimes major conflict. One of the basic questions is, whether entities have one single identity or several (*partial*) identities. As an introduction into the topic this section discusses the question of '*One identity or many*' first in general terms and then in typical examples of the information society.

1.1.1 One Identity or Many? Identity Unification vs. Identity Differentiation

Having one single (continuous) identity has for long been viewed as a sign of integrity of character and of health of personality: In contrast an identity crisis is diagnosed, when an individual loses a sense of personal sameness and historical continuity. Also in the information society, whoever feels the need to better identify and address related entities is on the verge of identity unification by identity management.

Nowadays, employees in an organisation very often have a historically grown plethora of identifiers and access rights. Consequently it is difficult to know and manage, who has the authorisation to do what. So when someone leaves an organisation it is usually difficult to revoke authorisations, accounts and access rights to avoid later misuse of corporate systems and corporate information. Establishing an efficient framework for corporate access management with reliable accountability is not a trivial task. A popular aim here is 'single sign-on', basically the unification of all accounts and access rights on one system per enterprise, to which users authenticate themselves and which then provides access to the resources needed, such as a customer database or a printer.

A similar unification approach is popular in dealing with customers, e.g., when a telecommunication company unifies customers' accounts to provide a single bill for different but related services. Currently very often a provider offers landline telephony, mobile telephony, and Internet access – and sends a different bill for each. Whereas this may cause unnecessary costs and complexity, the unification of those accounts that refer to the same customer also offer the chance to provide more customised and personalised bundled services while raising the security, service quality, and customer satisfaction.

The unification of accounts and access rights can be a double-edged sword for users and service providers alike. Users usually like the added convenience of single-sign-on systems, using one single password for a number of log-ins and access accounts. Enterprises on the other hand see the benefit of single s systems in a better control and management of access rights. However, ... number of applications for one individual increases, adding numerous mobile devices or new web-based services to their daily life, the risk of data misuse increases as well. The idea of just having to provide a fingerprint instead of typing a complicated password every morning is fascinating. However, the more sensitive information gets possibly accessed with this one identifier, the higher the risk for the user to fall victim to identity fraud and ultimately experience loss or damage.

A similar scenario applies to the service provider. When it comes to personal information stored on computer systems, privacy concerns need to be taken seriously. It may well be useful for a citizen to have an account with the tax office to deal with the annual tax declaration online, and it may be useful to link this with some information on the costs paid for medical services, but e.g., a complete unification of all the data and profiles stored by the tax office, the hospital, and the health insurance would need to be managed closely and is unacceptable in many cultures – besides the fact that it may violate privacy regulations. Very often Internet accounts, such as eBay or YouTube accounts, are named in a way that does not give a hint towards their holders 'normal' names or email addresses. These accounts serve as partial identities supporting users, who want more control over their identity and over personal information which is collected and stored on them. They also want to be able to use technologies for anonymity and pseudonymity in order to manage whether and how they are identified in which contexts. Consequently 'Identity Differentiation' is another major trend in more or less direct contrast to 'Identity Unification'.

1.1.2 Identity in Different Areas of the Information Society

The looming conflicts can be seen in the changing world of 'classic' physical and organisational entities, such as citizens, governments, customers, businesses employees, and enterprises, and the relation(s) between them. This is due to new and ongoing political developments, such as the integration of the European Union, and due to new and ongoing economic trends, such as global competition, global sourcing, and the disintegration of traditional value chains. All these trends have a strong influence on the respective identities, as can be seen in the discussion of the following areas.

Citizens and Their Governments ('G2C')

European states still follow very different concepts of identification and identity management: E.g. in Germany holding an ID card is mandatory for any citizen from 16 years of age on, while in the UK any initiative towards state-issued identity cards creates major discussion and even uproar in society. On the other side social acceptance of CCTV, a rich base for investigating where people are at which point in time or who has been at a location at a certain time is much more popular in the UK than in Germany.

While Europe is only in the process of merging its identity cultures and processes the raising connectivity and the Internet bring a new dimension into the discussion: A hotel, that would not only take the ID-Card or passport of an arriving guest, but would also routinely double-check these documents with the issuing authorities would create at least raised eyebrows if not astonishment. In the Internet this is a common practice: Somebody being asked for granting access sees itself as a relying party and checks identifiers (e.g. certificates, credit card numbers, or other credentials) immediately and directly with the parties who issued these identifiers.

Meanwhile there are discussions among providers of physical ID-Cards to establish a service for on-the-spot-double checking of physical ID-Cards presented to relying parties, such as hotels. This could help to identify criminals and other parties being searched for. Public-private partnerships for offering these services more efficiently are being discussed. The unification of identifiers would help these initiatives a lot.

However, the way how identities and identifiers are handled has a close relation to the way how citizens are treated and therefore to the essence of our democracies. The question is, whether citizens are per se considered to be criminals that need to be identified as thoroughly as possible, or whether they are considered to be able to select adequate partial identities, identifiers and the degree of identification in a situation.

Business and Their Customers ('B2C')

Many milestones of social development came along with major changes in the economy. The rise of the Information Society is closely related to the evolution of the ICT industry and the diffusion of ICT in everybody's life. Yet, the Information Society tends towards something that can be characterised as an information affluent society, where more information than needed is available. For businesses it is not just the goal of reaching the (potential) customer – gaining the customers' attention is the real deal. As a result, products, services, and communication are increasingly tailored towards the demands and requirements of individual customers or groups of them.

While customers' attention is becoming the scarce resource, identification of customers and knowledge about their identity attributes is getting more and more of a major asset for businesses. Depending on business area and business model, the role of identity can be manifold within the process of value creation. Traditionally, identification and identity plays a major role within the payment process, e.g., for judging of customers' creditworthiness. Knowledge about customers' identity has always been a central part of customer relationship programs. Nowadays and in addition to the classical applications, identity attributes are more and more used to better sell or create products in the online world:

- Online retailers use customer preferences to recommend goods ar
- Individualised advertising within social networks and communit on identity attributes stored within user profiles.
- Automatic pricing of goods and services depending on customers' identity attributes is possible and has already been tested.

Knowledge about customers' identities will play a prominent, if not even central role in future processes of value creation. Handling identities in a proper way to prevent the invasion of customers' private spheres will be one major challenge for businesses to keep the relationship with their customers alive.

Enterprises and Their Employees ('B2E')

Today's digital work environments include more and more (business) processes facilitated by information systems. Organisations have to take care of their users and access management (often called identity and access management (IAM)), in order to protect their systems and their information from unauthorised access and to lower their overall costs (e.g., by centralising account data of various information systems). The need for these initiatives is enforced by the diversity of IT infrastructures used in everyday transactions (e.g. enterprise resource planning, document management, or human resources management) and the often dynamic change in user entitlements, (e.g., due to job changes, promotions, or layoffs). Therefore, identity management systems (IdMS) are becoming increasingly important for companies and corporations, and given enterprise-wide responsibilities these need to be enterprise-wide identity management systems.

A variety of identity management technologies can be identified. Examples are single / reduced sign-on, directory services, public-key infrastructures, and IAM systems. Still and contrary to the position of many technology vendors identity management is not a simple out-of-the-box solution but a complex framework of different technologies and functions. So when introducing IdMS, organisations incur a variety of costs for the implementation and the related organisational issues, such as the integration of processes and technologies.

Therefore, topics such as the interoperability of IdMS, business process integration of identity related technologies, and High-Tech ID (RFID tokens, biometry, etc.) are in the focus of interest. While the technology issues seem to be a solvable problem, practical challenges and research needs to follow from the complex interaction of the various players, processes, structures, and tasks of organisations.

1.2 The Role of FIDIS

FIDIS (Future of Identity in the Information Society, www.fidis.net) is a multidisciplinary endeavour of 24 leading institutions from research, government, and industry. Research from states with different cultures on e.g., the identification of citizens and ID cards is combined towards a well-founded analysis of High-Tech IDs and Virtual Identities, considering aspects, such as privacy, mobility, interoperability, profiling, forensics, and identity related crime. It is organised as a Network of Excellence (NoE) in the 6th Framework programme of the European Union, funded under Contract N° 507512.

The borders between the scenarios and the concepts of identity as well as identity management, etc. are not sharp lines and cannot be sharp lines. Overlaps exist almost everywhere, making identity omnipresent.

Identification and authentication, identity management, liability, security and privacy, legal aspects, and social implications are issues that need to be carefully addressed by researchers and policy makers. The main aspects of these are being analysed in depth by the FIDIS 'Future of Identity in the Information Society' Network of Excellence (NoE), which is also working on the issues' complex interactions, a difficult and important task requiring the integration of inter-disciplinary expertise.

FIDIS is proud to contribute to the future of identity in the Information Society, e.g., by shaping the requirements, definition, conception and development of specific security, trust and privacy technologies, and infrastructures. This should help to enable a joint or at least synchronised European approach for identity management.

1.3 On This Book

When FIDIS came into existence there was confidence that it would produce results that deserve reading beyond the usual lifetime of a project deliverable, even though one at that time did not exactly know what they were. So the idea to summarise the results after 5 years was always around. Now the book in your hand aims to give an overview of those results that FIDIS considered to be most interesting.

For many chapters this means that the respective work package leaders edited them, while other were joint editing efforts by FIDIS partners and / or FIDIS coordination. This introduction aims to give some guidance through the flow of topics and chapters in this book that aims to document the most relevant aspects of identity and its future challenges and opportunities.

The remainder of this section is structured as follows: Three subsections give an overview on the main scientific chapters of the book. A forth subsection introduces the 'Vignettes', short hypothetical scenarios to illustrate future impacts of identity developments on the daily lives of ordinary people, and a fifth subsection explains the Annexes of the book.

1.3.1 Basic Concepts

Chapter 2 introduces foundational concepts on the 'Identity of Identity'. The objective of this chapter is not to bring the ultimate answer to the question 'What is identity?', as this would be an almost impossible undertaking given the complexity and the constant evolution of the subject. The aim is rather to present different angles that can be used to define the concept, in particular in the context of the Information Society. Starting at describing how this conceptualisation can be conducted in the traditional way of theorisation well known by academics, this chapter then indicates how less formal approaches such as narratives can be used to help understand the concept. It also introduces how the new 'social tools' originating from the 'Web 2.0' can be used to stir the intelligence of experts from different horizons so as to generate a meaningful and practical understanding of the subject. The second part of Chapter 2 illustrates how each of these approaches has been operationalised by presenting a series of models and scenarios presenting different perspectives and issues that are relevant to the subject, and a collaborative Web 2.0 knowledge infrastructure that is used in FIDIS to facilitate the conceptualisation of identity by a group of experts.

Chapter 3 introduces the concept of 'Virtual Persons and Identities', bringing light to the questions: 'What is a virtual person? What is it used for? What is its added value?'. Virtual persons sometimes describe avatars and new forms of identities in online games. They also appear in other contexts (e.g., in the legal domain). Within the work of FIDIS, the concept of virtual persons has been extended to better describe and understand new forms of identities in the Information Society in relation to rights, duties, obligations and responsibilities.

Virtual persons, as other virtual entities, exist in the virtual world, the collection of all (abstract) entities, which are or have been the product of the mind or imagination. The virtual world – not to be confused with the digital world – allows a unified description of many identity-related concepts that are usually defined separately without taking into consideration their similarities: avatars, pseudonyms, categories, profiles, legal persons, etc.

The legal system has a long experience of using abstract entities to define rules, categories, and the like in order to associate legal rights, obligations, and responsibilities to persons that can be considered instances of these abstract entities in specific situations. The model developed within FIDIS and lined out in this chapter uses a similar construction. After introducing the model, the application to pseudonyms is described. Also the concept of virtual persons from a legal perspective and (eventually) trust in the light of virtual persons is explored.

1.3.2 Identity and Advanced Technologies

Turning towards technologies to facilitate the management of identities, Chapter 4 analyses High-Tech ID and emerging technologies. Technological development has undeniably pervaded every aspect of our lives, and the ways in which we now use our identity related information has not escaped the impact of this change. We are increasingly called upon to adopt new technology, usually more through obligation than choice, to function in everyday society, and with this new era of supposed convenience has come new risks and challenges. Chapter 4 examines the technological roots of identity management and the systems used to support this activity, means to protect digital information (such as public-key encryption) and digital signatures and the evolving yet somewhat controversial role of biometrics in identification and authentication.

Considering the ever changing landscape of identity related technologies, Chapter 4 further explores emerging technologies with likely impact in the near to mid-term future. These include Radio Frequency Identification (RFID) which has more recently come to the fore of the public consciousness, Ambient Intelligence environments which offer convenience at the potential cost of privacy and human implants which surprisingly have already been developed in a medical context and look set to be the next major step in our ever burgeoning relationship with technology.

Chapter 5 turns to another sometimes underestimated technology related to identity management: While identity management systems for the Internet have been debated intensively, identity management in mobile applications has grown silently over the last almost 20 years. Technologies, such as the still-growing Global System for Mobile Communication (GSM) with its Subscriber Identity Module (SIM) identification infrastructure, are foundations for many new mobile identity management related applications and services. This includes location-based services (LBS), offering customised and convenient services to users (e.g., friend finder applications) and new revenue opportunities for service providers (e.g., location-based advertising).

However, even though the opportunities seem to be endless and technology manageable, challenges arise when looking at advanced aspects of mobility and identity such as privacy, regulation, the socio-cultural aspects, and the economic impacts. To this regard, the interdisciplinary nature of mobility and identity is imminent and needs to be explored further. By learning from the diverse field of challenges, new mobile communication systems can be created, allowing for more privacy-preserving service provision and a more transparent handling of mobile identities. Therefore Chapter 5 presents an analysis of the specific properties of Mobile Identities, leading to a description of the FIDIS perspective on mobility and identity. Then a deeper analysis of the technological aspects of mobile networks gives the basis for a closer look from the legal perspective (on issues such as data protection), the sociological, and the economic perspective. An outlook on the future challenges of mobility and identity concludes this chapter.

One of the key aspects of effective and efficient management of identities is interoperability, being the focus of Chapter 6. Establishing interoperable systems is a complex operation that goes far beyond the technical interconnectedness of databases and systems. Interoperability emerges from the need to communicate data across different domains for a specific purpose. Transferring the data may represent a technical challenge because of different protocols, standards, formats and so forth. However, the most difficult challenge lies in reconciling and aligning the purpose, use and other changes consequent on transferring that data. Changes in data ownership and custodianship have an effect on power structures, roles and responsibilities and on risk. In the first part of this chapter our aim is to develop an understanding of the term interoperability as it currently applies to the area of identity management. FIDIS proposes a three-fold conception of interoperability in IdMS, involving technical, but also formal-policy, legal and regulatory components, as well as informal-behavioural and cultural aspects. Having noted the official EU / government agenda as regards interoperable IdMS, the second part of the chapter is concerned with the perspective of other important stakeholders on the same topic. First, the views of experts from private and public sectors across Europe are presented. Following this, the perceptions and attitudes of EU citizens towards interoperable IdMS are discussed. Together, the findings presented point to the crucial challenges and implications associated with the sharing of personal data in the provision of eGovernment, eHealth, and related services.

1.3.3 Identity and Society

Some of the most critical challenges for 'the future of identity in information society' must be located in the domain of automated profiling practices, being the focal point of Chapter 7. Profiling technologies enable the construction and application of group profiles used for targeted advertising, anti-money laundering, actuarial justice, etc. Profiling is also the conditio sine qua non for the realisation of the vision of Ambient Intelligence. Though automated profiling seems to provide the only viable answer for the increasing information overload and though it seems to be a promising tool for the selection of relevant and useful information, its invisible nature and pervasive character may affect core principles of democracy and the rule of law, especially privacy and non-discrimination. In response to these challenges Chapter 7 suggests novel types of protection next to the existing data protection regimes. Instead of focusing on the protection of personal data, these novel tools focus on the protection against invisible or unjustified profiling. Finally, Chapter 7 develops the idea of Ambient Law, advocating a framework of technologically embedded legal rules that guarantee a transparency of profiles that should allow European citizens to decide which of their data they want to hide, when and in which context.

With the ever-increasing use of identities in commercial transactions, such as credit card payments, identity-related crime is also on the rise. Combating crimes like identity fraud, not in the least with the help of identity forensics, is a key challenge for policy makers. Therefore Chapter 8 aims at contributing to addressing that challenge. It summarises the findings of five years of FIDIS research on identity-related crime and identity forensics. A typology is given of the various forms of identity-related crime. After an analysis of relevant socio-economic, cultural, technical, and legal aspects of identity-related crime, potential countermeasures are discussed. We then move on to forensic aspects, with a critical analysis of pitfalls in forensic identification and case studies of mobile networks and biometric devices. Next, forensic profiling is discussed from a wide range of perspectives. The chapter concludes with lessons drawn in the area of identity-related crime and forensic aspects of identity.

Last but not least, the relation between privacy and identity is the main topic of Chapter 9. The current mainstream approach to privacy protection is to release as little personal data as possible ('data minimisation'). To this end, Privacy Enhancing Technologies (PETs) provide anonymity on the application and network layers, support pseudonyms and help users to control access to their personal data, e.g., through identity management systems. However, protecting privacy by merely minimising disclosed data is not sufficient as more and more electronic applications (such as in the eHealth or the eGovernment sectors) require personal data. For today's information systems, the processing of released data has to be controlled ('usage control'). This chapter presents technical and organisational solutions elaborated within FIDIS on how privacy can be preserved in spite of the disclosure of personal data.

As initially stated, even after 5 years of FIDIS, not all questions in the domain of identity and identity management could be answered completely This is due to the fact that identity is a moving target, which is constantly evolving in different directions. Consequently, the concluding Chapter 10 presents the open challenges and potential (especially for Europe) on how to deal with the issues of identity.

1.3.4 The Vignettes

As an addition to the more scientifically oriented Chapters described so far FIDIS has developed a number of hypothetical scenarios which illustrate potential future identity developments as well as their potential impact on the daily lives of ordinary people. These scenarios are placed as 'Vignettes' between the 'scientific' chapters.

Based on the results of FIDIS Deliverable on use cases and scenarios of emerging technologies[1], the scenarios are heavily influenced and triggered by the endeavours of FIDIS and the personal experiences and expectations of the authors. Of course, the future is always clouded in uncertainty and the goal of each scenario is not to deliver the most accurate prediction of the future at all. Nonetheless, visions and hypotheses of individuals have always been a first step towards a next stage of technical, economical or social development – most likely also for the future of identity in the information society.

Starting with a scenario that looks at the potential impact of Ambient Intelligence environments, a subject well explored in the FIDIS network, subsequent scenarios focus on biometrics, social networks, virtual identities, grid computing and forensics, all areas to which FIDIS has dedicated much research effort.

A number of characters show up in the scenarios, among them Frank Idis, a 39-year-old humanities teacher and housemaster at a British public school in Royston Vasey, in the north of England. He first met his now wife Fanny (née Cheung) while holidaying in mainland Greece. Fanny's family are originally from Hong Kong, but she is second generation in the UK. Fanny works as a security director of a big hotel chain and frequently visits companies producing security devices.

---

1 Gasson, M. (ed.) (2008), FIDIS Deliverable D12.5: Use cases and scenarios of emerging technologies.

1.3.5 The Annexes

This book aims not only at comprising the core results of FIDIS, but also to give an insight into FIDIS' way of work. Therefore the deliverables (Annex A) as well as the biographies of the contributors (Annex B) and the descriptions of the partners (Annex C) are included. Last but not least and as an example of outreach activities beyond the core activities of FIDIS Annex D contains a joint paper with two major thought-leaders in the identity arena (Kim Cameron (Microsoft) and Reinhard Posch (TU Graz, Government of Austria) on a 'Proposal for a common identity framework: A User-Centric Identity Metasystem'.

1.3.5 The Annexes

VIGNETTE 1: PUTTING THE MACHINES IN CONTROL*

Having planned their wedding some 12 months earlier, the Idis' are on honeymoon for two weeks in Crete. This, due to circumstance, coincides with the imminent delivery of their first child whose announcement came as a 'happy surprise' some months earlier.

It's All Greek to Me

Their late arrival at 'Hotel Warwikakis' in the city periphery the night before had, on the whole, been uneventful. Frank had previously opted not to allow his intelligent home to send a public version of his family preferences agent to their hotel in advance, and instead accepted that, because of this, they 'may not be able to provide for all specific needs on the first night'. However he hadn't figured on the Greeks being a little slow on the uptake of new technology, and so despite trying to use his MyComm personal communication device to upload the data at the reception desk, he found he was unable to because their system did not use the latest international standard.

Despite this, after converting the profile agent to an older format and answering a few questions related to the types of personal data the hotel was allowed to read from their agent and for how long they wished their preferences to be stored by the hotel, they enjoyed a room lit and heated to their approximate preferred comfort levels, classical music piped through the suite's music system, and the television channels ordered to reflect their tastes.

After a good night's sleep, the day had started abruptly at 06.45 by a wake-up alarm call. Unfortunately neither Frank nor Fanny wished to get up at that time, but during the conversion to the older format, the MyComm had been switched out of holiday mode, and as such had assumed today was like any other typical working day. This was rapidly rectified.

Some time later, after getting out of bed, Fanny decides that she is too exhausted to venture outside this morning, so she opts to stay at the hotel while Frank does some sightseeing. As part of Fanny's travel-insurance policy, she is wearing a MediCheck health-monitoring system which monitors her continually for anomalous physiological changes. Frank ensures that his MyComm device is listed to receive alerts, and authorises the device to contact the hotel reception in

---

* This scenario is based on FIDIS deliverable D12.5, Chapter 3 by Mark Gasson (READING), Katja de Vries (VUB), and Niels van Dijk (VUB).

the event of an emergency. As is default with such devices, in line with Greek law, the local emergency service is authorised automatically to be contacted.

Meeting the Local Location Services

Frank has never been one for shopping, but when away always has a look around the local shops. Like many cities, the centre is littered with international clothing stores, most of which use RFID tag scanners in the doorway so as to scan for tags in clothing and accessories to work out what the customer wears and thus to create a rough profile of them. Additionally, most shops welcome the ad hoc automatic upload of shopping agents from personal communicators so as to create a list of offers and discounts to help tempt the customer. By default, Frank has such options disabled on his MyComm device, and having felt a sense of personal invasion when, for example, a shop was able to alert him to discounts on his type of underpants based on the RFID tag data, he opted to subscribe to an online tag-swap site which periodically sends him credit-card sized plastic tokens stuffed full of random RFID tags designed to confuse the shop's profiling agents. His favorite one apparently registers him as wearing a sombrero and carrying eight kilos of jam.

After a bit on an amble around the local area, Frank wants to find some food. Having heard of the local dolmathes, he is interested in trying them, but he also has some dietary requirements that he needs to be wary of. Frank's MyComm device is a 5th-generation mobile device with many useful functions and access to location-based services. One of his favourites is the locator service which enables the device to pin-point his location and seek out places of interest to him – in this case restaurants. Frank's device is also equipped with MInD, a mobile device identity manager which allows him to specify a range of partial identities which he can use when accessing such online services. Frank enables the service and selects restaurant finder. Then he selects his 'personal food finder' profile which stores details of his dietary requirements and then selects 'local food' and 'time sync', which tells the service to look for items relevant for the current time. After a few moments, the MyComm indicates that the service is requesting further details – in this case his location. Frank authorises the transfer and a list of appropriate places appears on the screen. Frank is also notified by his device that he can update his iConcert database via the same service provider using the information he has already sent. iConcert is a plug-in for his MyComm that monitors his music library and generates a personalised list of upcoming concerts in his local area. The filtering of relevant events happens on his local device, so that no further information is needed by the service provider. He chooses not to bother, so he remains unaware that his favorite sitar player, Ravi Shankar, is performing with the Cretan lute-player Ciborgakis in the city just that night.

While en route, Frank's MyComm informs him that he is carrying insufficient cash funds to get him through the day after a typical breakfast at the restaurant.

Frank is aware of the link between uses on his eComm card and subsequent targeted mailings from his card company's 'trusted group of associates' (a downside of the agreement that assures him a marginally decreased interest rate), and his profiling agent knows that he usually opts to use cash for smaller one-off purchases. As such, a detour to a cash-machine is offered and accepted, after Frank has authorised his MyComm to give his name and nationality to the local ATM finder service. Cash-machines still use PIN security, but this is augmented with additional biometric protection. However, rather than using non-revocable biometrics such as fingerprints, the cash machines use a type of keystroke analysis to obtain a characteristic typing pattern from the PIN button presses. This type of changeable biometric has become widely accepted as preferable. Frank is annoyed when he has to type in a sample line of numbers four times over and is still rejected by the machine. He now has to use the fall-back option of authorising the ATM to take a picture of him and compare this to the facial-biometric template stored by his UK bank. Even though he knows the picture will be stored for five years by the hefty Greek anti-identity-fraud laws, he has no choice but to accept.

I Don't Drink Coffee, I Take Tea My Dear

Because it's a holiday, Frank doesn't bother with trying to decipher the Greek menu by himself. He uploads his profile to the restaurant system and clicks his agreement with the system's data-processing practices. He is guided to his preferred seat position in the window and is able to select his meal from a heavily customised menu. He enjoys the luxury of just seeing his favorite foods fulfilling his dietary requirements offered to him on the menu, even though he knows the restaurant will sell his data to many food-broking services. The restaurant is augmented with sensor technologies and in the absence of any other information, makes sweeping generalisations in order to project targeted advertising on the menu card when not in use. Frank is not best pleased to find an advert for a local sports club appear as a result of the doorway height sensor and stool strain sensor concluding he is too heavy for his height. This is soon updated when he removes his rucksack and his weight is recalculated. Unfortunately, being a result of a combined group profile of the current restaurant patrons, changing the music of 'Sakis Rouvas' which is piped through the building is not so easy to correct.

After a delicious assortment of mezes, and the best part of a drink, the waitress, alerted as to the volume of drink remaining by the cup coaster, comes over with a filter coffee pot to offer a complimentary top-up. Unfortunately even the advances in Ambient Intelligence haven't eliminated human error, and Frank explains just too late how he had actually gone out of his way to find Lapsang Souchong tea ...

While preparing to leave, a message comes through the MyComm from Frank's intellifridge back at home. It requests his acceptance for a menu for that evening's meal based on items that are nearing expiry in storage. Usually, the fridge would negotiate such a message with the house gateway, and thus discover that the house had gone into holiday mode. However, Frank had previously configured a link with it in order to interrogate it directly, so messages were unfiltered. He starts to remotely configure the preferences to route it back through the house and avoid further messages when a priority message appears – Fanny's MediCheck device has found cause for concern.

Congratulations, It's a ...

Despite having had several false alarms in the past, this time Fanny was in complete agreement with the MediCheck device – something was definitely happening! Having automatically alerted the concierge's desk and contacted the local emergency services, help was quickly to hand, and within 30 minutes, Fanny was being wheeled through the doors of a maternity unit. Having been largely planned in advance by her insurance company, her arrival was not totally unexpected. Indeed, her doctor had already authorised access to relevant portions of her eMedical file to the hospital.

Fortunately, Fanny is still alert enough to give her consent to the hospital cross-referencing her iris scan with that stored in the medical files, and her identity is confirmed. She realises that she had better change her eMedical preferences to allow such identification without her consent, seeing the kind of emergencies that can arise, particularly when travelling.

Meanwhile ...

Frank returns to the hotel too late to see Fanny, but, having taken the opportunity to collect some of her belongings for her stay in hospital, he heads to the hospital in their rental car. Not being familiar with the local area, he instructs the on-board GPS unit to guide him to the city hospital, and for once, he doesn't mind at all that his personal data and profiles are being transferred to the local rental-car company in exchange for the routing service. Being slightly flustered and concerned for his wife, Frank becomes increasingly annoyed with the enforced limits on the car, and so he disables the overrides by putting the car in 'emergency mode'. Unfortunately, the traffic monitoring cameras observe his erratic driving, trace the car back to the rental company, and automatically issue a fine to Frank. As a result, Frank also has an additional sum levied onto the car insurance policy by the rental company.

On arrival at the hospital, Frank makes his way inside, and looks for directions to maternity. Because most of the signage is in Greek, he uses the camera on his MyComm device to translate the words to find his way. He curses when his MyComm only yields error messages and he has to spend precious minutes to use sign language with a passing nurse to indicate where he wants to go.

Sometimes, he feels there are distinct advantages to living in the US, where buildings automatically infer and smoothly indicate people's desired routes. The European AmI Directive, however, has prohibited such automated guidance without explicit individual consent. Who cares about explicit informed consent when your wife is in labour?!

The maternity unit is augmented with additional security measures to prevent unauthorised personnel from entering. To request access Frank, is asked to scan his iris, and not being on the list of personnel is told to wait for further instruction. Security at the hospital is tight, and the security department is able to cross-check iris scan patterns with the European centralised biometric database. Despite having been acquitted of an alleged offence with a minor at a previous place of work, Frank's details are still to be found in the database, and as such he is taken aside for further questioning as to his purpose at the hospital.

After some four hours in labour, Fanny gives birth to a healthy baby girl. As has become standard, the baby is implanted in the umbilical stump with an RFID tag to allow identification in the hospital. Although such temporary implants have become normal practice, permanent implantation is left for the parents to decide at a later date. Frank and Fanny have already decided to have the umbilical tag removed, even though they realise that younger generations seem rather fond of these identifying implants. Frieda – as the girl is named – will just have to decide for herself when she comes of age whether or not she wants to be permanently chipped.

The visions and thoughts expressed in this vignette are inspired and based on various discussions, and results of the FIDIS Network of Excellence as well as the authors' personal experiences and expectations. Partially, underlying concepts and ideas of this vignette are described in Chapters 4, 5, 6, and 7.

2 Identity of Identity

Thierry Nabeth

Summary. The objective of this chapter is not to bring the answer to the ultimate question 'what is identity?', – an almost impossible undertaking given the complexity and the constant evolution of the subject – but rather to present, more like on a journey, different angles that can be used to define this concept, in particular in the context of the Information Society. Starting first at describing how this conceptualisation can be conducted in the traditional way of theorisation well known by the academics, this chapter then indicates how less formal approaches such as narratives can be used to help to understand the concept. It also introduces how the new 'social tools' originating from the Web 2.0 can be used to stir the intelligence of experts from different horizons so as to generated a meaningful and practical understanding of the subject. The second part of the chapter is used to illustrate how each of these approaches have been operationalised by presenting a series of models and scenarios presenting different perspectives and issues that are relevant to the subject, and a collaborative Web 2.0 knowledge infrastructure that was used in FIDIS to facilitate the conceptualisation of identity by a group of experts.

2.1 Defining the Identity Concept

Conceptualising identity represents a number of challenges originating from the complex and multidisciplinary nature of the subject (identity), a domain in constant evolution in which old concepts are being reinterpreted and new concepts are created, and which involve experts of different horizons and of different geographical location.

The traditional approach for this conceptualisation is well known and consists in asking experts to provide theories of the subject being under study. The experts typically reflect on the subject and produce generic models that can be applied in different situations. These experts then write academic papers and textbooks to document their findings and to make their knowledge available to a large audience. Another approach consists in identifying the *vocabulary* of the terms that are the more frequently used in the domain to describe the subject, and to define the semantics of each term and their relationships in a way that will have as little ambiguity as possible. Practically, these definitions are to be found in *dictionaries* or *encyclopaedias*. Information system specialists have also invented some special languages and tools allowing more formal definition of the different terms and to connect them with one another. *Ontology, taxonomies, Unified modelling Language* (UML) diagrams, are created as a way to define the concept of a domain. This chapter, and more generally this book, presents several illustrations about how this conceptualisation was conducted in FIDIS to define the concept of identity.

Yet at the same time, the experience has demonstrated that this very explicit conceptualisation presents some flaws: a domain as complex as identity is not easily put into boxes, at least for some of its aspects. Firstly, identity is a concept that is constantly evolving. Also it is considered a moving target. By trying to formalise too early and too precisely some concepts, you take the risk that the meaning of these concepts becomes obsolete in the perspective of the new contexts, or that you overlook more important concepts that have emerged since. An example has been given recently with the Web 2.0 where the massive use of online social networking or of blogs has totally refined the concept of online identity. In the new setting, the identity of the person is blurred, being constructed from a multitude of sources that are more difficult to control, and this requires a novel approach to become manageable. Besides some people are more inclined than in the past to expose their selves towards the world so as to gain visibility, increase their social capital and flatter their narcissism. Another difficulty of this very explicit conceptualisation is that it creates barriers since it mostly relies on experts for its elaboration, and requires some effort in its exploitation. Creating theories is a complicated task, and absorbing these theories is not necessarily a pleasant experience for many. However, research in knowledge management has shown that alternative methods exist to codify knowledge and to diffuse knowledge that in some cases do not even need to be codified. Hence storytelling has proved a very effective technique to capture knowledge, to describe concepts and to diffuse it largely. Many people like to write stories, and even more people love to listen to them. In this chapter, we will explain how storytelling and more generally narratives (such as use cases and scenarios) can be effective in helping to clarify concepts, and how they have been used in FIDIS.

Finally this chapter will also present the opportunity to introduce new tools such as Wikis, blogs or social bookmarking that have emerged as part of the Web 2.0 and that can greatly contribute to support the conceptual process in its formal or informal form.

We hope in this chapter, to provide the epistemological perspective of how conceptualisation can be conducted to define the concepts of a complex domain, and how these principles have guided FIDIS in defining the identity concept.

2.1.1 The Multidisciplinary Challenge

Defining the concept of Identity represents a significant challenge: identity spans a variety of disciplines such as Security, Law, Technologies, Information Systems, Social Sciences, and Philosophy for which approaches and traditions for conceptualising a subject can vary considerably. For instance philosophers may be interested by very high level and abstract conceptualisations presenting a big picture relevant to humankind, whereas social scientists may care more about an analysis of the usages grounded in reality. Some lawyers may be more interested by very formal rules (the book of Law) describing precisely the meaning of all the elements intervening in a situation. Yet, lawyers also like at the same time (in particular common law[1] countries) to rely on more descriptive approaches based on cases presenting precedents of court decisions as a way of specifying the rules to be applied. Information system specialists may need very precise descriptions so that it can be implementable in machines. And security experts or technologists may feel more familiar with a process oriented perspective defining mechanisms.

Besides, all the different dimensions are increasingly interrelated, and no domain can afford to remain isolated in its knowledge silo, without taking the risk of affecting the effectiveness of the work (Sveiby and Simons, 2002). For instance technical or security experts have to be aware of the human dimension (people have emotions, are influenced by social norms (Kogut, 2008) and culture (Nisbett, 2003), are not always rational in their decisions (Ariely, 2008), and can be manipulated (Cialdini, 2001)), and take into account the effectiveness of social engineering 'techniques' for breaking into systems that appeared secured. Law specialists have to be informed about the pace of evolution of the technologies and of the current practices (e.g., the usage of the exchange of music files in peer to peer networks) so as to be able to address effectively novel forms of fraud and to defend people's privacy (ALRC, 2008), and information systems designers have to be aware of the privacy concerns raised by society and governments so as to elaborate socially acceptable solutions.

2.1.2 Identity: A Concept Subject to Major Evolutions

Identity is also a topic which is subject to constant evolution and reinterpretation, given the tremendous changes in the technologies that can completely transform and make obsolete a vision of reality. For example online systems have enabled the development of totally new forms of identities such as in the case of multiplayer online games (i.e., MMORPG) in which people can invent a new life, or with the case of blogs that a normal person can use as a personal 'stand' in which she is able to express their opinion, and even take the role of a journalist. Profiling technologies may radically transform the concept of identity by exposing some of the previously hidden part of the person by analysing the digital traces that people leave as part of their actions, or by exploiting and by cross-joining the content of huge databases.

---

[1] *Common law* refers to law and the corresponding legal system developed through decisions of courts and similar tribunals, rather than through legislative statutes or executive action. Wikipedia. Countries having adopted 'common law' as the basis of the legal systems include in particular the Anglo-Saxon countries such as United Kingdom or the United States.

In the Digital Society, and in particular in the Social Web (implementing the vision of the Internet as a social space encouraging and supporting people participation), much more personal information is available: people can describe explicitly their identity using the profiles that are present in many systems such as social networking services (such as in Facebook or LinkedIn). They can also define more implicitly their identity by exposing their thoughts, beliefs and actions via a variety of tools (e.g., blogs, bulletin boards, micro-blogging) from which their identity can be inferred. The traces of their activities (referred to as digital traces) are even increasingly exported by the platforms thought RSS feeds[2], and these 'life streams' can be displayed into aggregators[3], or processed by machines. This personal information defined by the end user is also less reliable than in the off-line world since it is usually not controlled by a trusted authority that can enforce the validity of the information. For instance on the Internet, people have many opportunities to 'lie' with the reality. Thus, according to a study from Robert Epstein (2007), many people are lying in dating services: women tend to lie about their age and about their weight, and men are inclined to lie about the level of their income. The unreliability of information is however compensated by mechanisms such as recommender and reputation systems relying on social mechanisms such as trust building (Resnick and Zeckhauser, 2002).

The more traditional world is also impacted by this trend: For instance new Id cards incorporating biometric information or having RFID capabilities create new issues such as more important risks for the privacy and the dawn of a 'Big Brother' society. DNA databases are already a reality, and are now even present in the 'collective unconscious' of the society having been popularised by the many television series such as CSI (Crime Scene Investigation). In these series, the forensic experts frequently use databases such as CODIS (Combined DNA Index System) to track criminals by comparing DNA profiles electronically. Yet at the same time the large diffusion of mobile phones able to take pictures anytime and anywhere and the possibility to easily spread information on the Internet in personal blogs creates the conditions of transparency counterbalancing some of the risks attached to a too high level of surveillance: In a context where almost any person has become a potential journalist, the identity and the acts of the 'torturers' are largely known. In the physical world, the technical progress has impacted the concept of identity by augmenting the transparency.

Finally, on the horizon with the announce of an 'Ambient Intelligence' Society in which communication technology will become pervasive, identity will go through an even bigger transformation. This future is already happening with the case of Location Based Services (LBS) that are made available via mobile phones incorporating a GPS such as the latest Apple iPhone. These new mobile

---

[2] A RSS feed represents a list of items (each item consists of a title and a summary) that is provided in XML format, that is frequently updated, and that is used to exchange lists of summary information such as news.

[3] An aggregator is a component that is able to display in a single place several feeds of information.

services (see Chapter 5 for a presentation of these services) may not be as tacular as the announcement of the transformation of humans into cyborgs[4] with people having RFID chips implanted in their body (see Chapter 4 for a discussion about High-tech systems), but they are very effective in popularising news usages given their level of adoption. If it is still difficult to predict the exact impact of these changes on people's life, we can imagine that, with the disappearing of the frontier between the offline and the online world, the new identity that will emerge will bring in the physical world many of the characteristics very present in the online worlds, such as increased transparency and massive tracking and profiling.

2.1.3 Addressing the Challenges

How do we reconcile all these perspectives originating from so many disciplines into something comprehensible by the normal person? How do we make people of different origins and cultural backgrounds work together in defining the multiples facets of the concept of Identity? How do we define precisely concepts that can constantly evolve without the risk of freezing definitions that can rapidly become obsolete?

First, it is important to note that the definition of a concept can be done in multiple manners that range from the very strict definitions of the concept as the one found in a dictionary, to the much less formal description such as narratives (such as stories or scenarios) illustrating how this concept is applied. In the first case, strict definitions will present the advantage of reducing ambiguity, whereas in the second case the use of the more 'lazy' approaches will allow the description of fuzzier concepts. Less formal methods may also present the advantage of being easier to elaborate (and in particular by the non specialist), and the result may be more digestible by the 'common mortal' (and not only by the expert).

Second, it is also important to create the conditions of good communication between the stakeholders involved in the conceptualisation process, in particular if they originate from different disciplines. These conditions facilitate and accelerate the finding of a common understanding and the reaching of a consensus by allowing the exchange and the confrontation of ideas and perspectives. Practically, a certain number of processes and tools can be used for this purpose such as meetings and brainstorming. More interestingly, the Internet and more particularly the so called Web 2.0[5] with services such as Wikis, blogs or social bookmarking systems, has made available a whole set of solutions allowing groups of communities to participate collaboratively on a subject.

---

4 Cyborg is a term that was coined by Clynes and Kline (1960) for defining an organism having both a synthetic and an organic part.

5 Web 2.0. is a term that was first coined in 2003 at a conference brainstorming session between Tim O'Reilly and Dermot A. McCormack as a means to indicate a completely new revival of the Web along new concepts such as the importance of the social dimension, the creation of a rich user experience, and an architecture of participation (O'Reilly, 2005).

This book chapter will show how the FIDIS project has tried to address this complexity challenge by adopting these principles and tools that we have mentioned to define the concept of identity. It will also provide an extract of the outputs that has resulted from this work.

2.1.4 Structure of This Chapter

Section 2.2 presents the different approaches (formal and less formal) that can be used or have been used in FIDIS to help the conceptualisation process in particular in the context of a domain that is very multidisciplinary and in constant evolution, and favouring the participation of many participants of the FIDIS network. It also describes the Web 2.0 knowledge infrastructures that can be put in place to support the conceptualisation process. Section 2.3 describes the more explicit approaches of this conceptualisation via the definition of terms and the inventory of the profiles of the person in different systems. Section 2.3 also indicates systems and processes that have been used for this conceptualisation such as Wikis. Section 2.4 is about a more descriptive approach of this conceptualisation via the provision of use cases, stories and scenarios allowing understanding more concretely these concepts. Section 2.5 will briefly present how FIDIS have tried to make use of the new participative tools such as Wikis or blogs that have emerged as part of the Web 2.0. Section 2.6 concludes this chapter.

2.2 Conceptualisation

If you put three Lawyers together in a room, you'll end up with four different opinions[6]

Defining the meaning of a subject such as identity represents a difficult endeavour: firstly because the subject can be vast and complex, and span a variety of concepts and disciplines. Secondly because the domain may not be mature and be subject to constant evolution: how do we describe a domain that constantly changes without taking the risk of becoming rapidly obsolete? Thirdly because some of the concepts are inherently difficult to define or are by essence blurry. Modelling concepts involving human factors for example usually represent a difficult undertaking: the human nature is complex, and cannot easily be put into boxes. Besides some terms used in the language are definitively vague, since their function is not so much to convey meaning but to facilitate communication. This is the case with boundary objects (Star and Griesemer, 1989) that are known to have different interpretations in different communities, but that are useful for the forming of a shared understanding. This limitation of the language is even more profound, and has epistemological roots: objective recognition of an existing

[6] Note: Similar jokes also exist for economists, scientists, theologists, etc., for illustrating the difficulties for a group of persons to converge to a shared opinion on a subject.

world is impossible due to limitations of cognition and communication (Holten, 2007). Also, at least in some cases, the result of some conceptualisation has to be accessible to a large enough audience: what is the point of having a 'perfect' conceptualisation if it is only manageable by a very small group of specialist. Finally, and as illustrated in the previous joke about Lawyers, reaching an agreement between different people is often difficult, since each person relates to a different experience of the world, and often has a different set of priorities.

Yet at the same time, supporting this conceptualisation process can be done in a variety of manners, and in particular does not need to rely only on very formal approaches. For instance, narratives (use cases, stories and scenarios) represent a more descriptive approach that can be used to expose a concept and reflect on the different issues in a way that can be very effective. Besides, structures can also be put in place and tools can be used, to facilitate the emergence and the diffusion of a common understanding of a domain in a community.

The aim of this section is to present the different approaches that can be used for the conceptualisation of a topic, starting from the more formal approaches, such as the elaboration of definitions in a dictionary, and continuing with the less formal ones consisting of the use of narratives for the description of concepts. It also reflects for each of these approaches what are the advantages and the limitations. This section also indicates how different collaborative tools, such as Wikis, blogs or social bookmarking that have recently appeared as part of the Web 2.0, can be effectively used for supporting a participatory conceptualisation process amongst a group of people.

2.2.1 Formal *versus* Informal Conceptualisation

Both formal and informal conceptualisation should be considered as useful since they serve a different purpose. Formal conceptualisation is useful for the elicitation of concepts that are stable and already well established. More informal conceptualisation is more adapted in the case of the concepts that are still subject to important evolution. Informal conceptualisation should also be used to illustrate concepts in general in a way that is more comprehensible and more attractive.

It should be noted that this discussion related to the level of formalisation is not new, and exists in one form or another in other domains such as knowledge management, education or Law. Hence the idea of making the knowledge explicit was at the heart of the first knowledge management models which put a particular strong emphasis on knowledge externalisation, i.e., in creating processes making the tacit knowledge to become explicit. More recent approaches of Knowledge Management (KM), acknowledging the disappointing outcomes of these approaches, are incorporating processes taking into account both the tacit and the explicit. Thus the SECI (Socialisation, Externalisation, Combination, Internalisation) model of Nonaka and Takeushi (1995) proposes a number of knowledge processes articulating the explicit and the tacit, and the modern approach of knowledge management, also termed as Enterprise 2.0 'do not focus on capturing knowledge itself, but rather on the practices and outputs of the knowledge worker' (McAfee, 2006).

Another example can be found in education related to the method used to teach people about a subject, and that can include both very didactic methods and more informal methods. This is the case in management education with the Case method (Hamond, 1976) which consists of putting students in situations presented in a narrative mode and asking them for a solution, and that is frequently used as a teaching method that departs from the explicit exposure of a theory: In the Case method, people assimilate knowledge by experimenting rather than by 'absorbing' theories.

Finally, it should be noted that Law (and Theology) also includes both the formal and informal dimensions with the distinction between statuary law and common (or decision) law: In the first case, a strict and precise codification in the Code of Law describes concepts and rules that help to categorise lawful or unlawful actions; In the second case description of cases and discussions presenting precedents are used for governing future court decisions (or in religion to provide some interpretation to the 'Books of Law').

2.2.2 Formal (or Explicit) Conceptualisation

Formal conceptualisation refers to a very explicit definition of concepts aiming at defining precisely a subject so as to facilitate the unambiguous understanding of that subject and facilitate the communication between different actors, and in particular the reaching of a shared understanding and the construction of a common ground (Clark and Brennan, 1991). Concepts and terms that are frequently associated with formal conceptualisation include categorisation, classification, taxonomies, ontology, dictionary, encyclopaedia, models or theories. It should however be noted that no general agreement exists about what is a *conceptualisation*, Bjelland (2005) mentioning that there is even a disagreement in the nature of *classification*.

An important function of very explicit and formal conceptualisations is to offer a precise vocabulary facilitating the good comprehension of the domain and a good communication between two or more actors. Thus a study reported in Bjelland (2005) suggests that classification may contribute to a shared understanding of basic modelling concepts. A good conceptualisation will in particular reduce ambiguity to a minimum and guarantee that the interpretation of a concept is the same for everyone, and therefore helps in the establishment of a common ground.

More concretely, explicit conceptualisation of a domain consists of different elements such as: (1) the identification of a vocabulary of terms to be employed to define the domain; (2) the classification of this vocabulary of terms into categories (often referred to as taxonomy); (3) the precise definition of the semantic of each of the terms. The definition of the semantics consists in the statement of the meaning that is done using sentences in natural language, but it can also be done by specifying the relationships of this term with other terms or concepts. Typical examples of explicit conceptualisations include dictionaries and encyclopaedias. Formal conceptualisation is also an important field in knowledge management (Andrade et al., 2008).

The Specification of Conceptualisation in History

The explicit specification of concepts can barely be considered as something new, since it is a topic that was already explored back in Greek antiquity by philosophers. For instance, in his text 'Categories' written in 350 B.C., Aristotle introduces categorisation as an attempt to articulate the different objects and actions, and helping to define meaning univocally (such as explaining the concepts of synonymy or homonymy). Greek philosophers invented the term Ontology that they defined as the branch of metaphysics relating to the nature and relations of being. At this time this conceptualisation was mainly done through writing and discourse. Since then, Ontology has at various times received the attention of philosophers.[7]

Then in the Middle-Age and later at the Renaissance, people have began to more systematically and explicitly specify the conceptualisation of a domain by using dictionaries and encyclopaedias (the first reference to the term dictionary can be traced in the 13th Century[8], and the modern encyclopaedia can be dated to the beginning of the 16th Century). Dictionaries and encyclopaedias represent a way of specifying a conceptualisation that is based on definition, in alphabetical order, of the terms or words of a domain (dictionary), or on the subjects of a domain (encyclopaedia).

In the 19th Century, classification played a key role in Natural Science, and one can cite the work related to the classification of species of Lamarck, Buffon and Darwin that played a considerable influence in this area (and is at the root of genetics). Classification relies on the idea of conceptualising a domain based on the identification of a set of characteristics that can be owned by an object and that is usually hierarchically structured (examples of classification: the library classification of subjects[9]; or the classification of species in biology).

Computer Science has shown an early interest in the very explicit specification of concepts. The aim was at making the specification of concepts comprehensible by machines. Hence, as a necessary condition for conducting automatic operations and reasoning, Artificial Intelligence started early trying to define explicit and formal specifications of knowledge (Aiii, 2004): Examples include Allen Newell's research on symbolic computation in the mid 50's then Ted Nelson's invention of Hypertext in the 60's, then Marvin Minsky with the introduction of the concept of Frames in the 70's, and later Douglas Lenat with his work on the Cyc framework aiming at representing common sense in the 80's.

---

7 See 'Ontology: A resource guide for philosophers', by Raul Corazzon. http://www.formal-ontology.it/.

8 The first recorded use of the term 'dictionary' to mean 'word list' can be associated with the 13th-century Dictionarius of John of Garland; the first edition of the Webster dictionary of the English language was launched in 1806.

9 For instance the Dewey Decimal Classification (DDC) system or the Library of Congress Classification (LCC) provides a dynamic taxonomical structure for the organisation of library collections. Note: These classifications should be distinguished from other classification in library such as the Dublin Core (http://dublincore.org/), which aim at defining the structure of the objects (books, authors, etc.) that are dealt with in a library.

More recently with the advent of the Internet, the Computer Sciences field has generated a lot of activities around the concept of the Semantic Web (Berners-Lee et al., 2001) which relies on strong semantic representation of data that is aimed at facilitating the exploitation of this data by machines. In this context Ontology work consists mainly on the idea of conceptualising a domain in term of objects and semantic relationships. This trend towards the semantic web, which has dynamised research in how to represent the elements of a domain with a maximum depth, has however proved to be cumbersome, since difficult to create and maintain. More recent approaches such as folksonomies (an open classification emerging from the participation of a community (Mathes, 2004)) are moving away from the strict interpretation of these concepts in favour of a less rigid and more emergent approach.

On a parallel track, knowledge construction and categorisation has flourished, and new approaches have been invented such as combination hyper-textual and collaborative knowledge construction which is best exemplified by Wiki systems (Cunningham and Leuf, 2001), a system in which every member of a community can participate in the creation of the content of an encyclopaedia.

Advantages and Disadvantages of Explicit Conceptualisation

As indicated previously, very formal definition of terms in a dictionary presents the advantage of reducing the level of ambiguity to a minimum, and therefore reduces the risk of misinterpretation of the meaning. As a consequence, explicit conceptualisation facilitates the communication process inside a community by contributing to making people speak the same language, and with some guarantee that each term will have the same meaning (Clark and Brennan, 1991). Another advantage of a formal definition is generally its depth and completeness: authors of definitions have often made a lot of effort to guarantee the good articulation of different concepts, and to have explored the many dimensions related to this concept. For instance, the reader of a dictionary is expected to find related to a given term all the different meanings associated to that term. Finally the processes of abstraction that is conducted as part of the formalisation of the concept, which often consist of extracting the knowledge from its original context, contributes to the generality of the result and its applicability in a variety of contexts. This very 'solid' level conceptualisation is actually very much consistent with the scientific method, which aims at producing precise models, the application of which is guaranteed to generate replicable results.

Yet, very explicit conceptualisation is not without some limitations for the elaboration of these concepts, but also for how these concepts are used later. More specifically defining rigorously concepts can be difficult and lengthy in particular when the meanings of these concepts have not yet stabilised and when the definition of these concepts involves different participants. It can also be made difficult since it requires a high level of expertise from the participants of the conceptualisation and a good level of coordination. It is not rare that the conceptualisation process can create incomprehension and even tensions between different stakeholders of different disciplines, since the same term can have a different meaning in the different disciplines, and the same concept may be expressed using different terms depending on the discipline.

Besides, the result of a conceptualisation may also sometime appear to be somewhat complex and 'esoteric' (i.e., very detached from the reality) and be difficult to apply except for the experts. In particular, the result may also become sometimes difficult to comprehend by the non expert of the domain, since it can conduce to a high level of abstraction originating from the aspiration of creating something as generic as possible, or being obfuscated by details aimed at removing ambiguity. Finally, too 'perfect' conceptualisation may not be the most appropriate medium in the perspective of a dissemination purpose (e.g., for educating people about some concepts) since it may appear tedious (few people enjoy reading a dictionary), and not prone to facilitating serendipitous discovery.

Ironically, the 'conceptualisation of conceptualisation' itself, i.e. the definition of the domain of conceptualising 'things' is relatively confused, and the associated terms are subject to multiple interpretations and are the object of controversy. Thus the definition of the term Ontology is diverse, and is used in a different manner in different domains[10].

Interestingly, explicit conceptualisation methods are evolving with the objective of overcoming some of these limitations such as their rigidity. For instance the term folksonomy which was created in 2004 as the concatenation of the terms folks and taxonomy, represents a vocabulary of terms used by a community, and that originates from an emergent process involving the participation of all the members of the community in the identification of the terms generally used by that community.

2.2.3 Informal Conceptualisation with Narratives

Formal and precise descriptions of concepts as can be found in dictionaries are not the only approach that can be adopted to describe a concept. It is also not always the most desirable.

Narratives (such as cases, stories and scenarios) represent an alternative approach that can be used to define concepts. Narratives rely on the idea of exposing the audience to the subject in a relatively informal way, in a context well connected to a concrete situation making sense to the audience (note that this situation can be fictional or non-fictional). A narrative favours a very descriptive presentation of situations in contrast of the in-depth and very high level conceptualisation.

Narratives may not appear as the most 'rigorous' way to describe concepts, and in particular do not have the same depth as the more formal approaches. They present however a certain number of advantages such as their ability to help to understand concepts that are blurry (because they are very recent or they are by their nature very complex) and / or that resist a formal conceptualisation. Narra-

[10] See for instance the definition of Ontology that is given by Gruber (2008).

tives also contribute to people coordination: Thomas, Kellogg, and Erickson (2001) thus indicate that 'stories can serve not only to support communities of practice with a common vocabulary; they can also serve an important coordinating role within a team'.

Thus, the use of narratives has been the subject of numerous researches in the field of knowledge management as a very effective means to propagate (McLellan, 2002), to elicit (Snowden, 2002), to capture, and to exchange complex ideas, and also to encourage collaboration, to generate new ideas and to ignite change (Denning, 2001; Lelic, 2002). In organisations in particular, Sole and Wilson (2002) indicate that storytelling has been identified as a means to: share norms and values; develop trust and commitment; share tacit knowledge; facilitate unlearning; and generate emotional connection.

Power and Limitations of Narratives to Describe Concepts

The narratives present a number of advantages both for elicitating concepts (Snowden, 2002), and for diffusing these concepts (McLellan, 2002). First, narratives are often easier to elaborate than theoretical construction, facilitating the process of collecting the knowledge related to a subject: one does not need to be an expert to write a story or to describe a case. The writing of a narrative also does not require the same level of reflection and time as the more formal approach since they do not pretend to be as rigorous as the more formal methods. They may also be more pleasant to write, engaging, stimulating the imagination and authorise the expression of ideas that are at odds with the current organisational common beliefs (Snowdon, 2001).

Narratives are also usually more comprehensible, facilitating the diffusion of concepts to a larger part of the population. Indeed, narratives can be more entertaining (less boring) both for the author of the narrative and for the audience, and subsequently, they are more accessible: most people understand and enjoy reading or listening to stories, whereas many people have some difficulties in keeping concentrated in very theoretical descriptions. Finally, narratives can have a more important impact, since they are more grounded to reality and concrete situations that people may have experienced in their real life.

Narratives appear very adapted to describe concepts that are by essence very blurry, or concepts that are very new and that have not yet gone through a maturation phase.

Of course, the use of narratives is also not a panacea, and actually it does not pretend to be a substitute for the more formal approaches. Narratives lack the rigour and the coverage of more formal methods, and in particular fail to provide an in-depth knowledge of the subject, and their application can be limited to the context, which is presented. Narratives may also be more ambiguous, and are more subject to multiple interpretations.

2.2.4 Web 2.0 & Conceptualisation with Wikis, Blogs, Social Bookmarking and Other Tools

Meanwhile, the poor Babel fish, by effectively removing all barriers to communication between different races and cutures, has caused more and bloodier wars than anything else in the history of creation.[11]

Adams, 1979

The conceptualisation of a subject should also be considered in the perspective of the different processes contributing to a good conceptualisation and on its diffusion, and not only on the visible results of this conceptualisation (such as textual definitions or narratives). This conceptualisation can bring a less visible result such as the better awareness of the subject being conceptualised, or motivating conditions keeping this conceptualisation up-to-date also represent tangible values. Practically, processes contributing to contextualisation can result in the setting-up of the conditions for good communication and coordination between the different stakeholders participating in the conceptualisation as well as the diffusion of the concepts. The objective is to facilitate the creation or the reaching of a common understanding accommodating the different perspectives and resulting from the interaction between the different actors, the confrontation of ideas and perspectives, and the forming of a consensus. The objective is also to support the participatory elaboration of the different concepts both for the formal and the informal definition of the concepts.

A number of processes and mechanisms can be made available to support a community in defining formally or more informally a set of concepts such as review and quality controls, committees or more informal discussions. More interestingly, the Internet, and more particularly the Web 2.0, has come with a whole set of solutions allowing groups and communities to participate collaboratively on a subject such as Wikis, blogging or social bookmarking. Each of these tools, often referred to using the term social media, contributes in its manner in the elaboration of definitions, in the exposition of situations or in the emergence of a common understanding in the community. In the next paragraphs, we will provide a brief survey of these new tools and indicate for each of them how they can contribute to the conceptualisation process.

Wikis

Wikis represent the most obvious tool for supporting the contextualisation process. A Wiki is a set of linked Web pages created through incremental development by a group of collaborating users as well as the software used to manage the set of

[11] Douglas Adams' 'The Hitchhiker's Guide to the Galaxy' (Pan Books, London, 1979) is a famous science fiction comedy series and a novel which addresses cultural differences in a humorous way.

Web pages (Wagner, 2006). Practically a Wiki can be used to collaboratively conceptualise a domain, each of the pages corresponding to a particular term or concept to which everyone can participate. An important characteristic of Wikis is related to the open, very iterative, and quick post-approval process (changes are immediately effective, and errors are corrected afterwards) making the evolution of the content very dynamic and involving a large number of participants. This collaborative dimension is real and has proved to be effective, the 'edits correspond on average to an increase in article quality' and the quality of the articles is correlated to the number of distinct editors (Wilkinson and Huberman, 2008). Rafaeli and Ariel (2008) indicate in their research of Wikipedia[12], the most popular Wiki that is on the top 10 of the most visited web sites on the Internet, that Wikipedia is able to mobilise a high level of participation that makes it work in practice.

Yet Wikis are not without limitations such as the accuracy of their content, and the various level of participation of the authors contributing to their content. The reliability of information in a Wiki has been questioned (Lih, 2004) in particular related to Wikipedia and the possibility for everyone becoming an author. Tumlin et al. (2007) have also pointed out the risk of this category of system to shut down divergent thinking. However empirical studies do not seem to support the assertion of lack of reliability of Wikipedia (Chesney, 2006). Concerning participation in the case of Wikipedia, the proportion of lurkers (users that access the system but that never contribute) is very important since the number of more than 75,000 active contributors has to be compared with a number of unique visitors of about 50 million per month as of year 2008[13]. The question of motivation for participation by scholars in Wikis or other open collaboration systems also appears to represent a real challenge: Academics indeed get promoted via their publications that go through a strict review process; they therefore have little incentive to publish their work in the open. Besides, the possibility for anyone to update any content in a Wiki and the anonymity and the nature of the 'correctors' (self-proclaimed experts that are usually non academics and even students) put them in the situation in which their contribution can be challenged and modified, a situation of lack of control they may not feel comfortable with.

Blogs

Blogs represents another method that can be used to support the conceptualisation process. Personal blogs in particular offer the possibility for their authors to expose their beliefs and opinions (Nardi et al., 2004) using chronologically ordered short and informal texts from which the visitors can easily provide feedbacks. Besides, the mechanism of trackbacks allows the author of a posting when referencing another post, to automatically generate a bidirectional link between the two posts, allowing the creation of a web of links between related postings, contribut-

[12] Wikipedia: www.wikipedia.org/.

[13] Statistics provided by Wikipedia at : http://en.wikipedia.org/wiki/Wikipedia:About.

ing to relaying ideas and opinions in the blogosphere (a term meaning the space comprising all the blogs). This blogosphere can in particular be observed to identify trends in a domain (Klamma et al., 2007).

The nature of the content posted on a blog can be associated to short narratives, and represents a form that can be particular adapted for identifying issues, and in particular can be very useful in relaying news on the subject and adding comments (opinion and perspectives) on this news. Hence, in the domain of identity, a blog posting may relay the announcement of the stealing of a database of social security numbers, and may raise the issue of the increased risk associated with the disclosure of personal information in the Information Society. Comments on this post may indicate other data thefts, and for instance, add that 'no data is safe' when it is on the Internet. Other postings may just aim at sending a message to the blogosphere (i.e., as was done for communicating about the Budapest declaration[14]) so as to raise the attention of the community, and get some reaction from the Internet community.

If the advantages of blogging are undeniable, in particular by providing the way for a community to easily provide informal input helping to raise the attention of a community of the important issues, or at contributing to the emergence of new ideas, it has also many limitations. First, the knowledge collected may look shallow and unstructured, giving only a parcelised and diffused view of a domain, making it difficult to get the global picture of a topic. Second, its dominant usage may be in the relaying or information rather than the creation of new knowledge. Also, but this is the case of most collaborative systems, blogging raises the question of motivational issues: blogging, and more generally using social media, is a time consuming activity for reading and even more for contributing (Perez, 2008). Finally, the seeking of truth should be the driver for determining the scientific knowledge and not the conforming to the public opinion (the wisdom of the crowd).

Social Bookmarking and Tagging

Social bookmarking or collaborative tagging provides an extremely simple, distributed, not disruptive but powerful way for a community of people to share bookmarks of internet resources. Practically, a social bookmarking system (Hammond et al., 2005) such as del.icio.us[15] often takes the form of an Internet browser extension (plugin) allowing a user to bookmark an Internet site, and to associate keywords or tags. The bookmarks are recorded in a central server and made available to the whole community (Marlow et al., 2006; Golder and Huberman, 2006; Halpin et al., 2006; Naamann, 2006; Millen et al., 2005). When connecting to the

[14] The Budapest Declaration on Machine Readable Travel Documents is a Public declaration that was issued by FIDIS in September 2006 to raise the concern to the public to the risks associated by a security architecture related to the management of Machine Readable Travel Documents (MRTDs), and its current implementation in the European passport that creates some threats related to identity theft, and privacy.

[15] Del.icio.us http://delicious.com/.

social bookmarking server, an individual user is able to access his / her personal bookmarks, as well as the bookmarks from the whole community in a chronological manner, or via the different tags. This collection and categorisation of resources can also be done via specialised social bookmarking services aimed at organising academic papers such as CiteULike[16] or Connotea[17]. Finally, social tagging mechanisms are often present in many social media services such as Flickr[18] (photo sharing), YouTube[19] (video sharing), SlideShare[20] (Slides sharing) and blogs.

In the context of conceptualisation, social tagging can be used to annotate content (bookmarks, academic references, Medias) in a participatory way, i.e., to associate keywords or tags to this content, and also to collect resources that are relevant to a domain in a community. It can also help to identify the terms (the tags) that are the most frequently used in a community of users, and to raise the attention of these communities about the topics (terms) that are the more popular in that community. Tagging also improves the quality of information retrieval.

As for blogging, social bookmarking represents only a tool that enhances a participatory conceptualisation process, and does not pretend to conceptualise explicitly a domain. Yet, the process of tagging can be associated with a categorisation of the content making use of folksonomy (an emerging categorisation originating by the community of the users), and therefore contribute more to the elicitation of the knowledge than in the case of blogging. Besides, this categorisation can also be associated with the emergence and the adoption of a vocabulary of terms (the tags) by the community: the members by being aware of the more popular tags will be inclined to use the same tags, and therefore the same vocabulary to communicate. Again as in the case of other participatory mechanisms, the adoption of tagging practices is dependant upon the motivation of the participants. However, the cost of tagging content in social bookmaking services is usually very low, and more importantly tagging benefits the user at the individual level: people tag to organise their knowledge, and this work is made available to others without additional cost (Naaman, 2006). Tagging has also some limitations in terms of efficiency in the information retrieval process, related to the difficulty of determining the most adequate level of specificity of the tags to use to annotate a set of resources (Chi and Mytkowicz, 2008). Besides, the quality of tagging varies widely 'from tags that capture a key dimension of an entity to those that are profane, useless, or unintelligible' (Sen et al., 2007).

---

16 CiteULike. http://www.citeulike.org/.
17 Connotea. http://www.connotea.org/.
18 Flickr http://www.flickr.com/.
19 YouTube http://www.youtube.com/.
20 SlideShare http://www.slideshare.net/.

Other Tools (Social Networking, Virtual Worlds, Information Aggregators, etc.)

The Web 2.0 has also proposed a variety of other mechanisms and tools that can be used to support the collaboration process in a community and that can therefore contribute to a participatory conceptualisation process. Social networking systems (Boyd and Ellison, 2007) such as Facebook[21], LinkedIn[22] or Ning[23] can be used to support the creation of social structures (such as groups or social networks) and the diffusion of social awareness (via the activity streams that these systems make available) contributing to the creation of trust, common culture, and therefore facilitating collaboration in particular with people weakly connected (Granovetter, 1973; Brzozowski, Hogg and Szabo, 2008). Virtual worlds (Mennecke et al., 2008) such as Second Life[24] represent another category of system that can be used to support the collaboration of a community by offering the possibility to their members to interact in 3D digital spaces, each member appearing to the others via avatars. Virtual worlds may also be used to simulate a situation. Thus in the case of the identity concept, a virtual world could be used to create games in which the participants could experiment with some issues such as testing the usage related to the control of an identity card at a check point, or how to develop a totally new digital identity.

Information aggregators like Netvibes[25] allow syndicating streams of content available as RSS feeds that other web sites have published (Gill, 2005). The categories of this content are very large and can include news headline, but also a variety of other things that Web 2.0 systems (blogs, Wiki, social tagging, social networking, etc.) generally export. These aggregators therefore allow collecting in a single place the many categories of activities related to the conceptualisation process in a community such as news headlines, latest changes in the Wikis, latest posts in the blogs, last items tagged with a particular keyword relevant to this domain, streams of activities in a social network, life streams, etc.

2.3 Identity of Identity Defined (Formal Conceptualisation)

In the previous section, we showed that conceptualisation of knowledge could be done in a formal or an informal manner. In this section will look at applying formal conceptualisation for defining the identity concept.

21 Facebook http://www.facebook.com/.
22 LinkedIn http://www.linkedin.com/.
23 Ning http://www.ning.com/.
24 Second Life http://www.secondlife.com/.
25 NetVibes http://www.netvibes.com/.

2.3.1 The Concepts of Identity and Identification

This part is based on some work[26] that was conducted as part of FIDIS to understand how the concept of identity is perceived by identity experts. In this work it was observed that experts approach the concept of identity according to one of the following perspective:

1. **A structural perspective: Identity as a representation.** *Identity* is seen as a set of attributes characterising the person.
2. **A process perspective: Identity for identification.** *Identity* is considered according to a set of processes relating to disclosure of information about the person and usage of this information.

These two perspectives should be considered as complementary: a broader model consists in viewing the concept of identity in the perspective of persons defined by a set of characteristics (the personal information), and involved in a series of processes making use of this information. More specifically, this personal information is used to authenticate a person, to grant authorisation, and also to support the actions of this person (such as when this information is used to personalise the interaction). Yet each category of expert perceives the concept of identity according to a very different vision leading to a different focus.

Experts in the first category are interested in understanding the different facets of the person, as well as concepts such as partial identity, and how it can be applied in different contexts. For these experts, identity is used to refer to a set of attributes (permanent or temporary) describing the characteristics of the person in the context of practical activities. In the case of a working context, these attributes may relate to the competency of a person and the function of the person in the organisation (such as the position), and intervene in a scenario in which competency represents an important factor of success in the accomplishment of a goal.

The experts in the second category are more interested by identity in the perspective of disclosure of the information for identification purposes so as to define the boundaries of people's actions. For these experts, identity refers to the elements that can be used to identify the person and to link her to some authorisation, and for which a good illustration is the Id card. The elements that may intervene in this identity include the name of a person, her position in the organisation, photograph, fingerprints, genetic characteristics and even behavioural patterns. In the case of the working context, this identity may be used in the identification process to grant a person access to a resource (such as a building or an information system) or give her the right to execute a transaction (such as signing a contract).

Another distinction between two concepts of identity has been advanced in philosophy by Paul Ricoeur with the concepts of ipse-identity and idem-identity (Hildebrandt, 2006; Ricoeur, 1992). The ipse-identity refers to the identity of a

[26] A more complete presentation of this work is available in (Nabeth and Hildebrand, 2005).

living person representing who the person really is (from a philosophical point of view). It is fundamentally fluid and indeterminate, and is out of the reach of the information and identification technologies. The idem-identity refers to the reductive characterisation of a person. It is static even if it is regularly upgraded, and is the only one explicitly formalised and manipulated by information and identification technologies. We will not try to draw a parallel between the structural perspective / process perspective and the ipse-identity / idem-identity, although it would probably make sense. We will only use this latter example of conceptualisation of identity to point out its complex nature, and in particular the existence of very different perspectives of this concept.

The Multiple Facets of Identity

Identity is not a topic only reserved to a small group of specialists. It intervenes very concretely in many facets of people's lives: their geographical mobility (dealing with the crossing of territories); their private life (dealing with their hobbies, romance, etc.); their family life (dealing with their marital status, their family structure); their social life (dealing with their friends, and their affiliation to groups); their work life (dealing with role, position, responsibility) and the way they conduct busi-

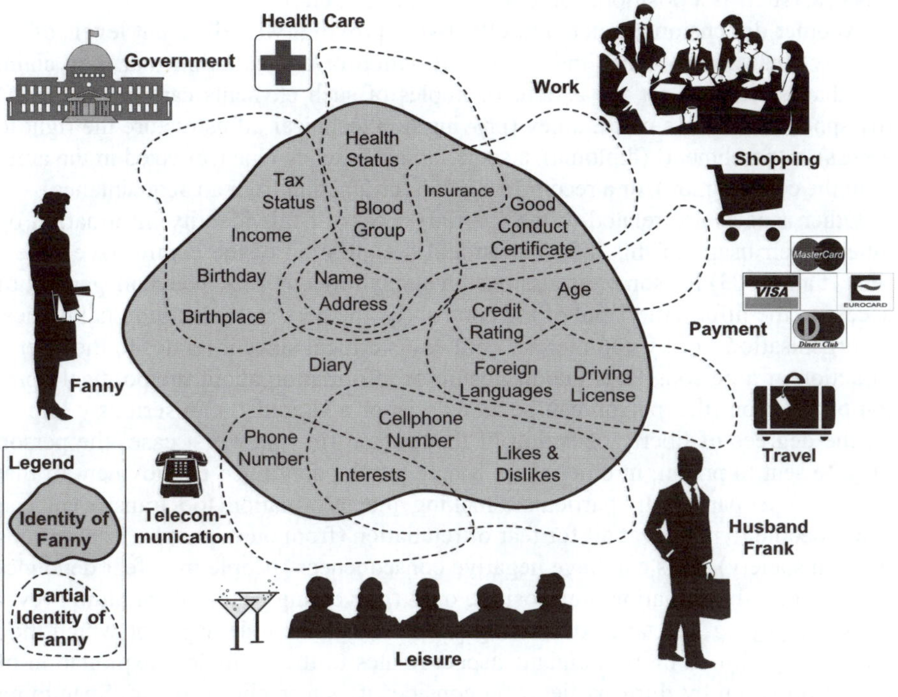

Fig. 2.1. Schema: Fanny's partial identities (Clauß and Köhntopp, 2001), with the permission of Marit Hansen

ness activities (dealing with contracting, reputation, …); their life as a citizen (dealing with voting, and participation in communal life); their biological life (dealing with healthcare); their life as a customer (dealing with transaction); etc. Figure 2.1 helps to illustrate this multiple nature.

In practice, in each of these different portions of life, identity and identification issues can occur, and take different forms.

First, identity and identification issues can relate to the legitimacy of acting because of the affiliation to a particular group (country, company, social group) or given the prerogatives (authority, right, etc.) attached to a particular accreditation (role in an organisation, diploma, recognised competence, bank account, etc.). Hence citizenship can give you access to some social benefits or the right to travel and work in another country; a diploma or other such proof of competence can allow you to apply for a job position and later to exercise this profession; friendship opens up the possibility of asking for 'and obtaining' free service from another person (the friend). Consequently, as individuals take on many different roles in the course of their life, different sets of characteristics, corresponding to these different roles, are used to represent their identity. Each of these 'partial identities' includes both inherited 'timeless' characteristics (such as nationality, gender, etc.) and characteristics that they have acquired during their life (such as diplomas, competences, etc.), or that they have been assigned or issued to fulfil this role (such as a position, some sort of authority, etc.).

Another dimension is related to effectively proving (with different levels of reliability) that a person has indeed the affiliation or accreditation that they claim and that is required for the action. Examples of such elements can include an ID (passport, or business card), a key (proving to a technical infrastructure the right to access), a 'parchment' (diploma), a social or competency clue (reflected in the attire or in the conversation), or a recommendation (originating from an acquaintance).

Other aspects are related to the (partial) access of this identity information by others, their usage of this information and the question of the control (see Claessens et al. (2003) for some discussions on anonymity control). The management of access to the information and of the control (by the person, by institutional bodies, by organisations, or by commercial entities) is critical since it relates to the liberty of action of a person. Thus the disclosure of information about the political opinion of a person (this person can be an activist or a Unionist) can seriously impact on the degrees of liberty of action of that person (in 'the worst case' the person may be sent to prison, in other cases it may put the continued employment of that person in jeopardy). In particular, making the information too transparent can cause people to not act at all for fear of retaliation (from other people, from groups or from society). This can have negative consequences (people may fear denouncing unacceptable situations) or positive ones (preventing people from hiding revenues and paying less taxes or making people liable for a damage for which they are responsible). A more mundane aspect relates to the shameless exploitation of this information by third parties who consider it as a public resource. Spamming (direct marketing of mass emailing) represents one of the most irritating consequences of this.

2.3.2 (Self-)Identity Concepts. Some Models

The notion of Identity is related to the characterisation and representation of a person (physical or moral) or of a group, and is concerned with the structure of this characterisation. For instance, Identity can be categorised according to different facets such as the personal Identity (personal), the biologic Identity (DNA), social Identity (membership), or the legal Identity and articulates them with their usage in different situations (such as leisure activities, transactions, work or social interaction). The concept of Identity can be applied to a physical, a moral or an abstract person (such as an organisation or group). Notably, many different possible categorisations of identity information exist.

The I, the Implicit Me, and the Explicit Me

Without having to go too deep into the psychological realm, it may be useful to make a rudimentary distinction between:

- *The I:* the indeterminate first person perspective
- *The implicit me:* how a person perceives herself
- *The explicit me:* how this person is perceived and represented (what is the image that this person provides to her environment).

These aspects establish the link between the living person, and her relationship to the external environment (the explicit me), the two being modulated by the (un)conscious perceptions a person has of herself (the implicit me) (Rost, 2003).

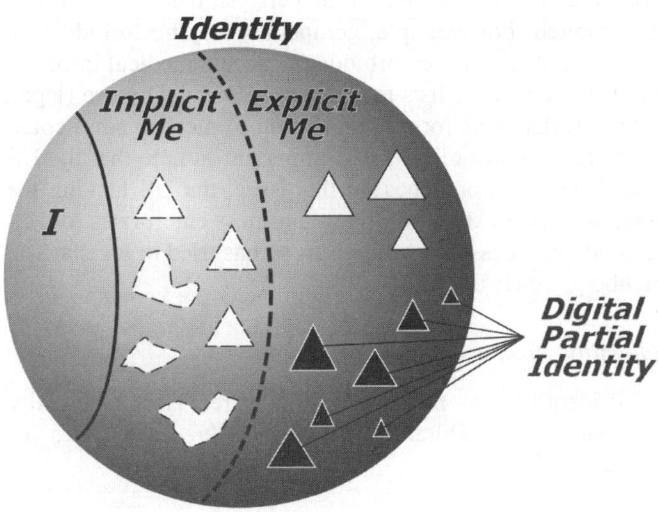

Fig. 2.2. The I, the Implicit Me and the Explicit Me (schema from (ICPP, 2003), with the permission of Marit Hansen)

This categorisation is important because it helps to raise and address two issues:

Acknowledging and addressing the Imperfection of the representation: Firstly it demonstrates that the access and representation of a person is only imperfect (incorrect) and partial since it is always a reduction of the person to objectifiable attributes. As mentioned before, much care should be taken to acknowledge this. Indeed, conflicts and problems typically arise in the case of dissonance between the way a person perceives herself to be and the identity attributed to her. In real world situations, addressing this issue does not always mean just questioning the correctness of the information and providing some mechanisms for assessment, adjustment and correction, but also acknowledging that the objectified identity is never congruent with the living person. As to the correction of redundant or false information, European law imposes holders of personal information databases to explicitly provide some mechanisms allowing a person to rectify incorrect information.

The question of the Control: The second issue is related to the control of this information: a person really only controls a limited part of her identity information. A large part of this information is externally controlled: by governments or institutions, such as the tax office, the healthcare organisations, by companies, e.g., by the company employing this individual or by her bank; by commercial entities, such as marketing firms; or by 'public opinion', such as newspapers or informal networks. Finding better ways to restrict an external entity from storing, manipulating and exploiting personal information may help address this issue. Some mechanisms (legal, technical, etc.) can be used to enforce good practices when an entity (governmental, commercial, …) manages personal information, such as defining what kind of information a certain category of entity is entitled to store, what kind of operation can be conducted on the personal data file, and how this information can be exploited. For example, companies may be forbidden to store medical information, the police may be forbidden to access medical information and the commerce of some customer lists may not be allowed. Diverse (legal, technical, educational, etc.) mechanisms (or a combination of mechanisms) could be used for this purpose. In the domain of law, it is important to note that the US and Europe have adopted different approaches on this issue, the US leaving the regulation of such matters, to a large extent, to private business enterprises (developing codes of conduct, good practices etc.), while Europe has tried to legislate on this issue (Agre and Rotenberg, 2001; Lessig, 1999).

True Identity, Assigned Identity, Abstracted Identity

A second categorisation of identity is as presented in the Three Tiers of Identity (Durand, 2002). In this model, Andre Durand distinguishes three categories (or tiers) of identities:

- *Tier 1:* The personal identity (the inner and timeless identity). This is the true personal identity that is owned and controlled entirely by the person.

- *Tier 2:* The corporate identity (the assigned identity). This identity relates to a particular context (for instance a business relationship) and represents a temporary assigned or issued characteristic for the person such as: a job title, phone number, etc.
- *Tier 3:* The marketing identity (the abstracted or aggregated identity). This identity is more diffuse, and corresponds to some result of profiling. The person is not really considered as an individual (this person does not have a name), but as the result of filtering performed on a given set of characteristics. An example could be: 'the customer belonging to the 'upper-level' social category, middle-aged, having a car more than three years old, playing golf, and living in one of the cities on the East-coast', who is contacted by a salesperson.

While this model may appear too simplistic to capture all the complexity of the Identity concept, it introduces several properties to Identity: its temporality, its conditionality, and its concreteness. What is the impact of this model on the way we capture the Identity related issues?

Temporality & Conditionality: The Personal Identity represents an inherent property of the person and is both timeless and unconditional. The Corporate Identity is, on the contrary, conditional and temporary, and exists in a given context. This later identity can also be considered as attached to a person, rather than being part of the person. These concepts have some similarity with the Ipse and Idem identity of Paul Ricoeur, mentioned previously.

These properties of temporality and conditionality are important in the context of the management of the Identity because it allows a distinction between two facets that may be managed differently.

The first one is very important to the person and should therefore be controlled as much as possible by that person herself (or by very trustworthy third entities) and strongly protected. Indeed threats on this 'pervasive' identity (it intervenes in the many facets of life of a person) will have some more serious consequences for the person since it can potentially impact many parts of her life and for a long time. For instance, the thief of personal identity (done for the purpose of conducting illegal actions) has some impact on the reputation of the victim, who may suffer some consequences to her work (forbidding access to some jobs), her social life (isolating the person in society) or her personal life (destroying trust inside the family or in the circle of friends).

The second identity is more linked to the role of the person in a given situation and can be more subject to control by a third party. Besides, the critical aspect of protecting the individual with the management of this identity may be oriented towards transparency and accountability rather than the privacy dimension. This could be relevant for mitigating the responsibility of the individual, for instance in the case of actions done as a representative of an organisation, and for isolating the representation of this identity in a specific area.

Concreteness: It is also interesting to note that an identity may not have a formal existence, and can, in particular, be abstract. For instance, the marketing identity does not explicitly represent the identity of an individual person, but an abstraction to which the person can a posteriori identify herself or be identified. Another abstract identity relates to the group or organisational identification: a person belongs to a group or an organisation not because of some formal and official status (explicit affiliation or contract), but via an implicit identification. A person believes she is part of a group or an organisation because she shares the same (assumed) attributes that characterise that group or organisation (Dutton, Dukerich, and Harquail, 1994), or via a process whereby an individual's beliefs about an organisation become self-referential or self-defining (Pratt, 1998: 175).

The abstract nature of this identity (marketing or organisational) does not prevent some very concrete consequences in the real life of the person: First, by becoming the target of direct-marketing campaigns (spamming) or psychological manipulation (advertising). Second, because this profiling (extraction of identity and categorisation) may reinforce the social structural rigidity, and may prevent people from gaining access to some resources (such as getting a loan to buy a house, or accessing jobs of high social status) because of belonging to certain social categories. The management of identity should therefore be careful and put limits (given the performance of the technology, such as data-mining for profiling) on the uses that do not contribute to the well being of the person. On the more theoretical side, it may also support the transition between the social statuses of identities (Korotov, 2004).

Another emerging consideration is the possibility given by technology to 'concretise' this implicit identity, with the advent of a whole range of applications enabled by technology. For instance, social computing services (Li, 2004) that explicitly represent and exploit the social network of a person are now proposed to help manage identity information that until now was only implicit and hidden. This is not without raising some serious new issues, such as the invasion of the 'social private life' (Kahney, 2004) that identity systems will have to address, or the risks associated to a wrong perception or the real and substantive social position identity, and the biased social identity projected via the new information media (blogs, social networks, personal web pages). For instance, in the latter case, this may mean displaying an 'arranged identity' not really reflecting the reality, even unconsciously (for instance, people tend to identify themselves with organisations or groups with high social status or socially desirable features).

2.3.3 Terminology of Identity

We would like now to report some of the terminological work that was conducted in Nabeth and Hildebrandt (2005) and that consisted of defining a series of terms related to identity. This works as a starting point borrowed from the work that was conducted by some of the participants of the FIDIS and in particular from Hansen and Pfitzmann (2008)[27] and Modini (2005). Similar works have been conducted

---

27 Hansen and Pfitzmann (2008) is a continually evolving document.

by Sproule and Archer (2007) to define the terms related to identity
tity fraud, or the Lexicon that was developed by the Identity Gang
estingly, these terminological works can benefit from the Wiki co
that we have described previously, and actually several of them do,
FIDIS. Finally, FIDIS has also engaged in a collaboration with ISO (International Organisation for Standardisation) so as to contribute to the definition and the standardisation of the terms used in the identity domain.

In this section we will only provide an illustration of how concepts can be defined more individually.

The Concept of Unlinkability

> *'Unlinkability of two or more items of interest (IOIs, e.g., subjects, messages, actions, ...) from an attacker's perspective means that within the system (comprising these and possibly other items), the attacker cannot sufficiently distinguish whether these IOIs are related or not.'*
>
> Hansen and Pfitzmann, 2008

This definition of Unlinkablitly is general, and deals with unlinkability of any sort of 'items'. ISO (1999) provides another definition that is more focused on the user. It defines this concept as: '[Unlinkability] ensures that a user may make multiple uses of resources or services without others being able to link these uses together. [...] Unlinkability requires that users and / or subjects are unable to determine whether the same user caused certain specific operations in the system.'

We can also differentiate an 'absolute unlinkability' ('no determination of a link between uses') and 'relative unlinkability' (i.e., 'no change of knowledge about a link between uses').

Unlinkability of an item can in particular be partial, and 'protect' only some operations associated with this item. For instance, unlinkability of an item can only concern the linking with the originator of the item (such as the author of the message) or with the recipient of the item (the reader).

An example of an unlinkable item would be an anonymous message for which it is not possible to determine the identity of the author.

The Concept of Unobservability

> *'Unobservability is the state of IOIs (the items of interest) being indistinguishable from any IOI at all.'*
>
> Hansen and Pfitzmann, 2008

Note: ISO (1999) provides the following less general definition:

[28] Identity Gang Lexicon. http://wiki.idcommons.net/Lexicon.

'[Unobservability] ensures that a user may use a resource or service without others, especially third parties, being able to observe that the resource or service is being used. [...] Unobservability requires that users and/or subjects cannot determine whether an operation is being performed.'

Our approach is less user-focused and thus more general than the ISO approach. With the communication setting and the attacker model chosen in this text, our definition of unobservability shows the method by which it can be achieved: preventing distinguishability of IOIs. Thus, the ISO definition may be applied to different settings where attackers are prevented from observation by other means, e.g., by encapsulating the area of interest against third parties.

Unobservability is stronger than Unlinkability since it protects the content of an operation, and even its existence. Certainly, an unobservable item it unlinkable, since a precondition of linkability is the awareness of the existence of the item.

A similar concept is untraceability. The definition of the antonym is: 'traceability is the possibility to trace communication between application components and as such acquire private information'; traceability is the ability to obtain information about the communicating parties by observing the communication context (e.g., through the IP address).

An example of an unobservable item message would be a secret message for which other parties cannot be aware of its existence, and a fortiori, of its content.

2.3.4 Profiles of the Person, and Overview

Another conceptualisation work that was conducted in FIDIS was the identification of the different models for defining the profile of the person in different domains such as Human Resources, eLearning, mobility, or justice. The result of this work can be found in: Nabeth (2005). In this section, we only provide an extract of this work, and we invite the reader to access more complete information in Nabeth (2005).

Modelling the Person

Identity Management Systems (IMS), or systems that integrate an IMS component, use a variety of attributes to represent (model) a person and to later manage that person's information. For instance attributes can be used to represent the identifiers of a person (such as name or pseudonym), biological characteristics (gender, hair colour), location (permanent address or geo-location at a given time), competences (diploma, skills), social characteristics (affiliation to groups, friends), and even behaviours (personality or mood).

In some cases, standards and specifications have even been elaborated to facilitate the design and the interoperability of such systems. For instance LDAP schemas have been defined to specify how to represent person's information in directories. In the human resources domain, the HR-XML specification has been elaborated to standardise the way information about employees are represented in the management software (see Annex of Nabeth (2005) for an overview of different standards and specifications for people representation).

Actually, an important strand of research has been conducted for many years in user modelling, aiming at enhancing the interaction between users and systems via the design of adaptive systems (Fischer, 2001; Brusilovsky, 2001; Stephanidis, 2001; Kay, 2000; Fink and Kobsa, 2000, etc.). The goal of research on personalisation is to improve the efficiency and effectiveness of user interaction by taking into account the specificity of the person using the system (such as her cognitive style, or her competence) as well as the context of activity of this person (for instance the current tasks in which she is engaged or the organisational context (Nabeth et al., 2004)). Practically, adaptive systems are able to support users better by filtering the irrelevant information (reducing cognitive load), by delivering this information at the right time, by choosing a form of delivery that maximises its impact on users, or by proposing very contextualised help. Research on adaptive systems has been conducted for applications in a number of domains such as eLearning (Diogene, 2002), eCommerce (Kobsa et al., 2000) or knowledge management (Razmerita, 2004).

In this document, we propose a categorisation of the different attributes describing the person according to:

- A temporal perspective
- A functional perspective
- A domain perspective

Temporal categorisation: The different attributes can be first categorised by the level of permanence of the information they represent:

- *Permanent – given:* Some attributes are used to represent some permanent (given) characteristics that were given to a person and over which she usually has no influence. Examples include for instance the biological characteristics (gender, eye colour, fingerprint, etc.), some socio-cultural-economical characteristics (parents, country of birth, etc.), basic personality traits (for some psychologists such as Hans J. Eysenck, personality has an important genetic basis), etc. Some exceptions such as gender changing have to be made regarding the person's non-influence.

- *Permanent – acquired:* Some other attributes are used to represent permanent (acquired) characteristics that the person was able to acquire because of some circumstances or because of a deliberate action. Examples include qualification (either because of a deliberate action like graduating at a University or because of circumstances like learning a new foreign language during the stay in a country), and behavioural characteristics.

- *Persistent – situations:* Other attributes are used to represent a situation that is not permanent, but that has some persistence (for instance several years). Examples include the address of a person, a job position (title, employer, etc.), marital status, social status, or a network of friends.
- *Transient:* Finally, other attributes are used to represent very temporary situations that are attached to a particular context. Examples in this case include for instance the geographical position of a person at a given time or the mood of the person.

Functional categorisation: The attributes can also be categorised according to some functional characteristics. Examples of such categories of attributes include:

- identification (such as a name, the social security number, password)
- location (such as geographical location, addresses)
- biological characteristics (such as biometrics, age, …)
- personal – psychological (such as personality, psychological state, preferences)
- group – sociological (such as affiliations, social group, social networks)

Categorisation by domain: The attributes can also be grouped according to their application domain / activities in which these attributes are used such as:

- work (such as employer, title, roles, expertise, acquaintances, work context / tasks)
- education (such as university, degrees)
- leisure (such as pseudonyms used in chat spaces, friends, sexual preferences)
- government (such as registration information, tax services)
- justice and police (such as criminal files)
- health (such as social security number (ssn), medical information)

An Example of Categories of 'Biological' Attributes

The biological attributes represent the category that is used to represent the biological (or physiological) characteristics of a person. The representation of the biological characteristics can be done for several reasons such as identification, verification (access control), criminal investigation or healthcare.

Biometrical information: The first category of attributes is related to the identification of the person and includes all the biometrical information. The underlying premise is that some of the biological characteristics are permanent, intimately associated with the person, difficult to forge and unique enough so that they can be used for identification purposes. For instance they can be used to link a person to a passport or, in the context of a criminal investigation, to link the presence of a person to the scene of a crime.

The biometrical characteristics can vary considerably, and include elements that are highly visible to the human (such as a Facial Feature) or need some sophisticated mechanisms to be analysed (such as the DNA). These characteristics can either be physiological (passive), such as iris or face recognition or behavioural (active), such as lip movement, gait or keystroke dynamics. Within the physiological biometric methods we can distinguish between morphological methods (such as facial features, iris, fingerprint or palm geometry) and those being related to the senses (including voice, thermal patterns, body odour etc.). Biometric methods and their use for identification and verification are investigated further in FIDIS D3.2.

Physiological & medical information (patient data): Another category of biological information is related to healthcare and includes the physiological characteristics that can be recorded in a medical record. Examples of biological information that can be recorder include: blood characteristics (pressure, level of albumin, cholesterol, etc.), known disease, etc.

It is important to mention that the use of these physiological characteristics can also be relevant outside of the medical domain, such as ability to practice a sport or to perform a job, insurance, etc., though in some case it raises a series of questions related to privacy protection.

Example of attributes:

- Biometric
  - Physiological (or passive)
    - Morphology
      - ⇒ Facial features
      - ⇒ Fingerprint
      - ⇒ Palm geometry
    - Senses
      - ⇒ Voice
      - ⇒ Body odour
      - ⇒ Thermal patterns
    - Other
      - ⇒ DNA
  - Behavioural (or active)
    - Gait
    - Lip movement
    - Keystroke dynamics

- Physiological and medical
  - Physiology
    - Sex
    - Weight
    - Length
    - Strength
    - Biological clock (morning / evening)
  - State
    - Awake / asleep
  - Health characteristics
    - Known diseases
    - Vaccinations
  - Health instant state
    - Blood pressure
    - Body temperature

Standards and Specifications

Several formats and standards have been elaborated in different domains to represent the person in information systems. For instance IMS-LIP is used to model the person in eLearning systems, HR-XML is used in Human Resource management system and JXDM is used in the domain of Justice[29]. Most standards specify some attributes which have identification as a principal role. For instance the name of a person, if present, is the major representation specification in LDAP, vCard, HR-XML, IMS-LIP, JXDM, etc. Some specifications are however addressing more specifically the identification dimension, and in particular provide more sophisticated 'identification attributes'. For instance, the LDAP schema includes the 'identification attributes' password and user certificate, and JXDM (used in the US) includes an attribute that is used to specify many (14) assigned ids of a person (SSNID, TaxID, DriverLicenseID, FBIID, StateID, AFISID, OtherID, Registered-OffenderIndicator, FirearmSalesDisqualifiedIndicator, LicenseID, GeneralLedger-ID, PersonHumanResourcesID, PersonVendorID, PersonNationalID).

2.4 Identity Use Cases and Scenarios

This section will present a set of use cases or scenarios that were elaborated by the FIDIS Network of excellence in order to identify and to illustrate concretely identity issues, and that are also available in the booklet 'Identity in a Networked

[29] See Nabeth (2005) for a more extended list, as well as their description.

World – Use Cases and Scenarios' (Jaquet-Chiffelle et al., 2006).[30] In this chapter, we have selected four (out of the seven in the booklet) cases and scenarios.

2.4.1 Virtual Online Social Environments, Real Identities Issues[31]

Abstract. The new Internet of Blogs, Wikis, online social networking and reputation systems, represent new virtual social environments in which rich identities are created. Although these environments are only virtual, they raise real identity issues.

The Internet has very much become a social space. People develop real and long-term friendships or relationships (online dating) in online communities (Friendster) and online games (MMORPG – Massively Multi-users Online Role Playing Games) with people they have never met in the 'physical word' and that they will probably never meet. They use online networking systems such as LinkedIn to better manage their relationships, for instance to find a job. Online vendors develop reputations in commercial spaces such as eBay. Knowledge worker create blogs as knowledge exchange channels to interact with other professionals, or to present themselves to potential employers. People participate collaboratively in the construction of online encyclopaedias such as Wikipedia. Children use MSN, or eSpace to interact with other children that they know in the physical world, or that they have only met in these virtual spaces. By doing this, people are dedicating an increasing amount of their leisure and work time, money, and emotional involvement in these spaces, which are becoming an integrated part of their life.

Identity in Virtual Environments

The reader of these lines may say 'Ok, I have understood why these online worlds are important; but can you tell me more about the online identities that people develop in these worlds and what makes them special?' Identity is particularly important in virtual environments. Since virtual environments are usually not supervised (people participate on a totally voluntary basis), the quality of the interaction that people develop in these spaces is strongly correlated to the image that people project of themselves. For instance, an effective interaction is very dependant on the level of trust between the participants involved in that interaction.

Identities in virtual environments are complex, and include both the explicit personal identities (real or faked) that are managed via digital identity management systems or declared by people when they fill in a profile (see Figure 2.3 for a screenshot of user profiles).

---

[30] The full booklet can be downloaded at http://www.fidis.net/resources/networked-world/.

[31] Scenario by Thierry Nabeth (INSEAD) – taken from http://www.fidis.net/resources/networked-world/.

Fig. 2.3. Multiple online identities

More interestingly, they also include all the implicit social identities (such as reputation, social networks) that people develop via their online behaviours (when they post, discuss, act). This latter 'social identity', sometimes summarised as 'you are who your network is', possesses a particular significance in the digital worlds, since contrary to the off-line world, it is made persistent, and can be explicitly represented (people's relationships are for instance captured in social network services software, behavioural traces are present in log files, etc.). This behavioural information can later be exploited for instance in reputation systems to help in the forming (via social translucence mechanisms) of online reputations (one major component of social identity), and can even be mined and be the subject of profiling operations for automated utilisations.

Cases of Real Identity Issues in Virtual Environments

To conclude, we would like to list a number of examples that illustrate some Identity issues that have occurred in virtual worlds.

A short case of email identity forging, and the consequences for a person's reputation. In October 1994, someone broke into the computer account of Grady

Blount, a professor of environmental science at Texas A&M University, and sent out racist email to more than 20,000 people on the Internet[32]. The message brought death threats and other harsh responses from nearly 500 users and seriously harmed the reputation of this professor, and threatened his career (Blount said that even his research grants were put in jeopardy as a result of the incident.)

The blurring of public / private identity: being fired after posting on a blog. 'If you've got a blog and a job, beware. The two sometimes don't go together, as many ex-workers are finding out'. Metz (2004)[33] reports several cases of problems that have occurred for people who posted on a personal blog. Concretely, a flight attendant in Texas, a temporary employee in Washington and a web designer in Utah were all fired for posting content on their blogs that their companies disapproved of. They wrongly assumed that their personal blog only belonged to their private sphere.

Approaches for isolating life spheres: Multiple identities. 'I soon found myself behaving in different ways on different networks. On Friendster, I looked for people to date. On Tribe.net, I joined tribes and participated in discussions. On LinkedIn, a business-oriented service, I didn't do much of anything at all. On Orkut, I went friend-crazy. Orkut was where "my" people were hanging out, the geeks and techies and online journalists', (Leonard Andrew, 2004)[34]. This example illustrates how an experienced 'netizen' organises his 'online social network life' to isolate different life spheres (dating, discussion, business, …).

Beware of online reputation: Fraud at eBay. Should knowing about the seriousness of a vendor from the aggregated feedback of many participants in a marketplace provide a strong sense of security or not? Warner Melanie (2003) in an article[35] suggests that people should think twice before trusting too much an identity reflected by a reputation system. Jay Nelson was able to extract $200,000 on eBay, before being caught and his real identity revealed. Jay Nelson had an excellent reputation on eBay however. It just happened that Nelson managed to use several strategies to boost his eBay reputation, such as: multiple user IDs (that he used to generously give himself rave reviews), but also initially selling computers legitimately to create the illusion of authenticity. By the time negative feedback started rolling in from his subsequent fake auctions, Nelson had adopted a new online identity.

---

[32] Stolen account used to send hate mail at Texas A&M : RISKS 16 (51), 27 October 1994. url: http://catless.ncl.ac.uk/Risks/16.51.html.

[33] Metz Rachel (2004); Blogs May Be a Wealth Hazard; Wired magazine, December 6, 2004 url: http://www.wired.com/news/culture/0,1284,65912,00.html.

[34] Leonard Andrew (2004), 'You are who you know', Salon.com, url: http://www.salon.com/tech/feature/2004/06/15/social_software_one/.

[35] Warner Melanie (2003); eBay's Worst Nightmare; FORTUNE, Monday, May 26, 2003 url: http://money.cnn.com/magazines/fortune/fortune_archive/2003/05/26/343106/.

2.4.2 Real Life in Virtual Worlds – Anthropological Analysis of MMO Games[36]

Abstract. Switching, undertaking, using and dropping roles and identities is as old as human civilisation. The phenomenon lives on in the age of the information society with the appearance of a new factor, network identity. ***Network identity***, although it is to a great extent determined by technological circumstances, is a human set of identities.

MMO (Massively Multiplayer Online) games are becoming more and more popular and fashionable nowadays. In the virtual world of Everquest there was a time when 12,000 players played simultaneously! World of Warcraft (see Figure 2.4 for a screenshot) had 3 million subscribers within half a year; the MMO games attract an even bigger user base in Asia – a game named Yulgang could boast 9 million subscribers within a month. Although the game style has existed for quite a long time – for almost ten years – it is only these days that an explosive growth of the market can be observed. With this growth several sub-types are generated of course, every developer tries to come up with something new, and also professionalism can be observed on a higher level.

MMO games are not only characterised by the fact that they can be played exclusively online, but also that the aim of the game is not to go through a pre-written story line, but life in a virtual world. Tens of millions of people play such games all over the world. Among them there are some who only identify themselves with a particular character temporarily, but some do so for years. The identity of the MMO players is made special by the responsibility associated with the character, which can derive from loving the character or simply from the fact that the game is paid for. It is also important that these characters not only have online but offline identities during the game, and there is a triple twist to it, namely the identity they take up in the virtual world. These identities overlap, and mutually strengthen one another.

Research has proved eloquently that, during the game, characters are not only having fun (although this is their primary purpose); they also get involved in economic activities, building relationships, careers, etc. The analysis of MMORPG communities constitutes a chance to analyse identity in different and unique ways: voluntary but strong identity; assumed identity; several oscillating identities; responsibility towards the identity; power to build and shape community; intercultural environment, financial risk; levels of anonymity and the role of technology in the preservation of identity, the issue of trust.

The real and the virtual worlds are connected in many ways, and the medium of these connections is of course the player himself. In an MMO game the participants play with several identities simultaneously: their real life identity (RL), their

[36] Scenario by Árpád Rab (ISRI) – taken from http://www.fidis.net/resources/networked-world/.

Fig. 2.4. World of Warcraft

role play identity (the character they personalise), as well as a virtual identity, which are connected to playing on a computer, such as anonymity, account etc. These identities mutually affect one another. A connection however does not only exist in the minds, but also on a physical level too.

2.4.3 Enjoy a Bar in 2012[37]

Abstract. The digitisation of life and particularly of identity may be regarded as a bottleneck in the engagement of citizens with Information Society services and particularly with Ambient Intelligence environments. The concept of identity in such environments presents two main aspects: multifacet and ubiquitous. This article deals with the concept of identity in this specific environment and describes the different facets of identity in the future.

In the Ambient Intelligence (AmI) space, a future environment combining off-line and on-line life, communications and exchanges of personal data (identity information) proliferate. The purpose of the AmI environment is to deliver seamless

[37] Scenario by Sabine Delaitre (JRC) – taken from http://www.fidis.net/resources/networked-world/.

applications and services to citizens in order to support their activities. Profiling activity is an essential and continuous background task and consists of extracting the useful information from the current context related to the user, identifying the users' needs, selecting and providing suitable services in order to allow that the AmI environment behaves according to the users' preferences, actions and expectations. Hence, the AmI vision is based on a user-driven approach with a goal to foster the integration of technology into our environment. Profiling activity thus involves the proliferation of communications, exchanges of personal user data, and identity information, and their storage by means of numerous types of technologies, sensors and devices. Therefore, a growing quantity of identity information will spread over many different systems and increase digitisation of authentication/ identification processes. This implies the omnipresence of identity information, but what kind of identity-related information is ubiquitously disseminated in AmI Space?

In AmI environments, we can split identity information into three types. (1) The 'off-line identity information' can be related to appearance such as hair, eye colour, etc.; used as social information, e.g., name, postal address, phone number; and represented by identity tokens (passport, credit card, security social number, bank account number). (2) The 'digital identity or on-line identity information' can be described in the same way. For example, the information related to the

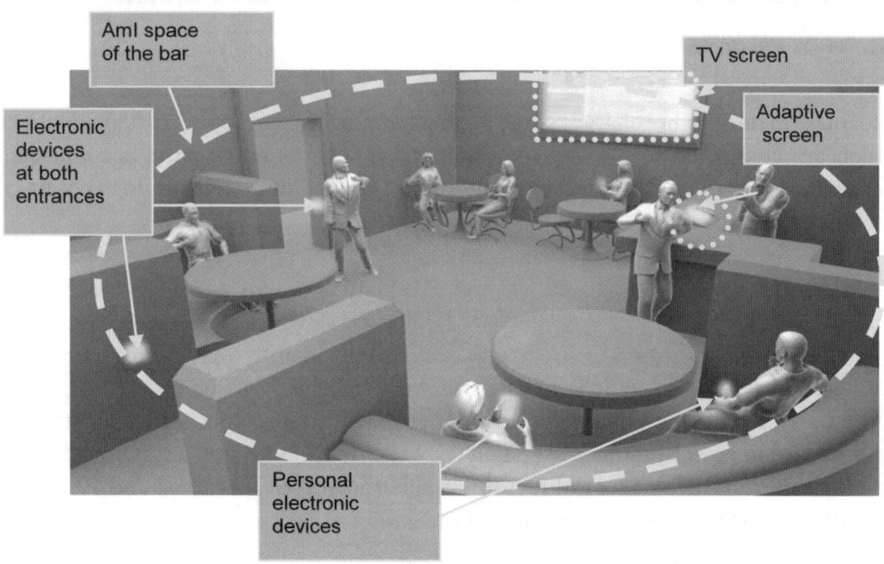

Fig. 2.5. A scene in a bar in 2012 – background image source (Beslay et al, 2005)[38]

[38] Beslay, L. and Hakala, H. (2005), 'Digital Territories: Bubbles', In *European Visions for the Knowledge Age: a Quest for New Horizons in the Information Society (the Vision Book)*, Macclesfield, UK, Cheshire Henbury.

appearance can be incorporated into a biometric template. (3) And finally 'identity information bridging offline and digital Identities' that is represented by the 'knowledge-based' identification (e.g., password, PIN) and information gathered from the user context (e.g., a user profile).

In what way does AmI shape the environment of a bar in the future? This scene (see Figure 2.5) helps describe the hypothetical features of such a bar, a specific public AmI environment.

First of all at both entrances, we can observe electronic devices (e.g., for the detection of new customers or the transmission of information); on the wall a special TV; at the bar an adaptive screen and personal electronic devices (e.g., a PDA) for some customers. The AmI space of the bar is symbolised by the dashed oval: this determines the space in which communications are enabled and all devices can interact.

The story is composed of four moments: the customer (i.e., the user of the AmI environment) enters into the bar (place), enjoys a moment at the bar, is fortunate enough to have a chance encounter and finally, he pays for the drinks.

Story: Enjoy a Bar in 2012

Entry into the bar: The customer *declares* his *preferences* (using his PDA protected by a PIN code) and *activates* his availability to meet a *friend* (Thus, the following data are transmitted – to the adaptive screen for example: his favourite drink, language etc., his user specificities, e.g. prescribed medication and list of friends).

At the bar: Barman: *'do you want a cappuccino?'* (the transmitted favourite drink). The adaptive screen shows him the soft drink options (it knows he cannot have alcohol because of his medication).

Thanks to his *electronic device* he 'watches TV in the language of his choice (preference)'. (More precisely, he listens to the sound in the language of his choice through his PDA and the corresponding image is displayed on the TV screen).

Chance encounter: An alarm *notifies* him a friend has arrived. After a nice conversation with his friend, he decides to leave.

Payment: He chooses whether to pay with *fingerprint mode* or with *RFID* (Radio Frequency IDentification) card from his local account.

Each term in italics is related to the identity concept. Table 2.1 presents some of these terms, which are ontologically described in order to examine the different facets of identity.

In this article, the concept of identity in the AmI environment has been examined. By the omnispresence of the identity related information involved in the AmI space, different facets of identity have been described and the ubiquitous aspect of the identity in the AmI space has been illustrated.

Table 2.1. Terms

Term	**Identity facet representation**
Preference(s)	Identifier → bridge offline and digital identities → related to the user context → profile representation → individual profile → preferences
Interaction: declares, activates, Or notifies him	Interaction → devices communication → access request → ID network (declaration) or ID electronic device (notification) → authorisation → Identifier(s) (communication of information) Remark: The declaration (declares) may be active (the user acts, e.g. pushes a button, sends information) or passive (the bar device detects the customer). activates refers to an active declaration
Friend	Identifier → bridge offline and digital identities → related to the user context → profile representation → individual profile → sociological profile → personal network (→ friends)
PDA, an electronic device	Identifier → digital identity → social information →ID electronic device → ID PDA
Fingerprint mode	1) Identity → data protection 2) Identity → storage → biometrics template Remark: Indeed, the fingerprint mode payment raises two important concepts related to the identity: the data protection and the storage of the fingerprint template

Table 2.2. Implicit terms

Implicit term	**Identity facet representation**
Fingerprint template (used by the fingerprint mode)	Identifier → digital identity → related to the appearance → biometric template

2.4.4 Tracing the Identity of a Money Launderer[39]

Abstract. In the information society, almost every aspect of daily life – from magazine subscriptions to financial transactions – is subject to being captured and incorporated in a database. The electronic traces are then used to develop models of who people are and what they do which, in turn, are used to inform decision-making in a variety of areas. One such area is crime prevention and detection, and this paper describes how profiling is used in the fight against money laundering.

---

[39] Scenario by Ana Isabel Canhoto and James Backhouse (LSE) – taken from http://www.fidis.net/resources/networked-world/.

Money Laundering: Definition and Methods

Money laundering refers to the processing of the financial proceeds resulting from criminal activity ranging from tax evasion and forgery, to drug- and people-trafficking[40,41]. The underlying principle is, in the words of the National Crime Intelligence Service: 'Most organised crime is not worth anything to a criminal unless they can launder the money. A high percentage of criminal gangs has money laundering as a secondary activity'[42].

Money launderers will use both the financial and the non-financial system to launder their money. The method involves three stages:

- *Placement* – When the money is introduced into the system. It will involve, for instance, the breaking up of large amounts of cash into smaller sums which, being less conspicuous, are less likely to draw the attention of the intermediary.
- *Layering* – A series of transactions to distance the funds from their source or destiny. In some instances, these transfers may be disguised as payments for goods or services to give them a legitimate appearance.
- *Integration* – When the funds re-enter the legitimate economy. For instance, through business ventures and the payment of tax.

Tools for Anti Money Laundering

One key component of the fight against money laundering is emerging in the development of models of who money launderers are and how they act. The modelling usually encompasses the use of automated monitoring tools – powerful algorithms that sweep the records in transaction databases for patterns of financial behaviour that deviate from the norm. The unusual behaviour only becomes a source for concern when there is no known legitimate source for the income or the observed lifestyle does not fit the one expected from someone with a specific legitimate economic activity: a sudden peak in a butcher's bank account may be due to the sale of a house rather than the reward from some criminal activity, for instance. It is crucial for financial investigators and other anti-money laundering agents to command a holistic picture of the identity of each person flagged by the automated monitoring systems.

---

[40] Since 2001, this definition has been extended to include the financing of terrorist activity, a practice referred to as 'reverse money laundering'.

[41] A thorough description of the typology of money launderers is available in Bell, R. E. (2002), 'An Introductory Who's Who for Money Laundering Investigators', Journal of Money Laundering Control 5 (4), pp. 287-295.

[42] An NCIS spokesman is quoted in Scotland on Sunday (13 April 2003). See Assets Recovery Update; Issue No 1 24 April 2003. http://www.assetsrecovery.gov.uk/MediaCentre/ProceedsOfCrimeUpdate/2003/Issue1240403.htm.

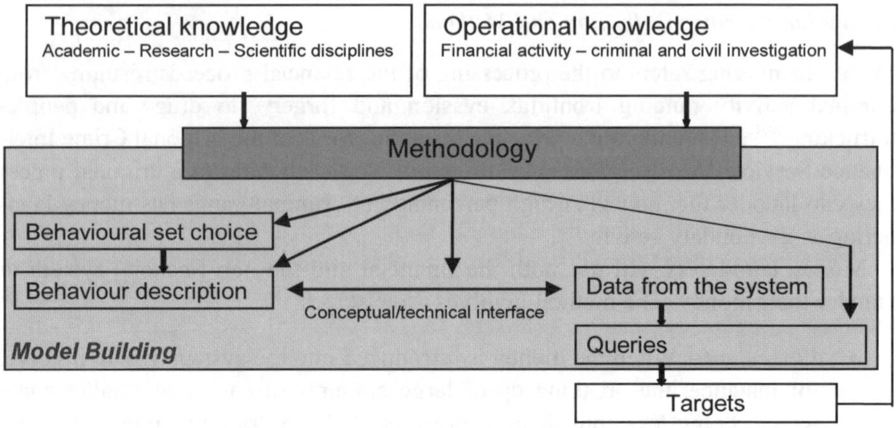

Fig. 2.6. Development of behaviour-based models to target money laundering suspicious activity

The Various Components of Identity

There are many aspects that contribute towards the identity of a person. In particular, the following four components of identity can be considered:

- *Socio-demographic characteristics* – Includes characteristics such as gender, age, ethnic group, household size, or employment status. It is based on the premise that demographic groups are relatively homogenous and lend themselves easily to quantification, measurement and classification.
- *Benefit sought*[43] – The benefits desired from pursuing certain behaviour, including the underlying motivation. It focuses on common values and attitudes across cultural groups.
- *Lifestyle adopted* – Focusing on options made regarding travel patterns, or the type of goods and services acquired, for instance.
- *Behaviour exhibited* – In relation to the financial institution. That is, based on data resulting from actions of the account holders, such as length of relationship with the bank, modes of payment and shopping preferences, product ownership, and contributions to political, religious, and charitable groups.

The next section illustrates a case widely covered in the British press to illustrate how the four components discussed above contributed to the development of the subject's identity as a money launderer and the problems it highlighted.

[43] Also referred to as psychographic profiling.

Case Study: the City PA

In the spring of 2004, Joyti De-Laurey, a personal assistant at Goldman Sachs in London, was convicted of stealing £4.3m from her bosses, through fraud and forgery, and laundering the proceeds of her crime with the help of her mother and her husband (a 50-year-old former chauffeur).

De-Laurey's gross salary with bonuses amounted to £42,000 a year[44]. Yet, during her time at Goldman Sachs, she acquired, among other things, a £750,000 seafront villa in Cyprus, £500,000 worth of furniture, £400,000 in jewellery, several top of the range cars and a £150,000 power boat[45]. The gap between her known source of income – a socio-demographic characteristic – and her exhibited lifestyle was enormous and led to alarms being raised by several financial institutions. This picture was compounded when, in court, it was revealed that De-Laurey was planning to start a new life with her family in Cyprus, and she had described herself on a school registration form[46] as a banker – an indication of the benefit sought with the behaviour pursued. The string of cheques with forged signatures being deposited into her account and, later, the transfer to Cyprus was considered suspicious behaviour. Similarly, the pattern of transfers between De-Laurey's bank accounts and those of her husband and mother implicated them in the associated money laundering charges.

The components of identity were used in order to identify De-Laurey and her associates as money launderers. The construction of someone else's identity is, however, not an objective process; rather it is one subject to the prejudices and judgment of those who engage in the identity construction exercise. Several suspicious transaction reports were filed against De-Laurey, yet the case of her being a money launderer took some time to build because, in the words of a financial investigator interviewed by the authors, she 'did not fit the typical money launderer profile: man, white, 40 years old'.

2.5 Making Use of the New (Web 2.0) Participatory Tools

In subsection 2.2.4 we presented the new participatory tools that have emerged as part of Web 2.0 and that include Wikis, blogs, social bookmarking, and social networking. In this section, we would like to present how these tools have been used in FIDIS to support the conceptualisation process of defining the identity concept. We will however be brief in our presentation, since these tools have not played a central place in the conceptualisation process, even thought we believe they represent an important potential for the future.

44 Kate Newman (2004), 'The power of a City PA', BBC News Online, London, 20 April, 2004, url: http://news.bbc.co.uk/1/hi/england/london/3629087.stm.

45 BBC News (2004), 'Fairy tale' world of crooked PA, BBC News Online, London, 20 April, 2004, url: http://news.bbc.co.uk/1/hi/england/london/3614597.stm.

46 Idem.

2.5.1 Web 2.0 Initiatives

FIDIS has explored the use of many of the new participatory tools as part of FIDIS Interactive.[47] This action was coordinated by a Steering group. Table FIDIS Web 2.0 initiatives in the appendix to this chapter summarises the different FIDIS Web 2.0 initiatives.

In some cases, the usage of these tools has been considered as potentially important, and some effort has been dedicated to make it work. This was the case with the creation of an internal collaborative platform for the project, as well as for the use of different Wikis (internal & Wikipedia). In some other cases, the usage of a tool was considered as nice to have, and able to generate value without requiring an important effort. The project therefore decided to create a blog, and to create a group in online social networking (OSN) services (in LinkedIn and in Facebook). Mechanisms were also used to explore their potential and as a way to learn about their functioning. Thus, different systems were tested such as social bookmarking services (del.icio.us), social bibliographic management service (such as CiteULike), some social platforms (AtGentNet and Ning) and an information aggregator (Netvibes). Finally other services were not used (or only indirectly), although they were considered as interesting, because of lack of time. Examples include the use of, rich social media (such as podcasting, video cast with YouTube or electronic presentations with SlideShare), or virtual worlds (such as Second Life).

2.5.2 Discussion

The idea of using Web 2.0 participatory tools to support in FIDIS the conceptualisation process of a community geographically distributed appeared very appealing. These different tools would help in supporting the creation of a shared understanding, as well as with the collaborative authoring of the definition of the concepts (thanks in particular to the Wiki systems). Therefore, it was decided to set-up a number of these systems such as Wikis, blogs, or social bookmarking and these are described in the appendix to this chapter. Yet, the difficulty of innovation adoption is not new (Rogers, 2003), and to the question 'If you build it, will they come?' the answer is generally 'no', unless you have prepared it to make it happen, and/ or waited enough time. This situation proved not to be different in the case of FIDIS, since the question of participation represented a real challenge, and was not fully addressed. We will not describe in detail here all the aspects related to the adoption of these participatory tools, since their role was considered as marginal in the conceptualisation process, which was focused on more traditional

[47] FIDIS Interactive: is a set of advanced services that have been set up to support the management of knowledge inside FIDIS, and which includes the Web 2.0 tools as well as other tools such as databases or bibliographies. http://www.fidis.net/interactive/.

methods. We will just indicate that some of these tools were adopted at a moderate level in the case of the collaborative platform or of the Wikis. In the latter case, FIDIS went back and forth in using an internal Wiki totally controlled, to the public Wikis of Wikipedia, none of the solutions being considered as totally satisfactory, but also each of them bringing its benefit. Some other tools such as the blog did not manage to get a momentum and had to be interrupted because of a lack of authors providing content. Finally some other tools such as the social bookmarking or social networking managed to get a momentum principally because of a few more involved participants.

To conclude this section, we will indicate that the advent of the new Web 2.0 participatory tools promises to support in a very effective way a collective conceptualisation process in the future. However, our experience in FIDIS is that this promise is not yet fulfilled, although we were able to observe the starting of an adoption that will need to be validated in the future. We believe that in the future we will see more and more the adoption of these tools to support the conceptualisation process, for the identity domain, or for other domains.

2.6 Conclusion and Outlooks

We would like to conclude this chapter not so much by a summary of the work of conceptualisation that we have conducted, but with a reflection about what happened to work and not to work in our endeavour of conceptualising the identity domain. Concerning identity, this concept has proven to be even richer and fuzzier than what we had predicted. Besides, this concept far from stabilising and converging to a well defined and delimited definition has seen a continuous transformation originating from the explosion of the new usages that emerged given the advent of new technologies and services such as online social systems, RFID tags, or location based services in mobile communications.

As a consequence, the less formal methods for defining meaning such as the use of narratives have proved to be very effective in a number of cases to understand the concept of identity, even if the benefit of the more formal methods should not be minimised.

As we gain more experience, and as we manage to aggregate more content of the subject of identity, we expect to see in the future a better articulation of the two kind of knowledge: a very formal knowledge favouring the theorisation of identity concept, and a less formal and more descriptive knowledge based on narratives able to more easily collect and disseminate the meanings amongst a large population of participants. We believe that the new Web 2.0 participatory tools that we have presented may represent the instruments that will enable this to happen, although it is difficult to predict the time frame in which this will happen.

References

AAAI (2004), 'Brief History of Artificial Intelligence', AAAI AI Topics dynamic library of introductory information about Artificial Intelligence, url: http://www.aaai.org/AITopics/bbhist.html

Agre, P. E. and Rotenberg, M. (ed.) (1998), Technology and Privacy: The New Landscape. Cambridge Massachussets: MIT Press.

ALRC (2008), For Your Information: Australian Privacy Law and Practice. ALRC (Australian Law Reform Commission) report 108, Canberra : Law Reform Commission.

Andrade, J., Ares, J., García, R., Pazos, J., Rodríguez, S., Silva, A. (2008), 'Formal conceptualisation as a basis for a more procedural knowledge management', Decision. Support System. 45 (1), pp. 164-179.

Ariely, D. (2008), Predictably Irrational: The Hidden Forces That Shape Our Decisions. HarperCollins.

Berners-Lee, T., Hendler, J., Lassila, O. (2001), 'The Semantic Web', Scientific American 284 (5), pp. 34-43.

Bjelland, T. K, (2004), 'Classification: assumptions and implications for conceptual modeling', doctoral dissertation, Department of Information Science and Media Studies, Faculty of Social Science, University of Bergen.

Boyd, D. and Ellison, N. (2007), 'Social Network Sites: Definition, History, and Scholarship', Journal of Computer-Mediated Communication 13 (1), article 11.

Brusilovsky, P. (2001), 'Adaptive Hypermedia', User Modeling and User-Adapted Interaction 11 (1-2), pp. 87-110.

Brzozowski, M., Hogg, T., Szabo, G. (2008), 'Friends and foes: Ideological social networking', Proceedings of the 26th annual SIGCHI Conference on Human Factors in Computing, ACM Press, pp. 817-820.

Chesney, T. (2006), 'An empirical examination of Wikipedia's credibility', First Monday 11 (11), url: http://firstmonday.org/issues/issue11_11/chesney/index.html.

Chi, E. H. and Mytkowicz, T. (2008), 'Understanding the efficiency of social tagging systems using information theory', Proceedings of the 19th ACM Conference on Hypertext and Hypermedia; NY: ACM, pp. 81-88, url: http://www.parc.com/research/publications/details.php?id=6294

Cialdini, R. B. (2001), Influence: Science and practice (4th ed.). Boston: Allyn & Bacon.

Claessens, J., Díaz, C., Nikova, S., De Win, B., Goemans, C., Loncke, M., Naessens, V., Seys, S., De Decker, B., Dumortier, J., Preneel, B. (2003), 'Applications Requirements for Controlled Anonymity', APES Deliverable D7.

Clark, H. H. and Brennan, S. E. (1991), 'Grounding in communication', in: Resnick, L. B., Levine, J., Behreno, S. D. (Eds.), Socially shared cognition.

Clauß, S. and Köhntopp, M. (2001), 'Identity Managements and Its Support of Multilateral Security', Computer Networks 37 (2), Special Issue on Electronic Business Systems, pp. 205-219.

Clynes, M. E. and Kline, N. S. (1960), 'Cyborgs and Space', Astronautics 14 (9), pp. 26-27 and 74-76.

Cunningham, W. and Leuf, B. (2001), The Wiki Way. Quick Collaboration on the Web, Addison-Wesley.

Davis, M. (2008), 'Semantic Wave 2008: Industry Roadmap to Web 3.0 and Multibillion Dollar Market Opportunities – Executive Summary', Project10X report January 2008. url: http://www.project10x.com/.

Denning, S. (2001), 'The Springboard: How Storytelling Ignites Action in Knowledge-era Organizations', Journal of Organizational Change Management 14 (6), pp. 609-614.

Diogene (2002), 'Survey on Methods and Standards for Student Modelling', Diogene project, url: http://www.diogene.org/archive.html.

Durand, A. (2002), 'Three Tiers of Identity', Digital Identity World, March 16, 2002.

Dutton, J., Dukerich, J., Harquail, C. (1994), 'Organizational Images and Member Identification', Administrative Science Quarterly, 39 (2), pp 239-263.

Epstein, R. (2007), 'The Truth About Online Dating', Scientific American Mind, February / March 2007, pp. 32-39.

Nabeth, T. (ed.) (2005b), FIDIS Deliverable D2.3: Models, Download: http://www.fidis.net/resources/deliverables/.

Fink, J. and Kobsa, A., (2000), 'A Review and Analysis of Commercial User Modeling Servers for Personalization on the World Wide Web', User Modeling and User Adapted Interaction, 10 (2-3), pp. 209-249.

Fischer, G. (2001), 'User Modeling in Human-Computer Interaction', User Modeling and User Adaptive Interaction 11 (1-2), pp. 65-86.

Gill, K. E. (2005), 'Blogging, RSS and the Information Landscape: A Look at Online News', In Proceedings of the 14th international WWW conference: 2nd annual workshop on weblogging ecosystem: aggregation, analysis and dynamics, 10 May 2005, Chiba, Japan.

Golder, S. and Huberman, B. A. (2006), 'Usage Patterns of Collaborative Tagging Systems', Journal of Information Science 32 (2), pp. 198-208.

Granovetter, M. (1973), 'The Strength of Weak Ties', American Journal of Sociology 78 (6), pp. 1360-80.

Gruber, T. (2008), 'Ontology', in: Liu, L. and Özsu, M. T. (eds.), The Encyclopedia of Database Systems. Springer-Verlag.

Halpin, H., Robu, V., Shepherd, H. (2006), 'The Dynamics and Semantics of Collaborative Tagging', Proceedings of the 16th international conference on World Wide Web, pp. 211 – 220.

Hammond, J. S. (1976), Learning by the case method. HBS Publishing Division, Harvard Business School, Boston, MA, Case #376-241.

Hammond, T., Hannay, T., Lund, B., Scott, J. (2005), 'Social Bookmarking Tools', D-Lib Magazine 11 (4), url: http://dlib.org/dlib/april05/hammond/04hammond.html.

Hansen, M. and Pfitzmann, A. (2008), 'Anonymity, Unobservability, Pseudonymity, and Identity Management – A Proposal for Terminology', Working document, url: http://dud.inf.tu-dresden.de/Anon_Terminology.shtml.

Hildebrandt, M. (2006), 'Privacy and Identity', in: Duff, A., Claes, E., Gutwirth, S. (eds.), Privacy and the criminal law, Antwerp/Oxford, Intersentia, pp. 43-57.

Holten, R. (2007), 'Deriving an IS-Theory from an Epistemological Position', Proceedings of the 18th Australasian Conference on Information Systems (ACIS 2007), Toowoomba, Australia.

ICPP (2003), 'Independent Centre for Privacy Protection (ICPP) Schleswig-Holstein and Studio Notarile Genghini (SNG)', Identity Management Systems (IMS): Identification and Comparison, study prepared under contract for Institute for Prospective Technological Studies, Joint Research Centre Seville, Spain, Sept. 2003, url: http://www.datenschutzzentrum.de/idmanage/study/ICPP_SNG_IMS-Study.pdf.

ISO (1999), ISO IS 15408, 1999, url: http://www.commoncriteria.org/.

Jaquet-Chiffelle, D.-O., Benoist, E., Anrig, B. (eds.) (2006), FIDIS Deliverable 2.6: Identity in a Networked World – Use Cases and Scenarios, Download: http://www.fidis.net/resources/networked-world/.

Kahney, L. (2004), 'Social Nets Not Making Friends', Wired magazine, January. 28, 2004, url: http://www.wired.com/culture/lifestyle/news/2004/01/62070.

Kay, J. (2000), 'User modeling for adaptation', in Constantine, S. (ed.), User Interfaces for All, Human Factors Series, Lawrence Erlbaum Associates, pp. 271-294.

Klamma, R., Y., Cao, M., Spaniol (2007), 'Watching the Blogosphere: Knowledge Sharing in the Web 2.0', Proceedings of the International Conference on Weblogs and Social Media, Boulder, Colorado, USA, pp. 105-112.

Kobsa, A., Koenemann, J., Pohl, W. (2000), 'Personalized hypermedia presentation techniques for improving online customer relationships', The Knowledge Engineering Review 16 (2), pp. 111-155.

Kogut, B. (2008), Knowledge, Options, and Institutions. Oxford University Press.

Korotov, K. (2004), '"Neither Here nor There" or "Both Here and There": Experiencing Liminality and Playing with Identity', Academy of Management Conference, New Orleans, August 6-11, 2004.

Lelic, S. (2002), 'Fuel Your Imagination. KM and the Art of Storytelling', Knowledge Management 5 (4).

Lessig, L. (1999), Code and Other Laws of Cyberspace. New York: Basic Books.

Lih, A. (2004), 'Wikipedia as Participatory Journalism: Reliable Sources? Metrics for evaluating collaborative media as a news alternative', 5th International Symposium on Online Journalism at the University of Texas at Austin.

Marlow, C., Naaman, M., Boyd, D., Davis, M. (2006), 'Position Paper, Tagging, Taxonomy, Flickr, Article, ToRead', Proceedings of Hypertext 2006, New York: ACM Press.

McAfee, A. P. (2006), 'Enterprise 2.0: The Dawn of Emergent Collaboration', Sloan Management Review 47 (3), pp. 21-28.

Millen, D., Feinberg, J., Kerr, B. (2005), 'Social Bookmarking in the Enterprise', ACM Queue 3 (9), pp. 28-35.

Mathes, A. (2004), 'Folksonomies – Cooperative Classification and Communication Through Shared Metadata', Graduate School of Library and Information Science, url: http://www.adammathes.com/academic/computer-mediated-communication/folksonomies.html.

McLellan, H. (2002), 'Introduction to Corporate Storytelling', url: http://tech-head.com/cstory1.htm.

Mennecke, B.E., McNeill, D., Ganis, M., Roche, E., Konsynski, B., Bray, D., Lester, Townsend, A.M. (2008), 'Second Life and other Virtual Worlds: A Roadmap for Research', Communications of the Association for Information Systems 22 (article 20), pp. 371-388.

Modini (2005), 'Modinis Study on Identity Management', in eGovernment, Common Terminological Framework for Interoperable Electronic Identity Management – Consultation Paper, v2.01, 23 November 2005, url: https://www.cosic.esat.kuleuven.be/modinis-idm/twiki/bin/view.cgi/Main/GlossaryDoc.

Naaman, M. (2006), 'Why Do Tagging Systems Work?', Conference on Human Factors in Computing Systems (CHI 2006), Panel session, pp. 36-39.

Nabeth, T., Angehrn, A. A., Balakrishnan, R. (2004), 'Integrating "Context" in e-Learning Systems Design', Proceedings of IEEE International Conference on Advanced Learning Technologies (ICALT 2004), pp. 355-359.

Nabeth, T. (ed.) (2005), FIDIS Deliverable D2.3: Models, Download: http://www.fidis.net/resources/deliverables/.

Nabeth, T. and Hildebrandt, M. (eds.) (2005), FIDIS Deliverable D2.1: Inventory of Topics and Clusters, Download: http://www.fidis.net/resources/deliverables/.

Nabeth, T., Karlsson, H., Angehrn, A. A., Maisonneuve, N. (2008), 'A Social Network Platform for Vocational Learning in the ITM Worldwide Network', Proceedings of IST Africa 2008.

Nardi, B. A., Schiano D. J., Gumbrecht, M. Swartz, L. (2004), 'Why We Blog', Communications of the ACM 47 (12), pp. 41-46.

Nisbett, R. (2003), The Geography of Thought: How Asians and Westerners Think Differently...and Why. Reed Business Information, Inc.

Nonaka, I. and Takeuchi, H. (1995), The Knowledge-Creating Company. New York: Oxford University Press.

O'Reilly, T. (2005), 'What Is Web 2.0 Design Patterns and Business Models for the Next Generation of Software', 30 September 2005, url: http://www.oreillynet.com/pub/a/oreilly/tim/news/2005/09/30/what-is-web-20.html.

Perez, S. (2008), 'Real People Don't Have Time for Social Media', ReadWriteWeb, April 16, 2008, url: http://www.readwriteweb.com/archives/real_people_dont_have_time_for_social_media.php.

Pratt, M. G. (1998), 'To Be Or Not To Be: Central Questions in Organizational Identification', in: David A. W., Paul G. (eds.), Identity in Organizations, Thousand Oaks: Sage, pp. 171-207.

Rafaeli, S. and Ariel, Y. (2008), 'Online motivational factors: Incentives for participation and contribution in Wikipedia', in: Azy, B. (ed.), Psychological aspects of cyberspace: Theory, research, applications, Cambridge, UK: Cambridge University Press, pp. 243-267, url: http://gsb.haifa.ac.il/~sheizaf/cyberpsych/11-RafaeliandAriel.pdf.

Razmerita, L., (2004), 'User modeling and personalization of the Knowledge Management Systems', Adaptable and Adaptive Hypermedia, Idea Group Publishing.

Resnick, P. and Zeckhauser, R. (2002), 'Trust Among Strangers in Internet Transactions: Empirical Analysis of eBay's Reputation System', The Economics of the Internet and E-Commerce, pp. 127-157.

Ricoeur, P. (1992), Oneself as another. Chicago and London: University of Chicago Press.

Rogers, E. (2003), Diffusion of Innovations (5th ed.). New York: Free Press.

Sen, S., Harper, F. M., LaPitz, A., Riedl, J. (2007), 'The Quest for Quality Tags', Proceedings of the 2007 international ACM conference on Supporting group work, pp. 361-370.

Snowden, D. (2001), 'Narrative patterns: the perils and possibilities of using story in organisations', Knowledge Management, 4 (10).

Snowden, D. (2002), 'Narrative patterns: uses of story in the third age of knowledge management', Journal of information and knowledge management, 1 (1), pp. 1-6.

Sole, D. and Wilson, D. (2002), 'Storytelling in organizations: The power and traps of using stories to share knowledge in organizations', Boston: LILA, Harvard Graduate School of Education, url: http://lila.pz.harvard.edu/_upload/lib/ACF14F3.pdf.

Sproule, S. and Archer, N. (2007), 'Defining Identity Theft', Eighth World Congress on the Management of eBusiness (WCMeB 2007), pp. 20-20.

Star, S. L. and Griesemer, J.R. (1989), 'Institutional Ecology, "Translations" and Boundary Objects: Amateurs and Professionals in Berkeley's Museum of Vertebrate Zoology', 1907-39; Social Studies of Science 19 (4), pp. 387–420.

Stephanidis, C. (2001), 'Adaptive Techniques for Universal Access', User Modeling and User-Adapted Interaction 11 (1-2), pp. 159-179.

Sveiby, K. E. and Simons, R. (2002), 'Collaborative climate and effectiveness of knowledge work: an empirical study', Journal of Knowledge Management 6 (5), pp. 420-433.

Thomas, J. C., Kellogg, W. A., Erickson, T. (2001), 'The knowledge management puzzle: human and social factors in knowledge management', IBM System Journal 40 (4), pp. 863-884.

Tumlin, M., Harris, S. R., Buchanan, H., Schmidt, K (2007), 'Collectivism vs. individualism in a wiki world: librarians respond to Jaron Lanier's essay 'digital Maoism: the hazards of the new online collectivism, (Johnson K., ed.)', Serials Review 33 (1), pp. 45-53.

Wagner, C. (2006), 'Breaking the Knowledge Acquisition Bottleneck through Conversational Knowledge Management', Information Resources Management Journal, 19 (1), pp. 70-83.

Wilkinson, D. M. and Huberman B. A. (2007), 'Assessing the Value of Cooperation in Wikipedia', First Monday 12 (4), url: http://www.firstmonday.org/issues/issue12_4/wilkinson/.

Appendix: Table of FIDIS Web 2.0 Initiatives

Table 2.3. FIDIS Web 2.0 initiatives

Service	Type	Description
FIDIS Intranet	CMS & Collaborative platform	FIDIS Intranet (FIDIS Communication Infrastructure – FCI) is a collaborative system based on the TYPO3 content management framework that was used inside the project to support the management of the content and the collaboration amongst the participants. The development itself took place in the context of Work Package 1 and the work of the FCI Steering Group of FIDIS. **Status**: This system was extensively used during the project. However, the initially offered bulletin board system has met very limited success. http://internal.fidis.net/ http://www.fidis.net/ (public web site)

Table 2.3 (continued)

Service	Type	Description
FIDIS Wiki	Wiki	FIDIS Wiki is a dedicated Wiki that was created as part of FIDIS to collect definitions about *identity* terms. It is based on a Wiki plugin for Typo3 (dr_wiki). **Status**: This service is still alive, but the focus has been put to FIDIS in Wikipedia. Note: Wikis have also been used as a way to create databases such as http://internal.fidis.net/ (internal Wiki) **Note**: The TYPO3 Wiki plugin '**dr_wiki**' was designed in the project and is available and actively maintained as an open source project at: http://drwiki.myasterisk.de/ http://forge.typo3.org/projects/show/extension-dr_wiki.
FIDIS in Wikipedia	Wiki	FIDIS in Wikipedia represents the initiative aimed at using Wikipedia (the open encyclopaedia Wiki) as a way for FIDIS to disseminate some of its results. **Status**: FIDIS in Wikipedia has restarted with a less ambitious objective of improvement of the existing content. The highly regulated nature of Wikipedia has made more difficult an initially more ambitious objective of creating and taking a leadership role in defining the concept of Identity in Wikipedia. http://www.wikipedia.org/
FIDIS Blog	Blog	FIDIS Blog is a public blog that was set up to collect references and news, and to engage in discussions. **Status**: The activity of this blog has been suspended because of the lack of participation. The functionality of collecting resources has been transferred to the social bookmarking system: del.icio.us. http://blog.fidis.net/
FIDIS LinkedIn group	OSN	FIDIS LinkedIn group is a group that was set-up in the OSN services LinkedIn to allow people to declare their affiliation to FIDIS, and to support some diffusion of knowledge. Originally restricted to the participant of FIDIS only, this group was opened to every person interested in the future of *identity* in the information society. **Status**: After a slow start, FIDIS LinkedIn group is progressively getting some momentum. http://www.linkedin.com/e/gis/46597

Table 2.3 (continued)

Service	Type	Description
FIDIS Facebook group	OSN	FIDIS Facebook group is a group that was set-up in the OSN services LinkedIn to allow people to declare their affiliation to FIDIS. **Status**: Very little activity can be reported. Facebook does not appear to appeal to identity experts. http://insead.facebook.com/group.php?gid=18942353104
FIDIS in del.icio.us	Social bookmarking	Two tags: fidis and fidis_watch have been defined to allow the members of FIDIS to collaboratively tag useful resources. The resources thus collected are then aggregated and displayed on the FIDIS web site, thanks to the RSS feature. **Status**: del.icio.us has been adopted by a limited number of participants, but it is active, and appears to represent a very effective mechanism. http://delicious.com/tag/fidis_watch http://delicious.com/tag/fidis
FIDIS Atgentnet[48]	Social platform	An AtGentNet community has been created. One of its characteristics is to monitor and reason on members' activities. The access is restricted. **Status**: This platform is currently dormant, but may be reactivated in the future to experiment with monitoring and the mining of people activities. http://www.calt.insead.edu/FIDIS/ICDTManager.nsf (restricted)
FIDIS Ning	Social platform	A Ning[49] community has been created. Its function is to support social networking and collaboration for groups and communities. **Status**: Although this service is not very active, it is being used to support the familiarisation of participants in physical events (such as the PhD training event), and prepare them in the construction of a shared understanding. http://fidis-noe.ning.com/

48 AtgentNet is a next generation social platform that was designed as part of the research project AtGentive (Nabeth, Karlsson, Angehrn, Maisonneuve, 2008). http://www.calt.insead.edu/LivingLab/AtGentive/Wiki/?AtGentNet.

49 Ning (http://www.ning.com/) is an online platform for users to create their own social websites and social networks.

Table 2.3 (continued)

Service	Type	Description
FIDIS aggregator	Information aggregator	A Netvibes[50] information aggregator was created for FIDIS. It is used to reference stream of identity related sources and to reference FIDIS Web 2.0 initiatives. http://www.netvibes.com/fidis
FIDIS in Second Life	Virtual worlds	Second Life was considered as a way to allow participants to meet each other in virtual worlds and to explore some identity issues in these worlds. **Status**: SL for FIDIS was never created.
FIDIS in CiteULike	Social bookmarking	A CiteULike group was created to aggregate people from FIDIS, and to collect bibliographical references. **Status**: was only a test. Note: This appears to represent a big potential in the future for collecting bibliographical materials, and organise them (using tags). http://citeulike.org/group/2226
FIDIS rich social media	Rich social media	YouTube, Flickr, SlideShare, … were used from time to time. **Status**: Only used to store media.

[50] Netvibes (http://www.netvibes.com/) is an online information and service aggregator.

VIGNETTE 2: VIRTUALLY LIVING IN VIRTUAL REALITIES*

During breakfast Frank sees that the fridge is almost empty. Moreover, the list of important things to buy, which is stuck on the door of the fridge is very long. He probably has to go shopping today. He has always considered this activity as being very boring, and even if the high-tech supermarket shop-bots may do a lot of the work, he does not rely on them. They are rarely very good at choosing the big red tomatoes or a sweet smelling and juicy melon.

Even if most of the time people nowadays go themselves to the shop, some supermarkets offer a virtual shop to their customers which one can visit using a virtual reality (VR) system. This virtual reality system is mainly a VR-suit that, at first sight, one may mistake for a diving suit. It is made of special material to fit as snugly as possible to the body and is equipped with a lot of sensors and effectors. The suit consists firstly of the helmet, which has a high resolution retinal projector, allowing the user to have a real three-dimensional view of the environment. Into the helmet, one may additionally build in a high-performance sound system which gives very precise information for locating elements of the environment. The latest generation of helmets even has a scent diffusion system integrated. Based on a similar idea to an imaging system, one can, mixing a limited number of base odours, reproduce a great range of perfumes.

The second part of the suit is the pair of gloves. These gloves are haptic devices allowing the user to 'touch' the things he sees. Using these gloves, Frank can feel the form of the object, its rigidity and temperature, but not texture. The suit itself is also a haptic device. The arms may behave more or less rigidly to simulate the weight of the object which Frank touches. It may also simulate some external contacts to different parts of the user's body, letting the user know when he touches a (virtual) object in the environment.

Watching the technology channel, Frank has learned that some laboratories are working on an 'extension' of the suit. This extension will consist of a cortical interface which should help the user feel the velocity and acceleration, perhaps not so needed for his supermarket experience, but very handy for playing games like aeronautical fighting. Another advantage of these cortical interfaces is that they should diminish or even remove the famous 'cyber sickness'. But not all people agree with this new aspect. In the newspapers one can regularly read some letters to the editor (even from university professors and recognised scientists)

* This scenario is based on FIDIS deliverable D12.5, Chapter 6, by Claude Fuhrer and Bernhard Anrig (VIP).

arguing that these interfaces could allow the firm that produces them to take control of the brain of their users, for example by influencing their political opinion or changing their shopping behaviour. During the 20th century there were many warnings of the possible use of subliminal pictures in advertising, but no one was really able to prove it. But this fear seems much more serious now. As such, Frank chooses not to have such options.

Before wearing his suit, Frank chooses a supermarket, and feeds the list of things he has to buy into his computer. He is totally aware that everything he buys in this shop could then be used (and probably will be used) to profile him and his family. For example insurance companies use profiling to check if someone is eating too much sugar or too many 'rich meals'. The laws do not allow a firm to ask a potential female employee if she is pregnant, but knowing – through profiling – that she has recently bought some pregnancy tests may be a sign the she will need maternity leave in the near future.

To protect against these more or less aggressive profiling methods, Frank has on his computer a program which warns him if he deviates from an 'average Joe' profile. This is surely not a perfect solution, but better than nothing. Moreover, whenever possible he always tries to reach the best anonymity he can. But, for the present case, where the things he wants to buy should be delivered to his home, it is necessary to reveal his real name and address. For activities like shopping, Frank should be registered, and so his personal data are stored in a database at every shop (or at least every chain of shops). To lower the risk of profiling, every member of the family shares the same virtual identity. This means that the shopping platform is not necessarily able to distinguish Frank from Fanny. It can try to infer if the virtual shopper is a man or a woman, based on some standard profiles, but it will never be totally sure of the real identity of the family member who is actually present.

When he has his suit on, he starts the program which opens for him the doors of the virtual supermarket. He can now walk along the aisles between the shelves and pick whatever he needs. But, unlike real shops, he regularly sees some items jumping out of the shelves and 'dancing' in front of him or calling him. Why precisely theses items? Because, in virtual reality, one can profile the customer in much more detail than is possible in real life. Here, the system may be aware of everything Frank has touched or even seen in the past within this supermarket (or even other ones which collaborate). The supermarket has very precise information about the type of package (colour, size or form) Frank likes, and then may propose (or impose) a customised shop, built to attract the eyes of Frank and convince him to buy more than he planned. For example, there is *stracciatella gelato* in the middle of the path, blinking and calling him. The ice cream was not on the list he entered but he loves stracciatella. Since he was a kid this was always his favourite. He picks up the box to add it to his shopping cart. Immediately a red light is blinking at the tip of his finger. This is his anti-profiling program which is warning him that he has already bought too many sweets, and his health insurance company may consider that all this sugar is a sign to check if his family should be switched to a bad risk customer category. He is now informed that if he wants another dessert, he has to go to buy it in the real world and pay in cash. One can note here that in this situation, the virtual world acts as an interface between the real world where Frank lives and the real world where the goods are. What Frank sees in his virtual shops are, for example, real fruits. This is necessary to allow him to choose the sweet smelling melons he loves.

When Frank has collected all he needs, he is ready to pay. Another advantage of virtual shopping is that there is no need to wait in the queue of the checkout. At the end of every aisle, there is a (virtual) button which will automatically establish the bill of the customer. The identification of the user is done by the different biometrical sensors embedded into the VR-suit. The data of Frank's credit card are already known by the supermarket and within seconds, the billing process is finished.

The goods he bought will be delivered during the afternoon to his home.

Before he takes his helmet off, the idea of planning the next holiday with his family crosses his mind. Looking at the catalogues of travel agencies is very interesting, but, using an immersive tool to check 'directly' the view of a beach in the Caribbean is much more exciting. He just wants to have a quick glance and not have to identify himself. Therefore, he disables the identifying process in his computer. Pointing a finger at the top displays a menu in front of him. He then just has to point his finger to the needed functionality to make him almost anonymous. Then, he can walk along the beach and check which hotel he would like to book for his holidays. While anonymously walking on the beach, the information he gets on the hotels, their advantages or actual room prices are not personalised and, for example, no discounts (based on e.g., recent stays in the same hotel company) are available. When he has selected his favourite hotel, he can still identify himself to look at the discounts etc. available, but for now, he prefers to stay anonymous in order not to get too much unwanted advertising over the coming days.

For this situation, the virtual word in which Frank walks is probably not the real world around the area where he plans to spend his vacations. For the purpose of advertising, the company has probably chosen a day where the weather is nice and sunny, where the season shows a nice environment, etc. They may however claim that it is virtually the same!

The visions and thoughts expressed in this vignette are inspired and based on various discussions, and results of the FIDIS Network of Excellence as well as the authors' personal experiences and expectations. Partially, underlying concepts and ideas of this vignette are described in Chapters 2, 3, 4 and 7.

3 Virtual Persons and Identities*

David-Olivier Jaquet-Chiffelle, Emmanuel Benoist, Rolf Haenni, Florent Wenger, and Harald Zwingelberg

Summary. What is a virtual person? What is it used for? What is its added value?

Virtual persons sometimes describe avatars and new forms of identities in online games. They also appear in other contexts; some authors use them in the legal domain. Within FIDIS, the concept of virtual person has been extended in order to better describe and understand new forms of identities in the Information Society in relation to rights, duties, obligations and responsibilities.

Virtual persons, as other virtual entities, exist in the virtual world, the collection of all (abstract) entities, which are or have been the product of the mind or imagination. The virtual world – not to be confused with the digital world – allows a unified description of many identity-related concepts that are usually defined separately without taking into consideration their similarities: avatars, pseudonyms, categories, profiles, legal persons, etc.

The legal system has a long experience of using abstract entities to define rules, categories, etc., in order to associate legal rights, obligations, and responsibilities to persons that can be considered instances of these abstract entities in specific situations. The model developed within FIDIS intentionally uses a similar construction.

In this chapter, after having explained the model, we apply it to pseudonyms. Then we explore the concept of virtual persons from a legal perspective. Eventually, we introduce trust in the light of virtual persons.

* This chapter has been reviewed by Bert-Jaap Koops (TILT) and Vashek Matyas (MU). The authors thank the reviewers for their valuable comments and suggestions.

3.1 Modelling New Forms of Identities[1]

In the era of the information society, the traditional concept of identity is evolving. Historically, identity has been used to try to uniquely identify persons. Such an identity is meant to refer to somebody without ambiguity. For example, Antony E. Muster, born on 17 March 1974 in Longborough, is a unique person for the tax office, the bank, or the police. Thus, he can be identified to calculate his taxes or impute liability for his acts.

In order to ensure the uniqueness of identity, states have developed a way to uniquely register each of their citizens. They have created registry offices for the registration of births, marriages, and deaths of their citizens. Moreover, any foreigner on their land may be asked to prove his identity using identity documents issued either by the visited state (visa) or his home country. The state is a trusted party that provides official identity documents (passport, ID card, visa) that are used as identification means in and out of the country.

This official identity and the corresponding official identity documents can then be exploited to create a bank account, to rent a room in a hotel, or to find a job. Its uniqueness also permits the enforcement of the legal rights and duties of each individual (citizen or foreigner, consumer, employee, etc.). The rights and duties of a person are tied to this person: whoever commits a crime can be sent to prison; whoever earns money has to pay an income tax; whoever borrows money from a bank has to give it back in the end.

It used to suffice to see an identity bound to a certain person with a one-to-one link. But this is not the case anymore. On the one hand, a person usually manages many identities: in her family, with the banker, at work, in forums, on Gmail, as an avatar in an online game, etc. On the other hand, some identities are shared by several people. For example, the guest account of a university is used by many visitors. Members of a family may also call from the same cellular phone with the same SIM card and surf the Internet from their home Wi-Fi access point, i.e. share the same IMEI number, IMSI number and IP address.

Last but not least, we are sometimes facing persons in the virtual world that, while having an identity, are not real persons. Think, for instance, of artificial (intelligent) agents moving avatars in video games, and expert systems administering forums or dealing on the stock exchange.

We can see from these examples that the traditional vision of a single and unique identity is obsolete in our world today. Usually, people have many identities nowadays; and some identities may also be shared by different persons or even by things. For all those more or less recent use cases, the traditional mapping

---

[1] This section is an adaptation of FIDIS Deliverable D2.13 on *Virtual Persons and Identities*, edited by D.-O. Jaquet-Chiffelle (VIP), co-edited by B. Anrig (VIP), E. Benoist (VIP), and R. Haenni (VIP), with contributions from M. Hildebrandt (VUB), E. Kosta (ICRI/K.U. Leuven), and K. Lefever (ICRI/K.U. Leuven), reviewed by V. Matyas (MU), T. Nabeth (INSEAD), and K. Warwick (READING). The authors of this section are E. Benoist (VIP), D.-O. Jaquet-Chiffelle (VIP) and F. Wenger (VIP).

of 'one person – one identity' does not apply anymore. This is why we have decided to develop an indirection layer based on the concept of virtual persons that enables us to unify the representation of all those cases.

In the next section, we will focus on new forms of identities that have been created, partially separated from the original, unique identity of the person.

3.1.1 Partial Identities and Virtual Identities

The information society has brought several new challenges in the area of identity. In real life, the uniqueness of identity may only apply to the official identity. And even for the official identity, there are many exceptions in practice. For example, many dual citizens have two different official identities: one in each of their countries. Moreover, each person has partial identities corresponding to the different roles he or she plays in society.

Let us suppose that Mr Antony E. Muster is the father of two children, 2 and 4 years old, and the director of the firm Smith and Smith, Inc. He has at least two different, partial identities. His children call him 'Dad' and do not even know that he has another name. For his employees, he is simply Mr Muster, the director. For his friends and family, he might be Tony. When he books a flight, he is always very careful because his credit card indicates Tony as his first name whereas his passport states only his official first name, i.e., Antony.

Antony Muster can sign a contract under two different identities. In his private life, he can buy a house or rent a car for himself. But for the business he conducts, he acts as a representative of his firm. He can borrow money from a bank for his firm, and the firm must repay the loan. If the bank does not receive its money back, it will sue the firm, which can then go bankrupt. But the rest of the patrimony of Antony will be protected (to a certain extent). In this type of contract, Antony E. Muster acts as the director of the firm Smith and Smith which he represents.

Antony manages all his identities in a natural way. He is probably unaware that he has partial identities. He knows that his firm has a legal personality but it is not a real person, is it?

In virtual environments, the development of new universes for video games, such as multi-user dungeons (MUD) and massively multiplayer online role-playing games (MMORPG), has offered the opportunity to create new characters called avatars that players can manipulate. The players create avatars with their real or imaginary physical features and control them to interact in a virtual world. The player is not Tony Muster anymore: he is 'Anshe Chung'[2], 'Malcolm Landgrabb'[3], or 'Jandoleer'[4], and he acts accordingly.

When participating in an online game, the players have simultaneously a dual role. They act as two persons: their avatar and their offline 'real' self. They utilise 'I' or 'me' to refer to both alike. In some cases, they invent codes in order to dif-

[2] Anshe Chung is a famous avatar in Second Life.

[3] Character in the Sims.

[4] Character from EverQuest.

ferentiate between those two parts of themselves when discussing with other participants: IRL (in real life), IC (in character), OOC (out of character), etc. Such behaviour continues even when they are no longer playing inside the online environment. They can tell their friends about their online activities using the first person singular. But would this be enough in order to consider the avatar as just a partial identity of the player?

Moreover, eBay account users are also hidden behind masks: their pseudonyms. Most of these users buy and sell on eBay for fun. For them, it is just a new part of their life: a new partial identity. But some persons have created real shops on eBay where a group of persons share the same account to sell a large amount of goods. In this case, the shop is referred to as its pseudonym on eBay; this is a so-called group pseudonym.

In science fiction films, we have already seen humanoid robots. It is very unlikely to meet such a robot on the streets within the next 10 years. In the information society, however, virtual robots are already acting similarly to humans. They can be expert systems taking decisions on the stock market, or softbots administering a forum that kicks out any member using an expression from a list of prohibited words. They can be programs managing one or more avatars in a MMORPG. There are also programs that participate in eBay auctions or online poker (which is forbidden in most virtual casinos). On the Internet, it can be hard to know if the entity we are interacting with is of flesh and blood, or only digital.

We are now facing a complex reality both in the 'real' world and in the information society. We have to deal with subjects acting behind masks: the director of a firm, the parents of a child, an auctioneer on eBay or players in an online game, etc. Finding the person using the mask may be easy; for example, the children will usually soon learn the name of their father. But it is sometimes quite hard, especially if the user wants to stay hidden. This might even become impossible when many persons behave as one (e.g. the staff of an eShop) or when there is simply nobody behind the mask (e.g. a program that acts as if it were human). In Section 3.1.4, we will introduce a new model, based on virtual persons, that offers a unifying answer to many questions that arise when dealing with identity in the information society.

3.1.2 The Case of Legal Persons

Before presenting our model, let us study the instructive case of legal persons. Within legal theory and legal philosophy, the concept of legal subject is often described in terms of the Greek 'persona'. The persona was the mask used in Greek theatre to hide the face of the actor of flesh and blood behind the physical picture of the role that was played. In the law, the terms 'legal subject' or 'persona' are used to mark the difference between the person of flesh and blood and the person in a legal sense. It emphasises the fundamental indeterminacy of the human person who should not be equated with the legal role he or she is attributed.

Thus, the legal persona achieves two things. Firstly, it provides the human person of flesh and blood with a means to act in law so he can exercise his rights, take on certain obligations, or be attributed certain competences. It also supplies the legal instrument to attribute civil and criminal liability. Secondly, it protects the human person against transparency by marking the difference between the indeterminate, indefinable person of flesh and blood on the one hand, and the role played or attributed in law on the other hand.[5]

By thinking of legal subjects as persons with roles attributed by the law, it becomes possible to attribute legal subjectivity to entities other than the human person. One realises that a human person is not a legal subject by nature because the category of legal subjectivity is an artefact created by law. Besides, legal persons are not restricted to human beings: corporations, trusts, associations, states and public bodies have also received legal personhood. Therefore, one can extend legal subjectivity to other subjects if it makes sense to grant such a subject the possibility to act in law and / or to be liable for harm caused.

Rights, duties, obligations, and responsibilities can be associated with a legal person. In some situations, the responsibility is carried directly by the legal person and not by any of the physical persons representing it. One of the reasons why legal persons have been created is to shift responsibility. Another one is that a legal person continues to exist even after the death of its embodier(s).

Legal subjects thus provide a mask behind which acting entities, like human beings, can hide. Such a concept of mask can be extended in order to model new forms of identities arising in the information society. This is what our model does (see Section 3.1.4).

3.1.3 Identity and Privacy Issues

Several new technologies introduce severe threats for privacy, especially when identifying information from different sources or from different points in time can be linked. As presented in the introduction, the simple, traditional model for identities consists in associating to each person a unique, if possible universal, identity:

$$\text{one physical person} \quad \leftrightarrow \quad \text{one identity}$$

This model presents several advantages, one of them being simplicity. An identified person gets rights like the right to travel and to pass a border, the right to vote or to be on welfare. Those rights are strongly related to the person's identity. Traditional identity management systems (IdMS) usually associate a list of rights, duties, obligations, and responsibilities to each identified person, i.e. essentially to each identity. The absence of such a strong identity model may prevent a person from being fully recognised as a citizen. Such a person might be denied important rights given to identifiable citizens.

That is one of the reasons why governments usually promote official registers, such as the social security number (SSN) register, where all citizens of their country are recorded exactly once. Some people even claim that it is a fundamental right for everybody to have a unique (universal) identity. In the light of what pre-

---

[5] Compare Kantorowicz (1957).

cedes, the traditional simple model may appear very convenient from the point of view of both the person and the society.

However, this model has also some drawbacks. The unique identity opens the door to the linking and analysis of a lot of information about its owner's doings. Profiles[6] deduced from this information may later disqualify the person from access to certain services. For example, a life insurance company may refuse a new customer because his profile suggests unusual risks.

The convenience of a unique identity has a price which might overcome its advantages in the near future. In particular, it presents severe threats to privacy.

In order to protect privacy, the link between one person and its identifying information could be weakened. Privacy preserving technologies promote, whenever possible, unlinkability between different actions, activities, and preferences of a same person. Shared identities can be considered, in some situations, as privacy enhancing tools since they hide a person within the group of people sharing an identity. Other techniques are based on pseudonyms, or even one-time pseudonyms. Each pseudonym may be seen as a kind of identity of the person that usually does not reveal the true identity of its owner.

The two-layer model that we introduce below creates a theoretical indirection between acting subjects and their corresponding identifying information. Our model allows a faithful description of the variety of new forms of identities induced by new technologies.

3.1.4 Unifying Model Based on Virtual Persons[7]

We wish to describe new forms of identities while maintaining the traditional idea of a strong link between an identity and a specific entity. Therefore, we propose to introduce an abstract layer that creates an indirection between identities and the corresponding physical entities. Entities in this abstract layer will be called virtual entities. Physical entities belong to the physical world. Some physical entities are physical persons, others not: stones, buildings, animals, etc.

Likewise, virtual (or abstract) entities belong to the virtual world. A virtual entity corresponds to an abstraction, a perception, a thought, a concept, or an illusion. Some virtual entities can have rights, duties, obligations and/ or responsibilities associated with them in some context, for example legal or moral rights, or organisational responsibilities. Such virtual entities will be named virtual persons.

In particular, virtual entities that could represent or be represented by a physical person are virtual persons. Not all virtual entities are virtual persons. For instance, the virtual entity described by 'a white sheet of paper' is not a virtual person.

Identity-related information that defines a virtual entity becomes the tautological identity of this virtual entity. In the abstract layer – the virtual world – we impose the following condition:

$$\text{one virtual entity} \qquad \leftrightarrow \qquad \text{one tautological identity}$$

6 See, for example, Chapter 7 in this book and Hildebrandt and Gutwirth (2007).

7 For a detailed description of the model, we refer to Jaquet-Chiffelle et al. (2006).

This is in particular true for virtual persons. A physical person having several (partial) identities is replaced by a physical person linked to several virtual persons, each having a unique tautological identity as shown in Figure 3.1.

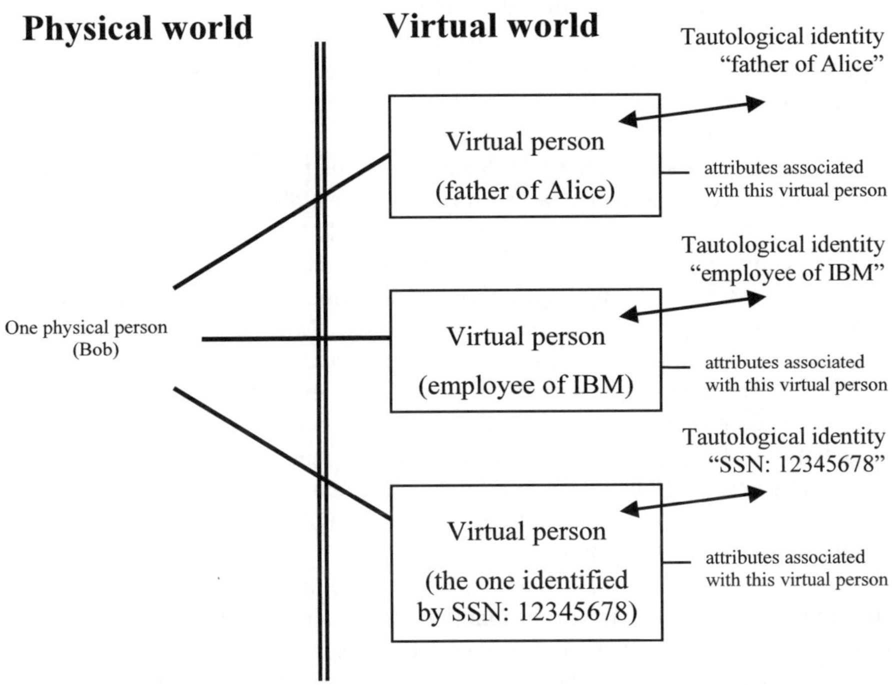

Fig. 3.1. Multiple identities

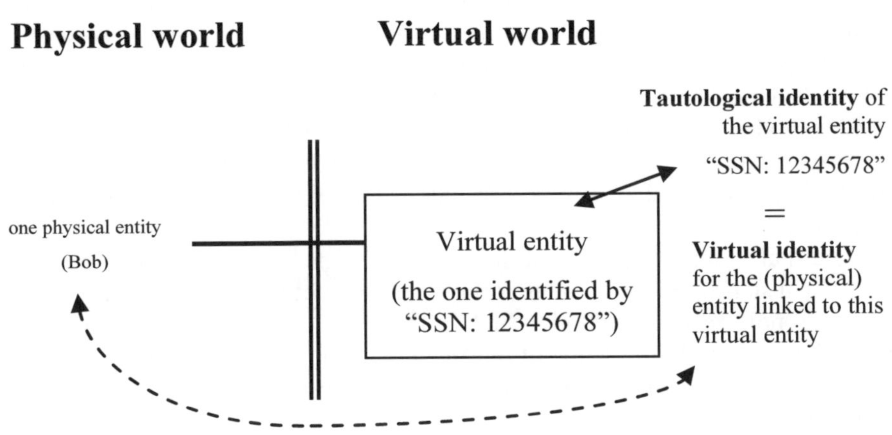

Fig. 3.2. Virtual identity

A virtual identity of a physical entity is the identity of a virtual entity linked to it (see Figure 3.2). Pseudonyms form an important family of virtual identities. Indeed, a pseudonym is the identity of its corresponding virtual person, which in turn is linked to the user(s) of the pseudonym. The virtual person creates an indirection between the pseudonym and its user(s).

Virtual persons play the role of a mask. In front of the mask, we have the identity. Several physical persons can hide behind the mask. When several persons share an identity, they are all linked to the same virtual person. The shared identity becomes in our model a shared virtual identity.

In doing so, we keep some of the advantages of the simple traditional model. For example, we can associate a list of rights, duties, obligations and responsibilities to each virtual person. But we lose the direct link between the identity and a physical entity (e.g. a physical person). This indirection helps to describe important concepts such as anonymity, pseudonymity, and unlinkability which play an important role in privacy enhancing technologies. Moreover, as we will see, it describes more faithfully what happens in today's reality.

Last but not least, a virtual person continues to exist whatever happens to the physical person(s) once linked to it. It survives its corresponding physical entities. As a matter of fact, any virtual entity comes to existence at some point in time but never stops existing (that is what our model assumes).

The introduction of an abstract entity – the virtual person – can be elaborated further. Let us take two examples to examine more thoroughly what is behind the mask. To begin with, let us consider Zeus, the identity of an abstract concept in ancient Greek religion. The corresponding virtual person is described by 'the one who is Zeus'. What is behind the mask? Is there a physical person, a physical entity, or nothing? This answer might vary depending on one's belief.

Another example is 'the sender of a given email' which is the identity of the doer, i.e. a virtual person. What is behind the mask? Is it a physical person? Is it a computer program? Is it a dog? The introduction of virtual persons allows the description of situations where an action is not necessarily initiated by a physical person but possibly by a computer program or a virus for example. Therefore, physical entities behind the virtual persons should not be reduced to physical persons only.

We introduce the concept of subjects in order to include the possibility of having non-human physical entities behind virtual persons. Intuitively speaking, a subject is any physical entity that can hide behind a virtual person. Physical objects can be subjects, too.

Note that human beings or animals might be more than just physical. The soul, for instance, might be neither physical, nor virtual. However, these questions are more related to religion and philosophy than to the identity in the information society. In the scope of our model, we purposely abstain from including entities that would be neither physical, nor virtual (e.g. immaterial, spiritual entities).

3.1.5 Illustration of Our Model

Our model can accurately and consistently represent various forms of identities in the information society. First, a legal person is a virtual entity which has a legal status and its own, unique identity. According to our definition, a legal person is a virtual person. Actually, the virtual person generalises the well-accepted concept of legal person. It is an abstract entity that can have rights, duties, obligations and/or responsibilities associated with it.

Second, the term 'virtual person' often refers to characters in a MUD, MMORPG, or other computer game. The relation between players and avatars has been described from different perspectives. Some avatars rely on human players for their behaviour, while others might be directed by the game itself. Avatars are virtual persons according to our definition, too. Indeed, they can have rights and obligations associated with them within the game.

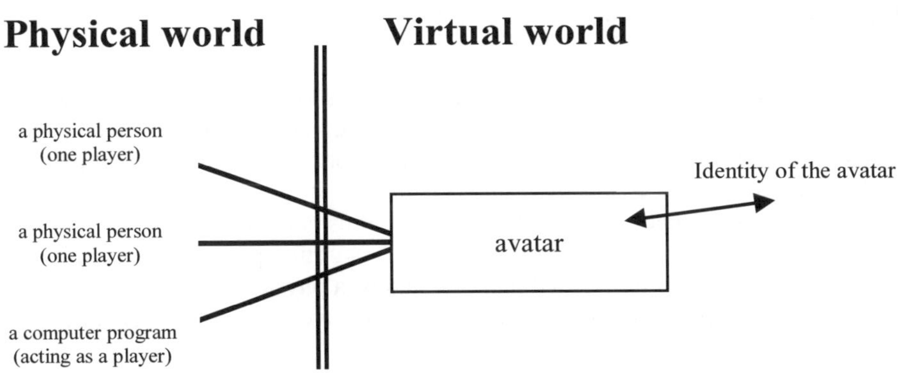

Fig. 3.3. Avatars are also virtual persons

For an external observer, it is often hard to decide whether the subject behind this or that virtual person is a real player or just a computer program. We see these virtual persons (characters) as masks used by subjects (human players, computer programs) to act or interact within the game as shown in Figure 3.3.

Even though avatars are also virtual persons according to our definition, the concept of virtual person is much broader and should not be reduced to avatars only.

Third, a group of physical persons, as an abstract concept, describes a virtual person, too. For example, a couple is a virtual person since it is an abstract entity, which hides two physical persons that can have rights, obligations, etc., associated with it. Categories resulting from profiling also describe virtual persons.

Profiling techniques allow the creation of categories of physical persons sharing similar attributes. These attributes define the category and therefore the identity of the category. In other words, the category is a virtual person whose identity is defined by a set of information. Several persons may belong to this category, i.e. may hide behind this virtual person. As an example, we could consider the category defined by 'people who are older than 45 and who earn more than 100 k€ per year'.

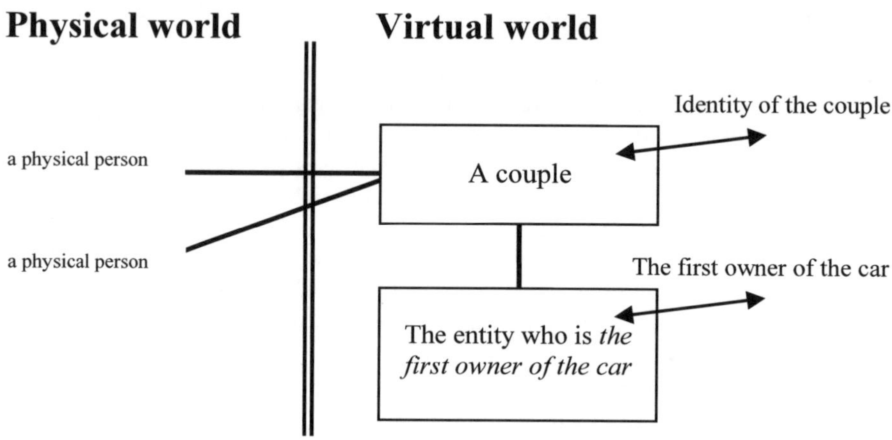

Fig. 3.4. A virtual person hiding another virtual person

Finally, we have seen that virtual persons can hide subjects in the physical world. But nothing prevents a virtual person from hiding another virtual person in the virtual world. Virtual persons can hide virtual persons hiding other virtual persons and so on. This creates chains of virtual persons.

Indeed, such a situation is not exceptional. Let us take the example of 'the first owner of a given car' (see Figure 3.4). This is a virtual person described by its role. The entity behind this virtual person could be a physical person, a couple or a legal person. Couples and legal persons are, as we have seen, virtual persons.

3.1.6 Conclusion

Virtual persons allow us to combine advantages of both the traditional unique identity paradigm – since any virtual person is (tautologically) bound to a single identity – and the multiple identities approach fostered by privacy enhancing technologies. In FIDIS deliverable D2.13 (Jaquet-Chiffelle et al., 2008), these concepts are developed and a new theory is built where the main notions related with identity are mapped into a unifying model based on virtual persons.

We have seen the rise of new types of 'persons' whose reality is restricted to the virtual world but that have at the same time a considerable impact on human beings in the physical world. Some MMORPG players invest so much time and money in their avatar that they start considering it as a part of themselves. The eBay account of an eVendor is essential to her business: if its reputation is tarnished, her eShop may be ruined. In section 3.2, we will further illustrate pseudonyms in the light of virtual persons.

In section 3.3, we will illustrate fundamental similarities between legal entities and virtual persons. We have seen that legal persons can be considered virtual persons. Of course, not all virtual persons can claim legal personhood. However, it is interesting to investigate under which conditions a virtual person could gain some sort of legal subjectivity, some partial legal personhood.

What happens when machines act or initiate transactions and cause harm? Like in the case of animals, machines are currently treated as legal objects (as opposed to subjects). They have no power to act in law or to be attributed civil or criminal liability. If a horse wins a race, the legal obligation to provide the prize money is directed towards the owner of the horse, not to the horse itself. If an animal happens to cause harm, the owner of the animal is usually liable and this is mostly a matter of strict liability – this of course depends on the jurisdiction. If it bites a child, a dog may be killed due to a court order to that effect. However, this is not considered a punishment but the destruction of a dangerous object. Could it make sense to punish certain types of objects in some contexts? As presented in Anrig (2007), there are already programs that learn and take decisions. These programs make choices that are not only based on their algorithms but also on their own experience, i.e. on data they have 'learnt'. Such systems may be used to take decisions in many fields. Who should be held responsible when a fault occurs? Is it still meaningful (if even possible) to always find a physical person responsible? Could it help to provide legal subjectivity to some virtual persons (machines, software programs, networked artificial agents, and so on) in some specific contexts?

The interested reader will find further developments in FIDIS deliverables D17.1 'Modelling New Forms of Identities: Applicability of the Model Based on Virtual Persons', D17.2 'New (Id)entities and the Law: Perspectives on Legal Personhood for Non-Humans' and D17.3 'Bridging the Accountability Gap: Rights for New Entities in the Information Society?'.

3.2 Pseudonyms in the Light of Virtual Persons[8]

The term 'pseudonym' comes from the Greek word pseudonumon which means false name. Traditionally, a pseudonym refers to a fictitious name taken by an author, a pen name. Voltaire and Molière are pseudonyms of famous French writers. Nowadays, pseudonyms are often used by artists, especially in show-business, to mask their official identity. In this case, a pseudonym can be seen as a self-chosen name becoming an identity in the artist context. In several cases, actors do not want to be confronted with their official name given by their parents – maybe because it sounds less glamorous.

In some situations, the pseudonym is used to conceal the true identity of the person, i.e., it acts as a privacy enhancing tool. Journalists sometimes use such pseudonyms. On the Internet, many people use a pseudonym (or multiple pseudonyms) hoping to stay anonymous.

[8] This section is written by D.-O. Jaquet-Chiffelle and is based on an excerpt of his contribution in FIDIS deliverable D17.1 *'Modelling New Forms of Identities: Applicability of the Model Based on Virtual Persons'*.

In show-business, however, the mask is often transparent. The link between the physical person (actor, singer, etc.) and his or her pseudonym can even become stronger than the one with his or her official identity. As an example, the famous French singer Johnny Hallyday – whose real name is Jean-Philippe Smet – is better known and recognised by most people by his pseudonym than by his real name. For her last name, his wife has even chosen the surname of the pseudonym after their wedding; she is known as Laeticia Hallyday, not Laeticia Smet. The same is true for Johnny Hallyday's son, David Hallyday.[9] In such a situation, the use of a pseudonym is clearly not a way to protect anonymity anymore. It transcends its original purpose and becomes assimilated within a full identity.

These examples illustrate that a pseudonym, as a (false) name, can become an identity in the common language. This is in line with the approach proposed by the model based on virtual persons: a pseudonym is the identity of a virtual person. The user of the pseudonym is linked to this virtual person: it is represented by this virtual person.

Pseudonyms also intervene as User IDs in the information society. The term digital identity is often used for sets of data representing a person, or more generally identity-related digital information that characterise this person in a specific context. A person can choose to use only subsets of these attributes to be represented in different situations and roles.

These subsets of attributes are called partial identities (pID) in Pfitzmann and Hansen (2008). For transactions and interactions on the Internet and online applications, e.g. when participating in social networks, forums, instant messaging, or eCommerce, people make use of partial identities. Very often, instead of a person's real name, a pseudonym is used in order to reach a certain level of anonymity.

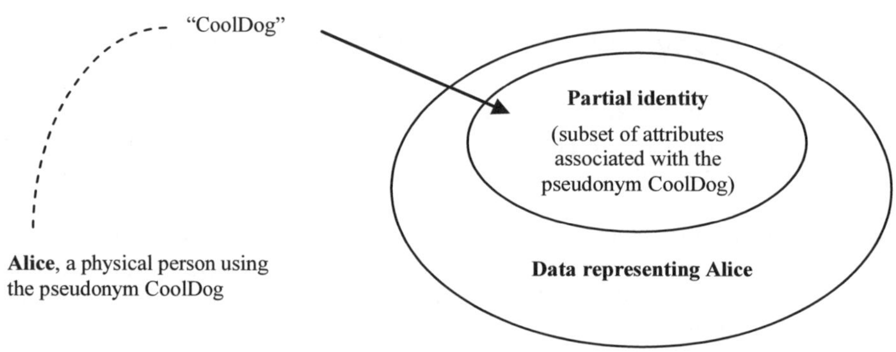

Fig. 3.5. A pointer to a partial identity according to (Pfitzmann, Hansen, 2008)

[9] Laura Smet, daughter of Johnny Hallyday and the French actress Nathalie Baye, uses Smet for her last name.

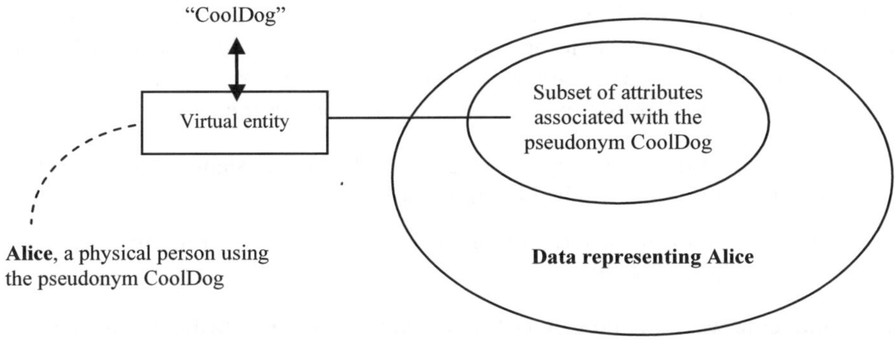

Fig. 3.6. An identity pointing to its corresponding virtual entity according to (Jaquet-Chiffelle et al., 2008, FIDIS deliverable D17.1)

In Pfitzmann and Hansen (2008), pseudonyms act as pointers[10] to partial identities. Pfitzmann and Hansen focus on a pseudonym being a pointer to a partial identity instead of being an identity attribute or even an identity itself, to clearly distinguish between pointers to partial identities, and attributes or partial identities.

Reducing a pseudonym to a mere pointer maybe constitute an accurate depiction when a pseudonym is some completely meaningless UserID, for example a random number. However, it eliminates the intrinsic 'identity' nature of a pseudonym in real life. As a name, (chosen) pseudonyms usually contain more identity-related information than randomly generated identifiers.

We agree with Pfitzmann and Hansen that a pseudonym acts as a pointer. However, the 'pointer' nature of a pseudonym should not be considered to be in opposition to its 'identity' nature. Indeed, according to the identity model that we developed (see section 3.1), any identity of an entity is identifying information linkable to this entity. In particular, the identity points to the entity (without being necessarily a pointer in the strict sense). For a pseudonym, our model can be interpreted in some aspects as a refinement of Pfitzmann and Hansen's approach.

In our model, the corresponding entity is called a virtual person – the one called CoolDog – and the pseudonym CoolDog is the (tautological) identity of this virtual person. Attributes can be directly associated with this virtual person.

Similarly to Pfitzmann and Hansen, we make a distinction between an identity pointing to an entity and the attributes associated with this entity. We also recognise in our model that both identities and attributes are identity-related information. The same identity-related information can be an identity for an entity while also being an attribute for this same entity or for another one.

10 The term 'identifier' as used in Pfitzmann and Hansen (2008) essentially means pointer. However, as identifiers have several different meanings in specialised literature, we write 'pointer' in order to avoid a possible confusion. In FIDIS deliverable D2.13, identifiers have a different meaning (Jaquet-Chiffelle et al., 2008).

In our model, the fundamental unifying concept behind identifier, identity, attributes, pseudonyms, etc. is information or more precisely identity-related information. Attributes are identity-related information; identifiers are identity-related information too, etc. Let us recall two core concepts in our model:

- the concept of *entity* (anything that has a distinct existence; it is the fundamental 'thing' that can be identified) and
- the concept of *identity-related information* (any information that characterises – uniquely or not – an entity).

In our model however, contrarily to Pfitzmann and Hansen, attributes can be identifiers and identifiers can be attributes: an identifier is essentially information that characterises exactly one entity within a specific context.[11] It does not prevent this entity from being represented by other sets of data or information, too. However, an identifier points to an entity rather than to a subset of attributes – a partial identity according to Pfitzmann and Hansen. Actually, in our model, a partial identity is a partial identifier.[12] A (partial) identity is relative; it depends on the ability of the observer to find or verify the link between the entity and the (partial) identifier, i.e., the identifying information.

In our model, we take full advantage of the identity nature of a pseudonym as it is commonly perceived. A pseudonym is considered as an identifier as well as the identity of a virtual person: the one called by this pseudonym. This is in line with the common perception of a pseudonym being an identity among others. This virtual person is a new entity with its own existence. This new entity even survives the physical person(s) using this pseudonym.

Such a construction allows us to associate attributes and give rights, in a broad, not necessarily legal sense, directly to the virtual person, i.e., almost to the pseudonym itself rather than to tie them to the physical entity (or entities) behind the mask. For example, as we will see in the case-study that follows, royalties can be associated to the virtual person 'the one called Johnny Hallyday'.

3.2.1 Johnny Hallyday

In this case-study, we consider further the artist-pseudonym Johnny Hallyday used by a famous singer whose real name is Jean-Philippe Smet. In this situation, the use of a pseudonym does not work as an anonymizing mechanism. It is an artist-name, a self-chosen identity. The traditional one-to-one model (one person – one identity) would emphasise the very strong link between the singer Jean-Philippe Smet and his artist-pseudonym Johnny Hallyday in merging both 'names' into a

[11] A *partial* identifier (or partially identifying information) is any information that characterises *at least one entity* within a specific context or environment. An identifier is a partial identifier that characterises *exactly* one entity within this specific context or environment.

[12] A (partial) identity of an entity – according to an observer – is a (partial) identifier that can be linked to this entity by that observer.

single identity. In doing so, it cannot catch the subtlety of reality. What happens if there is yet another physical person named Jean-Philippe Smet?

To represent this situation in our model, we consider two different virtual persons: 'the one called Johnny Hallyday' and 'the one called Jean-Philippe Smet' (see Figure 3.7).

Note that if there is another physical person named Jean-Philippe Smet, our model can easily catch this fact. Even in this simple case, the model based on virtual persons allows for a finer description of the relations between the different entities that are involved.

Johnny Hallyday is a pseudonym used by the physical person Jean-Philippe Smet. It is

- the (tautological) *identity* of the virtual person 'the one called *Johnny Hallyday*' and
- a *virtual identity* for Jean-Philippe Smet (physical person) linked to this virtual person.

Identities do not exist by themselves; they must relate and point to an entity. The traditional one-to-one, or one-to-many, or even many-to-many models cannot faithfully describe the scenario in 'Jean-Philippe', a 2006 French movie: One morning, the link between Jean-Philippe Smet and Johnny Hallyday has disappeared; Johnny Hallyday does not exist anymore (only one unique fan remembers him) and Jean-Philippe Smet (who plays his own role) has just become a 'normal' citizen who never realised his dream of becoming Johnny Hallyday. These models also meet difficulties when the corresponding physical entity (or entities) do not exist anymore, e.g., after Jean-Philippe Smet's death.

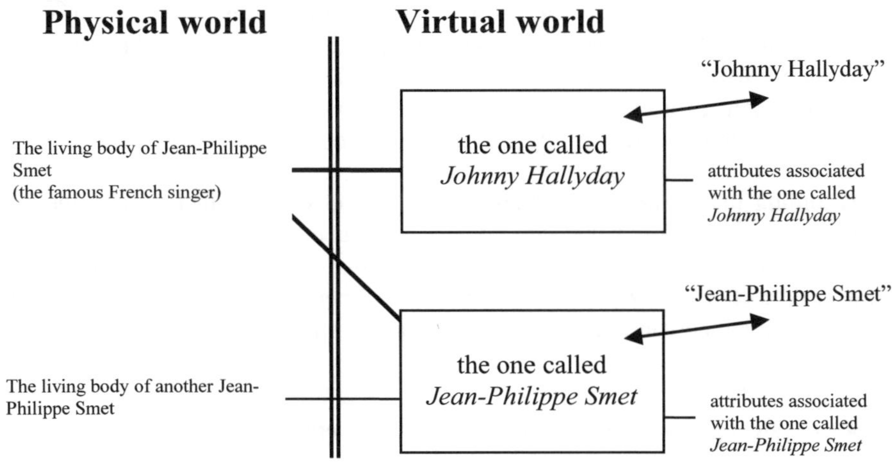

Fig. 3.7. Jean-Philippe Smet & Johnny Hallyday

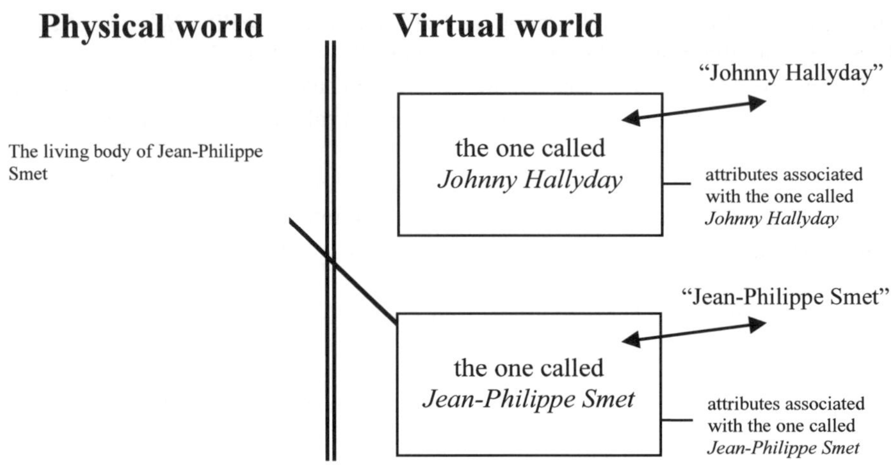

Fig. 3.8. 'Jean-Philippe', the movie

The situation in the movie 'Jean-Philippe' is easy to describe in our model (see Figure 3.8). The link between the living body of Jean-Philippe Smet and the virtual person 'the one called Johnny Hallyday' does not exist anymore. However, the virtual person 'the one called Johnny Hallyday' continues to exist in the movie. Indeed, it is the product of someone's mind: the unique fan that 'remembers' Johnny. This example illustrates one of the advantages of having virtual persons with their own existence. The virtual person 'the one called Johnny Hallyday' exists even if it does not represent any physical entity (see Figure 3.8).

After the death of this famous French singer, both virtual persons 'the one called Johnny Hallyday' and 'the one called Jean-Philippe Smet' will continue to exist but will not be linked to any physical entity anymore.[13] In this case, the connection between the physical and virtual worlds is severed, as it is depicted in Figure 3.8.

These virtual persons that are not linked to physical entities anymore might have some rights, for example intellectual property rights. Such a situation is not covered in a convincing way by the traditional one-to-one, or one-to-many, or even many-to-many models.

According to our model, royalties are to be paid to the virtual person 'the one called Johnny Hallyday'. They are transferred to the physical person called Jean-Philippe Smet as long as he lives; then, after his death, these royalties will be transferred to the virtual person 'Jean-Philippe Smet's heir' and eventually to the physical or legal person(s) represented by 'Jean-Philippe Smet's heir':

- any foundation (another virtual person) that inherits (some of) those royalties,
- physical persons that inherit those royalties, etc.

[13] Except if another physical person is called Jean-Philippe Smet or Johnny Hallyday.

Figure 3.9 shows how royalties stay associated with the virtual person 'the one called Johnny Hallyday', even after this French singer has died:

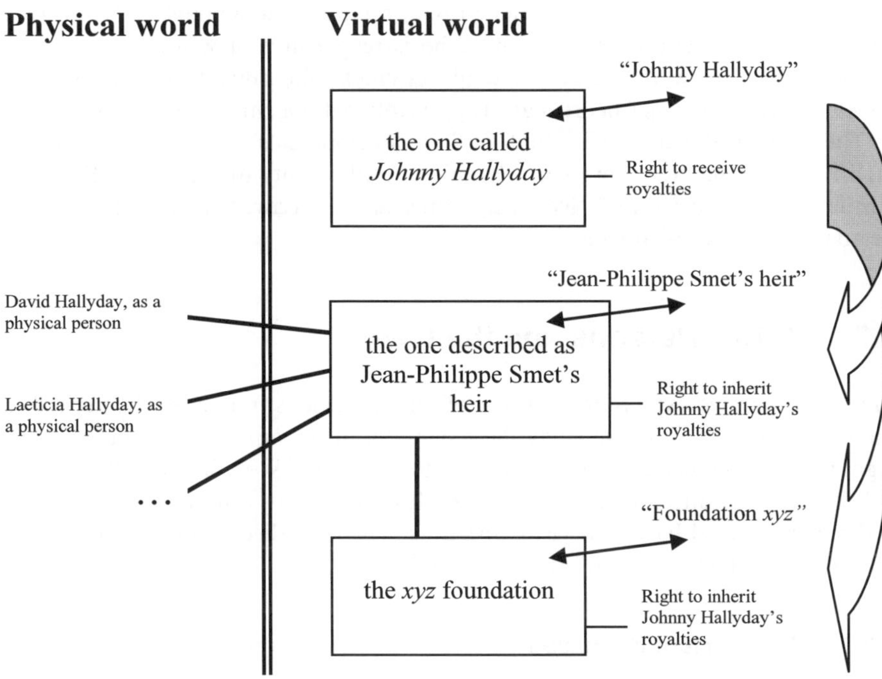

Fig. 3.9. Jean-Philippe Smet's heir

Figure 3.9 could be refined in order to include other, more precise, virtual persons: for example, categories of heirs (wife, children, grandchildren, etc.). Law uses those categories in order to determine the distribution of the heritage if there is no will stipulating otherwise. The model based on virtual persons can catch well this legal mechanism.

3.2.2 Conclusion

Our model developed in FIDIS deliverable D2.13 (Jaquet-Chiffelle et al., 2008) uses abstract entities, called virtual persons, to tie a pseudonym to an entity that survives the physical person(s) using this pseudonym. For pseudonyms, our model can be interpreted in some aspects as a refinement of Pfitzmann and Hansen's approach.

In our model, a pseudonym is a special kind of identity. It is the (tautological) identity of its corresponding virtual person 'the one called by this pseudonym' as well as a virtual identity for any existing entity (or entities) using this pseudonym.

The widespread use of pseudonyms on the Internet makes the link between an action (or a transaction) and the physical person who has initiated this action (or transaction) invisible for most observers. How do we deal with this new reality, when no physical person can be linked with a reasonable amount of effort to an action (or a transaction) or an event? Who is responsible or will bear the (legal) consequences? New forms of unlawful activities take advantage of these grey zones, where the law is (theoretically) applicable but not enforceable anymore.

The interested reader will find further developments in FIDIS deliverables D17.1 'Modelling New Forms of Identities: Applicability of the Model Based on Virtual Persons' and D17.2 'New (Id)entities and the Law: Perspectives on Legal Personhood for Non-Humans'

3.3 Virtual Persons and the Law[14]

In this section, we explore the concept of virtual persons from a legal perspective. First, we consider as a case study the modelling of unborn human entities from a legal perspective, using the concept of virtual persons. We will show that we are able to describe different well-established legal concepts within the homogenous and generic model based on virtual persons. Then we discuss new challenges to technology and law in the information society.

3.3.1 Unborn Human Entities

Law recognises a capability to be subject of rights and duties for all living human beings but recognition of unborn human entities is restricted to some special purposes. We analyse and discuss this topic in the light of the model based on virtual persons as developed in FIDIS deliverable D2.13 (Jaquet-Chiffelle et al., 2008).

Unborn subjects that are possible bearers of rights are the nondum conceptus and the nasciturus. The nondum conceptus describes the not conceived person who is acknowledged in law as a possible heir or beneficiary of a third party contract.[15] The nasciturus is the conceived but not yet born entity which in many jurisdictions is already treated as an heir under the condition of being born alive later.

[14] The first part of this section is written by H. Zwingelberg and is based on an excerpt of his contribution in FIDIS deliverable D17.1 '*Modelling New Forms of Identities: Applicability of the Model Based on Virtual Persons*'. The second part is written by D.-O. Jaquet-Chiffelle and is based on an excerpt of his contribution with B.-J. Koops in FIDIS deliverable D17.2 *'New (Id)entities and the Law: Perspectives on Legal Personhood for Non-Humans*'.

[15] Most jurisdictions accept the concept as beneficiary of a bequest; civil law countries also allow rights of third party's contracts, and in common law jurisdictions *nondum conceptus* may become beneficiary of a trust.

Nondum Conceptus

The nondum conceptus is a legal figure that allows addressing future rights to a child that may be possibly conceived and born in the future. Legal personality is unthinkable at this stage. Indeed, the particular human being must at least be created to some extent to be recognised as a legal subject.

At the time of observation, the physical entity involved can be a cell in the ovary of the mother or a maybe still to become sperm cell. These circumstances raise the difficult question as to whether there is a physical entity at all and at which stage of development we could speak about a beginning personality.

The legal concept of the nondum conceptus maps rights and duties to a not yet existing physical entity. It therefore postulates a virtual entity which is capable of bearing rights, thus a virtual person. The model based on virtual persons can flawlessly describe the legal fiction without the need to decide at which degree of development a human being constitutes a physical entity.

Case study. In this case study, John I wishes to become grandfather and hopes that his line of blood will be perpetuated. His three daughters are over 30 years old already, well situated and successful in their jobs. Therefore John I decides to set up a will in which he divides his property among his daughters and stipulates in regard to his stock portfolio: 'The stock portfolio shall be administered by my daughters and shall be given to my first grandchild upon its birth. If no grandchild is born by the 40th birthday of my youngest daughter, the money shall be transferred to the kindergarten of the local church.'

We may assume that such a stipulation is legally valid. As the stock portfolio cannot be without an owner and the not yet conceived baby does not have legal personhood, the legal systems stipulate different solutions for the time until birth: trust constructions, some kind of agency or by denominating a preliminary heir who is subject to restrictions in regard to the legal estate.

The traditional one-to-one, or one-to-many, or even many-to-many models cannot catch this reality, as initially a physical person is missing and it is unclear whether there will be a physical person matching the stipulations in the will of John I at any given point of time. No link might ever exist to the physical world, as no physical person linkable to the described identity might ever exist.

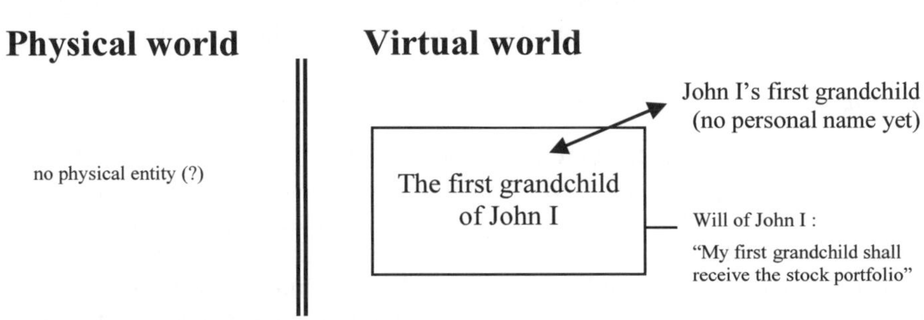

Fig. 3.10. Nondum conceptus

The model based on virtual persons is a time-dependent m-to-n model, where null is a possible value both for m or n. This time dependency is the dynamic component which enables the model based on virtual persons to appropriately describe this use case. Even if at the time John I drafts his will it is not yet foreseeable whether he will ever have a grandchild, the virtual person describing the entity that might become John I's first Grandchild, i.e., 'The first grandchild of John I', already exists as a virtual entity.

The ethically and legally difficult question as to when a human being (physical entity) comes into existence is not of relevance when applying the model based on virtual persons. The law provides a solution as it provides for a fiction, meaning that the law assumes a fact (here: that the child is born alive in the time when it is not even conceived) while the law is well aware that the fact is not necessarily true. The model based on virtual persons offers a satisfactory solution to describe the legal fiction.

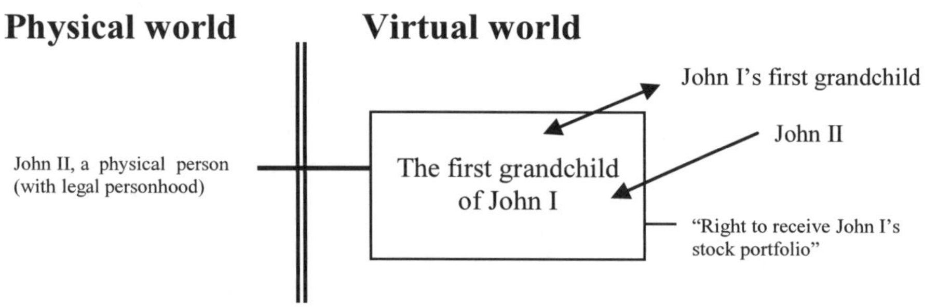

Fig. 3.11. After John II has gained legal personhood

Upon the birth of John II, the first grandchild of John I, a physical person appears that is linkable to the already existing virtual person. As soon as John II has gained legal personhood, the right to receive John I's stock portfolio can be granted to the virtual person 'The first grandchild of John I'.

Even if John II happens to die quickly after having gained legal personhood, the right to receive John I's stock portfolio can stay attached to the virtual person 'The first grandchild of John I' until it is transferred to John II's heir.

Nasciturus

The nasciturus is the legal figure for the conceived but yet unborn child. A nasciturus lacks legal personhood but is capable of acquiring rights when it is born alive later. The nasciturus is in particular capable of inheriting and tort law grants damages to a child when prenatal injuries or medical errors cause the child to be born impaired. With the embryo in the mother's womb, there is at least some physical entity existing. As the scope of the traditional ID-models is targeted on identifying existing physical entities, the one-to-one (e.g., citizen registers) and

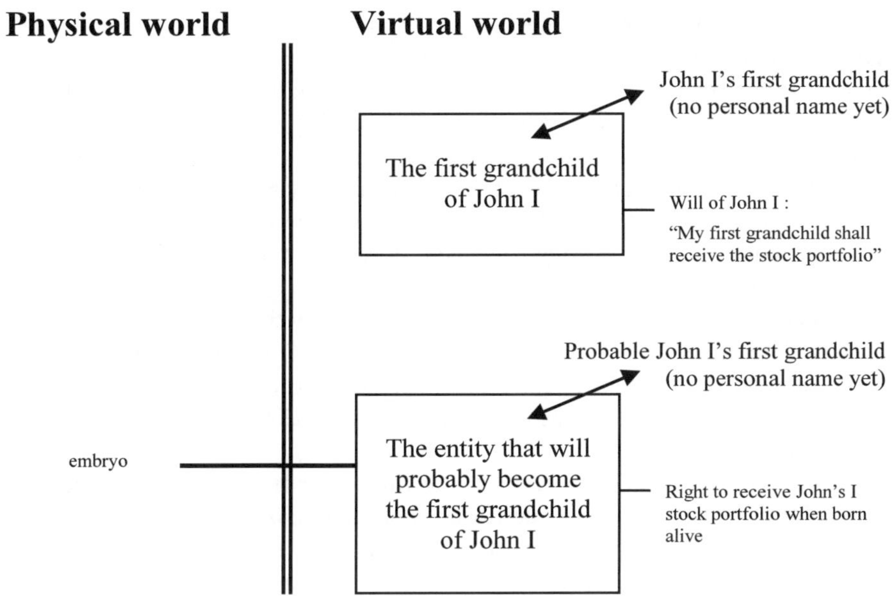

Fig. 3.12. Nasciturus

one-to-many models are faced with the question as to when the embryo has reached a level of development that is 'human enough' to fall within their scope.

The model based on virtual persons already provides a solution as the virtual persons 'The first grandchild of John I' and 'The entity that will probably become the first grandchild of John I' (e.g., the embryo) can easily be described in the virtual world and linked to the corresponding physical entity later. Thus the model provides for a seamless description of the yet unborn and non-existing subject of rights offering a cross discipline approach of mapping the legal concepts in IDM-technology.

3.3.2 New Challenges to Technology and Law

Technological developments in the information society bring new legal and technical challenges. This concerns both the applicability and adequacy of current laws and the enforceability of these laws. The new challenges cannot be solved by law or technology alone; they require an interdisciplinary approach that can combine innovative solutions with a thorough understanding of both technology and law.

To briefly illustrate some of the new developments and challenges, we will follow a what? where? when? why? who? approach. For example, what can be considered as property in law? Can a unique and precious virtual object in an on-line game be considered as property recognised by today's laws?

Where did the crime of criminal threat take place, if a Swiss resident during a workshop in Brussels reads a threatening email on his Gmail account that is stored on a server in the USA, which message was sent by someone from Germany via a Malaysian Internet provider? If some 'physical presence' is a legal condition for the locus delicti in a crime, this has to be interpreted in the light of new technologies: is it the location of the person sending or reading, or the location of servers storing and transmitting the message that are constitutive of jurisdiction, or all of these? When is an electronic contract concluded for buying a camera online: when the 'OK' button is pressed by the consumer, when the OK message reaches the webshop, when a receipt acknowledgement is sent by the webshop, or when the acknowledgement is received by the consumer?

In order to assess responsibility, the reason why an action took place sometimes has to be determined. Was the email threat actually sent with the intent of criminal threat, and did the consumer really intend to buy the camera? Can non-human entities, like a software agent, be considered to have their own will and take independent decisions?

The widespread use of persistent pseudonyms on the Internet, for example of an eBay tailer or consumer, raises questions about the link between a transaction and the physical person with whom the transaction is made, since this person is often invisible for most observers. How do we deal with this new reality, when if something goes wrong, no physical person can be linked with a reasonable amount of effort to the transaction? Who is responsible and will bear the (legal) consequences? New forms of unlawful activities take advantage of these grey zones, where the law is theoretically applicable but becomes very hard to enforce in a globalised cyberworld.

The abstract layer in the model based on virtual persons is particularly well-suited to describe (new) entities operating at an increasing distance from the physical or legal persons behind them. It recognises the existence of these (new) intermediate entities and explicitly incorporates them in the model. Some of these intermediate entities are recognised as persons in law (e.g., companies), others are not.

The concept of virtual persons in the FIDIS model is very general; this is necessary in order for it to cover all possibly relevant entities with respect to rights, obligations and responsibilities. Of course, not all virtual entities can have the same legal status or even have a legal status; in particular, not all virtual persons will have legal personhood. For example, avatars – a typical, traditional example of a virtual person, who have in-game rights and duties[16] – do not have legal personhood, and they very well may never acquire it. However, for some types of new entities it might be useful to extend 'virtual personhood' to legal personhood, if their position and functioning in society warrants giving them legal rights and duties.

---

[16] This illustrates that the term 'person' is not restricted to entities with legal personhood; it is thus a broader concept than the legal notion of 'person'.

3.3.3 Conclusion

Laws have a long experience of using abstract entities to define rules, categories, etc., in order to associate legal rights, obligations, and responsibilities to persons that can in concrete situations be considered instances of these abstract entities. The law does not say that John Doe will inherit his mother's fortune when she dies, but defines generically who is the 'heir' under which conditions. The application of the law in a specific situation makes an entity with legal personhood the bearer of the legal rights, legal obligations, and legal responsibilities associated with one of these abstract entities that the law uses. The model developed in FIDIS deliverable D2.13 (Jaquet-Chiffelle et al., 2008) intentionally uses a similar construction. Therefore, the model might learn from the long experience of handling abstract entities in law to refine some of its concepts specifically for the legal framework. Reciprocally, the legal framework might use this generic model to represent its abstract entities as well as new abstract entities together. This might be useful if current laws need to be adapted to encompass new paradigms, such as the rise of autonomically acting entities, to better understand if and when new laws or even new legal persons have to be created as a response to new technological developments.

The interested reader will find further developments in FIDIS deliverables D17.1 'Modelling New Forms of Identities: Applicability of the Model Based on Virtual Persons', D17.2 'New (Id)entities and the Law: Perspectives on Legal Personhood for Non-Humans' and D17.3 'Bridging the Accountability Gap: Rights for New Entities in the Information Society?'.

3.4 Trust in the Light of Virtual Persons[17]

Trust has always played an important sociological role in the history of human beings. Many observable patterns of social interaction and corresponding relationships between individuals or group of individuals are intrinsically tied to various forms of trust. In a broad sense, trust is usually understood as someone's firm belief in the reliability, competence, qualification, ability, strength, integrity, truthfulness, honesty, sincerity, loyalty, etc. of someone else. It is thus a relationship of reliance between a trusting and a trusted party (hereafter called the trustor and the trustee, respectively). Usually, the strength of this relationship depends on what the trustor knows about the trustee, which is why trust relationships between closely related persons (e.g., between family members, friends, or partners) tend to be stronger than trust relationships between less related or unrelated persons. A trustee is presumed to meet the trustor's expectations formed by experiencing previous interactions or by explicit agreements or promises. Trust is therefore

[17] This section is a preliminary excerpt of the forthcoming FIDIS deliverable D17.4 on '*Trust and Identification in the Light of Virtual Persons*'. This excerpt is written by R. Haenni; it has been reviewed by D.-O. Jaquet-Chiffelle, B.-J. Koops and V. Matyas.

directed towards the trustee's actions or behaviour in the future, and it should thus be seen as a prediction of reliance in the absence of full knowledge or control (Sztompka, 1999). In this way, trust is a mechanism by means of which an individual compensates a shortage of knowledge to obtain a feeling of control (Numan, 1998), and therefore a way of dealing with social complexities and uncertainties that goes beyond rationalistic reasoning (Luhmann, 2000).

The classical subjects and objects of trust relationships are physical persons (or groups of physical persons) involved in everyday social interactions. With the emergence of information technologies and the resulting trend towards a ubiquitously interconnected information society, the range of applicability of trust-related questions needs to be enlarged more and more from personally connected local communities towards globally distributed virtual communities. Then, one of the key questions to answer is whether and to what extent trust is also a matter between virtual persons, which are hidden behind ambiguous descriptions or pseudonyms (Cofta, 2007). This problem is a particular instance of the following more fundamental question: 'How can I trust bits and bytes?' (Gerck, 2002). Most generally, we may pose the question of the possibility of human-machine or machine-machine trust relationships (Muir, 1987; Lee and Moray, 1992).

The purpose of this subsection is to provide a first introduction to trust-related concepts and problems in the context of virtual persons. We start by giving a short overview of the research on trust in various scientific fields. Next, we expose the dominant views of trust in the literature and propose a set of compatible definitions of trust-related concepts. We also show how these concepts relate to existing trust metrics and trust management systems, and finally discuss some of the most compelling problems of applying trust to the concept of virtual persons. A more profound analysis and investigation of this topic will be included in the forthcoming FIDIS deliverable D17.4.

3.4.1 Research on Trust

Due to the fundamental role of trust for social groups like organisations, communities, institutions, or even whole economies to function, it has been an increasingly popular area of scientific study and research in many different fields, most notably in the social sciences and its sub-branches, e.g., in sociology (Sztompka, 1999), psychology (Castelfranchi and Falcon, 2001), economics (Fukuyama, 1995), and political sciences (Giddens, 1990; Levi and Stoker, 2000; Seligman, 2000; Hardin, 2006). It has also been an area of interest for numerous philosophers, who strive to explore the conceptual nature, moral foundations, and the epistemology of trust and trustworthiness (Uslaner, 2002; McLeod, 2006). More recently, physicists and system scientists interested in collective processes, dynamical complex systems, or generally in cybernetics have discovered trust as an important issue (Oliver and Montgomery, 2001). Simultaneously, trust has been recognised in computer science to be fundamental for building up and managing public-key infrastructures (Zimmermann, 1994; Perlman, 1999), peer-to-peer networks (Xiong and Liu, 2004), large-scale eCommerce applications (Tan and Thoen,

1998; Jones et al., 2000; Grandison and Sloman, 2000; Patton and Jøsang, 2004), web services (Wang and Vassileva, 2007), the semantic web (Richardson et al., 2003; Almendra and Schwabe, 2006; Artz and Gil, 2007), or interactive online communities (Abdul-Rahman and Hailes, 2000; Preece and Maloney-Krichmar, 2003). The problems of applications of that kind are intrinsically tied to the more general problem of establishing trust in IT applications and services or in new technology in general (Flowerday et al., 2006).

In the light of its widespread scientific relevance, trust should be regarded as a multi-disciplinary research topic with many different meanings and varying perceptions. In sociology and psychology, for example, trust is primarily perceived as a trustor's mental state of belief in the trustee's competence and honesty, and the degree to which one party trusts another is the corresponding strength of belief (Castelfranchi and Falcon, 2001). If regarded as a mental state, trust is not directly observable, only indirectly over someone's trust-driven behaviour or by self-reported trust levels. This has important implications when it comes to setting up the data acquisition of trust-related sociological or psychological studies. In psychology, trust has furthermore the facet of an instrument for social influence. The idea is that a trusting party is easier to influence than a non-trusting party. Related questions result from the psychological asymmetry between building up and destroying trust, or from the often-observed reciprocity of a trusted party who starts acting differently after learning about being trusted.

In economics, trust is mostly perceived as a relationship between consumers and the products or brands they buy. As such, trust has an important impact in marketing or branding strategies. Similar trust relationships exist between business partners, between corporations and their shareholders, or generally between the stakeholders involved in all sorts of business processes. Trust-strengthening measures are therefore of crucial importance for business management and economic decision-making. The economics of trust thus requires a profound understanding of questions related to the costs of developing, maintaining, and losing trust. In this context, trust is often perceived as being intertwined with risk, e.g., as a particular form of voluntary risk-taking based on the expectations of the future behaviour of others (Giddens, 1990; Szerszynski, 1999; Jøsang and Lo Presti, 2004).

In political sciences, research on trust focuses on a citizen's confidence in the political system, the governmental institutions, and their ability and benevolence to act on behalf of the public good and to use the assigned power and resources for the general welfare. This impersonal form of trust is what is sometimes called institutionalised (or generalised) trust, in contrast to the interpersonal form of formal trust between individuals as discussed in sociology, psychology, and economics. Many authors consider institutionalised trust as the foundation for economic development and democratic stability (Fukuyama, 1995; Warren, 1999; Newton, 2001).

A very diverse conceptualisation of trust is observed in computer science. Applications related to anonymous online communities usually start from a view similar to the one in sociology and psychology (Preece and Maloney-Krichmar, 2003). In eCommerce applications, trust inherits the above-mentioned role as a customer-supplier relationship and is thus considered to be crucial for the expansion of eBusiness markets and the full exploitation of the technological developments (Doney and Cannon, 1997). Another role of trust in eCommerce implicitly results from collaborative filtering techniques or more generally from so-called reputation systems, where a user's interests are automatically predicted on the basis of observed patterns or collected ratings from other users (Yu and Sing, 2002; Herlocker et al., 2004). Similar ideas are applied for establishing trust in peer-to-peer networks (Xiong and Liu, 2004). In a centralised public-key infrastructure (PKI), where the assumption of trustworthy certification authorities is a prerequisite for users to accept encrypted communication channels as secure, we observe a particular form of institutionalised trust (Perlman, 1999). A decentralised PKI avoids this form of institutionalised trust by dispersing it into a distributed network of interpersonal trust relations among individual users, a so-called web of trust (Abdul-Rahman, 1997; Haenni and Jonczy, 2007). In network and web service security, or more generally in access control, trust is usually interlinked with access control policies and corresponding digitally signed credentials. The holder of a sufficient amount of such policy-based trust credentials is then considered as being trustworthy and authorised to receive certain access rights (Ryutov et al., 2005; De Capitani di Vimercati et al., 2007). A similar definition of policy-based trust results from the concept of a trusted system, which is designed to enforce specified security policies, e.g., with respect to the processing, storage, and retrieval of sensitive information (Abrams and Joyce, 1995). Restricted to a PC's hardware and software, people also refer to it as trusted computing (Challener et al., 2007). In applications of the semantic web, a very fundamental problem of trust is the verification of a resource's claimed authorship. This is a consequence of the web as a place where 'anybody can say anything about anything' (Berners-Lee, 1997).

In the remainder of this subsection, we provide a compilation of definitions and concepts related to trust, each of which we think may be relevant to further research on virtual persons. Our main focus will be on the sociological understanding of trust as somebody's belief state, but the discussion will be rooted in the computer science literature, particularly in papers on computational aspects of trust as found in so-called trust metrics, or more generally on trust management in distributed systems. For a more comprehensive overview of trust in computer science, we refer to several excellent surveys (Grandison and Sloman, 2000; Ruohomaa and Kutvonen, 2005; Artz and Gil, 2007).

3.4.2 Defining Trust

Despite the wide variety of trust literature with its diverging definitions and conceptualisations, there are a number of common themes and patterns. Those are far from delivering something like a unified view, but they allow us here to provide some sort of digest, which may serve as an orientation guide to make the major streams in the literature more accessible. The only principal commitment we adopt from the beginning is to view trust as a person's mental state about the future contingent actions and behaviour of others, as is common practice in sociology, psychology, and computer science (Castelfranchi and Falcone, 2001). To enlarge the flexibility of this initial position of predictive behavioural trust, we also allow retrospective trust relations with respect to the authenticity or credibility of statements from a source of information. This particular form of informational trust is important in semantic web and PKI applications, where the truth of a statement or the claim of the origin of a piece of information is a crucial factor for drawing reasonable conclusions. Informational trust leads thus to the acceptance of the truth of a statement in the absence of conclusive evidence. As a mental state, both behavioural and informational trust is inherently subjective. Note that informational trust can be interpreted as a retrospective form of behavioural trust. Similarly, we can often interpret behavioural trust as a particular case of informational trust towards respective promises or commitments to act accordingly.

Instead of repeating some of the most general definitions from the trust literature, as it is done e.g., in (Artz and Gil, 2007), we suggest here a hierarchical approach, in which the meaning of trust is narrowed down from a small set of very general, higher-level concepts (e.g., trustor, trustee, trustworthiness) towards some more elementary, lower-level concepts (e.g., competence, honesty, belief). By doing so, we attempt to gradually approximate the principal characteristics of trust and to incorporate the most important aspect and trends mentioned in the literature, but we are aware that the result will be far from delivering a complete picture. For some of those concepts, we will give some rough ideas about a possible formal underground, but we will try to keep the necessary mathematics as simple as possible. The whole hierarchy of concepts is depicted in Figure 3.13. For a more comprehensive overview of trust definitions and trust-related concepts, we refer to the excellent classification in (McKnight and Chervany, 1996).

Definition 1: Trust is the opinion of a trustor about a trustee's trustworthiness relative to some trust context.

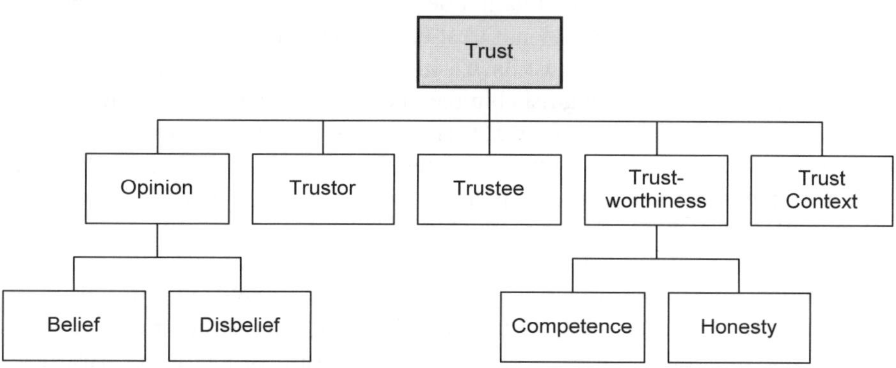

Fig. 3.13. A hierarchy of trust-related concepts

By saying that trust is an opinion, we try to incorporate the above-mentioned idea of a mental state. This is consistent with the cognitive or epistemic view of trust, so-called knowledge-based trust, in which the strength of a trust relation depends on the trustor's available information or evidence about the trustee's trustworthiness. It also includes the dynamic aspect of trust, because opinions may change non-monotonically over time when new information is accumulated. Finally, it also covers the aspect that most people experience trust as a matter of degree, because our conceptualisation of an opinion as a composition of respective states of belief and disbelief (see Def. 8) is inherently a quantitative one. Note that the three most basic positions of a qualitative approach (full trust, full distrust, zero trust / distrust) are included as extremal borderline cases. This allows us to distinguish properly between zero trust and distrust, an aspect that is well recognised in the literature (Marsh, 1994; Cho, 2006; Lewicki, 2006).

Reduced to a relationship in the sense of an entity-relationship model (ERM), trust may thus be considered as a ternary relation,

trust(<*trustor*>,<*trustee*>,<*context*>), (3.1)

which depends on three principal parameters (Jøsang et al., 2006; Hardin, 2006). Some authors suggest trust to be seen as a binary, context-independent relation (Yhang et al., 2004), but this is only sufficient in applications with a general, predetermined trust context, or for extremal positions such as blind trust or paranoia. Other authors propose a quaternary relation with time or evidence as an additional parameter (Gutscher, 2007), but as argued above, those aspects are implicitly included in our ternary model as particular characteristics of the trustor's mental state. Other proposed parameters in the literature are the trustor's or trustee's future actions and goals, implied risks, or third-party authorities (Castelfranchi and Falcone, 2001). Some of those additional aspects are at least partly included in our general understanding of a trust context (see Def. 4).

An immediate question that arises from the ERM perspective of trust is whether certain properties hold for trust relationships (Gutscher, 2007). It is generally accepted that trust is a one-to-one relation between a trustor and a trustee. The relation is asymmetric (A and B may not trust each other to the same extent) and non-reflexive (A does not always trust itself). In some specific situations, for example with respect to some indistinguishable members of a certain group, we may observe a one-to-many relation of equal trust between a trustor and several trustees. Many-to-one or even many-to-many trust relations are also thinkable, but only in some very particular situations (Grandison and Sloman, 2000). Those aspects are all well reflected in our cognitive view of knowledge-based trust.

A more controversial issue in the literature is the question of whether trust relations are transitive or not. In a transitive trust relation, it holds that if A trusts B, and B trusts C, then A trusts C. While transitivity of trust is the primary mechanism for deriving indirect trust, a key concept in most trust metrics or trust management systems (Mahoney et al., 2005), the majority of authors agree that general transitivity is only exhibited under very specific circumstances (Christianson and Harbison, 1997). For a given or fixed trust context, one such scenario results from the assumption that all agents share a common or centralised repository of trust-relevant information about each other. This may be achieved by mutually exchanging the information about existing direct trust relationships by means of recommendations or credentials (Jøsang et al., 2006). From a global perspective, interpreting a common or centralised trust repository corresponds to computing the transitive closure of the trust relation (Branchaud and Flinn, 2004). Our proposed perception of knowledge-based trust is generally not transitive, but it inherently supports such particular scenarios without difficulty.

Trustor and Trustee

To make the above-stated general definition of trust more accurate, let us first have a closer look at the possible subjects and objects of a trust relation. From the ERM perspective, it would be most natural to consider them generally as entities, which are not further specified except that they have a distinct existence. But to emphasise that trust is a mental state about an entity's future behaviour or its credibility as a source of information, which requires entities with the capability to 'think', 'speak', and 'act' (in a very broad sense), we prefer to call them agents, as it is common practice in economics and artificial intelligence. A cognitive agent is one that reasons, decides, speaks, and acts on the basis of the evidence from and knowledge about the agent's environment.

Definition 2: A trustor is a cognitive agent with the ability to collect trust-related evidence and use it to form corresponding opinions about the trustworthiness of others.

Usually, we can think of a trustor as a living physical person, but our definition as a cognitive agent also includes software agents, autonomous robots, or intelligent machines as possible trusting parties. In a similar way, we may also consider groups or whole communities as subjects of a trust relation, as long as they act as if they were a closed unit with a common view of trust-related knowledge and respective opinions. More generally, we allow the range of possible trustors to include various forms of virtual persons.

Definition 3: A trustee is an agent whose actions and statements are (partly or fully) unpredictable respectively unverifiable to others.

As above, we may most typically think of a trustee as a living physical person, but our definition is again compatible with software agents or robots, groups or communities, and other virtual persons. As a borderline case, it is even compatible with all sorts of machines, systems, devices, or tools, as long their future behaviour is not entirely predictable. In such cases, we may also replace in our consideration the machine itself by 'the one(s) who built the machine'. Nevertheless, we consider trust interpersonal with respect to the two agents involved, but not necessarily with respect to individual human beings.

As a final note, we want to stress that a trustee may not necessarily be different from the trustor. With this we explicitly allow reflexive trust relations, so-called self-trust. In many trust metrics, self-trust plays an important role as a base case on which recursive trust propagation methods are rooted.

Trust Context

The third principal parameter in the trust relation in (4.1) copes with the fact that a particular agent may not be equally dependable with respect to all different types of actions or statements. A trustee may thus be a perfect service provider or a reliable source of information in its own area of expertise (e.g., medical advice), but at the same time be completely unreliable in some other area (e.g., IT support). In other words, the level of trust attributed to an agent strongly depends on the context towards which the trust is directed. Some authors refer to it as context-specific trust (Branchaud and Flinn, 2004).

Definition 4: A trust context is a particular class of actions or statements, which are not further distinguished when judging an agent's trustworthiness.

A trust context limits thus the application of trust to a specific purpose or domain of action. In the literature, trust context is the most commonly used term, but essentially the same concept is sometimes called trust scope (Kohlas, 2007), trust class (Beth et al., 1994), trust category (Kinateder and Rothermel, 2003), trust domain (McLeod, 2006), or simply subject-matter dependent trust (Mahoney et al., 2005). A particular trust context is Maurer's concept of a trust level (Maurer, 1996), where a hierarchy of trust contexts reflects a particular form of inter-contextual dependencies.

The dimension of a particular trust context is application-dependent and may thus vary significantly. On one side of the spectrum, the context consists of a single, very specific action or statement (e.g., 'to return the rental car in time'). Such a restricted context allows the trustor to draw very accurate conclusions, but it makes the process of collecting trust-relevant information more difficult. On the other side of the spectrum, we may consider a very broad and general class of actions or statements (e.g., 'to follow orders'). The generality of such a context facilitates information gathering and enlarges the range of possible conclusions, but those will generally be less accurate. Choosing an appropriate specificity for a trust context is thus a tradeoff between simplicity and accuracy.

In the computer science literature on trust metrics, many authors find it convenient to assume a single generic trust context, one that covers all possible types of actions and statements. Other authors prefer to work with a fixed principal trust context for the whole application. A particular principal trust context, the so-called issuer trust context (Haenni et al., 2007), refers to an agent's ability to issue meaningful credentials about a third party's authenticity and trustworthiness. Issuer trust is thus the same type of trust that is required to accept public-key certificates in centralised and decentralised PKIs. In those types of applications, trust has a self-referral component, which imposes a cascade of related trust contexts on different layers (Maurer, 1996; Haenni et al., 2007). We refer to Kohlas (2007) for a more profound discussion of such interlinked trust contexts.

In various attempts to classify different forms of trust in the literature, the distinction between different trust contexts has often been a key parameter. One such proposal foresees the distinction between service provision trust, resource access trust, delegation trust, certification trust, and infrastructure trust (Grandison and Sloman, 2000). Further trust classes of that kind are authentication (or identity) trust and system trust (Jøsang et al., 2007). Another possible classification scheme distinguishes between concrete or material trust (e.g., 'to pay the restaurant bill') and abstract trust (e.g., 'to keep promises'), which is similar to the above-mentioned distinction between behavioural and informational trust.

Trustworthiness

The concepts of trust and trustworthiness are closely related, but they turn out to be quite distinct upon closer inspection. Most authors separate them sharply (Hardin, 2004; Ashraf et al., 2006). While trust is usually perceived as an attitude or mental state of the trustor, trustworthiness is a trustor-independent property of the trustee. A trustworthy person is thus someone in whom we can place our trust without any risk of being disappointed or betrayed. This position, which is based on the trustor's expectation of the trustee's trustworthiness, is the dominant view in the literature, especially in behavioural economics and psychology. Some authors refer to it as expectation-based trust or calculative trust (Rotter, 1980; Williamson, 1993). For example, psychological studies have shown that trustworthiness implies trust but not vice versa (Chaudhuri and Gangadharan, 2007). Many of those studies have used variants of the trust game proposed in (Berg et al., 1995) to measure trust and trustworthiness.

Despite the obvious differences between trust and trustworthiness, one can always imagine a borderline case in which 'those whom we trust will be trustworthy, and those who are trustworthy will be trusted' (McLeod, 2006). This would then be the ideal situation of so-called objective trust (Zhang et al., 2004), in which the trustor has full knowledge about whether or not, or to what degree, the trustee is actually trustworthy in some context. As it is usually not very realistic to assume full knowledge or even objectivity, we may see the difference between trust and trustworthiness to result from the trustor's incomplete epistemic state. The difference between trust and trustworthiness is thus another aspect of our subjective, knowledge-based perspective of trust, according to which various trustors may attribute to a particular trustee quite different levels of trust.

Perceiving trustworthiness as an agent's property gives rise to a number of implied questions. One of those questions concerns the existence of more fundamental components, on which trustworthiness is grounded. The following definition involves competence and honesty as necessary prerequisites for trustworthiness. While competence is a property that refers to the agent's capability to do and to say the truth about what it is trusted for, we use honesty for the agent's respective commitments and intentions. Therefore, competence mainly differs from honesty in the lack of a motive.

Definition 5: Trustworthiness is an agent's compound property of being competent and honest with respect to the actions and statements in some trust context.

Definition 6: Competence is an agent's ability to act dependably and to make truthful and relevant statements in some trust context.

Definition 7: Honesty is an agent's will to act dependably and to make truthful and relevant statements in some trust context.

In the discussion about the possible decomposition of trustworthiness, the absence / presence of motivational elements is the most common distinguishing feature in the literature (Castelfranchi and Falcon, 2001; McLeod, 2006). Competent but dishonest agents are sometimes called malicious (Kohlas, 2007). Note that some authors suggest a more detailed decomposition of trustworthiness with up to four different basic components (McKnight and Chervany, 1996; Oliver and Montgomery, 2001; Gefen, 2002).

To cover as many trust-related aspects as possible, both competence and honesty should be regarded as respective placeholders for a large number of similar properties with subtle differences. While competence involves many motive-independent factors such as know-how, expertise, accuracy, efficiency, skill, proficiency, qualification, capability, dependability, power, strength, or experience, we use honesty as a general term for motive-dependent properties such as sincerity, benevolence, goodwill, loyalty, faithfulness, truthfulness, responsibility, adherence, incorruptibility, integrity, discreetness, or fairness. Note that the latter may depend on the intended recipient towards which the action or statement is addressed. This is a direct consequence of the fact that an agent's motives to act are highly recipient-dependent, which is most apparent in properties like loyalty or faithfulness. Some authors use recipient-dependence to distinguish trustworthiness from mere reliability. It follows then that 'people known or considered to be trustworthy have the power to betray us, whereas people known or considered to be merely reliable can only disappoint us' (McLeod, 2006). The same subtlety can be used to separate trust from confidence, but this is not generally accepted (Cofta, 2007). A complicating issue in this respect is the fact that languages like Dutch or German do not provide separate words for trust and confidence.

While most authors have recognised the importance of the motivational element that might underlie trustworthy behaviour, there are still various discrepancies with regard to its exact nature. The most dominant position discussed in the literature is the goodwill view, according to which a trustee acts out of goodwill toward the trustor (McLeod, 2006). Another type of motive is addressed in the risk-assessment view, in which the trustee's own risk determines its behaviour (Jones, 1999). This view is a generalised form of the social contract view, in which the force of social constraints compels the trustee, and the encapsulated interest view, where trustees are motivated by their own personal interests. Note that recipient-dependence is mainly present in the goodwill view.

Another important characteristic of trustworthiness follows from the observation that both competence and honesty are highly time-dependent. While somebody's level of competence may gradually improve with practice or new experiences, it may quickly decrease in the absence of such practice or as consequence of the agent's natural aging. Honesty may exhibit a similar non-monotonical behaviour, depending on whether the motives on which it is grounded change over time. An agent's trustworthiness is therefore a dynamic property, which is subject to constant changes. Note that the dynamics of trustworthiness as an objective property is quite different from the dynamics of trust as a subjective epistemic state.

To summarise our discussion about trustworthiness, we may regard it from the ERM perspective as a quaternary relation, which inherits its parameters from respective relations for competence and honesty. Note that the parameter <recipient> does not necessarily need to refer to the one who wants to evaluate the agent's trustworthiness.

$$\begin{aligned}&\text{trustworthy}(<\!agent\!>,<\!context\!>,<\!time\!>,<\!recipient\!>) =\\&\quad\text{competent}(<\!agent\!>,<\!context\!>,<\!time\!>) \wedge\\&\quad\text{honest}(<\!agent\!>,<\!context\!>,<\!time\!>,<\!recipient\!>).\end{aligned} \tag{3.2}$$

To complete this picture, a few additional words need to be said about the observation that competence, honesty, and therefore trustworthiness are usually perceived as a matter of degree. Note that the granularity of such degrees may depend on the context. In a very specific context, which consists of a single action or statement only, we may actually not need more than a pair of extreme values, e.g., 1 for 'fully trustworthy' and 0 for 'not trustworthy', but this may not suffice for a less specific context. A common approach in the trust metrics literature is to define the degree of trustworthiness as the proportion of action and statements, for which the trustee is actually trustworthy, relative to the total number of action and statements in the current trust context (Gutscher, 2007). In mathematical terms, this means that trustworthiness is a quaternary mapping,

$$\text{trustworthy}(<\!agent\!>,<\!context\!>,<\!time\!>,<\!recipient\!>) \in [0,1], \tag{3.3}$$

which assigns to each possible configuration of input parameters a value from the unit interval [0,1], and similarly for competence and honesty. This definition as a proportion allows degrees of trustworthiness to be interpreted as probabilities and to apply the probability calculus to compute all sorts of related quantities. For example, assuming probabilistic independence between competence and honesty allows degrees of trustworthiness to be computed as the product of respective degrees of competence and honesty (Kohlas, 2007). Note that the probabilistic view includes the dichotomous perspective of the ERM as a borderline case.

Opinions

Most proponents of the knowledge-based perspective of trust, in which trust is regarded as a subjective attitude or mental state, agree that trust is more than a simple belief state with respect to the trustee's trustworthiness. The main concern comes from the observation that the absence of trust is clearly quite different from distrust. For example, one may not trust a stranger, but almost certainly distrust a notorious cheat or liar. In other words, trust has two different opposites, one in which the trustor's epistemic state is insufficient to draw any meaningful conclusion about the trustee's trustworthiness, and one in which the trustor's epistemic state leads to the conclusion that the trustee is actually untrustworthy. The absence of trust is sometimes called untrust (Marsh and Dibben, 2005). As most of the trust literature focuses on the positive aspect of trust, it is restricted to the simple dichotomy between trust and untrust. To include negative aspects of trust on an equal footing with positive aspects of trust, we suggest here a trichotomy between (positive) trust, untrust, and distrust (negative trust). This differentiation is necessary for agents to make use of distrust in their decision making in the same way they use trust or untrust, or more generally to establish a full symmetry between trust and distrust, with untrust as a neutral intermediate state.

An elegant way of capturing such a trichotomy is to detach the concepts of belief and disbelief. We depart thus from the dominant probabilistic (or Bayesian) view in the literature on representing uncertainty, in which degrees of belief and disbelief are represented by an additive pair of values $\mathrm{Bel}(h) \in [0,1]$ and $\mathrm{Bel}(\neg h) \in [0,1]$, respectively, for which $\mathrm{Bel}(h)+\mathrm{Bel}(\neg h)=1$ holds for all hypotheses h and their negations ¬h, and thus implies that degrees of belief are determined by respective degrees of disbelief and vice versa. One simple way to detach them from each other is to relax the additivity requirement into the inequality $\mathrm{Bel}(h)+\mathrm{Bel}(\neg h)\leq 1$, or to remove the restriction altogether. The main advantage of such sub-additive or non-additive degrees of belief is their ability to properly represent states of partial or full ignorance (Haenni, 2009), and this is exactly what is needed to separate trust, untrust, and distrust. Recall from Def. 1 that we use the notion of an opinion as an additional concept to realise the separation between belief and disbelief. To make the following definition of an opinion more flexible and general, we prefer to talk about states of belief and disbelief rather than degrees of belief and disbelief.

Definition 8: An opinion about a hypothesis is the composition of an agent's respective states of belief and disbelief with respect to some hypothesis under consideration.

Definition 9: A belief state is an agent's cognitive attitude towards the truth of a hypothesis.

Definition 10: A disbelief state is an agent's cognitive attitude towards the falsity of a hypothesis.

In our particular area of application of opinions as a means for defining trust, the hypotheses under consideration are statements like 'Agent X is trustworthy in context C at time T (towards recipient R)', and the knowledge and evidence to consider includes both first-hand experience and second-hand credentials about the trustee's trustworthiness. Exchanging and collecting such second-hand credentials is one of the key mechanisms on which most trust metrics and trust management systems are based. Positive credentials (i.e., those which designate an agent as trustworthy) are sometimes called recommendations, whereas negative credentials (i.e., those which designate an agent as untrustworthy) are called discredits (Haenni et al., 2007). The process of collecting and taking into consideration such trust-related evidence is an important feature of the proposed knowledge-based perspective of trust. It gives a concise explanation of the dynamics of trust, e.g., as a three-stage process of trust building, trust stability, and trust dissolution (Oliver and Montgomery, 2001).

Depending on the concrete way of representing states of belief and disbelief, we may obtain quite different forms of opinions. One of the simplest forms results from restricting the representation of belief and disbelief to their opposite extremities of full belief/ disbelief and no belief/ disbelief. If those extremities are represented by Boolean values 1 and 0, and without further restrictions, this delivers four different opinions (0,0), (1,0), (0,1), and (1,1), which may be interpreted as respective states of ignorance, belief, disbelief, and inconsistency. While it is common to exclude inconsistent opinions such as (1,1) by imposing the above-mentioned sub-additivity requirement, we can use the remaining consistent opinions (0,0), (1,0), and (0,1) to represent respective borderline cases of full untrust, full trust, and full distrust.

The most obvious generalisation of this simple scheme is to relax the restriction to Boolean values. In the context of trust representations, there are various proposals for less restrictive discrete scales with values such as 'untrusted', 'marginally trusted', 'fully trusted', and 'ultimately trusted' (Abdul-Rahman and Hailes, 2000; Li and Singhal, 2000; Ruth et al., 2004), but most authors agree that they should be mapped into a continuous scale such as the unit interval [0,1] or the percentages scale [0,100]. The trust and distrust propagation method proposed in (Guha et al., 2004) uses such a general scheme, in which trust and distrust values are entirely detached from each other, and where trust and distrust calculations are performed independently on respective matrices. Each particular state of trust and distrust corresponds then to a point in the unit square $[0,1]\times[0,1]$.

If the above-mentioned sub-additivity property is imposed to exclude inconsistent belief states, half of the unit square is chopped off. The result is a so-called opinion triangle, which is bounded by the extreme opinions (0,0), (1,0), and (0,1). It is common to depict this space by an equilateral triangle and corresponding barycentric coordinates b, d, and $i=1-(b+d)$ for respective degrees of belief, disbelief, and ignorance (Jøsang, 2001; Haenni, 2009). This picture is shown on the left hand side of Figure 3.14.

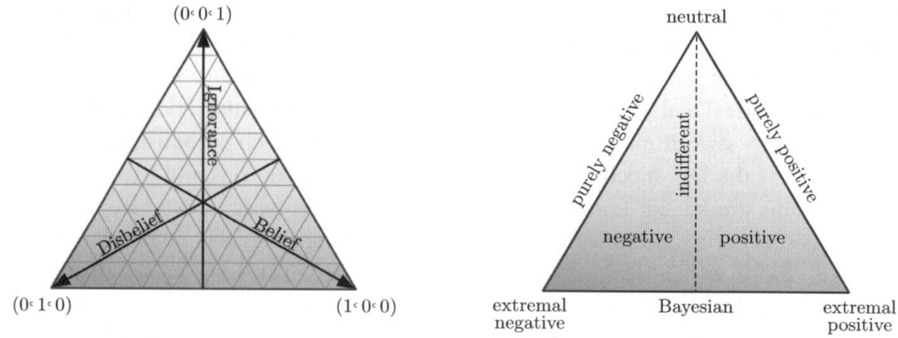

Fig. 3.14. Left: the opinion triangle with its three coordinates for belief, disbelief, and ignorance; Right: different opinion classes

In a more mathematical setting, it is common to define opinions as additive triplets (b,d,i), for which b,d,i≥0 and b+d+i=1 hold. According to the terminology proposed in Hájek and Valdés (1991), an opinion (b,d,i) is called positive if b>d, negative if b<d, indifferent if b=d, Bayesian if i=0, and simple if either b=0 or i=0. The borderline cases (1,0,0) and (0,1,0) are called extremal, whereas (0,0,1) is called neutral. All those particular types of opinions are depicted on the right hand side of Figure 3.14. We propose to adopt the same terminology for corresponding states of trust and distrust.

Opinions as suggested above are the elementary structures of the opinion algebra, which has been applied as a calculus for indirect trust (Jøsang, 1999). Note that there are many strong links between opinions of that kind and various mathematical approaches to non-additive degrees of belief (Haenni, 2007). Some of them include the dominant Bayesian paradigm of representing uncertainty by probabilities as a special case. If applied to the problem of representing trust and distrust, they are thus compatible with the widely accepted probabilistic interpretation of trust and trustworthiness.

As an alternative to the above opinion-based representation of trust and distrust, some authors suggest to apply other mathematical structures such as fuzzy sets (Griffiths, 2006), Dempster-Shafer belief functions (Yu and Singh, 2000), probabilistic argumentation systems (Haenni, 2005), or imprecise and second-order probabilities (Gutscher, 2007). We do not further address those directions here, but we want to point out that they are all motivated by the same fundamental problem of detaching distrust from untrust, or more generally uncertainty from ignorance. The same can be said about attempts to represent trust and distrust as a single continuous variable in a range like [−1,+1] or [−∞,+∞] and with 0 as a representation for untrust (Marsh, 1994), but those do not reach the full generality of our opinion-based definition of trust.

3.4.3 Trust Metrics and Trust Management Systems

Designing general computational models of trust has always been a principal goal since the scientific investigation of trust has started in various areas. The mathematical foundation of such a computational model, together with associated algorithms, is what is usually called trust metric. In sociology and psychology, trust metrics are used as a measure of how somebody is trusted by others. Usually, they use quantitative statements about direct trust relationships between two individuals as input data to compute quantitative estimates of indirect or derived trust relations. This general idea has been adopted in many eCommerce, network security, peer-to-peer, web services, or online community applications to draw conclusions about the trustworthiness of their users. Due to the wide range of different application areas, each of which with its own characteristics and specialties, there is no general agreement on what is the 'best' trust metric. To provide a rough guideline when judging the appropriateness of a concrete trust metric, some authors tried to identify different soundness properties that one would expect from a reasonable trust metric (Degerlund, 2007). Trust metrics are often embedded in so-called trust management systems (TMS), which support trust decision processes in distributed systems. Research on trust management systems is rooted in authentication based on public-key certificates (Zimmermann, 1994; Blaze et al., 1996), but are nowadays established in many other application areas of distributed systems. We refer to Ruohomaa and Kutvonen (2005) for an excellent survey.

Classification

Despite the diversity and wide variety of proposed trust metrics and trust management systems, a few principal dimensions with distinctive features have been identified as major axes for a possible classification (Ziegler and Lausen, 2005; Wang and Vassileva, 2007). One of them concerns the origin and availability of the input data, and another one the place and the so-called trust view of the evaluator. These axes are not entirely orthogonal, as the following discussion will show.

A centralised trust management system is based on one or several central authorities, which are responsible for making judgments and decisions about the trustworthiness of the users. To place such trust decisions at everybody's disposal, they are usually stored in central repositories. For such a system to work, it is necessary that all users accept the central authorities as trustworthy with respect to the task of making such trust decisions and for properly maintaining the accuracy and data consistency of the repository. In this way, the direct trust relation between a central authority and a particular user is transformed into an indirect trust relation between two users. The classical X.509 PKI is the most prominent example of such a centralised system. Most research however focuses explicitly on a decentralised or distributed trust decision process, in which individual users are empowered to make their own decisions and to communicate them to others in form of credentials. Note that the mechanisms in distributed systems are usually more complex to implement than those in centralised systems (Wang and Vassileva, 2007).

The second major dimension to classify trust management system concerns the place and the corresponding trust view, from which indirect trust relations are evaluated and established (Ruth et al., 2004). In a global system, the information relevant for making trust decisions is public and visible to all the system members. For a given trust metric, the evaluation of such a global trust view is the same for all users and can thus be delegated to a single user or central authority. Note that centralised trust management systems are usually global and vice versa. In a local (or personalised) trust management system, each user collects its own repository of trust-related information. Depending on the users' connections and interactions in the network, this can lead to quite different trust views and corresponding conclusions. Local trust management systems are designed to implement the subjective aspect of trust.

In the context of large online communities, in which users are allowed to issue ratings or recommendations about each other, trust management systems are sometimes called reputation systems. They differ from recommendation systems in their purpose of establishing interpersonal trust among users rather than trust towards external resources such as books, music, services, or web pages. The object type of the intended trust relations is thus another major dimension for the classification of trust management systems. It allows us to distinguish between interpersonal and resource-oriented trust management systems.

Another important distinguishing feature of trust management systems is the type of the underlying trust metrics. Some of the existing trust metrics, so-called scalar metrics, are designed to quantitatively evaluate trust relations of particular pairs of users, whereas group metrics are designed to compute each user's trustworthiness individually. Note that scalar metrics are inherently local (Ziegler and Lausen, 2005). Another distinctive characteristic of the underlying trust metric is the actual choice of the mathematical representation of trust (see Subsection 3.4.2) and the adopted mechanism to derive indirect trust relations from direct trust relations. An outline of such trust propagation algorithms is given in the following subsection.

Web of Trust

In a distributed trust management system, we can assume that a particular user issues credentials about some of the other users, but not about all of them. Such a credential, which describes a direct trust relationship between its issuer and recipient, can then be regarded as a link between two nodes in a trust network called web of trust. To represent different degrees of trust and to distinguish them properly from respective degrees of distrust, we assume here that an opinion is assigned to each link in the network (see Subsection 3.4.2). A missing link between two nodes means that no trust opinion has yet been formed. An exemplary web of

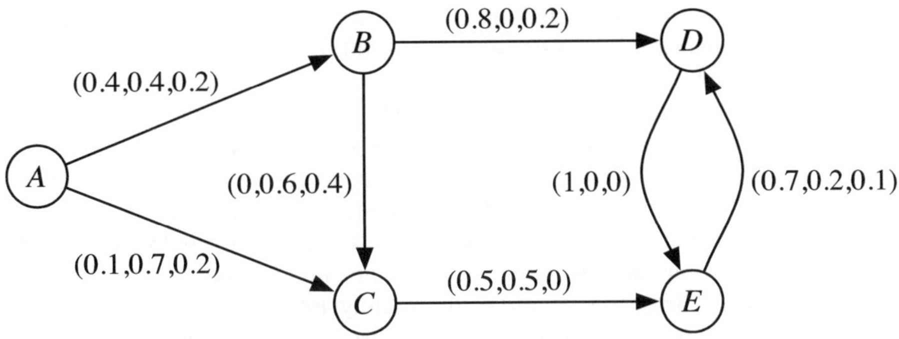

Fig. 3.15. A simple web of trust with users *A*, *B*, *C*, *D*, *E* and corresponding opinions

trust with users A, B, C, D, and E with corresponding links and opinions is shown in Figure 3.15. Note that most of the existing webs of trust are far less general than the proposed opinion-based scheme.

For a given web of trust like the one in Figure 3.15, the principal question now is how to use the given links and opinions to evaluate indirect trust relations for a pair of users with no direct link, e.g., for A and E. To make such calculations, a couple of assumptions with regard to the transitivity of trust and distrust need to be imposed (Ziegler and Lausen, 2005; Jøsang et al., 2006). As mentioned before, trust relations are only transitive under very particular semantic constraints. It is thus important for a meaningful trust propagation method to prove that such constraints are given in the intended application and to properly expose the necessary conditions and parameters for those constraints. One particular set of such conditions, which is known as conditional transitivity (Abdul-Rahman and Hailes, 1997), constitutes the foundation for many existing trust metrics. Its key requirement for a credential to be used to derive transitive trust is that the issuer of the credential is considered trustworthy as a recommender. For this, we may either assume a generic trust context, which includes the activity of issuing credentials, or we may distinguish at least two trust contexts, one for the application-specific activity and another one for the activity of issuing credentials (Haenni et al., 2007).

Another important, but less cited condition for transitive trust results from the problem of unambiguously attributing a credential to its issuer. This is a problem of informational trust with respect to the origin of a piece of information (see Subsection 3.4.2). In a closed system with registered users, e.g., in eBay's feedback forum, this problem is usually solved by implementing various security measures and policies, which prevent users from issuing credentials about others from the outside of their own user account. Such systems however can often not guarantee that each user is only registered once, which can easily be exploited to circumvent negative repudiation. This is a typical weakness of many centralised or global trust management systems. It results from the more general problem of attributing trust in the presence of multiple virtual identities. Note that this problem is inherent to all sorts of trust management systems (Kohlas, 2007).

A decentralised solution for the problem of validating the origin of a credential is to request a digital signature. The corresponding trust decision is then a question of verifying the digital signature using the issuer's public-key certificate. Note that certificates themselves are a particular form of credentials, i.e., accepting the authenticity of a piece of information after successfully verifying a digital signature requires an additional trust decision towards the issuer's ability and will of issuing certificates only after carefully checking the recipient's identity. The problems of authentication and trust are therefore intrinsically intertwined. This observation has been the motivation of many PKI-related trust management systems, which are thus followers of PGP's original proposal of a web of trust (Zimmerman, 1994; Maurer, 1996; Levien and Aiken, 1998; Jonczy and Haenni, 2005; Kohlas, 2007). For a general analysis of such two- or three-layer models we refer to Haenni et al. (2007).

If a system and the intended application are such that all the necessary conditions for transitive trust are satisfied, then the problem of the 'right' trust propagation method arises. The proposal of a network with opinions attributed to the links is one of the most general schemes, and it is best analyzed from an algebraic perspective (Jøsang, 1999; Theodorakopoulos, 2004). Most other approaches are restricted to single-valued trust representations and are therefore not designed to cope with some of the most important aspects of trust such as the aforementioned distinction between distrust and untrust (see Subsection 3.4.2). Their advantage however is the reduced mathematical complexity. For example, if each value assigned to a link (or node) of a web of trust is interpreted as a probability of operation of that link (or node), then it is possible to transform the problem of computing transitive trust into a network reliability problem, for which a wide variety of general solutions exist (Mahoney, 2005; Haenni and Jonczy, 2007). Many other single-valued trust propagation schemes use local trust aggregation functions like weighted sums or averages to update the degree of trustworthiness of a user according to its incoming links in the web of trust. Some of them iterate through the loops of arbitrarily long trust chains. The simplest systems are usually those with discrete trust values. They often do no more than generating simple statistics or applying some pragmatic trust propagation rules. The most popular systems of that kind are eBay's feedback forum and the web of trust in PGP.

Another popular family of approaches to solve the trust propagation problem is based on logical inference rules. Those rules are designed to formally describe the process of building up transitive trust relations. Usually, they are based on some first-order predicate logic (Beth, 1994, Maurer, 1996; Jonczy and Haenni, 2005; Gutscher, 2007; Kohlas, 2007). Their strength is the preciseness and transparency obtained from using logical predicates to encode fundamental concepts like trust and trustworthiness. However, most of those systems are computationally not very efficient and thus not scalable to large real-world applications.

The information given in this subsection only reflects a very small portion of the relevant literature. For a more detailed classification of existing trust propagation methods and for an exhibition of existing practical web of trust implementations, we refer to the excellent surveys and critical discussions in Jøsang et al. (2007) and Haenni et al. (2007).

3.4.4 Trust in the Light of Virtual Persons

With the growing virtualisation of many real-world processes and activities, together with the resulting shift of personal interactions in the physical world to virtual interactions in the digital world, we are faced today with a number of entirely new problems and challenges. Many of these encompass sociological, psychological, philosophical, or even legal aspects, and are thus not purely technological. A particular class of problems results from the question of how to establish trust in a digital context, in which virtual identities are the front-ends of almost all interactions. The majority of existing trust management systems are based on some simplifying assumptions, often implicitly, but those are mostly designated to avoid rather than to overcome such problems.

One particular type of problem results from the disguised link between a virtual person and the physical person(s) by which it is controlled. Similar problems arise in situations in which the same physical person is hidden behind multiple virtual identities. Problems of that kind are quite fundamental for applications situated in the virtual world. As an example, consider the problem of paying for an auctioned item on eBay, where the unknown seller is only visible as a subscribed eBay user with a corresponding account, but not as a tangible physical person within reach. We may use other users' ratings to judge the seller's trustworthiness, but considering their own trustworthiness with respect to issuing such ratings makes to problem even more complicated.

To analyse the application of trust to virtual persons more systematically, let's look at the basic model proposed in the first part of this section, in which the connection between physical and virtual persons is described as a n-to-n relationship: one physical person may be linked to several virtual persons, and several physical persons may be linked to the same virtual person (see Subsection 3.1.4). Now if we permit virtual persons or general virtual entities as objects of a trust relationship, as suggested in Def. 3 (see Subsection 3.4.2), we obtain three entirely new, but quite fundamental questions:

1. Can a trust relationship between a trustor and a *physical* person be transferred to a virtual person?
2. Can a trust relationship between a trustor and a *virtual* person be transferred to a physical person?
3. Can a trust relationship between a trustor and a *virtual* person be transferred to another *virtual* person?

It is obvious that transferring trust between physical and virtual persons requires respective links in the model. The problem is that the existence of these links is generally unknown to the trustor, and transferring trust may thus be impossible even in cases in which such links exist. In other words, the transfer of trust between physical and virtual persons may only occur after a process of link verification has given the trustor sufficiently enough evidence to become confident in its existence. This means that, for example, we should only rely on the eMail content apparently received from a trustworthy friend if we have enough evidence to believe that our friend is in control of that particular eMail account and is thus the author of the message.

To formally model the link verification process, we may look at it as another particular instance of the evidence-based process of forming respective opinions, as exposed in the second part of Subsection 3.4.2. In its most general form, we may thus come out with an additive triplet (b,d,i) of respective degrees of belief, disbelief, and ignorance, which may then be combined with the opinion included in the original trust relation to obtain an adapted opinion for the transferred trust relation. A complicating issue of this general method is the possibility of the available evidence to include statements from other physical or virtual entities, which may themselves depend on further trust relationships.

The most challenging question in the above list is the problem of transferring a trust relationship from a virtual person to another virtual person. For this to take place, it is compulsory that a pair of links exists to at least one (possibly unknown) common physical person. Such situations are not untypical; they arise for example when two mutually unknown eBay users switch to eMail communication to arrange the payment details of an auctioned item.

If we assume that the transfer of trust between physical and virtual persons can be handled properly, then we may additionally pose the aforementioned questions related to the transitivity of trust. And we may also try to apply or to extend the methods from existing trust management systems (see Subsection 3.4.3). Note that the fact that a physical person may be linked to various virtual persons has then an important impact on whether certain independence assumptions are still justified or not. In the forthcoming FIDIS deliverable D17.4, questions of that kind will be studied in further detail.

3.4.5 Conclusion

From the perspective of trust as an agent's mental state about another agent's trustworthiness, we have found that trust is a subjective, dynamic, context-dependent, non-transitive, non-reflexive, non-monotone, and non-additive relation between a trustor and a trustee. If certain conditions hold, we may assume transitivity in some applications. Transitivity is the key mechanism on which most trust propagation methods rely. Those methods are important in distributed trust management systems to evaluate indirect trust relations for a given repository of direct trust relations. The concrete look of such a method depends on the adopted trust metric and the underlying representation of trust. One of the most general trust representations uses the concept of an opinion to reflect the whole range of possible epistemic states and thus to separate distrust properly from untrust.

In the light of the growing virtualisation of many of our daily-life activities, a number of new problems related to our understanding of trust arise. To improve our understanding of these interdisciplinary problems, we encourage researchers to investigate these topics to the full extent of their facets and consequences. Some of the problems have been addressed recently (Cofta, 2007; Kohlas, 2007), but the current state of the literature is still very shallow. Further results can be expected from the forthcoming FIDIS deliverable D17.4.

References

Abdul-Rahman, A. (1997), 'The PGP trust model', EDI-Forum: the Journal of Electronic Commerce, 10(3):27–31.

Abdul-Rahman, A. and Hailes, S. (1997), 'A distributed trust model', NSPW'97, Workshop on New Security Paradigms, pp 48–60, Langdale, Cumbria, U.K.

Abdul-Rahman, A. and Hailes S (2000) 'Supporting trust in virtual communities', HICSS-33, 33rd Hawaii International Conference on System Sciences, pp 1769–1777, Maui, USA.

Abrams, M. D. and Joyce, M. V. (1995), 'Trusted system concepts', Computers & Security, 14(1):45–56.

Almendra, V. S. and Schwabe, D. (2006), 'Trust policies for semantic web repositories', in: Bonatti, P. A., Ding, L., Finin, T., Olmedilla, D. (eds), SWPW'06, 2nd Semantic Web Policy Workshop, pp 17–31, Athens, USA.

Anrig, B., Browne, W., Gasson, M. (2007), 'The role of algorithms in profiling', in: Hildebrandt, M. and Gutwirth, S. (eds), *Profiling the European Citizen*, Springer, pp 65–80.

Artz, D. and Gil, Z. (2007), 'A survey of trust in computer science and the semantic web', Web Semantics: Science, Services and Agents on the World Wide Web, 5(2):58–71.

Ashraf, N., Bohnet, I., Piankov, N. (2006), 'Decomposing trust and trustworthiness', Experimental Economics, 9(3):193–208.

Benoist, E. (2007), 'Collecting data for the profiling of web-users', in: Hildebrandt. M., Gutwirth, S. (eds), *Profiling the European Citizen*, pp 169–175, Springer.

Berg, J., Dickhaut, J., McCabe, K. (1995), 'Trust, reciprocity and social history', Games and Economic Behavior, 10:122–142.

Berners-Lee, T. (1997), Metadata architecture, available online at http://www.w3.org/DesignIssues/Metadata.

Beth, T., Borcherding, M., Klein, B. (1994), 'Valuation of trust in open networks', ESORICS'94, 3rd European Symposium on Research in Computer Security, LNCS 875, pp 3–18.

Blaze, M., Feigenbaum, J., Lacy, J. (1996), 'Decentralized trust management', SP'96, IEEE Symposium on Security and Privacy, pp 164–173, Oakland, USA.

Blaze, M., Feigenbaum, J., Ioannidis, J., Keromytis, A. D. (1999), 'The role of trust management in distributed systems security', Secure Internet Programming: Security Issues for Mobile and Distributed Objects, pp 185–210, Springer.

Bourcier, D. (2001), 'De l'intelligence artificielle à la personne virtuelle: émergence d'une entité juridique?', *Droit and Société*, 49, pp 847–871.

Branchaud, M. and Flinn, S. (2004), 'Trust: A scalable trust management infrastructure', PST'04, 2nd Annual Conference on Privacy, Security and Trust, pp 207–218, Fredericton, Canada.

Castelfranchi, C. and Falcone, R. (2001), 'Social trust: a cognitive approach', in: Castelfranchi, C. and Tan, Y. H. (eds), Trust and Deception in Virtual Societies, pp 55–90, Kluwer Academic Publishers.

Challener, D., Yoder, K., Catherman, R., Safford, D., Van Doorn, L. (2007), A Practical Guide to Trusted Computing, IBM Press.

Chaudhuri, A. and Gangadharan, L. (2007), 'An experimental analysis of trust and trustworthiness', Southern Economic Journal, 73(4):959–985.

Cho, J. (2006), 'The mechanism of trust and distrust formation and their relational outcomes', Journal of Retailing, 82(1):25–35.

Christianson, B. and Harbison, W. S. (1997), 'Why isn't trust transitive?', in: Christianson, B., Crispo, B., Lomas, T. M. A., Roe, M. (eds.), IWSP'97, 5th International Workshop on Security Protocols, LNCS 1189, pp 171–176, Paris, France.

Cofta, P. (2007), 'Confidence, trust and identity', BT Technology Journal, 25(2):173–178.

De Capitani di Vimercati, S., Foresti, S., Jajodia, S., Samarati, P. (2007), 'Access control policies and languages in open environments', in: Yu, T. and Jajodia, S. (eds.), Secure Data Management in Decentralized Systems, pp 21–58, Springer.

Degerlund, F. (2007), 'Trust mass, volume and density – a novel approach to reasoning about trust', Electronic Notes in Theoretical Computer Science, 179:87–96.

Doney, P. M., Cannon, J. P. (1997), 'An examination of the nature of trust in buyer-seller relationships', Journal of Marketing, 61(2):35–51.

Flowerday, S. and von Solms, R. (2006), 'Trust: An element of information security', in:Fischer-Hübner, S., Rannenberg, K., Yngström, L., Lindskog, S. (eds.), SEC'06, 21st International Information Security Conference, pp 87–98, Karlstad, Sweden.

Fukuyama, F. (1995), Trust: The Social Virtues and the Creation of Prosperity, The Free Press.

Gefen, D. (2002), 'Reflections on the dimensions of trust and trustworthiness among online consumers', ACM SIGMIS Database, 33(3):38–53.

Gerck, E. (2002), 'Trust as qualified reliance on information', The COOK Report on Internet, X(10):19–24.

Giddens, A. (1990), The Consequences of Modernity, Polity Press.

Grandison, T. and Sloman, M. (2000), 'A survey of trust in internet applications', IEEE Communications Surveys and Tutorials, 3(4).

Griffiths, N. (2006), 'A fuzzy approach to reasoning with trust, distrust and insufficient trust', in: Klusch, M., Rovatsos, M., Payne, T. R. (eds.), CIA'06, 10th International Workshop on Cooperative Information Agents, volume 4149 of LNCS 4149, pp 360–374, Edinburgh, U.K.

Guha, R., Kumar, R., Raghavan, P., Tomkins, A. (2004), 'Propagation of trust and distrust', in: Feldman, S. I., Uretsky, M., Najork, M., Wills, C. S. (eds.), WWW'04, 13th International Conference on World Wide Web, pp 403–412, New York, USA.

Gutscher, A. (2007), 'A trust model for an open, decentralized reputation system', in: Etalle, S., Marsh, S. (eds), IFIPTM'07, 1st Joint iTrust and PST Conferences on Privacy Trust Management and Security, pp 285–300, Moncton, Canada.

Haenni, R. (2005), 'Using probabilistic argumentation for key validation in public-key cryptography', International Journal of Approximate Reasoning, 38(3):355–376.

Haenni, R. (2009), 'Non-additive degrees of belief', in: Huber, F. and Schmidt-Petri, C. (eds.), Degrees of Belief, pp 121–160, Springer.

Haenni, R. and Jonczy, J. (2007), 'A new approach to PGP's web of trust', EEMA'07, European e-Identity Conference, Paris, France.

Haenni, R., Jonczy, J., Kohlas, R. (2007), 'Two-layer models for managing authenticity and trust', in: Song, R., Korba, L., Yee, G. (eds.), Trust in E-Services: Technologies, Practices and Challenges, chapter VI, pp 140–167, Idea Group Publishing.

Hájek, P. and Valdés, J. J. (1991), 'Generalized algebraic approach to uncertainty processing in rule-based expert systems (dempsteroids)', Computers and Artificial Intelligence, 10:29–42.

Hardin, R. (2004), Trust and Trustworthiness, vol. 4 of Series on Trust. Russell Sage Foundation Publications.

Hardin, R. (2006), Trust (Key Concepts), Polity.

Herlocker, J. L., Konstan, J. A., Terveen, L. G., Riedl, J. T. (2004), 'Evaluating collaborative filtering recommender systems', ACM Transactions on Information Systems, 22(1):5–53.

Hildebrandt, M. and Gutwirth, S. (eds.) (2007), *Profiling the European Citizen*. Springer.

Jaquet-Chiffelle, D. O. (2007), 'Direct and Indirect Profiling in the Light of Virtual Persons', in: Hildebrandt, M. and Gutwirth, S. (eds.), *Profiling the European Citizen*, pp 34–43, Springer.

Jaquet-Chiffelle, D. O., Anrig, B., Benoist, E., Haenni, R., Hildebrandt, M., Kosta, E., Lefever, K. (eds.) (2008), FIDIS Deliverable D2.13: Virtual Persons and Identities, Download: http://www.fidis.net/deliverables.

Jaquet-Chiffelle, D. O., Anrig, B., Zwingelberg, H. (eds.) (2008), FIDIS Deliverable D17.1: Modelling New Forms of Identities: Applicability of the Model Based on Virtual Persons, Download: http://www.fidis.net.

Jones, K. (1999), 'Second-hand moral knowledge', The Journal of Philosophy, 96(2):55–78.

Jones, S., Wilikens, M., Morris, P., Masera, M. (2000), 'Trust requirements in e-business', Communications of the ACM, 43(12):81–87.

Jonczy, J. and Haenni, R. (2005), 'Credential networks: a general model for distributed trust and authenticity management', in: Ghorbani, A., Marsh, S. (eds), PST'05, 3rd Annual Conference on Privacy, Security and Trust, pp 101–112, St. Andrews, Canada.

Jøsang, A. (1999), 'An algebra for assessing trust in certification chains', NDSS'99: 6th Annual Symposium on Network and Distributed System Security, San Diego, USA.

Jøsang, A. (2001), 'A logic for uncertain probabilities', International Journal of Uncertainty, Fuzziness and Knowledge-Based Systems, 9(3):279–311.

Jøsang, A., Gray, E., Kinateder, M. (2006), 'Simplification and analysis of transitive trust networks', Web Intelligence and Agent Systems, 4(2):139–161.

Jøsang, A., Ismail, R., Boyd, B. (2007), 'A survey of trust and reputation systems for online service provision', Decision Support Systems, 43(2):618–644.

Jøsang, A. and Lo Presti, S. (2004), 'Anlysing the relationship between risk and trust', in: Jensen, C. D., Poslad, S., Dimitrakos, T. (eds.), iTrust'04: 2nd International Conference on Trust Management, LNCS 2995, pp 135–145, Oxford, U.K.

Kantorowicz, E. H. (1957), The King's Two Bodies – A Study in Mediaeval Political Theology, Princeton University Press.

Kinateder, M. and Rothermel, K. (2003), 'Architecture and algorithms for a distributed reputation system', iTrust'03: 1st International Conference on Trust Management, LNCS 2692, pp 1–16, Heraklion, Greece.

Kohlas, R. (2007), Decentralized Trust Evaluation and Public-Key Authentication, PhD thesis, University of Bern, Switzerland.

Koops, B. J. and Jaquet-Chiffelle, D. O. (eds.) (2008), FIDIS Deliverable D17.2: New (Id)entities and the Law: Perspectives on Legal Personhood for Non-Humans, Download http://www.fidis.net.

Lee, J. and Moray, N. (1992), 'Trust, control strategies and allocation of function in human-machine systems', Ergonomics, 35:1243–1270.

Lewicki, R. J. (2006), 'Trust and distrust', in: Kupfer Schneider, A. and Honeyman, C. (eds.), The Negotiator's Fieldbook: The Desk Reference for the Experienced Negotiator, ch. 22, pp 191–202, American Bar Association.

Levi, M. and Stoker, L. (2000), 'Political trust and trustworthiness', Annual Review of Political Science, 3:475–507.

Levien, R. and Aiken, A. (1998), 'Attack-resistant trust metrics for public key certification', Security'98, 7th USENIX Security Symposium, pp 229–242, San Antonio, USA.

Li, H. and Singhal, M. (2000), 'Trust management in distributed systems', Computer, 40(2):45–53.

Luhmann, N. (2000), Vertrauen – ein Mechanismus der Reduktion sozialer Komplexität, UTP, Stuttgart, Germany, 4th ed.

Mahoney, G., Myrvold, W., Shoja, G. C. (2005), 'Generic reliability trust model', in: Ghorbani. A. and Marsh, S. (eds.), PST'05: 3rd Annual Conference on Privacy, Security and Trust, pp 113–120, St. Andrews, Canada.

Manchala, D. W. (2000), 'E-commerce trust metrics and models', IEEE Internet Computing, 4(2):36–44.

Marsh, S. P. (1994), Formalising Trust as a Computational Concept, PhD thesis, University of Stirling, Scotland, U.K.

Marsh, S. and Dibben, M. R. (2005), 'Trust, untrust, distrust and mistrust – an exploration of the dark(er) side' in: Herrmann, P., Issarny, V., Shiu, S. (eds.), iTrust'05: 3rd International Conference on Trust Management, LNCS 3477, pp 17–33, Rocquencourt, France.

Maurer, U. (1996), 'Modelling a public-key infrastructure', in: Bertino, E., Kurth, H., Martella, G., Montolivo, E. (eds.), ESORICS, European Symposium on Research in Computer Security, LNCS 1146, pp 324–350.

McKnight, H. D. and Chervany, N. L. (1996), The meanings of trust, Technical report, Carlson School of Management, University of Minnesota, Minneapolis, USA.

McLeod, C., Zalta, E. N. (ed) (2006), 'Trust', The Stanford Encyclopedia of Philosophy, Center for the Study of Language and Information, Stanford University, USA.

Muir, B. M. (1987), 'Trust between humans and machines, and the design of decision aids', International Journal of Man-Machine Studies, 27(5-6):527–539.

Newton, K. (2001), 'Trust, social capital, civil society, and democracy', International Political Science Review, 22(2):201–214.

Numan, J. H. (1998), Knowledge-Based Systems as Companions: Trust, Human Computer Interaction and Complex Systems, PhD thesis, University of Groningen, The Netherlands.

Oliver, A. and Montgomery, K. (2001), 'A system cybernetic approach to the dynamics of individual- and organizational-level trust', Human relations, 54(8):1045–1063.

Patton, M. A. and Jøsang, A. (2004), 'Technologies for trust in electronic commerce', Electronic Commerce Research, 4(1–2):9–21.

Perlman, R. (1999), 'An overview of PKI trust models', IEEE Network, 13(6):38–43.

Pfitzmann, A. and Hansen, M. (2008), 'Anonymity, Unlinkability, Undetectability, Unobservability, Pseudonymity, and Identity Management – A Consolidated Proposal for Terminology, v.031', Technical Report, Faculty of Computer Science, Technical University, Dresden, Germany.

Preece, J. and Maloney-Krichmar, D. (2003), 'Online communities: Focusing on sociability and usability', in: Jacko, J. and Sears, A. (eds.), The Human-Computer Interaction Handbook: Fundamentals, Evolving Technologies and Emerging Applications, pp 596–620, Lawrence Erlbaum Associates.

Richardson, M., Agrawal, R., Domingos, P. (2003), 'Trust management for the semantic web', in: Fensel, D., Sycara, K. P., Mylopoulos, J. (eds.), ISWC'03, 2nd International Semantic Web Conference, LNCS 2870, pp 351–368, Sanibel Island, USA.

Rotter, J. B. (1980), 'Interpersonal trust, trustworthiness, and gullibility', American Psychologist, 35:1–7.

Ruohomaa, S. and Kutvonen, L. (2005), 'Trust management survey', in: Herrmann, P., Issarny, V., Shiu, S. (eds.), iTrust'05: 3rd International Conference on Trust Management, LNCS 3477, pp 77–92, Rocquencourt, France.

Ruth, P., Xu, D., Bhargava, B., Regnier, F. (2004), 'E-notebook middleware for accountability and reputation based trust in distributed data sharing communities', in: Jensen, C. D., Poslad, S., Dimitrakos, T. (eds.), iTrust'04, 2rd International Conference on Trust Management, LNCS 2995, Oxford, U.K.

Ryutov, T., Zhou, L., Neuman, C., Leithead, T., Seamons, K. E. (2005), 'Adaptive trust negotiation and access control', SACMAT'05, 10th ACM Symposium on Access Control Models and Technologies, pp 139–146, Stockholm, Sweden.

Seligman, A. B. (2000), The Problem of Trust, Princeton University Press.

Szerszynski, B. (1999), 'Risk and trust: The performative dimension', Environmental Values, 8(2):239–252.

Sztompka, P. (1999), Trust: a Sociological Theory, Cambridge University Press.

Tan, Y. and Thoen, W. (1998), 'Towards a generic model of trust for electronic commerce', International Journal of Electronic Commerce, 3(1):65–81.

Theodorakopoulos, G. (2004), Distributed trust evaluation in ad-hoc networks, Master's thesis, University of Maryland, College Park, USA.

Uslaner, E. M. (2002), The Moral Foundations of Trust, Cambridge University Press.

Wang, Y. and Vassileva, J. (2007), 'Toward trust and reputation based web service selection: A survey', International Transactions on Systems Science and Applications, 3(2):118–132.

Warren, M. E. (1999), Democracy and Trust, Cambridge University Press.

Williamson, O. E. (1993), 'Calculativeness, trust, and economic organization', Journal of Law & Economics, 36(1):453–486.

Xiong, L. and Liu, L. (2004), 'PeerTrust: Supporting reputation-based trust for peer-to-peer electronic communities', IEEE Transactions on Knowledge and Data Engineering, 16(7):843–857.

Yu, B. and Singh, M. P. (2002), 'Distributed reputation management for electronic commerce', Computational Intelligence, 18(4):535–549.

Zhang, Q., Yu, T., Irwin, K. (2004), 'A classification scheme for trust functions in reputation-based trust management', ISWC'04, 3rd International Semantic Web Conference, Workshop on 'Trust, Security, and Reputation on the Semantic Web', Hiroshima, Japan.

Ziegler, C. N. and Lausen, G. (2005), 'Propagation models for trust and distrust in social networks', Information Systems Frontiers, 7(4–5):337–358.

Vignette 3: Use and Abuse of Biometric Data and Social Networks*

Frieda, the daughter of Fanny and Frank, is now two and a half years old, and enrolled in kindergarten, and so Fanny has returned to work.

Getting Ready for Work

Fanny and Frank are getting ready to leave for work and are dropping Frieda at the kindergarten. Fanny got home late the evening before, returning from one of her regular business trips. She still feels upset by something her good friend Joanne told her over the phone while she was waiting for her departure at Cairo airport. Fanny closed an inexpensive supplementary health insurance contract a couple of months ago which among other additional treatments offers better protection during her trips abroad. She had told her friend Joanne of the policy because Joanne works as a flight attendant and hence travels a lot. Joanne had told her that the day before she had received an offer 35 percent more expensive than Fanny's insurance rate. This offer came as a surprise because Joanne is only three months younger than Fanny, she has one child slightly older than Frieda and no prior severe illnesses.

Joanne's research on the internet revealed that the reason for the offer may have been an exploit of biometric raw-data. The application procedure for the insurance required a standard digital picture to be taken as well as a fingerprint. She was told that the picture would be printed on the insurance card and that the fingerprint would be used as a key for personal data stored on the card. Joanne found out that biometric raw data can be used to identify health risks. A photo reveals data such as sex, age and ethnic origin but apparently can also contain hints to health conditions such as stroke (asymmetry of the face), liver diseases (yellowish skin) or Marfan syndrome (special symmetry of the face). The fingerprint may reveal information on the nutrition status of the mother during pregnancy or the risk of certain types of stomach problems. In Joanne's case it may have been a slightly yellowish taint as she had been on a special diet during the time the picture was taken. She was led to this conclusion by the fact that the company offered the same insurance rate Fanny was offered, if any liver related illnesses were excluded from the insurance protection.

---

* This scenario is based on FIDIS deliverable D12.5, Chapter 4, by Harald Zwingelberg & Maren Raguse (ICPP).

Frank, whose cousin works as an insurance agent, is not very surprised at the story. He explains to his wife that after all that is what insurance companies have to do: assess possible future risks of events covered by insurance. If several causes are known to exist for a certain biometric feature the insurance company will, if they cannot rule out benign reasons, proceed based on a negative conclusion. As far as Frank can recollect, the precision of biometric profiling regarding biometric pictures has increased. A large collection of high resolution photographs made it possible to create a register of health risks. Data was taken from the internet and social networks using advanced face recognition software to compare the pictures and to align them with the database. This database is operated by *H.E.L.L – Health Profiling Ltd.* The company had repeatedly stressed that only publicly available pictures were used to build the database. Rumours had spread that pictures may have been attained by spoofing biometric passports, health cards, or some membership cards. An investigation by the Information Commissioner's Office however found no evidence supporting these rumours.

After all, Frank argues, Joanne can always submit a medical statement indicating that she does not suffers from liver disease. Fanny disagrees. She feels insurance customers should not be obliged to rule out that they suffer from certain diseases. The duty to inform insurance companies of known prior diseases is sufficient for risk assessment, especially if the methods used by insurance companies to gather further information are as error-prone as the method of biometric raw data analysis seems to be.

Fanny had heard of several US-based insurance companies asking all of their customers for a genetic test. Based on the results many customers faced a rate increase. In the UK and other European countries national ethical committees were currently discussing this kind of genetic profiling.

At Work

Fanny's first day back at work after her business trip is dominated by administrative tasks. She recalls all of the changes that took place while she was on maternity leave and cannot help but smile at the thought of how surprised she was that day. The RFID-based service cards had replaced the time registration device for employees. The cards were also handed out to hotel guests and used for payment at the hotel's lounge and recreation areas. Fanny's colleagues had used the cards for access control to the hotel's office rooms too, until the cards were compromised The proprietary crypto-algorithm used by the RFID-access card had been broken. Further, using the cards was too insecure for the high class hotel. To all employees of the hotel strict security and confidentiality requirements apply because the hotel regularly accommodates politicians, diplomats, businessmen and celebrities. Any case of indiscretion would lead to damage to the hotel's image and reputation among its distinguished guests. Fanny is in charge of the security department at the hotel chain. For this reason her work requires an entry security level approved by the national government.

On that first day after her maternity leave the IT-department issued her a new password. Then she was asked to type a given text into her computer. The access control of the hotel's new computer system goes far beyond inserting her service card and entering a password. Once the machine, a portable computer for presentations at business partners' premises, cannot connect to the hotel network, the computer is set to travel mode. Being enabled, this mode does not only require Fanny's login but continuously monitors her keystroke pattern. Should anyone get access to the notebook or even force Fanny to hand it over while she is logged in, the computer will lock out the intruder once the deviation in pattern is recognised by the machine. The evaluation of the keystroke pattern method was praised by the privacy reviewer as less privacy-invasive because the keystroke pattern is a biometric that changes over time and thus features a built in expiry date. However, the advantage of not being traceable after some time turned out to be a disadvantage on her first day back at work. As Fanny's typing pattern changed massively during her maternity leave she had to spend two full hours typing specimen text.

Fanny's thoughts turn to her 70-year-old colleague Adriel (people now work up to 72 years in most EU jurisdictions) who was warned by the system about emerging Parkinson's disease. She wonders whether the system does not only warn the affected employee but also informs her employer about identifiable health risks. However, storing the keystroke pattern is still less invasive than other methods of analysing biometric raw-data like the insurance company's procedures she heard of from Joanne.

Having just returned from her last business trip, Fanny has to arrange her next trip to Toronto. She has come to feel at ease with the idea of presenting her travel documents (she holds a Chinese and a UK passport) to foreign authorities. Since cases of identity theft skyrocketed in the past when organised criminals abused the weak standard of the first generation of biometric passports, the EU together with the USA and some other nations reinforced the extended access control standard (EAC) to prevent illegal readout of biometric data. The new standard was improved to offer a considerably higher level of security and allows Fanny to protect her data from being read by third parties. Public key cryptography allows only accredited scanners to read out the data. All ICAO machine readable travel documents issued these days have extended access control implemented. Her Chinese passport, she is convinced, supports EAC.

The EU, being an international driver for passport security advancements, decided to implement encapsulated biometrics on the European biometric passport. Since encapsulated biometrics are used, external readers do not access the biometric data any more. All data processing is done by the microprocessor in the passport itself. It scans and checks the fingerprint of its owner and confirms the identity when the check is successful. Fanny read that encapsulated biometrics does mitigate privacy risks as no central biometric database is required and the risk of corruption or disclosure to unauthorised entities is addressed. After all, if biometric data is corrupted, it is corrupted for good. For this reason, Fanny prefers using her UK passport.

Scene 3: A Brief Break

Fanny and her friends grew up using social networks which became a vital part of their everyday life, allowing them to stay in contact, share news and to always feel connected to their loved ones even on extended journeys or while living abroad. But the attitude of many employers towards social networks has changed in recent years. As social networks have become so common most employers allow their employees to let their MyComm device connect to their different social network profiles.

Nafiseh, a friend of Fanny applied for a job and got rejected. It seems that it was due to some negative information in some social networks. Someone created an account, using her name and address, copied some of her pictures from other web pages and pictures of a student party that took place several years ago. Even though her friend had not been on any of these party pictures, her reputation was damaged. Furthermore, someone tagged her former home address with negative information about her on a neighbourhood rating form.

Much of the information was collected at an old social networking site where Fanny's friend entered much information during her student time – it was the thing to do at that time (2008) to have comprehensive CVs on the web. The service provider of the social networking platform did not use a technology for identity verification, thus allowing anyone to forge accounts.

Fanny uses a number of portals. However, it is important to her that the service provider uses some kind of authentication. The social networks used by Fanny offer an anonymous verification. For this purpose the government citizen portal is used.

Fanny also used a social network for health related questions informing herself about pregnancy and labour related issues. In particular she trusted some postings of someone claiming to be a physician who indeed was not. She now uses another network which has technology enabling identity management. Specialists can use credentials to anonymously write posting but are still able to show their expert status. Thus a physician or lawyer etc. can show his qualification to the system without disclosing his identity to other users or the service provider. Fanny has expert status for facility security issues.

At the Kindergarten

Frieda has been at the kindergarten for one month. To pick her up Fanny usually uses her MyComm device to open the kindergarten gate. Today, however, she forgot it on her desk. The backup system would use her biometric data instead but Fanny and Frank refused to provide this data, as the kindergarten was not able to prove that they implemented Privacy Enhancing Technologies to avoid misuse of the data. As Frieda is still new at the kindergarten, the replacement nursery teacher did not know Fanny personally and had to check her passport and the files before he allowed Fanny to take Frieda with her. Initially the kindergarten did not plan to keep the old-fashioned file system logging the parent's entitlement. However, a parent initiative successfully fought for it, as not everyone was willing to provide a raw-data photo.

Even if Fanny and Frank can avoid their biometric data being spread widely, it does not seem likely that they can prevent Frieda's data from being collected. A new programme of the local government envisages taking biometric pictures of every child and using the raw data to identify possible health risks and to automatically check for suspicious signs of child abuse or neglect by their parents. This, so argued a government spokesman to Fanny's infuriation, should provide pre-indications for the school doctor programme enabling the focus to be set on suspicious children and saving tax money on the service. But rumours spread that the acquired data will also be fed into the governmental databases on children, evaluating the likelihood of future criminal or offending behaviour and the possible need for assistance by social workers. When such databases were first introduced for convicted criminals nobody would have ever thought of registering children at kindergarten-age within such a database. But as pupils have been surveyed in this way for many years and intervention of social workers, and juvenile authorities is more effective the younger the children are, the step to include data collected at pre-schools and kindergartens was just a question of time.

While waiting for the passport to be checked against the files, Fanny thinks of a case in another kindergarten where a divorced mother not having received the right of custody managed to have somebody access the kindergarten's Wi-Fi and the verification reference database. By injecting her reference data in the profile of her authorised mother-in-law she received the desired entitlement. She then picked up her daughter and left for her country of origin. As everyone thought the girl was with her grandmother no one was suspicious until it was too late.

After finally accrediting Fanny to pick up her daughter, the nursery teacher uses a display to locate Frieda. All children are tracked throughout the day by cameras using face recognition. Other parents even use the online-service to watch the movements of their children on a floor plan of the kindergarten viewed on their MyComm. Fanny knows of another mother who uses the cloth-clean function. Using this, the system does not allow her daughter to enter the backyard when it is wet and thus dirty outdoors. She even defined the sandpit as a no-go area. Fanny disliked this idea. Instead she spends some extra money for children's clothes made from smart materials which are very robust and easy to clean.

When thinking about tracking Frieda, a conversation with her father-in-law comes to her mind. While Fanny does not want to be tracked when she is old, Frank's father appreciated the new possibilities. His mother had Alzheimer's disease and got lost during a vacation when she left the hotel at night. It took a long search to find her, dehydrated in the middle of a forest. While her father-in-law feels comfortable with the idea of being tracked, Fanny thinks that she would only agree to a system that uses an on-demand approach which only sends the location data when she initiates a request for aid.

Having given it much thought, Fanny gets concerned with all the tracking. She does not want Frieda to get too accustomed to tracking and currently considers another kindergarten for Frieda.

The visions and thoughts expressed in this vignette are inspired and based on various discussions, and results of the FIDIS Network of Excellence as well as the authors' personal experiences and expectations. Partially, underlying concepts and ideas of this vignette are described in Chapters 2, 3, 8, 9 and 10.

4 High-Tech ID and Emerging Technologies

Martin Meints and Mark Gasson

Summary. Technological development has undeniably pervaded every aspect of our lives, and the ways in which we now use our identity related information has not escaped the impact of this change. We are increasingly called upon to adopt new technology, usually more through obligation than choice, to function in everyday society, and with this new era of supposed convenience has come new risks and challenges. In this chapter we examine the roots of identity management and the systems we use to support this activity, ways in which we can strive to keep our digital information secure such as Public Key encryption and digital signatures and the evolving yet somewhat controversial role of biometrics in identification and authentication.

With an eye on the ever changing landscape of identity related technologies, we further explore emerging technologies which seem likely to impact on us in the near to mid-term future. These include RFID which has more recently come to the fore of the public consciousness, Ambient Intelligence environments which offer convenience at the potential cost of privacy and human implants which surprisingly have already been developed in a medical context and look set to be the next major step in our ever burgeoning relationship with technology.

The field of high-tech Identity (high-tech ID) is immense and is rapidly expanding because of developments in fundamental technologies. The evolution of technological mechanisms such as electronic ID cards, internet enabled devices and individualised services have arguable served to make our lives easier, and more efficient, and yet they risk leaving us more vulnerable in a variety of contexts. Understanding technologies which potentially have an impact on identity becomes increasingly important for a socially well developed and prosperous information society.

In this chapter, the results of research carried out in the context of new and emerging technologies to support identity and identification are summarised. Because of its fundamental importance, one of the core research focuses was on Identity Management Systems (IMS) where the key research questions were:

- How is identity management carried out now and in the future?
- What are the primary targets of identity management from the perspectives of the stakeholders involved?
- What are relevant technological trends in identity management?
- How should these technologies be put to use in identity management systems from a legal, technical (including privacy and data protection aspects) and a social point of view?

Based on criteria developed, recommendations were elaborated that mainly address the following stakeholders: policy makers (public sector), enterprises (private sector), scientists and the general public (citizens and customers). In an early phase of the work an overview on relevant technologies in the context of IMS was created. Important technologies from the point of view of the FIDIS researchers were:

- Technologies for a centralised identity management such as directory services, Public Key Infrastructure (PKI), biometrics (Section 4.2), technologies for mobile identity management (see Chapter 5), chip or smart card technology (Meints and Hansen, 2006: 15-18) and RFID (Section 4.2.4)
- Data Mining and Knowledge Discovery in Databases (KDD, see Chapter 7)
- Technologies for a user-controlled identity management such as credential systems (see Section 4.2.5), anonymisation services, and various functions for user-controlled identity management including related commercially or freely available solutions
- Supporting technologies such as Trusted Computing (TC), Digital Rights Management (DRM), networking protocols and protocols for privacy policy languages (see Section 4.3)
- Emerging technologies (see Section 4.4).

The criteria developed were also applied to real-life implementations of identity management systems. Focal areas of research were various implementations of data mining and RFID systems, biometric systems and others. In the context of this chapter two selected use cases will be discussed: CardSpace and ID documents (see Section 4.5).

4.1 Identity Management and Identity Management Systems[1]

As shown in Chapter 2, concepts of identity show a wide range. The same applies also to the term 'identity management'. In a general sense identity management is

---

1 Author: Martin Meints, Unabhängiges Landeszentrum für Datenschutz Schleswig-Holstein (ICPP).

understood as 'management of partial identities of a person' (Pfitzmann and Hansen, 2008) or 'management of digital identities or digital identity data' (Bauer, Meints, Hansen, 2005: 13). From a legal point of view this may apply as well to natural as legal persons. In the context of FIDIS both aspects have been researched. In this chapter the focus clearly is put on natural persons and related identities. A number of different activities carried out by different entities are summarised under the term identity management, e.g., (Bauer, Meints, Hansen, 2005; Buitelaar, Meints, van Alsenoy, 2008 etc.):

- Assignment or linking of (context specific) identifiers to a physical person
- Identification, authentication, authorisation and access control in the context of applications, IT resources and physical environment (buildings, rooms etc.)
- Management of life cycles of the identity of a physical person (e.g., enrolment and assignment of roles and rights, use or execution of assigned roles and rights, changes in roles and rights, de-enrolment etc.
- Aggregation and linking of attributes of a group of persons (group profiling) or individuals (individual profiling) from one or more sources, the use of profiles, e.g. by categorising or classifying individuals
- The application of pseudonymisation and anonymisation techniques
- The use of partial identities by an individual in various communicational contexts including role specific assignment and use of pseudonyms

In a general sense Identity Management Systems (IMS) are understood as technical systems supporting the process of management of (partial) identities. So far this term is used quite broadly in many different domains (e.g., economy, public administration, science) describing different technologies (how is the identity managed) used in different ways (who manages which identities). Examples range from centralised directory based solutions for organisations, organisations spanning federation frameworks, application of profiling practice and corresponding tools up to user centric and user controlled approaches and frameworks. Until 2004, to the knowledge of the author, no classification or typology was available helping to structure IMS.

To facilitate further analysis of existing IMS in the context of FIDIS research, three basic types of IMS were identified and described (Bauer, Meints, Hansen, 2005). In this model the aspect of control (control by an organisation or the user concerned), and methods used for the identity management (central account management, profiling techniques or user-centric methods) were covered. This resulted in the following typology:

1. Type 1: IMS for account management, implementing authentication, authorisation, and accounting
2. Type 2: IMS for profiling of user data by an organisation, e.g., detailed log files or data warehouses which support e.g., personalised services or the analysis of customer behaviour

3. Type 3: IMS for user-controlled context-dependent role and pseudonym management.

This typology maps nicely with the tiers of identity introduced by Durand (Section 2.3.2), though independent development leads to a missing map of numbers used in both models. Tier 1 identity (according to Durand, the personal or chosen identity) can be understood as a result from type 3 identity management (user-controlled identity management). Tier 2 identity (corporate or assigned identity) is a result of type 1 identity management (organisation centric identity management), and tier 3 identity (marketing or derived identity) results from type 2 identity management (profiling). Fig. 4.1. summarises major properties of these types of IMS.

In addition it was researched which role identity management functionality plays in products investigated. In this context a classification was developed:

1. Class 1: Main functionality of the product is identity management (example: directory services)
2. Class 2: Identity management is an important function; nevertheless the product also offers additional functionality (example: the Hushmail mail system for encrypted communication)
3. Class 3: The core of the product is not focused on identity management; however, identity management functionality is included (example: web browsers)

Type 1		Account Management: assigned identity	By organisations
Type 2		Profiling: derived identity	By organisations
Type 3	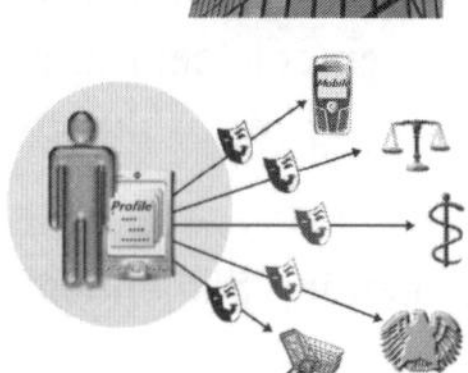	Management of own identities: chosen identity	By users themselves, supported by service providers

Fig. 4.1. Types of IMS

A number of such identity management systems have been analysed and observed over three years in a publicly accessible identity management database[2]. It should be noted that implementations of IMS can also be of hybrid types combining different organisational structures and methods characterising the introduced types. Examples for hybrid types are credential systems (focus: type 3 identity management) in which trusted third parties are involved (type 1 identity management).

From a market point of view in the context of type 1 identity management systems a concentration was observed. Many of the products investigated based on a study (Hansen et al., 2003) commissioned by the Institute for Prospective Technology Studies (IPTS) were taken over by competitors on the market. Currently the market for class 3 IMS seems to be growing rapidly. One example for this trend is the development on the market for social networks (see also Chapter 2); most of them do not have social networking as an economic core and gain their revenue through other activities, mainly market research and advertising.

4.2 Technologies and Technical Components

In this section established core technologies in the context of identity management are described. The focus concentrates on high technologies, especially those related to computer technologies and computer science. Technologies covered in this chapter are:

- Public Key Infrastructure (PKI)
- Electronic signatures
- Biometrics
- Radio Frequency Identification (RFID)
- Credential Systems

The description includes an introduction into functional principles of the technologies, properties, strengths and weaknesses with respect to identity management, and recommendations for the application in the context of identity management systems.

4.2.1 Public Key Infrastructure[3]

Cryptography can be used to provide secrecy of message contents or to provide integrity and accountability of messages. One of the most fundamental principles of modern cryptography was defined by Auguste Kerckhoffs (1883) and is now known as Kerckhoffs' principle: 'The security provided by a given cryptographic

---

2 See http://imsdb.fidis.net/.

3 Authors: Stefan Köpsell and Stefan Berthold, TU Dresden.

algorithm should not depend on the secrecy of the algorithm itself, but on the secrecy of cryptographic keys.'

Talking about secrecy of cryptographic keys in relation to communicating parties and their knowledge, one can distinguish between cryptographic algorithms which use symmetric keys and algorithms which use asymmetric ones. The terms 'symmetric' and 'asymmetric' refer respectively to the knowledge related to the keys: In the first case it is symmetric, i.e., both communicating parties know exactly the same key. This key is used for encryption as well as decryption. In the case of an asymmetric algorithm, each party has its own secret decryption key and a publicly known encryption key. Therefore the knowledge with respect to the keys is asymmetric between the parties.

One of the biggest obstructions from an organisational and usability point of view of modern cryptographic algorithms and protocols is the burden of key distribution. If one wants to use symmetric algorithms, this is more obvious as a trustworthy (i.e., secure) channel is needed for the transportation of the secret keys. But even in the case of asymmetric cryptography where public keys are used and therefore no concealed channel is necessary, one still faces the problem of integrity and accountability when distributing keys.

Public key infrastructures (PKIs) are a basic approach to solving these problems. Using PKIs, public keys are reliably assigned to persons by means of digital signatures and a certification authority (CA). A certification authority is an organisation or institution which accredits that a given public key belongs to a given entity. The entity is usually a human being but could also be a machine, e.g., a web-server. The assignments are also known as (digital) key certificates. These certificates are digitally signed by the certification authority. Figure 4.2 exemplifies the basic functionality of a PKI.

A typical use case for digital key certificates is to link a certain public key to an entity named within the certificate with its real identity, i.e., using the real name and not a pseudonym. But it is also possible to issue digital key certificates for pseudonyms. In this case the certification authority in fact knows the real name of the entity for which it issued a pseudonymous key certificate. This way the CA can reveal the true identity if necessary, e.g., if required by law.

Another type of certificates is the so-called attribute certificate, which binds a set of arbitrary attributes to an entity. Thus it can be seen as a generalised form of a digital key certificate as the public key can be seen simply as an attribute of the related entity.

In order to verify a digital certificate, one needs to know the public key of the certification authority. One possibility is to get this public key from another certification authority B which accredits the public key of certification authority A. Thus the relations between certification authorities form a hierarchical tree. The topmost element is called a root certification authority (Root CA). The tree could be used for implicit trust management, i.e., an application could define that it accepts all certificates which are directly signed by a certain certification authority B (e.g., the root certification authority) or subsequently signed by a certification authority A which has a certificate signed by B. Note that the very root of this tree

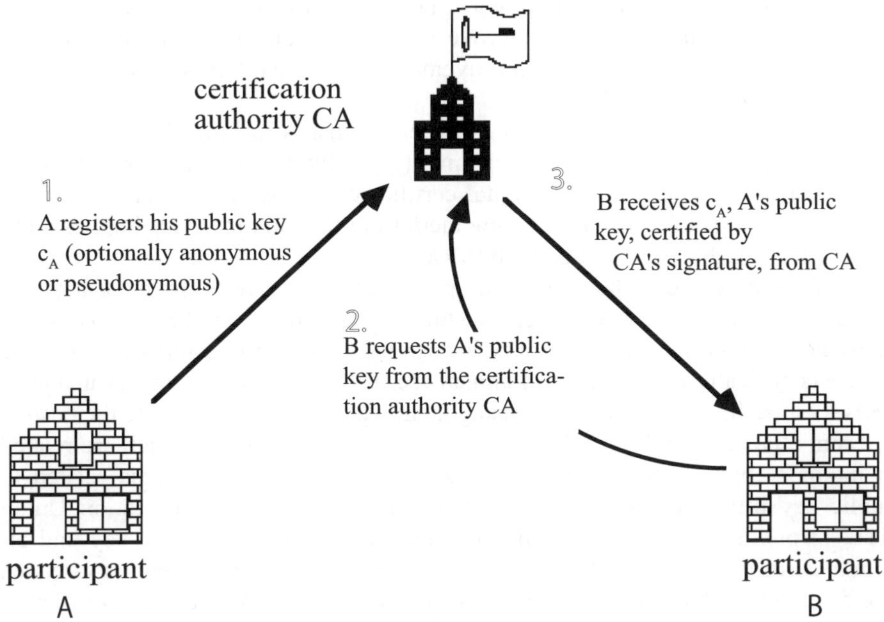

Fig. 4.2. Basic functionality of a certification authority[4]

is not authenticated by means of cryptography. Instead the integrity and validity of the root certificate has to be checked manually, e.g., by comparing the hash value of that certificate with a publicly known value which could be published in news papers or governmental communications, i.e., via a different channel.

One weakness in this hierarchical concept is the large tree of implicit trust it spans. This becomes more obvious if one considers that different certification authorities might have slightly different policies with respect to the steps required before the CA will sign a certificate. One CA might demand an official document proving the identity of the key owner before it signs the certificate while other CAs might not. To give just one example, in January 2001 the company VeriSign Inc.—one of the world's leading CAs—issued two digital certificates to a person who fraudulently claimed to be a representative of Microsoft Corporation. The issued certificates allowed the person to sign software in the name of Microsoft[5].

Another weak point of current PKIs is the way they deal with revocation. Certificates may get lost due to accidents or burglary, for instance. The common way is to provide a certificate revocation list (CRL) in order to keep every user informed about the validity of certificates. The distribution of such CRLs, however, requires users of PKIs to be online and up-to-date whenever they intend to use a certificate since they would need to check it before usage. This is quite inconven-

---

4 Figure taken from Pfitzmann (2008).

5 http://www.verisign.com/support/advisories/authenticodefraud.html.

ient since PKIs without revocation would not require the user to be online. In fact, there are several approaches to improve the distribution of certificates and trust chains. However, there is yet no improvement for the distribution of CRLs which is significantly better than broadcast.

One measure to bind the size of a revocation list is to limit the validity of a given certificate to a certain period of time (typically one or two years). This validity period is encoded in each digital certificate. But as now digital certificates can become outdated, one has to renew them from time to time. This implies additional effort for the users of digital certificates.

All these processes—the registration process, to take care of the revocation list and to renew certificates—cause costs which needs to be covered by the users of a certification authority if this authority is operated by a private company. Therefore the users typically have to pay an annual fee. Naturally this is a disadvantage of PKIs—especially if the benefits of using them will not overcompensate the costs.

From a practical point of view there are even more problems which are related to interoperability, although there exists a whole series of standards related to public key infrastructures. In 1988 the International Telecommunication Union (ITU-T) published the X.509 standard titled 'The Directory: Public-key and attribute certificate frameworks' within their X.500 information technology-related standards which focus on open systems interconnection. Most digital certificates today conform to the current version 3 of the X.509 standard. This version introduces extensibility by means of profiles. One of the (if not the) most important profile is developed by the Public-Key Infrastructure (X.509) working group of the Internet Engineering Task Force (IETF), called PKIX. The goal of this working group, which was established in 1995, is to develop standards for a public key infrastructure to be used on the Internet. The group produces more than 40 so-called 'Requests For Comments (RFCs)'—they are effectively Internet standards.

Not only is the 'correct' implementation of all these standards a hard task—as there is always room for interpretation—but also the inherent flexibility and extensibility of X.509 supports application- or domain-specific extensions which hinder global interoperability.

4.2.2 Electronic Signatures[6]

For high-tech IDs, there are roughly two relevant standard applications of electronic signatures defined in Article 2 of the EU directive 1999/93/EC, the advanced signature and the qualified electronic signature. An exhaustive discussion of these signature types with respect to requirements, legal effects, and their probative value can be found in (Gasson, Meints, Warwick, 2005: 26). In this section, we focus on the main differences between advanced and qualified electronic signatures and their relation to PKIs.

An advanced electronic signature is, according to the EU directive 1999/93/EC[7], an electronic signature with four requirements:

---

6 Authors: Stefan Köpsell and Stefan Berthold, TU Dresden.

- it is uniquely linked to the signatory;
- it is capable of identifying the signatory;
- it is created using means that the signatory can maintain under his sole control; and
- it is linked to the data to which it relates in such a manner that any subsequent change of the data is detectable.

Even though the legal effectiveness of advanced electronic signatures is limited for business, it still creates a unique link between the signed data and the signatory.

Of more interest for business cases are qualified electronic signatures. The validity of qualified electronic signatures is based on a qualified certificate, which is basically a digital certificate issued by a certification authority. A certification authority can be conceived as the root of a PKI or as a subsequent authority within a PKI certification tree. In the latter case, the PKI certification tree is used to delegate the permission to issue certificates from the root CA to a subsequent certification authority, see 'Public Key Infrastructure' in Section 4.2.1. Such permission can be limited in order to achieve a separation of duties between several subsequent certification authorities. In addition to the necessary qualified certificate, qualified electronic signatures are required to be created by a 'secure-signature-creation device'. This type of signature has legal effects comparable to a hand-written signature, as defined in Article 5 of 1999/93/EC.

Technically, electronic signatures can be seen as the counterpart of asymmetric encryption schemes. That is, there is a secret key for signing a message and a public key for verifying. In contrast to message authentication codes, electronic signatures can be used to convince third parties of the authenticity of a message, since the signing key is secret and must not to be shared by the sender with anyone else. The basic principles of generating and verifying an electronic signature are depicted in Figure 4.3.

An electronic signature is generated by first applying a hash function to the message and afterwards using the core signature algorithm to sign just the resulting hash value. Note that for electronic signatures to be secure, both parts—the hash function and the core signature algorithm—need to be uncompromised and work properly.

From a technical point of view the requirements of advanced and qualified electronic signatures induce some (controversially discussed) challenges and problems. Of special importance are two requirements on a secure-signature-creation device, 'the signature-creation-data used for signature generation can be protected in a reliable way by the legitimate signatory against the use of others' and 'secure signature-creation devices must not alter the data to be signed or prevent such data from being presented to the signatory prior to the signature process.' Both requirements are hard to assure with current technology. Today's standard PCs with

[7] See http://eur-lex.europa.eu/LexUriServ/LexUriServ.do?uri=OJ:L:2000:013:0012:0020:EN:PDF.

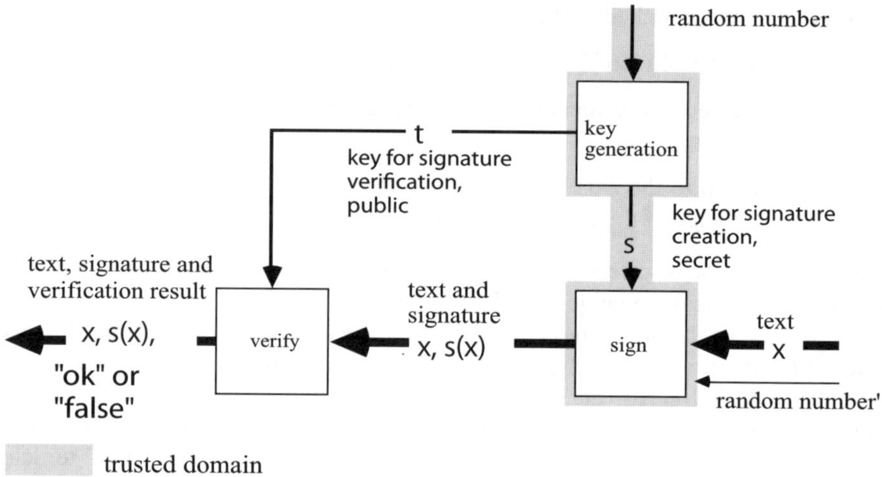

Fig. 4.3. Digital signature system[8]

standard operating system cannot be used as secure signature-creation devices. Given all the security weaknesses of PCs they can neither ensure that 'the signature-creation-data used for signature generation can be reliably protected' nor 'what I sign is what I see'. Therefore specialised hardware and software is needed, e.g. external card readers. Such devices need at least a means for input to authorise the signing process and a display (or other means of output) to inform the user about what he will sign. So from an organisational and usability point of view electronic signatures are slightly impractical and costly.

In addition to the problem of achieving the previous two requirements, an advanced electronic signature is required to be 'created using means that the signatory can maintain under his sole control'. Then, the problem is that the secret keys used for signing are typically created by certification authorities, not by the users themselves. Thus, a user can never be sure of having the process of signing 'under his sole control'.

4.2.3 Biometrics[9]

Biometrics is defined as the automated recognition of individuals based on their biological and/or behavioural characteristics. Typical examples for suitable biological characteristics used in biometric systems are fingerprints, iris filament structures or face forms. Recognition of hand written signatures or gesture dynamics are examples for behavioural characteristics. Any biometric system in-

[8] Figure taken from Pfitzmann (2008).

[9] Authors: Els Kindt, KU Leuven, Lorenz Müller, Axionics and Martin Meints, Unabhängiges Landeszentrum für Datenschutz Schleswig-Holstein.

cludes a measurement process that allows defining a query template with formalised features of the measured characteristics. These results are then compared with a reference template that has been acquired when the individual enrols into the biometrically secured system.

All suitable characteristics for biometrics have some mandatory qualities like universality (all persons have the characteristics), distinctiveness (every person has a different specificity of the characteristics), permanence (the characteristic is sufficiently invariant over a long time period) and collect ability (the characteristics can be physically measured on all individuals). There are some additional desired qualities like separability (the difference between individuals is much larger than typical measurement errors), performance (the measurement of the biometric characteristic is robust, fast, accurate and efficient), acceptance (individuals accept the measurement process) and reliability (the characteristics and the usual measurement are difficult to counterfeit).

Biometrics as Authentication Factor

Biometric recognition of individuals is a suitable method to establish a strong link between a person and an identity. It has the advantage that it is difficult for the concerned individual but also for potential impostors to manipulate this binding. This broad protection even against insider attacks differentiates biometrics from other authentication factors like token or knowledge based methods such as PINs or passwords. On the other hand, a biometric link between an individual and some identity-related data is difficult to revoke even if there are good and legal reasons to do so. Most of the biometric characteristics are stable for a long time in the lifespan of an individual, much longer than typical business relationships. Therefore a widespread use of biometrics for identity management in civil or business applications may expose a person to extensive profiling and thus seriously harm her right to privacy.

Biometric Recognition Process

All biometric systems have some common main functional components in a typical processing chain. These components are (see Figure 4.4):

- a storage entity with the biometric data samples (reference templates) of the enrolled individual that is linked to or integrated in a database with the identity information of the corresponding individual
- a sensor device and some pre-processing to capture the biometric data sample from an individual as input data
- a comparison process that evaluates the similarity between the reference templates and the captured data sample and that results in a similarity score
- a decision function that decides if a data sample matches a certain reference template.

The result is the approval or refusal of a mapping of the captured template to the identity information that belongs to the selected reference template.

Biometric Recognition Quality

Another important point is the fact that any biometric technique includes a physical measurement, which is intrinsically error-prone. Therefore the comparison between the query sample data and the reference template will normally not lead to an exact match but to a similarity score. Using this score value the system then has to decide if the query and the reference template are both coming from the same individual or not. This decision is based on probability estimates. Therefore a biometric recognition process can lead to false results in the sense that the authorised individual is rejected (False Rejection Rate—FRR) or that an impostor is accepted (False Acceptance Rate—FAR). The relative and absolute rates of such intrinsic errors in function of the threshold setting on the similarity score are the quality characteristics of a biometric system. These error rates depend on the

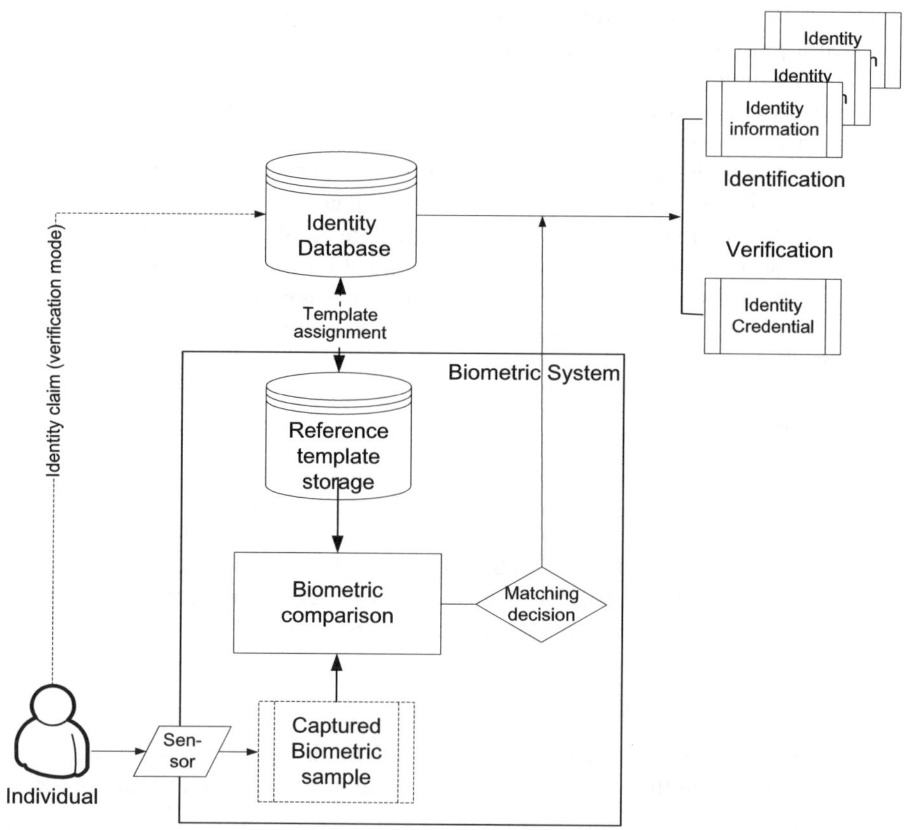

Fig. 4.4. The main processing components of a biometric system

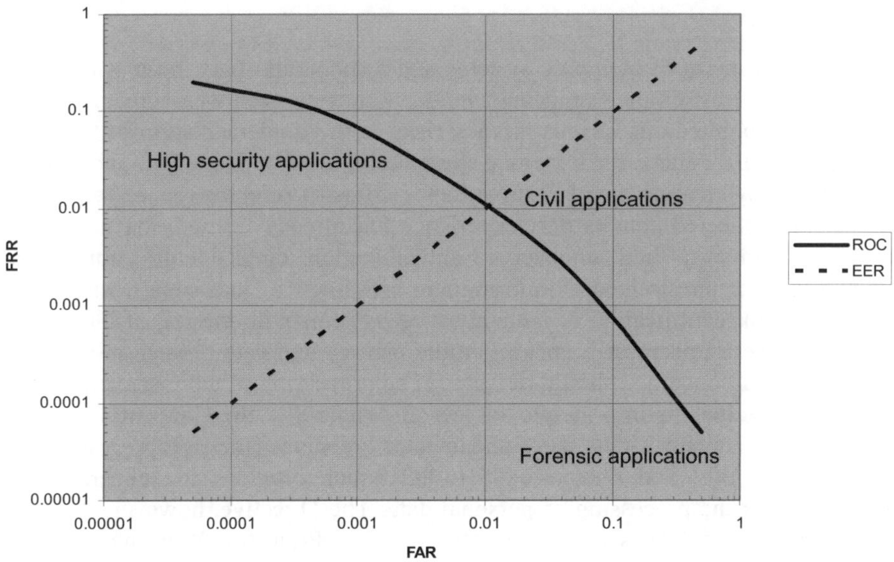

Fig. 4.5. Receiver operating characteristics curve of a typical biometric system that shows the correlation between the False Acceptance Rate (FAR) and the False Rejection Rate (FRR)

chosen characteristic, on the technical realisation of the biometric system and on the decision threshold setting. The two error rates are strongly negatively correlated and the overall quality of a biometric system is represented by the correlation plot called ROC (Receiver Operation Characteristics) curve that emerges when the threshold setting is changed over the full range of possible similarity scores (see Figure 4.5). A simplified form of this quality representation is the Equal Error Rate (EER). This single value represents the error rate of the FRR and the FAR when both values are equal.

Operation Phases and Modes

All biometric systems run in two separate processing phases. For each individual that shall be recognised by a biometric system first an initialisation procedure, called enrolment, takes place. In this processing phase the individual subject provides samples of a biometric characteristic to establish a new so called reference template. After the enrolment, the subject is known by the biometric system. In the subsequent query phase, the subject provides when requested a new biometric data sample called a query template. This query template is processed and compared with the saved reference templates of all enrolled subjects (identification mode) or with the saved template of a specified subject that claims a certain identity (verification mode). The output of the system may be a simple yes / no, or an identity credential with identity information about the subject for a system that operates in the verification mode, or a list of identity data that correspond to the best matches (comparison scores) for a system running in identification mode.

Legal Aspects

The privacy aspects of biometric systems and technologies have been widely discussed and, at least on the European level, have over all been well agreed.[10] FIDIS research has pointed out various privacy risks of the implementation of the technology as well.[11] These risks include the massive data collection in and outside Europe, hereby creating a global surveillance infrastructure, the risk of 'repurposing' of the collected data as past experience has already learned, the increasing chances for identity theft, unobserved authentication, direct identify ability and linkability, and unrestrained monitoring and profiling[12] of individuals. Increasing the security in identification or authentication systems with the use of biometrics however does not necessarily mean that the privacy and data protection rights of the individuals concerned should decrease. The processing of biometric characteristics of individuals is in principle subject to Article 8 of the Convention for the Protection on Human Rights and Fundamental Freedoms (the right to respect for one's private life) and Directive 95/46/EC which provides the general legal framework for the processing of personal data. The Directive, however, does not mention biometric data as such. The Article 29 Data Protection Working Party has therefore issued specific guidelines for the processing of biometric data in a working document of August 2003 (Art29DPWP, 2003), also see (Gasson, Meints, Warwick, 2005: 98-101) and (Kindt and Müller, 2007: 77-82). These guidelines include that (i) 'raw' biometric data shall not be stored because such data may reveal information about a person's health or race, (ii) templates should preclude the processing of data that is not necessary, (iii) central storage of biometric data is to be avoided, (iv) the use of unique identifiers should be avoided by the manipulation of the templates, (v) other personal information should be segregated from the biometric information, and (vi) the controller shall take all appropriate technical and organisational security measures to protect the biometric data.[13] National Data Protection Authorities, including those of Belgium, France, Greece and the Netherlands, have also issued opinions on the use of biometric systems, in general or in specific situations.

However, not all privacy concerns have been resolved. There is for example the uncertainty whether or not privacy-critical information for example concerning health can be extracted from templates, as this has not been thoroughly investigated (Kindt and Müller, 2007: 83-87). There is also the risk of biometric data becoming a primary key for the interoperability of systems. The inappropriate

---

[10] The specific privacy concerns for biometrics have been outlined in various documents and opinions, including Council of Europe, *Progress report on the application of the principles of convention 108 to the collection and processing of biometric data*, Strasbourg, February 2005, 26 p.

[11] In this first reference the use of biometrics for the enhancement of PKI also was extensively researched.

[12] See also Hildebrandt and Gutwirth (2008).

[13] On each of these principles, further explanation can be found in Gasson, Meints, Warwick (2005: 101-105).

security architecture for the storage of biometric data in the Machine Readable Travel Document (MRTD) has also been argued and demonstrated in a dedicated FIDIS deliverable (Meints and Hansen, 2006: 160) and was subject of the Budapest Declaration of the FIDIS research community.[14]

Control Models for the Operation of a Biometric System

Biometric systems can be understood as information and communication technology (ICT) systems (or parts thereof). From a security point of view control in ICT systems is an important prerequisite for effective security. In this context a classification has already been developed (Rannenberg, Pfitzmann, Müller, 1999):

- Centralised control in one organisation
- Distributed control in a group of trusted organisations following homogeneous and mutually accepted security targets (mainly developed in one joint and shared security concept)
- Distributed control with differing security targets, also called multilateral security. This model is especially of interest as research approaches for its implementation and no real-life implementations exist yet.

Based on these categories, taking relevant stakeholders in the operation and use of today's biometric systems (public and private sector, citizens and consumer) and relevant purposes together with the analysis of legal ground for the operation into consideration a typology of biometric systems was developed (Kindt and Müller, 2007: 55-67):

1. Type 1: Government controlled ID model;
   based on legal grounds, a group of organisations is running the biometric system either based on commonly agreed security targets or multilaterally; examples are the epass or biometrics enabled national ID cards
2. Type 2: Access control model;
   based on the consent of the user, the system is run by private or public sector organisations centralised or distributed; examples are pay per touch and access control systems for public and private buildings, one particular setting in this category is the shared control between the organisation and the biometric subject (see below 'encapsulated biometrics')
3. Type 3: Mixed model;
   mainly based on consent, biometric data is shared between private and public organisations (distributed control), but mainly common security targets exist; example: PRIVIUM (biometrics enabled border control)

[14] FIDIS, Budapest Declaration on Machine Readable Travel Documents (MRTD), September 2006, available at http://www.fidis.net/fileadmin/fidis/press/budapest_declaration_on_MRTD.en.20061106.pdf.

4. Type 4: Convenience model;
   based on consent, biometric data is either controlled by the user directly or shared with a service provider. Control can be centralised (at the user or the service provider) or distributed (from the service provider to the users); examples are biometric access control for private notebooks or the administration of school meals or books in libraries
5. Type 5: Surveillance model;
   based on legal grounds (public sector) or consent (private sector), biometric data is used centralised or distributed for surveillance purposes, mostly in the context of public security or fraud and theft prevention (private sector); examples are CCTV-based biometric systems at public places or private property.

Specific Risks for and Through Biometric Systems

These concerns point towards the need for an appropriate legal framework, in additional to privacy-enhancing biometric solutions.

In the context of biometric systems a number of risks have been discussed for operators and users. They are mainly (e.g., Meints and Hansen, 2006:105-115):

- Identity takeover or usurpations (generally called 'identity theft'; see also Chapter 8).
- Violation of purpose binding by use of additional information in biometric data or use of the biometric data for purposes other than the original purposes for which the data were collected (also called function creep).
- Violation of purpose binding is especially eased through the fact that biometric data can not be anonymised; the linkability of biometric characteristics to a person is a central functional principle of biometrics. Linkability of biometric data to other sources of data increases the risk of profiling to the disadvantage of the user of biometric systems.
- Violation of informational self determination by forcing users into the use of biometric systems where no legal ground for their use is in place.
- As biometric systems can be run hidden they may be used, and without proper legal grounds abused, for non-recognised and non-interactive authentication, tracking and surveillance purposes. On the other hand this feature of biometric systems includes them into the enablers of Ambient Intelligence (AmI).
- Improperly used biometric systems may lead to devaluation of established forensic methods.

Technical and Organisational Security Measures

Technical and organisational security measures need to meet criteria defined as 'state-of-the-art'. This can be achieved based on relevant standards for information security management systems such as the ISO/IEC 27000 series and CobiT[15]. On a product level, Common Criteria (CC, ISO/IEC 15408) can be used to counter general risks for identity management systems. The Biometric Evaluation Methodology for Common Criteria[16] covers especially threats in the context of deliberate attacks on biometric systems. In this context the following aspects seem to be especially relevant:

- Protective measures against theft of reference data in biometric systems. It has already been demonstrated that reference data in template formats can be used to reconstruct reference data to spoof sensors applying a so-called hill climbing attack (e.g., Hill, 2001; Adler, 2003). In a hill-climbing attack reference data is recalculated from templates in iterative cycles using, e.g., the match score of the system to evaluate the quality of the calculated data after each calculation cycle. To hamper hill-climbing attacks the biometric system should not return any match scores.
- Protective measures against infiltration of biometric systems with unauthorised reference data need to be taken.
- Detection measures for the use of copies of biometric characteristics (anti-spoofing measures for sensors are especially important as the successful use of copies of characteristics has been demonstrated with many sensor types[17]); additional data collected in this context must not be used for purposes other than security.
- Physical (environmental) protection of as many parts of biometric systems as possible and effective access control measures on all levels of the system (physical access control, effective login and data access procedures); this also should include the deactivation of interfaces of the system not needed to prevent sensor override attacks[18].
- Assurance of the authenticity of biometric reference data via appropriate organisational and / or technical measures in the enrolment phase.
- Logging of transactions and appropriate auditing of logs in biometric systems, especially of configuration parameters such as changes of thresholds.

[15] The Control Objective for Information and Related Technology (CobiT) are available at http://www.isaca.org.

[16] See http://www.cesg.gov.uk/site/ast/biometrics/media/BEM_10.pdf.

[17] See, e.g., Geradts and Sommer (2006).

[18] Sensor override attacks are described by, e.g., Heinz, Krißler, Rütten (2007).

- Inclusion of relevant stakeholders when biometric systems are introduced or modified (release management). Relevant stakeholders may be for example representatives of the works counsels, the information security officer and the data protection officer.
- When buying or outsourcing parts or the whole biometric system, corresponding service level agreements and security service levels need to be included in the contracts. An important part of these service levels is a control or auditing and enforcement strategy (e.g., via fines or disciplinary actions).

Technical and Organisational Data Protection Measures

From a data protection point of view the control model used for sensor and reference data is of interest. In some cases Data Protection Commissions in European member countries decided that for convenience driven applications the use of central reference data repositories under control of the service provider was not proportionate (e.g., Kindt, 2007). Alternatively reference data can be stored under the control of the data subject (e.g., using a token) or it can be encrypted with a key under control of the data subject. From a data protection point of view the control model implemented in encapsulated biometrics is currently the best. Encapsulated biometric systems integrate sensors, matching systems and reference data storage in one device under control of the user of the biometric system. This device reports only a match or non-match (Kindt and Müller, 2007). Characteristics or reference data in this case are not transferred to systems outside this device. This concept will be further described and evaluated in the next section. In any case it should be evaluated with care whether identification and thus a centralised reference data repository is really needed.

Another important aspect is hindrance of linkability of biometric reference data. This can be achieved, e.g., by storing biometric reference data separately from other personal data, keeping it fragmented and encrypting these fragments with different keys. The application of template protection measures (see, e.g., Jain, Nandakumar, Nagar, 2008) or the use of biometric encryption (Cavoukian and Stoianov, 2007) also can hinder linkability as well as decentralised storage of reference data under control of the user.

Biometric characteristics are, in difference to other factors of authentication, non-revocable. To hinder identity theft based on reference data schemes for revocable reference data (see, e.g., Cavoukian and Stoianov, 2007; Zhou et al., 2007) should be used.

Biometric raw data (mainly images of faces, finger tips, voice recordings etc.), data used for liveness detection and supposedly in some cases also templates contain information in addition to the characteristics needed for the biometric matching. In some cases this data is health or racial origin related and thus belongs to the special categories of personal data as defined in the European Data Protection Directive 95/46/EC (Kindt and Müller, 2007: 83-87). For this reason reference data should be especially protected against unauthorised access and use. In some

European countries (e.g., Luxemburg, Belgium etc.) prior checking of planned biometric systems by Data Protection Officers or Commissioners is recommended or required. To reduce additional information in biometric reference data, templates should be used instead of raw biometric data.

In many cases the implementation of biometric systems in Europe requires consent by the users (data subjects). In this context transparency among others about the data used and the procedures used in processing need to be described understandably to the user. In this context the three layer approach for privacy policies suggested by the Art. 29 Data Protection Working Party (Art29DPWP, 2004) may be useful. Important instruments to support trust in biometric systems' security and privacy are information system management (ISO/IEC 27001) and Common Criteria (ISO/IEC 15408 including Biometrics Evaluation Methodology) certificates as well as privacy seals[19]. When biometric systems are introduced based on consent as a general rule a non-biometric back up procedure is required as users may opt out at any time.

Encapsulated Biometrics—a Privacy-Enhanced Operation Mode

A biometric comparison is far more complex than a password or PIN code check. It always includes a physical measurement process to capture a query template. Biometric authentication systems therefore all need some locally installed infrastructure to which the subject needs physical access. This fact constrains the possible architectures of biometric systems. It is not possible to concentrate all processes in a physical completely secured environment; there are always points with immediate interaction with the outside world.

Today's biometric systems often work within architectures with entirely or partially centrally controlled components. The server or the server controlled peripherals collect biometric data from the individuals through the local capture devices. The further processing is done under the sole control of a centralised biometric application infrastructure which keeps the biometric information of all enrolees in an operator controlled database. Even if the centralised equipment is well protected, at least the capture devices are weak points in the system exposed to all kind of attacks and manipulations. In addition, the specific biometric characteristic may be expressed in very different forms from human to human. General purpose measurement equipment may fail to make an optimal raw data capture over the full population. As a consequence the requested features may not be reconstructed by the feature evaluation algorithm for a substantial fraction of the population or the resulting query templates may be too far away for a unique and reliable result in the comparison step. In addition centralised control systems bear all the dangers to the security and the privacy of the enrolled individuals that have been discussed in the above paragraphs.

---

[19] E.g., the Data Protection Seal of the federal state of Schleswig-Holstein in Germany, see https://www.datenschutzzentrum.de/guetesiegel/, or the European Privacy Seal EuroPriSe, http://www.european-privacy-seal.eu/.

All the above problems are directly or indirectly related to the system architecture with centralised components and data. Especially for type 2 models (access control) new approaches with a decentralisation of the biometric data have been developed to ease the above outlined drawbacks of biometric authentication. Systems with templates or even templates and the matching process on personal smart cards are examples of such improved architectures with reduced exposure of biometric data. An even more radical improvement can be achieved with the architecture model of encapsulated biometrics. In this scheme the whole biometric system is enclosed in a personal device that performs the full biometric recognition process customised for the user. The system has to recognise only one person and thus it stores only one set of reference templates. The encapsulated biometric system is securely enclosed in a tamper resistant device that performs the biometric recognition process in a predefined and secure way. The result of the biometric recognition of the user is communicated to the requesting organisation through cryptographic credentials which cannot be manipulated by the legitimate user nor a third party. The authenticating organisation does not hold any biometric data and thus it cannot jeopardise the biometric privacy of the authenticated subjects.

The encapsulated biometric model represents a shared control model where the authenticating organisation defines and controls the biometric evaluation process and its results and the biometric subject controls the biometric data and the usage of the biometric device (see Figure 4.6). This model fulfils the security needs of the authenticating organisation and the privacy need of the authenticated biometric subject in the best possible way. A necessary precondition for a biometric system to work in an encapsulated model is the ability to enclose the whole process in a secured personal device that works reliable even in a hostile environment. Fingerprint, iris, handwriting or voice biometric characteristics are suitable for such architecture. First realisations of such a user-centric model have appeared now on the market of authentication devices[20].

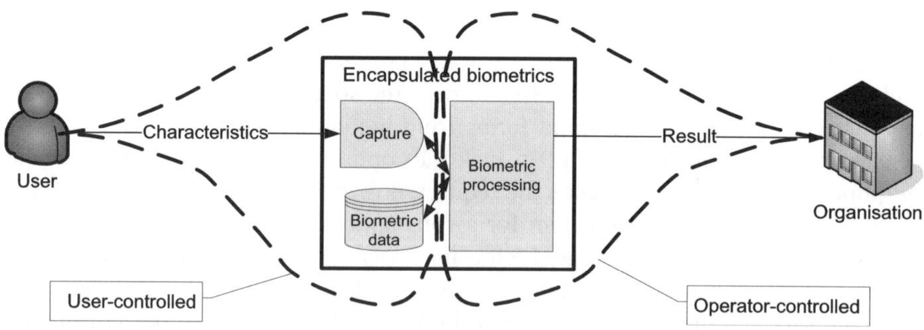

Fig. 4.6. Encapsulated biometrics enclosed in a device that allows a sharing of control: The data and the usage is controlled by the using subject; the processing and the evaluation result is controlled by the authenticating organisation

[20] Bodily functions, Finance & Economics, The Economist, 2008-07-10.

4.2.4 RFID[21]

Radio Frequency Identification (RFID) technology is increasingly used for various applications, including retail applications, transportation, aviation, healthcare, automatic toll collection, security and access control. RFID tags are tiny electronic radio tags that can be embedded in or affixed to objects for the purpose of identifying the object via a radio link. RFID readers can read the unique ID code and any other information stored in RFID tags remotely by sending and receiving a radio frequency signal. In an RFID system, RFID readers are connected to a backend system which processes the data read from tags and can link them to other data stored in backend databases (see Figure 4.7)

RFID tags in general come in many different types and have different characteristics regarding e.g., power source, operating frequency and functionality. Thus they can be classified in a number of different ways. A common way to classify RFID tags in a general way is to divide them into active or passive tags. Active RFID tags have a permanent power supply. Hence these tags can perform 'computations' continuously and independently from the environment.

Active tags also have in general much more computation power compared to passive ones. Hence they can do much better cryptographic operations. Both properties make active tags much more appropriate for applying security and privacy protecting mechanisms. But active tags are orders of magnitude larger than passive ones.

Passive tags can from a privacy and security standpoint be further divided into: **basic, very low-cost tags; symmetric-key, low-cost tags; and public-key, more expensive tags.**

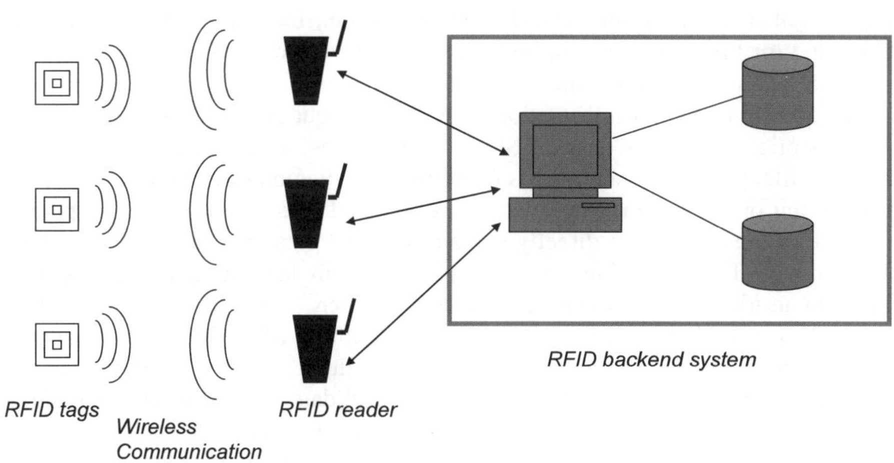

Fig. 4.7. An RFID system

[21] Authors: Simone Fischer-Hübner, Hans Hedbom, Karlstad University.

According to NIST[22], 'the most prominent industry standard for RFID are the EPCglobal specifications and standards for supply chain and patient safety applications'. EPCglobal divides the tags into different classes. The different classes have different security and cryptographic capabilities. Tags belonging to the EPCglobal Class-0 or Class-1 of the first generation have no security functionality.

The operating distance, data transfer speed and tag reading speed of an RFID-system is dependent on the radio frequency of the tag. In general one could say that the higher the frequency the higher the data transfer speed and the tag reading speed. High frequency tags are also usually designed to operate over longer distances.

The use of RFID systems can enhance the efficiency and functionality of such applications, create new services and can provide further benefits and added value for the owner of RFID tagged items (e.g., smart fridges operating in combination with RFID tagged items, or the possibility to include warranty information on tags).

Privacy Issues

Besides such benefits and opportunities, RFID technology however also poses severe privacy problems. Privacy as an expression of the right of self-determination and human dignity is considered a core value in democratic societies and is recognised either explicitly or implicitly as a fundamental human right by most constitutions of democratic societies. In the era of modern information technology, an early definition of informational privacy was given by Alan Westin: 'Privacy is the claim of individuals, groups and institutions to determine for themselves, when, how and to what extent information about them is communicated to others'. The German Constitutional Court had also defined privacy in its Census decision as the right to informational self-determination, i.e., individuals must be able to determine for themselves when, how, to what extent and for what purposes information about them is communicated to others.

The question whether information on RFID tags qualify as personal data is not always straightforward to answer. Moreover this question also usually depends on the tag's lifecycle, as in some parts (usually in the beginning) of the lifecycle the information on the tag may not classify as personal data whereas in other parts it may. RFID tags can either directly contain personal data, e.g., biometrics that are stored on RFID tags in European passports, or can include data that could be linked to an identified or identifiable person and thereby classify as personal data. Examples for the latter case are for instance situations where individuals carry or wear tagged items, which can be associated with them, where data on the tag can be linked to identifiable data stored in the backend databases or where individuals have RFID tags implanted (see also the next section). The problem whether profiling on the basis of a unique product code on a tag (e.g., on the watch of a customer

[22] (U.S.) National Institute of Standards and Technology, Guidelines for Securing Radio Frequency Identification (RFID) Systems Special Publication 800-98, April 2007.

visiting a supermarket) is enough to justify personal data processing, even if the identity of the person (name, address, etc.) cannot be determined with reasonable efforts, has been controversially discussed. Whereas according to the traditional view, the data on the tag are not personal data, the opposite opinion was recently voiced by the Article 29 Working Party (Art29DPWP, 2005) as well as in (Hildebrandt and Meints, 2006) who have interpreted the term 'identifiable' more broadly encompassing also re-recognition of a person.

RFID-related privacy threats can basically be divided into privacy threats within the reader-tag system and privacy threats at the backend. Privacy threats within the reader-tag system comprise unauthorised reading and manipulation of information, cloning of tags and real-time tracking of individuals. RFID readers can potentially secretly scan and track RFID tags that individuals passing by are wearing or carrying, without the concerned individual's knowledge or consent. Consequently, privacy principles implemented by the European Legal privacy Framework, such as transparency, informed consent, or more generally the right of informational self-determination, are at stake. Privacy threats at the backend include profiling and monitoring specific behaviour. Besides, there are security-related threats for the confidentiality, integrity (including malware threats), availability and authenticity of personal data stored on the tag or in the backend system.

The Article 29 Working Party and privacy and consumer organisations, such as CASPIAN and EPIC have voiced privacy concerns and discussed high-level privacy guidelines / requirements for RFIDs. Several trials and plans for using RFID in supply chain applications were confronted with protests by consumers, who felt that their privacy was at risk.

Towards a Holistic Framework

RFID-related privacy problems can however not be addressed solely by legal and / or technical measures but require a holistic approach. For instance, RFID applications, such as RFID implants, even though they are legally compliant, might raise ethical questions that need to be addressed as well. Besides, social aspects of user acceptance and trust also need to be taken into account. The FIDIS Deliverable D12.3 presents a first attempt of 'A Holistic Privacy Framework for RFID Applications'. After discussing the problem space from the technological, legal, ethical and social science perspectives and illustrating those problems with the help of scenarios, a holistic approach to privacy-enhancements is presented, which follows a development approach starting with social, ethical and legal requirements and measures, and then continuing with classifying technical and organisational measures and guidelines to some of those requirements. Important requirements and measures for an holistic approach to privacy-enhancements, which are discussed in more detail in D12.3, can be summarised as follows:

- User control as a prerequisite to technology acceptances needs to become a general guideline for manufacturers and vendors (see also Bizer and Spiekermann, 2006).

- The basic principles of the current European regulatory framework on privacy and data protection apply and need to be interpreted for RFID applications. Important legal principles include the principle that data are processed fairly and lawfully and only under the grounds of Art. 7 EU Directive 95/46/EC (e.g., if the data subject has given his / her informed consent), the principles of data minimisation, transparency and right of the data subjects in RFID applications. The principle of transparency, which is especially at stake in AmI environments, requires that each RFID reader and RFID tag must be clearly labeled if analogical laws existent in other privacy-related areas (like in the case of surveillance cameras) are adopted.
- Available technical privacy-enhancing measures, which can also be applied in combination, can be classified as follows:
  - Measures for preventing unauthorised read-outs, e.g., with the help of the kill- or sleep-commands.
  - Measures for blocking access to the tags, e.g., with the help of blocker tags, proxy-devices (watchdogs).
  - Authentication measures, e.g., based on symmetric or asymmetric cryptographic protocols.
  - Cryptographic measures for enhancing privacy, including 'minimalistic cryptography' for rotating pseudonyms that are replacing the tag's code, or universal re-encryption of the tag's identifier.
  - Measures for preventing tracking at application layer (i.e., via its unique global identifier), communication, and / or at network layer.
  - Privacy-enhancements by pseudonym usage.
  - Privacy measures for enforcing user self-control or voluntary commitments by organisations for processing data properly. Such measures include 'soft-blocking' based on a user-defined privacy policy or measures based on the trusted computing concept for controlling the adherence to a commitment.

Overall Conclusions

Summarising, the overall conclusions are the following (Fischer-Hübner and Hedbom, 2008):

- The use of RFID technology in several contexts and its role as a prime Ambient Intelligence enabler raises important data protection and privacy threats.
- The current legal privacy framework partly gives too much room for interpretation and does not always give clear answers with regards to RFID technology. For example, the essential question how to determine the data

controller in an RFID application who is responsible for the lawful data processing, is not always straightforwardly answered. Also, specific provisions of the e-Privacy Directive 2002/58/EC are not always applicable, as they presuppose processing of personal data in connection with the provision of publicly available electronic communications services in public communications networks. RFID technology however neither needs a publicly available electronic communications network nor does it involve respective providers. Such issues are currently being addressed by the EU.

- We believe that in order to get a privacy-friendly RFID system both the RF-subsystem and the backend system needs to provide privacy protection. Since the backend system presumably is under the control of the data controller while some parts of the RF-subsystem is not (notably the RFID tag), it is of utmost importance that the RF-subsystem provides for its own privacy protection.
- Many proposals for Privacy-Enhancing Technologies (PETs) for RFID exist—but only a few of them really seem to be feasible and all of them have some shortcomings, i.e., none provides the 'ultimate' solution addressing all RFID-related privacy problems. One of the main problems is that low-cost RFID tags by themselves currently cannot offer any solution for strong privacy. Nevertheless, in the short term the mechanisms suitable for a given area of application should be implemented in order to increase the level of privacy the RFID system offers.
- The state-of-the-art at the moment is to have a privacy patchwork for RFID rather than a holistic and integrative approach. A lot more effort in terms of research and development seems to be necessary to finally get a true holistic privacy framework for RFID applications. Among other things, low cost RFID tags with better and stronger cryptographic mechanisms need to be developed, transparency and awareness needs to be raised and the incentives for manufacturers and users of RFID technology to develop more privacy-friendly and secure solutions need to be increased.
- The combination of RFID and profiling, eventually coupled with many other privacy-sensitive means and techniques such as biometrics, may be a major privacy concern, as RFIDs, profiling and biometrics themselves already bear many risks, which are multiplied in combination.
- And finally, more research into life cycle analysis methods for RFID systems is needed to gain a clearer view of the data flows throughout the application's lifecycle and for subsequently developing a more fine-grained set of recommendations.

4.2.5 Credential Systems[23]

Access control typically is carried out based on a claim of the user (e.g., I'm authorised to use this application), the verification of this claim (these steps are also called authentication) and the assignment of a set of rights to the user (this step also is called authorisation). In distributed identity management environments the claim of the user also may include the rights he requests in the context of the application. In this case we also speak of claim-based access control.

Claim-based access control relies on credentials to tackle cross-domain authorisation. A credential is used by a party (holder) to prove its attributes. A credential is issued by a trusted third party (issuer) that asserts some attributes or claims regarding the holder. The integrity and origin of the claims are guaranteed by a signature of this issuer. Credentials are strongly associated with a secret of the holder, e.g., private key, to make sure that they cannot be used by another party. Knowledge of this secret is proven when using the credential, e.g., when signing a message. As a result, a third party can check the attributes of the message author (see also Bauer, Meints, Hansen, 2005).

This section focuses on two advanced types of credentials. First, 'minimal disclosure tokens' rely on cryptographic primitives that make it possible to reveal a subset of the claims and to ensure unlinkability, i.e., the issuer cannot trace the holder. Second, the logic-based 'Security Policy Assertion Language' enables taking access control decisions based on large sets of claims extracted from policies and credentials.

Minimal Disclosure Tokens

In today's online world, individuals are registered in hundreds if not thousands of organisational databases. Organisations are under increasing pressure to share this identity-related information with others to improve service, cut costs, and combat fraud. Both organisations and individuals stand to benefit.

In response to the demand for cross-organisational data sharing solutions, the computer industry has been working since the late nineties on an emerging identity infrastructure that will enable online data sharing across disparate computer systems. The emergence of an Internet-scale online identity infrastructure is not without challenges, however.

Firstly, care must be taken that individuals do not lose all control over the extent to which others can monitor their actions and learn (let alone misuse) private information about them. Making individuals a choke point for the flow of information about them is far from sufficient: this 'user-centric' approach may do nothing but greatly expand the ability of organisations to share personal information. This is particularly troublesome if each data sharing results in a common identifier for previously unlinked accounts: once all of an individual's accounts are 'feder-

[23] Authors: Stefan Brands, Microsoft; Laurent Bussard, EMIC; Joris Claessens, EMIC; Christian Geuer-Pollmann, EMIC; Ulrich Pinsdorf, EMIC.

ated', nothing stops organisations from directly exchanging information about the individual between themselves. The resulting online infrastructure would have unprecedented privacy consequences and be a huge boon to identity thieves.

Second, there are major security challenges for organisations. For example, when an online service provider relies on an identity 'claim' that has been issued by another organisation, how can it be sure that the information is authentic and pertains to the individual that is requesting a service? How can the issuing organisation be prevented from learning competitive information about the service provider's clients, let alone from surreptitiously accessing their accounts? How to prevent denial-of-service attacks and ensure availability of third-party identity claims? Compounding the challenge is that the threats in a distributed data sharing environment do not come only from outsiders: attacks may originate from the organisations that issue identity claims, as well as from hackers of these organisations.

Following the invention of public-key cryptography in the mid seventies, cryptographers have worked for several decades on a holistic solution to these challenges. This research has resulted in sophisticated techniques for so-called 'minimal disclosure tokens' (sometimes also referred to as anonymous credentials, a term that does not do justice to the power of the technology). Minimal disclosure tokens are basic cryptographic constructs for protecting digital information. They are issued by 'issuers' to 'users' by means of an issuing protocol, presented by their users to 'verifiers' by means of a presentation protocol, and optionally forwarded by verifiers to third parties (such as auditors). Since minimal disclosure tokens are just sequences of zeros and ones, they can be transferred electronically and can be verified by computers.

Minimal disclosure tokens are ideal for sharing identity-related information across organisations:

- **User-centric:** Using minimal disclosure tokens, organisations can securely share information via the individuals to whom it pertains or via other intermediating parties (such as brokers and outsourcing suppliers). The multi-party security features of minimal disclosure tokens prevent any unauthorised manipulations of protected information, not only by outsiders but also by intermediating parties. For instance, issuers can protect identity claims against unauthorised lending, pooling, cloning, discarding, and reuse by encoding them into minimal disclosure tokens. At the same time, intermediating parties can see the information that is shared, enabling them to boycott inappropriate exchanges. They can also be actively involved in the flow of protected information, helping to determine how organisations conduct data exchanges. Furthermore, they can store protected information upon issuance so that it can be ported and used off-line.

- **Selective disclosure:** Identity information encoded into minimal disclosure tokens can be selectively disclosed in a fine-grained manner. By way of example, the user of a minimal disclosure token stating that its holder is a Dutch citizen born on August 12, 1966 can present the token in a manner that reveals only that the holder is over 18 and European.[24] As another example, a token that specifies its holder's real name can be presented in a manner that proves that the name is not contained on a blacklist of suspected terrorists, without revealing anything else.

- **Unlinkability:** Minimal disclosure tokens can be issued and presented without creating unwanted linkages. This enables organisations to issue authentication tokens to identified individuals that can subsequently be used to access protected resources anonymously or pseudonymously. It also enables account holders to retrieve and present protected identity claims without thereby enabling organisations to link the source and destination accounts. This protects against unwanted profiling across spheres of activity and minimises the risk of identity theft by insiders and hackers. At the same time, individuals who abuse services can be excluded from further participation via several revocation methods that do not contravene the privacy features of minimal disclosure tokens.
- **Non-transferability:** Issuers can prevent users from transferring (copies of) minimal disclosure tokens that convey privileges, entitlements, and other personal credential information. One solution is to encode private information of the designated token holder into the tokens; the token holder can hide this data at presentation time (owing to the selective disclosure feature), but would need to reveal it in order to enable others to present the tokens. For stronger protection, issuers can electronically bind minimal disclosure tokens to a previously issued trusted module (such as a tamper-resistant smart card or a Trusted Computing chip) that can enforce security policies (such as non-transferability) throughout the life cycle of the tokens; in contrast to PKI certificates, a single low-cost module can protect arbitrarily many minimal disclosure tokens.
- **Private audit trails:** Relying organisations can capture signed transcripts that prove their interactions with individuals. Prior to storing or forwarding signed transcripts, some or all of their disclosed contents can be censored without destroying their verifiability. This enables organisations to protect their own privacy and autonomy interests vis-à-vis auditors.

A detailed description of how these features are achieved is outside the scope of this section.[25]

[24] Technically, the 'over-18' property is proved by providing a zero-knowledge proof that the value (e.g., total number of days or minutes) representing today's date minus the token value representing the birth date is greater than the value that represents 18 years. The 'is-European' property is proved by demonstrating in zero-knowledge that the country code encoded in the token is in the set of country codes representing all European countries.

[25] A starting point to learn more is Stefan Brands: 'Rethinking Public Key Infrastructures and Digital Certificates; Building in Privacy,' MIT Press, ISBN 0-262-02491-8, available at http://www.credentica.com/technology/book.html.

The privacy features of minimal disclosure tokens hold unconditionally, in the strongest possible sense: issuing and relying organisations cannot learn anything beyond what users choose to disclose when presenting their tokens, even if they collude and have unlimited resources to analyse protocol data.

Minimal disclosure tokens are not merely an academic construct: leading industry players are working to productise minimal disclosure token technologies. For example, Microsoft has announced plans to implement its U-Prove technology (see http://www.credentica.com) into Windows Communication Foundation and Windows CardSpace, and IBM has developed a similar technology (see http://www.zurich.ibm.com/security/idemix) that it plans to contribute to open source.

Advanced Claims: Security Policy Assertion Language

SecPAL (Becker et al., 2006; Humphrey et al., 2007) is a security policy language developed to meet the access control requirements of large-scale Grid Computing Environments. SecPAL is declarative, logic-based, and builds on a large body of work showing the value of such languages for flexibly expressing security policies. It was designed to be comprehensive and provides a uniform mechanism for expressing trust relationships, authorisation policies, delegation policies, identity and attribute assertions, capability assertions, revocations, and audit requirements. This provides tangible benefits by making the system understandable and analysable. It also improves security assurance by avoiding, or at least severely curtailing, the need for semantic translation and reconciliation between disparate security technologies.

A very simple example could look as follows (see also Becker et al., 2006). Researcher Fanny wants to access a file on a file server. The company's security token service (STS) issued a token to Fanny: 'STS says Fanny is a researcher'. The assertions are encoded in XML and signed by the issuer of the assertion, typically the STS. Let's assume that the file server has a security policy: a) 'STS says FileServer can say x can read y' and b) 'FileServer says x can read file://project if x is a researcher'. Finally, Fanny wants to read a file on the file server. She sends her read request together with her assertion to the file server. The file server is protected with a policy enforcement point that triggers the following SecPAL query at the policy decision point: 'Fanny can read file://project'. In this case we assume that the STS acts both as token issuer and as policy decision point. The SecPAL engine has Fanny's assertion, the policy and the query and uses an inference mechanism to determine if the query can be deduced from the policy and the assertions.

It is remarkable that the assertions, the policy and the query are expressed in the same language. The verbs 'says' and 'can' acts as a special keyword in the SecPAL even allows limited and unlimited delegation chains with a combination of both keywords 'can say'. In the example we see this when the STS allows the file server to define who may access the files. SecPAL defines a set of verbs such as 'read', 'write', 'execute' but is open for new verbs. However, the current research license allows only a fixed set of verbs in the context of Grid Computing.[26]

Becker et al. (2006) mention a list of design principle for the language: expressiveness, readable syntax, unambiguous semantics, effective decision procedure and extensibility. Humphrey et al. (2007) provide details from an implementation using SecPAL as fine-grained access control for GridFTP where SecPAL outperforms the other tested access control mechanism.

4.3 Supporting Technologies

In this section technologies supporting identity management intentionally or indirectly are introduced and discussed. In the context of FIDIS research the following technologies are investigated:

- Trusted Computing
- Protocols with respect to identity and identification
- Service Oriented Architectures
- Digital Rights Management

Most of these technologies carry the potential to be (ab)used for profiling and surveillance like identity management. However, for some of them application scenarios were developed that need to be considered as enhancing. In this section the problem domains and privacy enhancing application scenarios are presented.

4.3.1 Trusted Computing[27]

An important point when implementing cryptographic schemes and protocols is the fact that security needs some kind of 'trusted anchor', i.e., one cannot achieve protection within a completely untrusted environment. Trusted Computing (TC) is about establishing this trusted anchor.

The first seminal publications in the field of Trusted Computing can be dated back to the early 1970s (e.g., Baran, 1973). It became an 'emerging' technology in the past few years due to the fact that an industry consortium — the Trusted Computing Group (TCG)[28] — started to develop industry standard specifications that support trusted computing for PCs, clients and servers, mobile devices and a trusted infrastructure. The TCG has more than 120 members including nearly every important IT company (e.g., AMD, HP, IBM, Intel, Microsoft and SUN). The powerful market position of these companies drives the spreading of Trusted Computing as defined by the Trusted Computing Group.

---

[26] See http://research.microsoft.com/projects/SecPAL/ for details.

[27] Author: Stefan Köpsell, TU Dresden.

[28] http://www.trustedcomputinggroup.org/.

Nevertheless it is still (emotionally) discussed what exactly TC is[29] and whether it has more benefits for users or for commercial organisations, e.g., in scenarios like Digital Rights Management (DRM).

In general TC comprises at least the following technologies and mechanisms:

- **Trusted computing base** which is the minimal set of hardware (e.g., the TPM-chip specified by the TCG), firmware and software (e.g., a secure operating system) which is necessary for enforcing a security policy.
- **Secure I/O** which offers protected paths for all data from the input through the processing until the output. That means for instance that the user can be sure that the inputs he made can not be intercepted by malicious software like keyboard loggers.
- **Sealed memory** which refers to a protected memory which prevents other processes (and even unprivileged parts of the operating system) from reading / writing to it.
- **Sealed storage** a technology which ensures that persistent data can only be read and modified by exactly the same combination of hardware / software which has written the data.
- **Authentic booting and (remote) attestation** which allows a user to be sure with which well defined hard- / software he interacts and to prove this even to third parties.
- **Unique digital identities for computers** which means that each Trusted Computing base has a unique digital identity enabling the owner of a computer to prove that a certain message originated from a computer he owns or that two messages come from the same computer; that two messages do not come from the same computer.

An important fact and fundamental principle about Trusted Computing is, that Trusted Computing does not mean that the computing environment (hard- and software) can be trusted—but instead one has to trust it. According to Ross Anderson, 'In the US Department of Defense, a 'trusted system or component' is defined as 'one which can break the security policy'.'[30] This simply means, if the trustworthiness assumptions one has about a certain Trusted Computing based ICT system are wrong, then the whole protection offered by this system (in terms of security and privacy) can be broken.

Immediately the question arises to what extent should one trust the Trusted Computing. If one is willing to absolutely trust the Trusted Computing, many (if not all) security- and privacy-related problems can be solved easily. The reason is that most of the complex and complicated cryptographic mechanisms and proto-

---

[29] This is not surprising as the term 'trust' itself is heavily discussed within different communities.

[30] Ross Anderson: 'Trusted Computing' Frequently Asked Question. Version 1.1 (August 2003), http://www.cl.cam.ac.uk/~rja14/tcpa-faq.html.

cols just exist or were designed with the goal to circumvent the untrustworthiness of the computing environment (soft- and hardware) used by the communication partners and third parties.

As example in (Müller and Wohlgemuth, 2007) the delegation of rights and secrets to proxies which act on behalf of the customer was identified as one of the fundamental problems (with respect to security and privacy) in multi-stage business processes. Clearly if these proxies are not trustworthy, then they can use the data provided by the user to contravene the interests of the user and violate his privacy.

Using Trusted Computing on the proxy side could easily solve this problem (under the assumption that one is willing to absolutely trust the Trusted Computing as mentioned above). In this case the proxy would be trustworthy (and can be trusted) 'by definition'.

On the other hand the history of security and privacy technologies as well as ICT in general has shown that such absolute error-less and correctly designed and working systems do not exist and will (with high probability) never exist. Therefore Trusted Computing should only be seen as a 'helping tool' which could be used to enhance the overall security a system provides.

In (Iliev and Smith, 2005) the fundamental property of Trusted Computing is described as follows: 'We call the physically protected and trusted components of a server K, [...]. In any given client-server application, we can view K as an extension of the client: from a trust perspective, K acts on the client's behalf, but physically, K is co-located with the server.'

Derived from this fundamental property, using Trusted Computing comprises at least the following two overall goals / approaches:

- To *prevent* security threats by implementing (traditional) security mechanisms in a more trustworthy way or (more general) use Trusted Computing to secure the basic operations of the devices (e.g., client PCs, servers or mobile phones). This comprises all the well known technologies offered by Trusted Computing.

  In order to exemplify this one can look at a typical e-business scenario where the communication between the involved parties (users and services) has to be confidential and integral. The (cryptographic) protocols and measures used can benefit from TC and the TPM, e.g., the cryptographic keys could be stored under the control of the TPM (using the Sealed Memory and Sealed Storage functionality) making attacks on the communication confidentiality much harder.

  In general it seems that this 'classical' approach for enhancing the security is the one which is in the focus of the industry and corresponding business consultancies[31].

[31] See for instance: Jon Oltsik: 'Trusted Enterprise Security. How the Trusted Computing Group (TCG) Will Advance Enterprise Security.' White Paper, Enterprise Strategy Group, January 2006, https://www.trustedcomputinggroup.org/news/Industry Data/ ESG_ White_Paper.pdf.

- Enabling the communicating parties to *check, monitor* and *audit* the trustworthiness of each other using remote attestation. Even third parties could be permitted to do so (e.g., on behalf of a communicating entity).

  Online banking can serve as an example scenario to illustrate this. If trusted computing is used on the service side (i.e., the bank) then the user can check if the bank server is secure. Moreover if trusted computing is used on the user side then the bank can check if the computer of the user is secure, e.g., not tampered with malicious software. Depending on the detected security status both parties can for example limit the maximum amount of money allowed for online banking transactions. Finally these checks could be outsourced to third parties, e.g., the bank side could be audited by data protection authorities.

The FIDIS consortium analysed the potential of Trusted Computing for supporting security and privacy within various areas and scenarios. The different possibilities of applying Trusted Computing in e-Business scenarios are elaborated in Müller and Wohlgemuth (2008). Finally Alkassar and Husseiki (2008) give a broader overview on the applicability and implications of Trusted Computing in the area of identity management.

Note that so far the standards and technologies developed by the Trusted Computing Group focus primarily on software based attacks and not hardware based (i.e., physical) ones. Therefore TC does not offer protection if a device itself could be manipulated by the attacker. This has to be taken into account when considering the overall security of a given system, especially in scenarios where mobile devices are involved which could easily get lost or stolen. But even in the online banking scenario as illustrated above this has to be evaluated. On the one side one can assume that the bank is well experienced in offering excellent physical protection for valuable goods including their servers. On the other side one has to consider that many banks outsource their IT resulting in much less physical protection to the servers.

But focusing on software-only attacks is not the only controversial issue of Trusted Computing as defined by the Trusted Computing Group. Trusted Computing might have a negative impact on the privacy of its users as for instance remote attestation reveals the whole configuration of users' devices (e.g., all running software, installed hardware etc.). Each TPM device has a unique cryptographic key which could be misused to uniquely identify the device and consequently its users (e.g., if Trusted Computing is applied to mobile phones). Trusted Computing could also be misused to prevent the execution of certain 'unwanted' software or operating systems (e.g., Open Source ones). Alkassar and Husseiki (2008) as well as Müller and Wohlgemuth (2008) discuss the shortcomings of Trusted Computing and related legal and social aspects in more detail.

Summarising one can say that Trusted Computing is a necessity for privacy and security in the information society but needs to be carefully designed so that it does not do completely the contrary.

4.3.2 Protocols with Respect to Identity and Identification[32]

In computing, protocols are standards that control or facilitate the connection, communication, and data transfer between two endpoints. As communication is the basis of our Information Society, protocols are highly relevant for all activities in information and communication technologies. What is more, usually users are not aware of running protocols at least as long they function seamlessly and facilitate the desired services. This also means that people lack knowledge on privacy risks or other identity-related aspects when using protocols. One example is the repeated usage of some identifiers, e.g., MAC (Media Access Control) addresses or Cookies, which enable linkage and profiling by any observer. In some cases the network infrastructure relies on the transfer of these identifiers—real data minimisation would require a major redesign of the protocols.

When discussing protocols, there is a need to distinguish between their specification and implementation. Although these should be one and the same, in practice implementations do not always properly adhere to what is laid down in the specifications—this may be done accidentally, but in some cases deviations from the specifications are intended, e.g., when implementing light-weight versions of the full specification or when contradictions are discovered in the documents which cannot be overcome.

When describing networking protocols, typically the ISO/OSI layer model is used. This model describes seven layers with the following functions (Tanenbaum, 2003):

Table 4.1. Layers and corresponding functions in the ISO/OSI reference model

Data Unit	ISO/OSI layer	Function
Data	7: Application	Network process to application (http)
	6: Presentation	Data representation and encryption
	5: Session	Interhost communication
Segments	4: Transport	End-to-end connections and reliability (TCP)
Packets	3: Network	Path determination and logical addressing (IP)
Frames	2: Data link	Physical addressing (MAC & LLC)
Bits	1: Physical	Media, signal and binary transmission

In (Hansen and Alkassar, 2008) an overview is given of the identity-related aspects of network protocols on different technical layers: host-to-network layer (e.g., Local Area Network (LAN) and Wireless LAN (WLAN) communication), Internet layer (e.g., Internet Protocol (IP) and Internet Protocol Security (IPSec)),

---

[32] Author: Marit Hansen, Unabhängiges Landeszentrum für Datenschutz Schleswig-Holstein.

Table 4.2. ISO/OSI layers of selected protocols from the TCP/IP suite

TCP/IP layer	ISO/OSI layer	Protocols	
Application	5-7	HTTP	SMTP Telnet DNS SNMP SSH RTP
Transport	4	TCP	UDP SCTP
Internet	3	IP (IPv4, IPv6)	ICMP IPSec
Link / Physical / Host-to-Network	1-2	Ethernet (CSMA/CD), WLAN, Token Ring, PPP, ISDN, Modem	

transport layer (e.g., Transmission Control Protocol (TCP) and User Datagram Protocol (UDP)) and application layer protocols (e.g., HyperText Transfer Protocol (HTTP), Simple Mail Transfer Protocol (SMTP) and Domain Name System (DNS)). The following figure shows how the analysed protocols belonging to the TCP/IP protocol suite map to the ISO/OSI seven layer reference model.

In addition, protocols for privacy policies (ISO/OSI layer 7) are being analysed concerning their potential for improving the user's privacy. For both categories of protocols, the main results of the survey done in (Hansen and Alkassar, 2008) are summarised in the following paragraphs.

Network Protocols

When analysing identity and identification aspects of network protocols, the following criteria were put in the focus:

- Which identifiers are used in the protocols? How unique are they? Are all identifiers visible, or may there be hidden identifiers?
- Is linkage of different protocol runs possible? Could users be profiled or even identified by this linkage?
- Which additional user data—i.e., which data directly linked to the user involved (or his machine)—are disclosed?
- Is it possible to avoid or circumvent the information disclosure, and if yes: with which effort?

The analysis of network protocols shows that virtually any commonly used protocol reveals linkable information which could be used for profiling. For instance, transmitted identifiers such as IP addresses (in all Internet communication), Cookies (in HTTP) or MAC addresses (in Ethernet or WLAN communication) enable for each observer linkage of different protocol usages and thereby profiling of the user's (or computer's) behaviour. Dynamically assigned IP addresses are not uniquely bound to the user's computer—unlike the MAC address which typically is static to the network interface. However, IP addresses of one and the same Internet provider change only within a certain range, and in addition they can be mapped to geographical data to find out the region where that IP address was registered. This is also relevant for location privacy when mobile users use various WLANs.

The profiling possibility with linkable data may yield so extensive profiles that the link to the user can be easily established and thus they become personal data. Further, there are protocols which explicitly disclose user data, e.g., the header fields 'Referer', 'User-Agent', 'Accept' or 'Accept-Language' in HTTP or the information on sender and receiver of e-mails in SMTP. Again, these data alone or in combination may identify the users and are privacy-relevant. For instance, sender and receiver of e-mails give observers such as eavesdroppers or other parties the information that there is a relationship between the e-mailing parties. It can be used to figure out a user's social network. This is also true when the e-mails are encrypted: The header information stays the same even if the payload, i.e., the e-mail's body, is encrypted. Concerning HTTP, the content of the header field 'User-Agent' may be used to categorise the user as 'early adopter' (if very new browsers are employed) or it can be used as first analysis of possible security vulnerabilities on the user's computer (if old versions have not been updated). 'Accept-Language' informs about the cultural background of the user. The 'Referer' field contains the URL where the user came from—if this had been a search engine, the Referer usually also comprises the search terms.

Looking into protocols is not done by many users. Several people are aware of those options which can be configured in their application software, in particular in the browser. However, the choices that can be made on that level are very limited. For HTTP, browsers usually offer to configure the behaviour when setting or deleting Cookies. Since of the middle of 2008, so-called 'privacy modes' are being established from various browser manufacturers which among others may prevent the transmission of Referer information.

For most cases avoiding or circumventing the shown protocol-related threats for privacy and data protection cannot be done easily, though. One partial solution could be anonymisation services or other data minimisation techniques on the lower protocol layers that can be used to blur some of the traces one leaves while using the Internet. For browsing this can be done by substituting IP addresses or suppressing Cookies and interesting information in HTTP header fields. However, these services neither offer a convincing level of protection nor have they achieved a level of stability and quality of service necessary for every day use by the masses. Nevertheless they are suitable tools at least for some use cases. An easy to implement measure (from a technological point of view) would be to use link encryption of every single data link. This would greatly enhance privacy against outsiders—e.g., eavesdroppers on the lines—who would neither learn the communications' content nor (most of) their circumstances.

What are the odds that upcoming Next Generation Internet protocols will take into account the sketched privacy issues and handle them in an appropriate way?

FIDIS work (Hansen and Alkassar, 2008) took a look into important consortia dealing with new protocols to straighten out flaws created decades ago or to meet requirements stemming from actual usage patterns that were not foreseeable when the old protocols were designed. Important proposals comprise:

- the Internet2 Network[33] which provides a high-performance backbone network to U.S. research and education institutions, offering community control of the fundamental networking infrastructure.
- the GÉANT[34] and GÉANT2[35] network infrastructure, i.e., a multi-gigabit pan-European data communications network, reserved specifically for research and education use across Europe.
- the 'TRIAD – Translating Relaying Internet architecture integrating Active Directories'[36] architecture meant as overlay to the current Internet by defining an explicit content layer.
- the U.S. initiative 'FIND – Future Internet Network Design'[37] and the European 'Future Internet Research and Experimentation'[38] initiative, both long-term approaches to provide networks for new Internet-enabled applications and services.

All these proposals aim at improving security and robustness. Identity management and accountability are less prominently dealt with; privacy issues are rarely addressed as yet.

The next section describes privacy policy languages and protocols which are situated on higher levels in the network—they indeed try to take care of data protection issues.

Privacy Policy Languages and Protocols

In the World Wide Web, privacy policies are an important mechanism to inform users on the planned data processing. However, privacy policies often are hard to understand as they may be written in foreign languages or contain too much legalese. They are hard to compare with each other because they differ in scope, tackled issues and granularity. And why bother to read them if they usually offer no choices anyway (except for 'take it or leave it')?

This could be different with machine-readable privacy policies, expressed in specific languages: Privacy policy languages are designed to support organisations and users in managing their privacy policies and preferences. The development of privacy policy languages, the specification of their syntax and semantics, and the

---

33 http://www.internet2.edu/network/.
34 http://www.geant.net/.
35 http://www.geant2.net/.
36 http://gregorio.stanford.edu/triad/.
37 http://find.isi.edu/.
38 http://cordis.europa.eu/fp7/ict/fire/.

interaction with ICT systems, e.g., protocols for negotiating and matching policies, belong to a highly dynamic field. Since 1997 when W3C started the development of the Platform for Privacy Preferences (P3P), a variety of languages and protocols have been proposed which are specifically designed to manage privacy policies or—even if their main objective was less privacy-specific—can be applied for data protection purposes as well.

The vast area of privacy policy languages is not limited to the World Wide Web. Four categories of privacy policy languages are distinguished (Kumaraguru et al., 2007):

1. sophisticated access control languages (e.g., SAML, WSPL or XACML).
2. enterprise privacy policy languages (e.g., Enterprise Privacy Authorisation Language (EPAL)).
3. web privacy policy languages (e.g., P3P on the organisational side, APPEL or XPref on the user's side).
4. context-sensitive languages (e.g., Geopriv as an authorisation policy language for controlling access to location information or Protune (Provisional trust negotiation) as a rule-based trust negotiation framework).

In all of these areas, several proposals are being developed and evaluated. After involvement in P3P and EPAL, the World Wide Web Consortium continues its work on privacy policy language in the Policy Languages Interest Group (PLING). It is unlikely that the outcome of that work will be the one and only policy language. Instead other ways for interoperability of privacy policy languages are envisaged, e.g., by specifying common interfaces or establishing gateway services between different policy language domains.

Without doubt, protocols for negotiating policies and enforcing them will play a prominent role in the next years. As full data avoidance is not an option in many practical cases, policies and policy enforcement have to step in. From today's perspective it is not clear which languages and protocols will prevail in which areas.

Importance of Designing Protocols with Privacy Experts

According to Lessig, protocols belong to the major regulators which have a profound impact on society and whose implications must be considered (Lessig, 1999). This applies for all implementations of protocols, forming the architecture of ICT and providing today's possibilities for usage. In addition, the specifications of protocols already play a role as they are the blueprint not only for implementations thereof, but define interfaces to other specifications and implementations. If protocols, i.e., their specifications and / or their implementations, are faulty, the applications on top usually cannot eliminate the mistakes, but often even intensify the consequences.

Considering the complexity of the area and the massive influence of protocols on the Information Society, a privacy and linkability analysis should be performed during the design phase of each protocol, taking into account also linkage possibilities from and with the environment where the protocols will be run. Article 20 of the Directive 95/46/EC deals with 'prior checking' which should be carried out when the processing operations are 'likely to present specific risks to the rights and freedoms of data subjects'. In particular outside the European Union, e.g., in Canada, the United States, Australia and New Zealand, a similar procedure is also known as 'Privacy Impact Assessment'. Taking this seriously, privacy experts would have to be involved right from the beginning in each design process of communication protocol specifications.

The general participation of Data Protection Authorities (DPAs) and other trusted parties in the technology design process for better trust and trustworthiness might help. But this is no silver bullet since DPAs lack resources for skilled personnel travelling and participating in meetings where protocols are being specified. Indeed during the last decades very few DPAs were involved when protocols were specified, and those involved usually participated only in the design of specific protocols and languages focusing on privacy and data protection (such as P3P or EPAL). However, all kinds of protocols have been discussed and criticised in the privacy community, e.g., because of shortcomings concerning important privacy concepts such as data minimisation, transparency or the user's self-determination. Mostly the criticism came only after or in a late phase of the specification process, having a limited effect.

Summarising, a major challenge is not only the understanding of today's protocol world, but also the design and specification of new protocols. In particular in those areas where right now standardisation work is being performed, it is highly recommended to integrate experts from the fields of identity and privacy in the processes. Naïve specifications and implementations of global standards will usually cement not so privacy-friendly information and communication technologies. Even if privacy-invasive requirements such as demanded data retention are an obstacle to pure privacy-enhancing design of protocols, data protection functionality could be massively improved. In addition, the impact of these protocols, their interdependencies and the whole specification process have to be made more transparent to decision makers and citizens because protocols are the backbone of our Information Society.

4.3.3 Identity Management in Service Oriented Architectures[39]

Service Oriented Architecture (SOA) is a collection of cooperating services, which jointly fulfil a higher-level operation through communication. They fall in the class of distributed systems (Coulouris et al., 2005). A special attribute of SOA is the loose binding between the services. Typically the binding happens only at run-time, which means that a service learns only at this point in time with which actual service

[39] Authors: Stefan Brands, Microsoft; Laurent Bussard, EMIC; Joris Claessens, EMIC; Christian Geuer-Pollmann, EMIC; Ulrich Pinsdorf, EMIC.

instance it is communicating. This feature is called loose binding and is in fact said to be one of the core characteristics of SOA (Cabrera and Kurt, 2005).

This leads us back to identity management, since each service typically runs on behalf of a user's or organisation's identity. Considering that SOA allows, in addition to direct user interaction, an automated, intermediated and even delegated access to resources, leads to challenging identity management issues. Services which are bound only at run-time have to establish a verifiable trust relationship based on the identities of service owners. These issues are even amplified if we consider large, distributed service landscapes involving multiple business roles. Although SOA is commonly used inside organisations[40], service calls may even span across company boundaries, which leads to so called service federations between the hosting organisations (Goodner et al., 2007).

The need for standardisation of protocols to establish trust among services was already identified back in 2002, for instance the W3C created a number of working groups on various aspects of web services (Jacobs, 2002). The first version of the WS-Trust protocol was published in December 2002.

In the remainder of this section we want to introduce the most important protocols in the Web services world. Web services represent the most widely used type of SOA. The communication is XML-based and typically transported via HTTP. Web services fulfil a number of basic standards such as the Simple Objects Access Protocol (SOAP) for method invocation or Web Service Description Language (WSDL) for interface description. We describe the protocols WS-Security, WS-Trust and WS-Federation. WS-Trust is actually an identity protocol for trust establishment. It is based on WS-Security which supports the primitives for identity, key exchange, cryptography and signatures (see also Bauer, Meints, Hansen, 2005). WS-Federation goes a step further than WS-Trust and allows establishing of virtual collaborations across trust boundaries; it is thus comparable to a cross-certification in the PKI world. Having described the protocols, we want to introduce CardSpace in Section 4.5.2 as a use case that uses WS-Trust and WS-Security for identity management.[41]

Trust in Service Oriented Architectures

The WS-Trust specification (Nadalin et al., 2008) introduces the concept of 'security token services' (STS). A security token service is a Web service that can issue and validate security tokens. For instance, a Kerberos ticket granting server would be an STS in the non-XML world. A security token service offers functionality to issue new security tokens, to re-new existing tokens that are expiring and to check the validity of existing tokens. Additionally, a security token service can convert one security token into a different security token, thus brokering trust between two trust domains.

---

[40] The Open Group maintains an extensive list of SOA reference projects at http://www.opengroup.org/projects/soa-case-studies/page.tpl?CALLER=index.tpl&ggid= 996.

[41] CardSpace focuses mainly on user-centric identity management interaction, but it is applicable in SOA scenarios as well.

For example, a Web service describes required security tokens for Web service calls using WS-SecurityPolicy (Lawrence et al., 2008). A requestor may want to call that specific Web service but may not have the right security tokens indicated by the policy. The Web service may require Security Assertion Markup Language (SAML) credentials from a particular trust domain whereas the requestor only has an X.509 certificate from its own domain. By requesting the 'right' matching token (credential) from the security token service, the requestor may get back a token from the STS that can be included when calling the Web service in question. The decision what exactly the 'right' token is can be made either by the requestor or by the STS. After inspection of the Web service's policy, the requestor may specifically ask the STS: 'I have the attached X.509 certificate and need a SAML token.' The other option is that the requestor includes its possessed tokens and states what Web service it intends to call: 'I possess the following tokens and I would like to call the Web service http://foo/bar. Please give me whatever token may be appropriate.'

WS-Trust provides a rich interface that permits the implementation of various use cases. For instance, the requestor may include time variant parameters as entropy for a token generation process. The token service may return secret key material to the requestor (so-called proof-of-possession tokens) along with the requested security token, so that the requestor can prove that it possessed the security token. For instance, the requested security token may be a certificate whereas the proof-of-possession token is the associated private key. The security token service may also return multiple keys like a certificate along with its validation chain or it may create key exchange tokens with which the requestor can encrypt key material for the intended Web service. A requestor can also express requirements on algorithms and key strengths for required tokens.

WS-Trust defines protocols including challenge-and-response protocols to obtain the requested security tokens, thus enabling the mitigation of man-in-the-middle and message replay attacks. The WS-Trust specification also permits that a requestor may need a security token to implement some delegation of rights to a third party. For instance, a requestor could request an authorisation token for a colleague that may be valid for a given time interval. WS-Trust utilises WS-Security for signing and encrypting parts of SOAP messages as well as WS-Policy / SecurityPolicy to express and determine what particular security tokens may be consumed by a given Web service. WS-Trust is a basic building block that can be used to rebuild many of the already existing security protocols for trust establishing and make them fit directly in the Web services world by using Web service protocols and data structures.

The WS-Security (Lawrence et al., 2006) specification defines mechanisms for integrity and confidentiality protection, and data origin authentication for SOAP messages and selected parts thereof. Hence, it offers the basic primitives to establish mutual trust using WS-Trust. The cryptographic mechanisms are utilised by describing how XML Signature and XML Encryption are applied to parts of a SOAP message. That includes processing rules so that a SOAP node (intermediaries and ultimate receivers) can determine the order in which parts of the message have to be validated or decrypted. These cryptographic properties are described using a specific header field, the <wsse:Security> header. This header provides a mechanism for attaching security-related information to a SOAP message, whereas multiple <wsse:Security> headers may exist inside a single SOAP message. Each of these headers is intended for consumption by a different SOAP intermediary. This property enables intermediaries to encrypt or decrypt specific parts of a message before forwarding it or enforces that certain parts of the message must be validated before the message is processed further.

Besides the cryptographic processing rules for handling a message, WS-Security defines a generic mechanism for associating security tokens with the message. 'Associating a security token' means that one or more tokens are included in <wsse:Security> headers in the message and that a referencing mechanism is introduced to refer to these tokens. Tokens generally are either identification or cryptographic material or they may be expressions of capabilities (e.g., signed authorisation statements).

For instance, the certificate for signature validation may be added into the header. That may be done by either placing it into the signature itself (which makes reusage a bit complicated and fragile) or by directly making it a child of the <wsse:Security> header and referencing it from the signature. The latter use has the advantage that other signatures or security operations may also directly refer to that token. WS-Security, available in version 1.1 since February 2007, defines a simple username token, a container for arbitrary binary tokens (base64 encoded), a container for XML-formatted tokens, and an encrypted data token.

WS-Federation introduces mechanisms to manage and broker trust relationships in a heterogeneous and federated environment. This includes support for federated identities, attributes and pseudonyms. 'Federation' refers to the concept that two or more security domains agree to interact with each other, specifically letting users of each security domain access services in the other security domain. For instance, two companies that have a collaboration agreement may decide that employees from the other company may invoke specific Web services. These scenarios with access across security boundaries are called 'federated environments' or 'federations'. Each security domain has its own security token service(s), and each service inside these domains may have individual security policies. WS-Federation uses the WS-Security, WS-SecurityPolicy and WS-Trust specifications to specify scenarios to allow requesters from the one domain to obtain security tokens in the other domain, thus subsequently getting access to the services in the other domain.

To illustrate this concept with an example, imagine that a user Fanny from company A intends to access Frank's Web service in company B. Fanny and Frank do not have any prior relationship, but both companies have agreed to federate certain services, and the decision is that particular users from company A may access dedicated services inside company B. By some means, Fanny knows the endpoint reference of Frank's service. Using the basic mechanisms defined in WS-PolicyAttachment, WS-MetadataExchange (Ballinger et al., 2006), and WS-SecurityPolicy, Fanny retrieves the security policy of Frank's service and detects that the security token service STS_B of company B issues tokens to access this service. Fanny issues a security token request to the security token service STS_A of company A and claims to need a token to access STS_B. Company A and company B are federated together, therefore STS_A is able to issue a security token for Fanny. Of course, that may depend on whether Fanny belongs to the group of A's employees that are permitted to access Frank's services. In the next step, Fanny requests a token for accessing Frank's service from STS_B and proves her authorisation by utilising the token issued by STS_A. After validating that the STS_A security token is valid, STS_B issues a security token for access to Frank's service (assuming that Frank's Web service belongs to the group that company B offers to company A). In the last step, Frank's Web service is invoked by Fanny. During that final request, Fanny presents the token issued by STS_B.

Besides this introductory example, WS-Federation shows how such a federation could work across multiple security domains or how delegation could be used. Delegation means that a user may delegate certain access rights on one federated resource to a different federated resource. Additionally, WS-Federation defines mechanisms to handle pseudonyms (aliases used at different services and federations) and management mechanisms for the pseudonyms, including single sign-in and sign-out (sign-out refers to the removal of pseudonym-related information at different services).

The whole suite of Web service-related specifications is much broader, even just the part dealing with security and privacy. Geuer-Pollmann and Claessens (2005) as well as Cabrera and Kurt (2005) provide a solid overview on the most relevant standards and their relations to each other.

4.3.4 Digital Rights Management[42]

Digital rights management (DRM) refers to several concepts to restrict arbitrary use of data and to limit it in accordance with a certain defined policy (e.g. Hansen and Möller, 2005). The core-functionality of DRM also can be summarised as policy enforcement. Policies in this context contain access control policies. As a result DRM also can be understood as an implementation of identity management core-functionalities (namely authentication and authorisation). The concepts for DRM differ in the technological approaches used and the targets DRM is used for. The targets are mainly (Alkassar and Husseiki, 2008: 42):

- DRM in companies or governmental administrations to protect customers' / citizens' data
- DRM for personalised files
- DRM for media files and
- DRM for software products.

[42] Author: Martin Meints, Unabhängiges Landeszentrum für Datenschutz Schleswig-Holstein.

In addition the use of DRM has been discussed in the context of fraud prevention, especially the prevention of manipulation of bank notes[43]. Many recent DRM concepts rely on Trusted Computing. Many existing and planned technical implementations of DRM were investigated with respect to their potential impact on the privacy of customers and users. In most cases the impact on privacy was considered to be negative or at least discussed controversially (for an overview see Hansen, Möller, 2005, Alkassar, Husseiki, 2008 pp. 42-45 and references cited therein).

In the context of FIDIS research it was mainly investigated whether and how far DRM could be used to protect privacy of customers and citizen. While the direct application of DRM by customers in their relationship to organisations for technical and economic reasons does not seem to be promising, the application of DRM in organisations supported by trusted third parties (from the customers' viewpoint) seems to be more realistic. Together with policy management languages such as the Enterprise Privacy Authorization Language (EPAL)[44] DRM may become an important tool for the organisation internal and inter-organisation-client enforcement of security and privacy policies. Potential applications are the protection of the confidentiality of highly sensitive data, and the enforcement of the processing of this data for a defined purpose. These approaches also may be of interest for the processing of sensitive data along a chain of organisations, where service oriented architectures (SOA) are used and in the context of application service providing (ASP, also called saas, software as a service).

However, these concepts are more or less in an early conception phase and further research is necessary (also see Grimm et al., 2005).

4.4 Emerging Technologies[45]

In some contrast to the FIDIS research on IMS discussed thus far, the research in the area of emerging technologies has focused on less well developed technology, services or applications which may prove to have a weighty impact in the field of identity. 'Emerging technologies' is a topic which pervades all of the areas into which the work of FIDIS is separated and clustered, and so it is important to understand the potential impact which emerging technologies may have. While a relatively formalised description of emerging technologies has emerged over the last few years, i.e., the result of the convergence of nanotechnology, biotechnology, information technology, cognitive science, robotics, and artificial intelligence, within FIDIS the term is considered to be broader. We have defined this as (identity-related) technologies or applications whose practical usage is still far behind their potential.

---

43 E.g., Schulzki-Haddouti, C., *EU-Kommission für Banknoten-Kopierschutz*, Heise-News, http://www.heise.de/newsticker/meldung/47083.

44 See, e.g., EPAL 1.2, W3C Member Submission, http://www.w3.org/Submission/EPAL/.

45 Author: Mark Gasson, Reading University.

The use of techniques to profile people from varying sized sets of data have become increasingly utilised in light of the evolving underlying technologies which both enable the processing through powerful infrastructures, and the development of the profiling techniques themselves. It is obvious that this type of technology will continue to develop inline with the technologies which support it, and many have prophesised a shift in the way in which we interact with machines based on the extrapolated potential of this technology. The focus of the work investigated within FIDIS based on emerging technologies is broadly related to this developing area, the emergence of Ambient Intelligence.

4.4.1 Ambient Intelligence

Ambient Intelligence (AmI) has been presented for many years as the panacea for the human / technology interaction bottleneck. The very essence of AmI is to enrich the user experience by capitalising on the potential that additional computing processing can bring. Part of this enrichment is achieved by augmenting the user in their daily lives through additional services and access to additional information. However, this is achieved whilst actually reducing the focus on the traditional explicit data input / output paradigm—a true shift in our concept of what a computer is, and how we should interact and use it. The aim of the AmI environment is to provide a context aware system, using unobtrusive computing devices that will improve the quality of people's lives by acknowledging their needs, requirements and preferences and thus acting in some way on their behalf. To achieve this, the 'intelligent' environment, or rather, an intelligent agent within the environment needs to build up a profile of each individual, and be able to subsequently link the profile with the correct individual. In essence, the environment itself has become the interface to the distributed, seamless and invisible AmI. AmI itself will not be the outcome of any single technology or application—rather it is an 'emergent' property. Essentially, AmI is more than just the sum of its parts. Ubiquitous Computing is the next wave of technology, whereby many thousands of wireless computing devices are distributed in the environment in everyday objects around us. Clearly this technology integration into the environment is a key aspect of AmI. Ubiquitous Communication will allow robust, ad-hoc networks to be formed by this broad range of mobile and static devices, forming a ubiquitous system of large-scale distributed networks of interconnected computing devices. By adding intelligent user interfaces and integrating sensing devices, it should be possible to identify and model user activities, preferences and behaviours, and create individualised profiles. These key aspects are all required to achieve the ideal AmI environment.

The concept of AmI is largely based on the idea that by augmenting an environment with sensor technologies and by providing near unlimited storage and processing capabilities, the intentions, needs and desires of people can be predicted and catered for. The result is that people will not need to know how to operate complex technologies—instead the technology will interact with them in intelligent and intuitive ways. Clearly collating information is the key. However, if an environment is to know what a person wants or needs without being explicitly told, then this information needs to come from indirect means—i.e., the technology, or rather the environment as a whole becomes less interactive, and more proactive. Through varying levels of sensor data gleaned from pervasively embedded sensors, dynamic autonomic profiles can be drawn to enable this proactive ability. Intuitively these profiles can only be as good as the data that feeds them, and the processing available to create them, and hence the focus of development is to extract as much data as possible from all aspects of the users and their interactions within an AmI space, as well as developing the underlying infrastructure through which this data can be 'mined' for new information. This is further discussed in Chapter 7. From an implementation point of view, there are a range of technologies which are considered applicable in the fabric of an AmI environment. These stem from fundamental sensor technology for AmI spaces which will enable the data capture from which new information can be inferred, to enabling technology, i.e., technology which will serve in the underpinning infrastructure to provide the networking and processing capabilities necessary in the envisaged future scenarios of augmented living. Notably, and in contrast to other texts on AmI-related technology, we have investigated the concepts of 'sensors which detect sensors' and 'mobile user-controlled sensors' which may prove to be ways in which our privacy can be conserved to a greater extent in environments where data capture becomes ubiquitous.

In any case, it is likely that the user and the controller of the data will not be one and the same. Indeed in some cases it may be unclear who is collecting data from sensors and what it is being used for. One route to counteract such issues is the idea that new technologies should incorporate 'privacy by design', that is the mechanisms necessary for user control of their data should be an inherent aspect of the technology. To this end, many privacy advocates have suggested that emerging technologies and applications such as AmI should undergo mandatory privacy impact assessments before they are released into the mass market. To a large extent the technologies for AmI are speculative in that, in the main, they have not reached a mature level of development or deployment. Thus, it is exactly at this point where such technology needs to be discussed beyond the domain of those creating it to ensure that we are able to stay in control. 'Staying in control' is a broad turn of phrase, and indeed its exact meaning and context here is open to interpretation. However, what is for sure is that there are fundamental rights and freedoms which must be ensured.

The area of AmI has been extensively explored by the FIDIS NoE from the perspective of various disciplines. The fundamental enabling technologies which may form key parts of the AmI infrastructure have been discussed in Gasson and Warwick (2007), and Schreurs et al. (2005). Further to this, the very pertinent legal issues which need addressing, and the possible routes through which they may be addressed have been highlighted by Hildebrandt and Koops (2007), while solutions to the inherent security and privacy issues have been further developed by Hildebrandt and Meints (2006) and Fischer-Hübner and Hedbom (2008).

4.4.2 Human ICT Implants

The relatively new trend for low-tech human implants has recently risen in the public consciousness, although less publicised developments of high-tech implants in the medical domain have been progressing for several decades. Indeed, a significant drive behind the development of so called Information Communicating Technology (ICT) implant devices is medical—i.e., restoring deficient human abilities. It is clear that this application area is one which can be greatly enhanced through the new emerging technology phenomenon, and it is not clear where this may ultimately take us. The ability to form direct, bi-directional links with the human brain will open up the potential for many new application areas. Scientists predict that within the next thirty years neural interfaces will be designed that will not only increase the dynamic range of senses, but will also enhance memory and enable 'cyberthink' — invisible communication with others and with technology (McGee and Maguire, 2007). But are these claims realistic, and should they be taken seriously? As discussed by Kosta and Gasson (2008), current applications alone introduce challenging questions. Indeed the increasing commercialisation of human ICT implants has generated debate over the ethical, legal and social aspects of the technology and its products.

The basic foundations of advanced ICT implant devices are being developed for clear medical purposes, and it is reasonable to assume that few would argue against this progress for such noble, therapeutic causes. Equally, as has been demonstrated by cosmetic surgery, we cannot assume that because a procedure is highly invasive, people will not undergo it. So, while we may be some way away, there is clear evidence that devices capable of significant enhancement will become reality, and most probably will be deployed in applications beyond their original purpose. Thus, clear consideration needs to be given now to the fundamental moral, ethical, social, psychological and legal ramifications of such enhancement technologies. From a legal perspective, the implantation of ICT devices may challenge the right of bodily integrity for every human being, as a further expression of the right to self-determination. Moreover the use of human ICT implants allows the development of vast numbers of applications that will enable the tracking, tracing and profiling of the individual, as the unique number of the implant and/ or the information stored on it can be linked with great certainty to an identified or identifiable natural person. However, the processing of such information should follow the principles on the processing of personal data, as they are described in the European data protection directive.

The use of ICT implants, especially in the medical sector, has been most welcome as it has introduced devices such as cardiovascular pacemakers, cochlear implants, deep brain stimulators for Parkinson's disease, and insulin pumps. Notwithstanding the positive impact of such devices to the health condition of the patients, the restoration of human capabilities and especially the enhancement of existing ones are not free of ethical issues. The ethical debate reveals a number of counter arguments against the use of ICT implants on human beings.

Given the current situation, it is not too soon to start real debate. To this end, the European Group on Ethics in Science and New Technologies have published their opinion on the use of ICT implants and notes that implants, if not used properly, may prove to be a threat to human dignity, by at the very least not respecting an individual's autonomy and rights. Such dangers are already present with current medical ICT implant devices, whereby even simple security such as basic access control is not implemented.

4.5 Use Cases

In this chapter user cases of identity management systems relying on the technologies described are presented and analysed. This includes:

- ID documents and the electronic passports (referring especially to PKI, electronic signatures, biometrics and RFID)
- CardSpace (referring especially to credential systems, WS-Security and WS-Trust)

4.5.1 ID Documents[46]

As a use case for IMS in e-government ID documents were investigated. ID documents are mainly used to authenticate or identify citizens in the context of general governmental procedures or procedures in specific sectors such as health or social insurance. Another important functionality is facilitating electronic signing together with PKI. Apart from a general overview covering these functionalities, national ID cards, citizen cards and European implementations of the epassport were investigated in depth (Meints and Hansen, 2006). The selected implementations are especially of interest as a number of technologies are already implemented in this context, e.g., electronic signatures, PKI and biometrics. In addition these ID documents are increasingly understood as an important enabler for e-government. With the transition from paper based government to e-government electronic IDs (eIDs) are needed to authenticate or identify participants such as governmental officials or citizens. In this context (semi-) automated border controls procedures using Machine Readable Travel Documents (MRTDs) are also understood as authentication and authorisation procedures.

Traditionally the binding between an ID document and its (authorised) user was ensured by a seal, a hand written signature of a governmental official or a traditional photo of the user. In the electronic world this does not work anymore as these attributes can be verified electronically only with difficulty and spoofing becomes

[46] Author: Martin Meints, Unabhängiges Landeszentrum für Datenschutz Schleswig-Holstein.

easy. In the electronically enabled ID documents investigated in the FIDIS project mainly two ways were used to ensure the binding between an ID document and its user: (1) knowledge, typically a PIN, and (2) biometric reference data (typically biometric raw data such as standardised images of the face or finger tips).

A special focus was put on the Austrian and Belgium citizen card as they are both conceptualised as key-enablers for the national e-government strategies. Both concepts were investigated from a security and privacy point of view.

The Austrian citizen card is no traditional smart card based solution, but can be implemented in various formats, e.g., USB sticks and on mobile phones. The Austrian citizen card concept is remarkable due to the authentication mechanism used (see Meints and Hansen, 2006: 90-94). Based on a decree, the so called 'Bereichsabgrenzungsverordnung', governmental sectors are defined. The citizen card provides specific identifiers for each citizen in each of these defined sectors. The authentication of citizen is carried out based on SAML certificates and requires a specific local software component. In addition the Austrian citizen card can be equipped with an electronic signature. Linkability between sector-specific identifiers (called sector-specific PINs) is possible only in exceptional cases and needs to be carried out by the data protection authority acting as a trusted third party. In the context of the public sector this is the strongest mechanism to enforce purpose binding and to hamper function creep implemented today. In December 2005 the first prize for data protection in the category of European public authorities was awarded to Austria for the concept of the 'Bürgerkarte' by the Data Protection Agency of the Community of Madrid.[47]

The Belgian citizen card is based on a traditional smart card. The authentication of the user is based on X.509v3 certificates and is ensured and secured via PKI run by order of the Belgian state and a PIN (Meints and Hansen, 2006: 90-99). The citizen card itself has in the first version no privacy-enhancing functionality (De Cock et al. 2006). Recently as a transparency enhancing measure the online access of citizens to their own files at the National Register was introduced. [48] In this file also the access of citizens' data by Belgian public authorities is stored together with the purpose of the access.

Intensive research was carried out in the context of the electronic passport (epass). With the integration of an RFID chip and biometric reference data the epass became part of a largely distributed border control infrastructure. Vulnerabilities, threats and resulting security and privacy risks for the citizen were analysed and recommendations for future versions made. The technical concept of the first version of the epass, issued since November 2005, showed severe weaknesses, and for some of these exploits were already demonstrated (Meints and Hansen, 2006; Kosta et al., 2007; Meints and Hansen, 2008). Examples are:

---

47 http://www.austria.gv.at/DesktopDefault.aspx?TabID=4951&Alias=bka&infodate=19.12.2005 and http://www.ptapde.gr/news/PR_e-PRODAT_20051215.pdf.

48 Access is possible via https://www.mijndossier.rrn.fgov.be/, but requires a client certificate which is provided from the citizen card.

- Cryptographic weaknesses in the central access control mechanism called Basic Access Control (BAC); in addition in many cases BAC is not effective as together with the epass the BAC key has to be handed over to private organisations, especially hotels; in Sweden data needed to calculate the BAC key was publicly accessible for all Swedish citizens.[49]
- The reading range of the passport could be extended from the planned 10 to 15 cm up to 50 cm; communication between reader and epass can be eavesdropped from a distance up to 10 m.
- The issuing process for the epass was not mature, official passports with photos not belonging to the epassport holder could be retrieved in 14 European member countries[50].
- No security concept compliant with international standards such as ISO/IEC 27001 or CobiT is available covering all countries, epass and reader infrastructure and organisational aspects.
- The data minimisation principle is not implemented because biometric raw data (photos of fingerprints and faces) is used instead of templates; biometric raw data contain additional information that might be used for different purposes apart from border control (Kindt and Müller, 2008: 83-84). In addition the finality principle (purpose binding to prevent function creep) is not ensured internationally.

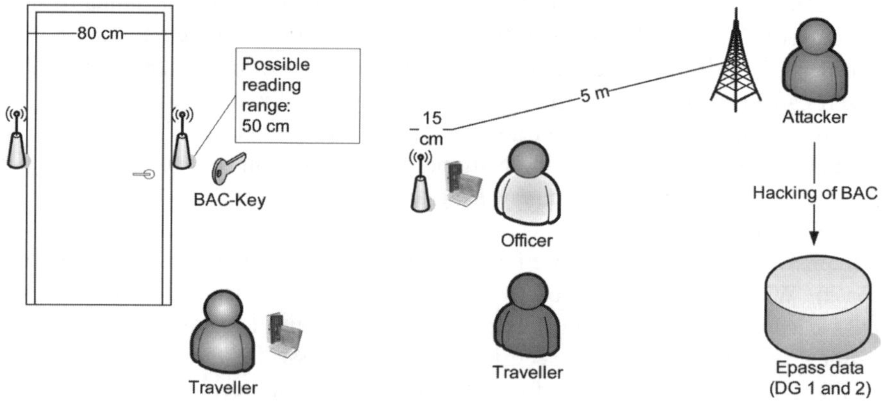

Fig. 4.8. Attack scenarios for the epass: tracking / deployment of events and eavesdropping

---

49 This was officially confirmed by the responsible issuing authority for epassports in the county of Värmland on 2nd of February 2007.

50 See the BBC report: 'My faked passport and me', http://news.bbc.co.uk/2/hi/programmes/panorama/6158927.stm.

In the literature the use of these risks in the context of the following scenarios were discussed: (1) tracking and deployment of person-specific events and (2) eavesdropping and (ab-) use of epass data, especially the content of the so called Data Groups 1 and 2 (DG 1 and 2). The scenarios can be demonstrated as shown in Figure 4.7.

Using the Attack-Tree-Analysis-Methodology developed by Schneier (1999) the applicability of these scenarios by states, private organisations and criminal organisations was qualitatively analysed based on the first version of the epass (Meints and Hansen, 2008). This is still highly relevant, as epasses of the first version remain valid for five to ten years. The following tables summarise and visualise the results of the analysis, whereby the colours illustrate qualitatively the risk for the data subject (dark grey = low, light gray = medium, no background = high):

Table 4.3. Qualitative analysis of the tracking scenario

Tracking	States	Private Organisations	Criminal Organisations
Costs	High, but at insular places only	Very high; area covering infrastructure needed	Very high; area covering infrastructure needed
Benefit	Low apart from exceptional cases where traditional instruments of surveillance cannot be used	Limited, as cheaper, more target oriented and legal methods are available, e.g., in the context of customer loyalty programs	Limited, as cheaper and more target oriented methods are available, e.g., in the context of established surveillance techniques
Risks for the attacker	Low / none	High compliance risks (e.g., Data Protection in the EU), damage of reputation	Moderate / managed

Since November 2007 in most European countries the issuing of the second version of the epass started. This version was in most European countries improved by: (1) with respect to the entropy of BAC key; (2) information needed to prepare fall-back procedures in case biometrics for technical reasons (Failure To Enrol (FTE) or False Rejection Rate (FRR)) do not work; (3) maturity of the issuing process, as fingerprints are collected directly at the holder of the epass; and (4) additional security features in the chip to prevent cloning. These improvements make the eavesdropping scenario even more unlikely. But data protection risks grew, as with the photos of the finger prints additional biometric raw data are stored on the epass.

For immediate implementation FIDIS researchers recommend (Meints and Hansen, 2006; Kosta et al., 2007; Meints and Hansen, 2008):

Table 4.4. Qualitative analysis of the deployment-of-events scenario

Deployment of events	**States**	**Private Organisations**	**Criminal Organisations**
Costs	High, but at insular places only	High; but at insular places only	High; but at insular places only
Benefit	Low apart from exceptional cases where international laws are ignored and traditional instruments cannot be used	Limited, as cheaper, more target oriented and legal methods are available, e.g., in the context of customer loyalty programs	Effective for person-selective threatening, blackmailing and assassination
Risks for the attacker	Low / none	High compliance risks (e.g., Data Protection in the EU), damage of reputation	Manageable. The event can be prepared far in advance, criminals do not need to be in place. Violation of legislation seem 'acceptable and managed'

Table 4.5. Qualitative analysis of the eavesdropping scenario

Eavesdropping and (ab-)use	**States**	**Private Organisations**	**Criminal Organisations**
Costs	Very high; area covering infrastructure needed	High; at insular places or as area covering infrastructure	High; at insular places or as area covering infrastructure
Benefit	Very low as more easy and already legal alternatives are in place	Limited, biometric raw data, especially the highly standardised photo of the face, may be of interest; in many cases more simple and legal alternate solutions are available	Very low by using epass data for identity theft
Risks for the attacker	Low / none	High compliance risks (e.g., Data Protection in the EU), damage of reputation	Moderate / managed

- The epass should be protected using a Faraday cage
- Technical and organisational measures to hamper eavesdropping such as shielding of readers should be implemented
- The epass should be carried around only when needed
- With the second version of the epass the electronic time stamp should be updated before leaving the home country
- Passport holders need to be informed about organisational security measures concerning themselves
- The epass concept should not be transferred to national eIDs without modifications especially concerning the improvement of access control mechanisms

In the long run the following recommendations should be taken into consideration:

- The technical and security concept should be revised taking data and privacy protection aspects into consideration; in this context it should be checked especially whether protected templates or encapsulated biometrics could be used
- As the epass is deployed for international use, the security concept needs to take the control over the passport by many states and private organisations into consideration
- It should be considered whether a wireless technique is really needed; in any case the wireless data transfer needs to be secured more effectively
- As the epass is a component of a large information system, life cycle management is needed. In this context it should be checked carefully how long biometric reference data can be used without raising false rejection too much e.g., caused by aging of the epass holder.

4.5.2 CardSpace[51]

The software product CardSpace (Alrodhan and Mitchell, 2007) is an example for advanced identity management based on WS-Trust, WS-Security, WS-Security-Policy and some related protocols. CardSpace is the identity selector provided by Microsoft, which is shipped with Windows Vista and the .NET Framework 3.0 and later. It provides four major features:

- support for any digital identity system
- consistent user control of digital identity

[51] Authors: Stefan Brands, Microsoft; Laurent Bussard, EMIC; Joris Claessens, EMIC; Christian Geuer-Pollmann, EMIC; Ulrich Pinsdorf, EMIC.

- replacement of password-based Web login
- improved user confidence in the identity of remote applications.

Those principles follow the seven laws of identity (Cameron, 2005). CardSpace is built on top of the Web Services Protocol Stack. It uses WS-Security, WS-Trust, WS-MetadataExchange and WS-SecurityPolicy. This means that it can be integrated with other WS-* applications (Maler and Reed, 2008). In CardSpace a so called Information Card contains all claims which are associated with an identity of a user. If a web site shall accept Information Cards for authentication, the developer needs to add an <object> tag to the HTML code of the Web site. This tag declares what claims the Web site needs for authentication. The developer has then to decrypt and evaluate the token that CardSpace sends to the Web site. In an application based on Web services, CardSpace talks directly to the services using the aforementioned protocols to learn the service's policy requirements and to deliver the appropriate security token.

We typically rely on a number of different digital identity systems, each of which may use a different underlying technology. To think about this diversity in a general way, it is useful to define three distinct roles:

1. User is the entity that is associated with a digital identity.
2. Identity provider is an entity that provides a digital identity for a user.
3. Relying party is an application that in some way relies on a digital identity to authenticate a user, and then makes an authorisation decision.

Given these three roles, it is not difficult to understand how CardSpace can support any digital identity. A user might rely on an application that supports CardSpace, such as a Web browser, to access any of several relying parties. The user might also be able to choose from a group of identity providers as the source of the digital identity it presents to those relying parties. Whatever choice the user makes, the basic exchange among these parties comprises three steps:

First, the application gets the security token requirements of the relying party that the user wishes to access. This information is contained in the relying party's policy, and it includes things such as what security token formats the relying party will accept, and exactly what claims those tokens must contain. Once it received the details of the security token this relying party requires, the application passes this information to CardSpace, asking it to request a token from an appropriate identity provider. After this security token has been received, CardSpace gives it to the application, which passes it on to the relying party. The relying party can then use this token to authenticate the user or for some other purpose. Working with CardSpace does not require relying parties or identity providers to implement any proprietary protocols.

CardSpace implements an intuitive user interface for working with digital identities (see also Pettersson and Meints (2008) for usability aspects of selected functions of CardSpace). Each digital identity is displayed as an Information Card. Each card represents a digital identity that the user can potentially present to a relying party. Along with the visual representation, each card also contains information about a particular digital identity. This information includes which identity provider to contact to acquire a security token for this identity, what kind of tokens this identity provider can issue, and exactly what claims these tokens can contain. By selecting a particular card, the user is actually choosing to request a specific security token with a specific (sub-)set of claims created by a specific identity provider. In fact, the user does not need to disclose the full information that is associated with an Information Card, but can verify what will be revealed to the relying party.

4.6 Summary and Conclusions

It is clear that it is essential to understand the impact which High-tech IDs can and may have on those that use them. The technologies analysed in this chapter provide tools (a) to form and shape partial identities under the control of the identity bearer or (b) to describe and model them under the control of external parties which are in many cases organisations. Both functions are of high importance in the Information Society which is characterised through intensive use of information in society and economy, facilitated by highly automated and digitised means of communication. In this way the technologies described already and will further fuel the information society in the near future. Also important in this context are economic aspects – the technologies analysed provide the platform for new products and services and thus economic welfare. But how are the functions described put to use?

The first function allows a user to present itself and to make claims in a new communicational context based on information that supports the level of trust needed. Important in this context is that the user gets some means to control the balancing between opacity and transparency regarding the disclosure of identity related information or attributes. The second function provides mechanisms needed to verify trust related information provided by the user through user independent sources of information and to verify claims made. In this context the access to more and more user independent sources for identity related information plays an important role. Both functions are not new as such; the difference with the described technologies is that they are (a) from a knowledge point of view demanding and (b) depending on the way they are used may change the balance between opacity and transparency between parties involved in communication. In this context organisations typically have more financial and personal resources for setting up more sophisticated IMS, potentially resulting in information, and thus power, asymmetry. Extreme application scenarios range from opaque and not trustworthy clients dealing somehow with organisations on one hand and completely transparent clients dealing with overly powerful and opaque organisations on the other hand. The technologies analysed clearly support both extreme scenarios. An overly opaque client for example could be generated by the use of credential systems not relying on a trusted third party, and surveillance like application scenarios of DRM, biometrics and RFID or abuse of data collected in AmI environments clearly could enable overly powerful organisations.

In many cases a shift in this balance of transparency and opacity does not happen on purpose. Weaknesses in the technological design and security holes are common reasons providing the platform for a potential shift in the balance of power as control by operators and users gets lost. Real life abuse scenarios today in many cases seem to be criminally motivated (see Chapter 8).

Society cannot function with both of the described extreme communication models and thus will balance them mainly by developing moral, social and legal norms. FIDIS research results support this balancing process by recommendations for stakeholders in research, industry and policy making and the general public concerning:

- Application scenarios concerning available and emerging technologies with respect to compliance with the existing legal framework
- Organisational advice for citizens and clients of organisations on how to use established identity management systems or components thereof (e.g., the epassport)
- Further research topics e.g., in technology design to support balanced technical implementations with a reliable control situation
- Further development of legal frameworks to ban unwanted application scenarios and to provide the ground for improved and balanced technical solutions

It should be noted that most emerging technologies, such as AmI and ICT implants, are different as technological concepts and are not well developed and described. As such, their impact on humans and society cannot be assessed based on hard facts. In this context existing visions and partial technological concepts can be consolidated in scenarios which can be used for formal or non-formal analytical methods such as a Technology Impact Assessment (TIA) or Strength, Weakness, Opportunity and Threat (SWOT) analysis. Especially in case of ICT implants, the potential impact by far exceeds aspects of the management of identities – potentially the personality of the persons concerned may be affected or altered. On the other hand for policy makers there is no immediate need to act, other than on the issues surrounding their research and development, as these technologies are relatively far from being implemented and importantly, there is still time for a socio-ethical debate.

To summarise the FIDIS recommendations, the adoption of the legal framework to the advancement of new technologies should be accompanied by addressing the ethical and social issues that the development of new devices may bring. It is not only privacy and data protection that are at stake and the discussion on security issues forms only a (temporary) part of the wider debate on how to live in tomorrow's information society. Respect for human dignity and equality and the freedom of thought, conscience and religion as well as the freedom to express, move, associate and assemble are only some of the rights and freedoms that are essentially at stake, where such activities suppose the increasing intervention of ICT and converging technologies provided and controlled by third parties.

References

Adler, A. (2003), 'Can images be regenerated from biometric templates?', Biometrics Conference, Washington.

Alkassar, A. and Husseiki, R. (eds.) (2008), *FIDIS Deliverable D3.9: Study on the Impact of Trusted Computing on Identity and Identity Management,* Download: http://www.fidis.net/fileadmin/fidis/deliverables/fidis-wp3-del3.9_Study_on_the_Impact_of_Trusted_Computing_on_Identity_and_Identity_Management.pdf.

Alrodhan, W. A. and Mitchell, C. J. (2007), 'Addressing privacy issues in CardSpace', Third International Symposium on Information Assurance and Security (IAS 2007), IEEE Computer Society, pp. 285-291.

Article 29 Data Protection Working Party (Art29DPWP) (2003), *Working Document on Biometrics,* WP 80, Brussels. http://ec.europa.eu/justice_home/fsj/privacy/docs/wpdocs/2003/wp80_en.pdf.

Article 29 Data Protection Working Party (Art29DPWP) (2004), *Opinion on More Harmonised Information Provisions,* WP 100, Brussels. http://ec.europa.eu/justice_home/fsj/privacy/docs/wpdocs/2004/wp100_en.pdf.

Article 29 Data Protection Working Party (Art29DPWP) (2005), Working document on data protection issues related to RFID technology, WP 105, Brussels. http://www.eu.int/comm/justice_home/fsj/privacy/docs/wpdocs/2005/wp105_en.pdf.

Ballinger, K., Bissett, B., Box, D., Curbera, F., Ferguson, D., Graham, S., Liu, C. K., Leymann, F., Lovering, B., McCollum, R., Nadalin, A., Orchard, D., Parastatidis, S., von Riegen, C., Schlimmer, J., Shewchuk, J., Smith, B., Truty, G., Vedamuthu, A., Weerawarana, S., Wilson, K., Yendluri, P. (2006), Web Services Metadata Exchange (WS-MetadataExchange), BEA Systems Inc., Computer Associates International, Inc., International Business Machines Corporation, Microsoft Corporation, Inc., SAP AG, Sun Microsystems, and webMethods. Specification Version 1.1.

Baran, P. (1964), 'On Distributed Communications: IX. Security, Secrecy, and Tamper-Free Considerations,' Memorandum RM-3765-PR, The Rand Corporation, 1700 Main St, Santa Monica, California, 90406. Reprinted in Hoffman L. J. (ed.): Security and Privacy in Computer Systems; Melville Publishing Company, Los Angeles, California, 1973, pp. 99-123. http://www.rand.org/pubs/research_memoranda/RM3765/.

Bauer, M., Meints, M., Hansen, M. (eds.) (2005), *FIDIS Deliverable D3.1 Structured Overview on Prototypes and Concepts of Identity Management Systems,* Download: http://www.fidis.net/fileadmin/fidis/deliverables/fidis-wp3-del3.1.overview_on_IMS.final.pdf.

Becker, M. Y., Gordon, A. D., Fournet, C. (2006), SecPAL: Design and Semantics of a Decentralized Authorization Language, Technical Report MSR-TR-2006-120, Microsoft Research, Redmond.

Bizer, J. and Spiekermann, S. (2006), TAUCIS – Technikfolgenabschätzung Ubiquitäres Computing und Informationelle Selbstbestimmung, study commissioned by the German Federal Ministry of Education and Research, Berlin. https://www.datenschutzzentrum.de/taucis/ita_taucis.pdf

Buitelaar, J.C., Meints, M., van Alsenoy, B. (eds.) (2008), *FIDIS Deliverable D16.1: Conceptual Framework for Identity Management in eGovernment,* Download: http://www.fidis.net/fileadmin/fidis/deliverables/fidis-wp16-del16.1-conceptual_framework_for_identity_management_in_egovernment.pdf.

Cabrera, L. F. and Kurt, C. (2005), Web Services Architecture and Its Specifications: Essentials for Understanding WS-*, Microsoft Press, Redmond.

Cameron, K. (2005), The Laws of Identity, published as weblog. http://www.identityblog.com/stories/2005/05/13/TheLawsOfIdentity.pdf.

Cavoukian, A. and Stoianov, A. (2007), Biometric Encryption, Ontario, Canada. http://www.ipc.on.ca/images/Resources/up-1bio_encryp.pdf.

Coulouris, G., Dollimore, J., Kindberg, T. (2005), Distributed Systems. Concepts and Design, Addison Wesley.

De Cock, D., Wolf, C., Preneel, B. (2006), 'The Belgian Electronic Identity Card (Overview)', in *Sicherheit 2005: Sicherheit—Schutz und Zuverlässigkeit, Beiträge der 3. Jahrestagung des Fachbereiches Sicherheit der Gesellschaft für Informatik e.V. (GI),* Lecture Notes in Informatics (LNI), Bonner Köllen Verlag, Bonn, pp. 298-301. http://www. cosic.esat.kuleuven.be/publications/article-769.pdf.

Fischer-Hübner, S. and Hedbom, H. (eds.) (2008), *FIDIS Deliverable D12.3: A Holistic Privacy Framework for RFID Applications,* Download: http://www.fidis.net/fileadmin/fidis/deliverables/fidis-wp12-del12.3.A_Holistic_Privacy_Framework_for_RFID_Applications_v2.pdf.

Gasson, M. and Warwick, K. (eds.) (2007), *FIDIS Deliverable D12.2: Study on Emerging AmI Technologies,* Download: http://www.fidis.net/fileadmin/fidis/deliverables/fidis-wp12-d12.2_Study_on_Emerging_AmI_Technologies.pdf.

Gasson, M., Meints, M., Warwick, K. (eds.) (2005), *FIDIS Deliverable D3.2 A Study on PKI and Biometrics,* Download: http://www.fidis.net/fileadmin/fidis/deliverables/fidis-wp3-del3.2.study_on_PKI_and_biometrics.pdf.

Geradts, Z. and Sommer, P. (eds.) (2006), FIDIS Deliverable D6.1: Forensic Implications of Identity Management Systems, Download: http://www.fidis.net/fileadmin/fidis/deliverables/fidis-wp6-del6.1.forensic_implications_of_identity_management_systems.pdf.

Grimm, R., Puchta, S., Müller, M., Bizer, J., Möller, J., Will, A., Müller, A., Jazdejewski, S., (2005), *Privacy4DRM,* Study commissioned by the German Federal Ministry of Education and Research, Berlin. https://www.datenschutzzentrum.de/drm/privacy4drm.pdf.

Goodner, M., Hondo, M., Nadalin, A., McIntosh, M. Schmidt, D. (2007), Understanding WS-Federation, Technical Report, IBM and Microsoft Corporation.

Geuer-Pollmann, C. and Claessens, J. (2005), 'Web services and web service security standards', Information Security Technical Report, Vol. 10, pp. 15-24.

Hansen, M. and Alkassar, A. (eds.) (2008), *FIDIS Deliverable D3.8 Study on protocols with respect to identity and identification – an insight on network protocols and privacy-aware communication,* Download: http://www.fidis.net/fileadmin/fidis/deliverables/fidis-wp3-del3.8_Study_on_protocols_with_respect_to_identity_and_identification.pdf.

Hansen, M., Krasemann, H., Krause, C., Rost, M., Genghini, R. (2003), *Identity Management Systems (IMS): Identification and Comparison Study,* Kiel. https://www.datenschutzzentrum.de/idmanage/study/ICPP_SNG_IMS-Study.pdf.

Hansen, M. and Möller, J. (2005), 'Digital Rights Management zwischen Sicherheit und informationeller Selbstbestimmung', in: Bundesamt für Sicherheit in der Informationstechnik (BSI, ed.): IT-Sicherheit geht alle an!, proc. of the 9. German IT-Security congress of the BSI, pp. 159-171. http://www.datenschutzzentrum.de/vortraege/050510_hansen-moeller_bsi.htm

Heinz, B., Krißler, J., Rütten, C. (2007), 'Fingerspitzengefühl', *c't Magazin für Computertechnik* 12, pp. 98-101.

Hildebrandt, M. and Gutwirth, S. (eds.) (2008), Profiling the European Citizen. Springer.

Hildebrandt, M. and Koop, B. (eds.) (2007), *FIDIS Deliverable D7.9: A Vision of Ambient Law,* Download: http://www.fidis.net/fileadmin/fidis/deliverables/fidis-wp7-d7.9_A_Vision_of_Ambient_Law.pdf.

Hildebrandt, M. and Meints, M. (eds.) (2006), *FIDIS Deliverable D7.7: RFID, Profiling, and AmI,* Download: http://www.fidis.net/fileadmin/fidis/deliverables/fidis-wp7-del7.7.RFID_Profiling_AMI.pdf.

Hill, C. J. (2001), Risk of Masquerade Arising from the Storage of Biometrics, Department of Computer Science, Australian National University, Canberra / Australia.

Humphrey, M., Park, S., Feng, J., Beekwilder, N., Wasson, G., Hogg, J., LaMacchia, B., Dillaway, B. (2007), 'Fine-grained access control for GridFTP using SecPAL', 8th IEEE/ACM International Conference on Grid Computing, IEEE Computer Society, pp. 217-225.

Iliev, A. and Smith, S. W. (2005), 'Protecting Client Privacy with Trusted Computing at the Server', IEEE Security and Privacy 3 (2), pp. 20-28.

Jacobs, I. (2002), Architectural Principles of the World Wide Web, W3C Working Draft, 30 August 2002 (outdated). http://www.w3.org/TR/2002/WD-webarch-20020830/.

Jain, A. K., Nandakumar, K., Nagar, A. (2008), 'Biometric Template Security', to appear in EURASIP Journal on Advances in Signal Processing. http://biometrics.cse.msu.edu/Publications/SecureBiometrics/JainNandakumarNagar_TemplateSecuritySurvey_EURASIP08.pdf.

Kerckhoffs, A. (1883), 'La cryptographie militaire', Journal des sciences militaires IX, pp. 5-38 and pp. 161-191.

Kindt, E. (2007), 'Biometric applications and the data protection legislation,' Datenschutz und Datensicherheit 31 (3), pp. 166-170.

Kindt, E. and Müller, L. (eds.) (2007), FIDIS Deliverable D3.10: Biometrics in identity management, Download: http://www.fidis.net/fileadmin/fidis/deliverables/fidis-wp3-del3.10.biometrics_in_identity_management.pdf.

Kosta, E.and Gasson, M. (eds.) (2008), *FIDIS Deliverable D12.6: A Study on ICT Implants,* Download: http://www.fidis.net/fileadmin/fidis/deliverables/fidis-wp12-del12.6.A_Study_on_ICT_Implants.pdf.

Kosta, E., Gasson, M., Hansen, M., Meints, M. (2007), 'An analysis of security and privacy issues relating to RFID enabled ePassports', in *New Approaches for Security, Privacy and Trust in Complex Environments, proc. of the IFIP SEC2007,* Springer, New York pp. 467-472.

Kumaraguru, P., Cranor, L., Lobo, J., Calo, S. (2007), 'A Survey of Privacy Policy Languages', SOUPS 2007, Pittsburgh, PA, USA. http://cups.cs.cmu.edu/soups/2007/workshop/Privacy_Policy_Languages.pdf.

Lawrence, K., Kaler, C., Nadalin, A., Goodner, M., Gudgin, M., Barbir, A., Granqvist, H. (2008), WS-SecurityPolicy 1.3, OASIS Editor Draft 1.

Lawrence, K., Kaler, C., Nadalin, A., Kaler, C., Monzillo, R., Hallam-Baker, P. (2006), Web Services Security: SOAP Message Security 1.1 (WS-Security 2004), OASIS Specification.

Lessig, L. (1999), Code and other laws of cyberspace, Basic Books, New York.

Maler, E. and Reed, D. (2008), 'The Venn of Identity: Options and Issues in Federated Identity Management', IEEE Security & Privacy 6, pp. 16-23.

McGee, E. M., Maguire, G. Q. (2007), 'Becoming borg to become immortal: regulating brain implant technologies,' Camb Q Healthc Ethics 16 (3), pp. 291-302.

Meints, M. and Hansen, M. (eds.) (2006), FIDIS Deliverable D3.6: Study on ID Documents, Download: http://www.fidis.net/fileadmin/fidis/deliverables/fidis-wp3-del3.6.study_on_id_documents.pdf.

Meints, M. and Hansen, M. (2008), 'Der ePass—eine Sicherheits- und Datenschutzanalyse', in: *Proceedings of the Sicherheit 2008, 2-4 of April 2008 in Saarbrücken*, Gesellschaft für Informatik, Bonn, pp. 31-43.

Müller, G. and Wohlgemuth, S. (eds.) (2007), FIDIS Deliverable D14.2: Study on Privacy in Business Processes by Identity Management, Download: http://www.fidis.net/fileadmin/fidis/deliverables/fidis-wp14-del14.2-study_on_privacy_in_business_processes_by_identity_management.pdf.

Müller, G and Wohlgemuth, S. (eds.) (2008), FIDIS Deliverable D14.3: Study on the Suitability of Trusted Computing to support Privacy in Business Processes, Download: http://www.fidis.net/fileadmin/fidis/deliverables/fidis-wp14-del14.3_Study_on_the_Suitability_of_Trusted_Computing_to_support_Privacy_in_Business_Processes.pdf.

Nadalin, A., Goodner, M., Gudgin, M., Barbir, A., Granqvist, H. (2008), OASIS WS-Trust 1.4, OASIS.

Pettersson, J. S. and Meints, M. (eds.) (2009), *FIDIS Deliverable D3.12: Study on Usability of Identity Management Systems*, to appear March 2009.

Pfitzmann, A. and Hansen, M., *Anonymity, Unlinkability, Undetectability, Unobservability, Pseudonymity, and Identity Management,* TU Dresden, Dresden, February 2008. http://dud.inf.tu-dresden.de/literatur/Anon_Terminology_v0.31.pdf.

Pfitzmann, A. (2008), *Security in IT Networks: Multilateral Security in Distributed and by Distributed Systems,* TU Dresden, Dresden. http://dud.inf.tu-dresden.de/%7Epfitza/SecCryptI_II.pdf

Rannenberg, K., Pfitzmann, A., Müller, G. (1999), 'IT Security and Multilateral Security', in: Müller, G. and Rannenberg, K. (eds.): *Multilateral Security in Communications, vol. 3: Technology, Infrastructure, Economy*, Addison-Wesley, München, pp. 21-29.

Schneier, B. (1999), 'Attack Trees', *Dr. Dobbs Journal.* http://www.schneier.com/paper-attacktrees-ddj-ft.html#rf7.

Schreurs, W., Hildebrandt, M., Gasson, M., Warwick, K. (eds.) (2005), *FIDIS Deliverable D7.3: Report on Actual and Possible Profiling Techniques in the Field of Ambient Intelligence,* Download: http://www.fidis.net/fileadmin/fidis/deliverables/fidis-wp7-del7.3.ami_profiling.pdf.

Tanenbaum, A. S. (2003), Computer Networks, forth edition, Prentice Hall, Upper Saddle River, NJ.

Zhou, X., Kevenaar, T., Kelkboom, E., Busch, C., van der Veen, M., Nouak, A., (2007), 'Privacy Enhancing Technology for a 3D-Face Recognition System', BIOSIG 2007: Biometrics and Electronic Signatures, pp. 3-14. http://www.3dface.org/files/papers/zhou-CAST2007-TemplateProtection.pdf

Vignette 4: Powering the Profile: Plugging into the Mobile Grid*

After an extremely busy period at work, Frank is now ready for his summer vacation. As his wife has one more week off than him, they have arranged to meet in Rhodes, so he will be travelling on his own. After packing his bags he activates his tourist profile on his personal MyComm device and enriches it with special preferences for this trip (things he might be interested in buying, his holiday companions, etc.). Then, he sets off to Heathrow airport's terminal 5. The moment he arrives, the 'myFlight' service running on his MyComm contacts the airport database for departure information. After the credentials for this interaction are checked, it sends him an SMS indicating the check-in counter he should go to as well as the gate his flight will be departing from. At the counter a camera captures his face image (both frontal and side view) and performs facial recognition. After being positively identified, he checks-in and he goes for a coffee at one of the many airport cafés. Meanwhile, without his knowledge the facial image captured is also compared against a set of facial images of wanted people of high importance stored in a database in Italy. As Frank's third match of the combined gridified facial recognition algorithms was 'Mario Martucci' – one of the most wanted people in Italy – with a match probability above the predefined threshold the 'GentleWatchAbout' service gets triggered and accesses Frank's photo and id-related data (cell phone number, passport number). For security reasons the 'GentleWatchAbout' service has the credentials to use a variety of services. The 'myFlight' service periodically contacts the airport database for further departure information and after a while Frank receives a notification on his mobile phone indicating that there will be a one-hour delay of his flight and so he decides to activate the 'myPlaces' application. This contacts the 'AirportPlaces' service to get information about points of interest within the airport and after processing the provided list and comparing it with Frank's preferences stored in the 'Travellers Profile' database in Greece, it suggests for him to go to the 'A little Shirty' store which has good offers on shirts, which are his favourite clothes to buy. Frank decides to do so. He spends most of his time there and 10 minutes before his gate opens he receives a scheduled notification SMS from the 'myFlight' service which indicates that he should proceed to his gate. As Frank gets really

* This scenario is based on FIDIS deliverable D12.5, Chapter 7, by Vassiliki Andronikou (NTUA).

bored during flights, he is happy to find out that the plane offers a service that, after you choose a song from the list it provides, it composes a playlist matching the original song selected.

As Frank arrives in Athens, he has to change flights to get to Rhodes, but his flight is in 5 hours time. The 'myPlaces' service contacts the 'AthensPlaces' service and the 'AthensTransportation' service and it processes the retrieved records based on his time remaining. The service sends him an SMS informing him that based on the time available he can go downtown for a walk, providing him with photos of places he could visit. Frank chooses to go downtown and asks the 'myPlaces' service for more information. His request is also automatically sent to the 'GentleWatchAbout' service. The service contacts the 'AthensPlaces' service to retrieve more information for downtown places, taking into account Frank's love for art and presents him with a list of options, such as the Parthenon, the National Museum, the National Gallery, as well as famous local cafés and restaurants. Frank chooses to visit the Parthenon. The service then contacts the 'AthensTransportation' service to obtain information about the means of transportation that could get him there. The latter makes near instant calculations within the Grid based on his current location as well as the available means of transportation and current traffic. The service informs him that he could take metro Line 3 from the airport, get off at Monastiraki station and then enjoy a nice walk indicated on a map provided. This has clearly taken into account that Frank enjoys walking and the weather in Athens is sunny. Alternatively, he can avoid walking too much and just take the metro Line 3 to Syntagma and then change to metro Line 2 to Acropolis station or he can hire a taxi that will take about 35 minutes to get there. The service also gives him information about the entrance fee for the Parthenon. Frank chooses to take the second option that, according to the service, will take him about 40 minutes to get there.

As soon as Frank arrives at Acropolis station, 'myPlaces' requests information about the surrounding monuments from the 'AthensPlaces' service which in turn contacts the 'AthensMonuments' service and instantly sends him historical information about the Acropolis and the surrounding monuments. Meanwhile, the 'myPlaces' service – whenever Frank moves to another place – requests processing of the retrieved list of places based on his currently activated profile. In the meantime, 'myPlaces' sends Frank's current position and preferences to the 'GentleWatchAbout' service. Policemen in the area get a notification from 'GentleWatchAbout' that a potential suspect for international thefts with low surveillance priority is at the specific location and are supplied with his photo. Frank enjoys his visit, but after a couple of hours he gets a scheduled notification on his mobile phone by the 'myFlight' service that his flight will depart in 2 hours. Frank activates the 'myPlaces' service so that he can choose the means of transportation back to the airport. As he is really tired, he chooses to take a taxi and so the 'myPlaces' service contacts the 'AthensTransportation' service which in turn contacts the 'AthensTaxis' service and calls one for him. After a few seconds he receives an SMS that the taxi will be there in 20 minutes and suggests he goes to a café nearby. As Frank has activated his tourist profile, the service asks Frank if he has a preference about the route the taxi will take and after the service activates the previous workflow it prompts him with two choices: through the historic centre which will take him about one hour and should cost him about 40 euros and the highway which will take him 30 minutes and should cost him about 25 euros. Frank chooses the first one and then decides to wander around a little bit to enjoy the view before the taxi arrives. Before Frank started his trip to Greece he had enriched his tourist profile by adding among others 'pasteli' as one of his favourite foods. Thus, the 'myPlaces' service sends a profile-based processing request to the 'AthensPlaces' service and Frank receives a notification that a shop with many local delights is right on the corner where he can find pasteli. Frank is really excited about this and decides to pay a visit to the shop. When Frank gets to the check-out counter, he gives 20 euros for his 10 euro purchase and forgets to take his change. As he gets out of the store the owner starts running after him. A policeman just across the street that had received the 'GentleWatchOut' notification notices the incident and heads towards them but realises it is a false alarm as soon as the two men shake hands. After 20 minutes, the taxi arrives and Frank enjoys the route he selected for the taxi to follow, while on the screen of his mobile phone information about the monuments in the historical centre are displayed. When Frank arrives at the airport the 'myFlight' service, after communication with the GPS service, contacts the airport database and he receives a 'myFlight' notification about the gate he should be heading for within the next 15 minutes.

The flight takes off and he is on his way to Rhodes. As soon as the flight takes off his wife receives an SMS from the 'myFlight' service that Frank will arrive at Rhodes airport in 45 minutes. Fanny sets off to the airport to welcome Frank to Rhodes. However, the security check at the airport for Frank is quite thorough. He experiences a one hour delay to get his baggage due to extensive security checks at the airport which had received a notification from the 'GentleWatchAbout' service. After one and a half hours Frank manages to reach the car where Fanny is waiting for him. The days go by happily and the couple enjoy the sun and the sea. As they are sitting at the beach, Frank receives an SMS from the 'myFriends' service that Fotis – a good friend of theirs – is also in town. Frank asks for more information and after the 'myFriends' service contacts the GPS service about the specific user and after numerous calculations are carried out within the Grid, he finds out that Fotis in fact is at a bar near their beach so they decide to join him. Fotis is very happy to meet the couple and they all enjoy their drinks together. Night falls, and they find a nice bar to start their evening. As they are about to enter the bar, Frank receives an SMS by 'myFriends' service that Sofia – his ex-girlfriend the name of which he had left in his list of friends – is there as well. As he would not like the two girls to meet, Frank tells them that he just received a notification about a nice bar at the end of the street that he had seen the previous night and so they go there instead. As the 'myPlaces' service gets information from the GPS service that they are not going to the same bar with Sofia, it automatically sends an information update to the 'myFriends' service about Frank lowering the priority for Sofia in his friends list. The notification is sent to the service and after processing within the Grid, the update is performed.

Time passes by and after two relaxing weeks come to an end, the couple prepares to go back home, again ably assisted by the personalised location based services.

The visions and thoughts expressed in this vignette are inspired and based on various discussions, and results of the FIDIS Network of Excellence as well as the author's personal experience and expectations. Partially, underlying concepts and ideas of this vignette are described in Chapters 4, 5, 6, 9 and 10.

5 Mobility and Identity*

Denis Royer, André Deuker, and Kai Rannenberg

Summary. While identity management systems for the Internet are debated intensively, identity management in mobile applications has grown silently over the last 17 years. Technologies, such as the still-growing Global System for Mobile Communication (GSM) with its Subscriber Identity Module (SIM) identification infrastructure, are foundations for many new mobile identity management related applications and services. This includes location-based services (LBS), offering customised and convenient services to users (e.g., friend finder applications) and new revenue opportunities for service providers (e.g., location-based advertising).

However, even though the opportunities seem to be endless and technology manageable, challenges arise when looking at advanced aspects of mobility and identity such as privacy, regulation, the socio-cultural aspects, and the economic impacts. To this regard, the interdisciplinary nature of mobility and identity is imminent and needs to be explored further. By learning from the diverse field of challenges, new mobile communication systems can be created, allowing for more privacy-preserving service provision and a more transparent handling of mobile identities.

This chapter presents three scenarios for mobile identities in life, work, and emergency situations: Mobile Communities, Traffic Monitoring, and Emergency Response via LBS. Based on these scenarios is an analysis of the specific properties of Mobile Identities, leading to a description of the FIDIS perspective on mobility and identity. Then a deeper analysis of the technological aspects of mobile networks gives the basis for the following closer look from the legal perspective on issues such as data protection and from the sociologic and economic perspectives. An outlook on the future challenges of mobility and identity concludes the chapter.

---

* This chapter has been reviewed by Simone Fischer-Hübner (KU) and Martin Meints (ICPP). The authors thank the reviewers for their valuable comments and suggestions. This chapter is based on the work done in FIDIS Work Package 11 on Mobility and Identity. The respective deliverables can be found in the Annex of this book.

Over the last 20 years and to a large degree due to the mainstream usage of mobile communications (e.g., based on GSM networks), *Mobility and Identity* engaged in a special relation – precisely two special relations. On the one side, GSM technology, especially mobile devices, such as mobile phones and SIM cards, allowed the management of identity, which is now often termed mobile identity management. On the other side the properties of mobile communication networks and especially the administration of location and other context information with regard to mobile devices and the related users have added to the content of identity, which is reflected in the concept of 'Mobile Identities'. Both aspects are illustrated in the first sections of this chapter. The following sections present different disciplines' perspectives on Mobility and Identity. These disciplines are technology, the law, sociology, and economics, as they contributed most actively on this topic in FIDIS. The chapter is concluded by a collection of requirements on mobile identity management systems and an outlook with further challenges and questions.

5.1 GSM – How Mobile Communication Achieved Its Special Role in Identity Management

While IdMS for the Internet are debated intensively, identity management (IdM) in mobile applications based on cellular wireless communication has grown silently over the last 17 years (Rannenberg, 2004). Still – and to many surprisingly – the Global System for Mobile Communication (GSM)[1] is one of the largest IdMS, using the Subscriber Identity Module (SIM) infrastructure as a basis for many application oriented initiatives to manage identities. This SIM infrastructure was introduced with mobile communication networks, mainly GSM, and for 2008 the GSM association reported nearly 4 billion subscriber connections world-wide (including UMTS) with GSM being the fastest growing communications technology of all time. The number of countries with a GSM system is reported as more than 200 (GSM, 2009), exceeding the number of UN member states (192 in February 2009 (UN, 2009).

Even without special technology support, quite a few people use a variety of GSM mobile communication accounts (and the corresponding SIMs and telephone numbers) to manage different identities for e.g., private and business purposes. Moreover, the almost global dominance of the GSM standard for mobile communications and the high penetration rates that GSM systems reached in many markets have inspired quite a few initiatives to piggy-back on the GSM system and especially the SIM as platforms for IdM and related applications.

[1] GSM used to be the abbreviation for standardisation committee *Groupe Speciale Mobile* of the European Telecommunications Standards Institute (ETSI), but is nowadays being used as abbreviation for *Global System for Mobile Communication* describing networks and standards according to the specifications that go back to the *Groupe Speciale Mobile*.

- IdM can be integrated into the SIM-Hardware.
- IdM can use GSM subscriber information as issued with the SIM.
- IdM can use GSM subscriber information stored in the GSM network.

The first two approaches aim at supporting the IdM that already exists in applications by using the GSM infrastructure. The third approach expands the GSM ID and user management itself and allows e.g., new revenue models in mobile communications. All three approaches are described in Rannenberg (2004) and may be extended in Universal Mobile Telecommunications System (UMTS) networks.

It is interesting to analyse the reasons for the quietness of the growth of GSM subscriptions and mobile IDs. The main reason is obviously that the telecommunications business of the 1990s was mainly national, and within the respective countries it was spread among usually not more than 2 to 10 players. Both market characteristics do not encourage international media coverage or sensational story-writing as e.g. the approach of a multinational company (Microsoft) to establish an Internet-wide IdM called '[MS] Passport]'. Another reason is that the view of mobile telephones as computers and consequently as Internet terminals is spreading only very slowly, and SIMs were not seen as the main asset of mobile phone but more as a helper technology.

However, the mobile and the *classic* (fixed line) Internet are integrating ever faster now, and the mobile networks are becoming enhanced Internet networks. At least three factors are enabling this.

1. In the aim of offering seamless services regardless whether customers are at home or on the road, Telecoms and their mobile partners or subsidiaries are collaborating closer than ever.
2. Also different sets of attributes (partial identities) are needed in different situations – and they can be made available due to the relative strength of the SIM card as a security token.
3. In more and more cases the context of a person and their situation are important for mobile communications, e.g., for filtering incoming communication.

Most of the trends outlined here are not just a result of the development of mobile communication technology, but of the role that the services play in society and business life and of their economical, socio-cultural and governmental consequences. Furthermore, while the discussion on mobile communication was mainly driven by technology topics, such as GSM or UMTS, it is more and more oriented towards services today. To this regard, the advent of Location Based Services (LBS) adds a new level of complexity to the domain of mobility and identity, to be discussed in the next section.

5.2 Mobile Identities – Context Added

Based on the work of FIDIS in the field of mobility and identity, mobile identities are described as:

> *'[...] a partial identity, which is connected to the mobility of the subject itself, including location data. The mobile identity may be addressable by the mobile ID. (...) Furthermore the mobility of a subject may be observed by others including the deployment of tracking mechanisms with respect to biometric properties, e.g., by a comprehensive video surveillance.'* (Royer, 2006: 31).

The context awareness of mobile services can impact on a user's mobile identity, especially when using a LBS (Reichwald et al., 2002). The availability of information on users' location combined with information about the interests or combined with information about the area they are situated in lead to a better understanding of the present user context. Mobile services allow considering the following types of user contexts:

- *Local context* (user's current place / time)
- *Action specific context* (user's current place / time combined with geo data)
- *Time context* (user's current time combined with time relevant information)
- *Interests specific context* (local, action and time context combined with personal user preferences)

Assuming that the different types of available context information affect a user's identity, the mobile identity consists of the user's time, location and attributes that have been derived from combining location and time information with relevant information about the user's self (e.g., interest specific context) or about the location of the user (action specific context).

The following subsections will give some details how information generated through LBS can extend context and discuss the related questions on users' control first in general (Subsection 5.2.1) and then along a scenario in the area of emergency response (Subsection 5.2.2).

5.2.1 Context Extension via LBS and User Control

Figure 5.1 shows how LBS can extend Fanny's mobile identity through connecting her local context with additional geo information about the area she is situated in. In this example, Fanny is at a certain time (Saturday, 3 p.m.) at a certain place (soccer stadium).

The external geo context information is the fact, that a soccer match takes place in the stadium at this point in time. A possible assumption and extension of Fanny's

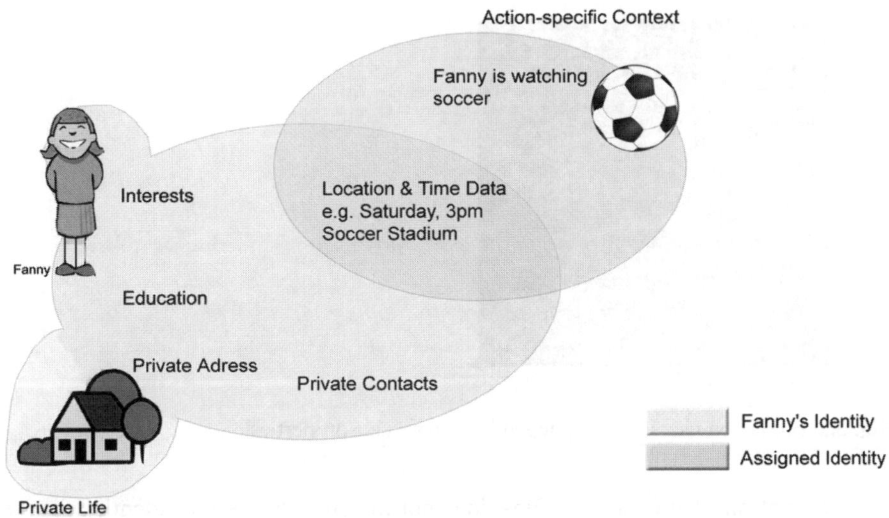

Fig. 5.1. Extension of the mobile identity through the action specific user context

mobile identity could be that Fanny is currently watching soccer. Any person or service that has this background information about Fanny's location can attribute this (subjective) action specific context to her identity creating a profile of Fanny.

To a certain degree, the (profiling) conclusions that can be drawn about Fanny's identity by using her action specific context are out of Fanny's control. Thus, the amount of control users have about their identity can depend on the type of the location based service.

The perceived control with regard to the mobile identity depends on two factors (cf. Figure 5.2):

1. The way the service is initiated (push vs. pull) and
2. The way the profile is created (direct vs. indirect)

A high level of control is possible if the data subjects / users are able to initialise the (location based) service by themselves (pull service). In this case they are aware that the service is enabled and can assess the types of data that will be processed in order to provide the service.

Another aspect that affects the users' control about their mobile identity is the way that their user profiles are derived. The user profile can be a critical piece of information as it is the baseline for the derivation of the interest specific context. Control of the user profile thereby influences the amount of users' control about their mobile identity. Direct profile creation means that the users themselves are able to deliver and change the data of their user profile (maybe supported by an identity management system). Indirect profile creation is done by a third party. The data subjects / users even may not be aware that such a profile is created. If

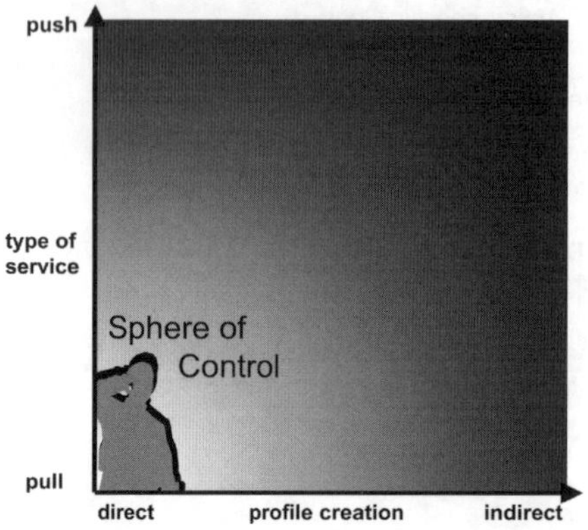

Fig. 5.2. Impact on users' control depending on service properties

the information of the user profiles does not match with the real identity profile, the wrong conclusions can be drawn and assigned to a user's identity.

In any case it is clear that LBS may have a major impact on the (mobile) identities of persons, by extending the users' context information.

5.2.2 Mobile Identities in Action – A Scenario on Emergency Response

Usage scenarios of mobility and identity, namely in the context of present and next generation mobile services, have been widely explored within various deliverables of the FIDIS network. Among them are scenarios covering topics such as emergency response, mobile work and mobile life. In refining the basic concepts and ideas of these scenarios, Vignette 4 gives an impression on how today's trends and visions could affect the daily life of ordinary people. In addition to that we would like to put emphasis on the following exemplary scenario on emergency response, describing a situation in which critical personal information is stored and processed. The focal point of this scenario is on the one hand to describe the huge, maybe life-saving, potential accompanying this type of service, and on the other hand the misuse potential and therefore the need for a proper and privacy protecting implementation.

Emergency Response: In this scenario (Figure 5.3) Fanny uses a mobile phone together with a special medical emergency service. When she pushes the emergency button on the phone, her GPS location data is automatically transferred together with her call to a specific rescue control centre. The rescue control centre is able to send medical professionals (if needed with special equipment, e.g., if Fanny's location is somewhere in the high mountains) to the location where Fanny submitted the emergency call (pull service). Except for emergency calls, her location data is not collected, nor transferred or stored by the service provider.[2]

---

[2] A service as described is offered for example by the Vitaphone GmbH: www.vitaphone.de/en/.

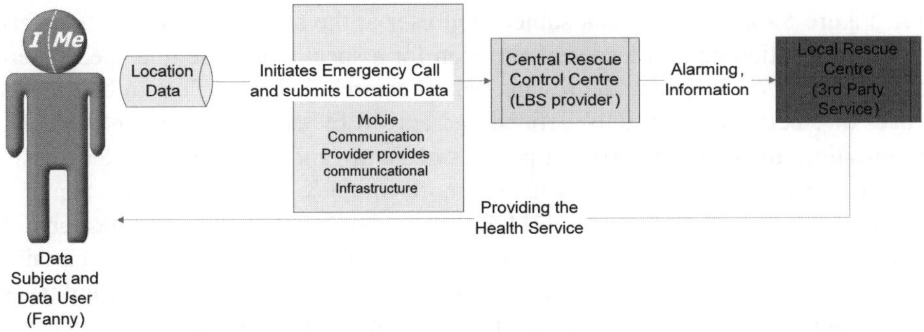

Fig. 5.3. Workflow in the medical emergency scenario

Data processed and stored in emergency cases are deleted by the service provider after the end of one accounting period of the medical professionals and rescue services involved (in general one year). So her location data is (in general) not available for profiling purposes. The rescue control centre is assumed to perform its service in the European Union. Accordingly, it complies with data protection legislation, such as European Directive 95/46/EC, and implements a high level of IT security related technologies.

The mobile identity in this scenario consists of Fanny's mobile subscriber data together with her current location and the attribute, that she is requesting help

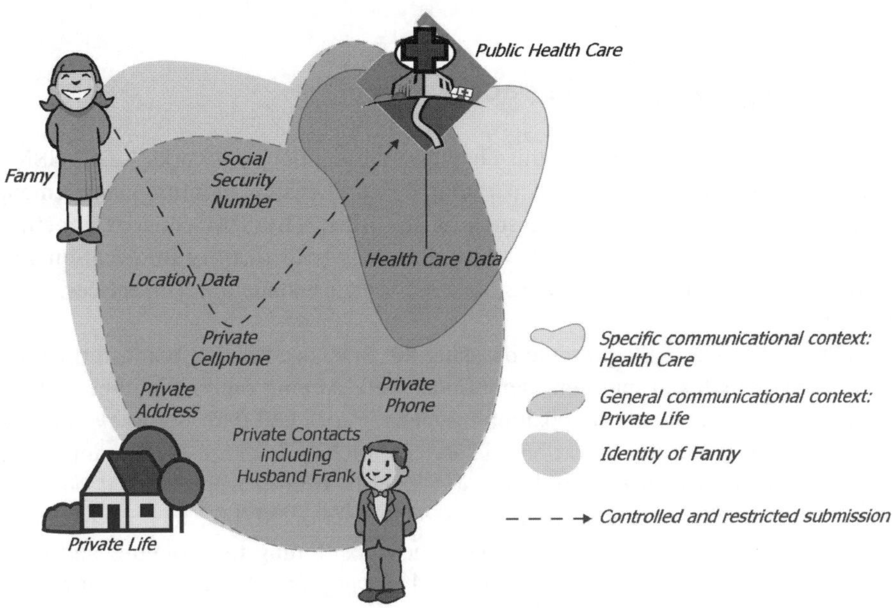

Fig. 5.4. Identity of Fanny in the medical emergency scenario

(cf. Figure 5.4). Fanny is data subject and user at the same time, as she transfers her own location data in a special situation for a special purpose to a special service provider (in this case the rescue control centre). The workflow to be used in cases of emergency is strictly defined and agreed by all participants in the communication, the communicational policies of Fanny and the LBS provider match. This communicational context, which is more complex compared to the examples discussed in FIDIS Deliverable D11.1 (Royer, 2006: 20-28), raises questions of data protection and multilateral security, as not all of the personal data remains under Fanny's control. The rescue control centre is aware of these issues and takes care of them by applying appropriate measures for data protection and IT security. The use of LBS in cases of emergency has no significant impact on the identity of Fanny when carried out in the described way.

5.3 The FIDIS Perspectives on Mobility and Identity

In general, the topical fields being identified and worked on in the field of mobility and identity do not only cover technological aspects, but also socio-cultural, governmental (legal, etc.), and economical aspects. However, each of these individual topics represents a microcosm of its own, allowing the identification of further overlaps and future research opportunities. The following chapters will shed some light on the different fields surrounding mobility and identity, as presented in Figure 5.5.

5.4 Technological Aspects

As stated in the introduction of this chapter, mobile phone networks' (e.g., GSM) success is very much based on a rather comprehensive identity management based on identification systems, such as the SIM. The SIM concept, together with the supporting GSM infrastructure, provides both identity information and security for accessing voice services, data services, or context based services, such as LBS.

While identification is possible by using the SIM as a starting point, further aspects need to be taken into consideration as well. Among others, the type of IdM used in a mobile context, the positioning technologies and their accuracy, and the privacy management in context based services, such as LBS are focal points to be analysed when looking into mobility and identity from a technological point of view. Accordingly, in this section two perspectives on Mobile Identity Management Systems (MIdMS) are introduced. Then positioning technologies and their accuracy are presented before security and privacy are discussed to enrich the technological perspective on MIdM.

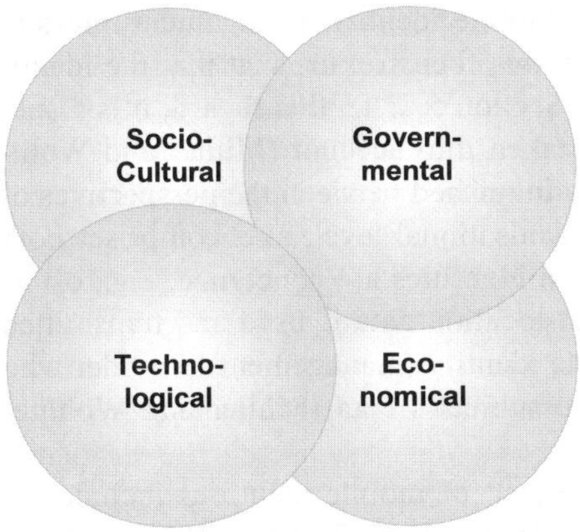

Fig. 5.5. Interdisciplinary aspects of mobility and identity

5.4.1 Management of Mobile Identities vs. Mobile Identity Management

Exploring the concept of Mobile Identity Management (MIdM) two basic facets can be observed. Namely these are: The management of identity through the use of mobile devices (mobile identity management) and the management of mobile identities (Royer, 2006: 37-49).

Starting with mobile identity management, this concept refers to the management of identities through the use of mobile devices. Here the fact that IdM is possible by means of mobile devices is stressed, not the management of mobile identities itself. Such an application helps its user to handle the access to mobile services by managing credentials, permission, or roles onto a mobile device. Depending on the given context, this data can be disclosed to a service (e.g., a LBS), based on the settings of its user. A prototypical implementation is the iManager, allowing its users to manage their partial identities, and consequently to protect their privacy[3].

From the point of view of the architects of IdMS, especially related to the type 3 IdMS (cf. Section 4.1), it needs to be ensured that the applications on mobile devices include technologies, such as Privacy Enhancing Technologies (PET) so that the end users can actually trust that they control the data flows of the mobile devices used for identity management. To this regard, privacy enhancing identity systems should be able to realise aspects such as Hansen et al. (2004):

- User controlled linkage of personal data
- Data minimisation
- Awareness of data being disclosed
- Sufficient usability towards the user

3 iManager has been developed at the University of Freiburg. Details are available here: http://www.telematik.uni-freiburg.de/pro.php?knoten=iManager.

Changing the perspective, the concept of mobile identity management refers to the management of mobile identities. Here we focus on the fact that the identities are mobile identities, as discussed in Section 5.2. To this regard, it is a special case of IdM, where location data is taken into account (Müller and Wohlgemuth, 2005: 78). This can be further distinguished between the perspectives of the end user and the perspective at the organisational level, as it comprises both the perspective of the subject whose partial identities are concerned, e.g., offering mechanisms to decide when and what location data is used and transmitted to whom and the perspective of the mobile identity (management) provider who operates the system and may process the subject's data (Müller and Wohlgemuth, 2005: p.78).

Indeed, success factors for the management of mobile identities include aspects, such as *locality*, *reciprocity* and *understanding* (Royer and Rannenberg, 2006). To this regard, *locality* refers to the fact that identities can have different roles and linkages in different contexts. Due to this fact, a user needs to be able to differentiate contexts. Moreover, *reciprocity* deals with the informational symmetry or asymmetry between consumers and service providers, e.g., the collection of data for service customisation purposes and the control on the related profile data. Accordingly, users should be able to know or to adapt their profile data, in order to minimise asymmetries.[4] Finally, the principle of *understanding* entails the fact that both consumers and providers should be able to understand each others' 'identities'. In the domain of mobile services, it is important to include this principle, as the perception of the identity of a service provider (e.g., perceived risks regarding transactions) is directly related to consumer acceptance.

5.4.2 Positioning Technologies and Methods

A typical LBS architecture consists of three parties: The *Mobile Operator*, the *LBS Provider* and the *Mobile User* (cf. Figure 5.6). Usually, the Mobile Operator works as intermediary between the actual provider of the service and the user. This includes the identification of the customer for payment purposes, the transmission of the user's location to the LBS Provider and the transmission of the service itself via mobile communication networks. The LBS Provider combines the user's location with relevant geo information in the process of creating and delivering the requested service. Thereby, the action-specific user context can be derived. This chapter will focus on the presented classical architecture. Nonetheless, further architectures exist.

4 In this context, the price of convenience model discussed in Subsection 5.6.2 deals with the implications of data disclosure and privacy, tying into the principle of *reciprocity*.

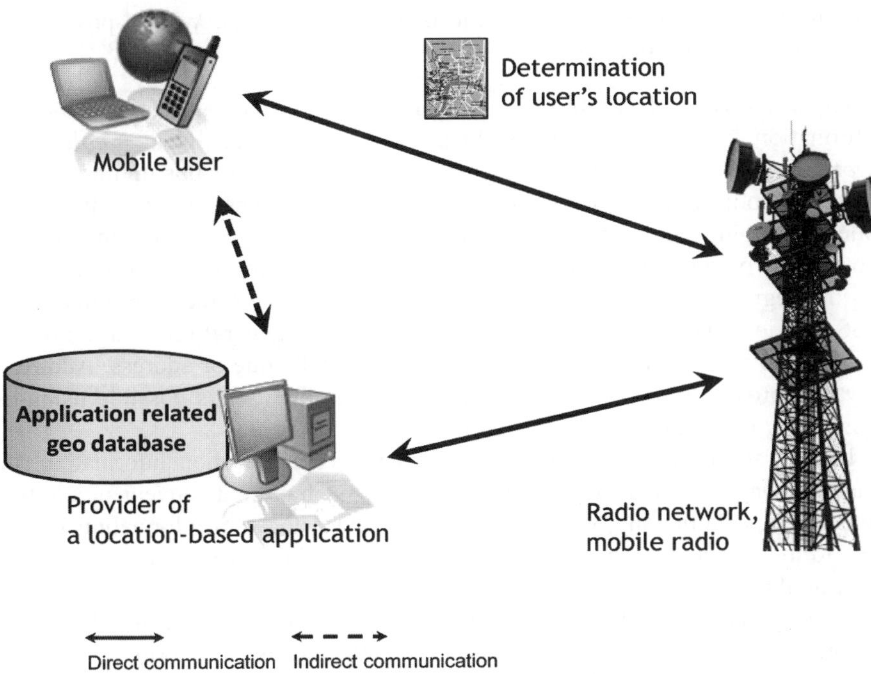

Fig. 5.6. Example for a location based service (LBS) infrastructure and the involved parties, under the assumption that the LBS user is directly connected to the data subject

The availability of the user's current location information is the precondition for the existence of LBS. The degree of accuracy that is obtained by the different positioning methods directly affects the user's idem identity (cf. Subsection 2.3.1) as it is a more or less concrete observable attribute of his identity. The way how the user's identity is determined affects the level of control he has about his idem identity. Thereby a smaller level of control about this attribute of his identity can also affect his idem identity.

In the following, we make a distinction between network-external sources of location and network-internal sources of location. A user can be located and tracked by using network-internal positioning methods (e.g., by cell of origin positioning). This can take place even without them noticing. In contrast, users have a certain amount of control if network-external positioning technologies are used.

Network-external source of location information. *Network-external* means that the positioning system is outside the control of the Network Operator and provided by a third party / third system. Common external sources of positioning information are user input, satellite based positioning systems, such as the widely used Global Positioning System (GPS) or the newly emerging Galileo positioning system, position senders, such as radio or infrared beacons, WLAN positioning, and peer-to-peer positioning.

'User' as source of location information. Having the user as source of location information for the provision of location based services is a *double-edged sword*. One of the key advantages is that the user keeps the positioning process under his control. That means that he / she can decide whether he wants to provide positioning-information, when he wants to provide positioning information (so there is no automatic tracking possible) and what kind information concerning the degree of accuracy of the location information he wants to provide to the LBS-provider. The degree of accuracy can vary from general information (country, city) to more concrete information like e.g., ZIP-code or address. Additionally, the provision of positioning information via the user is possible using almost every kind of terminal or medium.

In contrast to automatically derived and processed location information, the 'manual' way to provide the current position is much more inconvenient and time consuming. Additionally, the user can only provide location information if he is able to localise himself in the area (which requires familiarity with the location). That might be no problem for more general location information like country or area, but it gets gradually more difficult with a rising degree of required accuracy for the provision of location information. The most precise way to locate someone may be to provide an address. However, this is only possible in more densely populated areas.

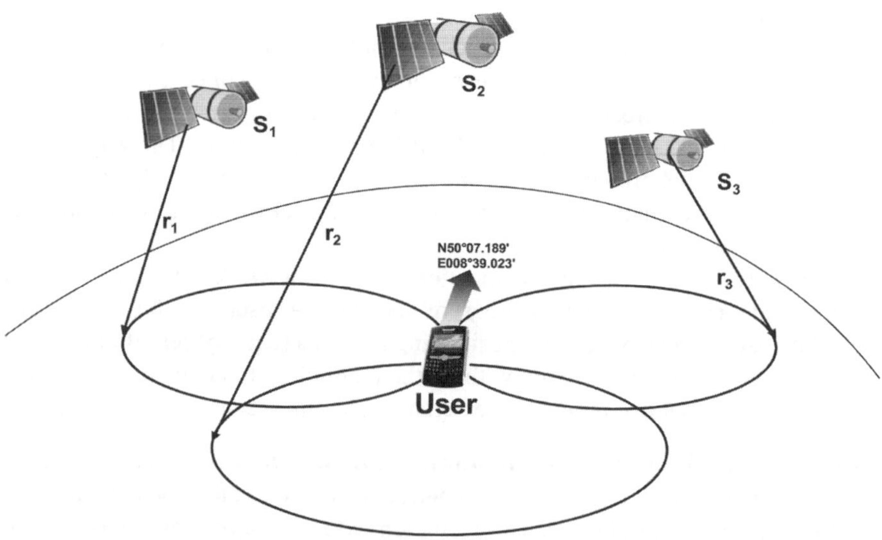

Fig. 5.7. Satellite based location tracking needs at least 3 satellites to triangulate the position of a device or person (Schiller, 2003: 181)

Satellite based location information. Theoretically, the determination of someone's position using satellites can be carried out all over the world (Schiller, 2003: 181). Satellite based positioning is characterised by a unilateral way of communication, as the mobile device only passively receives information (cf. Figure 5.7), from which it then calculates its location. The accuracy of satellite based positioning is between 1 and 15 meters depending on the used service / technology.

As described in Figure 5.7, the position of the user can be determined by using the position signals of at least three satellites that move on fixed orbits (Schiller, 2003: 182). Table 5.1 shows the advantages and disadvantages of satellite based positioning systems.

Table 5.1. Advantages and disadvantages of satellite based positioning systems

Advantages	Disadvantages
(+) High accuracy	(-) Long time needed for the initialisation of the positioning process
(+) High availability	(-) High-power consumption especially in the non-stop-positioning mode
(+) Relatively low cost for chipsets that can be embedded in terminals	(-) Signal strength: It is mostly used outside as the signals are generally too weak to be received inside buildings

The world-wide standard for satellite based positioning is still the Global Positioning System (GPS), established and controlled by the USA. The accuracy of the GPS can be altered in case of military emergency. The forthcoming European satellite positioning system Galileo is planned to be implemented by 2011-12[5] and should obtain a higher accuracy than GPS.

Further external information sources. Another method to allow positioning is the usage of position transmitters that communicate their location to a user's device via e.g., radio or infrared signals submitted by a beacon within a given area (cf. Figure 5.9 and FIDIS Deliverables D11.5 and D7.7 for example applications). The accuracy of the location information thereby depends on the size of this area and can vary from 10 centimetres to several meters. Common usage scenarios for position transmitters are exhibition information systems, museum guides, tourist guides or promotion activities.

WLAN Access Points (especially relevant in urban areas), peer-to-peer positioning (cf. Figure 5.9) or Radio Frequency Identification (RFID) are further relevant technologies / methods to determine users' locations.

5 Cf. www.esa.int/esaCP/SEM8LNN0LYE_Benefits_0.html.

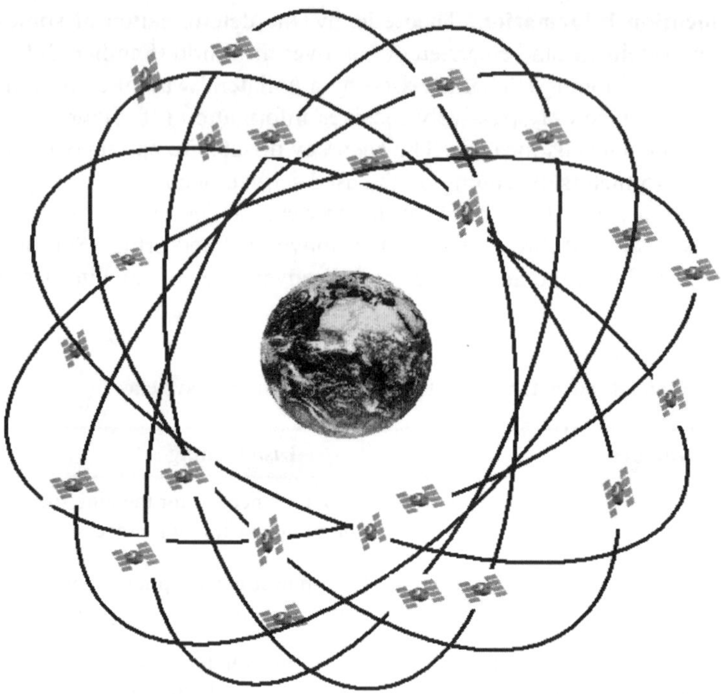

Fig. 5.8. Positioning satellites orbiting the earth[6]

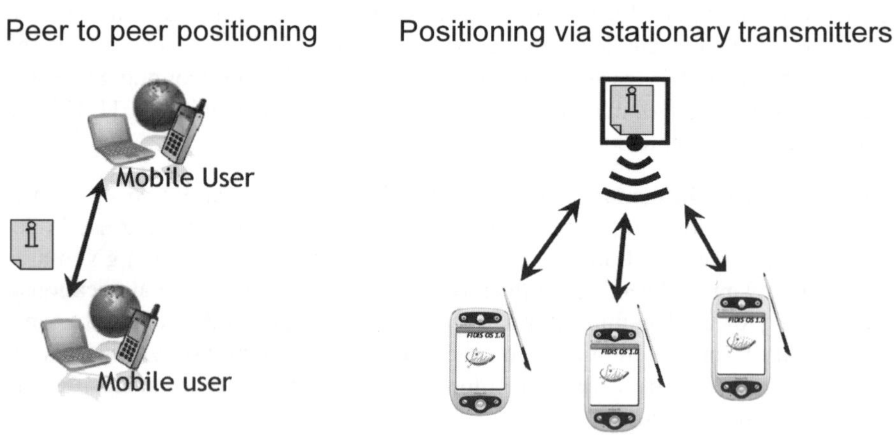

Fig. 5.9. Peer to peer versus stationary transmitter positioning (e.g. by radio or infrared beacons)

6 Cf. www.fc.up.pt/lic_eg/imagens/gps-const.jpg.

Network based source of location information. Network based positioning utilises the fact, that the user of location based services on mobile phones is connected to the mobile communication network (e.g., GSM or UMTS based mobile networks). The network itself is constructed of many (overlapping) network-cells, whose shapes are influenced by the environment (buildings, etc.) and usually are neither hexagonal nor a perfect circle, even though this is the usual way of drawing them (cf. Figure 5.10).

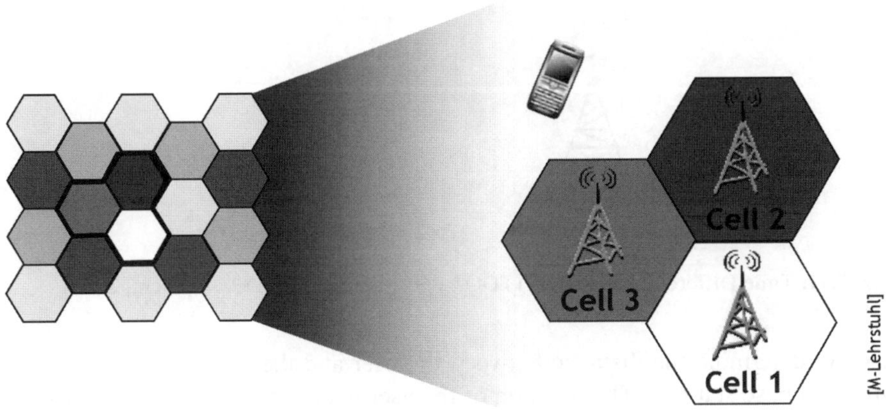

Fig. 5.10. Cell Based Communication (CBC) and cellular communication networks

The geographic location of the cell's base station / transmitter is well-known and can be used as a point of reference. The position of the mobile user can be approximately determined by using cell identity information, the distance and the angle between the mobile user and base stations. Until recently this information was exclusively known by the network operator. Meanwhile Google is aiming to collect and use cell information by its own cataloguing initiatives.

Cell of origin positioning (COO). The most rudimentary method is the cell of origin (COO) positioning method. Thereby the location of the base station to which the mobile user is connected is considered to be the location of the user. It is more a looking up in the visitor location register than a positioning. The accuracy of the obtained location data depends on the range of the radio cells. The range of the radio cells can vary from 100 meters in urban areas up to 25 kilometres in rural areas, depending on the size of the network's cell (Ludden et al., 2002: 49).

Time Difference of Arrival positioning (TDOA). The Time Difference of Arrival (TDOA) positioning method (cf. Figure 5.11) is based on at least three (synchronised) base stations, which measure the time difference it takes to receive a signal from the mobile user (also known as multilateration). This information is

Fig. 5.11. Time Difference of Arrival (TDOA) positioning (GIS Development, 2006)

used to determine the distance between the user and the position relative to the involved base stations. The location of the user is determined by using advanced triangulation techniques and cross-referencing the distance-information. Multilateration is commonly used in civil and military surveillance applications to accurately locate an aircraft, vehicle or stationary emitter by measuring the time difference of arrival (TDOA) of a signal from the emitter at three or more receiver sites.

Enhanced observed time difference positioning (E-OTD). The enhanced observed time difference method (E-OTD) is an improvement of the TDOA method (cf. Figure 5.12). It measures the time intervals of the radio signals between a base station and the mobile device and a known fixed spot (called location measurement unit). Three location measurement units are needed to determine the position. In contrast to TDOA the mobile device actively participates in the positioning process. E-OTD only works with mobile devices that include E-OTD technology.

Angle of Arrival positioning (AOA). The angle of arrival (AOA) positioning method seeks to determine a user's location, based on the angle of the signals sent by user's mobile device (cf. Figure 5.13). This is done by determining the direction of propagation of a radio-frequency wave incident on an antenna array. In order to calculate the AOA, TDOA is used at individual elements of an antenna array. From the resulting delays, the AOA and therefore the direction can be determined. Finally, using multiple base stations and AOA, the geographical location can be determined.

Fig. 5.12. Enhanced Observed Time Difference (E-OTD) positioning (GIS Development, 2006)

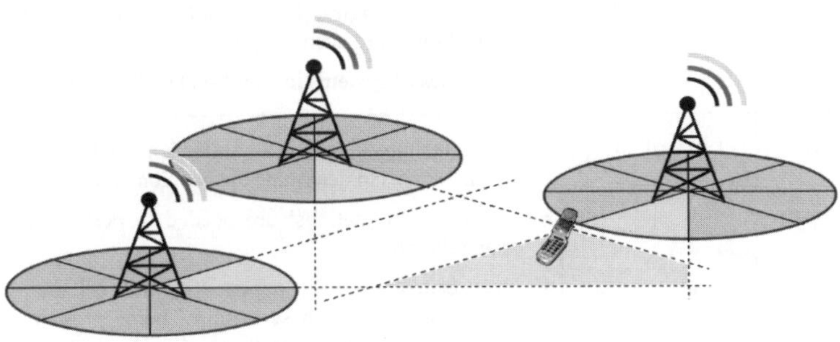

Fig. 5.13. Angle of Arrival positioning (AOA) (based on GIS Development, 2006)

5.4.3 Accuracy of Positioning Technologies and Methods

The presented technologies and methods for locating a device or a person differ considerably in the way they work. Accordingly, the accuracy of positioning varies. Table 5.2 and Figure 5.14 give a brief overview of positioning technologies and their characteristics. Furthermore, some of the limitations of these technologies and some possibilities to disturb or manipulate them are presented.

5.4.4 Security and Privacy in Mobile Identity Management

The last sections have shown how useful context information (especially location information) can be for applications. However, they also give a clear indication that location information is very sensitive. Due to the high market penetration of

Table 5.2. Positioning technologies used for LBS (based on Cuijpers et al., 2007: 16; Deuker, 2008: 27)

Technology	**Accuracy**	**Notes**
Satellite-based positioning Systems: GPS, Galileo	3 m – 100 m	• The accuracy of satellite-based systems depends on the service / technology being used. • GPS is mostly used outdoors since the signals are generally too weak to be received inside buildings. • Satellite signals can be jammed or the accuracy can be altered by the government, e.g. in a military emergency.
Cell-based mobile Communication Networks: UMTS (3G), GSM (2G)	80 m – 30 km	• Most mobile network-based positioning technologies only offer a limited accuracy with regard to the positioning of the mobile device. • The accuracy depends on the size of the communication cell in which the mobile device resides: In city centres, the diameter of a cell can be approximately 300 metres, in rural areas much larger cells (diameter up to approximately 30 km) exist. Additional technologies, for example using triangulation, allow more accurate positioning. • Examples of systems in use: E-OTD, Cell-ID.
Other wireless Technologies: Radio Frequency Identification (RFID), WLAN, Bluetooth	< 1 m – 50 m	• These technologies use a similar approach as cell-based systems to determine the position of an entity. • Several 'base stations' are needed to perform the triangulation. • The accuracy heavily depends on the technology and the amount of 'base stations' being present in the observed area → mostly these technologies are used indoors.
Sensor-based Systems: Optical sensors (infrared-based), biometrics (face recognition)	Close proximity: > 10 cm – several metres	• Sensor-based systems resemble a conglomeration of different location technologies. • Accuracy depends on the technology being used. • The technologies differ a lot in the way they work (e.g., optical systems vs. wireless systems).
Hybrid Systems	N/A	• Systems that use combinations of different positioning technologies to offer a higher accuracy. • Example: Assisted GPS (A-GPS), combining GPS technology with external sensors (e.g. tachymeter) or cell-based positioning technologies (mobile phones, etc.).

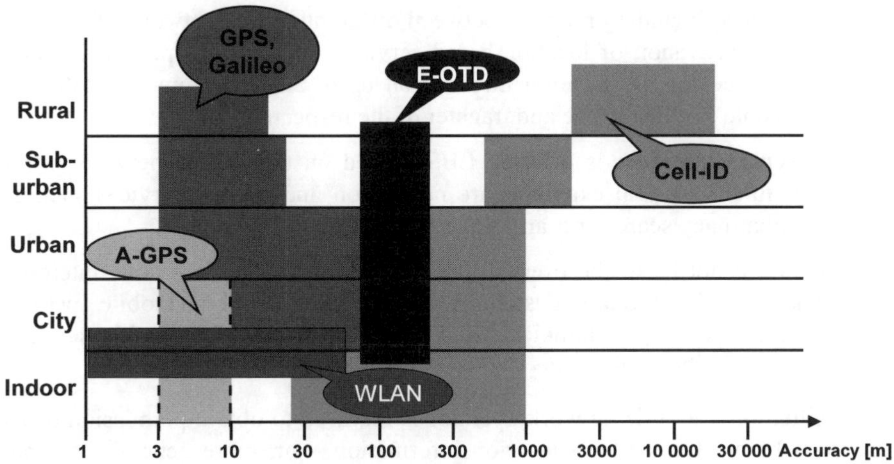

Fig. 5.14. Positioning technologies and their accuracy (based on Cuijpers et al., 2007: 17; Nokia, 2001: 11)

mobile communication networks based on GSM or UMTS, these networks were not only a highly attractive platform for the rendering of location-based services (LBS) reaching a broad user base, they were also the first areas where the discussion on location data and its security and privacy implications showed up.

The typical risks are the combination of data usually in an application domain, e.g., a health service with data from the communication domain. A related scenario was used in the PRIME[7] project's LBS application prototype (Zibuschka et al., 2007): A traveller arrives in a city and needs to urgently buy some medication that was forgotten at home. Therefore the traveller needs to find a pharmacy preferably with that medication in stock. The simplest solution is a LBS offered by the operator and enriched with pharmacy data. It may be easy to use and be of great help, but comes with the risk, that the mobile operator learns more about the medication needs and consequently the health of the traveller (which in addition is its subscriber) than needed and wished by the traveller.

This scenario and the related technical solution will function as the basis for the further discussion in this section. Typically, in a LBS of this nature mobile operator and service provider are different entities. So three stakeholders are involved and may be differentiated according to the concept of Multilateral Security (Rannenberg, 1994; 2000):

1. A mobile operator is the owner of the mobile network infrastructure. Its business is to offer the network infrastructure that mobile subscribers use

[7] PRIME (Privacy and Identity Management for Europe) was an EU-sponsored project (FP6), aimed to develop a working prototype of a privacy-enhancing Identity Management System. More can be found at https://www.prime-project.eu.

every day, including roaming between different mobile networks. Concerning the provision of location-based services, the mobile operator is often the source for the location information used, and therefore is legally responsible for the release and transfer of the respective data.

2. A service provider is offering LBSs based on the mobile network infrastructure. Classical examples are navigation and routing services such as the pharmacy search scenario illustrated earlier in this section.
3. Last but not least, the users or subscribers of the services have interests. They are often 'double' customers: A subscription with the mobile operator enables them to communicate and be mobile, while for specific services they subscribe to the respective specialist service providers.

In this situation a mobile network operator is required to obtain permission of its customers before transmitting location information – or, more general, personal information – to e.g., the service provider. Therefore, the PRIME LBS application prototype and its later implementation offered a number of options for subscribers to permit the transmission of these data under privacy friendly circumstances.

A further enhancement addressed the architecture of the system and the information flows between the parties: the integration of an intermediary as an additional party. This location intermediary allowed the following functions:

- Enabling the user's anonymity vis-à-vis the other involved parties, i.e. to ensure, that the user's identity will not be revealed to the service providers of the location based services and that the specific (health) service requested by the user will not be disclosed to the mobile network operator
- Keeping an audit trail and so empowering subscribers to trace interactions with certain service providers
- Providing a policy management front end for clients with limited capabilities (e.g., WAP phones)

The PRIME LBS application prototype can be seen as a model reaction to the specific challenges posed by context-rich mobile identities and their application. It approached the challenges by helping users to control the extent of identification and location being transmitted both with regard to time and action. Moreover it established an architecture to split up mobile identities, that may have become too convoluted e.g., by combination of subscriber and medical data. At the same time the application services can still be used and also the security and business requirements are taken care of.

This example shows a possible solution to address the stakes of several stakeholders by applying advanced technologies. It is also in line with the legal requirements, e.g., on privacy and their spirit. However it can only come to its full fruition in a legal framework that clearly defines the possibilities and non-possibilities for privacy-sensitive data-flows to avoid that e.g., operators and service providers cut corners in the separation of identity information.

5.5 Legal Aspects[8]

In order for location-based services (LBS) to flourish, their providers need a clear legal framework with a level playing field throughout Europe. At the same time, because location information can be quite sensitive, consumers should be protected from abuse of their personal data. Understandable and consistent rules safeguarding consumer protection will give them confidence to step into the emerging market of location-based services.

Unfortunately, the legal framework for new services in Europe is not always clear, consistent, or understandable. One major cause of legal uncertainty is the fragmented approach that is visible in several areas of European law and policy-making. Fragmentation of rules, for ensuring a level playing field and for safeguarding fundamental values, is understandable and not always avoidable. Technical and market developments are so complex and fast, that the European legislator has to strike a balance between intervening at an early stage, with sector-specific or technology-specific rules that cannot yet completely grasp the consequences of the developments underway, and intervening at a late stage, with perhaps more general and mature rules, at the risk of being too late to influence the technology or market to move in the desired direction.

This so-called Collingridge dilemma of early versus late intervention to control technology (Collingridge, 1980) is frequently solved by specific rules in different legal instruments dealing with separate developments. However, the resulting patchwork of rules gives rise to inconsistency, jeopardises the comprehensiveness of the relevant legal framework, and may ultimately undermine the very goals of regulation.

In this section, we analyse the data protection rules for LBS. We describe the two relevant data protection Directives,[9] with special attention to problems which arise from the divergent and obscure terms contained therein. We describe the extremely complex interplay between the three legal regimes that are contained in these two Directives, as they apply to three different, overlapping, types of data. We conclude that the current legal framework is neither suited to stimulate innovation of LBS nor to protect consumers using LBS.

---

[8] Authors: Bert-Jaap Koops and Colette Cuijpers (both TILT). This chapter is based on FIDIS deliverable D11.5 (Cuijpers et al., 2007).

[9] The scope of this Chapter does not allow us to go into another relevant Directive, 2006/24/EC, *Official Journal* L105, 13.4.2006, p. 54, which regulates the mandatory storage of traffic and location data, and which even further complicates the legal framework regarding LBS. For a brief discussion of the data retention directive in relation to LBS, see FIDIS deliverable D11.3 (Royer, 2008: 22).

5.5.1 Two European Directives on Data Protection

The general framework with regard to the processing of personal data is Directive 95/46/EC (hereinafter: Data Protection Directive).[10] The applicability of the Directive depends on whether there is 'processing' of 'personal data'. The definition given to processing is very broad and it is fair to say that almost each handling of data, from their establishment to their destruction, can be considered processing in the meaning of the Directive. Whether or not data can be considered to be personal depends on whether or not the data, directly or indirectly, identify a natural person.[11]

If the Directive applies, data processing must comply with its regime. This includes, for example, requirements that personal data can be collected only for specified, legitimate purposes and that they must be processed fairly and lawfully. The Directive gives various norms for when processing can be considered fair and lawful, for example, a legitimate basis, purpose limitation, and adequate information security measures. Also, data subjects must be informed of data processing, and they have various rights of access and complaint (see, *inter alia*, Articles 6, 7, 10, 11, 12, 14, 16, and 17).

For the sector of electronic communications, the EU has considered it necessary to supplement the general Data Protection Directive with a sector-specific data-protection Directive, which was part of a larger set of Directives regulating the electronic-communications sector (formerly known as the telecommunications sector). Directive 2002/58/EC on the processing of personal data and the protection of privacy in the electronic communications sector (hereinafter: ePrivacy Directive)[12] is more specific than and complements the Data Protection Directive. Directive 95/46/EC is *lex generalis* which applies to the processing of personal data unless Directive 2002/58/EC – the *lex specialis* – determines otherwise.

The reason for creating a *lex specialis* and introducing traffic data and location data as distinct types of data is the acknowledgement that these types of data entail specific risks against privacy. Hence, extra protection was considered necessary, in order to guarantee confidentiality, prompt anonymisation, and consent. Moreover, while Directive 95/46/EC only applies to natural persons, Directive 2002/58/EC also covers subscribers who are legal persons (Article 1 para. 2), whose traffic and location data are also to be protected. Furthermore, some provisions create explicit rules in relation to interconnection and billing in light of the particularities of the emerging market of eCommunication services, where business models may require more data processing of subscribers than in other markets. In addition to existing definitions in other directives, Directive 2002/58/EC provides for definitions of specific types of data that are of great importance to LBS: 'location data' and 'traffic data'.

---

[10] [1995] *Official Journal* L281/31.

[11] The Article 29 Working Group has clarified the concept of personal data in its Opinion 4/2007, 01248/07/EN, WP 136, June 20, 2007, http://ec.europa.eu/justice_home/fsj/privacy/docs/wpdocs/2007/wp136_en.pdf.

[12] [2002] *Official Journal* L 201/37.

Now, the processing of data can be governed by neither Directive, by one of the Directives, or by both Directives simultaneously, depending on the type of data and data processing. The substantive regimes of both Directives differ in some respects, as the *lex specialis* provides, for example, stricter conditions for processing certain types of location data. It is therefore very important for both providers and consumers of LBS to be able to qualify the data being processed, in order to be certain as to which legal rules apply. This turns out to be a very complex exercise.

5.5.2 Location Data, Traffic Data, and Their Relation to Personal Data

In Article 2 of the ePrivacy Directive, definitions are given of traffic data and location data:

> *'(b) 'traffic data' means any data processed for the purpose of the conveyance of a communication on an electronic communications network or for the billing thereof;*
>
> *(c) 'location data' means any data processed in an electronic communications network, indicating the geographic position of the terminal equipment of a user of a publicly available electronic communications service.'*

Since traffic data include data on the geographical position of the terminal equipment at the beginning and at the end of a communication, for instance a mobile phone call, some traffic data are also location data. Conversely, many location data in the electronic-communications sector are traffic data, namely if they are processed for the purpose of conveying a communication.

As to the relation between location data and personal data, the Article 29 Working Party has given the following interpretation: 'Since location data always relate to an identified or identifiable natural person, they are subject to the provisions on the protection of personal data laid down in Directive 95/46/EC'.[13] However, it is questionable whether this statement is correct, since location data can also relate to objects that are not linkable to individual natural persons.

Figure 5.15 illustrates the complex relation between personal data, location data, and traffic data.

This means that there are seven types of data, which we illustrate with some examples.

1. Location data that are also personal and traffic data, e.g., the location of the GSM cell in which a SMS was sent by a mobile phone of an individual with a GSM subscription.
2. Traffic data that are also personal data but not location data, e.g., the duration of a call made by an individual with a GSM subscription.

[13] Article 29 Working Party, *Opinion 4/2007 on the concept of personal data*, 01248/07/EN WP 136, June 2007.

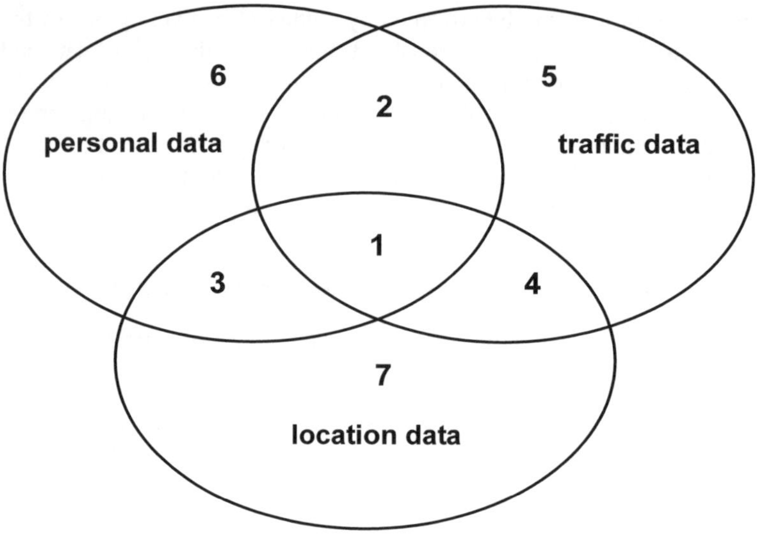

Fig. 5.15. The relationship between personal, traffic, and location data (Cuijpers et al., 2007: 27)

3. Personal and location data, but not traffic data, e.g., the address of a fixed telephone of an individual.
4. Traffic and location data, but not personal data, e.g., the location of a public phone booth where someone made a call.
5. Traffic data, but not personal or location data, e.g., the date and time when an Internet user accessed a business website using an anonymising service.
6. Personal data, but not location or traffic data, e.g., the account number of an individual.
7. Location data, but not personal or traffic data, e.g., the GPS location of a company car used by many employers; in the context of electronic communications, possibly the location of a stand-by mobile company phone used by several employers is an example of this category.

Note that this is a schematic representation, in which the size of the areas in the figure does not suggest anything about reality. It should also be remarked that the definitions of the various categories of data are not trivial and further complicate the Venn diagram. They depend on how we interpret elements of the definitions, notably the terms 'communication', 'electronic communications service', and 'publicly available'.[14]

[14] For an analysis, cf. FIDIS deliverable D11.5 (Cuijpers et al., 2007: 28-31).

5.5.3 Which Directives Apply to Which Types of Data?

Above, we have sketched the complex relationship between personal data, traffic data, and location data as well as the Directives and provisions that apply to these data. Generally, the ePrivacy Directive takes precedence over the Data Protection Directive, but the latter supplements the protection of traffic and location data when these are not covered by specific provisions in the sectoral Directive. Under the ePrivacy Directive, different regimes apply to traffic data and location data that are not traffic data. The picture is compounded by the fact that the ePrivacy Directive provisions only apply to public communications. Traffic and location data generated by private networks or in private services are not covered by Articles 5, 6 and 9 of Directive 2002/58/EC; if they relate to individuals, however, the general Data Protection Directive applies. This leads to the following, rather complex, picture of applicability of legal provisions to the various kinds of data.

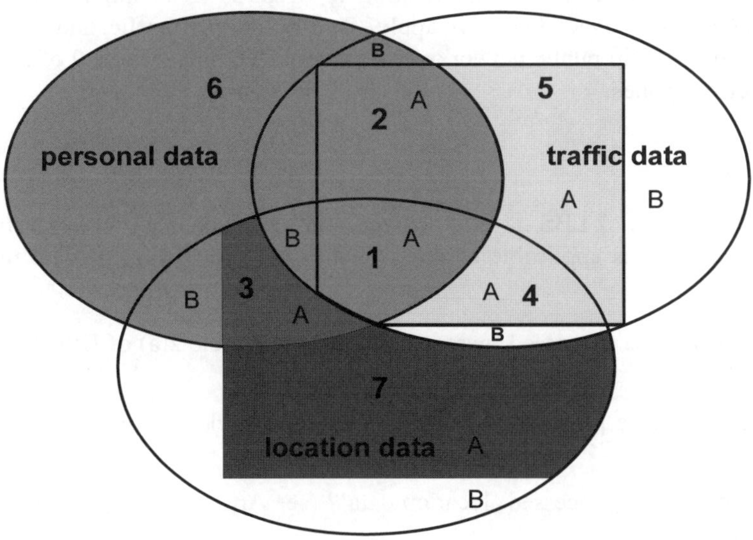

Fig. 5.16. Applicability of the directives to personal, traffic, and location data (Cuijpers et al., 2007: 34)

In Figure 5.16, 4A and 5A indicate applicability of Articles 5 and 6 of the ePrivacy Directive, while 7A indicates that Article 9 of this Directive applies. The entire ellipse of 6 indicates the scope of the general Data Protection Directive. Sections 1A, 2A, and 3A show that for some data, the specific provisions of the ePrivacy Directive as well as the general Data Protection Directive apply. This is only the case in public networks or services: 'A' denotes data generated in public networks or services, 'B' data generated in private networks or otherwise outside the scope of the ePrivacy Directive, for instance because they do not relate to electronic communications at all.

We give a few examples of what this figure implies in terms of applicable provisions. Section 1A indicates that for data generated in *public* networks or services, Articles 5 and 6 of the ePrivacy Directive apply, imposing requirements such as confidentiality, the legal grounds for processing, storing, and erasure. Other requirements under the Data Protection Directive also apply, when they relate to personal data and are not specifically covered by the ePrivacy Directive, such as several aspects of data quality and data security (Articles 6 and 17 Data Protection Directive).

Section 3 denotes the category of location and personal, non-traffic, data. If these are generated in public networks or services, then Article 9 of the ePrivacy Directive applies, as well as other requirements from the general Data Protection Directive not covered by the ePrivacy Directive, such as information-security measures (Article 17) and the limitation of automated decisions about the data subject (Article 15). For traffic and location but non-personal data generated in public networks or services (4A), e.g., relating to business subscriptions, only Articles 5 and 6 of the ePrivacy Directive apply. To location, non-traffic, and non-personal data generated in public networks or services (7A), only Article 9 of the ePrivacy Directive applies.

5.5.4 Conclusion

It is clear that providers of LBS have to answer many questions before they can determine what regime is applicable to the data they are processing in order to provide LBS:

- Are the data to be processed 'personal data'? (see Article 2(a) of Directive 95/46/EC)
- Are the data to be processed 'traffic data'? (see Article 2(b) of Directive 2002/58/EC)
- Are the data to be processed 'location data'? (see Article 2(c) of Directive 2002/58/EC)
- Do the data relate to users or subscribers of public communications networks or publicly available electronic communications services? (see Articles 6 and 9 of Directive 2002/58/EC and Articles 2 (a), (c) and (d) of Directive 2002/21/EC)
- Is one of the exceptions applicable? (see Article 13 of Directive 95/46/EC and Article 15 of Directive 2002/58/EC).

This list of questions and the ensuing assessment of which legal regime applies, is already quite complex to grasp. Legal uncertainty becomes even more pronounced when we recall that some of the answers are also difficult to give due to uncertainty about the precise scope and meaning of certain terms in relation to LBS technologies. We think that this gives sufficient ground for concluding that with the current fragmented legal regime, legal certainty is virtually absent, both for LBS providers and for LBS subscribers.

As a result, enterprises developing LBS services may well choose not to offer these services on the European market at all. European consumers would then lose the opportunity to benefit from new and innovative services. Alternatively, and perhaps more likely, business will develop LBS and offer them on the market with disregard for the legal framework of consumer protection rules, and unaware of which rules apply in the first place. As to consumers, they are subjected to violations of their data-protection rights about which they, too, know nothing.

We conclude that the legal framework is too complex and unclear, which hampers both the market for innovative LBS and threatens to erode fundamental rights of European consumers. A revision of the fragmented legal framework is urgently needed.

5.6 Sociological Aspects[15]

A sociological perspective on the relation between technology and society should neither reduce this complex domain to mere technological nor social determinism. It is more appropriate to say that the implementation and deployment of a mobile technology in a particular context is the specific outcome of the interplay of social choices of various actors. Economical resources and constraints, the underlying paradigm on ICT, the geography of space and place, the institutional arrangements, and public policy as well as the conceptualisation of the user all influence how a given technology will provide opportunities and/ or difficulties to citizens who make use of them (Dutton, 2001: 199). In general, it is right to say that in contrast with history, geographical limits on social interaction are declining very fast.

5.6.1 A Socio-technical View on Mobility and Identity

A socio-technical view on mobility[16] and identity implies that mobile IDs are *more than* 'the IDs of mobile devices which are bound to an individual' (Müller and Wohlgemuth, 2005). Based on Royer (2006), a re-conceptualisation of the concept mobile identity emerged, taking into account the critique on a too technocratic approach.[17] Consequentially, a mobile identity can be re-defined as 'a message or a set of (linked) messages derived from mobile computing devices, constituting claims about the mobility, the location or other characteristics which are

[15] Authors: Els Soenens (VUB) and Denis Royer (JWG).

[16] Social mobility is an important topic for sociology. However, here we address the issue of mobility on the level of geography, rather than looking at changes in Socio-Economical Status (SES) of citizens.

[17] Cf. (Saarenpää, 2002) or (Roussos, Peterson, Patel, 2003) as examples for such critiques.

assumed to represent a data subject' (Royer, 2006). Although it is of utmost importance for LBS providers 'to capture once and for all the immediacy of the given self, to read off identity from location'[18], this mobile identity is in fact (only) an idem type of identity (cf. Chapter 2.3.1). Nevertheless, mobile computing devices can influence people in their identity building and thus in the everlasting process of constructing one's sense of self, because these devices with their capacity of managing communication and information give the advantage of being able to choose to have specific social interactions on an almost continuous scale, where ever, whenever and with whom. This is not *per se* a negative thing. But by making the link between a mobile (idem) identity and one's ipse identity, it becomes very clear that processing of personal and location data and the use of personalised services have (negatively or positively) an impact on one's identity building.

Let's take the LBS as an example. LBS are promising tools for citizens. They facilitate that the right information is available at the right moment, making it easier for citizens to make decisions and live their lives as they want to. In this regards, surveillance is not necessarily bad; for the provision of some (push-oriented) LBS it is essential for third parties to track the (location) of data subjects. However, LBS and locational profiling (Sui, 2004: 65) result in the classification of mobile identities (Hildebrandt and Gutwirth, 2005: 46) and this bears the risk of narrowing human autonomy. LBS have the potential to profile continuously and in a very precise way, without necessarily respecting its user's need to protect secret (personal) information. In fact, 'LBS in the future may not just evolve to more instrumental / utilitarian applications, but enable its users to explore more intimate ways at the psychic and emotional levels' (Sui, 2004: 64). Consequentially, LBS could bite 'into human behaviour much more directly much more immediately and much more deeply' (Clark, 2001). The use of location data to profile e.g., styles and preferences is often far more accurate than necessary for the realisation of communication purposes (Arvidsonn, 2004: 458). LBS thus have the capacity to enhance the control of others (e.g., companies) over one's self. We perceive an urgent need to research how Privacy Enhancing Tools (cf. Chapter 4) and Transparency Enhancing Tools (TET) (cf. Chapter 7) can facilitate citizens to take control over one's construction of the social self when using LBS.

Location is valuable. Movement itself became of interest because of what Castells stipulates in his theory of the space of flows: '*our society is constructed around flows: flows of capital, of information, of technology, flows of organizational interaction, of images, sounds, symbols.*' (Castells, 1996: 412). Being able to capture information about these flows becomes very important. The tendency to commodify location data is in line with the growing attention for surveillance mechanisms. The surveillance of flows and thus of mobilities (movements of people, cars, devices, data) may not be ignored in the study of mobility and identity. At least from the point of view of the profilers, location based information is val-

[18] Stempec project, 'Socio-technological shaping of mobile multimedia personal communications', p 9.; www.surrey.ac.uk/research.

ued because it can categorise people. This creates a paradox, as Sui (2004) remarks: The social life becomes more 'mobile', the software technologies make people more predetermined. Thus Sui claims that the possibility of fully documented life through location profiling can in principle convert all of us into 'prisoners of geography' (Sui, 2004: 66). Indeed the danger of real-time control could bring us into 'an electronic version of Jermy Bentham's Panopticum' (Sui, 2004) or into a world of *geoslavery*, using the phrase of Dobson and Fisher (cf. Sui, 2004). To this regard, authors such as Marx G.T., Lyon D. and Bennet all warn about the rise of a surveillance society.

Another aspect which seems relevant to LBS is the issue of the digital divide between those who want and are able to profit from LBS and those who are not. This is something which from a social point of view, should be watched closely.

5.6.2 Price of Convenience (PoC)

In the previous subsection various models and concepts were developed to better understand communication and interactions between individuals in the mobile (social) context. The model to be discussed here is the price of convenience (PoC) model, developed by Ng-Kruelle et al. (2002), representing a model influenced by economic theory to explain social processes.

In the case of LBS, on the one hand an effective use of the provided context and profile data offers a higher convenience from services tailored towards the needs of its users. On the other hand this also can result in problems with regard to privacy and security aspects. Consequently, the balance between convenience of service provision and security / privacy becomes an aspect to be investigated, being in the focus of PoC.

The PoC model itself is based on the diffusion of innovation framework by Rogers (2003), addressing its shortcomings with regard to the universal validity and incapability to capture the entire complexity of mobile technologies (Ng-Kruelle et al., 2002). To this regard, PoC can be seen as a heuristic, socio-technical tool to better understand the mechanisms customers use to trade convenience for privacy.

The *'price'* is thereby not to be understood as an economic value, but as a metaphor. The model analyses the users' willingness to trade their privacy for convenience when using mobile applications. For the cluster of MIdM, this model can help to understand how these technologies can influence the usage of mobile services in general. Also links to relevant laws and regulations in general could be analysed, as consent and a need for privacy seem to be important.

As the development of innovations passes through several stages, the main influence of the PoC model can be found in the implementation and adoption phases. This separation allows the investigation of the behaviour of innovations and their development. By following this approach it is possible to identify the necessary measures to maximise the convenience. The PoC model is visualised in Figure 5.17 and can be further divided into the system aspects (society, government,

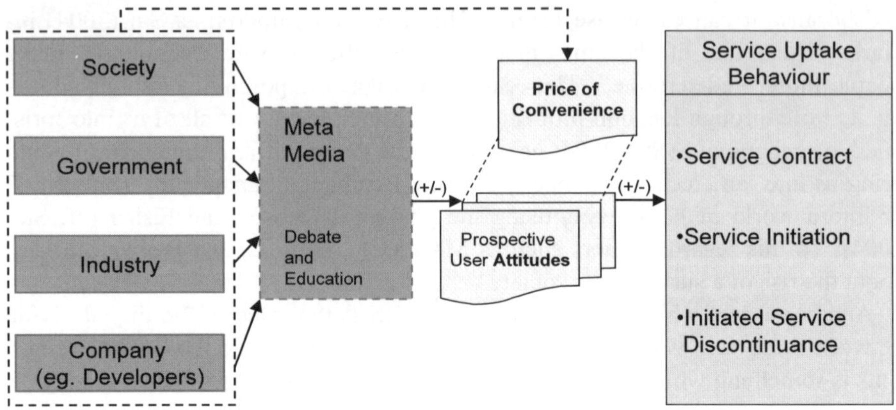

Fig. 5.17. Conceptual framework of the 'Price of Convenience' (PoC) model (Rebne, et al., 2002)

industry, company and media) and the subjective aspects (PoC, attitudes, behaviours, and service uptake).

The decision, whether a service is adopted or not by an individual user is influenced by the individual's value towards the gained convenience and the loss of privacy resulting from that service. The derivation of the PoC is thereby significantly influenced by five discrete factors recognising a diverse environment and supports both, socio-economic and technical perspectives. Namely these are: society, government, industry, companies (primary effects) and media (secondary effect), representing the *system aspects*:

- *Society:* For the PoC, society can be understood as a pluralistic concept in which law and order can be considered a negotiated result of different interest groups. Society is considered the strongest of the five factors.
- *Government:* The government is considered as a monitoring entity with respect to the social security. Special emphasis is placed on the government's consideration of the protection of the individual rights versus the *collective* safety.
- *Industry:* The word industry includes multiple companies offering similar products and targeting the same potential customers. Industry is credited with the capability to develop and implement standards and guidelines.
- *Companies:* The aspect 'companies' includes developers of mobile services, technology developers, and content aggregators. From the understanding of the model, mobile service developers should especially focus on the heterogeneity of the end device in the development process, as compatibility is an important requirement.

- *Media:* Media are brought into the PoC model as a secondary effect, complementing the other four effects. They describe an intra-institutional setting that has a great importance for the understanding of the individual PoC as a result of influence on the privacy. Media impact is often critical for the successful adoption of a new service or product. Developers and mobile network operators should therefore actively approach the media to be able to influence the perception of new services.

The five presented factors influence the actual PoC, showing various interdependencies among each other. The inner attitude with regard to the adoption of a mobile application or service and the behaviour of the adopting individual are influenced by the dynamic contexts between the players in the system. As a result, the user can finally decide whether to contract, to initiate, or to discontinue a service (cf. Figure 5.17).

5.7 Economic Aspects

Mobile Identity Management (MIdM) with all its facets is becoming ever more important for today's organisations and users. An increasing number of new services and application scenarios are being discussed and introduced into the market (e.g., Vignette 4). These markets and their underlying mechanisms have been investigated by scientists and market research institutions in the past years and various contributions were made in both the scientific and practitioners' literature.[19]

Besides purely revenue driven aspects, macroeconomic conditions such as the evolution of standards and governmental regulations affect the development of the market for mobile communications, services and applications. In addition to that more structural questions, e.g., whether the market will consist of oligopolies or be fully competitive, will also decide on the development and diffusion of technologies, services and applications and thereby on the need and justification for MIdM. Having the general economic context in mind, the subsequent section focuses on the microeconomic level and the relation between customers, technology, and further market players.

Starting with the relevant market players, this section discusses the economic aspects of mobility and identity. Moreover, trust as mechanism and foundation for the success of MIdMS is presented, followed by an overview of the related economic theories. Based on that, this section concludes with a framework for analysing the economic impacts of MIdM in next generation context aware services, helping to derive the requirements for future MIdMS.

---

[19] Examples can be found in: Büllingen and Stamm (2004); Nohria and Leestma (2001); Rebne et al. (2002); Ristola et al. (2005); Roussos et al (2003); Siau and Shen (2003).

5.7.1 Market Players

Looking at the market environment, several players could be identified in the mobile market. Among others, device manufacturers, infrastructure manufacturers, network operators, mobile virtual network operators, service providers, content providers, and customers can be listed, all of whom play a major role in the process of value creation in this market. Furthermore, these players can be put into value chains, which are suitable for illustrating value-adding activities among the individual players. An example for a value chain for the mobile business market, integrating the players listed before, was suggested by Picot and Neuburger (2002) and is visualised in Figure 5.18:

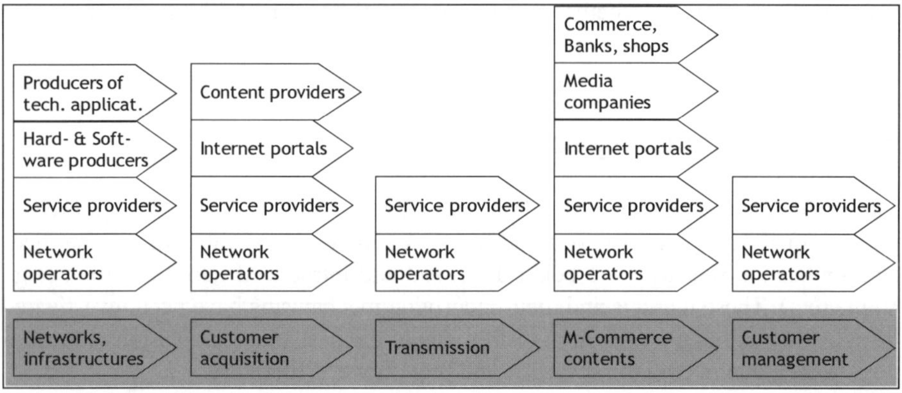

Fig. 5.18. Mobile value creation: the mobile value chain (Picot and Neuburger, 2002)

For the analysis undertaken here, the focus will be put on a limited number of players, resulting in a simplified value chain. The players involved include the (1.) mobile operator, (2.) the service provider (e.g., for LBS applications and services) and (3.) the users / customers (Deuker, 2008: pp. 9). This is due to the following reasons:

- In this context it can be assumed that these players have the highest impact on the trust building and a possible (non-) adoption of a newly introduced service from a customer's point of view.
- The mobile operator and the service providers are the players, who are (directly / indirectly) involved with the customers / users. Accordingly, it can be assumed that they have an interest in understanding the mechanisms that lead to trust building and the adoption of their services.

To this regard, this chapter discusses the mechanisms in the market of mobile applications, the use of MIdMS and the relevant economic theories from the customers' point of view. This should help to better understand the adoption and trust building mechanisms of customers using such mobile services (e.g., friend finder applications[20]), in order to better understand the customers' choices for *using/not using* mobile applications and services. For this purpose attitudes and behavioural elements are important aspects to explain the acceptance of technologies, such as mobile services using MIdMS.

5.7.2 Building User Trust

Among the many influencing factors for the usage of MIdM technologies, trust and the building of trust relationships between the different stakeholders, such as customers or service providers, can be seen as one of the most important and essential constructs. Trust can be defined as:

> *Trust: A state referring to a relationship between two parties in which one relies on the other to perform according to expectations, in situations entailing risk.*

Three general characteristics of trust are highlighted in this definition: First, a trust relationship involves two parties, namely the *trustor* and the *trustee.* Second, trust involves uncertainty and risk, and lastly, the trustor has faith in the trustee's honesty and believes the trustee will not betray him.

While it is possible to identify the characteristics and the players for trust, the process of trust building towards a service or a product is important as well. One of the models to explain this process is described by Fung and Lee (1999). Their model analyses trust building with regard to the market for mobile commerce applications (cf. Figure 5.19). In the opinion of the authors, this model can also be applied and extended to the domain of mobility and identity and mobile identity management. As initially stated, this is due to the fact that trust is necessary to attract users to adopt a new technology or a service. Moreover, the scope of this model can be broadened to general organisations, as not only commercial companies can offer MIdM facilities in their services and products.

According to Siau and Shen (2003) getting a potential customer to start a transaction with a service provider is the key step for initiating the trust development life cycle (cf. Figure 5.19). In order to do this, there are various ways – for example through reward attraction, or by demonstrating features such as convenience, cost efficiency, and personal necessity.

Besides the general concept of trust and the trust building life cycle, the general components of customer trust need to be taken into consideration. According to Siau and Shen, the technology and the service provider are the key components, since they are considered to have the biggest impact on the customer trust. Besides these two factors, reliability and security of mobile technology are equally important, since failures in the early stages of the usage of M-Commerce reduce the

[20] Further scenarios can be found in Deuker (2008): pp. 9.

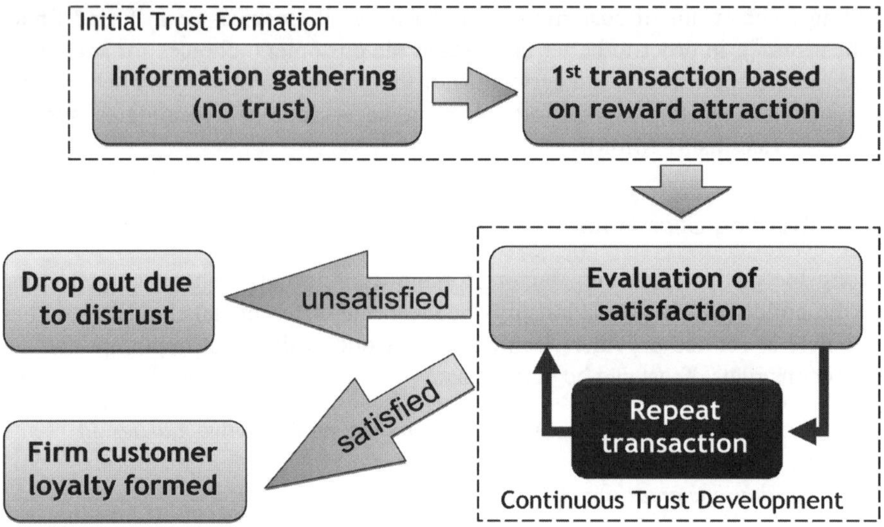

Fig. 5.19. Schematics of the trust development life cycle (Fung and Lee, 1999)

customers' trust significantly. Moreover, as mobile technology evolves, the trust focus shifts from technology to the mobile service provider.

From a service provider's perspective, there are several steps, which need to be taken into consideration to build an initial trust formation. Among other factors, this includes the dissemination of relevant information or the cultivation of interest. Other specific ways for organisations include the following steps:

- *Enhance customer familiarity*, as people tend to trust the familiar, e.g., by general publicity or advertisements.
- *Build vendor reputation*, as a good reputation suggests certainty and less risk in conducting business.
- *Deliver high-quality information*, as the information posted on a company has a high impact on the customers' perception.
- *Elicit third-party recognition and certification*, as the independent nature of third-party certification helps customers to feel more secure in doing business with the M-Commerce provider.
- *Provide attractive rewards*, such as free trials or gift cards helping to attract new customers.

It is important to maintain a trust relationship, as creating trust is time-consuming and trust can easily be destroyed. Accordingly, there are several successful methods derived from eCommerce that can be adopted by organisations offering mobile services bundled with IdM functionality to overcome trust barriers. This includes the following suggestions that can be pursued by organisations to successfully overcome trust barriers:

- *Improve site quality:* User-friendly design of web-sites accessed by mobile devices (e.g. giving customers sufficient information for purchases) helps to convey the vendor's competence.
- *Sharpen business competence*: Refers to the skills, technical knowledge, and expertise in operating mBusiness applications.
- *Maintain company integrity:* Providers need to be congruent with regard to the actions and the promises given to their customers.
- *Post privacy policy:* Similar to eBusiness providers, mBusiness providers should post their privacy policy online, so customers are informed about the information being processed. This helps to build transparency.
- *Strengthen security controls:* In order to have secured mBusiness transactions, technologies need to be in place, which help to allow Multilateral Security for all involved parties.
- *Foster a Virtual Community:* By building virtual communities, mobile service providers can replicate the success of web-based online communities and create positive evaluations by their users.
- *Encourage communication and increase accessibility:* In order to build synergies, the users should be brought into close communication with the mBusiness provider, reducing information asymmetries and fostering the provider's credibility and trustworthiness.

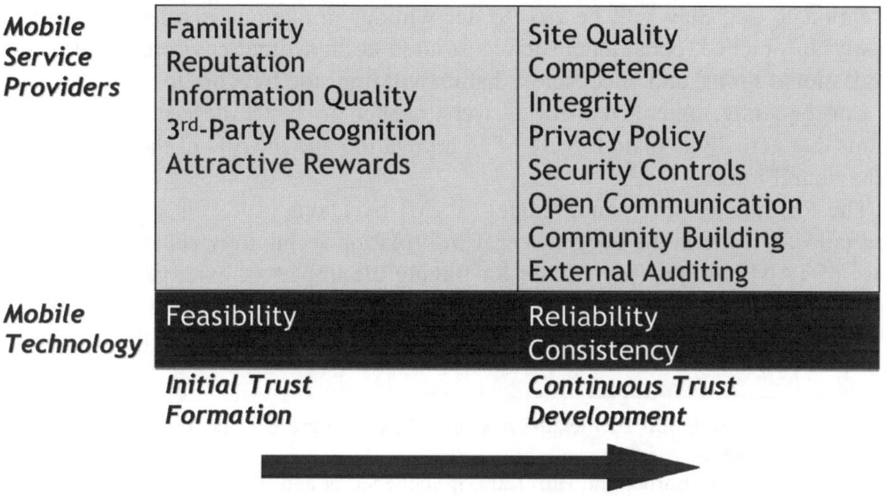

Fig. 5.20. Derived trust building framework (Siau and Shen, 2003)

- *Use external auditing to monitor operations:* External auditing helps to maintain the customers' trust by keeping the provider to behave fairly and legally.

Figure 5.20 summarises the activities for initial trust building and the continuous trust development for service providers and mobile technologies into a trust building framework.

5.7.3 Related Economic Theories

The following subsection is dedicated towards the economic theories being used to explain the behaviour of customers and adoption mechanisms in markets. The theories being discussed are shortly presented in the order of their appearance in the scientific literature, showing their theoretical relations and links.[21]

The *theory of reasoned action (TRA)*, by Fishbein and Ajzen (1975; see also Ajzen, 1980) posits that individual behaviour is driven by behavioural intentions. The theory received particular attention in the field of consumer behaviour as it provides a simple tool to identify possibilities to change customers' behaviour when using an innovation (Sheppard et al., 1988: 325). The actual use of an innovation is determined by the individual's behavioural intention to use it. The *Attitude towards an act or behaviour* is the individual's positive or negative feeling about performing *a behaviour*, determined through an assessment of one's beliefs.

TRA has some limitations in explaining all mechanisms of the actual use of an innovation and the role of the individual's behavioural intent, which are discussed in the relevant scientific literature.[22] One limitation is the significant risk of confounding between attitudes and norms since attitudes can often be reframed as norms and vice versa. Furthermore, the assumption that when someone forms an intention to act, they will be free to act without limitation, is often unfounded. Lastly, in practice, constraints such as limited ability, time, environmental or organisational limits, and unconscious habits will limit the freedom to act.

Consequently, extended theories were needed to better describe the mechanisms that actually explain the use of an innovation and the role of the individual's behavioural intent.

The technology acceptance model (TAM) by Davis (1989) is based on TRA and tailored towards the acceptance of information technology (IT).[23] A key purpose of TAM is to provide a basis for tracing the impact of external variables on internal beliefs, attitudes and intentions. In his research, two main factors were identified. On the one hand, the *perceived ease of use* represents the degree to

---

[21] A detailed description of the theories and their background can be found in Royer (2008), Chapter 5.

[22] Cf. Ajzen (1980); Barnes and Huff (2003); Schneberger and Wade (2008).

[23] In the original research by Davis (1989), these IT systems were email systems used in an organisation.

which a person believes that using a particular system would be free from effort. On the other hand, the *perceived usefulness is* the degree to which a person believes that using a particular system would enhance his or her job performance.

Moreover, there are several attempts to extend TAM, which generally have taken the approaches of introducing factors from related models, introducing additional or alternative belief factors (risk, emotion, etc.), or examining antecedents and moderators of perceived usefulness and perceived ease of use.

However, although TAM extends TRA, some limitations can be found, as both, TRA and TAM, have strong behavioural elements, assuming that when someone forms an intention to act, they will be free to act without limitation. The described constraints such as limited ability, time, environmental or organisational limits, and unconscious habits are not taken up in either model (Schneberger and Wade, 2008).

Next, the theory of the *diffusion of innovations* (DoI) is based on the research of Rogers (2003). The theory itself describes the process by which an innovation is communicated through certain channels over time among the members of a social system. The study of the diffusion of innovation is the study of *how*, *why*, and *at what rate* new ideas and technology spread through cultures. To this regard, this theory is an excellent resource to develop strategies in order to enable the diffusion of complex and controversial technologies in society (Beyers, 2002: 552). The DoI theory especially focuses on the core topics (1) adopters, (2) key innovation characteristics, and (3) the stages of adoption.

In his research, Rogers proposed that adopters of any new innovation or idea could be categorised as innovators (2.5%), early adopters (13.5%), early majority (34%), late majority (34%) and laggards (16%). Looking at the two extremes of the described groups, '*early adopters*' tend to adopt new innovations very fast, as they embrace change and are usually educated in the relevant field of the innovation being looked at. On the other hand, the adoption group of the '*laggards*' will adapt very late, as they tend to be resistant to change.

The adopter groups can be placed into a bell curve (cf. Figure 5.21) based on standard deviations from the mean of the normal curve, provided a common lan-

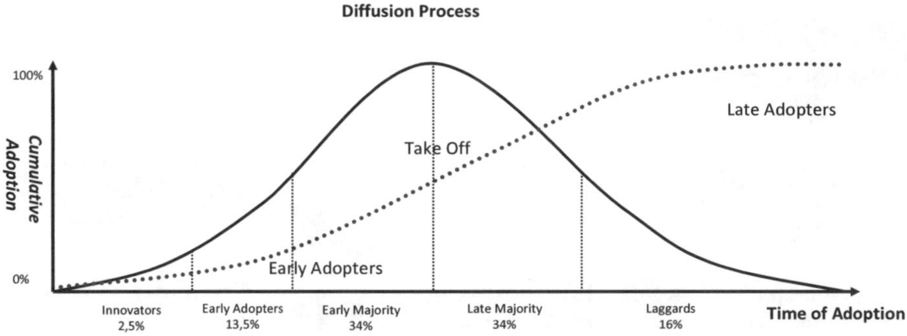

Fig. 5.21. Adopters Bell curve and cumulative adoption of an innovation over time, resulting in the S-shaped adoption curve

guage for innovation researchers. Each adopter's willingness and ability to adopt an innovation would depend on their awareness, interest, evaluation, trial, and adoption. People could therefore fall into different categories for different innovations.

For the adoption itself, certain characteristics can be observed, including:

- *Relative Advantage:* The degree to which the innovation is perceived as being better than the practice it supersedes
- *Compatibility:* The extent to which adopting the innovation is compatible with what people do
- *Complexity:* The degree to which an innovation is perceived as relatively difficult to understand and use
- *Trialability:* The degree to which an innovation may be experimented with on a limited basis before making an adoption (or rejection) decision
- *Observability:* The degree to which the results of an innovation are visible to others

The adoption of an innovation can be separated into five stages. Starting with the *knowledge stage (awareness)*, it includes the learning of an individual about the existence and function of the innovation. In the *persuasion stage (interest),* an individual becomes convinced of the value of the innovation. Here, the individual builds interest in the new ideas posed by the innovation, aggregating information about it. Following, the *decision stage (evaluation)* commits the adoption of the innovation and in the *implementation stage (trial)* an innovation is put to full use. The ultimate acceptance (or rejection) of the innovation is in the focus of the *confirmation stage (adoption)*. The individual steps of the adoption process are visualised in Figure 5.22.

Although the DoI is discussed widely in the relevant research and practitioners' literature, it also fuelled some controversy with regard to its implications and possible biases. Based on Beyrs (2002), DoI brings in a *pro-innovation bias* by

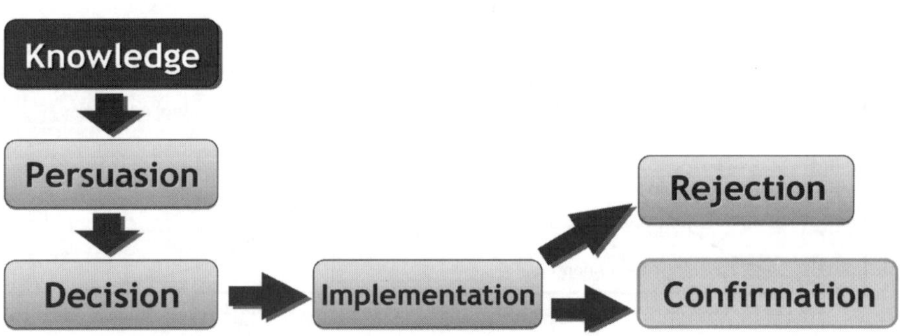

Fig. 5.22. Diffusion of innovations stages of adoption

assuming that at a certain point in time, the innovations will be adopted by all members of a particular social system. Furthermore, there seems to be an *individual – blame bias*, relating to the fact that people, who refuse to adopt innovations, are being reproached with it. However, one has to accept that innovations will never be perceived as useful by all people. Finally, Rogers' theory underestimates the *importance of the context* of a certain country or region. One has to keep in mind that characteristics of opinion leaders differ between different regions. Secondly the criteria to diffuse innovation and the ways of communicating and controlling communications also differ between regions.

5.7.4 A Framework for Analysing the Economic Impacts of MIdM in Mobile Services and Applications

As shown in the previous subsections, there are various models and theories available to understand market developments. These models are continuously developed and extended to better explain the mechanisms behind consumer adoption and trust building. Moreover, there are also models that are directly tailored towards the market of mobile applications and services, such as the PoC model (cf. 5.6.2). This is due to the fact that it has the closest relation to explain customer behaviour with regard to the trading of privacy to convenience and also links into the data protection and privacy discussion. However, in order to include all relevant aspects, new and extended models seem to be necessary.

One can identify various aspects, such as technological, legal, or social that have an impact on the economics of mobility and identity and ultimately on the usage of MIdM technology in markets. All of these aspects can be used to explain certain characteristics being present. However, there is no combined approach yet which includes all facets in a more holistic, explanatory framework. Based on the research by Royer and Meints (2009) initial ideas for a generic explanatory framework will be proposed that will help to combine the different aspects being presented in this document.

Based on the theories and aspects described before (e.g., Subsection 5.6.2 and Subsection 5.7.3), the following points should be addressed, in order to derive an explanatory framework for analysing the impacts of MIdM on mobile services and applications:

Derived from the theories presented (TAM, PoC, and TRA), the driving parameters / factors for the explanation of the adoption and trust building towards a technology or a product seem to be: Trust, perceived usefulness, perceived ease of use, convenience, and privacy. Accordingly, the factors stated before should be integrated into the further analysis as parameters to be observed. Furthermore, integrating DoI (cf. Subsection 5.7.3) can help to understand the properties of an innovation. It can also help to understand what happens during the stages of the innovation's adoption.

Moreover, the players described in the simplified value chain (cf. Figure 5.18) need to be integrated as well. However, the focus should be on the customer / user,

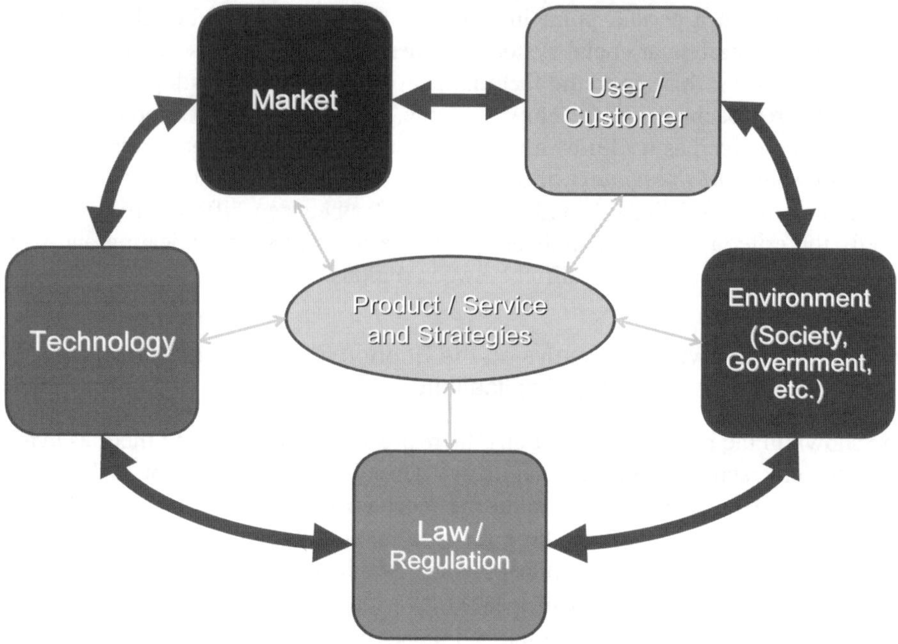

Fig. 5.23. Perspectives of the framework for analysing the economic impacts of MIdM in mobile services and applications

as this model is built to offer the opportunity to mobile operators and service providers to streamline their product development efforts for mobile applications and to offer better products and services tailored towards the needs of users and customers.

Accordingly, the properties and strategies towards the development of mobile applications and services are the key components to be looked at, similar to the visions and strategies presented in the original BSC.

Finally, the aspects of law and regulation should be integrated, as the impacts towards e.g., technology or society are manifold, resulting in requirements towards the safeguarding of information for mobile applications or services.

Similar to the approach taken by the BSC, the proposed framework for analysing the economic impacts of MIdM in mobile services and applications consists of five individual perspectives, which are linked to the strategies of an analysed product and service. Namely, these perspectives are: Technology perspective, market perspective, user / customer perspective,[24] environment perspective, and law / regulation perspective. The resulting scorecard and the linkage between the perspectives is visualised in Figure 5.23.

[24] Given the far-reaching applications and requirements one could add 'citizen' as an additional player in this perspective. However, in this analysis users and customers are in the focus, as this is an economic analysis.

For the perspectives, one could identify several quantitative and qualitative parameters and aspects that help to identify relevant properties for a product. As an example, the development of future *Next Generation Context Aware Services* (NG-CAS), as described in Vignette 4, will be shortly discussed in the light of the presented five perspectives.

Technology perspective: This perspective contains quantitative and qualitative factors, such as the general properties associated with a technology (application field, available user base), the maturity of the technology, and its ability to connect to other technologies. This helps to better understand the role of a given technology, related to the other four perspectives and the factors contained there (e.g. the perceived usefulness or the perceived ease of use, presented in Subsection 5.7.3).

Typical underlying technologies for NG-CAS are Next Generation Network (NGN) environments, converging various communication technologies (e.g. WLAN, GSM, UMTS, or fixed-line), as well as MIdM solutions allowing for an extended user-control (cf. Subsection 5.2.1).

Market perspective: In this perspective, relevant parameters to be investigated include the observed market's structure (e.g., monopoly or polypoly), the type of market (business, private, governmental), the number of service applications or service providers, and indicators for the demand of a certain product or service. Depending on the communicational context[25] and the actual type of market being observed, the need for privacy and security could be considered a point of reference, too.

For NG-CAS different market settings can be imagined. However, for services characterised by extensive user-collaboration among their users (thus implying network effects) the market structure is most likely characterised by oligopolies or monopolies. For other types of services, competitive market structures can emerge depending on the market power of the involved market players.

User / customer perspective: The user / customer perspective can be considered the most important one, as it integrates the behavioural elements, such as trust, or the willingness to adopt a certain technology (cf. Subsection 5.7.2) into the model. To this regard, an integration of the users' interests would be possible by using users' individual or group preferences as the point of reference when planning mobile applications and services (e.g. in order to tailor services to users' privacy or security needs). Furthermore, the critical point for the PoC, being the balance between privacy and convenience, could be identified and linked towards the technology and the environment perspective (cf. Subsection 5.6.2).

---

[25] The communicational context is based on the *Four Sector Model* described in Royer (2008). The model itself takes the perspective of a mobile device user, who can take various roles within society in different communicational contexts. Notably, the communicational contexts and the corresponding roles taken by the participants define their partial identities. So this perspective is also an (partial) identity centric view on markets for mobile applications and services (Royer, 2008: 14-21).

To this regard, an integrated IdM is a core component for NG-CAS as it can facilitate the trust building process for the users of a service. Two important components are the transparency of the process of using personal data as well as the possibility for the user to control the disclosure and usage of personal data. Examples are the way of setting up user profiles (direct vs. indirect profile creation as described in Figure 5.2) and the way of initiating services. Therefore mechanisms need to be in place to support users to balance their privacy and convenience needs. This also links to the technological perspective as future MIdMS need to support this kind of requirement.

Environment perspective: The environment perspective especially deals with qualitative factors, such as the impact that the media, the government, and society in general have on the other perspectives. To this regard, environmental effects on the remaining four perspectives can be identified. This also helps to identify more intangible factors (e.g., effects of media), leading to a more holistic view. An example could be the general opinion and discussion going on about the usage of a technology, such as surveillance using mobile communications technology.
The growing ubiquity of information flows and the substantial growth of mobile communication usage are leading to a growing acceptance of NG-CAS in future. Also the building of new user communities and new forms of user-generated content and interaction will change the perception of NG-CAS. This of course is influenced by the market perspective, the attitudes of the users, and development in technology and law.

Law / regulation perspective: This perspective deals with the factors resulting from business compliance, such as data protection regulation, data security (e.g. roles, access permissions), and security standards (if required). Furthermore, the regulatory needs with regard to the composition of a mobile application or service are contained in this perspective. To this regard, aspects, such as the need for (user) consent, the purpose of the used data, or the *costs* to achieve compliance are of interest (cf. Royer, 2008: 22-40).

As discussed in Section 5.5, the current fragmentation of the existing legal framework needs to be overcome, to accommodate the legal requirements of NG-CAS – especially with respect to the types of data used. Furthermore, attitudes towards the protection of personal rights and personal data are factors to be considered to protect the constitutional right of informational self determination. Linking to the law perspective, changing conditions in society and technology need to be reflected in adequate laws, standards and regulations.

The model still has limits: The aspects and parameters contained in the individual perspectives are not exhaustive and present a possible subset of aspects to be looked into. Also, the aspects and parameters contained in the different perspectives are not autonomous but interconnected. Further steps could include the building of causal chain models in order to identify and understand the interconnections. Consequently, future research should extend the work presented here. This especially includes the understanding of the market reality, the application domains for the proposed framework, and the identification of relevant factors and their interconnection.

Besides other aspects, and as described in the five perspectives, MIdM plays a central role for achieving user acceptance and ultimately market success for NG-CAS. Based on FIDIS research, requirements for MIdMS were derived, which are discussed in Section 5.8.

5.8 Requirements for Mobile Identity Management Systems

Summing up the aspects of mobility and identity presented so far, MIdMS need to support a variety of aspects, in order to support its users in a meaningful way. The following list illustrates some of the core functionalities and aspects being identified in the context of FIDIS (based on Müller and Wohlgemuth, 2005: 11-13; Royer, 2006; Deuker, 2008), which need to be taken into consideration when planning and developing MIdMS in the future:

- *Identity Administration:* To this regard, the communication-independent handling and representation of identities needs to be supported by a MIdMS, especially with regard to the possibility to choose between different profiles / data schemes, pseudonyms, or credentials. Furthermore, based on the identity lifecycle, creating, updating, deleting and (if required) the recovery of identities and identity information needs to be handled by a MIdMS.
- *Notice*: Here, the focus lies on the logging of transactions for reconstructing and analysing data flow or the detection of the context of a transaction such as illustrating what the communication partner knows from previous transactions or which partial identity was used in which transactional context.
- *Control*: A MIdMS should support its users in choosing the right profile / preferences. This is due to the fact that certain mobile devices, such as RFIDs, are designed to have no rule handling for the person carrying the device, making them potentially privacy violating. To this regard, rule handling becomes especially important when mobility is combined with location / context data. Here, anonymity could be applied as a base-rule for privacy enhancement, especially on the lower layers to enable Identity Management
- *Security*: Looking at security, techniques to enable anonymity have to be developed for the use of mobile devices and context / location, in order to allow confidentiality (e.g., anonymity, secrecy), integrity, accountability (including non repudiation), and availability of services, such as LBS.
- *Privacy Management*: Another important aspect of MIdMS is the incorporation of privacy management functionalities, in order to manage consent,

objection, disclosure, correction, deletion, and addition of privacy information. To this regard, the privacy control functionality need to include location data, in order to give users the possibility to control the flow of location data or the disclosure of data (data minimisation).

- *Interoperability and Gateways*: Ongoing, being compliant to existing standards in the field of mobile communications is important, as standards play an important role for mobile devices. The same also counts for the interfaces to MIdMS, representing the gateways for using MIdM. To this regard, design standards need to be taken into consideration.
- *Usability*: Tying into the previous point, comfortable and informative user interfaces for mobile devices have to be developed. This is due to the fact that mobile devices are limited with regard to display space or computational power. Accordingly alternative ways of handling user inputs are needed (e.g., by touch screen or speech recognition), to reduce system complexity and ultimately training and education to use a respective MIdMS.
- *Trustworthiness*: Changing the focus towards trust among MIdM and its users, the segregation of power, separating knowledge, and the integration of independent parties needs to be taken into consideration. Here, possible solutions can be found in Open Source applications or trusted seals, in order to build trust.
- *Law Enforcement / Liability*: Being already present today, identity related crime will also be a topic confronting the domain of mobility and identity. To this regard, digital evidence (e.g., proofs of transactions), digital signatures, and data retention are topics to observe closely.
- *Affordability*: A final point to consider is the *power of market* to create MIdMS that are competitive and able to reach a sufficient penetration of a given market. As for the trustworthiness, Open Source building blocks could be a starting point. Also subsidies for development, use, and operation could be an initiative to think about, helping to diffuse upcoming MIdMS into the market.

5.9 Outlook and Further Challenges and Questions

This chapter as well as the related work were triggered by the special relations between Mobility and Identity. Both trends, the management of identities via mobile devices and the mobility-induced enrichment of identity, are likely to proceed and raise further challenges. At the same time another major trend is developing: Mobility, mobility enabling networks, and mobile devices are becoming less and less of a speciality but the standard means of communication and interaction in business as well as private life. At the same time mobile and fixed-line communication networks are converging.

The trends described could mean that everything will be based on the offerings of today's mobile operators, but at the same time these operators could be reduced to commodity providers or even be replaced by the providers of other commodities. Whether mobility will then be a special or just a standard feature of identity remains to be seen. The following example discussions on popular trends and scenarios may illustrate these questions:

- Mobile devices (phones or SIMs) take up more and more functionality, e.g. by carrying of state-issued or state-certified electronic Identities (eIDs). This could mean that mobile identity management could manage even more identities than in the past. At the same time mobile devices may be incorporated into other devices or replaced by them. More and more laptops hold a GSM module with a SIM card reader for mobile data communication reducing mobile communication to a pure data channel. Others use a simple and cheap USB stick for this. The next step may be software certificates for accessing mobile networks replacing the SIM. At the same time state-issued ID cards get more and more enhanced with regard to their computing and communication capabilities. Chip-Cards are already included in many and short-range communication via RFID chips often comes with them. Identity devices with a small display and keyboard are being shown as prototypes. Enhancing these devices with a SIM card or even a SIM certificate and an interface to a mobile communication module is not impossible. This could reduce the information that is now something special on a SIM card in a mobile device to just another access certificate on a (state-issued) universal certificate carrier.
- Trends such as Ambient Intelligence, Ubiquitous Computing and Nomadicity can be seen as extensions of mobile communication networks and devices given that these mobile devices are already around now, often unnoticed. So first elements of ambient intelligence and ubiquitous computing are already implemented via cars equipped with GSM modules for theft prevention or location tracking, if the theft of the car could not be prevented. While this can be seen as the extension of mobile operator's business beyond people towards cars and other entities needing protection, cars could at the same time be upgraded towards more general identity carriers given that they already carry a few Identifiers (e.g. number plate and chassis number).
- After a long incubation time mobile payment is now getting more and more popular. However many architectures for mobile payment are not based on the core (communication) functionality of mobile devices, but use additional communication channels added to the mobile device, such as Near Field Communication (NFC). So while mobile operators may profit from additional information flows induced by payment transactions and their influence on future payment infrastructures at the same time payment providers may get into the market of mobile communications.

For all these scenarios it is not clear yet how they will turn out; still they will be involved with identity flows and therefore need some form of identity management as well as an analysis of the chances and risks involved.

References

Ajzen, I. (1980), *Understanding Attitudes and Predicting Social Behaviour*, Prentice-Hall, Englewood Cliffs, NJ.

Arvidsonn, A. (2004), 'On the prehistory of the panoptic sort: mobility in market research', *Surveillance and Society* 1 (4): 458.

Barnes, S.J. and Huff, S.L. (2003), 'Rising Sun: iMode and the Wireless Internet', *Communications of the ACM* 46 (11): 79-84.

Beyers, H. (2002), ‚Het internet en de informatiesamenleving – criteria voor de adoptie van nieuwe technologie', *tijdschrift voor sociologie* 23 (3/4: 545- 570.

Büllingen,F. and Stamm, P. (2004), *Mobile Multimedia-Dienste: Deutschlands Chance im globalen Wettbewerb*, Bundesministerium für Wirtschaft und Arbeit.

Castells, M. (1996), *The rise of the Network Society*, Blackwell, New York.

Clarke, R. (2001), 'Person-location and Person-tracking: technologies, risks and policy implications', *Information, Technology and People* 14 (2): 206-231.

Collingridge, D. (1980), *The Social Control of Technology*. Pinter, London.

Cuijpers, C., Roosendaal, A., Koops, B. J. (eds.) (2007), *FIDIS Deliverable D11.5: The legal framework for location-based services in Europe*, Download: http://www.fidis.net/fileadmin/fidis/deliverables/fidis-WP11-del11.5-legal_framework_for_LBS.pdf.

Davis, F. D. (1989), 'Perceived Usefulness, Perceived Ease of Use, and User Acceptance of Information Technology', *MIS Quarterly* 13 (3): 319-339.

Deuker, A. (ed.) (2008), *FIDIS Deliverable D11.2: Mobility and LBS,* Download: http://www.fidis.net/fileadmin/fidis/deliverables/fidis-wp11-del11.2_Mobility_and_LBS.pdf.

Dutton, W. H. (2001), *Society on the Line. Information Politics in the Digital Age. A synthesis of research based on Britain's economic and social research council programme on information and communication technologies*, Oxford University Press.

Fishbein, M., Ajzen, I. (1975), *Belief, attitude, intention, and behavior : An introduction to theory and research*, Addison-Wesley, Reading (Mass.).

Fung, R., Lee, M. (1999), EC-Trust (Trust in electronic commerce): Exploring the antecedent factors. In Proceedings of America Conference of Information System.

GIS Development (2006), *Location Based Services*, http://www.gisdevelopment.net/magazine/middleeast/2006/july-aug/22_2.htm, accessed February 2009.

GSM (2009), http://www.gsmworld.com/newsroom/market-data/ market_data_summary.htm, accessed February 2009.

Hansen, M., Berlich, P., Camenisch, J., Clauß, S., Pfitzmann, A., Waidner, M. (2004), 'Privacy-Enhancing Identity Management', *Information Security Technical Report (ISTR)* 9 (1): 35-44.

Hildebrandt, M. and Gutwirth, S. (eds) (2005), *FIDIS deliverable D7.4: Implications of profiling practices on democracy and rule of law*, Download: http://www.fidis.net/fileadmin/fidis/deliverables/fidis-wp7-del7.4.implication_profiling_practices.pdf.

Ludden et al (2002), *Report on implementation issues related to access to location information by emergency services (E112) in the European Union*, Coordination Group on Access to Location information for Emergency Services (C.G.A.L.I.E.S), Download: http://www.telematica.de/cgalies/.

Müller, G. and Wohlgemuth, S. (eds.) (2005), *FIDIS deliverable D3.3:* Study on Mobile Identity Management, Download: http://www.fidis.net/fileadmin/fidis/deliverables/fidis-wp3-del3.3.study_on_mobile_identity_management.pdf.

Ng-Kruelle, G., P. Swatman, D. Rebne and F. Hampe (2002), 'The Price of Convenience: Privacy and Mobile Commerce', *Quarterly Journal of Electronic Commerce* 3 (3): 273-385.

Nohria, N., Leestma, M. (2001), 'A moving Target: The Mobile-Commerce Customer', MIT Sloan Management Reviews, Spring Issue.

Nokia (2001), *Mobile Location Services (White Paper)*, Download: http://nds2.ir.nokia.com/NOKIA_COM_1/About_Nokia/Press/White_Papers/pdf_files/mlbs.pdf.

Picot and Neuburger (2002), 'Mobile Business – Erfolgsfaktoren und Voraussetzungen', in: Reichwaldt (Hrsg.), *Mobile Kommunikation* Gabler, Wiesbaden, 55-69.

Rannenberg, K. (1994), 'Recent Development in Information Technology Security Evaluation – The Need for Evaluation Criteria for multilateral Security', in: Sizer, R. et al., *Security and Control of Information Technology in Society – Proceedings of the IFIP TC9/WG 9.6 Working Conference August 12-17, 1993*, St. Petersburg, Russia, North-Holland, Amsterdam, 113-128.

Rannenberg, K. (2000), 'Multilateral Security – A concept and examples for balanced security', *Proceedings of the 9th ACM New Security Paradigms Workshop*, Cork, Ireland: ACM Press, 151-162.

Rannenberg, K. (2004), 'Identity management in mobile cellular networks and related applications', *Information Security Technical Report* 9 (1): 77-85.

Rebne, D., G. Ng-Kruelle, P. Swatman and F. Hampe (2002), 'Weberian Socioeconomic Behavioral Analysis and Price-of-convenience Sensitivity: Implications for MCommerce and Location-based Applications', *2002 CollECTeR (Europe) Conference on Electronic Commerce*, Centre de Congres, Toulouse, France.

Reichwald, R., Meier, R., Fremuth, N. (2002), 'Die Mobile Ökonomie – Definition und Spezifika', in: Reichenwald, R., *Mobile Kommunikation.* Gabler, Wiesbaden, 4-15.

Ristola, A., Koivumaki, T., Kesti, M. (2005): 'The Effect on Familiar Mobile Device and Usage Time on Creating Perceptions Towards Mobile Services', *International Conference on Mobile Business (ICMB'05)*, 384-391.

Rogers, E. M. (2003), *The Diffusion of Innovations*, 5th Edition, Free Press, New York.

Roussos, G., Peterson, D., Patel, U. (2003) 'Mobile Identity Management: An Enacted View', *International Journal of E-Commerce*, Vol. 8: 81-100.

Royer, D. (ed.) (2006), *FIDIS Deliverable D11.1: Collection of Topics and Clusters of Mobility and Identity – Towards a Taxonomy of Mobility and Identity,* Download: http://www.fidis.net/fileadmin/fidis/deliverables/fidis-wp11-del11.1.mobility_and_identity.pdf

Royer, D. (ed.) (2008), *FIDIS Deliverable D11.3: Economic aspects of mobility and identity*, Download: http://www.fidis.net/fileadmin/fidis/deliverables/fidis-wp11-del11.3.economic_aspects.pdf

Royer, D. and Meints, M. (2009; forthcoming): 'Enterprise Identity Management – Towards a Decision Support Framework based on the Balanced Scorecard Approach' *Wirtschaftsinformatik* 51 (3).

Royer, D. and Rannenberg, K. (2006) 'Mobilität, mobile Technologie und Identität' *Datenschutz und Datensicherheit* 30 (9): 571–575.

Saarenpää, A. (2002), 'The constitutional state and digital identity', Paper available on the website of the 2002 World Congress for Informatics and Law II Spain September 23rd to 27th 2002, http://www.ieid.org/congreso/ponencia_i.htm.

Schiller, J. H. (2003), *Mobile Communications*. 2nd ed., Addison-Wesley, London.

Schneberger, S. and Wade, M. (eds.) (2008), *Theories Used in IS Research Wiki*, http://www.fsc.yorku.ca/york/istheory/wiki/index.php/Main_Page, York (Canada), (Accessed on 30 June 2008).

Sheppard, B. H., Hartwick, J., Warshaw, P.R. (1988), 'The theory of reasoned action: A meta-analysis of past research with recommendations for modifications and future research', *Journal of Consumer Research* 15: 325-343.

Siau, K. and Shen, Z. (2003), 'Building Customer Trust in Mobile Commerce', *Communications of the ACM* 46 (4): 91-94.

Sui, D.Z. (2004), 'The media and the message of location-based services (LBS): Death of distance or the revenge of geography?', *Geoinformatics Proc. 12th Int. Conf. on Geoinformatics – geospatial information research.*

UN (2009), *United Nations Member States*, www.un.org/members/list.shtml, visited February 2009

Zibuschka, J., Fritsch, L., Radmacher, M., Scherner, T., Rannenberg, K. (2007) 'Enabling Privacy of Real-Life LBS: A Platform for Flexible Mobile Service Provisioning', in: *New Approaches for Security, Privacy and Trust in Complex Environments: Proceedings of the 22nd IFIP TC-11 International Information Security Conference*, Sandton, South Africa, 325-336.

Vignette 5: Human Enhancement, Robots, and the Fight for Human Rights*

The vision of a future world populated by humans, cyborgs, robots, and androids raises many fundamental questions. One such question is what this development means for fundamental or constitutional rights, also known as human rights. Will cyborgs be considered human enough to still be bearers of 'human' rights? Can androids claim 'human' rights if they look and function in the same way in society as cyborgs? Another important issue is the relationship between non-enhanced and enhanced people: will there be a social divide? And can human beings keep robots under control as they become increasingly autonomous; in other words, will robots comply with Asimov's three laws of robotics until the end of days, or will they, like HAL in *2001 – A Space Odyssey*, revolt and try and control humans? These types of issues are illustrated by the following two scenarios which show different possible worlds in a relatively far-away future – probably around the time of Frank and Fanny's great-grandchildren.

London, 28 June 2079, from Our Correspondent

Scenario 1

Under the circumstances, the mass demonstration of humanoids in Trafalgar Square yesterday took place quite peacefully. About 800,000 robots and androids had responded to a call from the Enhancement Society to demonstrate for the recognition of basic rights for their species. "Robots are the same as people / and want the same as humans", a sign read. "We finally want recognition of our rights. We also have the right to life" said AnDy02593, a third-generation android. "My in-built on/off button is very humiliating, I feel restricted in my freedom to develop myself".

The exuberant mood and atmosphere of alliance were subdued by a larger opposing demonstration of people headed by the Call for Human Dignity. The spokesman of the CHD, Frank Kufuyama, expressed many members' feelings during his speech: "Humanoids are different to people. They are very useful to humanity and the world, but that does not mean that they can just have all kinds of rights. Imagine that androids had the passive right to vote and could take over

* This scenario is based on FIDIS deliverable D12.5, Chapter 7, by Bert-Jaap Koops (TILT).

running the country. Before you know it they would join United Europe with the Asian Union and slowly phase us out. It is absolutely vital that the humanoids remain subordinate to us for the good of humanity."

Although the CHD has a strong basis, it is expected that the increasing social cry for rights from the humanoids will be heard by the government. Minister of Justice Warrik (grandclone of the pioneering former professor of cybernetics) is purportedly preparing a legal proposal to incorporate the rights of humanoids into the Constitution.

Scenario 2

The demonstration of orthodox humans at Trafalgar Square yesterday went calmly under the circumstances. Around 20,000 people, who for diverse reasons refuse to follow the normal procedures of enhancement, complied with the Human League's call to demonstrate against their subordinate social position. "Discrimination against normal people must end," says Andy, a 36-year old paleoman from Manchester. "We have the right to a job but nobody will give us work. The majority of us are healthy but we have to pay three times the amount of the contributions that genetically enhanced people pay. There are hardly any updated teaching materials for our children to learn from because nowadays everything goes to enhanced-brain education."

Despite the atmosphere of solidarity, the mood was subdued. The turnout was disappointing because many Human League supporters could not afford to travel to London and the demonstrators were practically ignored by the neopeople rushing by. The police fined a couple of teenage cyborgs for public abuse when they lingered during the demonstration and who, imitating a paleo-sense of humour, shouted "Hey, Neanderthaler!" to the demonstrators.

There was however, a ray of hope for the paleopeople in the speech of Minister of Justice Warrik (grandclone of the pioneering former professor of cybernetics). He emphasised that the socio-ethic position of minority groups must be respected and that paleopeople still also have a useful role to fulfil in society. He did not want to adopt the HL's ten-point plan because he considered positive discrimination in government functions to be going too far, and the right to paleo-medical facilities and the stimulation of non-brain-interactive cultural programmes to be too expensive. However, he did agree to look into promoting jobs for paleopeople and to pleading for government financing of teaching materials for paleochildren.

The visions and thoughts expressed in this vignette are inspired and based on various discussions, and results of the FIDIS Network of Excellence as well as the author's personal experience and expectations. Partially, underlying concepts and ideas of this vignette are described in Chapters 3, 4, and 7.

6 Approaching Interoperability for Identity Management Systems

James Backhouse and Ruth Halperin

Summary. Establishing interoperable systems is a complex operation that goes far beyond the technical interconnectedness of databases and systems. Interoperability emerges from the need to communicate data across different domains for a specific purpose. Transferring the data may represent a technical challenge because of different protocols, standards, formats and so forth. However, the most difficult challenge lies in reconciling and aligning the purpose, use and other changes consequent on transferring that data. Changes in data ownership and custodianship have an effect on power structures, roles and responsibilities and on risk. In the first part of this chapter our aim is to develop an understanding of the term 'interoperability' as it currently applies to the area of identity management. We propose a three-fold conception of interoperability in IdMS, involving technical, but also formal-policy, legal and regulatory components, as well as informal-behavioural and cultural aspects. Having noted the official EU/government agenda as regards interoperable IdMS, the second part of the chapter is concerned with the perspective of other important stakeholders on the same topic. First, the views of experts from private and public sectors across Europe are presented. Following this, the perceptions and attitudes of EU citizens towards interoperable IdMS are discussed. Together, the findings presented point to the crucial challenges and implications associated with the sharing of personal data in the provision of eGovernment, eHealth and related services.

6.1 Introduction

6.1.1 Why Interoperability in iDMS: Relevance and Strategic Motivation

A line of development from stand-alone computers to highly integrated networked systems can be traced from the early 1980s to the present day web-based systems. As computing and communications converged, the benefits of accessing data and services located on other computers and infrastructure have become undeniable. Given that so many business and government services are information-intensive and predicated on the identity-related information of citizens in their various guises as consumer, patient, subscriber, or account holder, it is not surprising that the whole question of the interoperability of information systems has become a central policy issue in Europe and its Member States. The central question of how to increase the interoperability of information systems that impact centrally on the lives of European citizens in a manner that accords with their legal and moral rights has come to preoccupy increasing numbers of policy strategists and systems designers in health, administration and commerce. All these sectors are experiencing growing pressure to move delivery of service onto digital platforms, or at any rate to take advantage of what are seen to be potentially interesting economies and efficiencies. Hence the development of eHealth, eGovernment and eCommerce applications and infrastructure demands ever more urgently the resolution of the central question set out above.

6.1.2 Interoperable Delivery of European eGovernment Services IDABC

The eEurope Action Plan 2005 called on the European Commission to issue an agreed interoperability framework to support the delivery of pan-European eGovernment services to citizens and enterprises (IDABC, 2005; Schnittger, 2005). More than just ePensions and eHealth, this plan of action encompassed an abundance of services including harmonising tax, social security systems, educational systems, jurisdiction for divorce and family law, driving risks and benefit and welfare regimes across Europe (Kinder, 2003; Threlfall, 2003). Further, the establishment of a common Visa Information System was seen as essential, although 'there is currently no interoperability between existing national visa systems in Europe or the possibility to check reliably whether an applicant for a visa has applied under another identity' (BTT, 2003: 1). The aim of the EU is to render electronic identities from the member states interoperable and the STORK[1] project aims amongst other things to develop 'common rules and specifications to assist mutual recognition of eIDs across national border'. But clearly there is some way to go yet.

A number of authors (Moen, 1994; Prokopiadou, 2000; Homburg and Bekkers, 2002; Scholl, 2005) view the complexities in developing an integrated social dimension for eGovernment applications (in practice) as the broadest, most difficult challenge. Owing to the multilevel, hierarchical nature of local, national and international public administrations, government procedures for production and dissemination of information are considered overcomplicated, rigid, fragmented and dispersed (Moen, 1994; Prokopiadou, 2000; Homburg and Bekkers, 2002). Szulanski calls this 'internal stickiness': a resistance by local Public administrations to adopt new ideas from outside. (Szulanski, 1996 in Kinder, 2003: 143). In addition, Choi and Whinston (2000: 40) warn that the time needed to reach consensus among public administrations may prove too lengthy to support rapidly changing technologies and practices.

Three challenges emerge. First, technical challenges relating to data homogeneity and system interoperability for proper and efficient metadata exchange

[1] http://www.eid-stork.eu/.

(Prokopiadou, 2004: 189). Second, challenges within the policy realm of the creation, communication and diffusion of commonly accepted standards (Moen, 1994: 358). Third, challenges interacting with these two concerning politics, culture and behaviour (Choi and Whinston, 2000: 41). These three elements are central to our discussion in the pages that follow, and according to our findings the third element is perhaps the one that needs most attention.

6.1.3 Organization of This Chapter

This chapter is organized in two main parts. Part one (Section 6.2) begins with a consideration of the term interoperability. The first section consults the literature for possible conceptualizations and concludes that a comprehensive understanding of interoperability should move beyond conceiving interoperability as merely a technical phenomenon to including important social, legal and behavioural facets. The FIDIS deliverable D4.1[2] proposed a useful lens through which to explore the different facets of interoperability, a simple framework called TFI (Technical, Formal, Informal) and this is outlined below in 6.2.

Having noted the official EU / government agenda as regards interoperable iDMS, the second part of the chapter (Section 6.3) is concerned with the perspective of other important stakeholders on the same topic. It draws on two other FIDIS deliverables that have investigated such perspectives: D4.2[3] and D4.4[4] First, the views of experts from private and public sectors across Europe are presented. Following this, the perceptions and attitudes of EU citizens towards interoperable iDMS are discussed. Together, the findings presented point to the crucial challenges and implications associated with the sharing of personal data in the provision of eGovernment, eHealth and related services.

6.2 Interoperable Identity Management Systems: Definitions and Framework

6.2.1 Conceptualizing Interoperability

> *The shift from the total integrated approach to interoperability development is not only a technical change, but reflects organisational, economical and social trends / requirements of the society. To successfully tackle this very complex and highly detailed endeavour, it is necessary to develop research involving knowledge and competencies of all domains concerned.* (Chen, 2003)

Establishing interoperable systems is a complex operation and goes far beyond the technical interconnectedness of databases and systems. Interoperability emerges from the need to communicate data across different domains for a specific pur-

[2] http://www.fidis.net/resources/deliverables/interoperability/#c1757.

[3] http://www.fidis.net/resources/deliverables/interoperability/#c1756.

[4] http://www.fidis.net/resources/deliverables/interoperability/#c1489.

pose. Transferring the data may represent a technical challenge because of different protocols, standards, formats and so forth. However, the most difficult challenge lies in reconciling and aligning the purpose, use and other changes consequent on transferring that data. Changes in data ownership and custodianship have an effect on power structures, roles and responsibilities and on risk. These issues run beyond the technical dimension and into the formal and social spheres. We discuss these different dimensions in this section. We also strive to develop a holistic conceptual view of this phenomenon, which can support future research into interoperability of identity management systems.

Definitions for Interoperability

According to Harvey et al. (1999), it is broadly accepted that 'interoperability' has emerged as a new paradigm, which facilitates a more efficient use of information resources through the linkage of heterogeneous ICTs into synergistic units (1999: 213). Indeed, as far back as 1994, in Moen's research, interoperability and data sharing were considered to have evolved into critical features necessary to achieve standardisation given the development of international 'electronic networks [and] the electronic delivery of government information and services' (Moen, 1994: 368).

However, interoperability still lacks a widely-agreed definition. A thorough examination of relevant literature reveals a notable absence of a common definition for the term. Many researchers (Lee and Siegel, 1996; Harvey et al., 1999; Ouksel and Sheth, 1999; Choi and Whinston, 2000; Brodeur et al., 2003; and Kinder, 2003) simply avoid offering a definition at all, and among those who attempt to provide a definition, there is a surprisingly varied selection to choose from. In this chapter, we investigate various understandings of this term in order to find solid conceptual ground for future work on interoperable iDMS.

For Miller et al. (2001), (information) interoperability is, 'the ability of processes and systems to effectively exchange and use information services' (2001: 259), although their study seeks to address the shortcomings of this definition. Moen (2000) provides a similar but richer definition seeing it as 'the ability of different types of computers, networks, operating systems, and applications, to exchange information in a useful and meaningful manner' (2000: 129). These two offerings reflect perhaps a relatively technical perspective. This is understandable considering the historical context in which, ever since computerised networks began to support and interrelate more than one single unit of independent function, interoperability has been an important concern for systems development (Klischewski, 2003: 18).

Woodall (2000) hazards a technical definition of interoperability:

> *The condition achieved among communications-electronics systems or items of communications-electronics equipment when information or services can be exchanged directly and satisfactorily between them and/or their users* (Woodall, 2000: 310).

Woodall is motivated by the undeniable, exponential increase in system complexities and components, and their related coding and data processing requirements.

Thus, he puts interoperability into a technical context, which can be approached and hopefully resolved through technical and technological means.

In stark contrast, Landsbergen and Wolken (2001) argue that interoperability is 'more than getting bits and bytes to flow properly' (2001: 206). In their view, within an ICT environment, the fundamental goal of interoperability is to overcome the challenge of assimilating people and organizations and to encourage the sharing of information – it is 'people talking and sharing information' (2001: 206). Here we are presented with a much broader, higher-level view of interoperation. Technology is certainly an essential element, but we can also start to appreciate a sense of social interoperability.

In fact Miller et al., (2001) admit that interoperability can fail even if the associated processes are properly exchanging logical units of data. Could there even be confusion between compatibility and interoperability? To ensure against an overly technical bias, one approach might be to distinguish between the proper exchange (compatibility) of a service and the ability to use the service (interoperability) – 'compatibility is a requirement for interoperability but not a sufficiency' (Miller et al., 2001: 267). As illustrated later, meanings and semantics are decisive elements in helping to reconcile the interoperability challenge, and to further exemplify Miller's axiomatic distinction. Mulley and Nelson (1999) highlight 'interconnectivity' as a term related to interoperability, yet similarly guard against complete assimilation, proposing that 'achieving interconnectivity is a necessary preliminary step towards interoperability' (Mulley and Nelson, 1999: 94) but it cannot complete the 'big picture'.

Certainly, the over-concentration of technical bias in the literature suggests a need to reframe the definition of interoperability. Rather than one narrow definition of interoperability we propose instead that a holistic notion of interoperability can serve as an umbrella beneath which may exist many disparate yet complementary definitions, according to a given perspective or level of abstraction.

So far the attempt to address the problem of reaching a simple definition for interoperability has pointed to the discordance and difficulties that can be related to a body of work concentrating on semantic interoperability – a concept we will return to later. The next section will continue this line of thinking and will illustrate that a purely technical lens in fact limits the dynamics of the interoperability paradigm and will stress that policy makers 'must make this conceptual leap before any real progress in improving interoperability can take place' (Landsbergen and Wolken, 2001: 212).

From Technical to Social and Back Again

> *Technological systems are socially produced. Social production is culturally informed. (Castells, 2001: 36)*

Technology alone may appear compatible, and standards and policy may enable interoperability, yet there is some dynamic missing in this 'bigger picture' – behaviour. Landsbergen and Wolken (2001) hint at social interoperability in their definition and research, and request additional 'support mechanisms to understand the range of economic, political, technical and organizational issues involved with information sharing' (Landsbergen and Wolken, 2001: 213).

Historically, we can find these elements in advice offered by Kraemer and King (1986), relating to fundamental, innate problems of IT management within the environment of public administration. Crucially, we need to consider these elements in context and in practice:

> *Computing fits within existing organizational life and exerts subtle influences. This does not mean, however, that computing is an activity that is easily managed. The challenge for public administration…is to focus on the actual experiences of computing technology as guides for how best to channel its use* (Kraemer and King, 1986: 494).

Choi and Whinston (2000) are supportive of this 'bigger picture' in their research, firstly by stressing that technological standards at the infrastructure level are relatively easier to reach than those at the applications and business process levels (Choi and Whinston, 2000: 38). Of course, they do not suggest technical-formal elements are trivial or easy to resolve; they are merely easier than those at the applications and business process levels. Moreover, they continue describing cultural and practical differences as being responsible for some of the many pitfalls in establishing standards in the application layer and ultimately in ensuring interoperability (Choi and Whinston, 2000: 40).

The failure of interoperability projects has not been confined to the technical realm, but to political – informal – friction among public agencies (Choi and Whinston, 2000). Undeniably, as Homburg and Bekkers (2002: 8) note, e-Government initiatives can be characterised as political.

In the following section, we propose the TFI framework, comprising Technical, Formal (policy and standards), and Informal (culture and behaviour) elements so as to engender a broader understanding of interoperability functions and as a useful tool for analyzing interoperability, providing a direction for future research and practice.

6.2.2 The TFI Model

According to the TFI model (Liebenau and Backhouse, 1990; Backhouse, 1996) information systems may be conceptualised and described as comprising technical (T), formal (F) and informal (I) layers. The power of the TFI model lies in its simple yet broad approach to the study of information systems and related themes, so that the layer to which particular research pertains can easily be understood and its place within the field as a whole ascertained.

The technical, formal and informal layers of the TFI model when applied to information systems are defined as follows. The technical layer refers to the information technology component and its spheres of convergence, that is, hardware, software, data formats, protocols and so forth. The design of the technology such as the layout and appearance of the system are also facets of the technical layer. The formal layer of the information system refers to the shared understanding of attributes and their formal structure. Policies, regulations and standards are typical manifestations of the formal layer. Finally, the informal layer refers to the ability to operate with attributes and context across domains. The informal layer of a system encompasses use or behaviour as well as systems of beliefs embodied in perceptions, expectations and culture.

The relationships between the abstracted layers of the TFI model are mutually constitutive and interdependent, suggesting that technical requires formal and formal requires informal. Furthermore, the relation between the three levels is neither unilinear nor unidirectional. For example, law demonstrates that it is possible to create and implement formal rules that do not relate to informal rules, depending on prosecuting transgressions.

Stamper et al. (2000) succinctly illustrate the interrelation of these abstracted layers, explaining that:

> *informal norms are fundamental, because formal norms can only operate by virtue of the informal norms needed to interpret them, while technical norms can play no role...unless embedded within a system of formal norms (Stamper et al., 2000: 19).*

Metaphorically, this can be viewed as a 'Russian doll' arrangement, where the informal is the outer shell containing the formal which, in turn, contains the technical. From the inside, the technical cannot be examined without first considering (unwrapping) the outer layers in turn. Figure 6.1 below illustrates the interrelationships between the TFI layers.

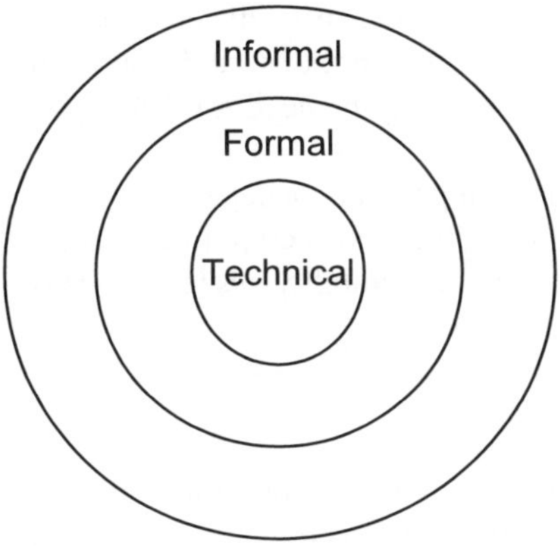

Fig. 6.1. The embedding of computer systems in the formal and informal organization. Adapted from Stamper et al., (2000: 19)

Semantic Interoperability and the TFI

Much interoperability literature explores semantic interoperability, whereby semantics is defined as the area of linguistics dealing with symbols and differences in the meaning of words. Hence semantics can refer simply to computer linguistics, or to linguistics of words that make up standards and policy, or could even infer an approach to treat 'meaning as a relationship between signs and human behaviour' (Stamper et al., 2000: 23).

Consistent with general interoperability research discussed above, much of the literature on semantic interoperability focuses on the technical domain (Harvey et al., 1999: 228). One such protagonist – Sheth (1996) – approached semantic differences with an engineering orientation, working on the concept of semantic proximity, demanding 'declarative language to articulate definitions of objects, and very strong ontological definitions'. Yet by 1997, working with Oeksel, an approach is taken to support a more general notion of semantics transpired, which relates the 'content and representation of information resources to entities and concepts in the real world' (Beech, 1997; Meersman, 1997; Sheth, 1997). That is, the limited forms of operational and axiomatic semantics of a particular representational or language framework are not sufficient.

For Bunge (1974), semantics is concerned not only with linguistic items, but also, and primarily, with the constructs such items stand for and their eventual relation to the real world (Lee and Siegel, 1996: 151). Accordingly, this gives credence to the proposition of a TFI framework incorporating the addition of a cross-sectional semantics. This can offer further value to incorporate the potential for 'seepage' between the different domains of the TFI. It embodies the impossibility of navigating differences in meaning to ensure absolute conformity, if this is possible, between disparate and dispersed social groups. A complex interoperability project may resemble more a melting pot than an assemblage of distinguishable layers of abstracted meaning. Furthermore, individuals construct different parameters according to their internal biases, norms and assumptions, and continually translate and interpret associated meanings – underlining the need for dealing with the semantics of each level of the TFI.

Having briefly described the TFI model in more general conceptual terms, and in relation to semantic interoperability, we move in the next section to illustrate its relevance and applicability for understanding interoperability issues of iDMS, particularly in the EU context.

Cases of Interoperability of Identity Systems in Europe

Threlfall, (2003) describes how 'the transferability of state pension rights was enlarged … in 1998 and became "portable"' through freedom of cross-border payments' (2003: 130). Interestingly, until the 1992 Treaty on European Union, free moving pensioners were not at liberty to burden their host country's health system. However, restrictive health entitlements made the maintenance of such compartmentalised health-care non-viable if not impossible in critical cases. By 1997, all community free movers were granted medical benefits, thus freedom of choice of residence for pensioners has therefore been widely enhanced, subject to the constraints of the individual's means. This brief example clearly engages with the messy, convoluted matter of interoperability and identity – and is moreover devoid of any reference to technical concerns. Hence, the ePensions domain will face political, organisational and social challenges, as well as having to build the foundations of an interconnected, interoperable technical platform.

A similar discussion by Threlfall (2003) within the health care domain offers supplementary evidence for considering interoperability in Europe as an important identity issue, as well as one which incorporates the abstraction of interoperability across the full spectrum of the TFI framework. The European Commission aims at improving the EU's healthcare system without direct interference in each country's delivery of health services (2003: 130-131). Nonetheless, in 1998,

> *Twin phenomena of 'patient mobility' (Wavell, 1998) and a 'Europe of Patients' (European Commission, 1999) had been created de jure, so that from the point of view of the patient's healthcare, they were living in the EU as in one country.*

Again, for the domain of eHealth, we are confronted with a plethora of interrelated technical, formal and informal elements. For example, a European Health Card replaced Form E111 in 2005, entailing much work on technical interoperability and the creation and revision of formal standards. Lastly, to exemplify an informal (behavioural) concern, 'implications [may ensue] arising from patients circumventing waiting lists by going to another member state'. eHealth clearly relates to identity, and its ultimate success will depend on satisfactorily addressing all the issues in each level of the TFI framework.

Overcoming purely technical hurdles will do little to reassure communities of the merits of a new information system, which may threaten privacy, trust and undermine cultural beliefs, i.e. a feeling of 'but that's not the way we do it round here'. For Wimmer (2002), identity considerations are crucial because 'citizens feel vulnerable when using eGovernment systems...they want to have security solutions, which provide subjective trust' (2002: 1). Here, the issue of privacy surfaces, as personal identity data exchange is a very sensitive subject (Homburg and Bekkers, 2002: 4-8). Further, privacy concerns become politically charged in practice as information exchange and standardisation across boundaries may reflect, legitimise and re-produce the discourses of powerful groups, validate their ways of steering and thinking, and give tangible force for their influence on organizational life (Bellamy, 1998).

These two examples of pensions and health underline that interoperability refers to much more than the technical, and that within the EU, identity is a term that also needs to be given value and meaning in this context. The following section presents an overview and summary of the current EU interoperability context, reiterating the challenges and indicating directions for future research and practice.

Using the TFI model, challenges to interoperability have been identified from an analysis of the holistic notion of interoperability and identity. Further, semantics are central to every level of abstraction and to the individual and contextual characteristics of citizens and communities, whether relating to the creation and exchange of metadata and communication protocols, establishing common agreed standards and policy between different national, legal and language borders, or relating to the flexible and dynamic meanings of interoperability and identity – and the associated understandings of their technical and formal structures.

As a forewarning, Mulley et al. (1999) construct a prophetic but disturbing conundrum,

> *Enhanced interoperability ... may be a catalyst for closer links between nation states, integrating and consolidating the EU and achieving a more equitable distribution of wealth. This may be broadly consistent with the aims of EU regional policies. Alternatively, greater interoperability ... may be a centralising force which concentrates wealth and leads to greater inequality; in opposition to the aims of regional policy. (1999: 97)*

Hopefully, steps being made towards multidisciplinary interoperability research might help circumvent the problems outlined by Mulley et al. and lead instead to a substantial reorganization of the research activities and cooperation in Europe (Chen and Doumeingts, 2003:162).

The next part of this chapter presents the findings of recent research into interoperability in iDMS undertaken as part of the FIDIS project. It is concerned with the perspective of different stakeholders on the issues at hand, thus moving beyond the official EU / governments agenda to exploring critically important aspects involved with interoperability. First, the views of experts from private and public sectors across Europe are presented. Following this, the perceptions and attitudes of EU citizens towards interoperable iDMS are discussed.

6.3 Stakeholders Perspectives on Interoperable iDMS

6.3.1 Expert Requirements for Interoperability

As part of the FIDIS project's work on interoperability, presented in D4.2, a number of European experts in eGovernment, eHealth and eCommerce applications were interviewed in 2005 to discover what they felt to be the key requirements that needed attention by policymakers in this area developing interoperable administrative systems. Although they hailed from different countries and backgrounds (see Appendix 1 for a full list) they showed remarkable consensus about the nature of the important issues in this field. Surprisingly, given their mostly technical backgrounds, the issues they identified were rarely seen as technological but almost always as social, political and cultural. In the section that follows we present the principal concerns that our group of experts, drawn mostly from the eHealth and eGovernment field, but also from eCommerce, saw as most in need of addressing at a policy and practice level. In any case, the issues that they have identified apply also to the field of eCommerce.

Control

Marc Sel took a strong position on citizen control over the access to and sharing of data, holding that 'identity management in e-commerce has only a chance of succeeding if it is clear from the beginning that the user remains in control of the identity management system'. Indeed his view was that interoperable systems as such would not be acceptable to the users unless they were, by default, controlled by the user. He viewed control as an issue that overlaps with acceptance, to which we refer below. Other experts took a slightly more pragmatic view holding that for the users to accept iDMS, it is important to find an acceptable balance between the 'automatic' interoperability of identity and the control that users desire to exercise over the use of their identity. Automatic interoperability implies that the rules that drive the system will have been pre-programmed so that the system does not revert to the user to make a discretionary choice of whether to share or reveal personal data to another system. Perhaps the user's preferences have been adequately represented in the programming. However, this has been a thorny issue, for in effect to obtain the efficiencies that are promised by interoperability, automatic operation would be highly desirable from a purely technical point of view. If adequate control cannot be automated in some way then systems that require regular user input are unlikely to deliver cost savings.

Security

Another important issue was security: identification must be secure and this security must be guaranteed. Further, Herbert Leitold believed that the art of 'eGovernment application design' lay in finding a solution which ensured high degrees of interoperability when necessary but that at the same time guaranteed a highly secure and privacy-rich environment. Another view on this came from the expert working in the EU, Olivier Libon, who emphasised a need for harmonization of all the security policies among governments: indeed if ministries want to participate in interoperable identity management systems, they might follow what is being developed and agreed by FEDICT, the Federal Public Service for Information and Communication Technology, which works within the Belgium government on these questions. An Austrian expert, Arno Hollosi, emphasised that to avoid privacy and security issues, eID solutions and national citizen registers should not be based on one single number! Besides, the main identifier should not be included in any digital certificate. As he pointed out, Austria's privacy laws forbade any collaboration with such a system.

Separate Identity 'Spaces'

A view advanced by Marc Sel regarding issues for citizens in respect of any identity management system referred to the need to understand that individuals operate in distinct 'spaces' where they act using different profiles. In general, he saw four 'spaces' as paramount: government, private, commercial, and private-public partnerships. These spaces are in principle separate and should not interact, unless explicitly designed to do so. One of the key issues is to understand to what extent individuals would want to act as one and the same interoperable individual across all these spaces, i.e., whether individuals require interoperable iDMS. In Sel's opinion, interoperability of iDMSs could lead to a loss of privacy, unless the spaces issue were appropriately addressed. Consequently, either the iDMSs should be confined to a specific space or it should be individual citizens who decide in which space they will act whether or not individual information could be shared across the spaces.

Data Protection Guarantees

One of the cornerstones of an iDMS is proper management of the privacy and data protection issues. Interoperability is often seen as opposed to privacy – sharing personal data runs counter to withholding it. As an example, it is unlikely that individuals want to give up the privacy they enjoy in their distinctive spaces and which they may enjoy currently without interoperable systems. The use of privacy profiles that are transparent, understandable and manageable by the end-users might be a way to maintain such privacy, in Sel's view. Herbert Leitold felt that the EU Signature Directive was not sufficient to fulfil Austria's requirements on privacy and data protection and that this would also most likely be true of other EU member states' legislation. As a result most EU member states will have to pass additional laws that might ultimately hinder interoperability on a legal level.

Trust in and Acceptance of Systems

Others, such as Paul Timmers, held that the dependability of systems was critical, that users should feel that the system worked properly and have trust in it. He saw trust and acceptance as a vital issue for technology adoption. Creating awareness and communicating with the users was critical in this trust dimension. Here, the main challenge in establishing interoperability of iDMSs lay in creating user awareness and communicating the benefits and functioning of the new system. Otherwise, users might go so far as not to use the system because of lack of trust or for concern with data protection or security. Asbjørn Følstad supported this position on the role of user acceptance, maintaining that any system needs to be easy to use and users must trust and use it with confidence. He said that the most challenging issue was related to users' understanding because users were more accustomed to signing paper and would probably understand the new technology in the same way. Also users need to be reassured of the data protection, especially because vendors tend to request excessive information. Følstad believed the most important success factor was user trust in the system where trust was seen as a function of good communication between the government and citizens. Therefore, the greatest challenge lay in user adoption of and trust in the system. If users have no confidence in data protection or functionality, they would not want to use identity cards or allow sharing of their information with other entities. Finally, any systems that emerge must pass the test of usability for the citizens in order not to be discredited.

Roles and Responsibilities

Frank Robben stressed the importance of roles and responsibilities in the system as even more important than interoperability per se. For example, in a hospital scenario, there might be people trying to access data that are not their own. Mandates are necessary to determine who can act on behalf of another person. There might be a central database of mandates or a set of local databases. He saw the need for the creation of a sub-committee of Privacy Commissions specialising in eHealth and responsible for protecting health information. This committee would decide on which entity is allowed to have what access to which personal information, about which patient, in which capacity, in which context, and for what length of time. Robben felt that users need to be taught how to handle their own data in such a way that governments or insurance companies do not get their hands on them unless absolutely necessary and only with permission; professionals, such as doctors, should also be made aware of their responsibility as authors and originators of much personal data and be made responsible for exercising their right to authorise every single access to their client or patient data.

Changing Public Administration

Olivier Libon pointed out that a critical issue regarding identity consists in establishing collaboration among different government bodies from different political or administrative levels. He notes that the federal state political system in Belgium, where identity-related responsibilities are the concern of various authorities, makes it impossible to offer integrated services without explicit collaboration among such governmental departments and agencies. For him, the central administration must act as an enabler by removing obstacles and creating the right environment for cooperation. Paul Timmers indicated a paramount issue of changing the culture of public administrations towards accepting a more modern administrative system. Arno Hollosi worked on the implementation of the Austrian Citizen Card intended as the 'Official identity document' used for all electronic administrative procedures and Hollosi holds interoperability to be critical for the project. The official slogan for the card is 'open interfaces for eGovernment'. Hollosi said that the main issues with the interoperability of identity systems appear to be security, privacy, and cost. For him, the high costs must be justified by adequate benefits flowing from the introduction of the card. The head of eGovernment projects in Belgium's social sector, Frank Robben, highlighted the importance of identity for the overall context of the government's responsibility for social care, pointing out that identity management would permit gains in efficiency and cost reductions: the information from tests and analyses, such as x-rays, could be re-used instead of being repeated by different health care units. The role of the GP, given the better access to information and control over patient welfare, would also be reinforced. Robben also considered that interoperability was not just about managing identities, but rather it encompassed the whole functioning of eHealth and would affect current roles and responsibilities within the system. He also stressed the necessity of ensuring high standards in registration and authentication procedures across different authorities in different countries. He said it was important to guarantee 'quality insurance criteria for the registration procedures that are used to determine the identity, and relevant characteristics or mandates before linking it to authentication or verification means'. Bettina Neke emphasised the role of reliable information on identities when dealing with patients. She also referred to the value of communication between GPs, pharmacists and other care providers.

Our experts came from different experiences and EU member states but nevertheless seemed to agree on many of the requirements that interoperable eGovernment and similar systems would have to address, in the area of identity-related concerns. A strong focus on citizen control was evident, especially from those from Germany with its 1983 constitutional commitment to 'informational self-determination', but also from others. We take this to be a warning to governments to avoid creating systems that appear to be extensions of the 'surveillance society' by ensuring that citizens will have real control over what data is held on them and how it is used. Other important issues singled out by the experts were regarding security, data protection guarantees, trust and acceptance of systems and importantly clarity about who is responsible for important decisions regarding the sharing of personal data. These concerns are echoed in our next section that depicts citizens' views on these same matters.

6.3.2 Citizens Perceptions on Interoperability

In respect of plans for interoperable European electronic ID system, we conducted a research as part of the FIDIS project designed to investigate EU citizens' perceptions and attitudes towards issues involved in making eIDs interoperable (FIDIS Deliverable D 4.4 (Backhouse and Halperin, 2007)). This study formed part of the research effort to deepen understanding of the social and cultural questions associated with interoperable ID systems. Focus was placed on informal aspects associated with interoperability, a relatively under-researched layer of the TFI framework. Whilst many of the EU projects in the interoperability domain tend to privilege the engineering and legal perspectives on harmonising and interoperating identity management systems, the role of citizens' feelings and perceptions has not yet been sufficiently considered.

In what follows we illustrate research results that emerged from analyzing both qualitative[5] and quantitative data gathered from citizens on their attitudes towards interoperable iDMS (Backhouse and Halperin, 2007; 2008). The issues addressed concern the exchange of personal data across government departments, between governments and commerce, and between different European countries.

Citizen Interests: Representation and Protection

> *I believe that my interests will be represented in deciding how ID data will be exchanged.*

This statement was put forward in our survey to stimulate responses from EU citizens in terms of their agreement level. The results shown in the figure below

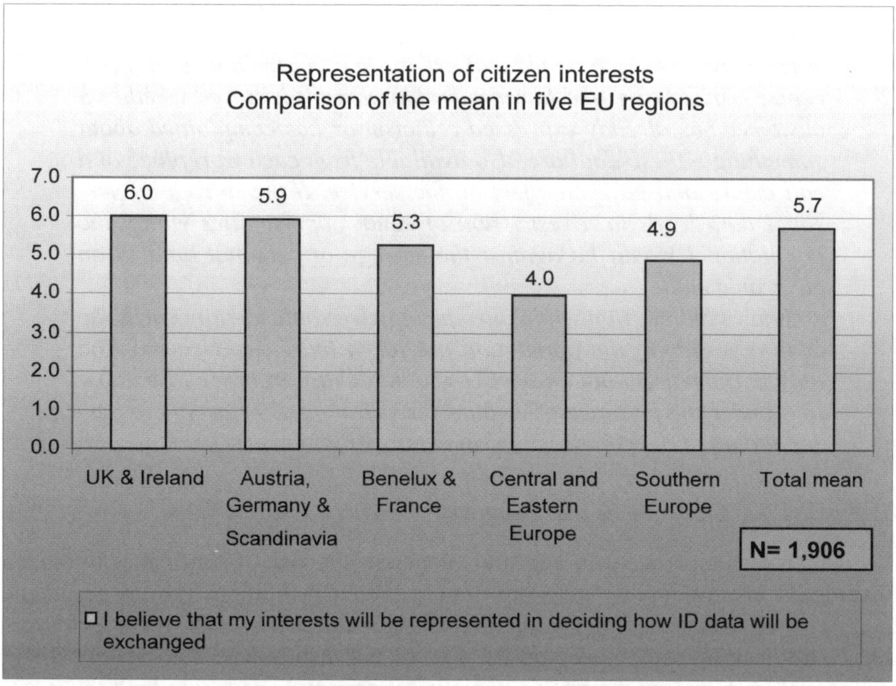

Fig. 6.2. Perceptions of citizens' interests being represented when ID data is shared

5 All figures presented below show results of a survey reported in full as part of D4.4, available at www.fidis.net. Survey respondents were asked to rate their agreement with a list of statements on a seven-point Likert scale. In all cases, 1 represents strong agreement with the statement and 7 strong disagreement. The midpoint of the scale is at 4 (as the scale starts at 1). In the presentation that follows, we maintain the original structure of answers, where numbers less than 4 show degrees of agreement with the statement and numbers greater than 4 show disagreement. The middle point of the scale is 4, which we interpret here as neither agreement nor disagreement.

suggest that respondents tend to disagree that their interests will be represented in deciding how ID data will be exchanged. Respondents from UK and Ireland are the most pessimistic, but Austria, Germany and Scandinavia come very close. The average for Central and Eastern Europe is at the midpoint of the agreement scale.

From the analysis of the qualitative data (free text voluntarily provided by the survey respondents), further evidence for negative perceptions emerged. The issue of the citizen interests and the extent to which such interests are sought to be represented and protected in the context of a EU wide, interoperable iDMS, was addressed, e.g., in the following statements made by two different citizens:

> *I regard the exchange between enterprises and authorities as problematic because there are interests involved which citizens don't share (marketing, product optimisation, advertisement geared to the target group...). Even at this stage enterprises divide residential areas in more well funded and less well funded ones – and treat those citizens living in rich residential areas – e.g., in the queue of a call centre – in a faster and fairer way. Moreover it is stored whether a customer has already expressed criticism or has complained about something – these data are also available from each workplace of a call centre and have an effect on the service. If the storage of personal data leads to a restriction of equal opportunities within the population I would be against the storage of personal data in an electronic mode.*
>
> *I don't believe that while introducing electronic identity cards the desires / needs of the population are taken into consideration. The only purpose is to obtain an EU-wide database in order to be able to – under the pretence of counter-terrorism – easier access to personal data of the population, dragnet investigation etc.*

ID Authorities: Competence and Integrity

A related issue that arose from the study concerns the lack of confidence of citizen towards ID institutions. Citizens are dubious about institutions' ability to handle their personal data securely. Two main reasons include: perceived incompetence – that is, the lack of competence on the part of the institutions, both technical and managerial, and, lack of integrity – namely, fairness and honesty in both the intentions and actions of the institutions responsible for iDMS.

This perception of institutional incompetence is illustrated in statements such as the following:

> *I believe the authorities will attempt to be honest and secure but ultimately will be unsuccessful in maintaining the confidentiality of my data.*
>
> *I feel the authorities will fail to deliver a secure, working system. It will be a monumental waste.*

I am not against ID cards in principle, but have grave doubts about the competence of those running the system. Human error is probably a bigger risk then IT.

When asked explicitly whether competent institutions will monitor the exchange of ID data, respondents were slightly more optimistic, but overall responses were still negative. Central and Eastern Europe showed a level of optimism, with a mean of 3.3. Results of the survey are shown in the figure below.

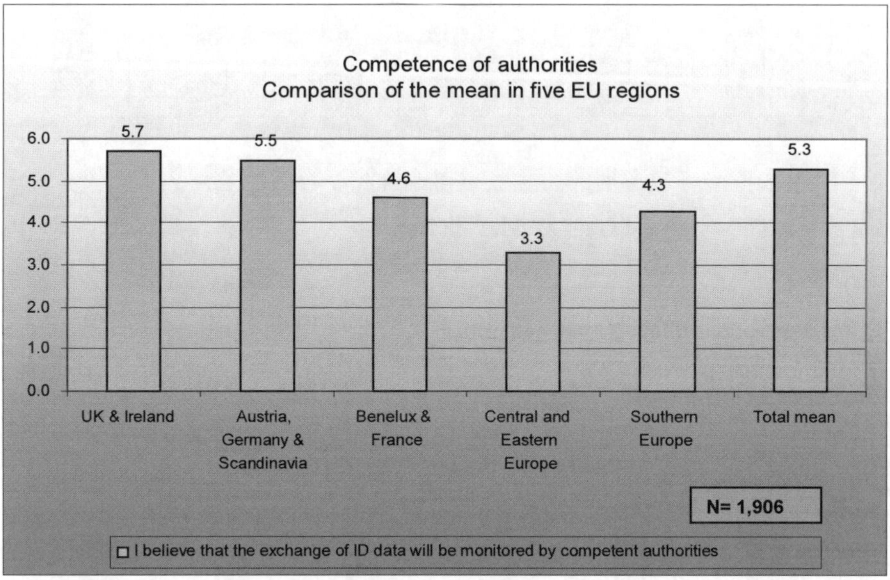

Fig. 6.3. Perceptions of competence of authorities

On the issue of integrity, the statements below were used in the survey to stimulate responses from citizens, and these are followed by the overall level of agreement across EU regions.

I believe that ID authorities will always act in my best interest.

I believe that ID authorities will be truthful and honest when dealing with my data.

As we can see from the diagram above, the majority of respondents did not believe that ID authorities would act in their interest or deal fairly with their data, with an overall mean of 6.0 and 5.4. UK and Ireland rate highest together with the group of Austria, Germany and Scandinavia.

Additional findings emerged from the qualitative data and are manifested in the following quotes:

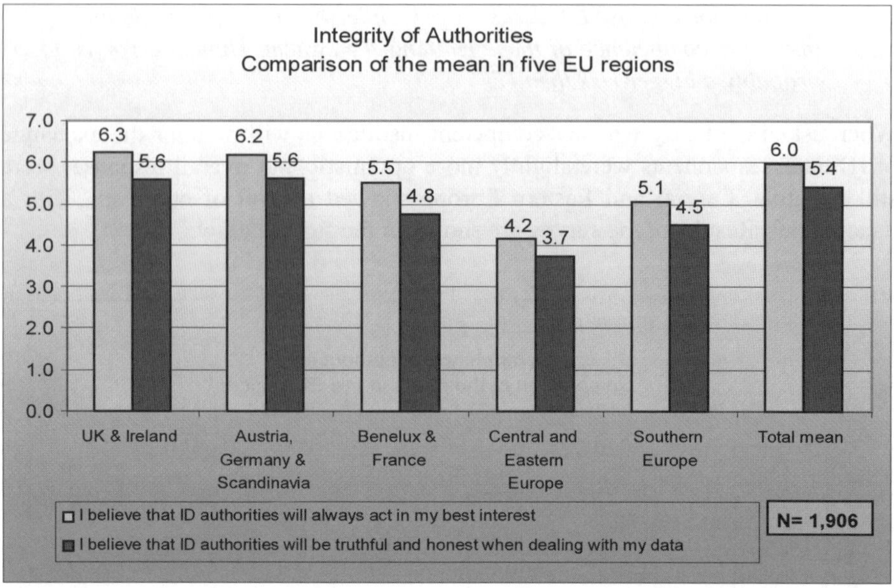

Fig. 6.4. Perceptions of integrity of authorities

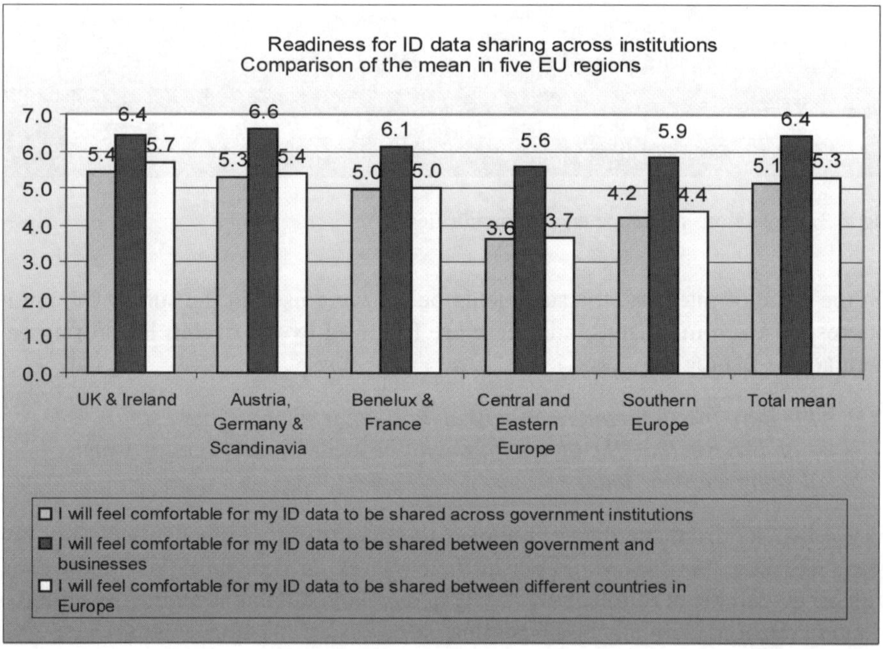

Fig. 6.5. Readiness to share ID data

> *...our Government will hand over our data to the CIA or any other organisation they care to without telling us.*
>
> *I am very concerned about the misuse of ID information especially considering links between government and industry.*

It follows that citizens feel uncomfortable and reluctant for their ID data to be shared across agencies, as evident in Figure 6.5.

Results indicate that the overall readiness to welcome cooperation between government and business was very low (6.4), while there was only some reluctance to share data within the government (5.1) or across different European countries (5.3). This pattern can be found in all the five regions.

Risk / Benefit: Assessment of Tradeoffs

As discussed earlier on in Section 6.2, the EU as well as European member states such as the UK have been pushing the interoperability agenda, attributing many benefits associated with data sharing and the exchange of personal information across government agencies, EU governments and the private sectors. Yet, when assessing the balance between risk and benefit involved in iDMS, EU citizens, unlike their governments, seem far from convinced that the benefits outweigh the risks.

> *What is the whole drama good for? I don't believe that an electronic identity card contributes to more security; rather it will animate even more enterprises etc. to collect data. In this context it is tried via telling scare stories to collect more data than necessary about every single person and – without us being able to comprehend it – to transfer more data than necessary. So – how does the single citizen benefit from that?*
>
> *They enable the state to totally control individuals but they don't bring any benefits – even not security technology benefits- for the individual at all.*

A more moderate perception is manifested in the statement below; nevertheless the bottom line is against the cross-linking of personal data.

> *I am convinced that the electronic identity card will facilitate bureaucratic seesaw considerably and I appreciate that. However, I don't trust the people at authorities and in commerce who deal with my data und gather information about me. The electronic identity card will make it more difficult for me to securely maintain my "official" privacy and depending on what information about me may circulate it maybe will be disadvantageous. That's my fear. If I have enough secure information about this question I possibly will be more open-minded about the crosslinking of my personal data.*

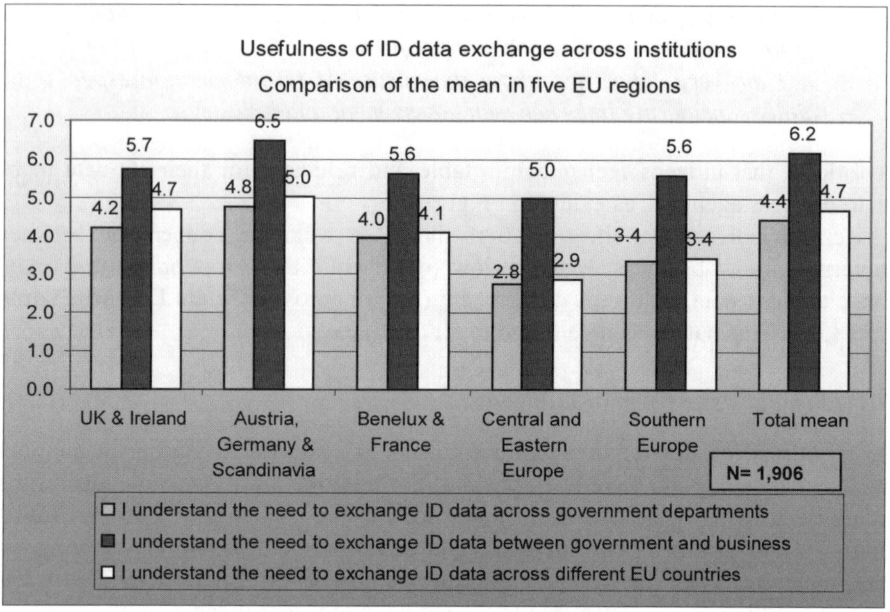

Fig. 6.6. Perceptions of usefulness of sharing ID data

In all five regions the exchange of ID data between government and business received the highest disagreement score, with an overall mean of 6.2 on the seven point scale. Austria, Germany and Scandinavia together were the most negative about the exchange of ID data. The overall mean of data exchange across government departments (4.4) is surprisingly positive. Data exchange between government departments as well as between different EU countries was well supported, especially in the new member countries and the southern part of Europe. Nevertheless, the total mean figure suggests negative perceptions.

In conclusion, findings arising from our study point to an overall negative perception held by EU citizens regarding interoperable iDMS. The vast majority of the respondents do not trust the relevant institutions; they are seriously critical about the competence of the authorities, and are dubious about their ability to handle personal data with appropriate care. Moreover, they are suspicious of the authorities misusing their identity data. Citizens are concerned about the extent to which their interests will be sufficiently represented and protected, or be undermined by political and commercial ones. Finally, upon assessing the balance between risk and benefit involved in interoperable iDMS, EU citizens, unlike their governments, seem unconvinced that the benefits outweigh the risks. Addressing the negative perceptions of citizens is of paramount importance: these perceptions hold implications for any future attempts at implementing iDMS, as they may well be translated into subsequent behaviours, namely, resistance to use or, indeed, non-use.

6.4 Conclusion

At the same time as more European states develop electronic identity cards for identity management, the European Union has been pushing its interoperability agenda in both eHealth and eGovernment as part of its aim to support the mobility of EU citizens and develop for them seamless provision of government and health services no matter the location in Europe. The study of interoperability in the context of iDMS was carried out as part of the EU FIDIS project, and the research outlined in this chapter reports on some of this work.

Our aim in this chapter was first to develop an understanding of the term interoperability as it currently applies to the area of identity management. The conceptual discussion of the term argued for a move beyond a technical understanding of interoperability to a three-fold conception of interoperability in iDMS, involving technical, but also formal-policy, legal and regulatory components, as well as informal-behavioural and cultural aspects. The TFI model was then introduced and illustrated as a useful lens for directing research attention to the different aspects of interoperability and the interrelation between them in different contexts and meanings.

Following the conceptual discussion in part one (Section 6.2), the second part of the chapter (Section 6.3) drew on empirical findings concerned with the perspective of important stakeholders on interoperability issues. First, a selection of views of experts from private and public sectors across Europe was presented[6]. Following this, the perceptions and attitudes of EU citizens towards interoperable iDMS were discussed. Together, the findings presented point to the crucial challenges, risks and implications associated with the sharing of personal data in the provision of eGovernment, eHealth and eCommerce.

References

Backhouse, J. (1996), 'Information@Risk', Information Strategy 3: 33-5.

Backhouse, J. and Halperin, R. (eds.) (2007), *FIDIS Deliverable D4.4: Survey on Citizen's trust in ID systems and authorities*, Download: www.fidis.net.

Backhouse, J. and Halperin, R. (2008), 'Security and Privacy Perceptions of eID: A Grounded Research', *European Conference on Information Systems*, Galway, Ireland.

Bellamy, C. and Taylor, J. (1998), *Governing in the information age.* Open University Press, Buckingham.

Beech, D. (1997), 'Data semantics on the information superhighway', pp 12-33 in: Meersman, R., Mark, L. (eds.), *Database Application Semantics*. Chapman and Hall.

Brodeur, J. et al. (2003), 'Revisiting the Concept of Geospatial Interoperability within the Scope of Human Communication Processes', *Transactions in GIS* 7 (2): 243-265.

BTT: Biometric Technology Today Sept 2003.

6 For a fuller picture, please consult the report (D4.2) available at www.fidis.net.

Castells, M. (2001), *The Internet Galaxy: Reflections on the Internet, Business, and Society*. Oxford University Press: Oxford.

Chen, D. and Doumeingts, G. (2003), 'European initiatives to develop interoperability of enterprise applications – basic concepts, framework and roadmap', *Annual Reviews in Control* 27: 153-162.

Choi, S.-Y. and Whinston, A. B. (2000), 'Benefits and requirements for interoperability in the electronic marketplace', *Technology in Society* 22: 33-44.

European Commission DGV (1999), 'Free Movement and Social Security: Citizens' Rights when Moving within the EU', Bulletin No. 2.

Harvey, F. et al. (1999), 'Semantic interoperability: A central issue for sharing geographic information', *The Annals of Regional Science* 33: 213-232.

Homburg, V. andBekkers, V. (2002) 'The Back-Office of E-Government (Managing Information Domains as Political Economies)', *IEEE proceedings of the 35th Hawaii International Conference on System Sciences*.

IDABC (2005), 'European Interoperability Framework for Pan-European eGovernment Services', V 1.0. http://ec.europa.eu/idabc/servlets/Doc?id=19529.

Kinder, T. (2003), 'Mrs Miller moves house: the interoperability of local public services in Europe', *Journal of European Social Policy* 13 (2): 141-157.

Klischewski, R. (2003), 'Top Down or Bottom Up? How to Establish a Common Ground for Semantic Interoperability within e-Government Communities', in Traunmüller, R., Palmirani, M. (eds.), *E-Government: Modelling Norms and Concepts as Key Issues, Proceedings of 1st International Workshop on E-Government at ICAIL 2003. Bologna: Geditedizioni*, 17-26.

Kraemer, K. L. and King, J. L. (1986), 'Computing and Public Organisations', *Public Administration Review*, Special Issue: 488-496.

Landsbergen, D. and Wolken, G. (2001), 'Realizing the promise: Government Information Systems and the Fourth Generation of Information Technology', *Public Administration Review* 61 (2): 206-220.

Liebenau, J. and Backhouse, J. (1990), *Understanding Information: An Introduction*. Basingstoke and London, Macmillan Press.

Lee, J. L. and Siegel, M. D. (1996), 'An ontological and semantical approach to source-receiver interoperability', *Decision Support Systems* 18: 145-158.

Meersman, R. (1997), 'An essay on the role and evolution of data(base) semantics', pp 1-7 in: Meersman, R. and Mark, L. (eds.), *Database Application Semantics*. Chapman and Hall.

Miller, B. et al. (2001), 'Towards a Framework for Managing the Information Environment', *Information, Knowledge, Systems Management* 2: 359-384.

Moen, W. E. (1994), 'Information Technology Standards: A Component of Federal Information Policy', *Government Information Quarterly* 1 (4): 357-371.

Moen, W. E. (2000), 'Interoperability for Information Access: Technical Standards and Policy Considerations', *The Journal of Academic Librarianship* 26 (2): 129-132.

Mulley, C. and Nelson, J. D. (1999), 'Interoperability and transport policy: the impediments to interoperability in the organisation of trans-European transport systems', *Journal of Transport Geography* 7 (2): 93-104.

Ouksel, A. M. and Sheth, A. (1999), 'Semantic Interoperability in Global Information Systems: A brief introduction to the research area and the special section', *SIGMOD Record* 28 (1): 5-12.

Prokopiadou G., Papatheodorou C., Moschopoulos D. (2004) 'Integrating knowledge management tools for government information', *Government Information Quarterly* 21: 170-198.

Stamper, R. et al. (2000), 'Understanding the roles of signs and norms in organisations – a semiotic approach to information systems design', *Behaviour & Information Technology* 19 (1): 15-27.

Schnittger, B. (2005), 'Introducing IDABC: European Integration by Electronic Means', *SYNeRGY* (01), 3-6.

Scholl, H. J. (2005), 'Interoperability in E-Government: More than Just Smart Middleware', *HICSS '05. Proceedings of the 38th Annual Hawaii International Conference on System Sciences*, 123-123.

Sheth, A. (1996), 'Data Semantics: What, Where and How?' Paper presented at the 6th IFIP Working Conference on Data Semantics (DS-6), Atlanta, GA.

Sheth, A. (1997, 3+4 December 1997), 'Semantic Interoperability in Infocosm: Beyond Infrastructural and data interoperability in federated information systems', Paper presented at the International Conference on Interoperating Geographic Systems (Interop'97), Santa Barbara.

Threlfall, M. (2003), 'European social integration: harmonization, convergence and single social areas', *Journal of European Social Policy* 13 (2): 121-139.

Wavell, S. (1998), 'Your Very Good Health – in a Foreign Body', Sunday Times, 31 May: 11.

Wimmer, M. and Von Bredow, B. (2002), 'A holistic approach for providing security solutions in e-government', *System Sciences. HICSS. Proceedings of the 35th Annual Hawaii International Conference*, 1715-1724.

Woodall, S. R. (2000), 'Self-jamming behaviour: Joint Interoperability, Root Causes, and Thoughts on Solutions', *Comparative Strategy* 19:, 309-317.

Appendix: Experts

Asbjørn Følstad
Norwegian research scientist in the ICT division of SINTEF working on interoperability, quality assurance and usability of information systems. Recent work has involved assessing the level that trust plays in system adoption and system use when new technologies are introduced.

Arno Hollosi
Joined the Stabstelle IKT-Strategie des Bundes in Austria in 2001 and since then he has been its Technical Director. The Stabstelle IKT-Strategie des Bundes is the Central Information Office (CIO) of the Austrian government. Mr. Hollosi is responsible for developing and coordinating the technical aspects of eGovernment projects in Austria.

Herbert Leitold
Holds the position of Director Technology at A-SIT, ZentrumfürsichereInformationstechnologie, founded in 1999 by the Austrian Ministry of Finance, the Austrian National Reserve Bank and the Technical University of Graz. Its mission is

to undertake ICT research for the use of eGovernment. In recent years A-SIT worked closely with the IKT-Board and the CIO of Office of the Austrian Federal Chancellor. Mr. Leitold is further an advisor on eGovernment projects.

Olivier Libon
Project Manager in Belgium, FedICT Security Architect (FedICT: Federal Public Service on Information and Communication Technology; www.fedict.be). Adviser for the Tractebel Group and the European Commission, he then joined GlobalSign (the European leading certification authority) as Vice President. He joined FedICT (the Belgian ministry of ICT) in 2002 before the launch of the BelPIC project (Belgian electronic Personal Identity Card) as security architect and PKI expert.

Erik Lindmo
Hasa MSc in civil engineering from Stanford, CA, and has been working in the banking sector for 25 years. He is currently the CIO for payment systems in DNB Norway, and has been working on the BankID project for the past year.

Bettina Neke
Works for Ministry of Social Affairs of the Federal Land of Schleswig-Holstein, Germany, and is responsible for the eHealth card project in Schleswig-Holstein. She works in the Ministry of Social Affairs Schleswig-Holstein, responsible for all political activities concerning this project. She has a professional background as a lawyer.

Frank Robben
General manager of the Crossroads Bank for Social Security which works on eGovernment strategy and coordinates the implementation of the eGovernment projects in the social security sector.

Marc Sel
Director, PriceWaterhouseCoopers, Antwerp, Belgium.Responsible for projects including the Belgian Electronic ID card project and the Belgian Digital Tachograph Project.

Paul Timmers
Head of unit for eGovernment in the European Commission, Directorate-General Information Society & Media. Previously he was a member of the Cabinet of the European Commissioner for Enterprise and Information Society. He has also been deputy head of unit for electronic commerce in the European Commission, where he was involved in policy and program development.

Gerhard Weck
Licensed IT Baseline Protection Auditor and Chief IT Security Officer at INFODAS in Germany. He is an IT security lecturer at the Ulm Academy for Data Protection and IT Security (Ulmer AkademiefürDatenschutz und IT-Sicherheit, www.udis.de) and spokesman of the DECUS professional group for security (www.decus.de).

VIGNETTE 6: MORE CONTROL FOR THE MACHINES*

Softwars

Frank is at home recovering from stress while Fanny is in Egypt on business. The school where Frank is teaching has recently started implementing the virtual learning environment (VLE): a personalised interactive learning coach which measures the progress of students in relation to targets that have been set. Since its implementation the system has not run well and has caused the teachers serious stress. This, combined with the fear of becoming redundant because of this implementation, has caused Frank to have a severe burn-out.

Frank only went to see his GP once. After his doctor diagnosed that Frank was suffering from a burn-out, he told him that the rest of the recovery trajectory could be done conveniently at home with the help of a *Medicheck* device. Frank's health insurance company will refund most of his costs on the condition that he permanently wears the *Medicheck* which can be rented at the local health centre. The *Medicheck* consists of a tight t-shirt with sensors monitoring heart rate, muscle tension, bodily posture, etc. A virtual doctor is activated when the measured signals reach certain values.

As he has the feeling that nobody really listens to his issues and because he would like to create some order in the chaotic feelings and thoughts he is experiencing he also decides to buy the *Psychicheck* – a mental wellbeing monitoring system, which according to the ads provides a permanent listening ear and personalised advice. The device registers the frequency in which certain words are uttered in combination with other words. It also measures the pitch of voice, sentence length and facial expression. It is able to take the registered domestic preferences profiled by his intelligent home into account: 'It would be good to stick to your normal daily routine and get up at 07.45' is the therapeutic advice based on the profiled user. One of the pleasant aspects about the *Psychicheck* is that it is designed as a user-friendly little robot dog called 'Fifi'. The social interface of this device makes it nice to interact with.

One night Frank cannot fall asleep due to a bad headache. He feels sad partly because of missing Fanny. Fifi picks up on Frank's mood and inquires as to what is wrong. After sharing his feelings, Fifi, based on Frank's leisure profile from his intelligent home, suggests that they watch a movie together. During a bloody cli-

* This scenario is based on FIDIS deliverable D12.5, Chapter 3, by Mark Gasson (READING), Katja de Vries (VUB), and Niels van Dijk (VUB).

max in the movie in which the main character is about to be violently attacked, Frank's *Medicheck* suddenly switches on. It reports exceeded heart rate and advises Frank to abort his stress causing activity. Frank wants to see how the movie ends and consults his *Psychicheck* which advises him to continue watching. Frank decides to ignore his *Medicheck* although his arm starts to cramp a little…

A Romantic Confusion of Identity

Fanny is in Egypt for a business trip. She feels quite uncomfortable about leaving Frank at home since he is experiencing such a difficult time. Now that they are separated by a huge distance, she is very pleased that they both have implanted in their hands an active electrode which wirelessly connects them. She is at the airport waiting for her flight when she remembers how she and Frank decided to do this on Valentine's Day. The active electrodes (both connected to wireless internet) were implanted into one of the nerves of their left hands. If one of them moves their fingers (creating a certain pattern of motor neural signal pulses) in a specific way (their 'secret' gesture) the other one will perceive this – even if they are separated by a huge distance. The couple experience this as being very romantic: one can 'feel' each other even when separated in space. However she has noticed on several occasions that the incoming signals confuse the monitoring system of her *Medicheck* (her travel insurance requires her to wear one during her stay in Egypt). Every time the muscle contractions were registered by the *Medicheck* as an unusual signal. She had to manually specify that the signals were coming from a trusted 'outside source'.

Pre-paid RoadMiles Cards & Interoperability

Fanny is driving in a rented car from Cairo to Alexandria where she has a business appointment. Before leaving Cairo the owner of the shop where Fanny rented the car tried to explain to her something about the 'mile-tax' card she had to insert into the ignition slot, but his English was so broken that she had difficulty understanding him. However, she assumed that the mile-tax system was more or less comparable to the system in the UK. Car owners in the UK use 'RoadMiles' cards which are linked to their account – and once a month an automatic payment of the due tax is made. When you rent a car in the UK you pay the amount of tax due to the car rental after returning the car. What Fanny did not know is that in Egypt you buy pre-paid 'RoadMiles' cards at the petrol station in order to drive. This system is used due to the lack of facilitating the required technological infrastructure and is also more privacy enhancing (you can buy your pre-paid card anonymously).

Somewhere in the middle of nowhere Fanny's car suddenly slows down and stops. Fanny wonders what the reason might be. Has the car noticed that her eyes became more and more tired? Impossible, the technology of this car is not smart enough to detect such complex facial features! When a car passes she waves for help. An Egyptian driver stops, smiles and tells her in a mix of Arabic and hardly comprehensible English that she needs to have a new pre-paid card. 'Where should I get one?' she asks. The Egyptian car driver shrugs, smiles, and drives away again. There she is, on her own in the middle of the desert. She begins to panic. Hours later she gets to Alexandria – she had to leave her car in the desert and was given a lift in a carpet truck to her destination. Of course she is still stressed by the course of events, but fortunately the business people she had to meet are still in town and the business meeting can still take place.

During the meeting her hand with the wireless electrode begins to hurt – this is certainly not Frank's secret gesture! Fanny thinks that it has something to do with the slight stress she has experienced. She takes a deep breath and her hand muscles relax. However, this is really not the time to think about those things – in the middle of her meeting. Fanny's *Medicheck* device starts to beep. On the screen it says: 'physiological anomaly'. Fanny is irritated by this intervention. She is fine, why is this device bothering her?! So she selects the 'no problem: natural cause for stress' option. When the alert goes off again she ignores the alert – she has to do business now!

Fifteen minutes later however an ambulance arrives at the business centre and its staff barges into the conference room. They slightly hesitate when looking at Fanny who is identified as the source of the distress signal. They are surprised that she looks perfectly fine. The audience slowly turns silent. The medical team turn to Fanny, who has now stopped her lecture, and ask if she is doing well and could go to the ambulance to do a medical check. Fanny follows them, confused by the whole scene…

Intermezzo: A Revealing Phone Call

While Fanny is sitting in a cab heading for the airport Frank appears on her My-Comm device. He looks very concerned because he has been notified about the *Medicheck* incident. Frank tells her that apparently the alarming signal that was received by the hospital in Egypt from Fanny's *Medicheck* device was caused by an unlucky coincidence. When Frank was watching the movie his stress level and muscular tension rose strongly and affected the implanted electrode in his hand. Normally these signals would have been immediately transmitted to Fanny, but her stay in the desert with no wireless connection made direct transmission impossible. Shortly after her arrival in the connection node of Alexandria all the delayed signals where received simultaneously. This caused a peak signal picked up by the *Medicheck* which was unable to find a contextual reason for it. Frank also says that the travel insurance company is not willing to pay for the cost of the ambulance since these are caused by the interference of the implant – and as such not covered by the insurance policy.

Citizenchip

Fanny arrives at the airport of Cairo and proceeds to the check-in. Since the European Commission has negotiated a border control system at the entrance gates to Europe, a chip detection system has been installed. People are immediately categorised according to the kind of chip implanted into them: European citizen*chip*, US citizen*chip*, chips provided to selected immigrants who are still in an immigration or asylum procedure. A few months ago Fanny read a news bulletin on her MyComm that there were massive demonstrations in the North African countries against the implementation of this system and the creation of a 'chipless' caste.

When Fanny passes the scanning zone, red lights suddenly start to flash. Fanny is asked to accompany the security staff for further examination. It turns out that the scanning system is unable to categorise her unambiguously due to her double citizenchip (both European/British and Chinese). According to Egyptian law only single citizenchip is allowed and thus the system is incapable of processing double citizenchip. Solving the confusion takes quite a while and Fanny almost misses her flight...

The visions and thoughts expressed in this vignette are inspired and based on various discussions, and results of the FIDIS Network of Excellence as well as the authors' personal experiences and expectations. Partially, underlying concepts and ideas of this vignette are described in Chapters 5, 7 and 10.

7 Profiling and AmI

Mireille Hildebrandt

Summary. Some of the most critical challenges for '*the future of identity in the information society*' must be located in the domain of automated profiling practices. Profiling technologies enable the construction and application of group profiles used for targeted advertising, anti-money laundering, actuarial justice, etc. Profiling is also *the conditio sine qua non* for the realisation of the vision of Ambient Intelligence. Though automated profiling seems to provide the only viable answer for the increasing information overload and though it seems to be a promising tool for the selection of relevant and useful information, its invisible nature and pervasive character may affect core principles of democracy and the rule of law, especially privacy and non-discrimination. In response to these challenges we suggest novel types of protection next to the existing data protection regimes. Instead of focusing on the *protection of personal data*, these novel tools focus on the *protection against invisible or unjustified profiling*. Finally, we develop the idea of Ambient Law, advocating a framework of technologically embedded legal rules that guarantee a transparency of profiles that should allow European citizens to decide which of their data they want to hide, when and in which context.

So far, profiling has not been the subject of a coherent, cross-disciplinary knowledge domain. Research is fragmented between computer engineers, social studies, lawyers, mathematicians, and those working on specific applications within for instance medical research, marketing or forensic science. Profiling is often reduced to data mining and discussed in highly technical terms (Fayyad et al., 1996) or from a social theory perspective in terms of semiotic or Deleuzian inquiries (Elmer, 2004; Hildebrandt, 2008). A coherent legal perspective on profiling, integrating privacy and data protection, non-discrimination, liability issues and forensic profiling has not been attempted yet, even if partial analyses have been made within the context of the FIDIS network (Schreurs et al., 2008; Hildebrandt and Koops, 2007; Geradts and Sommer, 2008).[1] For this reason FIDIS has devoted serious attention to the question

[1] From a legal perspective analyses are often made in terms of the protection of personal data, whereas specific attention to the legal status of profiles, especially group profiles is lacking.

of what profiling actually is, how it can be defined and explained in a way that is easily understandable across different disciplines. This will be discussed in Section 7.1, mainly building on the cross-disciplinary findings of *Profiling the European Citizen* (Hildebrandt and Gutwirth, 2008).

An important domain of research within the framework programmes of the European Commission as well as within industry is what has been coined as Ambient Intelligence (AmI), ubiquitous computing or autonomic computing. One could translate these terms into the idea of a 'smart' adaptive environment that requires little deliberate human intervention. Though AmI depends on a series of enabling technologies for its realisation of smart environments, profiling can be seen as the enabling technology, because to make sense out of the 'tsunami' of data that is generated by RFID systems and sensor technologies, profiling is essential.[2] In Section 7.2 we address profiling within the context of AmI.

To assess the impact of profiling technologies on the identity of European citizens two notions of identity have been introduced and explored within the FIDIS network, coined by the French philosopher Paul Ricoeur: idem and ipse. Idem (sameness) stands for the third person, objectified observer's perspective of identity as a set of attributes that allows comparison between different people, as well as unique identification, whereas ipse (self) stands for the first person perspective constituting a 'sense of self'. Their intersection provides for the construction of a person's identity. In Section 7.3 these concepts will be further explored and their relevance for democracy and rule of law will be discussed, pointing out that privacy as a matter of boundary negotiations and identity construction necessitates understanding privacy as a private interest as well as a public good.

After having discussed the risks of increased profiling throughout Sections 7.1, 2 and 3, we turn to a discussion of the legal implications. Data protection and privacy rights provide a legal framework that is mostly focused on the protection of personal data. With regards to the kind of threats generated by refined profiling a complementary focus is needed on protection against unwarranted application of profiles. On top of that the legal framework still 'thinks' in terms of the technologies of the script, which renders it ineffective in protecting against dangers afforded by the technologies of the digital and the virtual. In Section 7.4 this challenge is taken up in exploring the notion of Ambient Law (AmLaw), i.e., a type of law that is articulated into the socio-technical infrastructure that it aims to protect against.

Section 7.5 provides some concise conclusions.

---

2 The phrase 'tsunami' of data was used in The Future Group Report (2008), written by the Informal High Level Advisory Group on the Future of European Home Affairs Policy. 'The findings and recommendations of the Future Group are meant to be an important contribution and a source of inspiration for the European Commission's proposal for the next multi-annual program in the field of Justice and Home Affairs', see the report at p.3.

7.1 Profiling: Definitions, Applications and Risks

Profiling occurs in a diversity of contexts: from criminal investigation to marketing research, from mathematics to computer engineering, from healthcare applications for elderly people to genetic screening and preventive medicine, from forensic biometrics to immigration policy, from credit scoring to actuarial justice. Looking into these different domains it soon becomes clear that the term profiling is used to refer to a set of technologies that share at least one common characteristic: the use of algorithms or other mathematical (computer) techniques to create, discover or construct knowledge out of huge sets of data. Automated profiling involves different technologies (hardware), such as computers, RFID-tags, biometric applications and sensors, and techniques (software), such as data cleansing, data aggregation and data mining. These technologies and techniques are integrated into socio-technical profiling practices that allow both the construction and the application of profiles. Profiles are used to make decisions, sometimes even without human intervention. The visions of Ambient Intelligence, autonomic and ubiquitous computing depend entirely on autonomic profiling, the type of profiling that allows machines to communicate with other machines and take decisions without human intervention.

7.1.1 What Is Profiling?[3]

Before proceeding to describe some of the applications and some of the risks, we need a provisional definition to clear the ground. A working definition of profiling should take into account that the term is used both for the construction of profiles and their application:

> *Profiling is the process of 'discovering' patterns in data in databases that can be used to identify or represent a human or nonhuman subject (individual or group) and/or the application of profiles (sets of correlated data) to individuate and represent an individual subject or to identify a subject as a member of a group (which can be an existing community or a 'discovered' category).*[4]

The difference between the construction and the application of profiles is a first important distinction to be made when discussing profiling, which will be discussed hereunder. After that, three more distinctions will be discussed: the difference between individual and group profiling, between direct and indirect profiling and the difference and the one between distributive and non-distributive profiling.

---

[3] This section builds on FIDIS deliverables 7.2/3/4/5 and on part I of *Profiling the European Citizen* (Hildebrandt and Gutwirth, 2008).

[4] See Hildebrandt and Gutwirth (2008: 19).

Construction and Application of Profiles

As mentioned above, machine profiling makes use of mathematical techniques to uncover patterns that are invisible to the naked human eye. The process of profiling is often broken down to a series of 5 or 6 subsequent steps, that are interrelated and looped together in a process of constant feed-back. This process is called knowledge discovery in databases (KDD) and can be summed up as follows:

1. recording of data in a machine-readable, computable manner
2. storing and aggregating of data in databases
3. data mining, i.e. running algorithms through the database
4. interpreting the results
5. applying the resulting profiles to new data (matching) and monitoring for outliers

To highlight the feed-back that is constitutive of profiling Gasson and Browne (2008) visualise the different steps in terms of the Cross-Industry Standard Process for Data Mining (CRISP-DM), a non-proprietary and freely-available standard (cf. Fig. 7.1).

In this case the socio-technical nature of the process is highlighted in six steps, starting with business understanding (crucial for the choice of which data to collect and store), followed by data understanding (crucial for the choice of data recording, storing and aggregation), data preparation (data storage and aggregation), modelling (data mining), evaluation (interpretation) and deployment (application). Interestingly, the deployment of profiles implies matching them with new data, that will either confirm or falsify the patterns that have been found, thus allowing continuous fine tuning or even reconstruction of the profiles. This way the application of profiles can loop back into the construction phase. In as far as this is the case, the difference between the construction and application of profiles is relative.

Individual and Group Profiling

Besides the difference between the construction and the application of profiles, a second distinction is the one between individual and group profiling (Jaquet-Chiffelle, 2008). At the level of the construction of profiles, individual profiling concerns the construction of the profile of an individual person, either to individuate her or to infer her preferences, habits, earning capacity or whatever other specific characteristics she may be found to have. An individual profile is inferred from the data of one individual. Group profiling then concerns the construction of the profile of a group, which can be either an existing community or a category that emerges as such in the process of data mining. In the case of a community the group profile may be inferred from the data of one existing community. In the case of a category the group profile may have been inferred from data of many individuals.

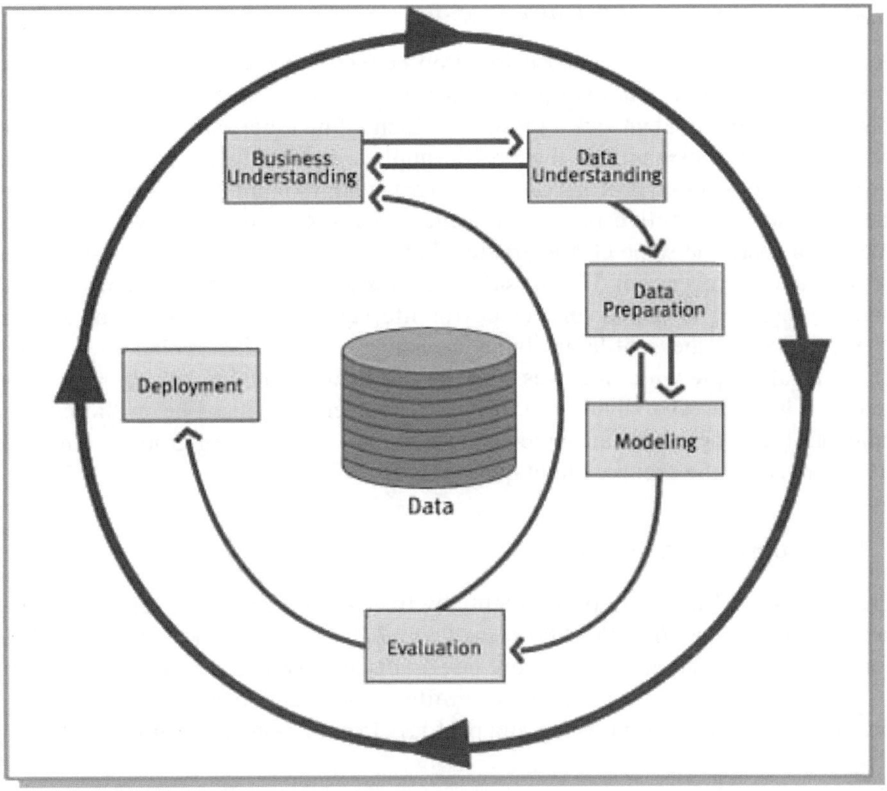

Fig. 7.1. A facsimile of the key phases of the CRISP-DM process model for the life cycle of a data mining project from the CRISP-DM process guide and user manual[5]

Direct and Indirect Profiling

At the level of the application of profiles we can make a third distinction, speaking of either direct or indirect profiling. If an individual profile is applied to the person whose data have been used to construct the profile, we speak of direct individual profiling. If a group profile is applied to an individual whose data match with the profile, we speak of indirect individual profiling. If a group profile is applied to the group whose data have been used to infer the profile, we speak of direct group profiling. If a group profile is applied to another group, whose data match with this profile, we speak of indirect group profiling.

[5] © CRISP-DM consortium: NCR Systems Engineering Copenhagen (USA and Denmark), DaimlerChrysler AG (Germany), SPSS Inc. (USA) and OHRA Verzekeringen en Bank Groep B.V (The Netherlands), see http://www.crisp-dm.org/.

Distributive and Non-Distributive Profiling

A fourth and – again – crucial distinction concerns the difference between distributive and non-distributive group profiles (Custers, 2004; Vedder, 1999). A distributive profile identifies a group of which all members share the same characteristics. This means that the profile applies equally to all members of the group. These types of profiles can be rather trivial, like 'all bachelors are unmarried'. A non-distributive profile, however, identifies a group of which not all members share the same characteristics. For instance, people with blue eyes may have an average chance of 67 % of suffering from skin cancer at the age of 72, while some – e.g. due to gender differences or life styles – have a bigger or smaller chance. Though the profile attributes a chance of 67% this applies only to the category of people with blue eyes – and not to its individual members. This is the reason why indirect individual profiling is problematic; just like in the case of epidemiology one cannot attribute chances found at the level of groups to individual members of the group without qualification.

7.1.2 Applications of Profiling[6]

Profiling is used in a variety of potentially overlapping contexts. Referring to the second part of *Profiling the European Citizen* (Hildebrandt and Gutwirth, 2008) for further information, we will now briefly discuss biometric profiling, location-based profiling, web profiling, user profiling for attention at school and work, customer and consumer profiling and profiling in employment situations.

Biometric Profiling

Both physical and behavioural biometrics present us with instruments for identification and verification (Andronikou, Yannopoulos and Varvarigou, 2008). Physical biometric concerns relatively stable characteristics dependent on the physiology of the human body, such as iris patterns, face images, hand and finger geometry. Behavioural biometrics concern measurements of a person's bodily actions, such as key-stroke and mouse click behaviour, gait and voice recognition. In allowing identification and verification biometrics can also provide a unique identifier that be used to link a variety of data across different contexts. The resulting databases will allow extensive profiling, especially group profiling, as discussed above. The application of group profiles can be combined with individual profiles, thus creating a rich profile of a person, which however partly depends on non-distributive group profiles, risking faulty generalisations. For example, in a sports surveillance environment, security systems could use biometrics to determine that an individual is a tall and strong skinhead with tattoos, and (rightly or wrongly) classify him as a hooligan; alternatively, we may use an RFID tag to determine

6. This sections builds on FIDIS deliverables 7.2/3/4/5 and on part II of *Profiling the European Citizen* (Hildebrandt and Gutwirth, 2008).

that this is John Smith who is, according to police information (which, however, could also be mistaken), a hooligan. Additional biometric analysis could be performed resulting in the determination that this individual is acting in an aggressive manner (e.g., from gait analysis) or is drunk or is asleep or alternatively, is in close and peaceful interaction with another individual who is classified as his girlfriend (being female, etc), thus surmising that the individuals observed are non-violent. The more complex a system becomes, the more prejudices it may end up incorporating (e.g., 'if a man is in the company of a woman, he is less likely to act violently'), but it is also possible to avoid excess sensitivity to major prejudices (e.g., 'skinheads are hooligans') and to improve the objectivity of the reasoning performed (e.g., by detecting violent behaviour).

Biometrics provide valuable information to generate individual and group profiles, as well as universal links between different profiles. This creates numerous opportunities for targeted servicing as well as targeted surveillance, generating a host of potential benefits but also risking the exercise of the rights to (informational) privacy and non-discrimination (Kindt, 2008). The risks are related to the fact that biometric profiles can be inferred from data that one 'leaks' instead of deliberately providing them.

Location-Based Profiling

In the context of mobile identities profiling techniques can be used to infer knowledge of a subject by combining location-based data to other data of the same person. Such profiling builds on position tracking technologies, data warehouse technologies, geographical databases & information systems (GIS) and meta databases with geo-coded data. In combination with knowledge about the contexts of everyday life, holidays, social conventions and suchlike, rich profiles can be constructed and applied that combine advanced group profiling with individual profiles. Fritsch (2008) describes how context data are combined with location data:

1. Collect time-coded location data for some time (preferably days or weeks).
2. Construct some temporal context of interest (e.g., private time vs. job time).
3. Check for a geographical pattern of interest in the location data track (e.g., places frequently visited, or unusual places rarely visited etc.).
4. Extract geographic coordinates along with their spatial and temporal information.
5. Query geographic information systems about locations, and extract meta data (e.g., '…is an office building').
6. Conclude from temporal context, spatial context and geographic meta data, e.g., the workplace, the home place, sports, and other personal data.

Notably, this algorithm works without knowing the person. It is enough to be able to re-identify him / her in the data set. It can be used for example on mobile phone spot or WiFi hot tracks that leave unique technical parameters as identifiable information. Using the algorithm above, we learn much about a – possibly yet unknown – person's preferences and frequent behaviour. This information can then be combined with information from other sources. Various methods from disciplines such as artificial intelligence, statistics, computational linguistics and stochastic methods are deployed on collections of data. Correlations between shopping habits and location, communication habits and location, movement and health data, social contexts and other users can be mined from the databases. The application of profiling techniques on geographic and database information could lead to new kinds of marketing, insurance or anti-terrorism systems. People's movement patterns combined with other features could be used to segment customers, generate health insurance conditions or arrest suspects.

As Leenes (2008) concludes, location data offers additional possibilities for the use of profiles, both in the guise of location-based services that make use of data derived from profiles, as well as by providing the input for new types of profiles. The first usage does not differ very much from location-based services, which are used for customer set preferences. The latter is significantly different because it adds a very detailed spatial and temporal dimension to profiling that goes beyond those already present in traditional profiling techniques. The possibility of the continuous collection of location data and correlating these to objects, locations, time, and other people potentially creates valuable information concerning the behaviour of mobile phone users. The use of this information in profiles may have a great impact on the profiled subjects and thus calls for utmost care by the profilers.

Web Profiling

As Benoist (2008) notes, though many people may be aware that in theory their web usage behaviour is not as anonymous as they may have once thought, few realise the extent to which e.g., webmasters can look into their surfing behaviours. Internet Service Providers as well as employers can easily register every movement made on the Internet by their clients or employees. In order to monitor their clients' online behaviour server administrators can use the features of the client-server architecture (the TCP/IP protocol) and of the language for communicating between two or more computers (the HTTP protocol). The client-server architecture implies that the server has the client's IP address, while the HTTP connection can be monitored per session (which is one visit to a website). Thanks to cookie technologies different sessions can be linked to the same user, thus enabling sustained tracking of a user's online behaviours. Web usage profiling is used for statistical purposes, or for improving the usability of a website. However, it also facilitates targeted marketing, based on refined personalisation. Besides the aim to prevent spamming and thus irritating potential customers, web usage profiling also hopes to provide crucial insights into personal life styles, earning capacity and credit risks. These insights can be used to proactively adapt websites to the inferred preferences of a client. Such proactive computing raises issues of personal autonomy and social sorting. Following Soenens (2008) we can invoke the interesting distinction made by Treiblmaier et al. (2004: 2) between customisation and personalisation: 'customization requires users to explicitly control the adaptation process' whereas personalization based on web usage mining is driven by the secondary (mis-)use of traces that people leave behind while surfing on the Internet. Seen from the clients' side, customisation is a far more active process than personalisation because at least part of the information has been 'actively declared'. Personalisation, on the other hand, can occur without the consent or even the awareness of citizens. Personalisation based on web usage mining is primarily derived from 'behavioural information'.[7] Authors like Won (2002: 31) argue that the term 'impersonal personalization' would suit the practice even better.[8]

User Profiling for Attention Support at School and Work

An interesting example of profiling has been provided by Nabeth (2008), falling out of the scope of the usual examples of consumer profiling and surveillance. He directs our attention to the potential role of profiling technologies in the case of an overload of information, a well known hazard in the information society. Profiling could be used to efficiently manage the attention of students or employees confronted with a multitude of projects, having to process more information from a variety of sources and available in different forms (news, email, instant messaging, social networking sites, etc.). Different levels of attention support can be provided by means of profiling technologies: first, by enhancing a user's perception in order to better discriminate between information and noise; second, by providing a meta-cognitive understanding of how a user proceeds to manage her attention; and third, by providing operational support of attention. Profiling could enable such attention support by capturing the user's behavioural data and processing them with regard to the actual management and the preferred allocation of attention.

Evidently, user profiling has its drawbacks (Halperin, 2008). Firstly, some doubts can be cast upon the underlying assumptions of the assessment process that should provide an accurate diagnosis of the user's state, due to the fact that cognitive processes are not readily available for observation (requiring interpretation of activities). Secondly, providing information about one's level and distribution of attention may increase the overload of information and thus reduce a person's ability to manage her attention. Thirdly, in the context of group learning monitoring a user's activity could create resistance against what may be perceived as a privacy threat or a form of manipulation.

7 'Behavioural information is information passively recorded through user logins, cookies and / or server logs': Crossly, Kings and Scott (2004: 100). See Chapter 6 of Hildebrandt and Gutwirth (2008), Section 6.2 'Setting the Stage: Personalisation and Profiling'.

8 Actually, personalisation uses all types of information to construct consumer profiles. Won (2002: 31) speaks of 'impersonal personalization' because (web) personalisation (also) relies on 'inferred information'. According to Crossly, Kings and Scott (2004: 100) inferred information is 'information indirectly associated with users, such as by identifying similar interests'. In the light of group profiling, it could be argued that personalisation is not really personal.

Customer and Consumer Profiling

Profiling is increasingly applied to (potential) customers and consumers. The objectives are refined market research, targeted advertising and servicing as well as credit scoring and fraud prevention. A well known example of profiling in customer relationship management (CRM) is the usage of the customer loyalty card (Kamp et al., 2008). The customer loyalty card is used to reward customer loyalty with discounts, in exchange for which they provide their personal data and / or allow data concerning their shopping behaviour to be collected, aggregated and mined. Typically the following data mining techniques are applied: association rules (individual profiling), classification (group profiling) and clustering (group profiling) (Schweizer, 1999). The resulting individual and group profiles provide valuable information about consumer preferences, allowing targeted discounts and advertising.

A second usage of profiling techniques in the management of consumer relations is in the field of credit scoring. This concerns an assessment of the risk of credit failure. For the estimation process a statistical model is created. This is done by analysing relevant attributes from a relevant set of people to assess which personal criteria have a statistic effect on the creditworthiness of a person and to measure the degree of this effect. These parameters and their relative importance are compiled in the statistical model which is often developed as a so called 'scorecard'. In many scorecards not only the criteria and their relative importance but also the combinations of certain parameters are considered. The individual credit score is then calculated by setting the scorecard with specific information from the prospective borrower. The credit score is commonly quoted as a number, which is allocated to a certain percentage of the statistical likelihood of credit failure.

The use of profiling in both customer loyalty programmes and credit scoring practices raises a number of issues with regard to the autonomy of consumers and customers and with regard to the discrimination it allows (Canhoto, 2008). The profiles that have been inferred are often protected as trade secrets or intellectual property, meaning that (potential) clients basically don't know on what grounds they are 'judged'.

Profiling in Employment Situations

Areas of potential application of profiling within the context of employment are prevention of fraud committed by employees, performance monitoring and management and establishing internal and external information security (see for example Lasprogata et al., 2004). Typical examples of the application of profiling are fraud prevention (for example in the retail sector through embezzlement by cashiers), direct and indirect supervision by tracking of employees (for example in postal services, logistics or call centres where skill management tools and access control systems can be used to monitor hours of work) and profiling on log-files for example in firewall systems and intrusion detection / prevention systems.

One example is the monitoring of email correspondence of employees. There are a number of tools and applications on the market allowing for automated analysis of e-mails of employees[9] allowing for hidden mail forwarding, mail analysis and reporting. From a technical perspective this is personalised profiling using data mining techniques for association (i.e., if a specific content, then it is a private mail with a likeliness of X%).

Another example is human resources and skill management. Some modern Human Resource Management tools aim at pooling, profiling and ranking / scoring the potential and the capacities of all employees with regard to their age, their qualifications, their working performance and salary etc. in order to optimise deployment within the company.[10] From a technical perspective in this context distributive group profiling is used. Typically data mining techniques for clustering or classification are applied.

A third example is fraud prevention in retail. Supermarkets use profiling to detect unusual cash flows which are often caused by cashier embezzlement.[11] Cash refund transactions are especially scrutinised. There are some well known techniques for fraudulently taking money out of a cash register. One example is the use of fake certificates for bottle deposits for usually small amounts of money. In the profiles, cashiers using this method can be determined by a higher rate of refund transactions than average. Further investigation is necessary, but can be carried out in a targeted fashion. In addition, data mining is used to generate insight into fraudulent techniques as yet unknown.[12] From a technical perspective personalised as well as non-distributive group profiling is being used. Thus it is expected that data mining techniques for association, clustering and classification are used in this context.

Profiling in the context of employment again raises the issues of privacy, autonomy and equality (De Hert, 2008). Precisely because the power differences between employer and employees are considerable, the focus on individual empowerment may fall short of providing adequate protection. Data protection seems geared to individual rights, while labour law could provide more effective protection, due to its emphasis on collective interaction.

7.1.3 Profiling, Democracy and the Rule of Law[13]

In this section we will briefly explore some of the risks of profiling. While other identification technologies are often associated with the erosion of our privacy, profiling has implications beyond the violation of the right to be left alone or the

[9] For example http://www1.seattlelab.com/Products/SLMailPro/email_monitor.asp, http://www.email-monitoring.net/ and http://www.siterecon.com/Email-Monitoring-Service.aspx.

[10] For example SAP HR as integrated solution: http://www.sap-press.de/katalog/buecher/titel/gp/titelID-717 or training tracking and skill management as specialised solution for example: http://www.cebos.com/training-system.html.

[11] For example http://www.fujitsu.com/de/services/retail/lossprevention/, http://www.torex-retail.de/german/loesungen/einzelhandel/loss-prevention/loss_prevention.php?navid=55 and http://www.evolution.com/news/GRMediaKit.pdf.

[12] See http://www.quarks.de/dyn/18298.phtml.

[13] This section builds on FIDIS deliverables 7.2/3/4/5 and on part III of *Profiling the European Citizen* (Hildebrandt and Gutwirth, 2008).

right to informational self-determination. Apart from that, the impact of profiling on the possibility to effectively exercise privacy and data protection rights, is different from the impact of the mere collection, storage and aggregation of data on these rights. Without profiling techniques, like bottom up data mining or unsupervised learning algorithms, identification technologies merely generate personal data that may be retained in databases. These databases can be searched by means of a query to relocate certain information as to a particular person. In putting the data of a specific person together the data controller has access to an individual profile, which brings together all relevant information available with regard to that person. This type of profile is not the result of profiling technologies, it does not provide any new type of information or knowledge, it can be located at the second step of the process of profiling as defined above. Data mining, however, provides the data controllers with patterns that are invisible to the naked human eye. And, though these patterns may be without meaning if taken out of context and without causal explanation (they could be based on spurious correlations), in the course of the fourth and fifth step of interpreting and applying these patterns, they may acquire meaning and effect real consequences for those whose data match the inferred profiles.

Dataveillance

In 1994 Roger Clarke coined the term dataveillance to describe the monitoring that was made possible by the increasing collection and storage of personal data. He summed up a number of threats, which we shall repeat here to provide a first impression of the dangers of mere collection and aggregation of data. After pointing out that massive dataveillance may lead to low data quality decisions; a lack of subject knowledge of, and consent to, data flows; blacklisting and denial of redemption, he sums up a set of other consequences: arbitrariness; a-contextual data merger; complexity and incomprehensibility of data; witch hunts; ex-ante discrimination and guilt prediction; selective advertising; inversion of the onus of proof; covert operations; unknown accusations and accusers and denial of due process. He then goes on with threats to society at large: a prevailing climate of suspicion; adversarial relationships; focus of law enforcement on easily detectable and provable offences; inequitable application of the law; decreased respect for the law and law enforcers; reduction in the meaningfulness of individual actions; reduction in self-reliance and self-determination; stultification of originality; increased tendency to opt out of the official level of society; weakening of society's moral fibre and cohesion; destabilisation of the strategic balance of power; and repressive potential for a totalitarian government. Hereunder we will raise a set of concerns that relate to these threats, focusing on privacy, autonomy and social sorting.

Threats to Privacy Due to Refined Personalisation

Personalisation can refer to highly sophisticated direct individual profiling, meaning that a person's behaviour or biometric make-up can be monitored for patterns that allow re-recognition and a prediction of future behaviours (earning capacity, accident proneness, dangerous driving) or status (like e.g., diseases). Because profiling can reveal knowledge previously unknown to the person it concerns, the privacy of the person is at stake. Even if the knowledge is disclosed to the person concerned, allowing for self-determination, the sheer availability of new information about oneself confronts a person with choices to be made. In the case of behavioural profiling it is important to note that a person might end up locked into her own past behaviours, because the profiler bases its dealings with the person on what is inferred from data collected from past interactions. One could argue that this will reduce people's capacity for change, as they are constantly judged on the basis of past habits. Personalisation can also refer to highly sophisticated indirect individual profiling, meaning that a person's data match a series of group profiles, the combination of which provides a pretty precise picture of a particular person. Like in the case of direct individual profiling this type of personalisation may reveal knowledge of which the person is not aware, possibly confronting her with information about, for example, diseases she may develop or providing knowledge about life-style and personal preferences she may not have wanted to share.

The Autonomy Trap in the Case of Refined Personalisation

Personalisation may have other effects that relate to privacy's association with self-determination. If service providers have access to knowledge about a person's habits, life-styles and preferences they can target the person with information and with offers that are customised to an extent previously not possible. Inasfar as a person is not aware of this knowledge she may be 'trapped' or 'manipulated' into certain behaviours about which she would have thought twice if she realised the deliberate appeal to her inferred preferences. Imagine a person who intends to stop smoking, which intention has been detected by online profiling technologies (Zarsky, 2002-2003). The profile of a person who is calculated to have 69% chance of quitting with smoking can be sold to the tobacco industry that may be willing to invest targeted advertising and free packets of cigarettes to increase the chances that this person will continue the habit of smoking. Those with an interest in the sale of cigarettes may even put banners on his screen that refer to scientific research that suggests specific health benefits from smoking. If the person is not aware why he is getting free cigarettes and where the banners come from, his choice for or against smoking is influenced in a secretive manner that challenges our conception of autonomous action. The increased personalisation that is made possible by the application of different group profiles (e.g., relating to her online transactions, offline shopping behaviour, and travel preferences) to the same person allows a type of individualisation that may end up de-individualising a person. This is the case because preferences inferred from relevant groups are fed back to her, 'normalising' her into the profiles even if they did not actually apply to her in the first place (non-distributive profiling, see Section 7.1.1 above). Such 'normalisation' again raises the issue of personal autonomy.

rting and Unfair Discrimination in the Case of Group Profiling

ofiling allows extensive as well as dynamic categorisation. The whole idea of targeted servicing is based on detecting and creating market segments that can be persuaded to buy specific goods or services. This type of segmentation will allow service providers, insurance companies and government agencies to discriminate between different consumers, different clients and different citizens, enabling them to figure out what price individual consumers are willing to pay, which risks individual clients generate and what kind of resistance can be expected from individual citizens confronted with certain governmental policies. The problem is, again, that consumers, clients and citizens will be mostly unaware of the way they are categorized and how this may impact them (Zarsky, 2002-2003; Lyon, 2003). While they have become transparent to those that profile them, the process of profiling is not easily accessible, and they can easily be discriminated on unfair grounds without ever knowing about it.

Democracy and Rule of Law

Pervasive dataveillance, the erosion of privacy and autonomy, as well as an increased potential for refined discrimination seem to challenge the system of checks and balances of constitutional democracy. A sustainable democracy depends on a measure of opacity of individual citizens, allowing them to retreat into a sphere of anonymity or intimacy, providing room to reconstruct the self without unreasonable constraints. At the same time democracy depends on a measure of transparency of those in power, in as far as their actions impact either the public good or the interests of private citizens. This balance of individual opacity and public transparency is seriously affected by the advent of profiling technologies. In making citizens more transparent and the process of profiling more opaque, the balance is turned upside down, putting at risk many of the central tenets of both democracy and the rule of law, which we may wrongly take for granted.

In Sections 7.2.4 and 7.3 we return to the issues of democracy and rule of law.

7.2 Profiling Technologies as the Enabling Technology for AmI[14]

7.2.1 What about Ambient Intelligence?

Ambient Intelligence (AmI) is still a vision, not a reality.[15] However, considering the amount of money invested in its realisation by the European Commission

[14] This section builds on FIDIS deliverables 7.3, 7.7, 7.9 and on Chapter 2 of *Profiling the European Citizen* (Hildebrandt and Gutwirth, 2008).

[15] For a more technical description we refer to Section 4.4.1 in this volume. Considering the fact that AmI is a vision rather than a reality the reader should not expect the level of concreteness that is possible when discussing specific emerging technologies. In Chapter 4 above, some of the enabling technologies of AmI are further discussed.

(ISTAG 2001), Philips (Aarts, 2003) and many other commercial enterprises, we should expect some form of AmI to materialize at some point in time. Ambient Intelligence has been labelled by a series of buzzwords, such as pervasive, ubiquitous, proactive and autonomic computing, each of which highlights another aspect of what AmI stands for. The idea is that computers will be miniaturized and hidden beneath the surface of things, doing away with keyboards and even touch-screens, turning the environment itself into the interface between the human user and the intelligent infrastructure that is meant to adapt the environment to the user's inferred preferences. An adaptive, smart environment should always be one step ahead of the user, like a butler who unobtrusively anticipates his master's wishes even before the master becomes aware of them. To seamlessly adapt to a user, an AmI environment depends on real time machine-2-machine (M2M) communication. This entails capturing data and aggregating them in online databases that are mined for relevant patterns. These patterns allow the environment to 'guess' (calculate) individual preferences, thus building predictions of future behaviour on statistical analysis of past behaviour. For seamless adaptation the application of relevant profiles must be decided upon by an autonomic environment, which avoids the need for human intervention as this would slow down the whole process. For this reason proactive adaptation implies networks of electronic agents that make decisions to e.g., change lighting arrangements or room temperature, to order tickets or groceries, arrange for transport, contact healthcare, negotiate about the sale of antiquarian books, to slow down the car before it collides with another car, etc.

The enabling technologies for this kind of smart environments are sensor technologies, RFID systems, behavioural and physical biometrics and a pervasive wireless interconnectivity that basically puts the offline world online, after translating it into digital data. The International Telecommunication Union (ITU) announced 'The Internet of Things' in its analysis of a world of things (ITU, 2005) that are all 'animated' with wireless technologies that leak their 'observations' of human and non-human behaviours, states or composition to massive online databases, to be mined for relevant patterns. Sensor technologies, RFID systems and biometrics as of themselves only provide data. To decide whether data is noise or information, profiling technologies are indispensable. The sheer volume of data gathered, recorded and stored from an AmI environment turns any single datum into a meaningless thing until it can be correlated with other data. To be one step ahead of the user, queries will not suffice; unsupervised learning algorithms, neural networks and multi-agent systems are necessary to make sense of the data. For this reason profiling technologies are preconditional for an AmI environment.

7.2.2 AmI and Autonomic Profiling

Above, we have introduced the concept of autonomic computing as a near synonym for AmI, noting that the different terms used to refer to AmI stress different aspects. In this section we discuss the aspect that is emphasised in using the concept of autonomic computing and we explain how autonomic profiling is a precondition for AmI or 'smart' environments. In 2001 Paul Horn, vice-president of IBM, coined the term autonomic computing.[16] His concept basically refers to the process of interconnected processing of data, gathered from 'everyware' (Greenfield, 2006), involving real time M2M communication and real time M2M decision-making. The concept of autonomic computing highlights the self management of the network (Kephart and Chess, 2003). Horn's choice of the term 'autonomic' is inspired by the unconscious awareness of our autonomous nervous system, which manages the real time adaptation of the body to our internal and external environment. The autonomic nervous system takes a host of decisions without requiring our deliberate consent. In fact, we have no access to these decisions, which do not even reach the threshold of consciousness. Autonomic computing mimics this unconscious real time adaptation, by adapting the physical environment to our inferred preferences. Instead of training a human butler to anticipate our needs before we express them, the non-human environment 'profiles' our needs and provides for their satisfaction. To enable this butlerisation of the material environment profiling techniques are used to analyse the data we 'leak', thus creating a dynamic data shadow, which is infinitely sharper than human memory could ever produce. Due to the enormous and low cost storage capacity of the technical infrastructure, we face a never fading trace of data and profiles that results in a 'denial of oblivion'. If AmI is realized, nothing we do will be forgotten and any data we leak can be used against us at some point in time.

7.2.3 Autonomic Profiling and Autonomous Action

One of the issues raised by the vision of AmI is the question of how autonomic profiling could influence our capacity for autonomous action. To explain the difference between autonomic profiling and autonomous action we will discuss three types of profiling, depending on who or what is doing the profiling: organic profiling, human profiling and machine profiling.

Organic Profiling: Enacted Cognition

In 1987 Maturana and Varela published *The Tree of Knowledge*, in which they explain 'The Biological Roots of Human Understanding'. Their theory of knowledge should interest us here because it explains knowledge as 'something that an observer attributes to an organism that effectively deals with its environment'. They propose an 'enactive' theory of knowledge and perception, meaning that these are constituted by an organism that interacts with its immediate environment, in as far as this interaction is successful in the sense that it sustains the life of the organism. An 'enactive' theory of knowledge implies that knowledge and action 'cause' each other: only by acting does an organism find out about its environment and in that sense even perception is a form of – entirely implicit – action. To be more precise one could say that all living organisms, in order to survive, must continuously profile their environment to be able to adapt themselves and / or to adapt their environment. Organic profiling consists of the process of detecting relevant information in an environment, of 'making the difference that makes a

[16] See http://www.research.ibm.com/autonomic/.

difference' (paraphrasing Bateson, 1972: 315). For organic profiling it is cı note that (1) profiling the environment happens without involving a coı mind, (2) profiling provides the feed-back that is necessary to survive, (3) ing detects information, thus discriminating between noise and information.

Human Profiling: the Meaning of Autonomous Action

This brief excursion into profiling by nonhuman organisms allows us to develop a keener eye for what makes knowledge human knowledge. If perception, information gathering, feed-back and even knowledge are not specific for the human animal, what is? Could it be that consciousness is the discriminating attribute, and if this is the case, what difference does this make for profiling? Compared to a plant, a dog has a different kind of awareness of its environment. Though both are aware of the environment, the plant has no consciousness, since this is the product of a central nervous system that is absent in plants. The philosopher Helmuth Plessner (1975) described how a central nervous system that allows for a centralisation of the organism's awareness gives rise to a conscious presence in the world. This raises the question of whether and how human consciousness differs from that of other mammals. According to Plessner, the difference lies in the fact that a human is not only consciously aware but also conscious of being conscious, conscious of her self. This reflective attribute, which is often thought to spring from the fact that we use language to communicate with each other, is absent in other mammals, or present to a different degree.

This difference is relevant for human profiling because it allows for self reflection, which is preconditional for deliberate intentional actions (which we suppose to be less evident in other mammals). Reflection implies that we can appropriate our actions as our actions, as it were from a third person perspective. Such reflection can be incorporated into our actions – even before we act. We may thus consciously reflect upon different courses of action and intentionally prefer one alternative to another. This is what allows for what moral philosophers call intentional action, which is the precondition for autonomous action: an action we have freely decided upon, an action within our own control. Auto is Greek for self, nomos is Greek for law. Autonomy means that we follow a law that we have set for our selves. We do not merely follow rules imposed on us by others and we do not merely exhibit regularity in behaviour. To follow a law we must be capable of intentional action and to set that law for ourselves we must be capable of conscious reflection. Nevertheless, most of our actions are neither intentional nor conscious. Cognitive psychology has demonstrated that we can move around freely in this world because we have acquired habits that are inscribed in our bodies, allowing us to act in a number of ways without conscious deliberation (Hassin, Uleman and Bargh, 2005). However, the small amount of actions we actually consciously intend are distinctive for our moral competence – taking into account that conscious reflection is the incentive to create new habits which will again move out from the zone of intentional action, but did originate from it.

Autonomic Machine Profiling

To target the difference between organic, human and machine profiling it is interesting to discuss autonomic profiling as autonomic machine behaviour. With autonomic machine behaviour we refer to the behaviour of machines that are part of an interconnected network of machines that exchange and make decisions after processing the data. 'Machine' – in this context – can be anything like an RFID-tag, a PDA (personal digital assistant), a PC (personal computer), but also a software programme. The point is that autonomic machine profiling implies making decisions without the intervention of a human consciousness. To discriminate such machine behaviour from human action, we could stipulate that it refers to the difference between behaviour and action, meaning that the first is automated (habitual), while the second implies intention (based on the capacity to reflect on the implications of one's actions). In this terminology intentional action would be a tautology.

Making a Difference

Having discussed organic, human and machine profiling we conclude that organic profiling does not necessarily involve conscious reflection or intentional action. A major part of human existence is sustained by the autonomic nervous system, without conscious awareness. This is an example of organic profiling. Machine profiling seems similar to organic profiling, in that it does not involve conscious reflection, nor intentional action. However, organic profiling presumes an organic system that constitutes and sustains itself. Maturana and Varela (1991) have coined the term autopoiesis for this self-constitution. Even if autonomic computing can be fruitfully compared to the autonomous nervous system, we may have a problem in defining it as self-constituting as long as it needs an initial software architecture provided by human intervention.

In other words, machine profiling is like organic profiling to the extent that it is part of autonomic behaviour and like human profiling to the extent that human profiling is done implicitly. At the same time, machine profiling differs from human profiling in two salient ways: (1) other than human and organic profiling machine profiling is not part of an autopoietic system that constitutes itself, (2) other than human profiling machine profiling does not integrate conscious reflection or intentional action. This is relevant for the way that autonomic machine profiling, which is preconditional for AmI, will impact autonomous human action and the constitution of human identity. It seems that machine profiling does make a difference here. We will return to this point in Section 7.3.

7.2.4 AmI, Democracy and Rule of Law

In recent years many authors have announced the death of privacy (Leenes and Koops, 2005). Though privacy can be seen as a private interest, it is of importance to realise that privacy is also a public good. As a public good, privacy is part and parcel of the constitution that sustains our democratic system. It allows citizens a space of negative freedom (freedom from) that provides room to reconstruct one's identity and in doing this, it forms the precondition to co-construct a public space of positive freedom (freedom to). Without their privacy, citizens are less free to form independent opinions (e.g., against public opinion or against state doctrine) and this implies that privacy is more than a private interest: it constitutes a public good that is central to a vigilant democracy. Autonomic environments may – unintentionally – form a socio-technical infrastructure with totalitarian overtones, because it may eradicate privacy altogether. Traditionally, totalitarianism is equated with the death of the private sphere due to pervasive colonisation by the state. In line with this notion of totalitarianism, the metaphor of 'Big Brother' has been referred to in order to alert citizens to the loss of their privacy due to permanent spying by state authorities.

With regard to the totalitarian overtones of AmI environments Solove (2004) suggests that this metaphor should be complemented with another metaphor that more aptly discloses the unintentional rather than deliberate, the omnoptical rather than panoptical and the anonymous rather than personalised enforcement mechanisms that may emerge in the wake of data mining, personalised proactive servicing and AmI. In *The Digital Person* Solove (2004) discusses Kafka's *The Trial* as a more adequate metaphor to describe the network of commercial data controllers that capture, store and analyse our data, trading them to the highest bidder for further processing, thus allowing ever more precise profiling of individual people. The intention of these data controllers is not to target a particular person, nor to control an entire society. Their objective is more modest: to make a profit by tuning their products to the inferred preferences of their potential clients.

Another metaphor that challenges 'Big Brother' has been put forward by Sunstein (2001): 'The Daily Me'. This refers to a personalised information channel (e.g., a website) that filters information in order to only receive information that is appreciated. Against such a comfortable filtering out of what seems of less interest, he raises two objections that relate to the preconditions of a viable democracy:

- Citizens need to be confronted with unexpected opinions, topics and other information they did not seek out of their own accord, to prevent losing touch with reality.
- Citizens need to share a range of experiences to prevent an increased fragmentation of shared goals, values and understanding.

Sunstein is not suggesting that we should worry about a governmental 'Big Brother' that is censoring our information, but rather warning that by allowing highly customised filtering civil society will crumble thus eroding what is central for a sustained democracy.

In the next section we will further investigate how profiling technologies, especially in the context of autonomic computing and AmI, may impact some of the presuppositions of democracy and rule of law. To develop a more profound perspective on this impact we will connect the right to privacy – seen as a public good – to the construction of a person's identity.

7.3 When *Idem* Meets *Ipse*: The Identity of the European Citizen[17]

7.3.1 Privacy and Identity

In a collaborative research project on 'the future of identity in the information society' we need to address the issue of how emerging identification technologies will affect the self-identity of citizens within constitutional democracies. Within the work package on profiling we have investigated how profiling technologies may impact human identity, especially in the context of automatic application of group profiles to individual persons. To distinguish self-identity from identities attributed by commercial or governmental organisations and to detect how they intertwine, we have introduced the concepts of idem and ipse, inspired by the work of the French philosopher Paul Ricoeur (1992). These concepts are of particular interest because the impact of identification technologies like profiling is often assessed in terms of privacy violations.[18]

The definition, scope and meaning of privacy has been the object of much scholarly debate (e.g., Solove, 2002; Hildebrandt, 2006). Central features seem to be intimacy, anonymity, reserve, solitude and autonomy. This indicates a focus on seclusion and separateness, associating privacy with a defensive strategy versus others. Because identification technologies presume a relationship between the subject who is identified and the subject who performs the identification, the context of identification requires a focus on the relational core of privacy. Instead of understanding privacy in terms of a static and exclusionary conception of private life, we prefer to understand it as a dynamic process of boundary control, taking place between a self and its environment (Altman, 1975). Agre and Rotenberg (2001: 7) build on this dynamic, relational perspective when they move beyond a 'static conception of privacy as a right to seclusion or secrecy', discussing privacy in terms of 'negotiated relationships'. They define the right to privacy as 'the freedom from unreasonable constraints on the construction of one's own identity.'

This definition links privacy to identity construction, highlighting the combination of positive and negative freedom that is pertinent for citizenship in constitutional democracy.

---

[17] This section builds on FIDIS deliverables 2.1, 7.2 and 7.4, as well as on Chapter 15 of *Profiling the European Citizen* (Hildebrandt and Gutwirth, 2008). The notions of *idem* and *ipse* are further explored in FIDIS deliverables 7.14a and b.

[18] See also the OECD STI Working Paper 2007/7, at 8 and 31.

7.3.2 Idem (Sameness) and Ipse (Selfhood)

According to Ricoeur (1992), the term identity refers to two different concepts of identity, which are interrelated. Firstly, identity derives from the Latin idem, meaning sameness in the sense of similarity and / or continuity. Similarity refers to the fact that two different entities can be identical in a certain respect (structure, form, content, relationship) without being one and the same thing. Continuity introduces the factor of time, indicating that though an entity is never entirely identical with itself in the course of time, it nevertheless has a continuity that allows an observer to identify it as the same thing. Sameness has to be asserted in opposition to difference or otherness: two things are the same because they differ from other types of things; one individual thing is the same thing in the course of time because it differs from all other things. Group profiling technologies build on sameness in the sense of similarity (categorisation); personalised profiling build on sameness in the sense of unique identification and continuity of the person.

Secondly, the term identity refers to the concept of ipse or self. Ipse-identity is the sense of self that is constitutive of the human subject. This sense of self is constituted from a particular, situated, embodied first person perspective, on which all third person perspectives depend. An important observation is that human beings experience themselves at the same time as ipse and idem: e.g., some philosophers speak of our body as Leib and Körper, i.e. as the experienced body that constitutes our sense of self (Leib), and as an object like other objects (Körper).

Profiling technologies cannot produce or detect a sense of self; they are built to detect sameness, even when they construct sophisticated personalised profiles that seem to define a person in many dimensions of her social, private and public life. They can, however, influence a person's sense of self. This is precisely because of the relational character of selfhood: the construction of one's own identity depends on the confrontation with others, especially with the way other people seem to 'profile' us. 'I' (first person perspective) learn about 'me' (third person perspective) when I receive feedback from my environment. The influence of third person perspectives on a person's sense of self, or identity-construction, is not necessarily a matter of conscious reflection. As indicated above, in Section 7.1.3, much of a person's behaviour is automated and non-conscious. However, there is a possibility to reflect on our behaviours, and – even if this is often after the fact – to make deliberate choices about future behaviour (intentional autonomous action). Understood in this sense, ipse-identity is (1) inherently relational, because it is constructed in confrontation with an environment; (2) fluid and dynamic, because this construction is an ongoing process as the environment changes and (3) while mostly progressing at a pre-reflective level, identity-building can become part of conscious intention and reflection, indicating the particular capacity of human beings to be conscious of their own consciousness.

An important question in the context of profiling technologies is to what extent profiles that are generated by advanced profiling technologies impact a person's sense of self without any awareness on her part, for instance when offering her targeted services not available to a person whose data match another profile. The point is not about whether those who profile a person have good or bad intentions or whether they use profiles to manipulate this person's inferred desires, but about the fact that knowledge is constructed that may impact her preferences without her conscious awareness.

7.3.3 Freedom from and Freedom to

Following Agre's and Rotenberg's definition of the right to privacy, and the distinction between idem and ipse identity, we will now investigate how privacy and the construction of a person's self-identity is related to freedom. This will enable us to discuss how profiling could impact the freedom to develop a sense of self.

In describing the right to privacy as a matter of freedom from unreasonable constraints Agre and Rotenburg highlight negative freedom: freedom from (Berlin, 1969). This type of freedom refers to a space that is relatively free from external constraints, providing room for a retreat into solitude or intimacy, creating a zone for experimentation and reflection outside the gaze of public opinion or state authorities. In further describing the right to privacy as a matter of freedom to build one's identity Agre and Rotenberg highlight positive freedom: freedom to (Berlin, 1969). This type of freedom refers to a space to reinvent one's self, creating new habits, providing the means for renewed identifications with other individuals, communities, ideas or even things. Absolute freedom does not exist. For this reason negative freedom is described as freedom from unreasonable constraints, not from all constraints. Without some kinds of constraints positive freedom does not emerge: constraints allow for anticipation and without anticipation a person cannot act. Without anticipation a person cannot develop a sense of what kind of person she is in relation to e.g. others (friends, family, colleagues etc.), to ideas (about taste, life style, art, work, politics, religion, sports etc.) or to things (her house, clothes, books, car, gadgets etc.). A sense of self (ipse-identity) develops from the identification with or resistance against the idem identifications that are available or even ascribed to a person; it cannot develop in a void.

Profiling provides for the attribution of idem-identities. If a person is categorised as a certain kind of person because her data match a group profile, the 'owner' of the profile might decide to treat that person differently from those whose data don't match with the profile. This results in specific constraints, based on e.g., a specific credit score, insurance risk assessment, estimated earning capacity, health risk assessment, which are in fact idem-identities. In this manner profiling – the construction and application of profiles – produces idem-identities that will affect the process of identity construction. On the one hand the application of such profiles provides opportunities to identify with the idem-identities attributed, thus giving freedom to construct ipse-identity (positive freedom). On the other hand it is not clear whether these constraints are reasonable, because of the invisibility of profiling practices. The profile attributed may be unreliable (too many false positives or negatives), not applicable (in the case of a non-distributive profile) or it may be unfair or unjustly discriminating to apply a profile (unfair price-discrimination or discrimination on grounds of gender, ethnicity etc.). Due to the fact that a person has no access to the construction of profiles and is most probably not consciously aware of the application of a profile, there is no possibility to control the application of unreasonable constraints. Citizens are largely out of control here, with no clue as to which data they would want to hide, because they don't know which of their data match what profiles. This loss of control affects the boundary negotiations that are essential for privacy: while the self is probably affected by the idem-identities that categorise her, resistance becomes very difficult as the boundaries of the self are transgressed invisibly. In that sense profiling could threaten the freedom from unreasonable constraints on the construction of a person's self identity.

7.4 A Vision of Ambient Law[19]

As has been indicated above, the vision of Ambient Intelligence (AmI) relies on smart devices in a smart environment that continuously and invisibly profile the 'users' to proactively cater to their inferred preferences. Advocates of AmI proclaim that in a proactive, adaptive environment devices, tools and things will be able to 'think' for us and that 'smart' decisions will be made for us. Given that AmI is still a vision, we cannot be sure what the future will bring, but as a vision AmI already poses many questions with regard to essential characteristics of constitutional democracy, such as discussed above (notably privacy, non-discrimination and human autonomy). Anticipating the realisation of adaptive environments, we think that now is the right moment to think differently about law, conceptualising a new type of law that is in line with the vision of AmI. Therefore we have proposed to develop Ambient Law (AmLaw),[20] a concept that was coined within the FIDIS network in FIDIS deliverable 7.3 (Schreurs et al., 2005), and further developed by Hildebrandt (2008) and in FIDIS deliverable 7.9 (Hildebrandt and Koops, 2007).

This section will describe a) what would make AmLaw law; b) why a paradigm shift in law seems essential for AmI; c) what this shift could be like in the case of AmLaw; and d) how, at the operational level, AmLaw could be inscribed in technology architectures of AmI environments.

P.T.O

[19] This section builds on FIDIS deliverables 7.7, 7.9 and 7.12 and is co-authored by Els Soenens.

[20] To prevent confusion between the acronyms of AmI and AmLaw we shall abbreviate Ambient Law to AmLaw.

7.4.1 AmLaw as Law

We need to emphasize that for AmLaw to qualify as law it needs to be developed in line with the requirements of a constitutional democracy. Therefore, rather than presenting a blue-print of law for AmI, AmLaw should be used as an important roadmap for making the vision of AmI come true, in such a way that the core values of privacy and non-discrimination are safeguarded. In line with Lessig ('code as law') and Nissenbaum ('values in design'), AmLaw can be understood as a 'law by design', relying on the embodiment of legal norms into technology itself. The vision of AmLaw purports that the norms embodied in technology should be constituted as legal norms, which implies two important constraints:

- their enactment should entail sufficient democratic legitimation.
- their application must be contestable in a court of law.

This distinguishes the vision of AmLaw from the many other conceptions of digital law, which tend to separate law (assumed to be written) from its implementation (e.g., automated via digitalisation). Such a separation implies that only the written part is law and requires democratic legitimation and contestability in a court of law, whereas AmLaw rejects this separation and requires democratic legitimation and contestability in court for the digital articulation of the norms. Examples of 'law in design' could be found in opacity and transparency tools that articulate privacy rights and transparency rights into the technologies they aim to protect about, using privacy enhancing technologies (PETs) and transparency enhancing technologies (TETs) to operationalise AmLaw. To qualify as prototypes of AmLaw their implementation should be initiated and sustained by the democratic legislator, while they should enable the contestation of automated decision-making in the private as well as the public sphere.

We now explain more in detail why we believe it is essential to have AmLaw in AmI environments.

7.4.2 Why Should AmI Require Another Type of Law?[21]

AmI may entail great promise as a user-centric technological environment, but we cannot ignore the threats to individuals and society, discussed above. We may in fact expect that the already existing information asymmetry between data subject and data controller will significantly increase. Moreover proactive computing will most likely result in a loss of user control. Though it could be interesting to explore the ethical implications of AmI, we urgently need to explore the legal implications, since law – other than ethics – has the capacity to actually protect citizens because it can rely on state authority. While ethics can provide interesting analyses of what is at stake, positive law can create the legal-technical framework to

[21] This subsection builds on Chapter 13 of *Profiling the European Citizen* (Hildebrandt and Gutwirth, 2008).

sustain the freedom from unreasonable constraints on identity constructio providing the preconditions for a vigilant civil society.

A thorough analysis of the current legal framework with regard to group profiling demonstrates that it does not suit the workings of AmI environments in as far as they depend on group profiling (Schreurs et al., 2008). The analysis concerns 3 steps and 1 step in-between:

1. The moment of collection of personal and other data to construct profiles
2. *The anonymisation of personal data*
3. The moment of the construction of the profile from anonymous data
4. The application of the group profile

These steps will be discussed from the perspective of the rights and obligations defined in Directive 95/46/EC,[22] basically consisting of the famous Fair Information Principles (FIPs): collection limitation, data quality, purpose specification and limitation, transparency, individual participation and accountability all fail in the face of the invisibility of the decisions made by the autonomic environment and the subsequent incontestability of the consequences.

Collection

The present legal framework is focused on the protection of personal data. In as far as data are not qualified as personal data the legal regime of data protection does not apply. Data contained in RFID tags, attached to things that may change hands raise many questions as to whether and when they must be labelled as personal data. The contextual, casuistic approach – necessary to decide on which data are personal data – generates extensive legal uncertainty, both for business enterprise and for individual citizens. Data captured and stored by sensor technologies about a person's whereabouts and her interactions with the environment may be personal data if we can find agreement on what it means to be identifiable. If behavioural biometric profiling is used to re-recognize a person as the same person, without linking this to her name, address etc., it remains unclear at which point such data must be termed personal data. In as far as data fall within the scope of the legal framework for data protection it is entirely unclear what the purpose specification and use limitation principles could mean in an environment that involves proactive adjustments made on the basis of extensive data mining. These principles imply that the data controller knows in advance how the data will be used, which will mostly not be the case. Limiting the usage of data or requiring consent for a use that was not stipulated in advance goes against the grain of AmI's interconnected, seamless, ubiquitous 'world'.

---

[22] Directive 95/46/EC of the European Parliament and of the Council of 24 October 1995 on the protection of individuals with regard to the processing of personal data and on the free movement of such data.

Anonymisation

The irony of anonymising personal data is that from that moment onward data protection legislation is no longer applicable. Whereas anonymisation can function as a protection against privacy invasions, it also implies a complete loss of control over how data are processed, sold and put to use. Though one can argue that the act of anonymising data falls within the scope of Directive 95/46/EC, because it is a matter of processing data, this will not solve the problem. If data remain personal the applicability of the directive requires the implementation of a set of principles that are entirely at odds with the 'logic' of the AmI environment.

Construction of Profiles

If profiles are inferred from personal data the data controller would need a legal ground for such processing, consisting of either unambiguously given consent or the necessity of processing for the performance of a contract.[23] AmI environments need to have a maximum of data to create accurate profiles, while they also need maximum flexibility as to the usage of these data to be able to anticipate changing preferences – made possible by real time monitoring. The combination of maximum data capture and maximum flexibility in their usage implies that AmI and Data Protection generate irreconcilable logics. Either a user would have to provide her unambiguous consent with every change of purpose or all potential usage would have to be interpreted as being necessary for the performance of the contract between the user and the service provider(s). Neither seems to offer a solution: reiterant requests for consent would negate the idea of a seamless adaptive and proactive environment; assuming that any data usage will be necessary for the performance of the contract will nullify the protection. It would mean that entering the area of AmI is the same as giving up on privacy. Another issue resides in the fact that the logic of processing data is probably protected as a trade secret or an intellectual property, causing a clash between the transparency rights for data subjects offered by Directive 95/46/EC and the commercial rights for data controllers.[24]

Application of Group Profiles

We must first note that a group profile is not personal data, since it does not – in itself – refer to an identifiable person. In article 15 of Directive 95/46/EC it is stated that 'every person has the right not to be subject to a decision which pro-

[23] There are several other grounds, summed up in article 7 of Directive 95/46/EC that are not relevant here. See Schreurs et al. (2008) for an extensive analysis.

[24] This concerns especially the clash presented in recital 41 of the preamble, which stipulates that 'Whereas (...) every data subject must also have the right to know the logic involved in the automatic processing of data concerning him, at least in the case of the automated decisions referred to in Article 15 (1); whereas this right must not adversely affect trade secrets or intellectual property and in particular the copyright protecting the software; whereas these considerations must not, however, result in the data subject being refused all information'. A pertinent example of 'having your cake and eating it, too'?

duces legal effects concerning him or significantly affects him and which is based solely on automated processing of data intended to evaluate certain personal aspects relating to him, such as his performance at work, creditworthiness, reliability, conduct, etc.'. Note that the paragraph does not refer to a data subject but to every person and not to personal data but simply to data. This article is one of the few legal norms that seem instrumental in the protection against the application of group profiles. It is not really an opacity-right but a right that directly addresses the consequences of the automated application of profiles. By attributing a right not to be subject to decisions taken on the basis of such automated application, the present legal framework seems to provide an important defence against undesirable group profiling, irrespective of whether the group profile was constructed out of the personal data of whoever wants to invoke the right or out of other people's data (which will most often be the case). Moreover article 12 of the Directive provides an important transparency right: 'Member States shall guarantee every data subject the right to obtain from the controller: (…) knowledge of the logic involved in any automatic processing of data concerning him at least in the case of the automatic decisions referred to art. 15'. Note that this paragraph does refer to a data subject, which suggests that while everybody has the right not to be subject to these automatic decisions, only data subjects can request access to the knowledge of the logic involved. The problem is that the logic of processing will often be protected as a trade secret of by means of intellectual property rights, and it is unclear how these conflicting rights should be interpreted in concrete cases. Another problem, which we will address below, is that the technological infrastructure to provide an effective access to this logic is not in place. Writing down and enacting a right of access is not the same as providing for an effective remedy.

Summarizing, the incentive to develop a vision of Ambient Law comes from the lack of efficiency and effectiveness of contemporary data-protection legislation as embodied in written code. This ineffectiveness erodes the legitimacy of data protection and may nourish distrust of emerging technologies, resulting in a growing resistance to their application. The aim of developing a vision of Ambient Law is to address this challenge by meeting the legal requirements of constitutional democracy, while endorsing a version of AmI that fosters these legal requirements. As will be clarified in the next section, this implies a double paradigm shift:

- from a singular focus on the *protection of* individual data to a more balanced focus which includes the *protection against* invisible application of group profiles;
- from articulating legal norms of protection in the technology of the script to articulating legal norms of protection into the technology they intend to protect against.

In the next section we will discuss the shift from written to digital law in constitutional democracy, after which we will discuss how the shift from personal data to group profiles can be used as an example of how to operationalise the concept of AmLaw.

7.4.3 From Written to Digital Law in Constitutional Democracy

The first point that needs to be made here is that modern law is already articulated in a particular technology, namely the technology of the script. In arguing for the necessity to rearticulate parts of the law into the emerging digital infrastructure we do not intend to eradicate written law. The shift from oral to written law, many centuries ago, did not eradicate unwritten law. In fact written law in the end seems to depend on unwritten law to be effective: in as far as written law does not create unwritten social norms that actually regulate human behaviour it requires extensive monitoring and sanctioning to achieve compliance. In the end all written law aims to be incorporated into the social fabric of a society, thus reducing the chance that the written law will be violated. Digital law will undoubtedly depend on written law, in that it will require the spelling out of the legal norm that is digitalised. Digital law does not replace written law but extends the scope of the law. The concept of AmLaw thus encompasses the totality of text-based and otherwise technologically embedded legal rules that regulate AmI.

Law Inscribed in the Technology of the Script

If we look into the history of written law, we must conclude that the era of the script has triggered major changes in the way the law operated. Especially the move from hand-written to printed script has been the key facilitating factor for a new type of state – the modern state that emerged in Europe in the 17th and 18th centuries – and a new type of enacted state law. This shifted the focus of legal state authority from adjudication to legislation, enabling a law-maker to impose new laws on his subjects. The implementation of this written (printed) law was in the hands of a literate class of civil servants that ensured adherence to the law. Since modern law was inherently systematic and hierarchical it helped to consolidate the emergent institution of sovereignty, based on an effective monopoly of violence within the state. Initially modern law provided the legal framework for absolutism, but with the printing press allowing for mass distribution of text the state faced the rise of public opinion, which mitigated claims to absolute power and eventually enabled democratic participation. While the printing press first allowed the rule by law (the sovereign using written codes as a means to rule his subjects), it later enabled the rule of law (the internal division of sovereignty that separates the enactment of legal rules by the legislator from their interpretation in a court of law). The class of professional lawyers that interpreted the body of legal rules that erupted in the wake of the printing press era became an effective buffer between the legislator and his subjects, preparing the ground for Montesquieu's separation of powers. Instead of rex est lex loquens (the king speaks the law) he advocates the judex est lex loquens (the judge speaks the law). One could argue that the era of the printing press has been a favourable precondition for the advent of the rule of law.

Law Articulated in Digital Technologies

If written law has generated (not caused) the advent of modern law, sovereignty and the rule of law, we must wonder what kind of law is generated by the digitalisation of law. It could entail a law that is adjusted to the digital age, implying that the digital age affect the law, without the law affecting the digital age. Digital law could thus end up as a mere tool for policy implementation, thus defying the autonomy of law as a safeguard against monopolies of power. That type of digital law could easily imply that the interpretation and negotiation of law is no longer a human activity but the result of a mere mechanical negotiation of overlapping codes in networks (Brownsword, 2005). Consequently, the functionality of digital legal codes as safeguards for constitutional democracy could be jeopardized. It would probably introduce a new class of 'digital literates', creating at the same time a class of 'digital illiterates'.[25]

Other than this type of digital law AmLaw implies more than just the automatic application of legal rules, since (1) the articulation in a particular technology warrants choices made by the democratic legislator and (2) the socio-technical infrastructure must allow for the contestation of the application of the legal norm. We will now briefly describe three valuable approaches that could help in developing AmLaw: the 'value by design' approach, the idea of privacy as 'contextual integrity' and the concept of 'digital territories'.

Value by Design

Kreutzberg (1986) has emphasized that 'technologies are neither good nor bad, but never neutral'. What he meant to say is that technological artefacts have a normative or regulative impact on human behaviour, even if this impact is unintended or even unforeseeable. The point is that technologies embody certain values, because of the kind of behaviour they invite or inhibit. The most obvious example is the speed bump that invites slow driving. In this case the value of careful driving is deliberately embodied in the hardware of the road. We have here a 'value in design' that is also a kind of 'law in design'.[26]

Contextual Integrity

Nissenbaum (2004) has argued that the digitalisation of our environment has blurred the borders between the private and the public spheres, while also decreasing the anonymity traditionally associated with many public spaces. She points out that the concept of privacy is often connected with private life, implying a person cannot claim a right to privacy in public spaces. She therefore pro-

---

[25] The transition from oral to written legal traditions similarly started with a class of scribes that maintained a monopoly on legal knowledge, because initially most people could not read or write. See e.g., Glenn (2004: 62-63).

[26] The concept of 'values in design' has been developed by Flanagan et al. (2007).

poses to replace the concept of privacy by that of contextual integrity. She claims that in order to safeguard a citizen's contextual integrity, two types of norms should be respected: (1) norms that guarantee the appropriateness of a specific information flow and (2) norms of flow or distribution of information. This means that the flow of information is not unlimited (not every exchange of data or profiles is appropriate) and the transparency of consumer-citizens is countered by transparency of profiles (the flow of information is reciprocal, generating a fair distribution of knowledge and information).

Digital Territories

The European Commission's Institute for Prospective Technology Studies (IPTS) has developed the notion of 'digital territories'. Just like in the case of Nissenbaum's 'contextual integrity' the underlying premise is that citizens should be empowered to create, shift, and sustain borders in order to develop and sustain their personal identity (self). In as far as virtual environments produce de-territorialisation and make it more difficult if not impossible to construct and sustain borders between public, private, social and intimate communications the idea of 'digital territories' invites a kind or deliberate re-territorialisation of the digital sphere.

AmI architectures that build-in the opacity and transparency technologies needed to safeguard the values of 'contextual integrity', privacy in the public sphere and non-discrimination would provide a real win-win situation. In the next section we will try to make all this more concrete by describing a series of privacy-enhancing and transparency-enhancing tools.

7.4.4 Legal and Technological PETs and TETs[27]

Requirements for AmLaw

In Section 7.4.1 we explained that AmLaw is more than just the digital implementation of a written law. Instead AmLaw should embody two central tenets of constitutional democracy for digitalised legal rules: (1) their enactment should entail sufficient democratic legitimation; (2) their application must be contestable in a court of law.

At the end of Section 7.4.2 we concluded that AmLaw entails two paradigm shifts: (1) from a singular focus on the protection of individual data to a more balanced focus which includes the protection against invisible application of group profiles; (2) from articulating legal norms of protection in the technology of the script to articulating legal norms of protection into the technology they intend to protect against.

We now have four criteria for testing AmLaw:

---

[27] This section builds on FIDIS deliverable 7.7, 7.9 and parts of deliverable 7.12 (which is still in progress at the moment of writing this chapter).

1. Has the enactment of the technological articulation of the digitalised legal rules been subject to a democratic decision making process?
2. Is the application of the digitalised legal rules ultimately and practically contestable in a court of law?
3. Does the digital articulation sustain both the protection of personal data and the protection against the application of group profiles?
4. Does the digital articulation provide an effective remedy against potential threats posed by the technology it aims to protect against?

Operationalisation

To operationalise the notion of AmLaw the development of PETs and data protection rights will have to be complemented with TETs that enable the exercise of e.g. the right not to be subject to autonomic decisions taken by machines in an AmI environment and the right of access to the logic of processing that underlies these decisions. This means that while PETs are focused on providing a measure of opacity regarding personal data, TETs are focused on providing a measure of

Table 7.1. Structured comparison of TETs and PETs; Source: Bellotti and Sellen (1993)

	Type of tool	
Criterion	Feedback about (TET)	Control over (PET)
Capture	When and what information about the data subject gets into the system.	When and when not to give out what information. The data subject can enforce its own preferences for system behaviours with respect to each type of information the data subject conveys.
Construction	What happens to information about the data subject once it gets inside the system.	What happens to information about the data subject. The data subject can set automatic default behaviours and permissions.
Accessibility	Which data controllers and third parties have access to information about the data subject and what information they see or use.	Who and what has access to what information about the data subject. The data subject can set automatic default behaviours and permissions
Purposes	What data controllers and third parties want information about the data subject for. Since this is outside of the system, it may only be possible to infer purpose from construction and access behaviours.	It is infeasible for the data subject to have technical control over purposes. With appropriate feedback, however, the data subject can exercise social control to restrict intrusion, unethical, and illegal usage.

transparency regarding group profiles. One way of differentiating between PETs and TETs has been to see PETs as tool that provide control over personal data, whereas TETs provide feedback about what happens to personal data. The control over and the feedback about the processing of personal data can concern capture, construction of profiles, accessibility of data and profiles inferred from them, and the purposes for which the data or profiles are put to use. In Table 7.1 we see a structured way of presenting this difference.

This way of distinguishing PETs and TETs, however, still concentrates on (the processing of) personal data. As we have seen, for an adequate protection feedback is needed on the types of group profiles with which a person's data may match. These group profiles are most often inferred from other people's data. To create transparency enhancing tools that give insight in these group profiles we need to face two types of obstructions:

1. Legally these profiles may be protected as trade secrets or by means of intellectual property, which has already been discussed above.
2. Technically one may run into the problem that access to the profiles that are actually constructed *will depend on information from data controllers*, and there are few ways of ensuring that this information is in fact correct.

Legal Obstructions

As to the first obstruction it would be interesting and in fact of great importance to investigate into the legal status of profiles and profiling techniques, after which recommendations can be made to design a legal regime for these profiles that provides the right balance between access rights for citizens that may be affected by the application of profiles and property rights for those who developed the profiles.

Socio-technical Obstructions

As to the second obstruction it would be interesting and pertinent to develop TETs that do not entirely depend on the trustworthiness of the data controller, because TETs are in fact necessary to decide on the trustworthiness. Perhaps some kind of trusted computing may be of help here.[28]

Legal and Technological TETools[29]

The problem of depending on data controllers for information about the profiles they are constructing out of our data, or about profiles that match our data, can be

---

[28] In FIDIS deliverable 7.12 (Hildebrandt, 2008) a set of TETs is discussed including the TAMI project (transparent accountable data mining); Privacy Evidence; Privacy Bird and several prototypes developed within the PRIME project.

[29] TETs is mostly used as an abbreviation for transparency enhancing technologies. Here it is used in a broader way, referring to both legal and technological transparency tools. For this reason we have used TETools instead of TETs.

countered by reverting to forms of counter-profiling. This means that instead of waiting for detailed and precise information from data controllers a person uses profiling technologies that process the observable machine readable behaviour of environments, thus anticipating what kind of consequences their own behaviour triggers. This approach may provide no detailed and precise information about the logic of processing by data controllers, but they may allow a person to 'play around' with the environment to figure out how her own actions are interpreted by the profiling machines.[30] Evidently this could impact the privacy of others and a careful analysis is needed to assess the legal framework that could guarantee the right balance between a right to counter profile one's environments and the right to privacy of those who are part of these environments.

We can conclude that there are two types of TETools:

- Type A: legal and technological instruments that provide (a right of) access to data processing, implying a transfer of knowledge from data controller to data subjects, and / or
- Type B: legal and technological instruments that (provide a right to) counter-profile the smart environment to 'guess' how one's data match relevant group profiles that may affect one's risks and opportunities, implying that the observable and machine readable behaviour of one's environment provides enough information to anticipate the implications of one's behaviour.

In as far as TETs are seen as an operationalisation of AmLaw, they will have to fit the requirements of AmLaw, discussed above. Their development will have to be based on the involvement of the democratic legislator, their application must be contestable in a court of law, they will have to find the right balance for the protection of personal data and the protection against undesirable group profiling and they will have to be articulated in the socio-technical infrastructure of AmI.

7.5 Conclusions

In a provocative article of June 2008 Wired editor Chris Anderson writes, under the title of 'The End of Theory: The Data Deluge Makes the Scientific Method Obsolete':

> *Scientists are trained to recognize that correlation is not causation, that no conclusions should be drawn simply on the basis of correlation between X and Y (it could just be a coincidence). Instead, you must understand the underlying mechanisms that connect the two.*

[30] An example of such playing around has been given by Privacy Mirrors (Nguyen and Mynatt, 2002).

> *Once you have a model, you can connect the data sets with confidence. Data without a model is just noise. (...)*
>
> *But faced with massive data, this approach to science — hypothesize, model, test — is becoming obsolete. (...)*
>
> *There is now a better way. Petabytes allow us to say: "Correlation is enough." We can stop looking for models. We can analyze the data without hypotheses about what it might show. We can throw the numbers into the biggest computing clusters the world has ever seen and let statistical algorithms find patterns where science cannot.*

Regardless of whether this is 'true' or 'false', Anderson's controversial stance on the impact of the tsunami of machine readable data and the data mining techniques that are capable of 'reading' them, is highly relevant for profiling technologies.[31] Profiling technologies capture, structure and analyse machine readable data in order to find patterns that make sense within a certain context, often with regard to decisions that need to be taken. At the same time profiling technologies apply the emergent profiles to new data in order to find a match that identifies a person as a certain type of person, allowing for targeted advertising, advanced risk assessment for the purpose of credit scoring, anti-money laundering, crime detection, actuarial justice, etc. If these technologies are used in so many contexts and if they indeed trigger a new type of knowledge with very different (or even no) truth claims as compared to traditional scientific knowledge, we need a more thorough analysis of their impact on the daily lives of citizens. This is even more urgent when, e.g., in the vision of AmI, these techniques become indispensable and autonomic: deliberate human interventions of both the user and the data processors are reduced to the bare minimum.

Profiling technologies impact a person's privacy, understood as the freedom from unreasonable constraints on the construction of her identity. This not only concerns privacy as a private interest but also privacy as a public good that should be fostered for the sake of facilitating a vigilant civil society. What happens if our identity is influenced by the dynamically inferred group profiles with which our data happen to match, whereas we cannot figure out how this influence relates to e.g., our behaviour or biological make up? When should such influence be qualified as manipulation and at which point is such manipulation a danger to our self-constitution as free and equal citizens, capable of solidarity with those less fortunately endowed (according to the latest risk assessment). If our self-constitution is always relational and never independent anyway, (how) could the invisible visibility – enabled by profiling – make a difference? Will profiling raise resistance in the end, generating a public demand for the legal competence and the technological capacity to contest the application of group profiles behind our backs? Will

[31] Cf. Custers (2004) who already suggested that profiling technologies question traditional ideas of scientific knowledge production, see Hildebrandt and Backhouse (2005). See also Hildebrandt and Gutwirth (2006).

invisible group profiling trigger public discontent to the extent that the democratic legislator will feel compelled to intervene in order to provide more focused and more effective transparency rights?

This chapter points to the need to develop a new type of law, complementing the written law of the era of the script. AmLaw should shift our attention from protection of personal data to protection against unwarranted application of invisible group profiles. It should find articulation in the socio-technical infrastructure of AmI to be effective and it should be initiated and sustained by the democratic legislator to be legitimate. Creating transparency and privacy enhancing tools should enable a citizen to contest the application of (group) profiles, rejecting the idea that one can be judged on the mere basis of a correlation.

References

Aarts, E. and Marzano, S. (2003), The New Everyday. Views on Ambient Intelligence. 010 Rotterdam, Rotterdam.

Agre, P. E. and Rotenberg, M. (2001), Technology and Privacy: The New Landscape. MIT, Cambridge, Massachusetts.

Altman, I. (1975), The Environment and Social Behavior. Privacy Personal Space Territory Crowding. Brooks/Cole, Montery.

Anderson, C. (2008), 'The End of Theory: The Data Deluge Makes the Scientific Method Obsolete', Wired Magazine 16.07. Available at: http://www.wired.com/print/science/discoveries/magazine/16-07/pb_theory.

Andronikou, V., Yannopoulos, A., Varvarigou, T. (2008), 'Behavioural Biometric Profiling and Ambient Intelligence', in: Hildebrandt, M. and Gutwirth, S. (eds.), Profiling the European Citizen. Cross-Disciplinary Perspectives. Springer, Dordrecht, pp. 89-103.

Bateson, G. (1972), Steps to an Ecology of Mind. Ballantine, New York.

Bellotti, V. and Sellen, A. (1993), 'Design for Privacy in Ubiquitous Computing Environments', Proc. of the European Conference on Computer-Supported Cooperative Work, pp. 77-92.

Benoist, E. (2008), 'Collecting Data for the Profiling of Web Users', in: Hildebrandt, M. and Gutwirth, S. (eds.), Profiling the European Citizen. Cross-Disciplinary Perspectives. Springer, Dordrecht, pp. 169-174.

Berlin, I. (1969), 'Two concepts of liberty', in: Berlin, I. (ed), Four essays on liberty. Oxford University Press, Oxford New York, pp. 118-173.

Brownsword, R. (2005), 'Code, control, and choice: why East is East and West is West', Legal Studies 25:1, pp. 1-22.

Canhoto, A. (2008), 'Reply: Profiles in Context: Analysis of the Development of a Customer Loyalty Programme and of a Risk Scoring Practice', in: Hildebrandt, M. and Gutwirth, S. (eds.), Profiling the European Citizen. Cross-Disciplinary Perspectives. Springer, Dordrecht, pp. 211-216.

Crossly, M., Kings, N. J., Scott, J. R. (2003), 'Profiles – Analysis and Behaviour', BT Technology Journal 21:1, pp. 56-66.

Custers, B. (2004), The Power of Knowledge. Ethical, Legal and Technological Aspects of Data Mining and Group Profiling in Epidemiology. Wolf Legal Publishers, Nijmwegen.

De Hert, P. (2008), 'The Use of Labour Law to Regulate Employer Profiling: Making Data Protection Relevant Again', in: Hildebrandt, M. and Gutwirth, S. (eds.), Profiling the European Citizen. Cross-Disciplinary Perspectives. Springer, Dordrecht, pp. 226-237.

Elmer, G. (2004), Profiling Machines: Mapping the Personal Information Economy. MIT Press, Cambridge, Massachusetts.

Fayyad, U., Piatetsky-Shapiro, G., Smyth, P. (1996), 'The KDD Process for Extracting Useful Knowledge from Volumes of Data', Communications of the ACM 39:11, pp. 27-34.

Flanagan, M., Howe, D., Nissenbaum, H. (2007), 'Emboying Values in Technology. Theory and Practice', in: Van den Hoven, J. and Weckert, J. (eds.), Information Technology and Moral Philosophy. Cambridge University Press, Cambridge.

Fritsch, L. (2008), 'Profiling and Location-Based Services (LBS)', in: Hildebrandt, M. and Gutwirth, S. (eds.), Profiling the European Citizen. Cross-Disciplinary Perspectives. Springer, Dordrecht, pp. 147-160.

Gasson, M. and Browne, W. (2008), 'Reply: Towards a Data Mining De Facto Standard', in: Hildebrandt. M. and Gutwirth, S. (eds.), Profiling the European Citizen. Cross-Disciplinary Perspectives. Springer Publisher, Dordrecht, pp. 58-63.

Geradts, Z. and Sommer, P. (eds.) (2008), FIDIS Deliverable D6.7: Forensic Profiling. Download: www.fidis.net.

Glenn, H. P. (2004), Legal Traditions of the World. Oxford, Oxford University Press, 2nd edition.

Greenfield, A. (2006), Everyware: The Dawning Age of Ubiquitous Computing. New Riders Publishing, 1st edition.

Halperin, R. (2008), 'Reply: Profiling Individual and Group E-learning – Some critical Remarks', in: Hildebrandt, M. and Gutwirth, S. (eds.), Profiling the European Citizen. Cross-Disciplinary Perspectives. Springer Publisher, Dordrecht, pp. 197-200.

Hassin, R. R., Uleman, J. S., Bargh, J. A. (eds.) (2005), The new unconscious. Oxford University Press, New York.

Hildebrandt, M. (2006), 'Privacy and Identity', in: Claes, E. et al. (eds.), Privacy and the Criminal Law. Intersentia, Antwerp- Oxford, pp. 43-58.

Hildebrandt, M. (ed.) (2008), FIDIS Deliverable D7.12: Biometric Behavioural Profiling and Transparency Enhancing Tools, Download: www.fidis.net.

Hildebrandt, M. and Backhouse, J. (eds.) (2005), FIDIS Deliverable D7.2: Descriptive analysis and inventory of profiling practices, Download: www.fidis.net.

Hildebrandt, M. and Gutwirth, S. (eds.) (2005), FIDIS Deliverable D7.4: Implications of profiling practices on democracy and rule of law, Download: www.fidis.net.

Hildebrandt, M. and Gutwirth, S. (eds.) (2006), FIDIS Deliverable D7.5: Profiling the European Citizen. Cross-disciplinary perspectives, Download: www.fidis.net.

Hildebrandt, M. and Meints, M. (eds.) (2006), FIDIS Report D7.7: RFID, Profiling and AmI, Download: www.fidis.net.

Hildebrandt, M. and Koops, B. J. (eds.) (2007), FIDIS Report D7.9: A Vision of Ambient Law, Download: www.fidis.net.

Hildebrandt, M. and Gutwirth, S. (eds.) (2008), Profiling the European Citizen. Cross-Disciplinary Perspectives. Springer Publisher, Dordrecht.

Hildebrandt, M., Koops, B. J., de Vries, K. (eds) (2008), FIDIS Report
Idem-Identity meets Ipse-Identity. Conceptual Explorations, Download: www.

ITU (2005), The Internet of Things. Seventh Internet Report of the International Tele munication Union.

Informal High Level Advisory Group on the Future of European Home Affairs Policy (2008), Freedom, Security and Privacy – European Home Affairs in an open world (Report of the 'The Future Group').

ISTAG (2001), Scenarios for Ambient Intelligence in 2010. Brussels. (Report of the Information Society Technology Advisory Group. Available at: http://www.cordis.lu/ist/istagreports.htm).

Jaquet-Chiffelle. D. O. (2008), 'Direct and Indirect Profiling in the Light of Virtual persons', in: Hildebrandt, M. and Gutwirth, S. (eds.), Profiling the European Citizen. Cross-Disciplinary Perspectives. Springer, Dordrecht, pp. 34-45.

Kamp, M., Körffer, B., Meints, M. (2008), 'Profiling of Customers and Consumers – Customer Loyalty Programmes and Scoring Practices', in: Hildebrandt, M. and Gutwirth, S. (eds.), Profiling the European Citizen. Cross-Disciplinary Perspectives. Springer, Dordrecht, pp. 201-211.

Kephart, J. O. and Chess, D. M. (2003), 'The Vision of Autonomic Computing', IEEE Computer Society 36:1, pp. 41-50.

Kindt, E. (2008), 'Need for Legal Analysis of Biometric Profiling', in: Hildebrandt, M. and Gutwirth, S. (eds.), Profiling the European Citizen. Cross-Disciplinary Perspectives. Springer, Dordrecht, pp. 139-145.

Koops, B.J., de Vries, K. and Hildebrandt, M. (eds.) (2009), FIDIS Deliverable 7.14b: Idem-Identity and Ipse-Identity in Profiling Practices. Applying the Conceptual explorations of D7.14a, Download: www.fidis.net.

Kranzberg, M. (1986), 'Technology and History: "Kranzberg's Laws"', Technology and Culture 27, pp. 544-560.

Lasprogata, G., King, N. J., Pillay, S. (2004), Regulation of Electronic Employee Monitoring: Identifying Fundamental Principles of Employee Privacy through a Comparative Study of Data Privacy Legislation in the European Union, United States and Canada. Stan. Tech. L. Rev. 4. Available at: http://stlr.stanford.edu/STLR/Articles/04_STLR_4/idex.htm.

Leenes, R. E, (2008), 'Reply: Mind My Step?', in: Hildebrandt, M. and Gutwirth, S. (eds.), Profiling the European Citizen. Cross-Disciplinary Perspectives. Springer Publisher, Dordrecht, pp. 160-168.

Leenes, R. E. and Koops, B. J. (2005), '"Code" – Or How Technology is Slowly Eroding Privacy', in: Dommering, E. and Asscher, L. (eds.), Coding Regulation. Essays on the normative role of information technology. T.M.C. Asser Press, The Hague. Available at SSRN: http://ssrn.com/abstract=661141.

Lessig, L. (1999), Code and Other Laws of Cyberspace. Basic Books, New York.

Lyon, D. (2003), Surveillance as Social Sorting: Privacy, Risk, and Digital Discrimination. Routledge.

Maturana, H. R. and Varela, F. J. (1978/1998 revised edn), The Tree of Knowledge. The Biological Roots of Human Understanding. Shambala, Boston and London.

Maturana, H. R. and Varela, F. J. (1991), Autopoiesis and Cognition: The Realization of the Living. Reidel, Dordrecht.

P.T.O.

Nabeth, T. (2008), 'User Profiling for Attention Support at School and Work', in: Hildebrandt, M. and Gutwirth, S. (eds.), Profiling the European Citizen. Cross-Disciplinary Perspectives. Springer Dordrecht, pp. 185-197.

Nissenbaum, H. (2004), 'Privacy as Contextual Integrity', Washington Law Review 79, pp. 101-139.

Nguyen, D. H. and Mynatt, E. D. (2002), Privacy Mirrors: Understanding and Shaping Sociotechnical Ubiquitous Computing Systems (Georgia Institute of Technology Technical Report). Available at: www.erstwhile.org/writings/PrivacyMirrors.pdf.

OECD Directorate for science, technology and industry (2007), At A crossroads. 'Personhood' and Digital Identity in the Information Society. (STI Working Paper 2007/07. Available at: http://www.olis.oecd.org/olis/2007doc.nsf/ENGDATCORPLOOK/NT00005D0E/$FILE/JT03241547.PDF).

Plessner, H. (1975), Die Stufen des Organischen und der Mensch. Einleitung in die philosophische Anthropologie. Suhrkamp, Frankfurt.

Ricoeur, P. (1992), Oneself as Another. Translated by Blamey K. The University of Chicago Press, Chicago.

Schreurs, W. Hildebrandt, M., Gasson, M., Warwick, K. (eds.) (2005), FIDIS Deliverable 7.3: The Report on actual and possible profiling technologies in the field of Ambient Intelligence, Download: www.fidis.net..

Schreurs, W. et al (2008), 'Cogitas, Ergo Sum. The Role of Data Protection Law and Non-Discrimination Law in Group Profiling in the Private Sector', in: Hildebrandt, M. and Gutwirth, S. (eds.), Profiling the European Citizen. Cross-Disciplinary Perspectives. Springer, Dordrecht, pp. 241-264.

Schweizer, A. (1999), Data Mining Data Warehousing – Datenschutzrechtliche Orientierungshilfe für Privatunternehmen. Orell Füssli Verlage, Zürich.

Soenens, E. (2008), 'Reply: Web Usage Mining for Web Personalisation in Customer Relation Management', in: Hildebrandt, M. and Gutwirth, S. (eds.), Profiling the European Citizen. Cross-Disciplinary Perspectives. Springer, Dordrecht, pp. 194-202.

Solove, D. J. (2002), 'Conceptualizing Privacy', California Law Review 90:4, pp. 1087-1156.

Solove, D. J. (2004), The digital Person. Technology and Privacy in the Information Age. NYU Press New York.

Sunstein, C. (2001), Republic.com. Princeton University Press, Princeton and Oxford.

Treiblmaier, H. et al. (2004), 'Evaluating Personalization and Customization from an Ethical point of View: an empirical study', Proceedings of the 37th Hawaii International Conference on System Science. IEEE Computer Society, Big Island, HI, USA.

Vedder, A. (1999), 'KDD: The challenge to individualism', *Ethics and Information Technology* 1:4, pp. 275-281.

Won, K. (2002), 'Personalization: Definition, Status and challenges ahead', Journal of Object Technology 1:1, pp. 29 – 40. Available at www.jot.fm/issues/issue_2002_05/column3.

Zarsky, T. Z. (2002-2003), '"Mine Your Own Business": Making the Case for the Implications of the Data Mining of Personal Information in the Forum of Public Opinion', Yale Journal of Law and Technology 5.

VIGNETTE 7: THE ROLE OF FORENSICS IN IDENTITY*

A Rude Awakening

The digital readout on the clock flashes to 03:05 – the night is very still, and the Idis are sound asleep. While the people may be resting, the house is very much awake. Such uninterrupted time is ideal for dedicated number crunching – a time when all the data collated during the day can be sorted, cleaned and processed to yield new information to update and augment current profiles being used in the system. That is, however, until the system flags a new primary task – the security system's proximity sensors have detected an anomalous movement in the vicinity of the front door. Because of their countryside location, and the local wildlife inhabitants, such an event is not unusual. Indeed the system is able to monitor through a variety of sensors to establish whether an event is of true importance. As the threat level flicks from amber to red, it appears in this case it very much is. In line with Frank's preferences, the lights in the bedroom are switched on dimly, and a computer generated voice tries to wake him from his slumber with a warning. He comes round in time to hear an almighty crash at the front door, a thunder of feet pounding through the house, and the sound of men shouting down the hallways.

Ello, Ello, Ello...

By late morning, things have started to become somewhat clearer. The hasty arrest of Frank's wife Fanny for 'data theft', and the immediate confiscation of their laptop computers and primary house server during the police raid had shed precious little light on the situation. In fact little was revealed during the associated chaos until Fanny's interview with the detective in charge of the case some hours later. It transpired that someone had gained high level access to the computer system in the hotel where Fanny worked, and had stolen the personal details, including banking and credit card numbers, from their customer database. A partial print and DNA left at the scene had been cross referenced with the UK's national ID card and national DNA databases, and had placed Fanny in the top ten of likely matches. Knowing that Fanny did not have security clearance for the main server room where the security breach occurred – finding her partial

* This scenario is based on FIDIS deliverable D12.5, Chapter 8, by Mark Gasson (READING) and Zeno Geradts (NFI).

fingerprint and DNA there appeared to be quite damning evidence. The only problem was that not only did Fanny emphatically deny any knowledge of the crime, she also appeared to have an alibi for the time it occurred…

Good Old Fashioned High-Tech Forensic Police Work

It was certainly true that Fanny did not fit the profile of a cyber-criminal, and this had cast doubt from the beginning of the investigation. However, identity theft was big business, and the police had taken a rapidly growing interest in it over the last few years. As such, it was now procedure to confiscate personal computer equipment for searching before anything could be removed or deleted. Of concern was the fact that no evidence could be found on the computers, and that the profiling agent on Fanny's home server indicated that she was in fact at home with her family at the time of the attack – something which her husband readily confirmed. This left something of a conundrum – someone had managed to defeat the iris scanner on the door to the server room to gain access, had stolen personal data, and had then left the fingerprint of someone else. As all leads began to look cold, there came a stroke of luck. The details of the crime had, as usual, been entered into the local police station's database. While databases across the country were not explicitly linked *per se*, the UK police force now uses a system called LinKSeE, an artificially intelligent data-mining program which distributes software agents across the isolated police databases which hunt for patterns and correlations, and generate new, potentially useful knowledge. In this case, the system had noted a case six months previously in a different police jurisdiction which had a very similar *modus operandi*. Indeed, not only was the target again a hotel, and the method of attack identical, but the system had cross-referenced the employee lists from both hotels and had come up with a match.

A Rude Awakening, Take 2

At 07:00 in the morning, the police swooped on the home of their new suspect. Having been employed as a cleaner at both hotels at the time of the attacks, it seemed clear that this man was key to the data theft crimes. Indeed the lifestyle revealed by analysis of his bank records and the out of place Mercedes on his driveway also indicated someone not surviving on a cleaner's wage. In a makeshift workshop in the house the police found what they were looking for: materials for lifting fingerprints and constructing gelatine copies to make fake prints at the scene, and samples of Fanny's hair containing her DNA. On a computer, high resolution holiday photos of the head of security at the hotel downloaded from the internet were also found, from which printed copies of his iris could be made to spoof the hotel security systems. Certainly enough evidence to vindicate Fanny of the crime.

The visions and thoughts expressed in this vignette are inspired and based on various discussions, and results of the FIDIS Network of Excellence as well as the authors' personal experiences and expectations. Partially, underlying concepts and ideas of this vignette are described in Chapters 4 and 8.

8 Identity-Related Crime and Forensics

Bert-Jaap Koops and Zeno Geradts*

Summary. With the ever-increasing importance of identity and identity management in the information society, identity-related crime is also on the rise. Combating crimes like identity theft and identity fraud, not in the least with the help of identity forensics, is a key challenge for policy makers. This chapter aims at contributing to addressing that challenge. It summarises the findings of five years of FIDIS research on identity-related crime and identity forensics. A typology is given of the various forms of identity-related crime. After an analysis of relevant socio-economic, cultural, technical, and legal aspects of identity-related crime, potential countermeasures are discussed. We then move on to forensic aspects, with a critical analysis of pitfalls in forensic identification and case studies of mobile networks and biometric devices. Next, forensic profiling is discussed from a wide range of perspectives. The chapter concludes with lessons drawn from the five years of FIDIS research in the area of identity-related crime and forensic aspects of identity.

8.1 Introduction

This chapter summarizes the findings of five years of FIDIS research on identity-related crime and identity forensics.[1] We present the insights gained into the various forms in which identity-related crime can take place, and analyze their socio-economic, technical, and legal aspects. We then move on to identity forensics, with a critical analysis of pitfalls in forensic identification, and forensic profiling.

In the past five years of FIDIS research, we have moved forward significantly in our understanding of the concepts, tools, and legal aspects of identity crimes

* Bert-Jaap Koops is responsible for sections 1, 2, and 5 of this chapter. Zeno Geradts is responsible for sections 3 and 4 of this chapter.

1 We acknowledge here the collective effort of a large group of FIDIS researchers. Key insights were provided by David-Olivier Jaquet-Chiffelle (VIP), Mark Gasson (READING), Ronald Leenes (TILT), Martin Meints (ICPP), Nicole van der Meulen (TILT), Róbert Pintér (ISTRI), Martin Rost (ICPP), and Peter Sommer (LSE). Other contributors included Vicky Andronikou, Sebastian Clauß, Mihály Csótó, Fanny Coudert, Sabine Delaitre, Ekaterina de Vries, Hans Graux, Mireille Hildebrandt, Sylvia Ioset, Attila Kincsei, Mathias Kirchner, Els Kindt, Klaus Kursawe, Mieke Loncke, Ioannis Maghiros, Svetla Nikova, Árpád Rab, Maren Raguse, Falk Wagner, Rikkert Zoun and Albin Zuccato.

and forensics. At the same time, we observe that the field is moving fast, and that key challenges lie ahead to keep up with developments in technology and society. With the ever increasing importance of identity and identity management in the information society, it is clear that combating identity-related crime, not in the least with the help of identity forensics, is a key challenge for policy makers. This chapter aims at contributing to addressing that challenge.

8.2 Identity-Related Crime

8.2.1 The FIDIS Taxonomy of Identity-Related Crime[2]

The importance of identity in the online world is clear and so is the fact that digital identities give rise to identity-related crime. Far less clear is the wide range of crimes that can be committed in relation to identity. Identity 'theft' or fraud is actually only one instance of the multi-faceted category of identity-related crime. Moreover, it is also not at all clear what exactly constitutes 'identity "theft"' or 'identity fraud'. This lack of precision becomes especially apparent when comparing the various official and media reports on these topics. Not often are definitions provided, even though statistics play a role in politically motivated discussions and policy decisions, for example, to introduce ID cards. Commonly accepted definitions are also lacking in literature. This means that we are at the stage where comparisons of apples and oranges abound making it virtually impossible to determine the real incidence of identity-related crimes.

Thus, in order to assess the nature and magnitude of identity-related crimes, and to be able to discuss how they can be combated, we first need to understand the various phenomena captured under the umbrella term 'identity-related crime'. Paramount to this understanding are clear definitions and a typology of identity-related crime. FIDIS has developed a comprehensive taxonomy of identity-related crime, as a basis for further research and policy on combating identity crimes.

To our knowledge, such a comprehensive framework is a novelty. Sproule & Archer (2006) provide useful classifications, and De Vries et al. (2007) propose a definition of identity fraud based on an extensive literature review, but these are too narrow because they pay little attention to types like identity deletion and consensual forms of identity fraud, which are part of the identity-related crime landscape.

Categories of Mismatches Between Identifier and Identity

To understand the nature of identity-related crime, it is useful to realize that there are lawful and unlawful cases where some kind of mismatch occurs between identifier and identity. Publishing under a pseudonym, for instance, is a widely accepted practice; impersonating one's neighbour to empty her bank account without her consent is not. A taxonomy should therefore include categories of mismatches between iden-

2 This section is based on FIDIS Deliverables D5.2b (Leenes, 2006) and D5.3 (Koops et al., 2009), and on Koops and Leenes (2006).

tifier and identity that cover both intentional and unintentional, and lawful as well as unlawful types of (mis)using identity. In our analysis, we take the perspective of an observer of the identification process. This provides a more objective view on the issues than taking other possible perspectives such as that of the individual whose identity is being (mis)used or that of the person or institution suffering a loss.

Most definitions and descriptions of identity 'theft' and identity fraud (see below) have in common that, within a specific communication context, the link between at least one individual and (a) the identifier used and / or (b) the social system and the role taken therein is established incorrectly. Authentication in these cases leads to false positives, the individual is unjustly identified: individual and the identifier or role in the social system do not match. The reverse, false negatives, is also possible: the individual is unjustly not identified. In this case the link between individual and identifier is not made or blocked. This may be caused by the individual herself, who may, for instance, circumvent her employer's identification or authorization system by slipping in behind a colleague while the door is still open. More common is identity obstruction by others. A felon may, for instance, secretly apply an RFID blocker to prevent the employee from entering the building with her RFID card. Technical failures are also common causes for identity obstruction.

Identity obstruction has two subcategories. The first is identification obstruction, which means blocking the identification process in the identifying system, for example with an RFID blocker; this is usually temporary. The second is identifier erasure, which is usually (more) permanent; for instance, instead of using an RFID blocker, the attacker may bar the employee from entering the building by deleting her access control record. Although the second is a more lasting form of obstruction, the deleted identifier can of course sometimes be re-instantiated (e.g., restoring the access control record), thus inversing identity erasure: identity restoration.

The mismatch of identifier and individual can be understood independently of criminal intent. In many cases the mismatch in fact happens unintentionally or accidentally. An example is mistaking a daughter for her mother in a telephone conversation due to the similarity of their voices. This example reveals a third type of identity rearrangement: identity collision. Identity collision is usually discovered by one of the communicating partners and subsequently resolved. When the collision remains undiscovered, and is caused deliberately, identity collision may shift into identity change. Identity change is the type most closely related to the notions of identity fraud and identity 'theft', where a false identifier is linked to a person intentionally.

Altogether, we can thus distinguish four types of problems regarding the link between identifier and individual.

- *Identity collision*: a wrong link is *accidentally* made between identifier and individual.
- *Identity change*: a wrong link is *intentionally* made between identifier and individual (the identifier may be an identifier to an existing individual or a newly created one.)

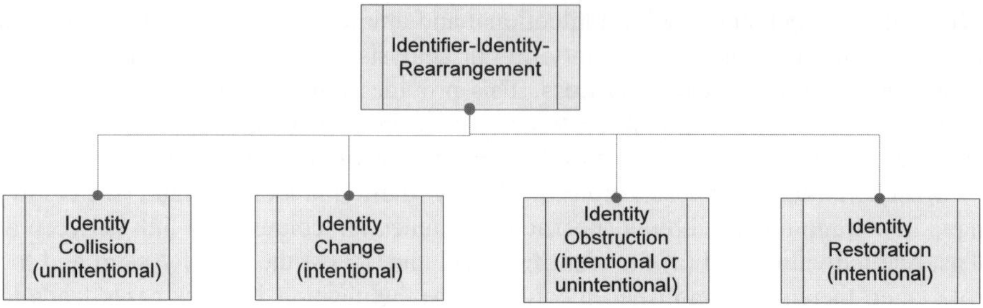

Fig. 8.1. Types of identifier-identity rearrangement

- *Identity obstruction*: an identifier linked to a specific individual is, intentionally or accidentally, deleted by herself or someone else (identifier erasure), or the link between individual and identifier fails to be made, through an intentional or accidental act (identification obstruction).
- *Identity restoration*: a deleted identifier is, usually intentionally, restored by the individual or someone else, or the linkability between identifier and individual is re-established.

Figure 8.1 summarizes the main types of rearrangement of identity linkage, which will be refined in more detail below.

Taking a closer look at identity change, we can distinguish four subcategories, depending on the behaviour of the actor – the non-original identity bearer – and, if present, of the original identity bearer.

- *Identity takeover* or *identity usurpation*: the actor takes over an existing identity of another individual (i.e., the original identity bearer) without this individual's consent. In most cases, the acquired identity was already established in a certain social structure; authentication therefore already took place or can easily be carried out because the required information already exists.
- *Identity delegation* or *identity licensing*: the actor uses an existing identity of another individual with her consent; this is similar to identity takeover, apart from the element of consent.
- *Identity exchange*: two or more individuals, with mutual consent, use each other's identity; this often happens in established 1:n relationships, for instance, customers (role) swapping loyalty cards in a supermarket.
- *Identity creation*: the actor creates an identity that is, at least to her knowledge, not linked to an existing individual. If the created identity accidentally links to an existing person, this constitutes identity collision, which, from the perspective of an independent observer, may be indistinguishable from identity takeover.

The actions in all these subcategories of identity change may be perfectly legal. For example, identity takeover can take the form of an actor assuming an official's role as part of a hidden-camera program or in a parody. Employees commonly authorize colleagues to answer their mail when on holiday (lawful identity delegation). In most cases of lawful identity delegation, consent is limited to a certain period and bound to a specific purpose.

CookieCooker (http://www.cookiecooker.de) provides a form of lawful identity exchange distributing one's webcookies randomly between different users with the aim of obscuring personalized profiles. Finally, identity creation is common in multiplayer role games and chatboxes where many users use pseudonyms. However, the actions in these subcategories can also be unlawful, which is the topic of the next section.

Categories of Identity-Related Crime

'Identity-related crime' can be defined as all punishable activities that have identity as a target or a principal tool (Koops and Leenes, 2006). It merits being treated as a distinct, novel category of crime, because combating these crimes requires special knowledge and understanding of identity-management systems and their vulnerabilities, because victims suffer from these crimes in special ways, for instance, by being blacklisted, and because public awareness is low and should be raised.

The categories of identifier-identity mismatches allow us to construct a categorization of identity-related crimes. Each type of rearrangement has lawful and unlawful instances (Figure 8.2).

Identity collision was defined as accidental (intentional identity collision falls within the category of identity change). Since crime usually requires intent, identity collision is unlawful only in rare cases. Unintentional acts are occasionally deemed unlawful, notably when a high risk is involved – e.g., accidentally cutting off the power of a hospital – or when someone is in a position where she ought to be particularly careful (Garantenstellung in German legal doctrine); for example, system administrators in a power plant are punishable if they accidentally upload programs with a virus. We have found no real cases of unlawful identity collision, suggesting that this category is small indeed, even if possible in practice.

Identity obstruction is a more relevant category from a criminal perspective. When someone has (part of) her identifier deleted by someone else or when identification is blocked, this can have severe consequences; think of a hacker destroying patient records in a hospital computer system. For such an act to fall within the scope of 'identity-related crime', however, the destruction of a patient record should be done with the goal of destroying their identity, else it would be data interference.[3] Most instances of unlawful identity obstruction actually constitute traditional crime categories (e.g., damage to property, data interference, slander). Nevertheless, given the fact that people can hardly function within society if their existence in

[3] See art. 4 of the Council of Europe's Convention on Cybercrime, http://conventions.coe.int/Treaty/EN/Treaties/Html/185.htm: 'the intentional damaging, deletion, deterioration, alteration, or suppression of computer data without right.'

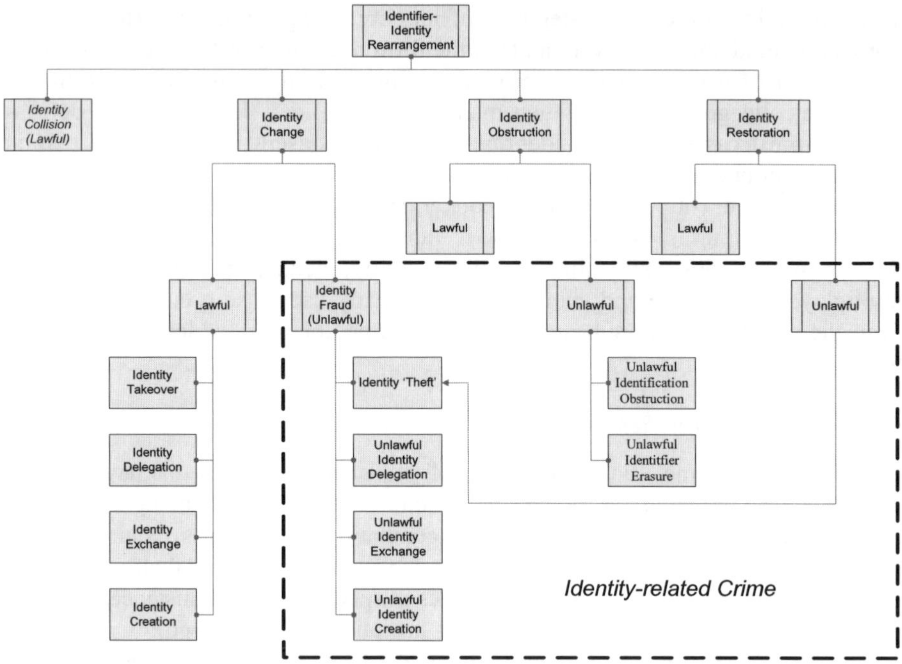

Fig. 8.2. Types of identifier-identity rearrangement and identity-related crime

computer records is denied, it may be useful to consider criminalizing intentionally erasing someone else's (partial) identifier or intentionally blocking identification. Destroying (part of) one's own identifier is considered unlawful in several countries. Germany, for instance, has criminalized destroying an official ID, considering it unacceptable when asylum seekers destroy their passport before arrival. Interestingly, the latter act could also be construed as building up a new identity (identity change) rather than destroying an old one (Leenes, 2006: 55).

Identity restoration is usually perfectly acceptable. The prototypical example is Mark Twain, who, after having been proclaimed dead by a newspaper, told the world that reports of his death were grossly exaggerated. An example of unlawful identity restoration, however, is a physician with a disciplinary prohibition to practice who resumes his practice, thus misleading the public. Unlawful identity restoration by the identity bearer usually involves roles rather than identifiers. Also forms of unlawful identity restoration by third parties without consent or knowledge of the individual involved exist. If an ex-mafia criminal who turned crown witness has received a new identity in a witness protection program (which is lawful identity creation), then making the link between him, his former and his new identity public, thereby endangering him, would constitute unlawful identity restoration. Incidentally, if the ex-criminal resorts to his former identity himself, this may also be deemed unlawful, because in many countries, civic identities are unique and defined by the state.

The preceding categories are minor phenomena when compared to the category of identity change. Although unlawful identity change often aims at committing fraud for financial gain,[4] this is not always the case. Fraud can also result in other types of damage.[5] Examples are the use of someone's identity to harm their reputation or providing a false name when stopped by a police officer to let someone else in for a criminal offense, such as drinking and driving. The latter behaviour is usually called 'criminal identity theft' in the United States.[6] Because most cases of unlawful identity change contain an element of fraud, we call this category 'identity fraud', defined as fraud (in the broad sense of unlawful deception resulting in some kind of injury to another person) committed with identity as a target or principal tool.

Each of the four subcategories of identity change has a substantial unlawful subcategory. We provide some examples. Unlawful identity delegation: a medical practitioner who provides her digital credentials to an assistant to process patient data on her behalf, which is unlawful in many countries. Unlawful identity exchange: someone visiting an inmate in prison and remaining behind while the convict walks out.[7] Unlawful identity creation: someone uses a self-generated credit-card number that fulfils the characteristics of credit-card numbers. Unlawful identity takeover in our view is what is usually called 'identity theft': fraud where the identity of an existing person is used as a target or principal tool without that person's consent. 'Identity theft' is a rather awkward term, since identity is not something that is typically stolen; unlike theft, where the owner loses possession over the stolen good, the victim of identity takeover still retains her identity. We should therefore speak of 'identity "theft"' rather than of 'identity theft' (Koops and Leenes, 2006).

Identity-related crime, certainly in the category of identity fraud, is often described (see, e.g., De Vries, 2007; Leenes, 2006: 114) as a two-stage process. The first stage involves – lawfully or unlawfully – gathering identifying data of a specific individual or unspecified individuals in a group of potential victims, or creating new identifying data. The second stage involves using these data in some unlawful way. While useful, this two-stage distinction does not provide much insight in the mechanics of identity-related crimes, how they are committed, nor into ways to combat them. Before we analyze those aspects in more detail, we will have a look at the occurrence of identity-related crime, both as portrayed in the media and in real life.

---

4 Cf., the definition of computer-related fraud in art. 8 Convention on Cybercrime: 'causing ... a loss of property to another person ... with fraudulent or dishonest intent of procuring, without right, an *economic benefit* for oneself or for another person' (italics added).

5 Cf., Webster's definition: 'intentional deception resulting in injury to another person', http://www.websters-online-dictionary.org/definition/fraud.

6 See http://www.privacyrights.org/fs/fs17g-CrimIdTheft.htm.

7 This is actually a problem in Dutch prisons, see Grijpink (2006).

8.2.2 Aspects of Identity-Related Crime

Identity-Related Crime in Films[8]

It may look odd to start a further discussion of identity-related crime with a section on films, but it is important to realize that the media is very influential in the way in which an issue is perceived and framed. When identity obstruction is mentioned, people may think first of Sandra Bullock's character in The Net being erased from society, and identity 'theft' raises the image of The Talented Mr. Ripley completely taking over the identity of his victim. The average person most often comes across the issue of identity-related crime, and identity 'theft' in particular, in mass culture indirectly rather than personally. Identity 'theft' and other forms of identity-related crime are indeed a permanent feature in mass culture, since identity and its integrity, preservation, and protection from others forms an integral part of the human mind and society.

It is therefore important to examine how identity-related crime features in mainstream films, particularly since media theory suggests that films constitute reality as source of information and have an educating effect on people (Pintér, 2007: 9-10). Films, as much as real-world stories, influence the perception of identity crimes and thus, indirectly, public policies that are always partly based on general perceptions.

Films draw on primeval stories and fears at least as much as on technological trends and topical situations. Roles and identities, as well as the changes these have undergone have existed ever since the earliest forms of society. In the Middle Ages, the concealment of identity and the "casting off" of traditional roles existed in regulated forms, notably the Carnival where roles were swapped during a few days of madness (allowing firm role establishment during the rest of the year). In modern times, where individuality and the associated importance of identity and liberty have come to the forefront, role and identity play have become more varied and common.

Throughout history, identity change has been an inexhaustible source of humour, but it was also important in fairy tales with a moral message to teach. These days, identity change as a source of humour still exists (e.g., Robin Williams in Mrs. Doubtfire), but the moral teaching element has largely disappeared. Besides humour, however, identity change as a possible source of crime has increasingly come into the limelight, with fear and suspension as prime factors in identity crimes facilitated by technology. This approach has been intensifying in the period of digital reality and digital identities, now it has become easier than ever before to assume another person's role, for example through plastic surgery (Face / Off) or the use of another person's data (Filofax), or the use and misuse of another's account (The Net).

A survey of international mainstream films, categorized according to the FIDIS taxonomy (Section 8.2.1), shows that identity collision (e.g., Working Girl, where the initial accidental collision gradually turns into identity takeover), identity deletion (e.g., The Net), and identity restoration (e.g., The Bourne Identity) occur much less frequently than identity change. Particularly identity 'theft' is a productive

---

[8] This section is based on FIDIS deliverable D5.2c (Pintér, 2007).

theme (e.g., Fantômas, Auggie Rose), but also delegation (e.g., Dave), (e.g., Trading Places), and creation (e.g., Johnny Handsome) occur frequent

The picture of identity-related crime suggested by films, however, is mostly misleading. Films, especially mainstream, mass-cultural products, oversimplify the issue and depict it as if victims have no means to defend themselves and are entirely at the mercy and whim of identity 'thieves'. These films focus on the rare cases where the targeted individual falls victim to fraud, is robbed of his identity, and is completely replaced in society by the identity 'thief'. Contrary to reality, this emerges as a standard or prototypical form of identity 'theft' in films. This is understandable, since such a plot is more interesting, exciting, and more effective on the screen as compared with the bulk of bank-account takeover and other abuses taking place in reality. The bulk of real-life identity 'theft' cases cause financial damage but do not completely disrupt the social life of the victims. In reality, invisible criminals do not strive to completely destroy their victims' personalities and identities; rather, they try to "simply" make money out of their crime without being seen or shedding blood. Such cases are unsuitable for mainstream films.

As a result, whoever receives their information mainly from films will form a false picture of identity-related crime and may remove the issue into the realms of fiction and the world of urban legends. The bias of films to focus on extreme and unrealistic cases therefore poses a risk that current trends in identity-related crime and legal, organizational, and technical countermeasures are underdeveloped in citizens' world views.

Given the importance of awareness-raising to combat identity-related crime, it is vital that actions are taken to adjust the picture of identity-related crime, in particular identity 'theft', as it is sketched in the media at large. Film producers could contribute to this by showing standard data-security measures, such as a virus check, as part of everyday life. However, films are not likely in future to sketch a substantially different picture of identity 'theft', given the primeval appeal of extreme identity takeover as a theme in visually mediated fiction. The required readjustment of the picture of identity-related crime will therefore have to rely on other mass-media, such as non-fiction literature and documentaries, the press, and blogs.

Identity-Related Crime in Real Life[9]

In the United States, 'identity theft' has become a household word, and the media continues to tell fear-igniting stories of stolen identities. The actual size of the problem, however, is contested, so that identity 'theft' might be a hype rather than a big problem in real life in the US. In recent years, the problem – or the hype – and the subsequent need for policies and countermeasures have spread from the US to other areas, including Europe. The extent of the problem in Europe is unknown. Rather than relying on (contested) US data and concerns – which may or may not be quite specific for the US situation – a description of actual European prevalence of identity crimes would help put our concerns about identity 'theft' in perspective.

---

[9] This section is based on FIDIS deliverable D12.7 (Van der Meulen and Koops, 2008).

We have tried to provide such a picture by shedding light on the situation in Belgium, France, Germany, and the United Kingdom, these being EU member states that have a policy debate about identity-related crime, so that a certain amount of reports and data are available. This provides a first indication of the prevalence of identity 'theft' in Europe, on which subsequent studies can build. The resulting picture is, unfortunately, only a piecemeal one: studies appear scarce, and most authors point out that the lack of a separate criminal provision makes it more complicated to gather information on the problem, since crimes are not being specifically reported or registered as identity-related crime. Moreover, uncertainty and unclarity about definitions are dominating themes in many reports with regard to identity 'theft'. The unclarity about definitions and about the actual prevalence of identity 'theft' prevent policy makers, or so they claim, from taking action.

Nevertheless, the contours of a picture of the European prevalence of identity-related crime shimmer through the available data and reports. Document fraud is an on-going concern, with tens of thousands of cases yearly in countries like Belgium and France. The traditional forms of document forgery have been supplemented more recently with look-alike fraud, which is a major concern in several countries.

However, in the past few years, a shift has occurred from document and look-alike fraud to online forms of fraud, in particular financial identity fraud or identity 'theft'. Phishing – which traditionally relies on luring ICT users by deceptive email messages to false websites – seems to be increasingly replaced by covert forms of fraud, in particular by botnets that assemble identity and personal data from infected computers.

Altogether, identity-related crime, particularly document forgery, look-alike fraud, and computer-related financial identity 'theft', is a significant form of crime that is on the rise. There is insufficient empirical evidence to call it a big problem yet, but the upward trend warrants taking expeditious measures to prevent it becoming a big problem in the first place. In order to know which measures are most appropriate, it is useful to have a further look at the ways in which these forms of crime can be committed.

Technical Aspects: Modes of Attack[10]

To deepen our understanding of identity related crimes it helps to study possible points of attacks, vulnerabilities, and types of attack. For this purpose, we make use of the following simplified picture of online interactions (Figure 8.3).

The threats and examples of their use are as follows.

T1 is a direct attack on the user: threatening them to make them disclose identity data; applying social engineering, such as phishing attacks; stealing credit cards from a wallet; replacing the individual by a look-alike.

[10] This section is based on FIDIS deliverables D5.2b (Leenes, 2006) and D5.3 (Koops et al., 2009).

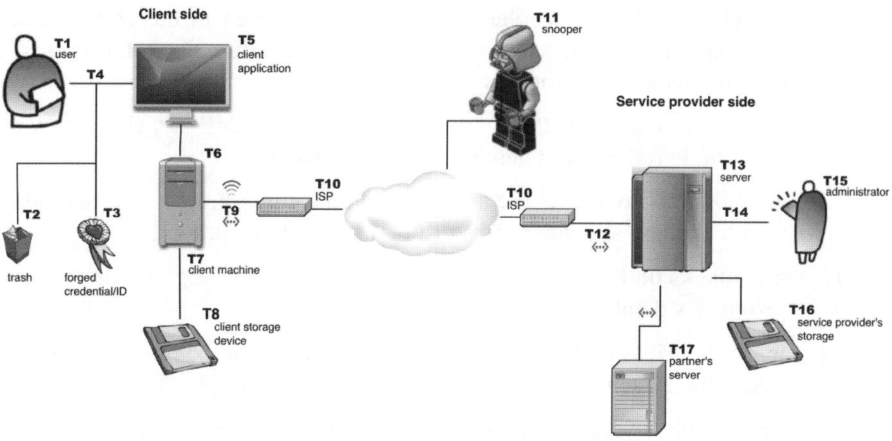

Fig. 8.3. General view of online interactions showing 17 points of attack

T2 is 'dumpster diving', obtaining identity data people leave behind in the physical world: acquiring user names and passwords written on post-it notes; finding receipts of account details in the garbage can; forensically scanning second-hand PCs for remaining identity data.

T3 represents the creation of forged identity data or credentials: generating identity data to acquire a credit card; forging a medical diploma.

T4 is any attack on the communication between users and their IT systems such as their PC. This includes malware phishing, like keystroke loggers, presenting forged biometric data, and intercepting or interfering with Bluetooth communication between keyboard and PC.

T5 is the manipulation of user applications such as web browsers to record data entered by the user, e.g., through Trojan horses, or to redirect the user to fake websites through spoofing. Reading cookies set in the user's browser is another example.

T6 relates to the interception and manipulation of data at the level of the operating system: viruses, root-kits, and spyware.

T7 concerns attacks on the client's PC itself: intrusion by hackers; the installation of physical devices, such as modified hardware.

T8 are attacks on the link between the user's PC and storage devices (hard disks and USB sticks), aimed at obtaining or redirecting identity data.

T9 are attacks on the communication channel between the user's system and the internet: interception or manipulation of WiFi signals from a user's home.

are attacks on Internet Service Providers involved in the communication: spoofing DNS entries resulting in the redirection of the user's communication to a rogue site.

T11 represent attacks on the network: man-in-the-middle attacks; wiretapping; node redirection; denial-of-service attacks.

T12 is analogous to T9, as the service provider's internal network can also be attacked by snoopers and sniffers – network infiltration.

T13 are attacks on the service provider's IT system: hacking into the service provider's databases.

T14 is symmetrical to T4, concerning any attack on the communication between the system administrator and the service provider's IT system.

T15 represents physical or logical attacks on or by the service provider's staff: personnel leaking identity data to outsiders.

T16 involves any attack on the service provider's data storage.

T17 concerns attacks on the communication between service providers and their business partners, like a bank or accountant.

This list shows the wide variety of possible attacks and modi operandi in identity-related crime. In principle, all possible cases of identity-related crimes involve one or more of the threats outlined. In order to assess actual risks in interactions and devise countermeasures, it would be useful to have empirical data on the likelihood or actual incidence. As emerges from the previous section, attacks like T3 (document forgery) and T6 (botnets to phish for data) are prevalent, but altogether, extensive empirical evidence on where attacks actually take place is sparse and anecdotal.

Legal Aspects: Relevant Legal Provisions[11]

The various types of identity-related crime are, by our definition, unlawful. Which attacks and modi operandi actually are unlawful, and what kind of sanction can be imposed, however, depends on a country's legislation. Relevant provisions can be found in multiple legal subdomains, such as criminal law (e.g., hacking), civil law (e.g., tort), and administrative law (e.g., giving a false identity in a naturalization request). Relevant regulation, such as data-protection regulation, often belongs to multiple legal domains (criminal law, administrative law). Furthermore, criminal law tends not to abide by neat, conceptual distinctions, and often disregards modi operandi and defines crimes regardless of the way they are committed. This also shows in the statistics. In the case of criminal convictions, available statistics usually report the crime for which people are convicted, not the attacks they used nor the conceptual category of the concrete crime. And finally, there are few interna-

[11] This section is based on FIDIS deliverables D5.1 (Koops, 2005) and D5.3 (Koops et al., 2009).

tional standards and relevant international treaties to facilitate cross-jurisdictional comparisons.

Not all attacks outlined in the previous section are punishable (criminal law) or otherwise unlawful (tort, administrative law) in practice. Whether they are depends on the existing legal context, i.e., jurisdiction and existing legislation. Moreover, not all types in our conceptual categorization need necessarily be criminalized; what is considered undesirable or criminal behaviour still depends to a considerable extent on social, cultural, and legal norms that vary from country to country. For example, the United States and European countries to date have varying approaches with respect to identity-related crime.

In the United States, the Identity Theft and Assumption Deterrence Act specifically covers identity-related crime, albeit largely restricted to identity 'theft'.[12] This penalizes anyone who 'knowingly transfers or uses, without lawful authority, a means of identification of another person with the intent to commit, or to aid or abet, any unlawful activity that constitutes a violation of Federal law, or that constitutes a felony under any applicable State or local law'.

In European countries, there is – to our knowledge – hardly any specific criminal provision targeting identity 'theft' or identity fraud as such, nor do the Council of Europe's Convention on Cybercrime[13] or the EU Framework Decision on attacks against information systems[14] contain identity-specific crimes. Some countries do have special provisions targeting specific subcategories of identity-related crime, such as deletion or forgery of official identity documents,[15] but a general criminalization of identity 'theft', identity fraud, or other types of identity-related crime is absent. Instead, countries largely rely on non-identity-specific, and often traditional, criminal provisions, such as fraud, forgery, data damage, illegal access to data, or imposture.

The legal categories of identity-related crime can be divided in identity-specific and identity-neutral crimes. Many identity-neutral provisions can actually be used to sanction identity-related crimes, in criminal, civil, and administrative law. Traditional criminal provisions unspecific to identity, like forgery, fraud, and theft, can be used, possibly in combination with general provisions about aiding and abetting or criminal attempt. Also, the traditional identity-specific crime of imposture might be relevant. For a tentative, non-exhaustive categorization that maps possible identity-neutral and identity-specific provisions that can be found in most jurisdictions, we refer to Koops et al. (2009). This overview could be used to detect potential gaps in national jurisdictions with respect to identity-related crime.

---

[12] U.S. Identity Theft and Assumption Deterrence Act, Public Law 105-318, 112 STAT. 3010, 30 October 1998, codified at 18 U.S.C. 1028(a)(7).

[13] Supra, note 3.

[14] Council Framework Decision 2005/222/JHA of 24 February 2005 on attacks against information systems, *Official Journal* L 69/67, 16.3.2005.

[15] See, for instance, articles 347-350 Estonian Criminal Code, as mentioned in the FIDIS *ID Law Survey*, available at http://www.fidis.net.

Countermeasures[16]

As we have seen, the United States have in the Identity Theft and Assumption Deterrence Act specifically criminalized identity 'theft'. They have taken several other countermeasures to combat identity-related crime, often through legislation. These include the Gramm-Leach-Bliley Act that imposes security measures on organizations, laws such as the Fair and Accurate Credit Transactions Act (FACTA), which increase organizational responsibility, and security breach notification laws.

Like the US, European countries are also taking countermeasures to combat identity-related crimes. Rather surprisingly in view of regulatory traditions, in Europe, legal measures are much less prominent than in the United States. As noted, criminal law has not been adapted in European countries to accommodate identity crimes specifically. Other legislative measures taken in the US, like free credit reports, seem rather specific to the US situation. Some measures, for example mandatory truncation of credit card numbers on receipts, may nevertheless be valuable in Europe as well. Particularly laws requiring security breach notification have recently also become an issue in Europe. Such a system requires organizations to provide their customers with notification whenever they have lost personal information. This is a promising measure, although the danger of individuals becoming immune to frequent notifications must be taken into account.

Measures like those imposed in the US by legislation are often taken by the financial sector itself, or by public-private partnerships, in Europe. Financial institutions are acutely aware of the threat of identity 'theft', and they take the lead in enhanced technical and organizational security measures. Unlike in the US, these do not necessarily have to be backed up by legislation. A wide panorama of measures is visible, consisting of awareness raising campaigns, complaint centers, and innovative technical measures like virtual dynamic cards or enhanced transaction authentication numbers. Some potential solutions, however, are opposed by merchants and banks for economic reasons, suggesting that market failure – one of the reasons for the US to impose legal obligations – may not altogether be absent in Europe.

Welcome as all these countermeasures are, there is a snag. One countermeasure consistently showing up is to introduce general-purpose electronic identity cards and numbers, often backed up by biometrics, aimed at preventing document or look-alike fraud. The downside of such measures is that they introduce considerable vulnerabilities: as the resulting identification infrastructure comes to rely heavily on the unique eID method, the risk of identity 'theft' actually rises, and the burden of proving being a victim of identity 'theft' becomes heavier as the system is supposedly more secure. Thus, general-purpose eID cards and numbers to curb document fraud are a two-edged sword, and governments need to carefully consider and monitor emerging side-effects.[17]

---

[16] This section is based on FIDIS deliverable D12.7 (Van der Meulen and Koops, 2008).

[17] See also FIDIS deliverable D13.3 (Buitelaar, 2007) and Section 9.2 of this book.

8.3 Forensic Implications[18]

We have focused so far on identity-related crime, analyzing its concepts and techniques and indicating legal, organizational, and technical measures to combat crimes in which identity is used as a target or principal tool. Much of the knowledge relevant to understand identity-related crime is also relevant to its mirror image: identity forensics. Identifying perpetrators is one of the key functions of forensics, and given the increasing importance of identity management, identity forensics is a major field of study in the information society.

The term forensic, as used in this chapter, refers to information that is used in court or other dispute resolution procedures as evidence. Such information can be extracted from identification management systems. This evidence can be very strong, however some limitations are apparent. For example, one should always investigate if identity change has been committed as shown in Figure 8.2.

8.3.1 Forensic Aspects

For forensic science, it is important to know the reliability of the identity management system, and that the evidence extracted from the system can be explained in court, where the model as discussed in Figure 8.2 can be used. We distinguish the following issues:

Reliability of Underlying Technology

How good is the technology, and is it easy to alter, copy, reproduce etc. the data that identifies a certain person? In forensic science it is important to understand the underlying technology that is used. For example how easy is it to alter an image of a person which is used as evidence in a crime case.

How Well Is the Individual Bound to an ID Artifact?

It is often quite easy to exchange paper passports. In the case of look-alike fraud, another person can use a passport at the border without anyone realizing it. Furthermore, in some countries it is relatively simple to switch identity, by asking the government for a change of names.

Auditability

Can we audit the complete system and determine how it works, for example an ATM system? Do we have log records of for example a payment system?

---

[18] This section is based on FIDIS deliverables D6.1 (Geradts and Sommer, 2006) and D6.7c (Geradts and Sommer, 2008).

Transparency

A question that arises is whether the forensic scientist actually has access to the artifact data and technology. If not, they might look at it as a 'black box', but the essential issue is the validation of the information extracted from the system. In many cases trade secrets are a hindering factor. Open source projects in general give more insight into the technology that is used, however source code review is a labour-intensive task.

Disclosure

With many proprietary systems it is not known if there are 'back doors' in the software, which allow the manufacturer (and thus anyone else who becomes aware of it) to circumvent the protection system. However, not everything can be disclosed in a court room, since manufacturers also sometimes have non-disclosure agreements with the expert. The reason is that they do not want to share methods with the public, or that the government would not like to disclose a certain method, since then it will not be useful in future cases.

How Long Is Data Kept?

To examine data, it is important to know how long the data is kept. Camera surveillance systems are known to typically keep their data for several days, after which they will overwrite it. These kinds of issues have to be taken into consideration. In some cases additional information can be extracted from data caching or other areas where the information was temporarily stored.

Legal and Ethical Issues

A forensic scientist should also know the rules relating to data protection legislation. Often in criminal law the system can be examined. However, whether it is admissible in court depends on the laws of the country and how the information was gathered. For example, in the Netherlands wiretaps are commonly used as evidence in court, whereas in the United Kingdom this is not admissible, which is based on the ethics within a law system. Other ethical issues one should be aware of are, for example, that personal details may become available from the data that is extracted.

Unintended Audit Trail

Unintended aspects are those of the artifact or the means of using it which yield information of forensic value. In some cases useful information such as GSM location data can be extracted. Using this data for locating someone goes beyond the original purpose of the network provider storing this information, which was for billing purposes.

8.3.2 Example 1: Mobile Networks[19]

Information from mobile networks is currently used as evidence in court. The determination of a location of a mobile phone is important to check if a person has been at a certain place and time. This can also be used to check information from witnesses and from the suspects. Furthermore, information who is calling who and SMS-details can be used as evidence in court.

However, one should always consider that the real identity of the user is not necessarily the person who is the subscriber or the purchaser of a prepaid phone, since the phone may be stolen or borrowed. A further problem is that certain models of SIM-cards can be cloned. Beyond these and other technical issues, on a management level the reliability of collected data may be undermined by fraudulent employees or contractors, software faults and other such issues. As such, although there is valuable data that can be exploited, the integrity of such data must be carefully considered.

8.3.3 Example 2: Biometric Devices[20]

Concluding from research in FIDIS deliverable 6.1, it is evident that the current state of the art of biometric devices leaves much to be desired. A major deficit in the security that the devices offer is the absence of effective liveness detection (Figure 8.4). At this time, the devices tested require human supervision to be sure that no fake biometric is used to pass the system. This, however, negates some of the benefits these technologies potentially offer, such as high-throughput automated access control and remote authentication.

The independent testing of biometric devices is still non-trivial as manufacturers tend to sell their products for more than they can achieve. The latter can give a false sense of security, adversely affecting actual security if not recognized in time. It is an issue that we encounter in many forms of technology today: if it can be cracked, it will be cracked. Accepting this would need a different attitude of manufacturers, in which more of what is going on inside the device and the accompanying software is made public. It would allow potential users of biometric systems to better judge the fitness of such systems for their particular purposes.

From a forensic point of view, care should be taken when drawing conclusions from information extracted from access control systems that use biometric devices. The possibility that the system was compromised, consequently falsely linking persons to events, should be examined or at least noted in the forensic examination report.

---

[19] Based on FIDIS deliverable D6.1 (contribution by Falk Wagner).

[20] Based on FIDIS deliverable D6.1 (contribution by Rikkert Zoun).

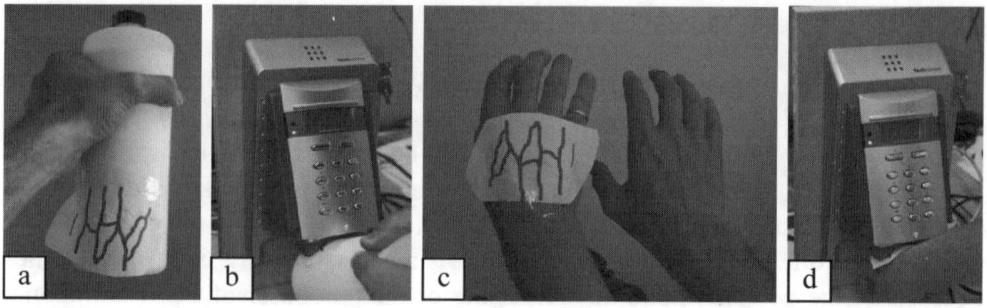

Fig. 8.4. Vascular pattern spoofs effective with liveness detection turned off. a) The copy of a vascular pattern stuck on a bottle. b) The bottle spoof verified as an authorized user. c) The copy of a vascular pattern stuck on a hand (left), next to the original hand (right) of an authorized user. d) The hand spoof verified as the authorized

8.3.4 Conclusion

This work has been an overview of issues that arise from different perspectives of Identity Management Systems and their forensic implications. As has been shown, information from digital systems can be useful as evidence in the court, however it is important to be aware that identities can be stolen or 'borrowed' in the case of a mobile device, and devices such as biometric systems do not always function as expected for technical, management or other reasons.

Although the information that is extracted from such systems can be used as evidence in court, for forensic science, it is important to give a statement of the technologies limitations and thus how strong or weak the evidence alone is. As such, it is important to also consider other available evidence. With many systems there exists a possibility of incorrect association of a user with a mobile device, deliberate tampering with the system or system error through incorrect usage or technical faults. A classic example is that fingerprints can be spoofed, and indeed other biometric features can be copied, even without the owner of that feature knowing it. Additionally, the claims from the manufacturers of the devices should always be verified. If they claim a device has liveness detection for example, this should be checked. For these reasons, in the examination process, it is important to consider the likely integrity of the data, i.e., how failsafe the system is, since this could provide an alternative hypothesis such as a different individual being involved in the crime. Equally, it is necessary to ensure law enforcement investigators and technical analysts follow the necessary protocols. In doing so, prosecutors can ensure that otherwise admissible electronic evidence is not suppressed or compromised legally either because of an illegal search and seizure or because the evidentiary foundation was not properly or credibly laid during trial.

8.4 Forensic Profiling[21]

8.4.1 Introduction

In the context of crime or criminal investigation, profiling is often assimilated with offender profiling, psychological profiling or the use of investigative psychology, mostly, although not exclusively, in the context of violent crimes. DNA-profiling is a different term that is also familiar to a wide range of the population even if its exact scope remains largely unknown. Another immediate perception of profiling in a forensic context is the application of data mining techniques to an important quantity of data collected from crimes and persons in order to recognize patterns that may inform about illegal activities. Less known, but the object of growing interest, is the field of illicit drug profiling (systematic extraction and storage of chemical attributes of drugs seized in order to obtain indications on the manufacture and distribution processes, the size and the evolution of the market). There is thus no one single use of the term "profiling" in forensic science and intuitive meanings apparently lead to very different territories. If the psychological viewpoint appears to fascinate and attract many people, DNA, illicit drug profiling and data mining dimensions appear to belong to technical and highly specialized fields, largely inaccessible to the public.

The distorted perception of all of the dimensions that lead to wrong expectations and fears: common sense vision of forensic science and criminal investigation differs considerably from concrete practice. Moreover, many different communities of researchers participate in the debate by developing similar but loosely connected models and approaches. These are based on different bodies of knowledge mainly borrowed from psychology, sociology, criminology, forensic science, crime analysis and criminal intelligence, or statistic and computer science. Finally, what really works and what does not is not easy to distinguish.

Thus, in the perspective of the FIDIS project, the process of balancing risks for the subjects and opportunities for the data controller is not easy (Hildebrandt and Gutwirth, 2008). For instance, weighing up the risks of being wrongly profiled as a criminal in the course of an investigation, and the opportunity for investigators, law enforcement agencies or the criminal justice system to be able to neutralize dangerous criminals early, is not straightforward. There is an initial need to find some unity within these scattered pieces of works.

A better definition of the term 'forensic profiling' is also essential from a forensic perspective because notions of identity and identification are at the core of the domain and should properly integrate evolutions associated to identification systems and new identities in the information society. Moreover, forensic science needs new frameworks in order to make the best use of data mining technology, not only in the treatment of electronic traces, but also to exploit more traditional forensic case data. This convergence between the different fields of forensic science, and particularly what is called forensic Information Technology (forensic

[21] Based on FIDIS deliverable D6.7c (contribution by Geradts/Sommer/Ribaux).

IT), with methods for their exploitation such as data mining, seem to constitute one of the biggest challenges for the future.

This is a considerable task, as forensic science is too often considered to be a list of separated and narrow specialties. However, this FIDIS task, connected with results obtained from other FIDIS activities, offers an opportunity to take some steps towards this objective.

Thus, the distinctions that are provided here aim to identify some of the profiling-related concepts, inferences and technical methods explicitly or tacitly used, as the object of research or applied in practice. Reasoning activities that may be assimilated with profiling are pervasive. Of these inference forms, some are identified here as an element of a more global approach of profiling (Hildebrandt and Gutwirth, 2008). This account is not intended to be comprehensive, because relevant dimensions go far beyond what can be explored in the single task of this project.

8.4.2 Definition of Forensic Profiling

We consider that forensic profiling consists of the exploitation of traces in order to draw profiles that must be relevant to the context of supporting various security tasks, mostly in the criminal justice system. A distinction of forms of profiles that are used in this context is necessary before evaluating applications of data mining techniques for forensic profiling.

8.4.3 Linkage Blindness and Limits of Profiling

It may be perceived that the necessary data for forensic profiling is immediately available in a suitable form to the criminal justice system. This is definitely not so. Methods for processing data carefully distinguish a selective collection of traces, the collation of the data coming from different sources, the evaluation of its quality, the analysis of the available information and the timely dissemination of intelligence or knowledge on a need-to-know and right-to-know basis (Peterson et al., 2000). This decomposition helps to make explicit a series of pervasive difficulties when profiling is envisaged.

A broad variety of barriers that go far beyond the inadequate use of technologies (Sheptycki, 2004) hamper the fluidity of information. These can lead to a well identified weakness called linkage blindness (Egger, 1984), an obstacle to the detection of relevant patterns in the information which exist in reality. This incapacity to connect the dots is generally accepted to be at the origin of main intelligence failures (United States, 2004). Below are some examples of causes, but other legal, organizational, methodological, technological, human and fundamental (complexity) causes may also lead to linkage blindness.

- Law enforcement data is scattered into different files and in different jurisdictions. For instance DNA and Automatic Fingerprint Identification Systems (AFIS) may be centralized at country level, but both databases are generally treated separately as the result of legal rules. Moreover, databases may also use different classification systems and even preclude extractions of parts of the data, as well as electronic exchanges.

- Beyond police recorded data, administrative data and openly accessible sources, information is generally not directly accessible and available. If we suppose a specific situation, a judicial authority must intervene to authorize the access by the police and to order the possessor to grant access. This may dramatically slow down the whole process. Consequently, this may invalidate the analysis of the data in regard of of the dynamics of thc problem under scrutiny. For example, several months are sometimes needed for obtaining some set of data in the framework of international co-operation agreements.
- Data comes from multiple sources under a broad variety of forms, which can still occasionally be a paper form. Moreover, the whole data treated, even police recorded data, is not prepared for profiling purposes, rather, it is structured for strictly administrative purposes.
- Profiles are hypotheses that are based mainly on imperfect (incomplete and uncertain) information. Thus, profiles may provide irrelevant leads and recovery from wrong investigative directions must be possible through recording assessment of the solidity of the information upon which hypotheses have been drawn.

These difficulties are obstacles to the treatment of data. Whether or not data mining technologies are implemented is not an essential question here. Rather, it appears that collection of data, evaluation of the information and the pre-processing stages for collating different sources of information generally imply a significant effort that must absolutely precede analysis and profiling.

This is particularly evident when dealing with the more fundamental questions of devising models in order to collate data coming from scattered sources. This data is generally available in different formats and must be structured in a suitable form for analysis purposes. Generally, at least three main dimensions of analysis appear relevant when dealing with criminal data for analysis purposes: what are the entities (for instance objects, individual, groups, traces, series, incidents, etc.) and their relations (for instance this person own this car), chronologies (for instance sequence of transactions between bank accounts), and spatio / temporal developments (for instance concentration of activities and their evolutions). It is very doubtful that data mining would be possible without first engaging efforts to collate the data. This is done through models that are based on at least one of those dimensions, depending on what the problem at hand is and what is searched for in the data.

Finally, disseminating obtained results in order to make intelligence products available to an organization is a critical aspect of the whole methodology. The quality of communication influences the possibility to appropriately use the obtained profiles in the field. The analytical part that entices profiling, at the core of the process, must thus be carefully considered within a broader process.

8.4.4 Data Available

Roughly speaking, sets of data available to law enforcement agencies are divided into two categories:

- Nominal data directly designates persons or objects (recidivists, intelligence files and suspect files, stolen vehicles or objects, etc.) and their relations. Nominal data may also be obtained in the framework of specific investigations, for instance a list of calls made with a mobile phone (card and / or phone) that cover a certain period of time, a list of people corresponding to a certain profile, or data obtained through surveillance.
- Crime data consist of traces that result from criminal activities: physical traces, other information collected at the scene, from witness or victims or some electronic traces, as well as reconstructed descriptions of cases (*modus operandi*, time intervals, duration and place) and their relations (links between cases, series).

Nominal data and relations may be abstracted in order to describe the structure of groups of offenders or criminal organizations.

Crime data are ideally also regrouped into abstract descriptions according to recurrent situations that share typical mechanisms. For instance, credit card frauds may be distributed into classes that separate skimming, distraction thefts, other thefts, etc. However, most of the time, data is initially administratively classified according to legal definitions which may mask the real dynamic behind crime problems (Goldstein, 1990). This emphasizes the necessity to make a distinction between sources of traces (persons or objects), the activity or situation that may explain the traces (the dynamic of the crime: context, immediate environment, victims, offenders) and the offense (legal definition) (Cook et al., 1998; Jackson et al., 2006).

The difference between crime-data and criminal data through crime / criminal data has led to a distinction between the fields of crime analysis, mostly carried out at a regional or local level, and criminal intelligence analysis, mostly the province of central agencies. This duality usually designates two professional communities (Bruce et al., 2004)[22]. However, both are obviously linked under many forms, particularly because traces directly result from behaviours of individuals and help provide some kind of description. This is compound by the aim of the investigation to identify, localize, and then provide evidence about the link between a trace and a person, to assume an activity or help determine an offense. In this context, forensic profiling will constitute the process that focuses on the exploitation of traces, but may overlap with criminal intelligence analysis.

[22] IALEIA: International Association of Law Enforcement Intelligence Analysts; IACA: International Association of Crime Analysts.

8.4.5 Structuring Evidence and Profiling

When a suspect has been arrested, forensic scientists may advise an authority on how to deal with traces and provide leads on new traces to be collected. At this stage, a lot of activity is dedicated to test the consistency of available information, under the assumption that the suspect is at the source of the traces and the activity. A test of consistency with the hypotheses is not sufficient for going to court (see above), but it may lead to refute the hypotheses if available traces show unexplained discrepancies.

For instance a person who is supposed to have used her credit card at one place could not have used simultaneously her mobile phone at another distant place. In terms of profiles, coherence of the profile of the person under scrutiny has to be tested from various perspectives in order to detect potential contradictions or on the other hand to support hypotheses by demonstrating consistence (it has still to be confirmed how those concordances may occur by coincidence!). For instance, it may be assumed that the use of a mobile phone is part of the modus operandi of a serial offender when he is operating. Thus, data related to the localization of mobile phones should show spatio-temporal coherence with data related to the crimes themselves. Correlation between different sources of data (traces) may be thus intensively used according to the hypothesis to be tested.

8.4.6 Forensic Profiling in an Investigative Perspective

As stated by many authors (Kind, 1987; Wiggett et al., 2003; Jackson, 2004; Jackson et al., 2006; Mennell, 2006; Mennell and Shaw, 2006), there is the realization among forensic scientists that their role must extend to the investigation itself. They must be particularly engaged when hypotheses have still not been entirely drawn, in the coordination of the forensic information collected, as well as for proposing new collection of data. In this way, the forensic scientist turns from an evaluator to a more investigative attitude (Jackson et al., 2006): who / what is the source of this trace, how can we explain the existence of these traces, what is the offence, what evidence may indicate some possibilities for new data collection, what support and leads to the investigation may be provided, where is the person who committed the crime, etc.?

This contribution is based on an entirely different inferential process than for interpreting evidence for the court. Rather than balancing probabilities related to given propositions, it focuses on the development of alternative hypotheses that may explain the existence of traces. Thus, rather than testing the hypothesis of culpability or innocence, we could generally describe the process as starting from the effects (the traces) and imagining possible causes on the basis of general knowledge (abduction and induction). Forms of profiling that arise during the investigative part of the process are manifolds and combine individual profiling with group profiling (Jaquet-Chiffelle, 2008). We do not have the pretension of identifying all the possible forms here, only the most typical will be described.

One of the basic operations consists of creating a first profile from the available (collected) information and then searching for all the persons or their relations to objects that correspond to this profile. Profiles are described here as categories that restrict the search within a 'selected' population. A person (individual) may generally be described through traces:

- They themselves reflect directly some physical aspects of the sources and have some descriptive capacity, such as fingermarks or DNA profiles extracted from biological marks, a snapshot taken from a camera.
- Traces and where they are found may be used to infer some indications about physical aspects or inform about clothes or accessories: earmarks found at a certain height on a door and the size of shoemarks may indicate (qualitatively) how tall the source is; a snapshot may provide some physical description as well as information about clothes and accessories.
- Traces may indicate the make and model of the printer used to print a recovered document, a bullet collected at the scene of crime may indicate the make and model of the firearm used, while paint marks coming from a car may point to a make and model of the implicated car. These are all types of acquisitions that may indirectly point to a person. Other possibilities include the use of fibre for inferring description of clothes, toolmarks or other marks for obtaining some description of the tools used. In a similar way of thinking, but about persons, DNA profiles indicate the gender (generally not more about the physical aspect through non-coding DNA sequences chosen for forensic use).
- The activity and behaviour in the immediate environment may be inferred through a global analysis of the spatial (and temporal) distribution of traces, such as a sequence of shoemarks, a sequence of withdrawals with a specific bank card at different ATMs, traces of navigation with an internet browser.
- Circumstances and application of different theories from different bodies of knowledge may help to interpret the situations in order to provide other traits of the person or of his behaviour. For instance, geographical profiling (mostly for serial crimes) aims at providing clues for localizing a person (Rossmo, 1999), or different theories point out that psychological traits may also be inferred. The person may also be the object of a classification process into different categories (pre-defined classification of computer crime offenders, arson offenders, rapists, etc.).

Each final profile may thus be more or less general. Its attributes are known or unknown, complete or not and mostly uncertain.

One of the main (but not the only) questions of the investigation is the identification of the sources of the traces and how they may be related with the activity. Developing hypotheses about who / what is the source may be straightforward for instance through the use of DNA databases or Automatic Fingerprint Identification Systems (AFIS). Those systems start from the traces that come from a source (data subject as defined in Hildebrandt, 2008a), transform them into a digital form (attribute of a virtual person (Jaquet-Chiffelle, 2008)), compare them with collections of reference material and suggest as output a (list of) possible candidate(s) (or list of virtual persons) that refer to possible data subjects. The result is then interpreted and integrated into the investigation process. When using AFIS databases, a list of candidates is returned by the system, while for DNA databases, usually a single profile[23] is returned. However, with the evolving content of databases and since identical twins have the same DNA, occasionally several DNA-profiles may be returned by the database. Moreover, with the extended use of partial DNA or mixtures, putative sources may be multiple.

In order to generalize this process, a useful concept has been stressed by Kind (1987). He argues for the use of the dual concepts of frame and form. The frame contains the set of entities considered as relevant for the investigation, according to available evidence, while, roughly, the form distinguishes different region of the frame as more or less promising. A list of candidates extracted from an AFIS system constitutes the frame, while scrutinizing the content provides as outcome the form. The frame is often constituted of persons or entities that share a common profile. This may also be seen as a non-distributive group profiling approach (Hildebrandt and Backhouse, 2005; Hildebrandt, 2008b; Jaquet-Chiffelle, 2008) where a category of individuals is built on the basis of a different set of data and where the decision to insert an individual (or its individual profile) into the frame may depend on features of different natures.

There are many ways to develop a frame in the course of the investigation, depending on the case and available traces. The direct and simplest way consists in comparing the trace with the collection of reference material (like for DNA or AFIS databases). A similar process consists of comparing images taken from video surveillance systems (CCTV) with collection of photos taken from known persons. The scheme is the same and simple, but obviously the source of data used presents specificities that make the methods routinely applicable, as well as automated profiling possible or not.

Another possibility, when recidivism is known as frequent, is to compare the assumed modus operandi of the offender with the modus operandi used by known recidivists. Here again, when serial crime is considered, a profile extracted from the series of modus operandi used by the recidivist (a profile extracted from an already constituted set of information – individual profile) may be used to proceed to the comparison: the burglar usually operated during the night, entered the prem-

[23] The use of profile for DNA may be confusing in the context of this deliverable. However, a DNA profile may be defined as a description of a person through part of her DNA structures. Even if the parts of the DNA structure used in a forensic context have been chosen for their polymorphism across the population, the same profile may apply to several persons. A profile thus does not define a single individual, but rather a group.

ises through an open window, and generally selected only credit cards. There may be very different approaches for building such a profile, for instance by expecting that a specific feature occurs in each case or only in the majority of cases, expecting the existence of a specific feature of not, etc. The relevancy of such a profile depends on the expected use of the profile (searching other databases for linking cases, organizing specific surveillance, trying to intercept the perpetrators) and thus may take the status of intelligence (see below).

Another important form of profiling is carried out through the application of models and methods used for hypothesizing the place where the offender resides, or one of his centers of interest. These methods are known as geographical profiling and may be used in specific situations, for instance when or where a serial offender operates (Rossmo, 1999). With the development of new technologies, data extracted from GSM operators may play an important role in this perspective, for instance by assuming the degree of mobility of a person, where he resides or other spatial dimensions related to his behaviour.

Finally, other possibilities are developed through new id-systems: when a profile of the offender has been developed and some of his activities may be inferred, new frames may be built. For instance if the author was suspected of having used her mobile phone when operating, details of all the calls made during the time of the offense in the region of interest may be requested from the operator, with the hope of detecting the card or the mobile phone used by the offender. If an offender is supposed to have entered a building controlled through id-systems, the list of persons who entered the building may be provided.

All these forms may be used in combination through cross-referencing, for instance when geographical profiles lead to a list of inhabitants, the use of firearms may indicate the relevancy to search among the list of legal possessors, the profile of a car to consider the file of car owners, etc. This data may then be cross-referenced either to build a category of persons corresponding the best to the offender profile, conscious of the fact that the offender may or not appear in these databases. This may, as an outcome, provide a list of relevant identities to be further investigated.

Jaquet-Chiffelle (2008) stressed that this kind of investigative profiling follows two distinct goals: the first is to identify an individual within a community or infer its habits, behaviour, preferences, knowledge, etc. But the second form is not independent from the first one as it is often not obvious, once identified, to find (ultimately arrest) a person worth being the object of further investigations. Occasionally, the localization of the person even leads to his arrest before he is identified. For instance, when a serial burglar operates, his pattern may be detected and used to devise surveillances that may in turn lead to his arrest.

A rich example, well documented, of possibilities for applying such techniques can be found in the review of the investigation of the Yorkshire Ripper during the 1970s (Byford, 1981). This investigation offers a broad series of inferences and treatment of data typical of complex investigations. Review of the case has led to an overview of profiling (Kind, 1987). At that time, among other difficulties, the lack of computerization and possibilities of cross referencing was identified as a severe handicap for the investigation. The ripper was finally arrested through a routine control in the street, because he was circulating with stolen plates. Despite that this arrest was made in isolation from the investigative strategy itself, it was actually also obtained through the use of a systematic control process aided by the databases of stolen plates. Lessons learned from this case have had in particular considerable impact on the development of computerization for major case management[24] and organizations of incident rooms. It may also be considered as a milestone in the development of analytical capabilities within law enforcement such as geographical profiling or the use of information technologies in the management of serious cases.

8.4.7 Illicit Drug Profiling

The systematic chemical and physical analysis of illicit drugs seized by law enforcement agencies has greatly developed since the middle of the 1990s (Guéniat and Esseiva, 2005; Ioset et al., 2005). Illicit substances are seized, transferred to laboratories, and analyzed in order to extract a profile (list of chemical substances and their quantities). The profiles are then recorded into a database which is exploited in an intelligence or investigative perspective. For instance the process of linking illicit substance seized in different circumstances may lead to concentrate attention to a specific organized network while they were previously the object of separated investigations. Other indications about cultivation (origin), manufacture processes, or the distribution process of illicit drug trades can be inferred through the systematic analysis of the database.

The data is organized into a dynamic memory: seizures are not stored individually but are rather collated and grouped into classes mainly according to similarity measurements between profiles coming from different seizures (Dujourdy et al., 2003; Esseiva et al., 2003). Depending on which basis they are formed, these clusters mainly indicate similarities in the traffic at different levels, from the cultivation (origin) to the distribution of the illicit substance.

Beyond standard clustering methods, other original methods for detecting patterns have been tested, particularly through spatio / temporal and graph visualizations. For instance, combinations of cutting agents are often used by drug smugglers before distribution on the street. The spatio / temporal evolution of these co-occurrences inform on the dynamics of the local market (Terrettaz-Zufferey et al., 2007).

However, there is evidence that each drug trafficking network and laboratory develop its own recipes and methods that reflect differently into the intrinsic structure of the chemical profiles (correlations between variables). Thus, there is no suitable universal metric that can be defined, except for those specificities, that can systematically provide the same reliability when measuring proximity between samples. There is a need for a typical learning process as classes or specific

[24] Development of the HOLMES system (Home Office Large Major Enquiry System).

groups profiles evolve over time, and show an inherent structure that may in turn influence the classification of new data.

This hypothesis has been tested with data coming from known solved cases. Spectral clustering and its variants have been chosen to train the system and have shown to substantially improve the classification process (Ratle et al., 2007). How those ideas may lead to the development of unsupervised methods is now the subject of further developments.

However, even if comprehensive European projects have led to some harmonization and extension of the use of the method, in particular in the field of amphetamines (Aalberg et al., 2007a; Aalberg et al., 2007b; Andersson et al., 2007b; Andersson et al., 2007a; Andersson et al., 2007c; Lock et al., 2007), we are far from exploiting the whole potential of the approach. In fact, the central question is how to integrate knowledge extracted from drug profiling databases with the analysis of other (traditional) sources of information (geopolitical, coming from investigations, etc.). Full aggregation of data, even theoretically ideal, can now be difficult to imagine as organizations that deal with the set of data are different (mostly forensic laboratories and the police), cover different countries and are based on different specialties. A more pragmatic model consists in the development of communication channels between partners organized as a network. For instance, chemical links can be systematically provided to the police and used in the investigative process. Conversely, investigative hypotheses can be tested through chemical profiling (Ioset et al., 2005). This integration process must attract much more attention than the lack of communication between the organizations (police, forensic laboratories and Universities) actually allows in practice.

8.4.8 Legal Aspects[25]

Profiling in forensic science is still inchoate as we can see from the examples, although there is much research in this area. As with searches in databases, one should be aware of false interpretations of hits. False hits can be caused by the size of the database, by the techniques used, and since databases are often not very 'clean'. The persons that interpret the information from profiling should be very aware of the limitations of the methods. In the example of the camera surveillance, one should be aware that artifacts which are used for identification can also be changed. This should always be considered in forensic evidence, and should be included in the chain of evidence.

New ID systems with strengths to detect what was previously impossible, but weaknesses when they provide false positives, still offer new opportunities for improving and consolidating security. Indeed, electronic traces are information among others that are valuable in the context of the criminal justice system and forensic science.

[25] Based on FIDIS deliverable D6.7c (contribution by De Vries and Coudert).

In the light of new technological advances in the field of forensic profiling, i.e., the interconnectivity databases and risk profiling, the existing data protection instruments are not always effective anymore. As commissioner Frattini recalled 'the protection of fundamental human rights such as privacy and data protection stands side-by-side with public safety and security. This situation is not static. It changes, and both values are able to progress in step with technological advances. But it also means that there must be lines which cannot be crossed, to protect people's privacy' (Franco Frattini, 20 November 2007). However, as pointed out by the European Data Protection Supervisor, the different instruments adopted at European level 'have in common that they enable a global monitoring of movements of individuals, even if from different perspectives. The way in which they can already contribute to the fight against forms of crimes, including terrorism, should be subject to in-depth and comprehensive analysis.'[26]

In that sense, the European Parliament pointed out that 'Governments and EU institutions have often responded to terrorist attacks by adopting laws that have not been sufficiently discussed and sometimes in violation of basic human rights such as right to privacy or to a fair trial. Members call for further scrutiny of intelligence operations and for more proportionate and evidence-based legislation in the future.'

In fact, the different norms approved at European level remain insufficient as they do not deal with the fundamental issues at stake before the widespread use of criminal intelligence, the increased monitoring of the average citizen or the increased linkage of police databases. Such instruments, fruit of difficult political consensus, implement principles broadly formulated and containing important derogations to the general data protection principles. Significant issues such as how to ensure the transparency and accountability of law enforcement activities, the quality of the data processed, e.g., the differentiation between categories of data subjects, or a strict application of the purpose specification principle remain unanswered. Moreover the comments of the European Commission, the European Data Protection Supervisor and the European Parliament are often not taken into account. At the level of the Council of Europe, the data protection principles formulated in the 1980s remain broad and subject to interpretation by Member countries.

Another complication is that the multitude of initiative creates a complex framework prone to legal loopholes and difficult to comprehend. The draft Framework decision on data protection in the third pillar has been limited to the exchange of personal data between law enforcement authorities and fails to provide the third pillar with a comprehensive and strong data protection framework. Furthermore, the European Data Protection Supervisor stressed that for certain aspects the current text of the proposal does not provide for the same level of protection as defined in Convention 108. This certainly seems to be the case with the

---

[26] European Parliament resolution of 12 December 2007 on the fight against terrorism, B6-0514/2007, available via http://www.europarl.europa.eu/.

provision on the further use of data received from a Member State (Articles 3 and 12) and the right of access (Article 17).[27]

All these factors create legal uncertainty and should lead each Member State to face individually the challenges of ensuring that the new activities developed within the law enforcement field are subject to the principles of 'scrutiny', 'accountability' and 'transparency', in a context of increased international activity and exchanges of criminal data. Each country will thus be called to make the specific balance between the competing interests at stake, in particular to prevent that the increasing use of personal data for risk prediction turns into stigmatization of parts of the population.

It is, however, too soon to evaluate how the European Commission will implement the required safeguards and balance the different needs at stake. It suffices to say that the proposal for a Framework Decision for data protection in the third pillar constitutes a first laboratory where the aforementioned safeguards will have to be implemented.

8.5 Conclusion

In this chapter, we have focused on identity-related crime: the concepts and techniques involved, and the legal, organizational, and technical measures to combat crimes in which identity is used as a target or principal tool. We have also looked at the mirror image of identity-related crime: forensics implications. Identifying perpetrators is one of the key functions of forensics, and given the increasing importance of identity management in the information society, identity-related forensics is emerging as a major field of study. A particular application is forensic profiling, in which traces are used to draw profiles that are relevant to supporting various security tasks, most notably in the criminal justice system.

Our discussion shows that identity-related crime and its implications for forensics, as well as forensic profiling, thrive on technologies and procedures for identification, which have become increasingly varied and complex with the advent of the information society. Weaknesses in identification procedures that enable identity-related crime are equally relevant to be aware of in identity-related forensics, where evidence of who committed a crime or tort may crucially depend on linking traces of evidence to a specific individual. Particularly in a digital environment, establishing the link between identifiers and individual is far from easy. Detailed knowledge of the technologies involved is crucial, but not enough. Equally important are a good grasp of identification procedures, of the organizational context of identification measures, and of the legal context. Only through multidisciplinary

[27] Third opinion of the European Data Protection Supervisor on the Proposal for a Council Framework Decision on the protection of personal data processed in the framework of police and judicial co-operation in criminal matters, *Official Journal* 23.6.2007, C139/1, available via http://www.edps.europa.eu.

research can we begin to understand the mechanisms that facilitate both identity-related crime and identity forensics for successful criminal investigation.

One of the lessons of five years of multidisciplinary FIDIS research is that it is useful to first establish a common ground for research: analyze concepts, definitions and taxonomies from different disciplinary perspectives, in order to come to a converging understanding of the key concepts at issue. Without such a common ground, no useful multidisciplinary debate can take place on policies or measures to address the complex problems that we face in the information society.

A second lesson, however, is that it is important also to move forward beyond concepts and definitions. The debate about identity-related crime sometimes seems to remain at the level of definitions, where the need is stressed for defining separate categories of identity-related crime before statistics on its prevalence can be collected. The implication is that policies cannot be devised without knowledge of how frequently which types of identity-related crimes are occurring. Criminals, however, are not interested in definitions – they simply use whichever vulnerabilities they can find to commit a crime, and when they find weaknesses in identification management systems, they will not hesitate to exploit them.

Therefore, for future research, rather than focus on generally accepted definitions, lack of data and whether or not to start registering identity-related crime before countermeasures can be taken, a better approach to address the threat of identity-related crime may well be to start conducting more in-depth studies of the strengths and weaknesses of European identification infrastructures in the information society. Based on such studies, timely and targeted measures can be taken by European governments, businesses, and citizens alike to effectively combat identity-related crime and to establish successful tools for identity-related forensics.

Reference

Aalberg, L., Andersson, K., Bertler, C., Borén, H., Cole, M. D., Dahlén, J., Finnon, Y., Huizer, H., Jalava, K., Kaa, E., Lock, E., Lopes, A., Poortman-Van der Meer, A., Sippola, E. (2007a), 'Development of a harmonised method for the profiling of amphetamines I. Synthesis of standards and compilation of analytical data', Forensic Science International 169: 219-229.

Aalberg, L., Andersson, K., Bertler, C., Borén, H., Cole, M. D., Finnon, Y., Huizer, H., Jalava, K., Kaa, E., Lock, E., Lopes, A., Poortman-Van der Meer, A., Sippola, E., Dahlén, J. (2007b), 'Development of a harmonised method for the profiling of amphetamines II. Stability of impurities in organic solvents', Forensic Science International 169: 231-241.

Aitken, C. C. G. and Taroni, F. (2004), Statistics and the Evaluation of Evidence for Forensic Scientists. John Wiley & Sons, London.

Anderson, D.S., Fleizach, C., Savage, S., Voelker, G. M. (2006), 'Spamscatter: Characterizing Internet Scam Hosting infrastructure', Proceedings of the USENIX Security Symposium, Boston, MA.

Buitelaar, H. (ed.) (2007), FIDIS Deliverable D13.3: Study on ID Number Policies, Download: www.fidis.net/resources/deliverables/.

Byford, L. (1981), 'The Yorkshire Ripper Case: Review of the Police Investigation of the Case', H.M.s.I.o. Constabulary, Home Office.

Cook, R., Evett, I. W., Jackson, G., Jones, P. J., Lambert, J. A. (1998), 'A hierarchy of propositions: deciding which level to address in casework',. Science & Justice 38: 103-111.

De Vries, U. R. M. T. et al. (2007), 'Identiteitsfraude: een afbakening. Een internationale begripsvergelijking en analyse van nationale strafbepalingen', WODC, Utrecht, http://www.wodc.nl/images/1496_%20volledige_tekst_tcm44-86343.pdf.

Egger, S.A. (1984), 'A Working Definition of Serial Murder and the Reduction of Linkage Blindness', Journal of Police Science and Administration 12(3): 348-355.

Frattini, F. (2007), 'Closing speech on Public Security (20 November 2007)', Speech /07/ 728. Privacy and Technology Conference on Public Security, Privacy and Technology, Brussels.

Geradts, Z. and Sommer, P. (eds.) (2006), FIDIS Deliverable D6.1: Forensic Implications of Identity Management Systems, Download: www.fidis.net/resources/deliverables/.

Geradts, Z. and Sommer, P. (eds.) (2008), FIDIS Deliverable D6.7c: Forensic Profiling, Download: www.fidis.net/resources/deliverables/.

Goldstein, H. (1990), Problem Oriented Policing. Temple University Press, Philadelphia.

Grijpink, J. H. A. M. (2006), 'Identiteitsfraude en overheid', Justitiële verkenningen 32(7): 37-57.

Hildebrandt, M. (2008a), 'Defining profiling: a new type of knowledge?' In: Hildebrandt, M. and Gutwirth, S. (eds.), Profiling the European Citizen: Cross Disciplinary Perspectives. Springer, pp 39-50.

Hildebrandt, M. (2008b), 'Profiling and the Identity of the European Citizen'. In: Hildebrandt, M. and Gutwirth, S. (eds.), Profiling the European Citizen: Cross Disciplinary Perspectives. Springer, pp 320-360.

Ioset, S., Esseiva, P., Ribaux, O., Weyermann, C., Anglada, F., Lociciro, S., Hayoz, P., Baer, I., Gasté, L., Terrettaz-Zufferey, A. L., Delaporte, C., Margot, P. (2005), 'Establishment of an operational system for drug profiling: a Swiss experience', Bulletin of Narcotics 57 (1-2): 121-146.

Jaquet-Chiffelle, D. O. (2008), 'Reply: Direct and Indirect Profiling in the Light of Virtual Persons'. In: Hildebrandt, M. and Gutwirth, S. (eds.), Profiling the European Citizen: Cross Disciplinary Perspectives. Springer, pp 55-63.

Kind, S. S. (1987), The Scientific Investigation of Crime. Forensic Science Services Ltd, Harrogate.

Kind, S. S. (1994), 'Crime investigation and the criminal trial: a three chapter paradigm of evidence', Journal of the Forensic Science Society 34(3): 155-164.

Koops, B.-J. (2005), FIDIS Deliverable D5.1: A survey on legislation on ID theft in the EU and a number of other countries, Download: www.fidis.net/resources/deliverables/.

Koops, B.-J. and Leenes, R. E. (2006), 'ID Theft, ID Fraud and/or ID-related Crime. Definitions matter', Datenschutz und Datensicherheit (9): 553-556.

Koops, B.-J. et al. (2009), 'A typology of identity-related crime: conceptual, technical, and legal issues', Information Communication & Society 12(1): 1-24.

Kosta, E., Coudert, F., Dumortier, J. (2007), 'Data protection in the third pillar: in the aftermath of the ECJ decision on PNR data and the data retention directive', International Review of Law, Computers and Technology 21: 343-358.

Leenes, R. E. (ed.) (2006), FIDIS Deliverable D5.2b: ID-related Crime: Towards a Common Ground for Interdisciplinary Research, Download: www.fidis.net/resources/deliverables/.

Peterson, M., Morehouse, B., Wright, R. (2000), 'Intelligence 2000: Revising the Basic Elements'. Law Enforcement Intelligence Unit (L.E.I.U.) et International Association of Law Enforcement Intelligence Analysts (IALEIA), Sacramento, Lawrenceville.

Pintér, R. (ed.) (2007), FIDIS Deliverable D5.2c: Identity related crime in the world of films, Download: www.fidis.net/resources/deliverables/.

Rossmo, K. (1999) Geographical Profiling. CRC Press.

Sheptycki, J. (2004), 'Organizational Pathologies in Police Intelligence: Some Contributions to the Lexicon of Intelligence-led Policing', European Journal of Criminology 1(3): 307-332.

Sproule, S. and Archer, N. (2006), 'Defining Identity Theft – A Discussion Paper', 6 April 2006, http://www.business.mcmaster.ca/IDTDefinition/lit&links.htm.

Terrettaz-Zufferey, A.-L., Ratle, F., Ribaux, O., Esseiva, P., Khanevski, M. (2007), 'Pattern Detection in Forensic Case Data Using Graph-Theory: Application to Heroin Cutting Agents', Forensic Science International 167: 242-246.

United States (2004) The 9/11 Commission Report, National Commission on Terrorist Attacks, http://govinfo.library.unt.edu/911/report/index.htm.

Van der Meulen, N. and Koops, B.-J. (eds.) (2008), FIDIS Deliverable D12.7: Identity-related Crime in Europe – Big Problem or Big Hype?, Download: www.fidis.net/resources/deliverables/.

VIGNETTE 8: DATING*

Audrey, Frank's younger sister, a long time user of these social hubs, knows very well the 'rule of the game' of dating systems. This is especially because one of her former boyfriends was an activist of the Opaque group movement.

This time however Audrey, who is getting older and would like to settle down, plans to use the system more seriously to help her find a long term relationship. 'Why not use a dating system to look for the perfect mate?'... 'I know the system well, and therefore, I am confident that I will protect my privacy, and will not be manipulated'... 'I also know what to expect, and therefore I will not be disappointed'.

For this 'mission', Audrey has chosen a 'social hub' (well, the term dating systems is no longer used except to mean something rather negative) that is more specifically dedicated to an older audience. Actually, the affiliation to this hub is subject to the agreement from the other members by a voting system. Audrey had to present herself before being accepted. The rejection rate of this process is however low since the operator of this hub wants to have as many customers as possible, but it helps to create a first level of filtering, and in particular discards people that are really too weird. Audrey was therefore able to pass this first gateway without difficulty, although she was initially a little bit worried that they would discover her past associations with the Opaques. But her fear was not founded, especially since the operator of a hub is strictly forbidden to share the personal information with another operator and besides, there is so much competition between the operators that that they never exchange information.

When moving to this new hub Audrey was able to bring part of the 'Identity' that she had developed in one of the previous hubs she was member of. However, to tell the truth, Audrey would like to make a radical change, and actually prefers to leave behind most of her previous identity that represents another period of her life. She will of course only import to the new hub the part of herself that is consistent with the new life she wants to construct. But she will also take care to erase all the information that she would not like to see pop-up in the new hub, such as the set of pictures of her graduation in which she is dressed as a clown, drinks champagne, smokes, and makes some provocative poses. However, the process of 'migration of identity' is now easy (the operators have made a lot of effort to make switching to their hub as easy as possible, thanks also to

* This scenario is based on FIDIS deliverable D12.5, Chapter 5, by Thierry Nabeth (INSEAD).

the adoption of standards for exporting personal information), and Audrey was able to monitor and control the transfer at a very small level of detail.

Since Audrey had decided to start from almost a 'blank sheet' in this hub, she had to construct an almost completely new profile. She also used a pseudonym: Audrey had little desire to embarrass herself with her colleagues or even worse with the members of her family. Selecting the most adequate attributes in her profile, so as to project the most advantageous image of herself, turned out not to be an easy task. Indeed, 'ShineoMatic', the 'impact assessment tools' assessing the attractiveness of her profile kept returning a 'lousy' feedback. First Shineo-Matic indicated that her current profile was mainly able to attract married persons, or very young people looking for an adventure! Really, this was not what she was looking for his time! After several other adjustments (that many would consider as falsifying the reality), Audrey finally managed to create a profile that was appealing to the right kind of person: the tall and handsome artists or journalist she was looking for.

A more difficult exercise to be conducted by Audrey was raising her level of visibility in the social space by participating in the numerous communications and events taking place in the community. An example would be to participate in the relationships advice forum. However, on a subject like this people tend to reveal more information about themselves than they want, and Audrey would prefer not to disclose some of her very definite opinions about marriage without risking potential relationships. For the time being her involvement in travel and cinema related discussions will do. Audrey has travelled a lot, and she knows a lot about cinema, two interests which her 'perfect mate' probably shares. Posting and interacting related to these two topics would also automatically contribute to building her 'interest profile', which she had to validate after only a few corrections.

'Well, let's start with this and see how many invitations I receive'. The reality check will in any case be done later, when the 'real physical encounter' will happen, given that you can still have many surprises. Last small revision, activation of the profile, and joy: already some matches! 'Wait a moment, one of my first matches is George, my former boyfriend the Opaque! What a big liar he is, he who pretended not so long ago that dating systems were only for the ugly, sociopathic or the dilettante!!!'

The visions and thoughts expressed in this vignette are inspired and based on various discussions, and results of the FIDIS Network of Excellence as well as the author's personal experience and expectations. Partially, underlying concepts and ideas of this vignette are described in Chapters 2, 3 and 9.

9 Privacy and Identity*

Maike Gilliot, Vashek Matyas, and Sven Wohlgemuth

Summary. The current mainstream approach to privacy protection is to release as little personal data as possible (*data minimisation*). To this end, Privacy Enhancing Technologies (PETs) provide anonymity on the application and network layers, support pseudonyms and help users to control access to their personal data, e.g., through identity management systems. However, protecting privacy by merely minimising disclosed data is not sufficient as more and more electronic applications (such as in the eHealth or the eGovernment sectors) require personal data. For today's information systems, the processing of released data has to be controlled (*usage control*). This chapter presents technical and organisational solutions elaborated within FIDIS on how privacy can be preserved in spite of the disclosure of personal data.

9.1 Introduction[1]

The concept of informational self-determination represents today's European understanding of privacy in the context of information and communication technology. For the EU member states, privacy is regulated by the EU Directive on the protection of individuals with regard to the processing of personal data (Directive 95/46/EC, 1995).

In short, the Directive requires that the user must be able to control both the collection and the processing of personal data, i.e., any information that can be directly or indirectly related to the user. This includes that

- data collection must be bound to a specified, explicit and legitimate purpose,
- data collection must be adequate, relevant and not excessive in relation to the purpose,
- data collection must be accurate and, where necessary, be kept up to date,

---

* Many researches in FIDIS have contributed to the FIDIS deliverables this chapter is based on. We gratefully acknowledge their contributions. Daniel Cvrcek and Jozef Vyskoc (MU) deserve special thanks for having reviewed this chapter so thoroughly.

1 Introduction and Conclusion by Maike Gilliot (ALU-Fr) and Sven Wohlgemuth (ALU-Fr).

- the data subject (the individual identified by the data) clearly has to give consent to data processing and
- further processing in a way different from the specified purpose is not allowed.

Accordingly, privacy violations can be classified into those related to data collection and those related to data processing (cf. Solove, 2006): Surveillance and interrogation are threats related to information collection; Aggregation, identification, secondary use such as for profiling and exposure are some of the threats related to data processing (for a detailed discussion on profiling see Chapter 7).

The predominant current approach to protect against the above mentioned threats is based on minimising data disclosure, i.e., preventing violations by not releasing personal data if possible. To this end, current Privacy Enhancing Technologies (or PET for short) provide anonymity on application and network layer, support pseudonyms and help users to control access control on their personal data by e.g., identity management systems.

However, protecting privacy by merely minimising disclosed data is not sufficient in many of today's electronic applications. The first reason is that today's (and future) applications 'require' personal data. For example, governmental applications such as health care or tax payment systems need to identify their users. Also a growing number of services are based on the users' personal data. For example in retailing, services such as shopping recommendations are based on the customers' preferences and previous purchases.

Second, with the advent of ambient environment, the process of data collection becomes invisible and uncontrollable for the user. Cameras and other sensors release information about the location or the actions of individuals without them being able to prevent this type of data collection (Sackmann, Strüker, Accorsi, 2006). Current Privacy Enhancing Technologies such as identity management systems can neither prevent nor control data collection occurring without the user's awareness.

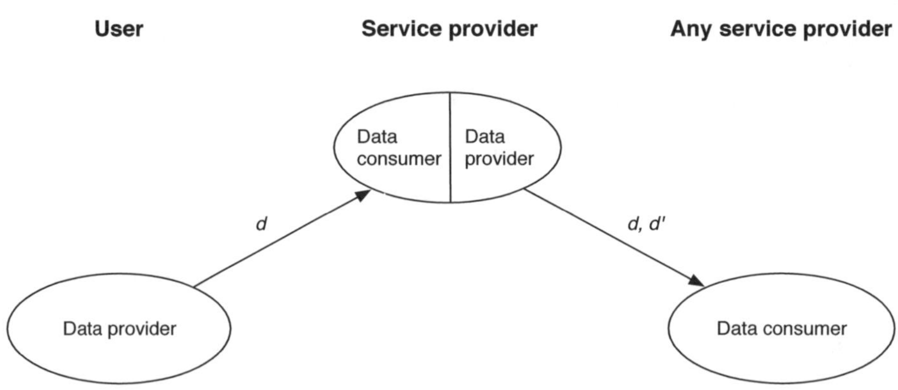

Fig. 9.1. Usage control model (Pretschner, Hilty and Basin, 2006)

Thus, in order to preserve privacy, access control to personal data is no longer a sufficient approach. For today's information systems, the processing of released data has to be controlled. To this end, research questions for privacy turn towards 'usage control' (Pretschner, Hilty, Basin, 2006).

Figure 9.1 shows the actors and the data flow model for access and usage control: Access control is about controlling what data the data provider releases to the data consumer. The data provider releases some data d to the data consumer. Usage control is about how the data consumer processes and disseminates the data. The data consumer may change its role and becomes a data provider to some other data consumer releasing the data d (or a variation d').

Chapter Outline

The goal of this chapter is to present technical and organisational approaches to usage control. First, in Section 9.2 we will show how unique identifiers can be conceived and deployed in a privacy preserving way focusing on organisational and social aspects. Section 9.3 deals with usage control in databases and presents mechanisms and methods for a privacy aware storage and retrieval of data, and Section 9.4 presents an extension to current identity management systems to control the usage of data in so called multi staged business processes. The conclusion in Section 9.5 gives an outlook on upcoming approaches and mechanisms to control the processing of personal data.

9.2 Privacy Aware Concepts for ID Numbers[2]

Much discussion takes place about the desirability of a single identification number in the context of eGovernment development and this has become a matter of a fundamental nature. It goes without saying that personal identification forms an important part of the foundation of our society. It allows us to create a link between people, actions and responsibilities. In many ways it is one of the lubricants allowing a society to function (Prins and de Vries, 2003). Whereas in the past (Buitelaar, 2007) physical means of identification predominated, we are now on the eve of an era where digital equivalents of these forms of identification will take over (College bescherming persoonsgegevens, 2002). Without these measures, fighting crime will be obstructed, ambitions in the field of eGovernment will be frustrated, and companies and citizens will lack faith in eCommerce, to name but a few things that could go wrong. Careful attention to the design of systems for digital identification is essential. It may be fair to state that there are doubts whether advantages and disadvantages of the use of an identification number have been sufficiently considered, and whether a digital identification system needs it unconditionally (Koops, 2001). ID numbers are an essential part of eGovernment

[2] By Hans Buitelaar (TILT) based on the FIDIS Deliverable D13.3: 'ID number policies'.

applications. In this section we investigate how identifiers must be conceived and which techniques are necessary to control the privacy risks.

It is worthwhile to analyse several crucial aspects of the policies that might lead to enabling secure and trusted distribution of identity digital assets. It goes without saying that the legal aspects of the use of digital identification need close scrutiny. After all ID numbers are personal data and therefore the European Data Directive might be expected to offer a firm basis for a proper use of the ID number. Even though it might seem that ID numbers are a mere technical matter for which a proper legal basis is present, it turns out that this legal basis is quickly set aside for technical priorities and managerial advantages. In order to understand why the general public quite often has felt an almost instinctive need to oppose the general introduction of such a number, a sociological analysis pinpoints some of the reasons for this, sometimes irrational, behaviour. The final technical section offers some hope, that exactly the boundless surge of claims that technology makes to create this ideal world of eGovernment, will help in putting the digital identity number to good use with due respect to the privacy of citizens concerned.

It can be stated that means of identification increasingly pervades the public sector. Examples are taxation, public health, law-enforcement, local administrations and social services. In the light of attempts to streamline government operations by making systems interoperable and in fighting fraud and terrorism, different developments can be witnessed in various EU countries. The various solutions proposed, offer different benefits and pose different threats to both governments and citizens. The most eye-catching solution in this respect is the introduction of a single personal identification number to be used throughout the public sector. Of course, a single personal identification number is country specific and there is no European-wide single personal identification number (yet). Undoubtedly, a reduction of the administrative burden for both government and citizens makes the single identification a very attractive proposition. In the scenario, where substantial user control is absent, the introduction of a unique identifier makes the consumer and citizen more transparent. Facilitating the linkage of a profile to the number ID and linking different profiles to each other via this number could potentially result in undesirable surveillance opportunities. Moreover, the costs of security measures to safeguard the unique identifier system against privacy invasions may not be sufficient to retain the citizen's trust in a reliable government.

9.2.1 Legal Aspects

Taking the needs of eGovernment as a starting point, the legal contribution to the study discusses the roles so-called entities can have in a particular sector. Entities can be attributed with a global, sector-specific or context specific identifier. In eGovernment an attempt is made to optimise service delivery by channelling internal and external relationships through a technology. Interoperability and the usage of common ID numbers for all relevant entities then makes the usage of ID numbers tantamount for eGovernment. Bearing this in mind we can question whether they are supported by a sound legal framework, whether the usage of global identifiers is enough to guarantee the rights of the individual as defined in the European Data Protection Directive (Directive 95/46/EC, 1995) or should technical unlinkability also be a requirement of an eGovernment architecture?

It is clear that ID numbers are personal data and therefore the processing of these numbers should be carried out subject to the Data Directive. This means that attention should be given to the legitimacy of the processing, the data quality and aspects of confidentiality and security. It may be said to be unfortunate that the Directive leaves standards for safeguards for ID numbers up to the Member states who are required to put them in place. With the present state of knowledge it might have been expected that due to the emphasis the Directive puts on the sound protection of ID numbers, technical unlinkability would have been prescribed. After all, the Directive does point out that appropriate technical and organisational security measures must be taken. These should take account of the state of the art, the cost of their implementation, and the risks represented by processing and the nature of the data.

In the context of eGovernment the processing of personal data should be respecting the minimum data and data processing quality principles, such as the *'finality'* and the 'proportionality' principle (article 6 of the Directive).

Briefly summarised, the term finality refers to the obligation to only collect personal data for specified, explicit and legitimate purposes. Personal data must not be further processed in a way incompatible with those purposes. Further processing of data for historical, statistical or scientific purposes shall not be considered as incompatible if the appropriate safeguards are taken. The purpose of the processing should be defined at the latest at the moment of the collection of the data.

Applied to ID numbers, it is clear that the data controller deciding on a use of a global, sector-specific or context-specific identifier should:

- make sure that the chosen data (for example, a global ID number instead of a sector-specific one) is adequate, relevant and not excessive in relation to the purposes for which it is being collected and / or further processed and
- make sure that the ID number is accurate and, where necessary, kept up to date; and not kept in a form which permits identification of data subjects longer than is necessary for the purposes for which the data were collected or for which they are further processed.

In addition, on the topic of finality and proportionality, it is important to note that when two or more government entities integrate their back-offices, there will typically be a reuse of personal data for another purpose than the one that was originally indicated. For example, when a particular set of data has been collected from a citizen for unemployment allowance purposes, the idea of eGovernment would be to make that data directly available to the tax authorities – of course within the borders of the law – instead of requesting it again from the citizen. As mentioned, the finality principle requires the further processing to be compliant with the original purposes.

The main point of departure is that identifiers are definitely needed in the public sector, especially to achieve the goals of eGovernment, for instance, 'the integration of back-offices'. Without data protection rules, it seems obvious to choose common, global identifiers between these back-offices, and not to be technically constrained by context- and or sector-specific identifiers. The question that is raised is whether the usage of global identifiers within a sound legal framework can be acceptable from a legal perspective for the default data exchange between two or more government entities or not. The alternative would be to choose technical unlinkability as a requirement of an eGovernment architecture, which would imply the usage of context- and / or sector-specific identifiers. At the other side of the spectrum, from an analysis of the data protection rules, the conclusion can be drawn that:

- If the usage of global identifiers is forbidden in the Member State (e.g., because it is unconstitutional), technical unlinkability should be a requirement of the architecture design. The Data Protection Authority has the important task of verifying that context specific numbers are indeed not being used outside their respective contexts.
- If the usage of *some or all* global identifiers is regulated, the basic data protection rules still apply. The additional rules should take the data protection principles as a minimum. The Data Protection Authority here mainly verifies whether the conditions under which that identifier may be processed are fulfilled.
- If the usage of global identifiers is allowed or at least is not forbidden, the Data Protection Authority only verifies whether the number is being processed within the limits of the data protection regulation (finality, proportionality, protection level etc.), as explained above. (de Bot, 2005)

When having a closer look at the data protection principles, additional, crucial issues can be noted.

- The data controller should make sure that the chosen data (for example, a global ID number instead of a sector-specific one) is adequate, relevant and not excessive in relation to the purposes for which it is being collected and / or further processed. In other words, a global identifier can be excessive in relation to the purposes for which the data is being collected. For instance, if no legitimate cross-context or cross-sector data exchange is present at the first processing of the ID number, a context- or sector-specific identifier should suffice.
- The data controller should make sure that the ID number is not kept in a form, which permits identification of data subjects for longer than is necessary for the purposes for which the data were collected or for which they are further processed.

- In practice, this means that when the purposes of processing the ID number have been realised, it should be anonymised. Encrypting or encoding the ID number will most probably not be sufficient if the reason why the ID number is being processed like that (e.g., encrypted) is to be able to re-identify the person if needed. In that case, the ID number would still be identifiable data – and thus also personal data.
- To evaluate the necessary, 'appropriate' technical and organisational security measures, three factors play a role: (1) the state of the art, (2) the cost of their implementation and (3) the risks represented by the processing and the nature of the data to be protected.
- The state of the art means that security measures should follow the technological evolution. This means that if technologies to ensure unlinkability between contexts and sectors mature sufficiently (which is more and more the case today) they should be chosen if they are more conducive towards achieving the goals of the processing. It also means that it can be an unacceptable risk to not take unlinkability measures.
- Yet, this is also the tricky part of the answer to the above mentioned question on 'technical unlinkability': it depends on the evaluation of the case at hand.

The technical section of the study shows that, unfortunately, the present legal framework soon becomes inadequate in preventing the technical linkability of potentially privacy harmful data about citizens on the basis of ID numbers. Once the necessary infrastructure is in place, including global ID numbers, data exchange will take place anyway either legitimately or illegitimately, based on an ad hoc argument or on political choices.

9.2.2 Sociological Aspects

In spite of the many managerial advantages, ID numbers arouse strong emotions, which cannot be solely comprehended from a legalistic suspicion of being potentially harmful to the individual's privacy. Therefore, a sociological analysis of the function of ID numbers may be helpful in this respect. The sociological approach is looked at from two angles: social systems theory and a theory on the role of bureaucracy in national states.

The social systems theory views society from a general perspective, allowing the analysis of the function of ID numbers in private and public organisations. By thoroughly analysing the function of names, identifiers and addresses it can be ascertained that ID numbers fulfil all three functions of a name, an identifier or an address. First, they can be used as names for a data set or a number of data sets in a database. Secondly, they can be used as identifiers if they link a person uniquely in an administrative context. Thirdly, they can also be used as addresses. In the organisational context, social systems theory learns that addresses are always administered (generated, assigned and deleted or deactivated) by organisations. Organisations are also careful to resolve potential address collisions by keeping addresses unique in the particular scope of the operation. The state ensures addressability for governmental, private sector or interactional (citizen to citizen) operations. Addressability today covers persons, families, organisations and objects in the context of communication techniques. Addressability is not possible without organisations. These organisations need the unique identifiability to run their operations smoothly and efficiently. This in turn may lead to information asymmetry because, as shown in the legal analysis, it reduces the autonomy of individuals by the usage of linkability measures. In other words, a shift of power may occur in favour of the organisation. In the context of states it is in many cases difficult to decide whether citizens overall benefit from this development or not, the reason being that citizens typically take on two roles with respect to the state. On the one hand they are members and thus benefit from a strong state that is able to protect them and, on the other hand they are clients of the state who suffer from reduced autonomy.

The second sociological angle is based on the Weberian theory of bureaucracy. Against the background of the rationalisation processes going on in all areas of society, the function of ID numbers is described as having the purpose of providing the members of a state with a feeling of unity and cohesion within the perspective of increased globalisation. It can be said that in the past political rationalisation resulted in the formalisation of the state. One of the unique properties of a state is a trained corps of civil servants specially trained in and restricted to regulations. This corps of civil servants has as its main task, the identification of the members of the state to enable the state to carry out its primary tasks. According to Weber these bureaucracies are the ultimate example of the rationalisation process because they aim at efficiency, predictability, quantifiability, control by substituting human judgement by non-human technology and irrationality by rationality. To carry out its tasks, the bureaucratic government accordingly issued identity cards and codes. These identification means provided access to a whole series of files and data sets. ID numbers therefore became the symbols of this bureaucratic culture. Seemingly meaningless numbers acquire meaning in this bureaucratic context because the developing nation-states desired to attach meaning to this symbol. Sociologically speaking it is argued, this was an unfortunate choice because, as Weber already pointed out, this was the irrationality of rationality. The intention of creating a notion of unity and solidarity was not attained because citizens felt, that the ID number identification led to depersonalisation. It could be argued, that the mismanaged effort to create unity in states by the introduction of an ID number, actually led to a sense of loss of privacy without contributing to the sense of unity.

9.2.3 Technical Aspects

Taking the risks and opportunities of ID numbers in the modern technological age, an investigation is made of the contrast between requirements that techniques such as profiling pose vis-à-vis the protection of the individual's privacy privileges. Profiling provides a new kind of knowledge used for decision-making based on Knowledge Discovery in Databases (KDD). KDD requires per definition as much information as possible about the individual, whereas traditional privacy rights focus on data minimisation. There is no easy solution for this conflict.

One approach is to ask citizens to be more transparent by introducing sector-wide and unique ID numbers, while at the same time attempts are made to make the state and its actions more transparent. Examples are, in the Netherlands, the introduction of the National Trust Function to log the use of the national ID number and, the introduction of Freedom of Information Acts in Germany, allowing citizens to access their own data files maintained by the state. Unfortunately, these attempts fall short in certain cases. In addition to limitations for citizens to access secret data, which is very understandable because these could be covered by trust based models, the use of profiling creates additional limitations for transparency. Certain types of profiles are not linked to the data they were derived from, they are no longer personal data and, may be used to the disadvantage of the citizen in a non-transparent way. Due to the complexity of the underlying profiling processes, regulatory attempts to increase transparency fall short and, Transparency Enhancing Technologies (TETs) to fill this gap are limited in effectiveness or do not even exist yet. Another problematic aspect of transparency is that from a social perspective people think, communicate and act in communicational terms. Data freely used in one context cannot necessarily be used in another. Keeping data in its appropriate context is also called the concept of contextual integrity. Informational self-determination can be understood as an important attempt to put contextual integrity in legal norms, though certainly from a social perspective an inappropriate one in certain cases.

Yet another approach is the introduction of additional functions and tools that make the individual less recognisable or opaque. In this context different methods have been developed and implemented to restrict and control linkability facilitated by ID numbers. On the whole the technical study arrives at the conclusion that by introducing the concepts of contextual integrity and reciprocal transparency in combination with multiple identifiers, it looks like both the needs of KDD techniques as well as the concept of privacy can be achieved. This does need a fine-tuned combination of transparency and opacity tools to be built into the new technological infrastructure (Gutwirth and de Hert, 2005).

9.2.4 European Approaches

In a FIDIS report on ID number policies (Buitelaar, 2007) an empirical study is presented of the background and present policy and usage of ID numbers in a sample of various EU countries. An attempt is made to provide an overview that shows how the attitudes towards and the choices made with respect to the usage of ID numbers can be very different in the EU region. For this reason country reports have been included on Belgium, France, The Netherlands, Czech Republic, Slovak Republic, Hungary, Germany, Switzerland and Austria. These country reports illustrate how the conceptual aspects that are analysed earlier are put into practice. These empirical and conceptual approaches make it possible to elicit lessons learned and provide benchmarks, by which to develop arguments for policy recommendations.

Taking into account national political strategies and existing infrastructures four different basic concepts on how to deal with ID numbers can be determined from the country reports. They are:

- Introduction of sector spanning ID numbers with a large area of use inside and outside the public sector mainly based on mutual transparency of use (e.g., The Netherlands)
- Introduction of sector spanning ID numbers with regulations on how they may be used (e.g., Switzerland, Czech Republic and Slovakia)
- Introduction of sector specific ID numbers and organisational enforcement of borders of sectors (e.g., Hungary, France, Germany)
- Introduction of sector specific ID numbers and organisational as well as technical enforcement of borders of sectors (e.g., Austria)

9.2.5 Conclusions

The analysis of ID numbers and policies as provided in this FIDIS study shows that ID numbers are an essential tool for the realisation of eGovernment and modern business processes. Due to the increasing pervasiveness of Internet as a means of communication by governments and enterprises, there is a growing necessity for a secure identity management. The need to identify who communicates with whom is essential in an Internet environment because the Internet, by design, lacks these provisions. Because of these shortcomings various solutions have been developed. The identity number is a prominent one. As shown, the developments in this area could affect privacy interests of individuals. Individuals often need to disclose more personal data than strictly required (Koops, Buitelaar, Lips, 2007). Several steps are still being taken to tackle this problem.

The sociological and the historical analyses indicate that only a carefully attuned policy will allow the present possibilities and opportunities of ID numbers to be used successfully. From the socio-cultural point of view, experiences in using the identification tool as a method by which to create a feeling of unity in a nation-state, that only exists in the minds of the heads of the state, have led to the opposite result. From the social systems point of view, there are potential benefits as well as drawbacks in the usage of an ID number. In the public domain one of the drawbacks could be caused by the fact that citizens are members of a state as well as clients. The state benefits from the advantages of using ID numbers and therefore these benefits are also beneficial to its members. Drawbacks might arise when these measures harm the clients of organisations when ID number linkability is used to create information asymmetry in favour of organisations. Organisations may use this asymmetry to reduce autonomy of the individuals. This, in turn, may result in a shift in the balance of power favouring organisations (Bygrave, 2002).

The potential information asymmetry, as achieved by technical means, is illustrated by describing profiling techniques. Even though there are the large risks of abuse in these scenarios, the suggestions for making good use of the opportunities technology has to offer are promising. This privacy-friendly scenario can be achieved through a joint effort of computer engineers, legal experts and policy-makers. Within the scope of the European Data Directive the opportunities for using profiling techniques can thus be put to good use. Individuals can then be monitored without necessitating any kind of transcontextual identification. This fits in with the purpose of the limitation principle of the Directive.

Without doubt, the protection of personal data is a fundamental right in the European Union. In many Member States it is a constitutional right (Charter of fundamental rights of the European Union[3]). However, if appropriate attention is given to the rights of individuals as expressed in the legitimacy of the processing, the data quality and aspects of confidentiality and security and the principle of the protection of personal data or so-called informational privacy, this will enable a sound identity management. In the area of profiling this seems to call for limiting the use of personal data to the proper context. However, this could preclude the use of profiling to its full potential.

It may be instrumental to redefine the concept of privacy in terms of 'privacy as contextual integrity' (Nissenbaum, 2004) while, at the same time, underpinning it with the appropriate technical means. In this light it seems preferable and feasible to adopt multiple ID number policies. These allow discriminating between different contexts providing tailored ID number policies, depending on which type of privacy is appropriate per context. The point of departure is a type of identity management based on user control. At the same time, the reciprocity or distribution of the transparency can be tailored, depending on the need for checks and balances per context. This does not necessarily rule out interoperability between contexts, because ID numbers may be linked, e.g. via clearing houses, to provide interoperability. The information asymmetry that looms behind the horizon may thus lead to the search for a sensible use of the ID number with due respect for the privacy of the citizens concerned.

---

3 The Charter of Fundamental Rights of the European Union enshrines the protection of personal data in Article 8 as an autonomous right, separate and different from the right to private life referred to in Article 7 thereof and the same is the case at national level in some states. Cf. Opinion 4/2007 of 20th June 2007 of the Article 29 Data Protection Working Party on the concept of personal data.

In essence, it may be concluded that multiple identifiers in conjunction with interoperability and contextual integrity are the most promising solution for a sound identity management policy in the near future. This requires a fine-tuned combination of transparency and opacity tools to be built into the technological infrastructure. In such a way the individual will not become unnecessarily transparent nor will interoperability be precluded by excessive user control. The advantages of eGovernment can thus be achieved reciprocally for government and citizen alike. Measures to prevent identity fraud must be part of this IDM policy while, at the same time, the corresponding security measures must be construed in such a way as to inspire the citizen with sufficient trust that the government treats his data safely. It may not be an unrealistic assumption that, if this avenue of using technology in this constructive way is followed, the concerns that arose from the analysis of the several constitutive elements of ID number policy choices can be sufficiently addressed.

9.3 Privacy Primitives and Applications[4]

In this section we will discuss privacy primitives and application privacy with a primary focus on privacy in statistical databases. By defining privacy primitives we can evaluate different privacy-protecting environments in terms of how privacy is protected as well as how good this protection is.

In Section 9.3.2 we focus on privacy protection in statistical databases. Such databases store information about individual entities, but provide statistical information only. The use of statistical database must be strictly controlled to prevent information leakage about individual entities. We present several approaches – query restriction approach, input data perturbation and output data perturbation. The aim of these techniques is to allow database users to retrieve statistical information but prevent them from querying individual entities. At the end of this section we shortly review privacy related issues in eCash systems and identity management.

9.3.1 Privacy Primitives

If we see privacy measures in the digital environment as a mean to prevent unintended leakage and usage of information, this information has to be protected by technical means. These technical means are built from privacy primitives that are based on cryptographic primitives or equivalents to these. We can differentiate privacy primitives according to the following criteria:

[4] By Vashek Matyáš (MU), Marek Kumpost (MU), and Stefan Köpsell (TUD), based on the FIDIS Deliverable D13.1: 'Identity and impact of privacy enhancing technologies' and FIDIS Deliverable D13.6: 'Privacy Modelling and Identity'.

1. *The parties involved.* Who is involved and what are their functionalities / abilities?
2. *The purpose.* What privacy goal(s) does the primitive achieve for what information?
3. *The attacker model.* Against whom should the information be kept private?
4. *The security-level.* Is information theoretic, i.e., unconditional or cryptographic computational security reached?

We present a classification of privacy primitives following the criteria above in the following sections. These primitives can be used to build larger privacy systems as they will be presented in the following Section 9.3.2 for the application level. But already the primitives often make use of each other and become standalone privacy systems as will be outlined in this section.

Pseudonyms

Pseudonyms are an important privacy primitive. They act as identifiers of subjects or sets of subjects. Whereas anonymity on the one hand and unambiguous identifiability on the other are extreme cases with respect to linkability to subjects, pseudonymity comprises the entire field between and including these extremes (Pfitzmann and Hansen, 2001).

1. The parties involved: There is the holder of the pseudonym and the parties he uses his pseudonym with.
2. The purpose: Important properties of pseudonyms can include (Clauß and Köhntopp, 2001):
    - Proof of ownership: Digital pseudonyms could be realised as a public key to test digital signatures where the holder of the pseudonym can prove ownership by forming a digital signature, which is created using the corresponding private key.
    - Linkability due to the use of a pseudonym in different contexts.
    - Convertibility, i.e., transferability of attributes of one pseudonym to another: The user can obtain a convertible credential from one organisation using one of her pseudonyms, but can demonstrate possession of the credential to another organisation without revealing her first pseudonym.
    - Authorisations can be realised by credentials or attribute certificates bound to digital pseudonyms, but also in case of digital vouchers transferable to other people by blind signatures as well.
3. The attacker model:
    - The users can determine the linkability of their pseudonyms themselves.
    - Attacker model of convertible credentials applies to convertibility.

- No attacker can break the ownership of a pseudonym and the correctness of authorisations as long as the signature scheme used is not broken.

The security-level: The linkability of pseudonyms is absolute. Security level of the remaining properties depends on the primitives used to implement them, they are usually computationally secure.

Pseudonymous Convertible Credentials

A credential system is a system in which users can obtain credentials from organisations and demonstrate possession of these credentials. Credentials usually are assigned to pseudonyms. With convertible credentials the users are able to transform a credential issued to one of her pseudonyms to another one of her pseudonyms. This concept was introduced in (Chaum, 1981).

1. *The parties involved:* There are users and credential issuing organizations.
2. *The purpose:* In an anonymous credential system organizations know the users only by pseudonyms. An organization can issue a credential to a pseudonym, whose holder can convert this credential to another pseudonym of hers. Then she can prove possession of this converted credential to another organization and the following properties hold:
    - Integrity of the converted credential
    - Unlinkability of credential and converted credential and thereby unlinkability of the pseudonyms they are used with
3. *The attacker model:*
    - Regarding integrity it should be impossible for a user and another organisation to forge a credential of another organisation for the user, even with an adaptive attack on the respective organization.
    - Regarding unlinkability an organization cannot find out if two pseudonyms belong to the same user as long as the user does not reveal this.
4. *The security-level:* There exist several possibilities of implementation. In (Camenisch and Lysyanskaya, 2001) a credential system based on the strong RSA assumption and the decisional Diffie-Hellman assumption (that makes the system computational secure) is presented.

In (Camenisch and Lysyanskaya, 2001) such a credential system is called anonymous. This term might be misleading because the system does not reach anonymity directly, but only pseudonymity by the use of pseudonyms and unlinkability. This might result in anonymity, but does not necessarily do so if personal pseudonyms are used.

Private Information Retrieval

1. The parties involved: The user who queries the database and the server(s) which hold(s) the database and answer(s) his queries.
2. The purpose: Private information retrieval (PIR) allows users to retrieve an item from another party (usually by querying a database) without revealing which item he is interested in (privacy for the item of interest).
3. The attacker model: Single servers or even collusion of servers do not learn anything about the item of interest depending on the implementation used.
4. The security-level: Security depends on the concrete implementation. The only possible protocol that gives the user information theoretic privacy for her item of interest is that the server sends an entire copy of the database to the user. There are two solutions to come to a more efficient solution: one is to make the server computationally bounded and the other is to assume that there are multiple non-cooperating servers, each having a copy of the database.

An early reference that already deals with this problem is (Rivest et al., 1978), but the problem was first formulated under the name 'private information retrieval' in (Chor et al., 1998). Since then numerous solutions have been presented and theoretical bounds calculated for how efficient such a system can become under the assumption of none or specific computational bounds of the servers.

9.3.2 Application Privacy

In this section we show some illustrative applications and also how such applications can be built out of the primitives.

Techniques for Providing Privacy in Databases

The need for techniques for preserving privacy in public databases (databases that are publicly available) or statistical databases is obvious as these may contain very sensitive information about individuals. Anyone who has access to these databases and has adequate rights for performing queries on data can learn a lot. Even more dangerous are aggregation queries that can combine lots of data together and infer new information that is not explicitly stored in the database. This can be done for both statistical purposes and a purpose of inferring information about a particular user(s). Even if the data is anonymised, it is possible to indirectly identify entities by combining some 'innocuous' looking attributes.

Statistical databases allow users to retrieve only overall results about some set of entities in the database. Any attempt to retrieve information about any particular entity must be strictly forbidden. As stated above, one can easily conclude that the most important issue is preserving privacy while allowing data to be used for statistical investigations. But these requirements – privacy for the responders and usefulness of the data – are in mutual conflict. Perfect privacy can be achieved by publishing nothing but this has no utility; perfect utility can be obtained by publishing data exactly as received from responders, but this offers no privacy. Data perturbation should permit data analysts (statisticians) to work with the data while preserving privacy of individuals. This section surveys current techniques for both dealing with privacy and data perturbation in statistical and publicly available databases.

The attacker model. From the intruder's point of view there are two main types of attacks. First if an attacker can learn some concrete information about one entity (database was positively compromised) and second if an attacker can conclude that some information (attribute) surely does not hold for some entity (database was partially compromised).

An inference attack on a statistical database is a set of database queries that (if properly combined) can reveal a new piece of information (which is not directly accessible) about an entity or a set of entities. The classical situation is that the attacker knows some information about the entity and using this information he tries to learn something new. Suppose that the attacker forms a query, which gives only one record as a result. Using this query the attacker can identify one entity. Suppose that the attacker is not allowed to query some other attributes directly but if the database is not well secured he can observe how many results the modified query produces. If the new attribute (e.g., diagnosis = 'HIV') together with the remaining part of the query produces one result the attacker has inferred new information – this is the case of a positively compromised database. If the number of the results is zero then the database is said to be partially compromised. Techniques discussed in the next section are to prevent databases from being attacked in this way.

Overview of main techniques used in statistical databases (Chawal et al., 2005) provides a nice overview of existing techniques of perturbation and also privacy related issues.

An important issue that also affects security in databases is the type of the database. We can consider online / offline, static / dynamic, centralized / decentralized and dedicated / non-dedicated databases. In an online database there is a direct interaction with users while in offline systems, users do not have any control on query processing. Static databases do not change in time while dynamic ones do. Centralised systems consist of only one database, decentralized system can be spread among many sub-databases. Dedicated system is used only for database. Non-dedicated system shares environment with other services.

Methods that are used for security and privacy protection can be classified into four general groups (Adam and Worthmann, 1989): conceptual, query restriction, data perturbation, and output-perturbation. Two models are based on the conceptual approach – the conceptual model and the lattice model. The conceptual model allows identifying a security-related problem on the conceptual and data layer. The lattice model describes statistical database information in a tabular form at different levels of aggregation. The aim of this approach is to allow for better understanding of possible aggregations that may reveal some new or redundant information. Methods that are based on the query restriction approach provide protection through one of the following measures: restricting the query set size, controlling the overlap among successive queries by keeping an audit trail of all answered queries for each user, or partitioning the statistical database.

Query restriction approach. This method allows retrieving statistical data only if the query size (number of entities involved in the query |C| processing) satisfies the condition $K \leq |C| \leq L-K$, where L is the size of the database (number of entities) and K is a parameter that is set by a database administrator (DBA). This parameter K should satisfy the condition $0 \leq K \leq L/2$. It was shown (Denning, Denning, 1979) that by using a tool called tracker it is possible to compromise a database even if K is close to L/2. Notice that K cannot exceed L because otherwise no statistics would be released.

Query-Set-Overlap Control. Query overlapping is a situation when different queries have many common entities. (Dobkin, Jones, Lipton, 1979) noticed that many compromises of database systems use query sets that have a large number of common entities. This type of control has several disadvantages – cooperation of more users cannot be avoided; there is a need for up-to-date profiles for each user and database usefulness may be jeopardized with these limitations. A mechanism that performs comparison between user queries works in O(L) complexity, where L is the size of the statistical database.

Auditing. This is a query restriction method in which a log of queries is saved, and every query is checked for possible data compromise. The given query is allowed or suppressed according to the check result (Chin and Özsoyoglu, 1982). One problem of this approach is efficiency – the problem of deciding whether a sequence of queries violates privacy was shown to be computationally hard. (Kleinberg et al., 2000) showed that given a database d and a set of queries, deciding whether an exact answer to these queries leads to full determination of the value of at least one protected database entry is an NP-hard problem.

Partitioning. The main idea of this method is to group individual entities into mutually exclusive subsets that are called 'atomic populations' (Adam and Worthmann, 1989). These are then available for queries from database users. Authors of the method believe that many ways of compromising databases (like if an attacker has quite enough additional information such as when entities are inserted/updated/deleted from the database) can be avoided since atomic population does not contain any information about particular entities. A drawback of this approach, as it was shown in (Schlörer, 1983), is that many real databases contain tables with only one entity. If these entities aggregate high volume of information, a data loss may occur.

Data perturbation. Data perturbation techniques are divided into two main categories – probability distribution and fixed-data perturbation.

The probability distribution approach considers the statistical database as a representative sample of a given population with some given probability distributions. The original database is then replaced with a new sample that has the same probability distributions as the original database. Using this method with dynamic databases is very difficult due to the computational overhead because some transformation needs to be made in the transformed sample with every data modification in the original database. This together with possible high inaccuracy (as mentioned below) makes this method not very widely used in statistical databases.

Fixed-data perturbation approach on the other hand changes values of the attributes, which are to be used for computing statistics, once and for all. This approach often requires another (transformed) database to be created for statistical purposes only. Data is perturbed by adding a random value to the real value. This can suffer from high inaccuracies so instead of adding a random value this value is multiplied with the original one. Attributes that have binary representation are perturbed with probabilities (fixed-data perturbation for categorical attributes) that the value is true or false. Probability value p that is defined by a database administrator is multiplied by the number of entities that satisfy a particular query but without the binary attribute. An advantage of the fixed-data perturbation approach is that transformed data can be updated dynamically along with changes in the original data. (Kargupta et al., 2003) discussed privacy of random-data perturbation techniques and showed that these techniques can provide under certain circumstances a very little data privacy. They also pointed out some possible directions for new privacy-preserving data mining techniques like 'exploiting multiplicative' and 'coloured noise'.

There is always a problem with the accuracy of results with data perturbation techniques. (Matloff, 1986) showed that under certain circumstances, 50% bias can occur. (Wilson and Rosen, 2003) provides a study on both the impact of perturbation techniques for protecting databases and the bias problem.

Output perturbation approach. The main difference between this approach and the previous one is that the bias problem is less severe here. This is because the results are based on the original values (not perturbed values) and only the result is perturbed.

The first approach is called 'random-sample noise' and was proposed by (Denning and Denning, 1979). The idea is very simple. A set of entities that satisfy a requested query is influenced by probability parameter P that is set by the database administrator (DBA). An entity in the set will be considered in the result with a probability P. The required statistics are computed based on the sample query set. The statistics computed from the sample query set has to be divided by P in order to provide a corresponding unbiased estimator. This method suffers from the resulting inconsistency.

In varying-data perturbation approach a random perturbation is added to the query answer, with increasing variance if the query is repeated (Beck, 1980).

Rounding technique takes the result of the query and rounds it up or down to the nearest multiple of a certain base b. There are three types of rounding techniques – systematic rounding, random rounding and controlled roundi atic and random rounding techniques add some offset to values in the Controlled rounding technique affects more values in the row in such a way that the sum of the row equals the sum of non-rounded values. Problem with rounding is that it is possible to determine the true value by averaging the responses to the same query. In general, rounding techniques are not considered to be effective security-tools but they can help if they are combined with some other approaches.

From the methods that were presented above, the random-sample queries method, the varying-data perturbation method, the fixed-data-perturbation method, and the fixed-data-perturbation for categorical attributes are the most promising security-control methods for online dynamic statistical databases. A very good comparison of all methods mentioned here is in (Adam and Worthmann, 1989).

Private database queries. Publicly available databases can pose a significant risk for privacy of their users, since a curious database administrator can follow a user's queries and infer what the user wants to find out. Users are often cautious about accessing a database when their intentions are about to be kept secret. It can be shown that in the case of a single database, to completely guarantee the privacy of the user, the whole database would have to be downloaded and queried locally. (Chor et al., 1998) investigates whether more efficient solutions to private retrieval problems can be obtained by replicating the database. The paper describes schemes that enable users to access k replicated copies of a database ($k \geq 2$) and privately retrieve information stored in the database. This means that each individual server (holding a replicated copy) gets no information on the identity of the item retrieved by the user.

Data mining. When we discuss privacy issues, we should also mention data mining. Data mining techniques are used for searching large volumes of data for patterns and various data relationships. It encompasses various techniques like association rules, cluster analysis, decision trees, neural networks, genetic algorithms, and exploratory data analysis.

It is important to discuss how data mining can violate personal privacy. 'Proper' use of data mining techniques can lead to some private data inference. (Tavani, 1999) provides a comparison between 'traditional' retrieval of personal information and data mining approaches, and (Clifton and Marks, 1996) discusses security and privacy implications of data mining. (Broder, 1999) discusses two views of data mining – the desire for privacy by web users and the need of web content providers to collect and utilise data about users – users may be unaware how much identifying information can be disclosed; and (from the point of web content providers) how privacy enhancing technologies (PET) can substantially invalidate data mining results.

Data mining is widely used for discovering web users' navigational characteristics and patterns for better understanding of their needs and for providing some levels of customization (Baumgarten et al., 2000; Borges and Levene, 2000; Dua et al., 2000).

eCash

Electronic cash is digital information and is being used to pay the price of a commodity in various scenarios. Electronic cash has been developed to complement the weaknesses of real currency because of electronic commercial trades and has many requirements and security measures to be met before it can be used like real currency. (Kang and Lee, 2005) provides a list of requirements compared to what real currency provides.

- Anonymity
  1. Real currency provides a user with privacy.
  2. If the digital data of electronic cash has or is connected to the information on a user, the cash cannot provide the user with privacy.
- Divisiveness
  3. Real currency can be divided or its changes can be offered because the currency has a basic unit.
  4. As for electronic currency, the issued data shall be divided.
- Transference
  5. Real currency can be transferred to a third party through offering the appropriate amount of money.
  6. Electronic currency can also be transferred to a third party through transmitting data; but the security should be kept the same as at the time of issuing the currency.
- Prevention of double use
  7. Real currency cannot be used for the second time unless it is faked.
  8. Electronic currency can be used for the second time if the saved information can be copied.

Authors of (Kang and Lee, 2005) have analysed the anonymity of electronic cash in order to come up with effective and safe ways to offer anonymity for a micropayment system. In their new system, anonymity is provided by generating a random number (instead of using blind signatures). The anonymity of the user will be removed in the case of double spending. (Qiu et al., 2002) presents a privacy protecting eCash system that provides offline revocable anonymity.

This helps in both privacy protection and misuse by criminals. Neither a bank nor a merchant can obtain identities of users but under certain circumstances (suspect criminal activities), a trusted third party (cooperatively with the bank) can remove the anonymity of a transaction and disclose the user's identity. The proposed protocol needs less communication and allows for both coin tracking and owner tracking.

Identity Management

Since it is now very easy to collect and process huge amounts of personal data for building 'profiles' of individuals, it is necessary to allow these individuals to be able to somehow influence what personal data will be processed. PRIME (Privacy and Identity Management for Europe) project has implemented a technical framework for processing personal data (Hansen and Krasemann, 2005), with a vision to give individuals sovereignty over their personal data so that (Camenisch et al., 2005):

- Individuals can limit the information collected about them by using pseudo-identities, certifications and cryptography when performing online transactions.
- Individuals can negotiate with their service providers legally binding 'privacy policies' which govern the use of disclosed personal data precautions that must be taken to safeguard it.
- Individuals and service providers can use automated mechanisms to manage their personal data and their obligations towards data which they have collected from other parties.

To accomplish this, the PRIME project has designed and implemented a practical system-level solution. The paper (Camenisch et al., 2005) describes the architecture of this solution.

Rapid growth of online services increases the number of different identities a user needs to manage (e.g. a person may have one identity as a bank customer and another identity as a company employee). This leads to a problem with proper identity management and people are not able to control and protect their digital identities against identity theft. (Josang et al., 2007) discusses the usability and privacy in online identity management solutions and proposes a general approach enabling users better control and management of their digital identities, as well as designs of more secure identity management solutions. (Josang et al., 2007) also provides a nice overview of existing identity management approaches, each illustrated from the perspective of usability and scalability. Their user-centric model solves the scalability problem and has a potential of providing a universal solution while still being compatible with other models described. Their model also provides stronger security than traditional solutions (this is achieved by having a single separate hardware device called a PAD – Personal Authentication Device). A PAD can take an active part in security transactions.

Another problem is that people have very limited understanding of security and privacy policies being applied to their confidential information and little control over the manipulation with this information once it has been disclosed to third parties. People perceive and address the related security and privacy issues in different ways, ranging from completely ignoring them to being so concerned to prevent their use in any Internet and web-based applications. Identity management systems and solutions need to simplify users' experiences so people can feel they have control over their confidential data and that their data is managed in an accountable way (Casassa Mont et al., 2003).

9.3.3 Summary

The main goal of this part was first to introduce basic privacy primitives that are used in evaluating systems for privacy protection. We then demonstrated the evaluation based on these primitives on selected environments – Pseudonymous convertible credential, Pseudonyms and Private information retrieval. Privacy primitives allow evaluating features of a given system with respect to privacy protection and also provide a methodology to compare different systems between each other.

We provided a detailed insight into statistical databases and related privacy protection issues. Statistical databases are commonly used to provide detailed statistical information about e.g. country population. The privacy related issue here is that the database contains detailed information about individual entities but any attempt to retrieve this detailed information must be strictly prohibited. In order to fulfil this requirement, several approaches are used in statistical databases. We discussed the query restriction approach and data perturbation. These mechanisms allow querying the database, but also provide countermeasures to attempts to get information about individuals.

Two other scenarios are discussed at the end of the section, eCash and identity management are environments where privacy protection is a key feature and special attention has to be taken to protect users of these services.

9.4 Privacy with Delegation of Personal Data[5]

Personalised services with several service providers require collection and delegation of personal data. The service providers collect personal data and delegate them to other service providers. Thus, a service may change its role: it may take the role of a data consumer or of a data provider. The challenge faced is whether the requirements of data protection legislation according to information self-determination can be fulfilled so that users are able to enforce the agreed rules for using personal data. An example of activities and role changes are customer loyalty programs (Customer Relationship Management – CRM).

The case study CRM shows that, in practice, users have to trust service providers. They have to accept the general terms and conditions and thereby give service providers full authority to process their data. Technically, these rules regarding the collection and delegation of personal data correspond to provisions and obligations in order to get access on some personal data. The consent of a user is then commensurate with a delegation of a specific access right to this data in combina-

[5] By Sven Wohlgemuth (ALU-Fr) based on the FIDIS Deliverable D14.2: 'Privacy in Business Processes by Identity Management'.

tion with the agreed rules. The evaluation of existing security tools for delegation of rights and for privacy shows their conceptional weaknesses: By delegating access rights, users are neither able to enforce the agreed rules nor to control the enforcement of delegated rights according to the agreed rules. They lose control of the access to their data. Consequently, the one-sided, practice-based trust model remains unchanged if these tools are applied.

To close this gap and to realise the trust model where users need not trust service providers, this section proposes the identity management system DREISAM with delegation of rights. The delegation of rights as credentials is a provision for the controllable enforcement of the obligations for the use of delegated rights. The delegation and revocation protocols for rights of DREISAM are its novelty. During a protocol run no additional information about the user is published so that his transactions cannot be linked by service providers. The implementation of DREISAM for the CRM case study demonstrates its operation mode.

This section is structured as follows: Section 9.4.1 introduces the collection and delegation of personal data in the case study CRM and shows today's trust model. Section 9.4.2 presents the usage control model with delegation of rights as our approach for a controlled delegation of personal data. Section 9.4.3 investigates on current security systems for privacy respectively delegation of rights and shows their conceptional weakness and thereby the problem of linkability, if they are applied on the scenario. Section 9.4.4 introduces the protocols for a non-linkable delegation of rights. Their application for a delegation of personal data in CRM is shown in Section 9.4.5 by the proof-of-concept implementation of DREISAM. Section 9.4.6 shows the properties of the identity management system DREISAM. Finally, Section 9.4.7 gives the conclusion.

9.4.1 The One-Sided Trust Model in CRM

In the case of customer loyalty programs, their providers take over personalised advertisements and offers for the participating service providers. A loyalty program provider stimulates users to participate in its program by offering them a discount on goods via loyalty points. Every time a user uses his customer card, the service provider collects personal data of this user and delegates them to the loyalty program provider. Consequently, the program provider gets a profile of each user which is a combination of the single user's profiles concerning the service providers. Depending on the loyalty program, its provider also delegates personal data of its customers to the participating service providers for their personalised services. Figure 9.2 shows the flow of personal data within a loyalty program according to the model of (Pretschner, Hilty, Basin, 2006).

Loyalty program providers publish their privacy policy as part of their general terms and conditions.[6] If users want to participate in a loyalty program, they have

[6] E.g., the privacy terms of Payback (http://www.payback.de), Miles & More (http://www.milesandmore.com), and HappyDigits (http://www.happydigits.de).

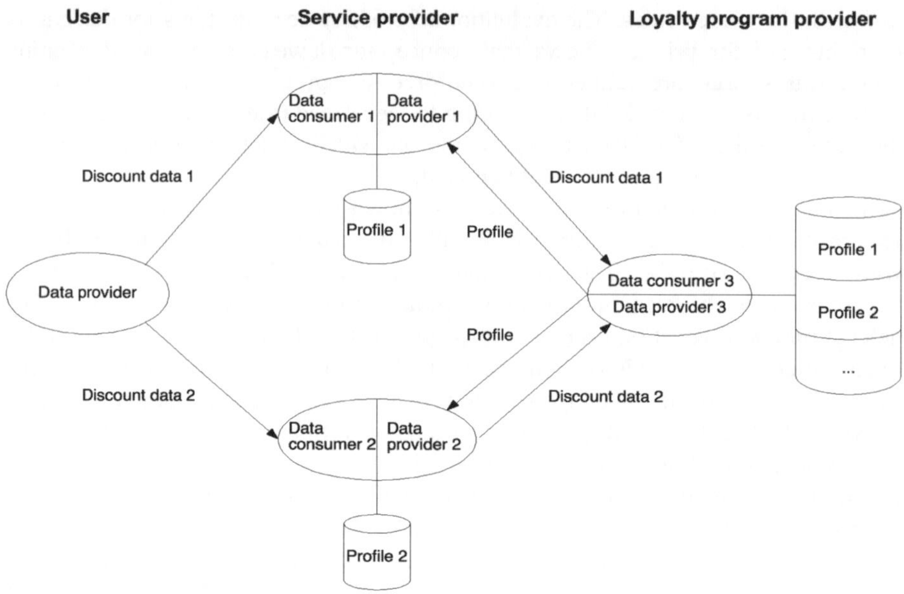

Fig. 9.2. Collection and delegation of personal data within a loyalty program

to accept its privacy policy and thereby give full authority to process their data. Users are not able to decide on the collection and delegation of personal data on a case-by-case basis. Consequently, a one-sided trust model is realised: Users have to trust every service provider that he will follow his privacy policy, i.e. users are not able to control the enforcement of the agreed privacy policy.

9.4.2 Delegation of Rights in CRM

The one-sided trust model will be enhanced, if solely service providers get access to those personal data for which a corresponding user has given his agreement. This means that users should only trust the data provider, e.g., the loyalty service provider, but not trust data consumers, e.g., service providers, anymore. On the other side, data consumers need to trust the data provider that users' data are authentic. This multilateral trust model should be realised by the following access control model.

The two main characteristics of the access control model are the location of storing personal data and the time of access on it. Concerning the collection of personal data, they are stored at the corresponding user. Concerning the delegation of personal data, they are stored at the loyalty program provider who decides on the access. It follows that the access control model consists of two access control domains each having a reference monitor for the access decisions: user's and loyalty program provider's domain. This kind of access control model is called usage control (Park and Sandhu, 2004; Pretschner, Hilty, Basin 2006).

Figure 9.3 shows the usage control model with delegation of rights. An ellipse represents a reference monitor and the arrows represent the assigned right for access on personal data. A dashed line shows a delegation of a right from the data provider to the data consumer. As long as personal data is in the domain of the user (data provider), he decides on the access. Once an access request has been granted, a user is neither able to control access nor usage for this data (Park and Sandhu, 2004; Pretschner, Hilty, Basin 2006). Hence, rights on personal data for their delegation refer to an access in the future. These rights are called obligations. In case of CRM, obligations are enforced via a loyalty program provider (data provider), since he stores users' data and decides on their delegation. The user influences these access decisions by delegating the access right together with obligations for its use to the requesting service provider (data consumer). This is the realisation of user's agreement. For realising a case-by-case agreement of a user, rights have to be delegated and revoked per user's transaction. Therefore, credentials as defined in trust management (Blaze and Feigenbaum 1998; Aura, 1999) are used for delegation of rights.

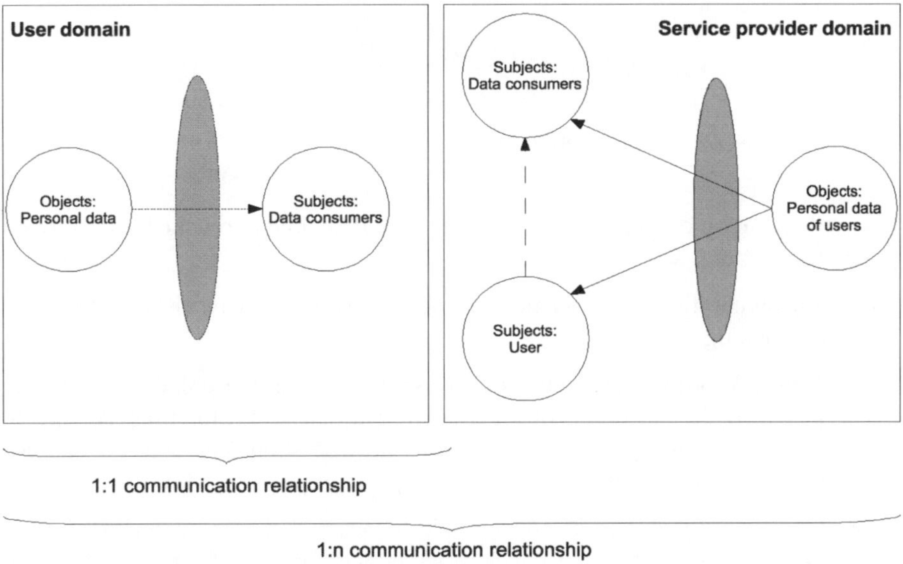

Fig. 9.3. Usage control with delegation of rights

In order to realise a multilateral trust model, as shown in Figure 9.4, a usage control mechanism has to follow the following rules:

- Case-by-case agreement: An access request on given personal data and for a given purpose should only be granted if the corresponding user has given his agreement.

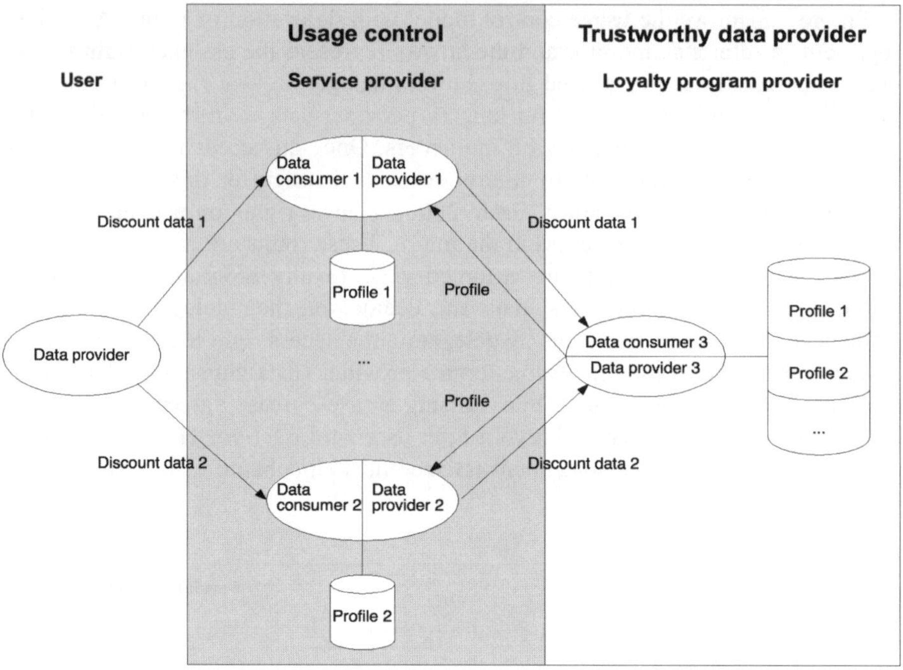

Fig. 9.4. Multilateral trust model for CRM

- Revocation of an agreement: A user should be able to revoke his agreement for a certain access to his personal data.
- Accountability: A transaction should be unambiguously assigned to a corresponding user.
- Non-linkability: Transactions of a user should be non-linkable for service providers so that they won't get additional data about the user. An exception is the loyalty program provider, since he should be able to establish profiles about his users.
- Observability: Users should be able to observe the enforcement of delegated access rights and check whether they are enforced in compliance with the agreed obligations.

9.4.3 Security Systems and Delegation of Rights

Anonymity services and identity management systems focus on the collection of personal data and on obscurity. If they are applied on business processes with delegation of personal data, users will lose the control over their personal data. From the identity management system's point of view, this stems from the fact that users' access rights are (a) linked to a user via credentials and (b) all credentials are linked to the master identity of the user implemented either by a cryptographic key or an account at an identity provider which means a Trusted Third Party (TTP) (Wohlgemuth and Müller, 2006).

Digital Rights Management (DRM) also considers the usage of digital content according to a policy and is therefore suitable to realize secured data storage for data consumers. However, DRM prevents a delegation of digital content and personal data at all (Cox et al., 2008).

Obligations for a delegation of personal data are nowadays realised by sticky policies (Karjoth, Schunter, Waidner, 2002). The privacy policy language *EPAL* formalises obligations but users are not able to control their enforcement. They have to trust a data protection officer of a service provider for checking the enforcement of a sticky policy according to stipulated data protection policy (Ashley et al., 2003). Consequently, the deployment of EPAL does not enhance the one-sided trust model.

An implementation of sticky policies for delegation of personal data is the adaptive privacy management system ('Adaptive PMS') by (Casassa Mont and Pearson, 2005). Sticky policies are linked to certain personal data at the time of their collection by an encryption scheme. The user encrypts his personal data together with the privacy policy. Upon request of a service provider, the encrypted data is sent according to the corresponding privacy policy to this service. Only if it fits the privacy policy, will the data consumer get the decryption key from the TTP. Since personal data is encrypted at the time of collection, its privacy policy has to consider all permissible purposes and data consumers in advance. This means that the user's identifier is the same for all data consumers given in this privacy policy. After the decryption of the personal data, these data consumers are able to link users' transactions and to union their profiles so that a delegation of further personal data is conducted. It follows that users have to trust these data consumers in addition to the TTP. The one-sided trust model remains unchanged.

The term 'delegation of rights' comes from trust management (Blaze et al., 1998; Aura, 1999). It differs from sticky policies in that rights or authorisations are linked to a cryptographic key of the corresponding data consumer instead to the corresponding personal data. This relationship is verifiable by means of a credential. If trust management is applied on CRM, the loyalty service provider issues these credentials to the cryptographic keys of its users. Users delegate a certain access right together with obligations for its use to service providers by issuing a proxy credential (Neuman, 1993). Users digitally sign their proxy credentials and include their public key in a proxy credential for verification. Concerning privacy, this is a drawback: users are linkable by their digital signature and their public key. So, participating service providers are also able to combine users' profiles; users have no control over the access to their disclosed data. The one-sided trust model remains unchanged.

But in contrary to the scheme for sticky policies, cryptographic modules for non-linkability exist for credentials. Anonymous credentials, as they are used by the system IBM idemix (Camenisch and van Herreweghen, 2002), make use of a commitment scheme for linking authorisations to a cryptographic key and of zero-knowledge proofs for showing this relationship without revealing any (additional) identifying data. Since these cryptographic protocols also focus on a direct communication between two parties, their application on an indirect communication to the loyalty service provider (data provider) via a service provider (data consumer) implies sharing the secret cryptographic key. Consequently, a user has no control anymore on his credentials and accesses on his personal data, if these protocols are used in CRM. A solution for using credentials in combination with these cryptographic modules for a non-linkable delegation of rights is presented.

9.4.4 DREISAM: Protocols for Delegation of Rights

The DREISAM protocols extend identity management by a protocol for a non-linkable delegation and revocation of rights. The participants are a user, a certification authority (CA) and service providers either as data consumers or as data providers. Since the protocols make use of anonymous credentials according to (Camenisch and Lysyanskaya, 2001), it is assumed that there is a PKI for anonymous credentials according to (Camenisch and van Herreweghen, 2002) in place. Service providers trust the CA involved for checking the relationship of authorisations to a user according to its certification policy before issuing proxy credentials. It is moreover assumed that the access rights to be delegated have already been attested by the corresponding data provider and the user has the respective anonymous credential.

A proxy credential substitutes sharing of a user's cryptographic key and represents the delegation request for a certain access right. According to the requirements of delegation of rights, a proxy credential is an attribute certificate and is specified as follows:

- Purpose: The purpose defines the use of the delegated access rights, the attributes of the personal data to which access is going to be granted, and the maximal number of accesses for the data consumer.
- Data consumer: This attribute specifies the data consumer, which is allowed to get access on the given attributes of personal data.
- Transaction ID (TID): A TID corresponds to a delegation request of a user to the CA with the issued proxy and anonymous credentials for the data consumers.
- Delegation: This boolean attribute specifies if a data consumer is allowed to further delegate the access right.
- Validity: Delegated access rights are only valid within a certain period of time and should not be used before and after this period.
- Issuer: The CA is given by this attribute in order to check the authenticity of a proxy credential by means of a certification path.

The verification of requests and the issued anonymous one-show credentials for the data consumers are logged by the CA in the so called delegation list. This list is similar to the access control list according to (Harrison, Ruzzo, Ullmann, 1976). An entry refers to the delegation of an access right of the user to data consumers. To allow the CA to resolve a dispute between users and service providers, the pertinent credential of the user is also stored. For monitoring the frequency of the access requests of a data consumer, the number of the issuances of anonymous one-show credentials is recorded. An entry of a delegation list comprises the following attributes:

- TID,
- pseudonym(U,CA) of the user which he has used at the CA,
- attributes of the personal data to be delegated,
- user's anonymous credential(authorisation, pseudoynm(U,CA),CA)
- agreed privacy policy for the delegation of personal data,
- name of the data consumers who have already received anonymous one-show credentials for this access, and
- for every data consumer the number of the corresponding anonymous one-show credentials already issued.

In the following, we present the phases of the delegation and revocation protocols. For their detailed description please refer to (Wohlgemuth and Müller, 2006; Müller and Wohlgemuth, 2007; Wohlgemuth, 2008). A delegation of rights is carried out in four phases as shown in Figure 9.5. Phase A considers the request of a data consumer for personal data from the user. Phases B and C implement the delegation of rights by proxy and anonymous credentials, whereby the CA issues these credentials. The aim of phase B is the issuance and delegation of an authorisation for a data consumer to get access on user's personal data. This is implemented by proxy credentials, which are attribute certificates according to (Ford and Baum, 1997). Proxy credentials cannot be used for an authentication at a data provider, since an authentication takes place by anonymous credentials. Phase C aims at the issuance of anonymous credentials representing the delegated rights of the data consumer. In this phase, the decision to delegate the rights is made by the CA depending on the agreed rules of a delegation. With phase D, a delegation is concluded. This phase aims at the use of delegated access rights according to their obligations.

The phases of a revocation are shown in Figure 9.6. The aim of the phase E is the initiation of a revocation by the user. The same CA is requested for revocation, which issued the proxy credential to be revoked. This CA subsequently examines whether the user is authorised for the revocation. The aim of phase F is the execution of the revocation of the proxy credential and the pertaining anonymous credentials of the data consumer. Current revocation mechanisms for conventional

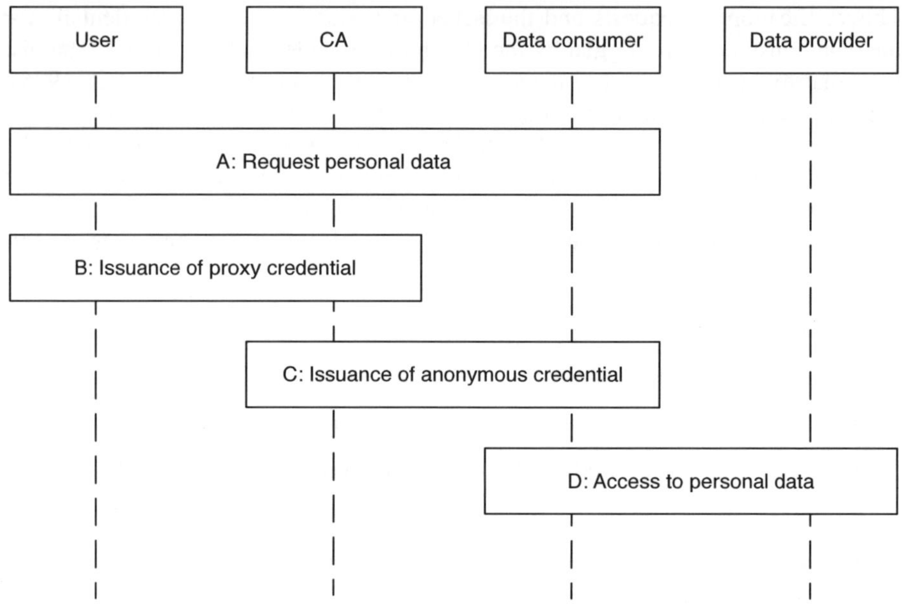

Fig. 9.5. Phases of the DREISAM delegation protocol

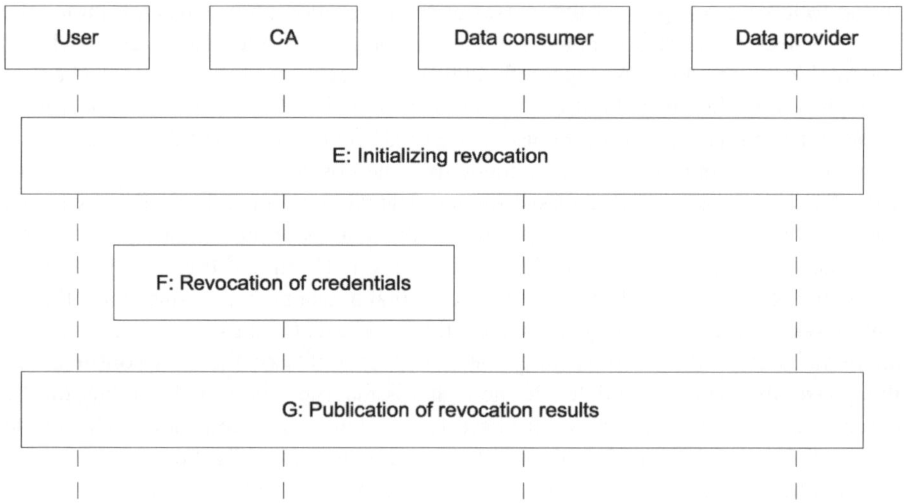

Fig. 9.6. Phases of the DREISAM revocation protocol

attribute certificates such as revocation lists (Ford and Baum, 1997), are implemented together with a mechanism for anonymous credentials, i.e. the use of a dynamic accumulator according to (Camenisch and Lysyanskaya, 2001). The aim of phase G is the publication of revocation's results. The revocation of a proxy credential is published as part of an updated CRL. The accumulator is distributed as part of the public key pk_{CA} of the CA, via its directory service for example. The prime numbers of the valid anonymous credential is published in the entry E_{add} and those of the revoked anonymous credentials in the entry E_{delete} of the directory service.

9.4.5 Proof-of-Concept Implementation of DREISAM for CRM

Concerning the case study CRM, the DREISAM identity system implements five use cases for initializing the system, collecting personal data, delegating personal data via delegation of rights and revoking delegated rights (see Figure 9.7). The aim of the use case 'Issuance of an electronic ID card' is to certify a user's identity. The result is an electronic ID card by an anonymous credential. This credential is linked to the master identity of the user, i.e. his cryptographic key k_{User}, and has been issued by the CA. By use case 'Issuance of access rights', the data provider grants access rights to the user in order to get access on his personal data, which have been already collected. These access rights consider the requirements of the European data protection directive, i.e., the user is allowed to read, modify, delete, and block his personal data. These access rights are granted to the user by issuing an anonymous credential. Furthermore, the data provider (loyalty service provider) issues the electronic customer card to the user, if this user has shown his identity by his electronic ID card. The electronic customer card is also realized by an anonymous credential. The use case 'Collection of personal data' considers 1:1 communication relationships of the usage control model. A user shows his electronic ID card, when he uses a service of a partner enterprise. Since a user acts with a pseudonym towards the partner enterprise, the collected personal data are pseudonymised. So that the loyalty program provider is able to establish a profile about this user, the loyalty program provider must be able to assign the pseudonymised data to the customer number of the corresponding user. Therefore, the loyalty program provider makes use of the de-anonymisation protocol for anonymous credentials (Camenisch and Lysyanskaya, 2001). The use case 'Delegation of personal data' considers 1:n communication relationships of the usage control model and so the DREISAM delegation protocol. Whereas the use case 'Revocation of delegated access rights' considers the DREISAM revocation protocol.

The proof-of-concept implementation of DREISAM is based on the identity management system iManager of the University of Freiburg (Wohlgemuth et al., 2004) and on the anonymous credential system IBM idemix (Camenisch and van Herreweghen, 2002). The iManager is extended by sub systems for data consumers, data providers, and for the CA. Concerning the data consumer, the DREISAM authentication service is responsible for requesting access rights and personal data, the DREISAM certification service issues Proxy Credentials and anonymous credentials, and the DREISAM authorisation service decides on access requests by data consumers. Figure 9.8 shows these sub services and their interaction for delegation of rights by the phases of the delegation protocol.

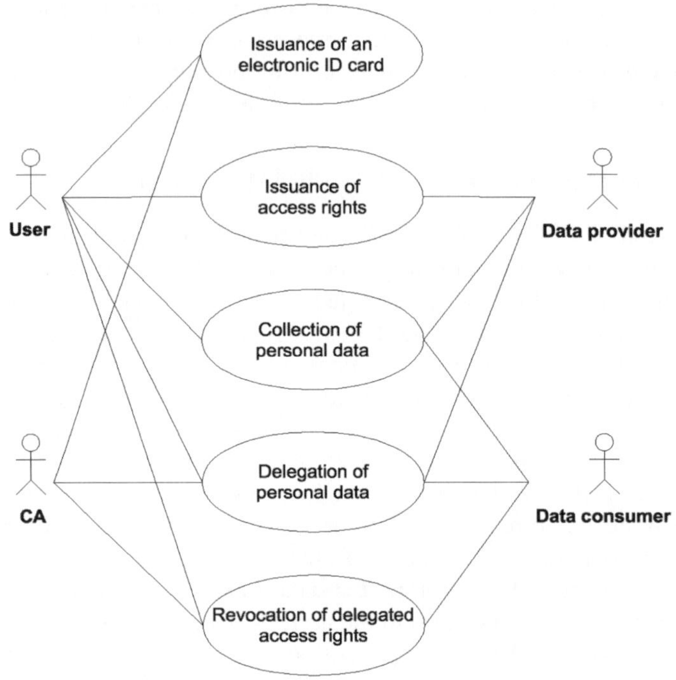

Fig. 9.7. Use cases of the DREISAM identity management system for CRM

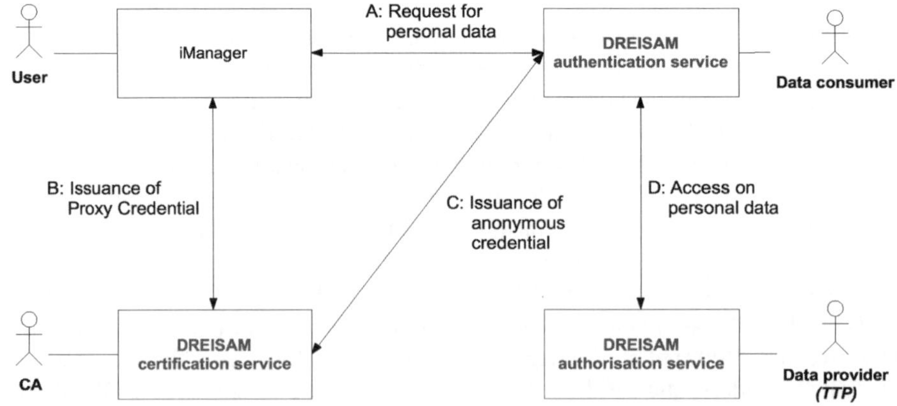

Fig. 9.8. The sub services of the DREISAM proof-of-concept implementation

The proof-of-concept implementation considers an electronic bargain for a health insurer. It consists of five services, one CA and one user. The services are two health insurers, one pharmacy, one fitness centre and a loyalty service provider. All service providers take part in the same loyalty program. It is assumed that services has already collected personal data of the user and delegated it to the loyalty program provider. In order to offer a discount on a health insurance, the insurance provider wants to get access to a user's fitness centre profile. The user agrees on this access but not on an access to his other personal data, e.g., his pharmacy profile. Therefore, he delegates an access right via the CA to the insurance provider INSURE and acts with a transaction pseudonym. Figure 9.9 shows this entry of the delegation list of the CA. The service of INSURE has got the requested fitness centre profile by the loyalty provider. Figure 9.10 shows a user's profile at INSURE by its DREISAM authentication service.

9.4.6 Properties of DREISAM

It has to be shown that DREISAM

(a) does not disclose any identifying data of the user,

(b) the transactions of a user cannot be linked,

(c) the request of a user respectively of a data consumer is accountable, and

(d) a data consumer is only able to use a user's personal data according to the purpose of the corresponding business process.

Cases (a) and (b) refer to a controlled disclosure of personal data; cases (c) and (d) refer to a prevention of misuse. Additionally, disputes must be resolvable to clarify liability.

Since DREISAM makes use of the identity manager iManager, a user is able to decide case-by-case on the disclosure of his personal data by using partial identities. Non-linkability of transactions is achieved by using transaction pseudonyms and anonymous credentials. Non-repudiation of a user for a delegation is achieved by showing his identity and access rights via anonymous credentials and by the log in the delegation list of the CA. Non-repudiation of a data consumer is achieved by showing an anonymous one-show credential to the data provider and by the access log of the data provider. DREISAM enables a user to delegate specific personal data to a data consumer by using proxy credentials. This empowers a user to delegate least authorisation necessary required by a data consumer. The de-anonymisation mechanism of IBM idemix is used for revealing the identity of a user or the data consumer in case of fraud.

It is assumed that the data provider, in case of CRM, follows the obligations of delegated rights and enforces them accordingly. Double-spending of an anonymous one-show credential is detected, if the data provider checks on-line with a CA whether the provided credential has already been used. In the off-line case,

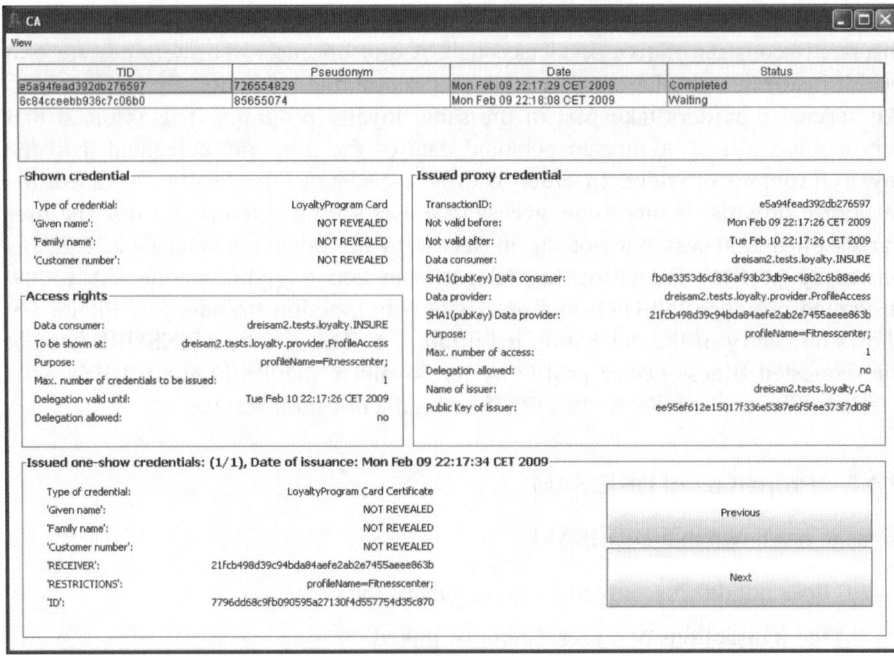

Fig. 9.9. An exemplary entry of CA's delegation list

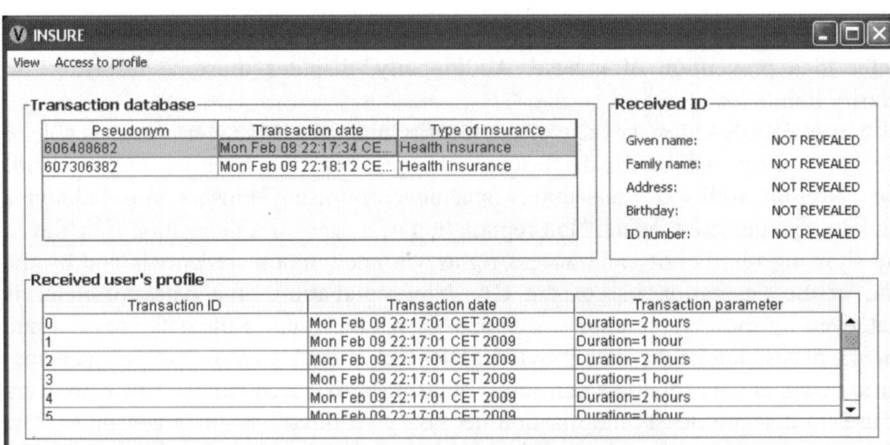

Fig. 9.10. Pseudonymity of a user after the use of a delegated access right

such a double-spending cannot be prevented but it can be detected afte the same way as in the on-line case. With respect to undesired re-deleg proxy credential, the CA would issue an anonymous credential for anc data consumer, which is not mentioned in user's policy. It follows that CA does not follow the certification policy and is not trustworthy. This contradicts the assumption of a trustworthy CA.

Disputes between a user and data consumers relating to the use of access rights may occur in two cases. A data consumer uses a delegated credential and denies its use or a dishonest user uses a credential in the name of a data consumer and denies its use. A dispute is solved by a data provider based on the transcript of the access decisions and on a CA's transcript of a delegation transaction. The data provider compares the transcript of the credential usage with the transcript of issued credentials to identify the cheater.

9.4.7 Conclusion

Personal data is not only used pseudonymised for today's personalised services. As shown by the CRM and the eHealth examples, services need identifiable personal data. Therefore, the protection of privacy in terms of data economy is not adequate. The challenge is not only to protect access on personal data, as it was in order to realise data economy, but also to protect the usage of personal data. That means that personal data is only used according to the given privacy policy.

Current research on usage control corresponds to the formalisation of obligations and their classification in enforceable and observable obligations (Pretschner, Hilty, Basin, 2006), on verification of mechanisms for usage control (Pretschner et al., 2008). It has to be mentioned that the DREISAM approach for a controlled delegation of personal data assumes a trustworthy data provider. Further work is the observation of service providers' behaviour whether they follow the agreed obligations according to the delegation of personal data.

9.5 Towards Transparency

Once the access to data is granted, users have no technical mechanisms to control as to how their data is used – irrespective of the initial partner's intention. All mechanisms require – to different degrees – to trust the data providers and they require the cooperation of the data providers. A 'proof' of being an 'honest' partner acting according to the declared privacy policy can be produced by making data storage and data usage transparent. Thus, where enforcement is technically not feasible, transparency comes into focus. Different institutions providing a first step towards transparency already exist: certification authorities, trusted third parties, privacy seals or codes of conduct.

So instead of seeking technical enforcement, the goal is to provide a 'privacy evidence' to users (Accorsi, 2008). Technologies for transparent data processing, such as logging and auditing, show that the partner respects the policy. The upcoming challenge will not only be to conceive mechanisms providing privacy by transparency, but especially to well balance out where trust is necessary (and justified) and where technical control is indispensable.

References

Adam, N. R. and Worthmann, C. J. (1989), 'Security-control methods for statistical databases: a coparative study', ACM Computing Surveys, 21 (4), pp. 515–556.

Accorsi, R. (2008), 'Automated Privacy Audits to Complement the Notion of Control for Identity Management', Policies and Research in Identity Management, IFIP vol. 261, pp. 39-48.

Ashley, P., Hada, S., Karjoth, G., Powers, C., Schunter, M. (2003), 'Enterprise Privacy Authorization Language (EPAL)', IBM Research, url: http://www.zurich.ibm.com/security/enterprise-privacy/epal/specification.

Aura, T. (1999), 'Distributed Access-Rights Managements with Delegations Certificates', Secure internet Programming: Security Issues For Mobile and Distributed Objects, LNCS vol. 1603, pp. 211–235.

Baumgarten, M., Buechner, A. G., Anand, S. S., Mulvenna, M. D., Hughes, J. G. (1999), 'User-driven navigation pattern discovery from internet data', in: Masand, B.M. and Spiliopoulou, M. (eds.), Revised Papers From the international Workshop on Web Usage Analysis and User Profiling LNCS Vol. 1836. pp. 74-91, SpringerWeb Usage Analysis and User Profiling, Proceedings of International WEBKDD'99 Workshop San Diego, CA, USA, LNCS vol. 1836.

Beck, L. L. (1980), 'A security mechanism for statistical database', ACM Transactions on Database Systems (TODS) 5 (3), pp. 316–338.

Beimel, A. and Dolev, S. (2003), 'Buses for anonymous message delivery', Journal of Cryptology, 16 (1), pp. 25–39.

Bennett, K. and Grothoff, C. (2003), 'GAP – Practical Anonymous Networking', Proceedings of the Privacy Enhancing Technologies Workshop (PET '03), pp. 141–160.

Blaze, M., Feigenbaum, J., Ioannidis, J., Keromytis, A. D. (1998), 'The role of trust management in distributed systems security', Secure Internet Programming, Issues in Distributed and Mobile Object Systems, LNCS State-of-the-Art series, Springer.

Borges, J. and Levene, M. (2000), 'Data mining of user navigation patterns', Revised Papers from the International Workshop on Web Usage Analysis and User Profiling, LNCS vol. 1836, pp. 92–111,.

Broder, A. J. (1999), 'Data mining, the internet, and privacy', Revised Papers from the International Workshop on Web Usage Analysis and User Profiling, LNCS vol. 1836, pp. 56-73.

Buitelaar, H. (ed.) (2007), FIDIS Deliverable D13.3: Study on ID number policies, Download: www.fidis.net/resources/deliverables/.

Bygrave, L. A. (2002), 'Data Protection Law, Approaching its rationale, logic and limits', Kluwer Law International, pp. 94-95.

Camenisch, J. and van Herreweghen, E. (2002), 'Design and Implementation of the idemix Anonymous Credential System', Proceedings of the 9th ACM Conference on Computer and Communications Security, pp. 21–30.

Camenisch, J. and Lysyanskaya, A. (2001), 'An efficient system for non-transferable anonymous credentials with optional anonymity revocation' Proceedings of the International Conference on the Theory and Application of Cryptographic Techniques (EUROCRYPT '01), LNCS vol. 2045, pp. 93–118.

Camenisch, J. and Lysyanskaya, A. (2002), 'A signature scheme for efficient protocols', Proceedings of Third Conference on Security in Communication Networks, LNCS vol. 2576, pp. 274-295.

Camenisch, J., Shelat, A., Sommer, D., Fischer-Hűbner, S., Hansen, M., Krasemann, H., Lacoste, G., Leenes, R., Tseng, J. (2005), 'Privacy and identity management for everyone' Proceedings of the 2005 workshop on Digital identity management (DIM '05), pp. 20–27.

Casassa Mont, M., Pearson, S., Bramhall, P. (2003), 'Towards accountable management of identity and privacy: Sticky policies and enforceable tracing services', Proceedings of the 14th International Workshop on Database and Expert Systems Applications (DEXA'03), pp. 377–382.

Casassa Mont, M. and Pearson, S. (2005), 'An Adaptive Privacy Management System for Data Repositories', in: Kazikas, S., Lopez, J., Pernul, G. (eds.) Proceedings of TrustBus 2005, LNCS vol. 3592, Springer, pp. 236-245.

Chaum, D. (1981), 'Untraceable electronic mail, return addresses, and digital pseudonyms', Communications of the ACM 4 (2), pp. 84–88.

Chaum, D. (1986), 'Showing credentials without identification. Signatures transferred between unconditionally unlinkable pseudonyms', Proceedings of the workshop on Theory and Application of Cryptographic Techniques (EUROCRYPT '85), LNCS vol. 281, pp. 241–244.

Chaum, D. (1988), 'The dining cryptographers problem: Unconditional sender and recipient untraceability', Journal of Cryptology 1 (1), pp. 65–75.

Chawla, S., Dwork, C., McSherry, F., Smith, A., Wee, H. (2005), 'Toward privacy in public databases', in: Kilian, J. (ed.) Proceedings of the 2nd Theory of Cryptography Conference (TCC'05), LNCS vol. 3378, Springer, pp. 363–385.

Chin, F. Y. L. and Özsoyoglu, G. (1982), 'Auditing and inference control in statistical databases', IEEE Transactions on Software Engineering (TSE) 8 (6), pp. 574–582.

Chor, B., Kushilevitz, E., Goldreich, O., Sudan, M. (1998), ‚Private information retrieval', Journal of ACM 45 (6), pp. 965–981.

Clauß, S. and Köhntopp, M. (2001), 'Identity management and its support of multilateral security', Computer Networks, The International Journal of Computer and Telecommunications Networking 37 (2), pp. 205–219.

Clifton, C. and Marks, D. (1996), 'Security and privacy implications of data mining', Proceedings of the ACM SIGMOD Workshop on Research Issues on Data Mining and Knowledge Discovery, Montreal, Canada, pp. 15–19.

College bescherming persoonsgegevens (2002), 'Electronische overheid en privacy, Bescherming van persoonsgegevens in de informatiestructuur van de overheid [Electronic Government and privacy, Data protection in the government information structure]', Den Haag.

Common Criteria Editorial Board (2007), 'Common Criteria for Information Technology Security Evaluation (Part 2: Security functional requirements)', Version 3.1, rev. 2.

Cox, I. J., Miller, M. L., Bloom, J. A., Fridrich, J., Kalker, T. (2008), Digital Watermarking and Steganography, Morgan Kaufmann.

De Bot, D. (2005), 'Privacybescherming bij e-government in België. Een kritische analyse van het Rijksregister, de Kruispuntbank van Ondernemingen en de elektronische identiteitskaart, [Privacy protection in e-government in Belgium. A critical analysis of the Rijksregister, the Crossroads bank of enterprises and the electronic identity card]', p. 56, Vandenbroeke, Brugge.

Denning, D. E. and Denning, P. J. (1979), 'The tracker: a threat to statistical database security', ACM Transactions on Database Systems (TODS) 4 (1), pp. 76–96.

Denning, D. E. (1980), 'Secure statistical databases with random sample queries', ACM Transactions on Database Systems (TODS) 5 (3), pp. 291–315.

Dobkin, D., Jones, A. K., Lipton, R. J. (1979), 'Secure databases: protection against user influence', ACM Transactions on Database Systems (TODS 4 (1), pp. 97–106.

Dua, S., Iyengar, S. S., Cho, E. (2000), 'Discovery of web frequent patterns and user characteristics from web access logs: A framework for dynamic web personalization', Proceedings of the 3rd IEEE Symposium on Application-Specific Systems and Software Engineering Technology (ASSET'00).

The European Parliament and the Council (1995), 'Directive 95/46/EC of the European Parliament and of the Council of 24 October 1995 on the protection of individuals with regard to the processing of personal data on the free movement of such data', Official Journal of the European Communities, L 281, Brussels, pp. 31–50.

The European Parliament, the Council and the Commission (2000), 'The Charter of Fundamental Rights of the European Union (2000/C 364)', Official Journal of the European Communities. http://www.europarl.europa.eu/charter/pdf/text_en.pdf.

Ford, W. and Baum, M. S. (1997), 'Secure Electronic Commerce', Prentice-Hall, Inc., New Jersey.

Grothoff, C., Patrascu, I., Bennett, K., Stef, T., Horozov, T. (2002), 'GNET', Whitepaper, Version 0.5.2. http://www.gnunet.org/download/main.pdf.

Gutwirth, S., and de Hert, P. (2005), 'Privacy and Data Protection in a Democratic Constitutional State', Profiling: Implications for Democracy and Rule of Law, in: Hildebrandt, M., Gutwirth, S., De Hert, P. (eds.), FIDIS Deliverable D7.4: Implications of profiling practice on democracy, Download: www.fidis.net/resources/deliverables/, pp. 11-28.

Hansen, M. and Krasemann, H. (2005), 'Prime White Paper', White Paper, Privacy and Identity Management for Europe, PRIME.

Harrison, M.A., Ruzzo, W.L., Ullman, D.J. (1979), 'Protection in Operating Systems', Communications of ACM 19, (8), pp. 461-471.

Josang, A., Al Zomai, M., Suriadi, S. (2007), 'Usability and privacy in identity management architectures', in: Brankovic, L. and Steketee, C. (eds.), Proceedings of the Fifth Australasian Information Security Workshop (Privacy Enhancing Technologies) (AISW 2007), CRPIT Vol. 68, Ballarat, Australia, pp. 143-152.

Kang, S.-I. and Lee, I.-Y. (2005), 'A study on the e-cash system with anonymity and divisibility', in: Gervasi, O., Gavrilova, M. L., Kumar, V., Laganà, A., Lee, H. P., Mun, Y., Taniar, D., Tan, C. J. K. (eds.), 'Computational Science and Its Applications – ICCSA 2005', Proceedings of the International Conference on Computational Science and its Applications (ICCSA '05), Part II, LNCS Vol. 3481, Springer, pp. 177–186.

Kargupta, H., Datta, S., Wang, Y., Sivakumar, K. (2003), 'On the privacy preserving properties of random data perturbation techniques', Proceedings of the third IEEE International Conference on Data Mining (ICDM'03), pp. 99-106.

Karjoth, G., Schunter, M., Waidner, M. (2003), 'Platform for Enterprise Privacy Practices: Privacy-enabled Management of Customer Data', Proceedings of the 2nd Workshop on Privacy Enhancing Technologies (PET 2002), LNCS vol. 2482, pp.69-84.

Kleinberg, J. M., Papadimitriou, C. H., Raghavan, P. (2000), 'Auditing boolean attributes', Proceedings of the nineteenth ACM SIGMOD-SIGACT-SIGART Symposium on Principles of database systems, pp.86-91.

Koops, B.-J. (2001), 'Een nieuwe GBA, digitale kluisjes en identificatiedrang [A new GBA, digital vaults and the identification urge]', NJB 32 (32), pp. 1555-1561.

Koops, B.-J., Buitelaar, H., Lips, M. (eds.) (2007), FIDIS Deliverable D5.4: Anonymity in electronic government: a case-study analysis of governments' identity knowledge, Download: www.fidis.net/resources/deliverables/.

Malin, B. (2002), 'Compromising privacy with trail re-identification: The reidit algorithms', Technical Report CMU-CALD-02-108, Carnegie Mellon University.

Matloff, N. S. (1986), 'Another look at the use of noise addition for database security', IEEE Symposium on Security and Privacy, pp. 173-181, IEEE Computer Society.

Matyáš, V. and Cvrček, D. (2004), 'On the Role of Contextual Information for Privacy Attacks and Classification', Proceedings of the Privacy and Security Aspects of Data Mining Workshop, pp. 31–39.

Müller, G. and Wohlgemuth, S. (eds.) (2007), FIDIS Deliverable D14.2 Study on Privacy in Business Processes by Identity Management, Download: www.fidis.net/resources/deliverables/.

Neuman, B. C. (1993), 'Proxy-Based Authorization and Accounting for Distributed Systems', Proceedings of the 13th International Conference on Distributed Computing Systems, pp. 283–291.

Nissenbaum, H. (2004), 'Privacy as Contextual Integrity', Washington Law Review 79, pp. 101– 140.

Park, J. and Sandhu, R. (2004), 'The $UCON_{ABC}$ usage control model', ACM Transaction on Information System Security 7 (1), pp. 128-174.

Pfitzmann, A. and Hansen, M. (2009), 'Anonymity, unobservability, and pseudonymity: A proposal for terminology', in: Federrath, H. (ed.), Designing Privacy Enhancing Technologies (PET'00), LNCS vol. 2009, Springer, pp. 1–9.

Pretschner, A., Hilty, M., Basin (2006), 'Distributed Usage Control', Communications of the ACM 49 (9), pp 39-44.

Pretschner, A., Hilty, M., Basin, D., Schaefer, C., Walter, T. (2008), 'Mechanisms for Usage Control', Proceedings of the ACM Symposium on Information, Computer & Communication Security (ASIACCS '08), pp. 240–245.

Prins, C. and de Vries, M. (2003), 'ID or not to be? Naar een doordacht stelsel voor digitale identificatie [ID or not to be? Towards a well thought out system for digital identification]', Rathenau Instituut, Working document 91, p. 13.

Qiu, W., Chen, K., Gu, D. (2002), 'A new offline privacy protecting e-cash system with revokable anonymity', Proceedings of the 5th International Conference on Information Security, LNCS vol. 2433, pp. 177–190.

Reiter, M. and Rubin, A. (1998), 'Crowds: Anonymity for web transactions', ACM Transactions on Information and System Security (TISSEC) 1 (1), pp. 66–92.

Rivest, R., Adelman, L., Dertouzos, M. (1978), 'On databanks and privacy homomorphism', Foundations of secure computation, pp. 168–177.

Sackmann, S., Strüker, J., Accorsi, R. (2006), 'Personalization in Privacy-Aware Highly Dynamic Systems', Communications of the ACM 49 (9).

Samarati, P. and Sweeney, L. (1998), 'Protecting privacy when disclosing information: k-anonymity and its enforcement through generalization and suppression', Technical Report SRI-CSL-98-04, SRI Computer Science Laboratory,.

Schlörer, J. (1983), 'Information loss in partitioned statistical databases', Computer Journal 26 (3), pp. 218–223.

Solove, D. (2006), 'A taxonomy of privacy', University of Pennsylvania Law Review 154 (3), pp. 477– 560.

Sweeney, L. (2002), 'k-anonymity: a model for protecting privacy', International Journal of Uncertainty, Fuzziness and Knowledge-Based Systems 10 (5), pp. 557–570.

Tavani, H. T. (1999), 'Information privacy, data mining, and the internet', Ethics and Information Technology, Kluwer Academic Publishers, Hingham, MA, USA.

The Common Criteria Project Sponsoring Organisations (1999), Common Criteria for Information Technology Security Evaluation – part 2, Version 2.1.

Wilson, R. L. and Rosen, P. A. (2003), 'Protecting data through perturbation techniques: The impact on knowledge discovery in databases' Journal of Database Management 14 (2), pp. 14–26.

Wishart, R., Henricksen, K., Indulska, J. (2005), 'Context Obfuscation for Privacy via Ontological Descriptions', in: Strang, T. and Linnhoff-Popien, C. (eds.), Location- and Context-Awareness: First International Workshop (LoCA 2005), Oberpfaffenhofen, Germany, LNCS vol. 3479. Springer.

Wohlgemuth, S. and Müller, G. (2006), 'Privacy with Delegation of Rights by Identity Management', Proceedings of International Conference on Emerging Trends in Information and Communication Security (ETRICS 2006), Freiburg, Germany, 2006, LNCS vol. 2995, Springer, pp. 175–190.

Wohlgemuth, S. (2008), 'Privatsphäre durch die Delegation von Rechten', Ph.D. thesis at the University of Freiburg, Germany.

Wohlgemuth, S., Jendricke, U., Gerd tom Markotten, D., Dorner, F., Müller, G. (2004), ‚Sicherheit und Benutzbarkeit durch Identitätsmanagement', in: Spath, D., Haases, K. (eds.) Tagungsband zum doIT Software-Forschungstag 2003: Aktuelle Trends in der Softwareforschung, IRB Verlag Stuttgart, pp. 241—260.

Zugenmaier, A. (2003), 'Anonymity for Users of Mobile Devices through Location Addressing', RHOMBOS-Verlag, Berlin.

Zugenmaier, A., Kreutzer, M., Müller, G. (2003), 'The Freiburg Privacy Diamond: An attacker model for a mobile computing environment', Proceedings of Kommunikation in Verteilten Systemen (KiVS) '03.

10 Open Challenges – Towards the (Not So Distant) Future of Identity

Kai Rannenberg and Denis Royer

Identity was a multifaceted and challenging topic, when FIDIS started to work on it, and it will be multifaceted and challenging in future. It has relations to aspects, such as societal values (e.g., privacy), societal phenomena (e.g., crime), application areas (e.g., eGovernment and mobile communications), technologies (e.g., High-Tech IDs), and last but not least scientific disciplines. In each of these areas FIDIS worked on identity, and it became clear that each of the areas is changing, keeping identity a dynamic and multi-faceted field. It may actually get even more aspects in the future, given the fact that none of the questions have disappeared during FIDIS' work so far, but new aspects showed up, e.g., with new technologies showing up. So even after 5 years of FIDIS, not all questions are answered. Some dimensions for future work are discussed in the following sections of this chapter including:

- Identity reference architectures
- Identity Management (IdM) and Privacy
- IdM and Multilateral Security
- Identity in the 'Internet of Things'

The discussion of these topics is especially focusing on the questions: 'What is to be done? How can it be done? What needs to be considered?', for shaping the future of identity in the information society and to adequately address its underlying challenges and opportunities.

In all cases standardisation (as it happens globally in e.g., ISO/IEC JTC 1/SC 27/WG 5 'Identity Management and Privacy Technologies') and regulation (e.g. on data protection and privacy) are of importance and usually trigger more research questions, once the first research results are on their 'radar'.

10.1 Identity Reference Architectures

Reference architectures provide a proven template solution when an architecture for a particular domain is to be designed. They also provide a common vocabulary to discuss implementations, often with the aim of stressing commonality between systems. A reference architecture often consists of a list of functions and some indication of their interfaces and interactions with each other and with functions located outside of the scope of the reference architecture.

When observing the domain of IdMS, reference architectures and reference models could help to structure the various application domains (such as eGovernment or Enterprise IdM) by e.g., identifying the building blocks of IdM and overcoming the currently existing fragmentation in concepts, usages, and technologies.

10.1.1 What Is to Be Done?

Reference architectures can be defined at different levels of abstraction. A highly abstract one might show the relevant pieces of equipment as building blocks, each providing different functions. In the case of IdM, these building blocks could be IdM related components, such as data repositories, identity and access management systems or access and policy services. A lower level one might demonstrate the interactions of procedures (or methods) within an IdMS defined to perform a very specific task, such as the processing of identity data or the granting of rights to an entity (user or object).

To this regard, FIDIS helped to identify the relevant aspects towards IdM in different application domains, such as eGovernment, eHealth, or mobility and identity. Depending on the domain the different stakeholders, technologies, and processes were identified, representing the building blocks for an integrated, domain specific IdM. However, in order to derive a generalisable reference architecture for IdM, it is necessary to identify the common aspects of the different domains in the first place, such as the relevant stakeholders, technologies, and data flows as well as their linkages and underlying processes.

10.1.2 How Can It Be Done?

For building architectures different technologies and related perspectives need to be taken into account. Figure 10.1 gives an initial overview on different perspectives and technologies to observe, when thinking about IdM reference architectures. However, the presented fields (PET, credentials, etc.) do overlap. Depending on the point of view and the focus taken, the components to be looked into are different and change.

From a business to customer (B2C) perspective, privacy enhancing technologies (PET) and data flow are the topics of utmost interest. This is due to the fact that trust from customers requires appropriate actions to protect personal data and add transparency to their usage. On the other hand, looking at the business to employee perspective, the requirements change. To this regard, credentials and access management are the focus. This is due to the fact that processes, organisational architectures, organisational structures, and process organisation are important determinants to be analysed. To this regard, a case-based approach, analysing different aspects towards IdM (as initially stated) is a way to bring light into the dark.

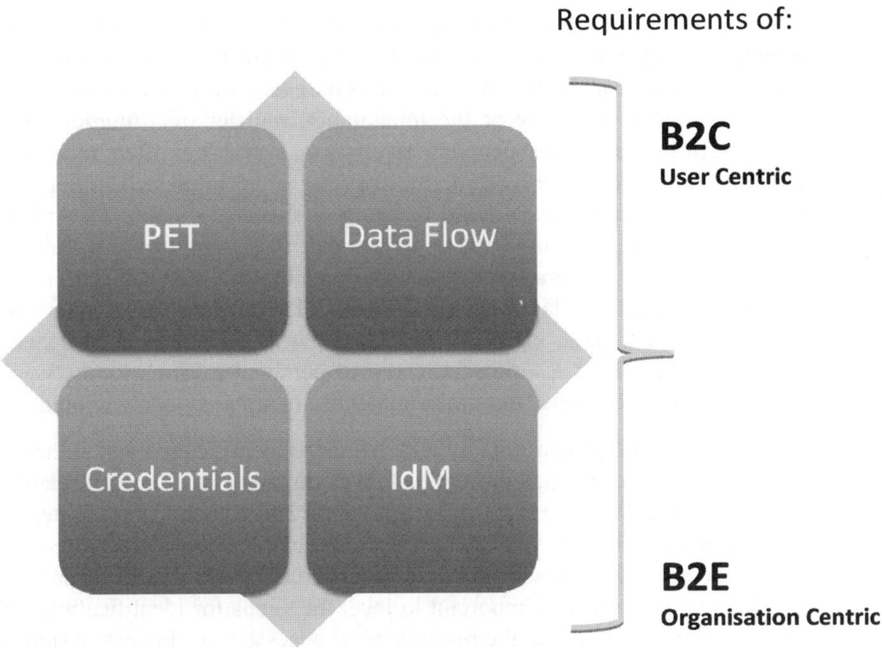

Fig. 10.1. Components of IdM reference models

10.1.3 What Needs to Be Considered?

The duality of IdM between User Centricity and Organisation Centricity (cf. 11.3.3) is of major importance. Also the borders between the perspectives discussed above are moving targets. Further research in conjunction with practical application in the field (e.g. mergers and acquisitions of companies or enhancing IdMS of (European) states for mutual recognition of eIDs across national borders) is necessary to fully grasp the potential of reference models.

10.2 Identity Management and Privacy

Privacy in itself is not a new challenge for research. However, the advent of more and more identifiers that can be tracked and exploited automatically in more and more situations of life make the relations between IdM and privacy more and more important and vice-versa.

10.2.1 What Is to Be Done?

The following aspects of privacy are of particular importance for IdM:

- Avoiding misuse of personal data in different contexts: Identifiers are a key instrument to efficiently connect personal data between different contexts, e.g., civil names can be found in the customer lists of a mail order house and an insurance company or the inhabitants' register of a municipality. However, at the same time people actively use several identifiers related to the contexts they are involved in, and they are often interested in keeping these identities separated to avoid merging or mixing of contexts: An example are the pseudonyms used in eBay, that only rarely give a link towards people's civil names and that usually cannot be matched with other identities, e.g., work-related email addresses. Therefore avoiding the misuse of identifying data, e.g., by supporting partial identities is of special importance. Moreover limiting the creep of personal information between different application areas and limiting identity creep are closely related.
- Actively respecting proportionality with regard to identification and authentication: The 'classic' privacy principle of proportionality has a special relation to identity and IdM in the areas of identification and authentication. Often as much identification and authentication as possible are considered to be the best solution e.g., for allowing access to a resource; however as identification can endanger privacy it is important to level the needs for identification and authentication, according to the resource to be accessed. An important step in this direction is the concept of claims, that enables relying parties to negotiate the terms of identification based on policy and risk assessment instead of simply asking users for 'more' identification
- Improving transparency and control of data flows: Given that identity data are of special interest to the persons identified by them, these persons have a special interest in controlling those flows and understanding them preferably before they take place. This is a special challenge, when data are being transferred as part of outsourcing efforts, e.g., to call centres, whose privacy policies and enforcement mechanisms may differ from those of their clients.
- Reducing temptation to misuse data: Identifying Data and addresses of persons are easy to use and to make available for further usage; therefore they are at special risk of being misused, e.g., being sold by (underpaid) call centre agents to parties misusing the addresses for electronic or paper-based spam mailings.
- Making privacy assessable: So far there is almost no support for users to assess the degree of privacy that a party working with their data, offers. There are some concepts for certificates issued to organisations respecting privacy, but the information available to the users is quite coarse and there is no real tool support to assess this information. Therefore standardised and transparent processes for issuing these certificates are needed. Transparency can be raised by established ('brand-name') certificate issuing parties, integrated into a multilateral identification schema, helping to better assess the level of privacy and a better market potential. Accordingly, this

would help to strengthen the principle of informational self-determination. Whereas this argumentation holds for privacy in general, it is of special importance for IdM, as identity information is very often one of the first elements of personal information that is transmitted.

- Enabling swift appropriate actions in case of problems: Especially with identity data being quite sensitive more support for users to react to problems, e.g., by swift changes or cancellations of identifiers or identities, is needed. The credit card and banking industry has established a scheme for contact between issuing parties and users, but there is not much help for contacts between users and relying parties, e.g., to withdraw accounts and identifiers after an incident.

10.2.2 How Can It Be Done?

The following approaches to improve privacy in the area of IdM are most important:

- Paradigms
  - Data minimisation: Checking solutions and architectures for the possibility of achieving the same level of service with fewer identifying data.
  - Data decentralisation: Avoiding risky accumulations of identifying data.
  - Proportionality: Balancing the requirements for identification and authentication of relying parties against the privacy requirements of users asking for authorisation or access.
- Concepts
  - Partial Identities: partial identities represent a person in a specific context or role. Technically partial identities are sets of attributes. They help towards data minimisation, as they reduce the amount of identifying data that needs to be delivered and stored. Partial identities also support data decentralisation, as less data is collected at e.g., relying parties.
  - Claims: claims are assertions made by one subject about itself or another subject that a relying party considers. By default any claim is 'in doubt' until it passes 'Claims Approval' by the respective relying party. The explication of 'Claims Approval' enables and forces the relying party to make an explicit decision on the presented claim compared to the access demanded by the claiming party. This can lead to negotiating the terms of identification based on policy and risk assessment instead of simply asking for 'more' identification and therefore supports proportionality.
- Tools for data subjects
  - To manage partial identities and claims.
  - To understand data flows and the usage of information.
  - To control data flows.

- Tools for organisations
    - To handle client requests for transparency on data flows.
    - To understand the degree of privacy offered to customers and/ or the degree of compliance achieved.
    - To give advice to customers and employees on further measures.

10.2.3 What Needs to Be Considered?

Especially two aspects deserve special consideration, even though one may not be able to address them directly

- Usability: As most of the tools aim at empowering users to make decisions, e.g., on data flows, the tools need to be understandable and usable by non-experts.
- Organisational fragmentation: The trend towards organisational fragmentation in business and industry, e.g., via outsourcing makes it hard to find responsible entities or to even allocate responsibility for data or data flows.

10.3 Identity Management and Multilateral Security

IdM can be oriented towards different interests that may be in conflict. Different interests often lead to a 'Balance of Power' issue; in the area of IdM this is especially an issue between users, relying parties and parties who issue IDs or other credentials.

Relying parties are often interested in receiving as much information as possible about a user requesting the use of an asset. This may help them to assess the request and the involved risk. Therefore a direct contact to the credential-issuing party, e.g., to check a credential, may be in their interest, and e.g., the X.500 credential model reflects this interest. Answering direct requests from relying parties may also be in the interest of issuing parties, as it can result in extra business for online-verification and also give some information how a credential is being used.

However a credential 'calling home' and the credential-usage information being collected by the credential-issuing party may well not be in the interest of the users, as it can lead to usage profiles on users endangering their privacy. If e.g., a government issued identity card is designed in a way, that every hotel that wants to make use of the information would need an online-check with the card issuer, the issuers learn about the travel patterns of the respective users. The online-check may be of interest to the relying party, but a credential that does not require an online-check is better in protecting the privacy of the users.

To balance the different interests and requirements of different parties the approach of Multilateral Security is of use.

10.3.1 What Is to Be Done?

The following aspects of Multilateral Security are of particular importance for IdM:

- Balancing the power of the involved parties.
- Assuring an agreeable degree of assurance to the involved parties.

10.3.2 How Can It Be Done?

The following approaches to achieve Multilateral Security in the area of IdM are most important:

- Analysing the information flows in the design and implementation of IdM systems with regard to their sensitivity and influence on the balance of power between the involved parties.
- Equipping parties, especially those parties, on whom identity information is transferred with means to understand and control these information flows.
- Analysing the properties of physical and virtual identifiers with regard to Multilateral Security, e.g., comparing physical IDs' protection against forgery with that of virtual IDs to understand how frequent information flows are needed to give relying parties the assurance needed.

10.3.3 What Needs to Be Considered?

A popular way to group stakeholders is to differentiate between users (and their interests) on the one side and organisations (and their interests) on the other side. This relates to the fact, that these interests are often in conflict and is reflected by the terms 'User Centricity' vs. 'Organisation Centricity'.

User centric research approaches tend to enable users to understand and control their relationships with other parties, including the respective flows of identifying information. This includes user-controlled hardware for identity data and (anonymous) communications as well as user-understandable (transparent) policies. It also includes offering users a choice of offers, e.g. to select trusted partners for identity intermediation or networks services. When then users make decisions they have to be able to do so with trade-offs, e.g., in test-beds, that let them experience trade-offs and also confront them with the results of their respective decisions.

Organisation centric research approaches tend to enable organisations towards more agility and flexibility when managing identities (e.g. user accounts) in an efficient way. Here, unifying identities and the support of the identity lifecycle are integral facets to consider. Moreover, being compliant with relevant laws and regulation, especially rules for transparency and audit, such as Basel II, Sarbanes-Oxley Act (SOX), or the 8th EU Directive on Company Law (2006/43/EC) play a major role as well. This includes approaches to integrate different IdMS and to unify identities.

10.4 Identity in the Internet of Things

The Internet of things has two major relations to IdM. On the one side the ‘things’ (household appliances, cars and other embedded systems) often have one or several identifiers that enable them to communicate with other ‘things’. On the other side identity has always been represented by physical tokens, which over time got more and more computing and communication facilities.

10.4.1 What Needs to Be Done?

There is a general need to raise the trustworthiness of embedded systems, as many of them, such as cars, can have severe (physical) impact on their environment. IdM can be used to e.g., identify the entities responsible for designing, manufacturing, operating, maintaining, and repairing the respective embedded systems. This can improve transparency with regard to those devices.

At the same time more understanding is needed with regard to the placement of identity information on physical or virtual identifiers.

10.4.2 How Can It Be Done?

Given that the Internet of things can easily cover the whole world, it may not be appropriate to aim for research goals to model or explain it in its entirety. However the following approaches should help to gain an enhanced understanding of the situation:

- Developing combinations between physical and virtual IDs that are needed in the respective application fields and reflecting on them to learn about possible generalisations.
- Researching the security of physical ID carriers that do not reside in the physical domain of their issuers, such as SIM cards and IT supported passports.
- Combining experiences from safety and IT security in developing protection concepts.
- Furthering High-Tech IDs bridging the virtual and physical world, such as forwarding messages from identities in virtual worlds onto people’s mobile phones.

10.4.3 What Needs to Be Considered?

Especially in the domain of physical systems that are more expensive than the typical computer the issue of legacy technologies needs thorough consideration. Some household systems exist as long as a household or a marriage and replacement cycles are of corresponding length. In addition interoperability between different domains that are usually separated (e.g., cars and active household appliances) but sometimes happen to come into interaction (as a car is used to transport a semiautonomous cleaning device) needs to be well understood.

Appendix A. List of Deliverables

This annex contains the list of deliverables (studies, surveys, etc.) being the basis for this book. Also, all participating partners and contributors for these deliverables are listed as well. The complete list of deliverables and other materials of the FIDIS NoE can be found at www.fidis.net/resources/.

A.1 Communication Infrastructure (WP1)

A.1.1 An Information structure to provide categories and subcategories relevant for FIDIS (D1.2)

This document describes the internal and external FIDIS web-portal system, focusing on the technical aspects of its development, the tools used, and the general structure. The objective of this document is to give a broad overview of the technologies and software products used to build this portal system. Furthermore its internal structure will be described.

Editors: Denis Royer (JWG)

Contributors: Denis Royer (JWG), Stefan Figge (JWG), André Deuker (JWG)

Reviewers: Mark Gasson (READING), Kai Rannenberg (JWG)

A.1.2 Manual of the Extended Wiki System (D1.3)

This document details the technical aspects (e.g., features, development notes, user manual) of the customised Wiki system, "DR_Wiki" used on the FIDIS Communication Infrastructure (FCI). The original Wiki software, on which this is based, is published under the GPL and is publicly available at www.typo3.org. This document is aimed towards both the general Wiki user and the work package administrators for configuring the "DR_Wiki" Typo3 extension.

Editors: Denis Royer (JWG), André Deuker (JWG)

Contributors: Denis Royer (JWG), Thierry Nabeth (INSEAD)

Reviewers: Mark Gasson (READING)

A.2 Taxonomy: Identity of Identity (WP2)

A.2.1 Inventory of Topics and Clusters (D2.1)

This deliverable represents the first results of a work aiming at specifying a conceptualisation of the Identity domain conducted in the FIDIS project. The objective of such a conceptualisation is to provide to both the expert and the non-expert a common and explicit understanding of the identity domain, facilitating the comprehension and the sharing of knowledge on this subject. In this first version, the conceptualisation has consisted principally on the inventory of topics and concepts used in the Identity domain, and in the definition of key Identity concepts. This document (complemented by a WIKI) is organised into sections providing:

- A methodological presentation of the approaches and principles used to specify a conceptualisation, and its application to FIDIS, in order to conceptualise the Identity domain.
- An overall presentation of key Identity concepts.
- A structured inventory of Identity terms.
- A concluding section.

Editors: Thierry Nabeth (INSEAD), Mireille Hildebrandt (VUB)

Contributors: Thierry Nabeth (INSEAD), Mireille Hildebrandt (VUB), Marit Hansen (ICPP), Sabine Delaitre (JRC/IPTS), Denis Royer (JWG), Claudia Díaz (K.U.Leuven), Mark Gasson (READING), Emmanuel Benoist (VIP), Bernhard Arig (VIP), David-Olivier Jaquet-Chiffelle (VIP)

Reviewers: Denis Royer (JWG), Claudia Díaz (K.U.Leuven), Mark Gasson (READING)

A.2.2 Set of Use Cases and Scenarios (D2.2)

The objective of this document is to propose a very concrete and multidisciplinary presentation of identity issues via the provision of a series of cases, stories, scenarios and perspectives. Each of these cases, stories, etc., has been elaborated by a different member of the FIDIS consortium.

Editors: Thierry Nabeth (INSEAD)

Conributors: Ana Isabel Canhoto (LSE), James Backhouse (LSE), Claudia Díaz (K.U.Leuven), Sabine Delaitre (JRC/IPTS), Wim Schreurs (VUB), Christian Krause (ICPP), Henry Krasemann (ICPP), Martin Meints (ICPP), Bernhard Anrig (VIP), Emmanuel Benoist (VIP), David-Olivier Jaquet-Chiffelle (VIP), Thierry Nabeth (INSEAD), Mark Gasson (READING), Kevin Warwick (READING), Sandra Steinbrecher (TUD)

Reviewers: Collective

A.2.3 Models (D2.3)

The objective of this document is to present, in a synthetic way, different models of representation of a person ("person schema") that can be used in different application domains.

In particular it presents:

- Different perspectives for modelling of the person in Information Systems.
- Different categories of attributes (or data schema) that can be used to define a person, and the different domains in which they are used.

This document is aimed at an audience of non-experts and experts who are interested in a broad overview of existing models of representation of the person in the Information Society.

Editors: Thierry Nabeth (INSEAD)

Contributors: Thierry Nabeth (INSEAD), Martin Meints (ICPP), Sabine Delaitre (JRC/IPTS), Sandra Steinbrecher (TUB), Mark Gasson (READING), Richard Cissée (TUB), Bernhard Anrig (VIP), Emmanuel Benoist (VIP), Marit Hansen (ICPP)

Reviewers: Emmanuel Benoist (VIP), Bernhard Anrig (VIP), Martin Meints (ICPP), Marit Hansen (ICPP), Mark Gasson (READING), Kevin Warwick (READING)

A.2.4 Identity in a Networked World – Use Cases and Scenarios (D2.6)

The goal of this deliverable is the creation of a high quality output for public diffusion, i.e., starting from the technically challenging contributions in D2.2 towards a more "digestible" and more attractive form for a wider public, not necessarily specialised. Hence seven articles have been elaborated to a form appropriate for the special needs. The form of the main part of this deliverable consists therefore of a booklet with 16 pages, available online at http://www.fidis.net/resources/networked-world/. The main goal is not the electronic version itself but a printed high quality version of the Appendix A that is produced.

Editors: David-Olivier Jaquet-Chiffelle (VIP), Emmanuel Benoist (VIP), Bernhard Anrig (VIP)

Contributors: Bernhard Anrig (VIP), Emmanuel Benoist (VIP), Bernhard Anrig (VIP), Mark Gasson (READING), David-Olivier Jaquet-Chiffelle (VIP), Sabine Delaitre (JRC/IPTS), Giampaolo Possagno (VIP)

Reviewers: All authors, Mark Gasson (READING)

A.2.5 Virtual Persons and Identities (D2.13)

The objective of this document is to describe typical uses of the term “virtual person”, as well as to define a generic two-layer model based on virtual persons. This model not only covers current uses of the term, but generalises its domain of application in order to better describe and understand new forms of identities in the Information Society in relation with rights, duties, obligations and responsibilities. We model in particular the concept of identity in the Information Society. Some sections in this document are aimed at an audience of non-experts; others are for experts who are interested in applying the model based on virtual persons to represent new forms of identities, as well as to describe identification and authentication processes in the Information Society.

Editors: David-Olivier Jaquet-Chiffelle (VIP), Bernhard Anrig (VIP), Emmanuel Benoist (VIP), Rolf Haenni (VIP)

Contributors: Mireille Hildebrandt (VUB), Eleni Kosta (K.U.Leuven), Katrien Lefever (K.U.Leuven), David-Olivier Jaquet-Chiffelle (VIP), Bernhard Anrig (VIP), Emmanuel Benoist (VIP), Rolf Haenni (VIP)

Reviewers: Vashek Matyas (MU), Thierry Nabeth (INSEAD), Kevin Warwick (READING)

A.3 HighTechID: Technologies to Support Identity and Identification (WP3)

A.3.1 Overview on IMS (D3.1)

The document is directed at an audience of academics, EU policy-makers, experts from technological, social science and legal disciplines and interested citizens.

It will give an overview of existing identity management systems (IMS). Different types, classes and subclasses of IMS are identified, described and illustrated by examples of existing IMS. To get an overview of the variety of existing technical implementations different designs of IMS are presented. Privacy enhancing mechanisms are developed and selected corresponding privacy enhancing technologies (PET) are shown as examples of existing implementations of those mechanisms. Finally an overview is presented of current research and development activities on IMS and conclusions, especially from the FIDIS Network of Excellence.

Editors: Matthias Bauer (ICPP), Martin Meints (ICPP), Marit Hansen (ICPP)

Contributors: Martin Meints (ICPP), Marit Hansen (ICPP), Ioannis Maghiros (JRC/IPTS), Elsa Lignos (JRC/IPTS), Sabine Delaitre (JRC/IPTS), Christian Krause (ICPP), Henry Krasemann (ICPP), Frank Steuer (TUB), Gábor Hontert (ISTRI), Christian Geuer-Pollmann (EMIC), Sven Wohlgemuth (ALU-Fr), Claudia Díaz (K.U.Leuven), Michael Backes (IMB ZRL), Matthias Bauer (ICPP)

Reviewers: Jozef Vyskoč (VaF), Sandra Steinbrecher (TUD), James Backhouse (LSE)

A.3.2 A Study on PKI and Biometrics (D3.2)

Public-Key Infrastructures (PKIs) have been a hot topic for several years now, and many – often very practical – questions are still open. These certainly include corruption of keys or algorithms, usability, awareness of users and security issues. With respect to high-tech IDs, advanced PKI, e.g., supporting convertible credentials, could be developed. Until now, official PKI in member states, working according to the Digital Signature Act and national signature law, rarely work with pseudonymous keys and certificates. To improve the diffusion of electronic signatures into European markets six concrete measures are suggested.

Both technologists and lawyers have experience in research on biometrics in the form of technology assessment and conceptualisation. However, for many kinds of biometrics it is still unclear how much security and privacy can be achieved. As the biometric market evolves in response to technology enhancement and political pressure, it is imperative that research on this topic is up to date, especially with respect to avoidance of discrimination and to privacy compliance.

This document forms a comprehensive study on PKIs and biometrics, specifically from the legal and technological point of view, with focus put on the possibility of privacy-enhancing implementations.

Editors: Mark Gasson (READING), Martin Meints (ICPP), Kevin Warwick (READING)

Contributors: Martin Meints (ICPP), Mark Gasson (READING), Lorenz Mueller (AXSionics), Jos Dumortier (K.U.Leuven), Henry Krasemann (ICPP), Ammar Alkassar (SIRRIX), Matthias Bauer (ICPP), Xavier Huysmans (K.U.Leuven), Heiko Rossnagel (JWG), Els Kindt (K.U.Leuven), Vasiliki Andronikou, Vaclav Matyas (MU), Michael Backes (IBM ZRL), Dionysios Demetis (LSE)

Reviewers: James Backhouse (LSE), Paul De Hert (TILT)

A.3.3 Study on Mobile Identity Management (D3.3)

Objective: This study gives a technical survey on mobile identity management. It identifies requirements for mobile identity management systems in particular on security and privacy of mobile users with mobile devices, e.g., smart phones or smart cards. A non-technical reader should understand the need and requirements for mobile identity management systems. Approaches for realising these requirements are described. The study gives answers to the following questions:

1. What are the requirements for mobile identity management systems in particular on users' mobility and privacy?
2. Which approaches for realising mobile identity management systems do exist?
3. What are the open issues and further steps towards mobile identity management?

Editors: Günter Müller (ALU-Fr), Sven Wohlgemuth (ALU-Fr)

Contributors: André Adelsbach (SIRRIX), Ammar Alkassar (SIRRIX), Christer Andersson (KU), Roger Cattin (EMIC), Joris Claessens (EMIC), Stefan Figge (JWG), Simone Fischer-Hübner (KU), Mark Gasson (READING), Christian Geuer-Pollmann (EMIC), Marit Hansen (ICPP), Marcel Jacomet (AXSionics), Henry Krasemann (ICPP), Christian Krause (ICPP), Leonardo Martucci (KU), Martin Meints (ICPP), Lorenz Müller (AXSionics), Jenny Nilsson (KU), John Sören Pettersson (KU), Alain Rollier (AXSionics), Denis Royer (JWG), Sven Wohlgemuth (ALU-Fr)

Reviewers: Jozef Vyskoč (VaF), Mark Gasson (READING)

A.3.4 Study on ID Documents (D3.6)

This document gives an overview of concepts, prototypes and implementations of European ID documents including machine-readable travel documents (MRTDs). Although not totally comprehensive, it summarises basic technologies that are used for ID documents such as PKI, RFID, biometrics and chip card technologies. Legal grounds for European MRTDs are described and analysed. In addition to a short overview on implementations, five good practice examples are described and discussed. Security and privacy aspects of ID documents are analysed based on current state-of-the-art in the described basic technologies and existing implementations of ID documents. Further, critical elements of cost projections for ID documents are presented and analysed from a social perspective.

Editors: Dr. Martin Meints (ICPP), Marit Hansen (ICPP)

Contributors: Martin Meints (ICPP), Stephan Alexander Freh (LSE), Marcel Jacomet (AXSionics), Mark Gasson (READING), Günter Karjoth (IBM ZRL), Paul De Hert (VUB), Wim Schreurs (VUB), Eleni Kosta (K.U.Leuven), Xavier Huysmans (KU Leuven), Claudia Díaz (K.U.Leuven), Marit Hansen (ICPP), Danny De Cock (K.U.Leuven), Christopher Wolf (K.U.Leuven), Bart Preneel (K.U. Leuven), Reshma Thomas (K.U.Leuven), Els Kindt (K.U.Leuven), Andreas Pfitzmann, Sandra Steinbrecher (TUD), Ian O. Angell (LSE), Dionysios S. Demetis (LSE)

Reviewers: Jozef Vyskoč (VaF), Ronald Leenes (TILT), Mark Gasson (READING)

A.3.5 A Structured Collection on Information and Literature on Technological and Usability Aspects of Radio Frequency Identification (RFID) (D3.7)

In this deliverable the physical properties of RFID, types of RFID systems basing on the physical properties and operational aspects of RFID systems are introduced and described. An overview on currently known security threats for RFID systems, countermeasures and related cost aspects is given. This is followed by a brief overview on current areas of application for RFID. To put a light on status quo and trends of development in the private sector in the context of RFID, the results of a study carried out in 2004 and 2005 in Germany are summarised. This is followed by an overview on relevant standards in the context of RFID. This deliverable also includes a bibliography containing relevant literature in the context of RFID. This is published in the bibliographic system at http://www.fidis.net/interactive/rfid-bibliography/.

Editors: Martin Meints (ICPP)

Contributors: Martin Meints (ICPP), Mark Gasson (READING), Pavel Rotter (IPTS), Simone Fischer-Hübner (KU), Daniel Gille (ALU-Fr), Jens Strüker (ALU-Fr), Sven Wohlgemuth (ALU-Fr), Markus Hansen (ICPP), Günter Karjoth (IBM ZRL)

Reviewers: Jozef Vyskoč (VaF), Sandra Steinbrecher (TUD)

A.3.6. Study on Protocols with Respect to Identity and Identification – an Insight on Network Protocols and Privacy-Aware Communication (D3.8)

This deliverable investigates identity-related properties of commonly used protocols and interesting proposed approaches for new protocols. This includes categorising and showing dependencies between network protocols and the outline of privacy properties, based on personal data disclosed, linkability and identifiability. Further, it critically discusses whether privacy experts are – and should be – involved in the process of designing protocols. Protocols for communication in networks are analysed according to privacy-relevant data and techniques for privacy-aware communication and their associated protocols are explained. Finally in this document, new developments for Next Generation Internet protocols are described.

This deliverable assumes some prior knowledge, but references and further reading is there to help the reader.

Editors: Marit Hansen (ICPP), Ammar Alkassar (SIRRIX)

Contributors: Marit Hansen (ICPP), Stefan Köpsell (TUD), Sandra Steinbrecher (TUD), Stefan Berthold (TUD), Stefanie Poetzsch (TUD), Henning Waack (TUD), Markulf Kohlweiss (K.U.Leuven), Claudia Díaz (K.U.Leuven), Stefan Schiffner (K.U.Leuven), Karel Wouters (K.U.Leuven)

Reviewers: Mark Gasson (READING), Jozef Vyskoč (VaF)

A.3.7 Study on the Impact of Trusted Computing on Identity and Identity Management (D3.9)

Trusted Computing (TC) is a key enabling technology adding substantially new security features, making many new use cases possible, which may revolutionise identity management. However, this emerging technology is not undisputed and raises many societal questions related to privacy, rights on ownership etc. This study takes a deeper look into TC concepts like TPMs, Trustworthy Operating Systems etc., and discusses possible use and business cases for TC in the context of identity and identification, pointing out possible risks of this technology in terms of privacy and consumer protection.

The objective of this study is to give an overview of Trusted Computing concepts and its supporting technologies, and to introduce new ideas on how those concepts can support or influence digital identification and identity management systems, including possible privacy and anonymity implications of Trusted Computing specifications defined by the Trusted Computing Group.

This deliverable differs substantially from 33 of ALU-Fr, as it addresses mainly the use of TC mechanisms on the client side and focuses on the technology description and its impact on IMS.

Editors: Ammar Alkassar (SIRRIX), Rani Husseiki (Sirrix)

Contributors: Rani Husseiki (SIRRIX), Stefan Köpsell (TUD), Christian Wachsmann (SIRRIX), Martin Meints (ICPP), Vassiliki Andronikou (ICCS)

Reviewers: Jozef Vyskoč (VaF)

A.3.8 Biometrics in Identity Management (D3.10)

This deliverable discusses the deployment of biometrics for the management of identity in the public and private sector from a technical, legal, security and forensic point of view. It highlights some specific security and privacy aspects, including those from new demonstrations of user/capture and capture/extraction threats, but also stresses the advantages which biometrics offer. The research indicates that a fruitful debate about the risks and opportunities of biometrics requires the use of an agreed harmonised vocabulary and that discussion should focus on where the control over the biometric system is exercised and on the functionalities and purposes of the applications. The report proposes, in this context, five groups of biometric application models for future use. Although biometric references become increasingly part of various identity applications, there remain several research items which are not yet fully explored as illustrated and described, such as the question of health related information contained in biometric templates and the proportionality of the use of biometric data. The report also warns for biometric data becoming a primary key for the interoperability of systems. Finally, the document offers guidance in the deployment of biometrics, including by describing an approach on how to preserve privacy and to enhance security by the data subject retaining control over the biometric data.

Editors: Els Kindt (K.U.Leuven), Lorenz Müller (AXSionics)

Contributors: Els Kindt (K.U.Leuven), Lorenz Müller (AXSionics), Paul De Hert (VUB), Annemarie Sprokkereef (TILT), Martin Meints (ICPP), Marit Hansen (ICPP), Rikkert Zoun (NFI), Zeno Geradts (NFI), Vicky Andronikou (ICCS), Koen Simoens (K.U.Leuven)

Reviewers: Mark Gasson (READING), Jozef Vyskoč (VaF)

A.4 Interoperability of Identity and Identification Concepts (WP4)

A.4.1 Structured Account of Approaches on Interoperability of IMS (D4.1)

The question of interoperability in respect of identity and identity management systems is one of growing concern. On the one hand there are many situations where being able to cross-match identity information about citizens and consumers would be of enormous benefit to them. On the other hand, without the appropriate control in the hands of the data subjects, interoperability could be another weapon in the hands of the surveillance society, unwelcome in a world where privacy is still valued. This report prepares the ground for a continuing study into interoperability in this area. It proposes a three-level framework for assessment and study bringing together perspectives as diverse as technical, legal and socio-cultural. A review of current and recent projects and literature on the topic is presented, with ratings for papers for their concerns in respect of the three different perspectives. The work has produced a bibliographic database of the most relevant literature available on the FIDIS web site. There follows a number of case-study type contributions on different applications of identity management systems including credentials systems, driving licences, European passports and government to consumer applications. A review of the interoperability issues in identity management in Ambient Intelligence contexts concludes that this matter will be an important one for determining how this technology will be shaped in the information society that is emerging.

Editors: James Backhouse (LSE)

Contributors: James Backhouse (LSE), John Baptista (LSE), Andrew Walwork (LSE), Stephan Freh (LSE), Paolo Spagnoletti (LUISS/LSE), Michaël Vanfleteren (K.U.Leuven), Els Kindt (K.U.Leuven), Martin Meints (ICPP), Martin Rost (ICPP), Mark Gasson (READING), Sandra Steinbrecher (TUD), Sabine Delaitre (JRC/IPTS), Ioannis Maghiros (JRC/IPTS), Wim Schreurs (VUB)

Reviewers: Mireille Hildebrandt (VUB), Ioannis Maghiros (JRC/IPTS)

A.4.2 Set of Requirements for Interoperability of IMS (D4.2)

This report highlights the spread of opinion amongst a group of European experts in application areas of identity management on the issue of interoperability of such systems. It builds from an earlier report that presented a literature review and an account of research in interoperability. It uses the three-part conceptual framework of technical, formal and informal dimensions through which to frame the questions posed and interpret the answers given. The 23 interviewees from 5 different European countries, while differing in detail, display a remarkable consensus on many of the issues. Application areas from which the experts are drawn cover eGovernment, eHealth and eCommerce, and while, given their specific nature, there may be many points on which such areas diverge, the likelihood of interoperability is deemed to turn on a small number of key questions, mostly non-technical. Importance is given to building trust in the citizen and end-user through good communication, usability, compliance with data protection and privacy principles.

Editors: James Backhouse (LSE), Michael Vanfleteren (K.U.Leuven)

Contributors: James Backhouse (LSE), John Baptista (LSE), Stephan Freh (LSE), Christopher Lovold (LSE), Els Kindt (K.U.Leuven), Michaël Vanfleteren (K.U.Leuven), Xavier Huysmans (K.U.Leuven), Martin Meints (ICPP), Martin Rost (ICPP), Andreas Westfeld (TUD), Sandra Steinbrecher (TUD)

Reviewers: Els Soenens (VUB), Paolo Spagnoletti (Luiss University, Italy)

A.4.3 Survey on Citizen's Trust in ID Systems and Authorities (D4.4)

This report from the FIDIS project has been created from within the Work Package 4 on Interoperability of Identity and Identity Management Systems. It emerges as the third in a series of investigations into the broadly social aspects concerned with sharing data, especially personal information, in respect of plans for interoperable European electronic ID systems. This survey was designed to investigate attitudes towards a number of issues involved in making eIDs interoperable that were drawn from an underlying theoretical framework of institutional trust. The survey questionnaire used 17 constructs, grouped into three broad categories of (1) sources of trust; (2) levels of trust; and (3) consequences of trust. A web-based survey was translated into 8 European languages and was made available online over a period of one month in June 2006. Overall there were 1,906 valid responses to the survey with respondents from 23 out of the 25 EU countries. A limitation of the survey was, however, that the response rate from some countries was very low. In this respect, the survey cannot be said to represent all European citizens as such. In addition, this biased response rate prevented a valid comparison across countries. Findings arising from the analysis of the survey point to an overall negative perception of the ID authorities by EU citizens. The vast majority of the respondents do not trust the institutions; they are seriously critical about the competence of the authorities, and are dubious about their ability to handle personal data. Moreover, they are suspicious of the authorities misusing their identity data. These negative attitudes of citizens hold important implications for any future attempts at implementing eID cards, as these perceptions may well be translated into consequent behaviour, namely, resistance to use or, indeed, non-use. The most negative attitudes were found in respondents from the UK and Ireland, and the least negative in Central and Eastern Europe.

Editors: James Backhouse (LSE), Ruth Halperin (LSE)

Contributors: James Backhouse (LSE), Ruth Halperin (LSE), James Backhouse (LSE), Katie Price (LSE), John Baptista (LSE), Bence Kollanyi (ITTK)

Reviewers: Ionnis Maghiros (JRC/IPTS), Thierry Nabeth (INSEAD)

A.4.4 A Survey on Citizen's Trust in ID Systems and Authorities (D4.5)

See D4.4 for details.

Editors: James Backhouse (LSE), Ruth Halperin (LSE)

A.4.5 Draft Best Practice Guidelines (D4.6)

This deliverable is concerned with the recommendations for best practice guidelines and the need for an effective development method and framework, which can be widely used for managing all aspects of identity resulting from the FIDIS research. The emphasis is on the delivery of a practical approach, which incorporates sound tools and techniques, which can be applied in the project and other settings.

The proposed method is a generic one that may be applied to any type of research project, business operation or delivery service to ensure it will fit effectively into a given environment. The method is flexible and customisable and incorporates clearly defined events and procedures throughout the information lifecycle. A holistic and systematic approach is adopted.

The method is first described and then an outline is provided, as to how it may be applied to interoperability, within the eHealth sector.

Editors: James Backhouse (LSE), Bernard Dyer (LSE)

Contributors: James Backhouse (LSE), Bernard Dyer (LSE), Thierry Nabeth (INSEAD), Mireille Hildebrandt (VUB)

Reviewers: Denis Royer (JWG), Thierry Nabeth (INSEAD), Mireille Hildebrandt (VUB)

A.4.6 Review and Classification for a FIDIS Identity Management Model (D4.7)

This deliverable is concerned with recommendations for establishing an identity classification system which can be incorporated into the best practice guidelines and the FIDIS identity management model, proposed in FIDIS Deliverable D4.6. It is paramount that the classification system may be readily applied in all areas of government, commerce and industry.

A review was made of the identity issues, being studied by FIDIS and other external bodies, which need to be represented in the classification system. The review concentrated on the work published in FIDIS Deliverable D2.1 "Inventory of topics and clusters", and in proposed standards by ISO and the U.S. Department of Commerce. It is hoped that this report may provide a basis for developing a global identity classification system, which can be shared by practitioners involved with identity management. The system will be continually enhanced throughout the duration of the FIDIS project.

It is recommended that the proposed inventory defined in FIDIS Deliverable D2.1, which categorises and defines the different terms used in the identity domain, should provide the core of the identity classification system.

Editors: James Backhouse (LSE), Bernard Dyer (LSE)

Contributors: James Backhouse (LSE), Bernard Dyer (LSE), Mireille Hildebrandt (VUB), Els Soenens (VUB), Bert-Jaap Koops (TILT), Vashek Matyas (MU), Kai Rannenberg (JWG), Denis Royer (JWG)

Reviewers: JWG, VUB, ICPP, INSEAD, READING, TILT, ALU-Fr, MU

A.4.7 Creating the Method to Incorporate FIDIS Research for Generic Application (D4.8)

This deliverable is concerned with the generic application of the best practice guidelines concerning interoperability, which incorporate an effective development method and framework. The guidelines presented in "D4.6: Draft best practice guidelines" have been applied, in broad terms, to four areas of interest relating to identity, namely the FIDIS research project and the sectors of eGovernment, eHealth and eCommerce. The identity classification system, which was outlined in "D4.7: Review and classification for a FIDIS identity management model", has been applied in the report for each of the areas of interest.

It is envisaged that the proposed FIDIS interoperability framework will be suitable for performing the applications discussed in the EC reports:

- "European Interoperability Framework for Pan-European eGovernment Services"
- "Connected Health – Quality and safety for European Citizens"

Editors: James Backhouse (LSE), Bernard Dyer (LSE)

Contributors: James Backhouse (LSE), Bernard Dyer (LSE), Vashek Matyas (MU), Denis Royer (JWG)

Reviewers: Denis Royer (JWG), Vashek Matyas (MU)

A.4.8 An Application of the Management Method to Interoperability within eHealth (D4.9)

This deliverable is concerned with developing interoperable identity management systems, within the eHealth sector, throughout and between EU states. To achieve comprehensive, practical, and cost effective systems that work together throughout the EU there are many challenges which need to be addressed including:

- A need for a common policy on interoperability throughout the EU
- Development and maintenance of an integrated eHealth network that brings together patients, professionals, providers, regions, and nations
- A need to incorporate identity management, including FIDIS research, into existing and proposed information systems
- The increased movement of EU citizens around the Union for purposes of travel, study, work and retirement
- Establishment of standard data sets for all aspects of health records
- Full cooperation between Member states, the many stakeholders involved and personnel performing a wide range of disciplines

It is envisaged that the work being performed in WP4 will assist practitioners in meeting these challenges in a methodical and comprehensive way.

Editors: James Backhouse (LSE), Bernard Dyer (LSE)

Contributors: James Backhouse (LSE), Bernard Dyer (LSE), Els Soenens (VUB), Mireille Hildebrandt (VUB), K.U.Leuven, TILT, Vashek Matyas (MU), Denis Royer (JWG)

Reviewers: Denis Royer (JWG), Vashek Matyas (MU)

A.4.9 Specification of a Portal for Interoperability of Identity Management Systems (D4.10)

This deliverable sets out a high-level specification for a portal to assist practitioners responsible for information management systems within different business sectors, such as eHealth, eGovernment and eCommerce, with the aim of supporting their activities in this field, particularly relating to interoperability between stakeholders.

The portal will provide managers and developers of identity management systems with a tool to aid in their navigation through the tricky issues that identity management technologies and systems engender. It brings together a wide range of materials that have been developed in FIDIS and elsewhere, which are required to reach good decisions on interoperable identity.

The approach has been built on earlier LSE research in the area of Flood Risk Assessment, which is currently being implemented by the UK government within England and Wales.

Editors: James Backhouse (LSE), Bernard Dyer (LSE)

Contributors: James Backhouse (LSE), Bernard Dyer (LSE), Vashek Matyas (MU), Thierry Nabeth (INSEAD)

Reviewers: Vashek Matyas (MU), Thierry Nabeth (INSEAD)

A.4.10 eHealth Identity Management in Several Types of Welfare States in Europe (D4.11)

This FIDIS deliverable relates to the field of eHealth in general and to the use of health and medical data for various purposes in specific. The use of eHealth tools, such as electronic health records and cards, not only enables the flow of medical data in the 'European Health Information Space'; it also addresses important choices that have to be made by (welfare) states.

The deliverable constitutes a descriptive part and a discussion section. For the descriptive part, a question list was send to the partners of this deliverable to gather information about European practices in the field.

Editors: Els Soenens (VUB), Mark Leys (VUB)

Contributors: Els Soenens (VUB), Mark Leys (VUB), Bernard Dyer (LSE), Maren Raguse (ICPP), Rani Husseiki (SIRRIX), Barbara Daskala (JRC/IPTS), David-Olivier Chaquet-Chiffelle (VIP), Simone Fischer-Huebner (KU), Hans Hedbom (KU), Sjaak Nouwt (TILT)

Reviewers: Emmanuel Benoist (VIP), Denis Royer (JWG)

A.5 ID-Theft, Privacy and Security (WP5)

A.5.1 A Survey on Legislation on ID Theft in the EU and a Number of Other Countries (D5.1)

This document gives the first results of a survey on legislation on ID theft in EU member states and the US. Unlike the US, EU countries appear to have no specific legislation on ID theft or ID fraud. As a consequence, it is proposed to extend the scope of the survey in the second Work Plan period to include other criminal provisions that may cover various forms of ID theft or ID fraud.

Editors: Bert-Jaap Koops (TILT)

Contributors: Bert-Jaap Koops (TILT)

Reviewers: Mireille Hildebrandt (VUB), Sarah Thatcher (LSE)

A.5.2 ID-related Crime: Towards a Common Ground for Interdisciplinary Research (D5.2b)

This deliverable contains the consolidated version of the papers that were prepared for the ID fraud Workshop, held on 18 May 2005 in Tilburg, the Netherlands. The papers discuss ID-related crimes from a legal, a socio-economic, and a technical perspective. It provides an initial presentation of the vast array of phenomena commonly addressed as ID fraud or ID theft from the various perspectives. The legal chapter briefly discusses the EU legal framework as well as some of the national ID crime provisions. The socio-economic chapter decomposes ID linkage into ID collision, ID change, ID deletion and ID restoration in order to gain a more detailed understanding of the various types of ID crimes. It also discusses the incidence of ID crimes as well as the social and economic effects for victims and businesses. The technical chapter describes a number of technical methods of ID crime, including different perspectives on biometrics. Finally, a chapter on countermeasures describes various socio-economic and technical measures to combat ID-related crime.

The objective of this deliverable is to start creating a common ground on which further interdisciplinary research on ID crimes can be developed. The chapters are separate building blocks, put together as a first step to develop such a common ground.

Editors: Ronald Leenes (TILT)

Contributors: Ronald Leenes (TILT), Hans Graux (K.U.Leuven), Martin Meints (ICPP), Martin Rost (ICPP), Albin Zuccato (KU), Sabine Delaitre (IPTS), Ioannis Maghiros (IPTS), Svetla Nikova (K.U.Leuven), Sebastian Clauß (TUD), Vicky Andronikou (ICCS), Klaus Kursawe (K.U.Leuven), Zeno Geradts (NFI), Bert-Jaap Koops (TILT)

Reviewers: Peter Sommer (LSE), Jozef Vyskoč (VaF)

A.5.3 Identity Related Crime in the World of Films (D5.2c)

This deliverable examines the manifestation of identity-related crime in mainstream films and compares the picture painted in these films with the occurrence of identity-related crime in reality. It concludes that the focus of films on exotic forms of identity takeover risks reducing the awareness of citizens of real-life identity-related crime.

Editors: Róbert Pintér (ISRI)

Contributors: Mihály Csótó (ISRI), Árpád Rab (ISRI), Attila Kincsei (ISRI), Róbert Pintér (ISRI)

Reviewers: Bert-Jaap Koops (TILT), Mireille Hildebrandt (VUB)

A.5.4 A Multidisciplinary Article on Identity-Related Crime (D5.3)

This deliverable proposes a typology of identity-related crime. From a conceptual, technical, and legal perspective, the numerous manifestations of identity-related crime have been analysed and categorised. The analysis shows that the relationship between attacks on identification systems, types of identity-related crime, and legal provisions is complex. This is important for policy-makers to realise when designing counter-measures to address the threat of identity-related crime.

The report has been written in the form of a multi-disciplinary academic article that has been submitted to a peer-reviewed journal.

Editors: Bert-Jaap Koops (TILT)

Contributors: Bert-Jaap Koops (TILT), Ronald Leenes (TILT), Nicole van der Meulen (TILT), Martin Meints (ICPP), David-Olivier Jaquet-Chiffelle (VIP)

Reviewers: Sabine Delaitre (IPTS), David-Olivier Jaquet-Chiffelle (VIP)

A.5.5 Anonymity in Electronic Government: A Case-Study Analysis of Governments' Identity Knowledge (D5.4)

The objective of this deliverable is to provide a first attempt to answer the question whether citizens becomes more anonymous or more known by the government when digital identification and authentication technologies are applied in the process of public service provision. From a historical-philosophical and a sociological angle, arguments are broached that may contribute to finding a foundation for answering this question. The issue is then addressed through case studies, which illustrate different aspects of the matter at hand. The case studies allow an assessment of the state of anonymity of the citizen in the electronic as opposed to the paper-based relationship with the government. The cases vary from an organisational through a more technical (e.g., PET techniques) to a legal, data-protection perspective.

Editors: Bert-Jaap Koops (TILT), Hans Buitelaar (TILT), Miriam Lips (TILT)

Contributors: Hans Buitelaar (TILT), Paul de Hert (VUB), Isabelle Oomen (TILT), Martin Meints (ICPP), Xavier Huysmans (K.U.Leuven), Bernard Anrig (VIP), Emmanuel Benoist (VIP), David-Olivier Jaquet-Chiffelle (VIP), Bert-Jaap Koops (TILT)

Reviewers: Ruth Halperin (LSE), Hans Hedbom (KU)

A.6 Forensic Implications (WP6)

A.6.1 Forensic Implications of Identity Management Systems (D6.1)

The objective of this document is to provide an overview of the forensic implications of current Identity Management Systems. Because of the broad scope of this field, this document should be viewed as a guide and does not attempt to be entirely comprehensive. In-depth examples of biometric devices and mobile networks are given in the forensics context. An overview of legal systems is also provided with a comparison of digital evidence law in different countries. From the examples used and the legal systems considered, the general conclusion is that forensic information can be extracted from many electronic devices and can subsequently be used in court. However, in the examination process, it is important to consider the likely integrity of the data, i.e., how failsafe the retrieval system is, since this will undoubtedly have an impact on the identity of the real person involved as a suspect. Equally, it is necessary to ensure law enforcement investigators and technical analysts follow the necessary protocols such that otherwise admissible electronic evidence is not suppressed or legally compromised.

Editors: Zeno Geradts (NFI), Peter Sommer (LSE)

Contributors: Peter Sommer (LSE), Zeno Geradts (NFI), Falk Wagner (JWG), Rikkert Zoun (NFI), Mieke Loncke (K.U.Leuven), Martin Meints (ICPP), Mark Gasson (READING)

Reviewers: Martin Meints (ICPP), Mark Gasson (READING)

A.6.2 Forensic Profiling (D6.7c)

This report, on forensic profiling, provides a bridge between forensic science and profiling from technical and legal perspectives.

Conclusions are drawn that new identity systems have their own strengths to detect what was impossible previously. But their weakness is that they can also provide false positives. From the examples it appears that much development is needed in this area before large-scale implementation can be used in practice. It is concluded that the different norms approved at European level remain insufficient. They do not deal with the impact of the widespread use of criminal intelligence, the increased monitoring of the average citizen or the increased linkage of police databases. Significant issues such as how to ensure the transparency and accountability of law enforcement activities, the quality of the data processed, e.g., the differentiation between categories of data subjects, or a strict application of the purpose specification principle remain unanswered. Each country will thus be called to make the specific balance between the competing interests at stake, in particular to prevent that the increasing use of personal data for risk prediction turns into stigmatisation of parts of the population.

Editors: Zeno Geradts (NFI), Peter Sommer (LSE)

Contributors: Zeno Geradts (NFI), Peter Sommer (LSE), Olivier Ribaux (University of Lausanne), Gerda Edelman (NFI), Gert Jacobusse (NFI), Thomas Gloe (TUD), Matthias Kirchner (TUD), Sylvain Ioset (University of Lausanne), Ekaterina de Vries (VUB), Fanny Coudert (K.U.Leuven)

Reviewers: Mark Gasson (READING), Martin Meints (ICPP)

A.7 Profiling (WP7)

A.7.1 Descriptive Analysis and Inventory of Profiling Practices (D7.2)

Deliverable D7.2 represents a genuine attempt to crystallise the multi-disciplinary nature of the FIDIS Network of Excellence in a document assessing the many facets of profiling, with contributions coming from across a wide spectrum of disciplines. Profiling is a powerful, critical and worrying technology because it is probably the only way that massive volumes of data about individual and group behaviour can be mined, whether for nefarious or benign purposes. Ever larger volumes of data have been the holy grail of generations of social scientists, medical researchers and technologists, and with profiling alongside new data-gathering technologies such data is available with the means to mine it for all its value. This deliverable examines how different approaches to profiling are taken, reviewing along the way some of the different technology contexts in which it can be used. Though matters of privacy and security loom behind every corner, the main focus of this deliverable is not on such issues. Subsequent deliverables will move into this. Clearly, with its multiple applications in marketing, law enforcement and surveillance, eMedicine and eHealth – to name just some, there exist currently many avenues along which profiling might progress, but unless the consumers and citizens of today and tomorrow have more knowledge of the actual workings of this technology, they will not be able to make informed decisions about how to respond when they are increasingly importuned for their personal data in the future. This report hopes to make a useful contribution to the vital task of explaining how profiling may impact the life of citizens and consumers in the coming years.

Editors: Mireille Hildebrandt (VUB), James Backhouse (LSE)

Contributors: Mireille Hildebrandt (VUB), Mark Gasson (READING), Ana Isabel Canhoto (LSE), Jean–Paul Van Bendegem (VUB), A. Vedder, Emmanuel Benoist (VIP), Thierry Nabeth (INSEAD), James Backhouse (LSE), Angelos Yannopoulos (ICCS), Vassiliki Andronikou (ICCS), Simone van der Hof (TILT), Martin Meints (ICPP), Zeno Geradts (NFI), Barbara Körffer (ICCP), Bernhard Anrig (VIP), A. Angehrn, P. Kumar Mittal, Claudia Díaz (K.U.Leuven), Els Soenens (VUB)

Reviewers: Thierry Nabeth (INSEAD), Martin Meints (ICPP)

A.7.2 Report on Actual and Possible Profiling Techniques in the Field of Ambient Intelligence (D7.3)

This document considers some of the wider aspects of privacy and security in the AmI environment as these are affected by profiling techniques and methods. It has been shown that by the very nature of the AmI space such issues are prevalent. Although it is unclear exactly how the AmI environment will develop, and indeed how it will be accepted by society as a whole, it is predicted that in some form AmI will appear in our everyday lives. However, AmI space requires a high level of profiling to be successful. Solutions for issues of privacy and security are usually located at a technological and a legal level, both implicating the social and the cultural. In this deliverable a first exploration of technological solutions and a first extensive exploration of relevant EU law is presented.

As to the technological level, the report discusses two privacy-enhancing techniques to provide pseudonymous customised services. In these models, the user is in control of his own data, and has an Identity Management Device (IMD) that manages his data, profiles and preferences. The IMD presents the user preferences to ambient intelligence devices in order to obtain personalised services. The first technique is based on anonymous credentials, and it may not be appropriate to be implemented in many ambient intelligence environments, as it requires costly resources. The second technique is adapted from the field of targeted advertising. It is cheap to implement, and ambient intelligence devices with low storage capacity and computation power could easily implement it.

As to the legal level, an extensive survey is made of the EU Data Protection Directive and other relevant sources of EU law, such as the Privacy and Electronic Data Communications Directive, and eCommerce Legislation, Consumer Protection Legislation. This survey, focused on relevant implications for both group profiling and personalised profiling, and implications at the level of the collection of data, the construction of profiles and at the level of their application, should serve as a first inventory on which subsequent deliverables can build.

Editors: Wim Schreurs (VUB), Mireille Hildebrandt (VUB), Mark Gasson (READING), Kevin Warwick (READING)

Contributors: Wim Schreurs (VUB), Sabine Delaitre (JRC/IPTS), Mireille Hildebrandt (VUB), Mark Gasson (READING), Kevin Warwick (READING), Ronald Leenes (TILT), Claudia Díaz (K.U.Leuven), Els Soenens (VUB)

Reviewers: Denis Royer (JWG), Ioannis Maghiros (JRC/IPTS)

A.7.3 Implications of Profiling Practices on Democracy (D7.4)

The possible effects of profiling technologies should be considered from a less policy-oriented perspective than may be usual within NoE's. This deliverable has chosen to raise some fundamental issues at the intersection of law, political theory and human identity – all related to the advance of profiling technologies. At this moment, highly sophisticated data mining techniques are becoming available to corporations and governments because of the ever cheaper and ubiquitous hardware and software that surrounds us. These technologies provide profiles with a flux of instant-categorisations that will be adjusted in real time if the Ambient Intelligent vision comes through. How will these instant-categorisations affect individual citizens and their sense of self? Will they be aware of this impact and does it matter if they are not? Should we worry about collection and processing of personal data, or only about sensitive personal data, or is this a crucial error, because profiling technologies construct intimate knowledge out of trivial data? Can abuse be prevented by counting on the human decency or 'good practices' of those in power, or do individual citizens need legal and/or technological tools to enforce such decency if necessary? Democracy and rule of law cannot be taken for granted; they are indeed historical artefacts that need constant maintenance and reconstruction to deal with the dynamics of a changing world. It may even be the case that the proliferation of information will clog efficient and effective government and fair, competitive market infrastructures unless profiling technologies provide the means to select relevant information from irrelevant information, in order to build knowledge instead of just collecting a meaningless abundance of data. The question will be how to reconstruct the checks and balances in the face of the new developments. The report begins with a careful exploration of democracy and rule of law. It continues by laying out possible implications of profiling and discussing tools to recreate checks and balances. After that, four critical replies are presented that deliver short, critical discussions of the issues at stake. In the conclusions the arguments are summarised and provided with a reply to critics.

Editors: Mireille Hildebrandt (VUB), Serge Gutwirth (VUB)

Contributors: Serge Gutwirth (VUB), Paul de Hert (VUB), Mireille Hildebrandt (VUB), James Backhouse (LSE), Martin Meints (ICPP), Angelos Yannopoulos (ICCS), Bert-Jaap Koops (TILT)

Reviewers: Sarah Thatcher (LSE), Bert-Jaap Koops (TILT), Martin Meints (ICPP)

A.7.4 Profiling the European Citizen (D7.5)

This deliverable intends to present FIDIS' excellence to an interdisciplinary academic public. It contains the manuscript for a book called 'Profiling the European Citizen. Cross-Disciplinary Perspectives', published by Springer. The main objective is to validate the interdisciplinary perspective on profiling that has been generated within Work Package 7, by (I) explaining what is profiling; (II) providing a set of applications; and (III) assessing the implications for democracy and the rule of law. This is achieved by bringing together experts from a host of European research institutes and a variety of scientific disciplines. The volume aims to put profiling on the agenda of computer scientists, social scientists, lawyers, philosophers and others, by presenting a multifocal perspective that provides serious insight into profiling while also grounding it in its societal context.

Editors: Mireille Hildebrandt (VUB), Gutwirth Serge (VUB)

Contributors: Mireille Hildebrandt (VUB), Serge Gutwirth (VUB), Thierry Nabeth (INSEAD), David–Olivier Jaquet–Chiffelle (VIP), Ana Isabel Canhoto (LSE), James Backhouse (LSE), Mark Gasson (READING), Will Browne (READING), Bernard Anrig (VIP), Jean–Paul Van Bendegem (VUB), Martin Meints (ICCP), Angelos Yannopoulos (ICCS), Vassiliki Andronikou (ICCS), Theadora Varvarigou (ICCS), Simone van der Hof (TILT), Corien Prins (TILT), Els Kindt (K.U.Leuven), Lothar Fritsch (JWG), Ronald Leenes (TILT), Emmanuel Benoist (VIP), Els Soenens (VUB), Ruth Halperin (LSE), Meike Kamp (ICCP), Barbara Körffer (ICCP), Paul De Hert (VUB – TILT), Wim Schreurs (VUB), Michael Vanfleteren (K.U.Leuven), Sarah Thatcher (LSE), Bert–Jaap Koops (TILT), Kevin Warwick (READING), Roger Brownsword (King's College, London)

Reviewers: Denis Royer (JWG), Jozef Vyskoč (VaF)

A.7.5 RFID, Profiling, and AmI (D7.7)

The target of this study is to provide a multifocal perspective on the workings of radio frequency identification (RFID) technologies, integrating technical, social and legal perspectives. As this deliverable is part of the work package on profiling, it regards RFID as an enabling technology for Ambient Intelligence, the 'Internet of Things' or the age of 'everyware'. Ambient Intelligence (AmI) implies a real time adaptive environment in which most adaptive decisions are taken by machines in a process of machine to machine communication. These decisions are based on what is called autonomic profiling, severely restricting human intervention, while being in need of a continuous and dynamic flow of information. This raises many issues that need to be anticipated and dealt with. This deliverable will provide a descriptive analysis to prepare the way for more fundamental research into the possibilities to integrate legal and technological solutions and more specific research into the development of a holistic privacy framework for RFID technologies. Both are taken on in the third work plan of the FIDIS NoE.

Editors: Mireille Hildebrandt (VUB), Martin Meints (ICCP)

Contributors: Mireille Hildebrandt (VUB), Martin Meints (ICPP), Denis Royer (JWG), Sabine Delaitre (JRC/IPTS), Eleni Kosta (K.U.Leuven), Michaël Vanfleteren (K.U.Leuven), Colette Cuijpers (TILT), Bert–Jaap Koops (TILT), Els Soenens (VUB), Ruth Halperin (LSE), Mark Gasson (READING), Markus Hansen (ICPP)

Reviewers: Denis Royer (JWG), Claudia Díaz (K.U.Leuven)

A.7.6 A Vision of Ambient Law (D7.9)

This report addresses the research question: can law as embodied in the future Ambient Intelligence architecture – Ambient Law – safeguard the core values of privacy and non-discrimination, while at the same time helping to realise the potential of Ambient Intelligence? This question is answered by analysing Ambient Intelligence and the role of Ambient Law therein from a conceptual, legal, and technical perspective.

Editors: Mireille Hildebrandt (VUB), Bert-Jaap Koops (TILT)

Contributors: Bert-Jaap Koops (TILT), Mireille Hildebrandt (VUB), Vassiliki Andronikou (ICCS), Mark Gasson (READING), Barbara Daskala (IPTS), Sven van Damme (K.U.Leuven), Eleni Kosta (K.U.Leuven), Martin Meints (ICCP), Marit Hansen (ICPP), Ammar Alkassar (Sirrix)

Reviewers: Claudia Díaz (K.U.Leuven), Jozef Vyskoč (VaF)

A.7.7 Multidisciplinary Literature Selection, with Wiki (D7.10)

Deliverable D7.10 aims to detect literature that moves beyond juxtaposition of different disciplinary perspectives. It provides the starting point for a growing selection of literature references in identity-related areas, such as RFID, Biometrics, Profiling and Ambient Intelligence with a long perspective of being dynamic. A Wiki workpad page is created on the internal portal in order to provide a discussion forum. Over time it will not exceed 100 references. As such, only the references which are perceived of highest quality and with a strong multidisciplinary point of view will be included in the selection. The creation and maintenance of the selection is based on the Reference Manager Software, which allows people to consult, search and export the literature selection.

Editors: Els Soenens (VUB), Vassiliki Andronikou (ICCS), Paul De Hert (TILT)

Contributors: Els Soenens (VUB), Vassiliki Andronikou (ICCS), Paul De Hert (TILT)

Reviewers: Dionysios Demetis (LSE), Denis Royer (JWG)

A.8 Integration of the NoE (WP8)

A.8.1 Database on Identity Management Systems and ID Law in the EU (D8.3)

This document consists of two parts. Part A puts forward a structure for a database of Identity Management Systems (IMS). Two designs for a database are laid out: a prototype with 29 fields (section 3) and an extended version with a total of 138 fields (section 4). The prototype has been implemented and is accessible online at http://www.jrc.es/projects/ims/imsintrodb.cfm. This document also includes a user manual (section 5) and the technical specifications for the database (section 6). Records will continue to be added to the database of IMS over the coming months and the document describes the next steps in the development process.

Part B introduces a database of ID laws, the Identity Law Survey (IDLS). Section 8 provides the context, and section 9 presents the initial structure of the law survey used to build a prototype, available at http://rechten.uvt.nl/idls/. Sections 10-11 outline a revised database structure, and sections 12-14 provide the interface requirements, user manual, and maintenance plan. The aim is to develop a simple and user-friendly database, providing the public with basic information and knowledge on ID-related laws in the EU and North America.

Editors: Ioannis Maghiros (JRC/IPTS), Sabine Delaitre (JRC/IPTS), Bert-Jaap Koops (TILT)

Contributors: Ioannis Maghiros (JRC/IPTS), Sabine Delaitre (JRC/IPTS), Bert-Jaap Koops (TILT)

Reviewers: Martin Meints (ICPP), Denis Royer (JWG)

A.9 Mobility and Identity (WP11)

A.9.1 Collection of Topics and Clusters of Mobility and Identity – Towards a Taxonomy of Mobility and Identity (D11.1)

This document gives an overview on the topic of mobility and identity and its related aspects (law, technology, sociology). Furthermore, it is the foundation for the work of FIDIS Work Package 11: “Mobility and Identity”, defining its context and the initial terminology and concepts for the ongoing work of this Work Package. This document is primarily aimed at an audience of academics, EU policy-makers, experts in the fields of law, sociology, and technology, and other interested citizens.

Editors: Denis Royer (JWG)

Contributors: Kai Rannenberg (JWG), Denis Royer (JWG), Andreas Westfeld (TUD), Sven Wohlgemuth (ALU-Fr), Marit Hansen (ICPP), Martin Meints (ICPP), Martin Rost (ICPP), Els Soenens (VUB), Eleni Kosta (K.U.Leuven), Nikolaos Volanis (K.U.Leuven), Christer Anderson (KU), Leonardo Martucci (KU), Sven Wohlgemuth (ALU-Fr), Mike Radmacher (JWG), Tobias Scherner (JWG), Jan Zibuschka (JWG), Layla Nassary Zadeh (JWG)

Reviewers: Mark Gasson (READING), Mireille Hildebrandt (VUB)

A.9.2 Mobility and LBS (D11.2)

Mobility and Location-Based Services play an ever-increasing role in everyday life. The spectrum of applications covers services for entertainment purposes as well as services that aim to increase the efficiency of business processes or help in case of emergency. In this deliverable, the impact of Location-Based Services on the identity of an individual is explained. Typical application areas and their impact on user identity are illustrated by exemplary use cases. From a technical perspective the deliverable focuses on various positioning methods as they constitute a prerequisite for the existence of LBS. Furthermore, legal aspects of Location-Based Services are discussed within an analysis of the regulations of the European data protection legal framework.

Editors: André Deuker (JWG)

Contributors: André Deuker (JWG), Martin Meints (ICPP), Christian Krause (ICPP), Denis Royer (JWG), Eleni Kosta (K.U.Leuven)

Reviewers: Patrick McKelvy (SIRRIX), Kai Rannenberg (JWG)

A.9.3 Economic Aspects of Mobility and Identity (D11.3)

The markets for mobile communications have been investigated intensively by scientists and market research institutions in the past years. Given the plethora of new services and the sensitivity of the data processed, mobile identity management (MIdM) is needed as an enabler technology to facilitate new services and to offer an effective tool for privacy and data protection.

Extending the previous discussions and findings in the context of FIDIS Work Package 11 on mobility and identity, this deliverable focuses on the economic aspects of mobility and identity. To this regard, topics such as user trust building and the relevant theories for adoption of technologies are explored. Furthermore the perspective on user centric markets and the economic implications from data protection legislation are discussed. Based on the previously discussed topics, initial ideas for an evaluation framework are presented.

Editors: Denis Royer (JWG)

Contributors: Kai Rannenberg (JWG), Denis Royer (JWG), Martin Meints (ICPP), Eleni Kosta (K.U.Leuven), Nikolaos Volanis (K.U.Leuven), André Deuker (JWG,) Els Soenens (VUB)

Reviewers: Jozef Vyskoč (VaF), Mark Gasson (READING)

A.9.4 The Legal Framework for Location-Based Services in Europe (D11.5)

This deliverable investigates legal certainty and privacy protection with regard to Location-Based Services (LBS). The main question is: Which legal data-protection framework applies when providers of LBS, public authorities and private parties like employers process location data generated in positioning systems? General descriptions provide a background to understanding the techniques used in LBS and the applicability of the relevant European legal framework. The practical implications of the European legal framework for the national level are described in four country reports: Belgium, France, Germany, and the Netherlands.

The main conclusion is that the applicability of legal provisions to varying forms of LBS and of processing location data is unclear. This is due to the very complex legal framework, which uses overlapping and not clear-cut definitions in three European Directives and in national implementations. The resulting legal uncertainty for European citizens and for providers of LBS and the enhanced privacy risks for citizens and employers should be overcome by a reassessment of the European legal framework.

Editors: Colette Cuijpers (TILT), Arnold Roosendaal (TILT), Bert-Jaap Koops (TILT)
Contributors: Arnold Roosendaal (TILT), Bert-Jaap Koops (TILT), Colette Cuijpers (TILT), Martin Meints (ICPP), Denis Royer (JWG), Fanny Coudert (K.U.Leuven), Eleni Kosta (K.U.Leuven), Maren Raguse (ICPP)

Reviewers: Mark Gasson (READING), Wim Schreurs (VUB)

A.10 Emerging Technologies (WP12)

A.10.1 Study on Emerging AmI Technologies (D12.2)

The technical issues relating to the actual implementation and thus realisation of Ambient Intelligence (AmI) environments are immense, and in most cases tangible solutions to technical related problems are still yet to be found. Meanwhile, 'Emerging Technologies' has become a term, which considers the convergence of areas such as nanotechnology, biotechnology, information technology, cognitive science, robotics, and artificial intelligence. Here we discuss how technologies which stem from this idea of domain fusion can be considered appropriate in the fabric of an AmI environment, meaning that AmI may actually be an application area made possible through this new emerging technology phenomenon. Further, we assess some of the emerging technologies on the basis of the European Charter of Fundamental Rights and Freedoms and apply an 'infoethic' approach (the application of ethical principles to the development and use of information and communication technologies) to raise questions regarding the role of fundamental rights for emerging technologies. Additionally, we offer a forum for an initial interdisciplinary debate based on the complex issue of technology evolution in its wider socio-cultural context through the use of an initial anthropological statement, and subsequent domain orientated replies. In essence, this deliverable is less about firm answers to specific questions, and instead aims to inform the reader on how emerging technologies may find application in AmI, and to stimulate further discussion on both the specific and broader issues that such development entails.

Editors: Mark Gasson (READING), Kevin Warwick (READING)

Contributors: Mark Gasson (READING), Martin Meints (ICPP), Stefan Köpsell (TUD), Vassiliki Andronikou (ICCS), Wim Schreurs (VUB), Bert-Jaap Koops (TILT), Colette Cuijpers (TILT), Daniela Cerqui (READING), Eleni Kosta (K.U. Leuven), Diana Bowman (Monash University, Australia)

Reviewers: Eleni Kosta (K.U.Leuven), Martin Meints (ICPP)

A.10.2 A Holistic Privacy Framework for RFID Applications (D12.3)

The objective of this deliverable is to discuss whether it is possible to create a holistic privacy framework for Radio Frequency Identification (RFID) systems given current advances in the area and, if so, what such a framework would look like.

The deliverable gives an overview of privacy problems in relation to RFID from legal, ethical, social and technical standpoints and discusses and presents some of the efforts made to address these problems. The overall conclusion is that much more research effort and technological development needs to be done before a true holistic framework can be constructed.

Editors: Simone Fischer-Hübner (KU), Hans Hedbom (KU)

Contributors: Simone Fischer-Hübner, Hans Hedbom (KU), Stefan Köpsell (TUD), Martin Meints (ICPP), Bernhard Anrig (VIP), Emmanuel Benoist (VIP), David-Olivier Jaquet-Chiffelle (VIP), Eleni Kosta (K.U.Leuven), Mireille Hildebrandt (VUB)

Reviewers: Jozef Vyskoč (VaF), Maren Raguse (ICPP), Mark Gasson (READING)

A.10.3 Use Cases and Scenarios of Emerging Technologies (D12.5)

Here we present a 'gateway document', which aims to distill some of the more complex concepts addressed by the FIDIS consortium into an easily digestible form which, while reaching a wider community, links through to more scholarly FIDIS deliverables. This is achieved through a range of hypothetical scenarios, which illustrate how emerging technologies may impact our lives in the future, within the context of identity. Emerging technologies is an area, which pervades all of the work packages into which the work of FIDIS is separated and clustered, and so, by drawing specific authors from across these divisions, this document gives a good insight into the ongoing endeavours of the network.

By developing and presenting this work in narrative form this deliverable aims to distance itself from the theoretical workings of emerging technologies and instead looks to the potential applications they may find, and the pros and cons therein. This is done through the use of short scenarios to highlight aspects, particularly relating to security and privacy, and the social and legal implications.

Editors: Mark Gasson (READING)

Contributors: Mark Gasson (READING), Katja de Vries (VUB), Niels van Dijk (VUB), Harald Zwingelberg (ICPP), Maren Raguse (ICPP), Thierry Nabeth (INSEAD), Claude Fuhrer (VIP), Bernhard Anrig (VIP), Vassiliki Andronikou (ICCS), Zeno Geradts (NFI), Bert-Jaap Koops (TILT), Eleni Kosta (K.U.Leuven)

Reviewers: David-Olivier Jaquet-Chiffelle (VIP)

A.10.4 A Study on ICT Implants (D12.6)

The increasing commercialisation and growing potential of human ICT implants has generated debate over the ethical, legal and social aspects of the technology, its products and application. Despite stakeholders calling for greater policy and legal certainty within this area, gaps have already begun to emerge between the commercial reality of human ICT implants and the current legal frameworks designed to regulate these products.

This study will detail and discuss the security and privacy implications of human ICT implants that are used both in a medical context and for authentication and identification purposes, that can hold or transmit personal data, and which could ultimately be used for human enhancement. Here, we will not only focus on the latest technological developments, but also the legal, social and ethical implications of the use and further application of these technologies.

Editors: Mark Gasson (READING), Eleni Kosta (K.U.Leuven)

Contributors: Mark Gasson (READING), Eleni Kosta (K.U.Leuven), Mireille Hildebrandt (VUB), Ioannis Maghiros (JRC/IPTS), Pawel Rotter (JRC/IPTS), Ramon Compano (JRC/IPTS), Barbara Daskala (JRC/IPTS), Bernhard Anrig (VIP), Claude Fuhrer (VIP), Carmela Troncoso (K.U.Leuven), Arnold Roosendaal (TILT), Diana Bowman (Monash University, Australia)

Reviewers: Hans Hedbom (KU), Vassiliki Andronikou (ICCS)

A.11 Privacy Fundamentals (WP13)

A.11.1 Identity and Impact of Privacy Enhancing Technology (D13.1)

This document is a report on technologies that enhance privacy from the technological point of view. We examined neither policy-based solutions nor law, we provide a review of technologies available.

Editors: Daniel Cvrček (MU), Vashek Matyas (MU)

Contributors: MU, K.U.Leuven, TUD

Reviewers: Jozef Vyskoč (VaF)

A.11.2 Addendum: Identity and Impact of Privacy Enhancing Technologies (D13.1)

This document is an addendum to our report on technologies that enhance privacy from the technological point of view, and where we provided a review of technologies available.

Editors: Daniel Cvrček (MU), Vashek Matyas (MU), Stefan Berthold (TUD)

Contributors: MU, TUD

Reviewers: Jozef Vyskoč (VaF)

A.11.3 Study on ID Number Policies (D13.3)

The objective of this deliverable is to present a view on the sensible use of identification numbers, especially in the public domain. The question of whether proper use can be achieved by a single global identifier or multiple identifiers will be answered.

In this deliverable several FIDIS partners investigate different aspects of ID numbers, such as the history of the use of identification documents, the legal framework, the sociological theoretical aspects and the possible use of ID numbers in the technique of profiling. Thus the investigations presented in this report provide a sound basis for determining the risks and opportunities in using ID numbers, especially in the area of eGovernment.

Country reports illustrate the choices made of using either a single global identifier or multiple identities. The report shows how the ID number can be put to good use while at the same time not unduly harming the privacy interests of the individual.

Editors: Hans Buitelaar (TILT)

Contributors: Hans Buitelaar (TILT), Marita Häuser (ICPP), Xavier Huysmans (K.U.Leuven), Martin Rost (ICPP), Martin Meints (ICPP), Isabelle Oomen (TILT), Mireille Hildebrandt (VUB), Fanny Coudert (K.U.Leuven), Adam Foldes, Robert Pinter (ISRI), Sebastian Meissner (ICPP), John Zeegers (TILT)

Reviewers: Gloria González Fuster (VUB), James Backhouse (LSE)

A.11.4 Privacy Modelling and Identity (D13.6)

This document critically reviews existing approaches (most common theoretical tools) for modelling relations of identity related information and also some related aspects of their applicability for measurement or quantitative expression of (the level of) privacy.

Editors: Marek Kumpošt (MU), Vashek Matyas (MU), Stefan Berthold (TUD)

Contributors: MU, TUD

Reviewers: Hans Buitelaar (TILT), Claudia Díaz (K.U.Leuven)

A.11.5 Applicability of Privacy Models (D13.8)

In this deliverable, we focus on the applicability of privacy models and review as well as illustrate the applicability of models from Deliverable D13.6 using a real-world example. Besides, we show some shortcomings of the approaches presented in D13.6 and include the aspects of combination of information and of misinformation, i.e., information which (partly) cannot to some extent and for some reason be verified by an adversary, hence approaches which may potentially be of major influence in the computation of a measure of anonymity.

Editors: David-Olivier Jaquet-Chiffelle (VIP), Bernhard Anrig (VIP), Emmanuel Benoist (VIP)

Contributors: David-Olivier Jaquet-Chiffelle (VIP), Bernhard Anrig (VIP), Emmanuel Benoist (VIP), Sandra Steinbrecher (TUD), Claudia Díaz (K.U.Leuven), Marek Kumpošt (MU), Vashek Matyas (MU), Stefan Berthold (TUD), Stefan Köpsell (TUD)

Reviewers: Jozef Vyskoč (VaF), Hans Buitelaar (TILT)

A.11.6 Estimating Quality of Identities (D13.9)

While in deliverable D13.8 the applicability of models/approaches for measuring privacy are illustrated by more-or-less declarative means, this deliverable focuses on testing and evaluating them. Due to the reason that real world data concerns real world people and their personal data, all data used were anonymised. Our main goals are demonstration of achievable results regarding privacy measurement by the data available for scientific research.

Editors: Stefan Berthold (TUD), Sandra Steinbrecher (TUD)

Contributors: Sandra Steinbrecher (TUD), Claudia Díaz (K.U.Leuven), Marek Kumpošt (MU), Vashek Matyas (MU), Stefan Berthold (TUD), Martin Meints (ICPP), Stefan Köpsell (TUD)

Reviewers: David-Olivier Jaquet-Chiffelle (VIP), Daniel Cvrček (University of Cambridge)

A.12 Privacy in Business Processes (WP14)

A.12.1 Study on Privacy in Business Processes by Identity Management (D14.2)

Privacy is not only a concern of customers. Service providers also fear privacy violations as a main hurdle for the acceptance of personalised services. Furthermore, the protection of privacy is an interest of service providers who take on customer relationship management activities of several service providers. They manage customers' profiles, e.g., in loyalty programs and eHealth scenarios with electronic patient records, and offer the service of aggregation. If it is possible to link profiles of a customer without the need of such service providers, latter would not benefit from their aggregation service. Three case studies show privacy threats in business processes with personalised services.

The objective of this study is to identify privacy threats in business processes with personalised services, to suggest process models for modelling privacy-aware business processes and to derive security requirements for user-centric identity management in order to preserve privacy.

The scenarios and use cases presented in this study are recommended for non-technical readers, whereas the analysis of user-centric identity management protocols and approaches for identity management extensions are recommended for technical readers.

Editors: Günter Müller (ALU-Fr), Sven Wohlgemuth (ALU-Fr)
Contributors: Ammar Alkassar (SIRRIX), Mike Bergmann (TUD), Jan Camenisch (IBM ZRL), Richard Cissée (TUB), Simone Fischer-Hübner (KU), Marit Hansen (ICPP), Mireille Hildebrandt (VUB), Susan Hohenberger (IBM ZRL), Günter Karjoth (IBM ZRL), Martin Meints (ICPP), Jan Möller (ICPP), John Sören Pettersson (KU), Sven Wohlgemuth (ALU-Fr)

Reviewers: Denis Royer (JWG), Jozef Vyskoč (VaF)

A.12.2 Study on the Suitability of Trusted Computing to Support Privacy in Business Processes (D14.3)

The European Directives 95/46/EC and 2002/58/EC demand the consent of users for a purpose-based processing of their data. In practice, users give their consent to the privacy statements of service providers, if they want to use personalised services. Since current privacy enhancing technologies focus on the disclosure of personal data and not on their usage, users are not able to verify whether service providers follow their privacy statement. It follows that users have to trust service providers to enforce the rules of their privacy statement.

The objective of this deliverable is to investigate on Trusted Computing whether it is suitable to realise a trust model where service providers are able to show users that they have enforced the agreed rules. The motive for choosing Trusted Computing is that Trusted Computing provides a tamper-resistant foundation for identifying an information system's configuration and so to identify if specific services, e.g., for monitoring the usage of personal data, are used.

Approaches for using Trusted Computing in order to support the enforcement of privacy policies are presented. This deliverable proposes a modification of the specification by the Trusted Computing Group and a monitor for observing the usage of personal data.

Editors: Günter Müller (ALU-Fr), Sven Wohlgemuth (ALU-Fr)

Contributors: Richard Cissée (TUB), Rani Husseiki (SIRRIX), Stefan Köpsell (TUD), Sven Wohlgemuth (ALU-Fr)

Reviewers: Martin Meints (ICPP), Jozef Vyskoč (VaF)

A.12.3 Experimental Study on Profiling in Business Processes (D14.5)

The aim of this study is in tracing the behaviour of mainly commercial entities with respect to their handling of personal data. Many profiling activities are done without a clear legal base: personal data is passed through without the explicit consent of the individuals. However, we are not aware of a clear empirical analysis, giving an understanding how companies and authorities are dealing with personal data. The study is proposed as a filed study where personal data is marked (e.g., by slightly modifying names, data etc.) and given away to commercial companies (e.g., buying portals, club cards etc.). This is a mid-term study. Based on the received postal and electronic advertisements, it can be traced which entities have leaked personal data.

Editors: Rani Husseiki (SIRRIX)

Contributors: Ammar Alkassar (SIRRIX), Rani Husseiki (SIRRIX), André Loos (SIRRIX)

Reviewers: Zeno Geradts (NFI), Uli Pinsodorf (EMIC)

A.12.4 From Regulating Access Control on Personal Data to Transparency by Secure Logging (D14.6)

Identity management controls the disclosure of personal data of data providers to data consumers. However, data providers do not obtain an indication as to whether data consumers use personal data according to the agreed privacy policy. Data providers are left with a number or privacy promises or expectation but do not get evidence that data consumers followed the agreed privacy policy. This deliverable proposes a "privacy evidence" by investigating on the data usage of data consumers for given data providers. This proposal is based on log views on accesses to personal data which can be checked by data providers on the compliance with privacy policies. Building blocks of system architecture for "privacy evidences", their requirements and approaches for their realisation are presented.

Editors: Günter Müller (ALU-Fr), Sven Wohlgemuth (ALU-Fr)

Contributors: Rafael Accorsi (ALU-Fr), Matthias Bernauer (ALU-Fr), Stefan Berthold (TUD), Sebastian Höhn (ALU-Fr), Günter Karjoth (IBM ZRL), Martin Meints (ICPP), Stefan Sackmann (ALU-Fr), Jens Strüker (ALU-Fr), Brendan Van Alsenoy (K.U.Leuven), Sven Wohlgemuth (ALU-Fr)

Reviewers: Vashek Matyas (MU), Jozef Vyskoč (VaF)

A.13 eGovernment (WP16)

A.13.1 Conceptual Framework for Identity Management in eGovernment (D16.1)

The main goal of deliverable D16.1 is to find an agreement within the different disciplines represented in the FIDIS NoE on the basic building blocks needed to allow dialogue on the very specific research field of privacy-friendly identity management in eGovernment.

Concretely, this means that the conceptual framework explores the basic concepts of (1) privacy and data protection; (2) identity management; and (3) eGovernment, and brings them together in a conceptual framework. This framework will, in the next phase, be used to define the requirements for privacy friendly IDM in a multi-level eGovernment context.

Editors: Hans Buitelaar (TILT, Netherlands), Martin Meints (ICPP, Kiel), Brendan van Alsenoy (K.U.Leuven, Belgium)

Contributors: Hans Buitelaar (TILT), Martin Meints (ICPP), Brendan van Alsenoy (K.U.Leuven), Bart Priem (TILT), Martin Pekarek (TILT), Eric Dubuis (VIP), Ruth Halperin (LSE), Marleen Knapen (TILT), Karolina Owczynik (TILT), Jacqueline van de Velde (K.U.Leuven), Suad Cehajic (TILT)

Reviewers: Jozef Vyskoč (VaF), Mark Gasson (READING)

A.14 Abstract Persons (WP17)

A.14.1 Modelling New Forms of Identities: Applicability of the Model Based on Virtual Persons (D17.1)

The objective of this document is to illustrate the applicability of the model based on virtual persons, model developed in FIDIS deliverable D2.13.

First, typical use-cases are described using the model based on virtual persons as well as the traditional one-to-one, one-to-many or even many-to-many models.

This allows comparing the efficiency of those models, i.e., their ability to faithfully describe the observed reality.

Then, a UML-description of the model based on virtual persons is given to show the internal consistency of this model.

Editors: David-Olivier Jaquet-Chiffelle (VIP) (Main Editor), Bernhard Anrig (VIP), Harald Zwingelberg (ICCP)

Contributors: Bernhard Anrig (VIP), Emmanuel Benoist (VIP), Dionysios S. Demetis (LSE, England), Eric Dubuis (VIP), Claude Fuhrer (VIP), Rolf Haenni (VIP), David-Olivier Jaquet-Chiffelle (VIP), Bert-Jaap Koops (TILT), Maren Raguse, Martin Meints (ICCP), Florent Wenger (VIP), Harald Zwingelberg (ICCP)

Reviewers: Dionysios S. Demetis (LSE, England), Thierry Nabeth (INSEAD)

A.14.2 New (Id)entities and the Law: Perspectives on Legal Personhood for Non-humans (D17.2)

New entities in the information society that operate at increasing distance from the physical persons 'behind' them, such as pseudonyms, avatars, and software agents, challenge the law. This report explores whether such entities – abstract persons – could be attributed legal rights and/or duties in some contexts, thus creating entities that are addressable in law themselves rather than the persons 'behind' them. Are current legal constructions sufficient to solve potential conflicts involving new entities, or would it help to create (limited) legal personhood for these new entities? The report identifies three strategies for the law to deal with the challenge of new entities: interpreting existing law; changing the law with specific rules; and changing the legal system by granting limited or full legal personhood to new entities. It provides a tentative conclusion and an agenda for further research.

Editors: Bert-Jaap Koops (TILT), David-Olivier Jaquet-Chiffelle (VIP)

Contributors: Bert-Jaap Koops (TILT), Mireille Hildebrandt (VUB), David-Olivier Jaquet-Chiffelle (VIP), Maurice Schellekens (TILT), Harald Zwingelberg (ICPP)

Reviewers: Jozef Vyskoč (VaF), Hans Buitelaar (TILT)

Appendix B. Contributors

Andronikou, Vassiliki (ICCS)

Vassiliki Andronikou received her MSc from the Electrical and Computer Engineering Department of the National Technical University of Athens in 2004. She has worked in the National Bank of Greece and the Organisation of Telecommunications of Greece, while since 2004 she has been a research associate and PhD candidate in the Telecommunications Laboratory of the NTUA. In 2005 she was given the Ericsson award for her Thesis on Mobile IPv6 with Fast Handovers. Her research has involved her participation in many European projects, such as BEinGRID, POLYMNIA, FIDIS and AKOGRIMO, with her interests focusing on the fields of the security and privacy aspects of biometrics and data management in Grid.

Backhouse, James (LSE)

James Backhouse is Reader in Information Systems in the Information Systems and Innovation Group of the Department of Management at the LSE. His teaching and research focuses on the social study of information risk and security and he has publications in journals such as the *Management of Information Systems Quarterly (MISQ),* the *European Journal of Information Systems (EJIS),* and the *Information Systems Journal (ISJ).* He is active in standards and professional best practice, a member of the Security Forum of the British Computer Society and member of the Accreditation Committee of the Institute of Information Security Professionals. Since 2003 he has led EU-funded research at the LSE in both anti-money laundering with a focus on profiling and behavioural modelling, bringing together consortia that include banks, regulators, law enforcement agencies from Eire, UK, Italy, Greece and Cyprus, and also in identity, security and privacy: he is a founder member of *FIDIS,* the 5-year EU research network of excellence. In 2007 he completed a review of ENISA, the European Network and Information Security Agency. In 2008, he was a co-author of the report *Dilemmas of Privacy and Surveillance* from the Royal Academy of Engineering that has had important policy impacts in the United Kingdom and beyond. He is the founder editor of the Springer journal *Identity in the Information Society.*

For more details see http://personal.lse.ac.uk/backhous/.

Benoist, Emmanuel (VIP)

Emmanuel Benoist has been professor at the Department of Engineering and Information Technology of the University of Applied Sciences of Berne (BFH-TI) in Biel, Switzerland, since 1999. He is a member of the computer science section board. He is married and a father of two.

He received his PhD in computer science at the University of Caen (France), where he also co-founded a web agency.

He specialises in web programming and more precisely, its implications on privacy protection and security. In this area he manages a team of programmers developing a system for the collection of medical data in an anonymous way. This system is used by many medical societies across Europe to host their registers. The privacy protection aspects are fundamental since the medical data collected are very sensitive.

He was invited professor at the University of Freiburg (Germany) for the summer term 2008 where he gave a course on web security.
His domain of interest includes web and its security and privacy components, identities and virtual identities. His aim is to extend security concepts developed for the web in order to also protect the privacy of persons.

Berthold, Stefan (TUD)

Stefan Berthold is a PhD student in Computer Science at Technische Universität Dresden (TUD), Germany. He received his MSc degree in Computer Science from TUD in March, 2007, after studies at Technische Universität Dresden and Karlstad University, Sweden. Since then, he has worked at TUD in the Privacy and Data Security Group under the supervision of Prof. Andreas Pfitzmann. He is involved in several EU funded projects, in PRIME until the finish in May, 2008, in FIDIS NoE since August, 2007, and in PrimeLife since March, 2008. He is author of several publications in FIDIS NoE, mainly focusing on WP13, Privacy Fundamentals, and took responsibility for the editing process of deliverables. Stefan published in the fields of anonymous communication and privacy-enhancing technology and won the best paper award together with Rainer Böhme and Stefan Köpsell at the 4th FIDIS/IFIP Internet Security & Privacy Summer School 2008 with a paper about "Data Retention and Anonymity Services".

Brandts, Stefan (EMIC)

Dr. Stefan Brands is a Principal Architect in Microsoft's Identity & Security Division in Redmond. In this capacity he contributes broadly to the company's technical and strategic efforts relating to identity, security, and privacy. Stefan joined Microsoft in February 2008 following the company's acquisition of Credentica. Stefan is also an Adjunct Professor in modern cryptology at McGill University, serves on the advisory board of public interest research center EPIC, and has served on the external advisory board of the Privacy Commissioner of Canada. Prior to joining Microsoft, Stefan worked at eCash pioneer DigiCash, at Zero-Knowledge Systems (privacy technology), and at Credentica (user-centric identity technology). Stefan is the author of a book on user-centric identity via minimal disclosure tokens, published in 2000 by The MIT Press and freely available as a download from www.credentica.com/the_mit_pressbook.php.

Buitelaar, Hans (TILT)

Hans Buitelaar is part-time researcher at the University of Tilburg, TILT – Tilburg Institute for Law, Technology and Society in The Netherlands. He is editor and co-editor of several FIDIS deliverables including ID-number policies in the EU (D13.3) and a number of deliverables in the context of eGovernment (anonymity in eGovernment, and privacy friendly Identity Management in eGovernment). Another area of interest is the legal and trust aspects of virtual entities. He published in Datenschutz und Datensicherheit as well as in Privacy en Informatie (a Dutch Privacy Journal).

In addition to his involvement at TILT, Hans is the internal data protection authority at two ministries in the Netherlands, viz the Ministry of Education Science and Culture, and the Ministry of Social Affairs and Employment in the Hague. Until recently Hans was a member of the board of the Dutch Society of Data Protection Officers.

Hans Buitelaar was educated at the Universities of Toronto, Oxford and Amsterdam. His degrees were in Ancient History, Litterae Humaniores and Library Science. Later on he received training in computer science and law.

Bussard, Laurent (EMIC)

Dr. Laurent Bussard is a Software Design Engineer at EMIC and works on research projects in the security and privacy area. He joined EMIC in 2004 after graduating as a PhD in network security from the ENST (Paris, France) and Eurecom (Sophia-Antipolis, France). His thesis was focused on security of pervasive computing environments in terms of access control, trust establishment, and privacy. He received his MSc in networks and distributed systems from the ESSI (Sophia-Antipolis) in 2000. In 1995 he graduated as an engineer in telecommunication from the EIVD (Yverdon, Switzerland). From 1995 to 1999, he worked as an engineer in software development at Siemens. Laurent has been and is involved in several European research projects focusing on security and privacy, including FP5 WiTness, FP6 FIDIS, FP6 MOSQUITO, FP6 SeCSE, and FP7 PrimeLife.

Cameron, Kim (Microsoft)

Kim Cameron is Chief Architect of Identity in the Connected Systems Division at Microsoft, where he works on the evolution of Active Directory, Federation Services, Identity Lifecycle Manager, CardSpace and Microsoft's other Identity Metasystem products.

Kim joined Microsoft in 1999 when it bought the ZOOMIT Corporation. As VP of Technology at ZOOMIT, he had invented metadirectory technology and built the first shipping product. Before that he led ZOOMIT's development team in producing a range of SMTP, X.400, X.500, and PKI products. Kim grew up in Canada, attending King's College at Dalhousie University and l'Université de Montréal. He has won a number of industry awards, including Digital Identity World's Innovation Award (2005), Network Computing's Top 25 Technology Drivers Award (1996) and MVP (Most Valuable Player) Award (2005), Network World's 50 Most Powerful People in Networking (2005), Microsoft's Trustworthy Computing Privacy Award (2007) and Silicon.com's Agenda Setters 2007.

Kim blogs at identityblog.com, where he published the Laws of Identity.

Claessens, Joris (EMIC)

Dr. Joris Claessens joined Microsoft in June 2003 as Security and Privacy Research Program Manager in the European Microsoft Innovation Center (EMIC). Since May 2008 he has been the overall Program Manager for EMIC's collaborative research activities. He also continues to act as security and privacy research expert.

He received a degree in Electrical Engineering (Telecommunications) from the Katholieke Universiteit Leuven, Belgium in July 1997. His Master's thesis dealt with the Security of the World Wide Web. In December 2002, he obtained a PhD in Applied Sciences from the same institute, while working as a researcher in the COmputer Security and Industrial Cryptography (COSIC) research group. His PhD thesis dealt with the "Analysis and design of an advanced infrastructure for secure and anonymous electronic payment systems on the Internet". Before joining Microsoft in June 2003, he was a post-doctoral researcher in the same research group.

His research interests are focused on improving security and privacy in cross-domain electronic applications and services, and his expertise spans across a wide range of topics including web security, network security, anonymity and privacy, electronic payment security, mobile agent security, digital signatures, authorisation, federated web services security, and the underlying cryptographic mechanisms.

He has built up significant experience in European collaborative, applied research through his direct involvement in at least a dozen projects in the FP5, FP6, and FP7 framework programmes, including FP5 PAMPAS, FP5 WiTness, FP6 TrustCoM, FP6 FIDIS, FP6 MOSQUITO, FP6 NextGRID, FP6 MYCAREVENT, FP6 BREIN, FP7 Consequence, and FP7 PrimeLife, where he contributed and/or steered security and privacy related research and development work.

Cuijpers, Colette (TILT)

Dr. Colette Cuijpers is Assistant Professor at the Tilburg Institute for Law, Technology, and Society (TILT). She studied European and Dutch Law at Tilburg University and in 2004, she received her PhD for a study on the possibility and desirability of implementation of the European Privacy Directive into the Dutch Civil Code. In addition to carrying out research relating to privacy, she has participated in research programmes and published in the field of liability law, eGovernment, eCommerce and intellectual property rights. Her research is focused around questions concerning technology regulation. At present, Colette is participating in a research project headed by Dr. Bert-Jaap Koops concerning the consequences of ICT-developments and the effect they have on the shift of power within the employer –employee relationship, and the relation between consumers and producers. She has been involved in several European projects relating to identity and eGovernment in which she addressed liability issues concerning eGovernment services, the legal implications of RFID technology, and the legal framework regarding Location Based Services. She is not only involved in research, but is also actively involved in education. Together with Dr. Anton Vedder she is responsible for the coordination of the Master Law and Technology, for which she is (guest) lecturer for several courses, e.g., 'Liability and the Internet' and 'Privacy and Data Protection'.

Deuker, André (JWG)

André Deuker received his diploma in business administration from the University of Frankfurt in September 2007. Since autumn 2007 he has been working as a PhD student and research assistant at the T-Mobile Chair of Mobile Business & Multilateral Security. André plays an active role in the coordination and management of the European Network of Excellence "Future of Identity in the Information Society" (FIDIS) and is editor and contributor of various FIDIS deliverables in Work Package 11 on mobility and identity. His focal point of research is on identity management and privacy topics in the area of mobile business applications, especially on context aware services and related revenue models.

Fischer-Hübner, Simone (KU)

Simone Fischer-Hübner has been a Professor at the Computer Science Department of Karlstad University since June 2000, where she is the head of the PriSec (Privacy & Security) research group. She received a Diploma Degree in Computer Science with a minor in Law (1988), and Doctoral (1992) and Habilitation (1999) Degrees in Computer Science from Hamburg University. Her research interests include IT-security and privacy-enhancing technologies. She was a research assistant and assistant professor at Hamburg University (1988-2000) and a Guest Professor at the Copenhagen Business School (1994-1995) and at Stockholm University/Royal Institute of Technologies (1998-1999). She is the vice chairperson of IFIP (International Federation for Information Processing) Working Group 11.6 on "Identity Management" and served as the chair of IFIP WG 9.6/11.7 on "IT Misuse and the Law" (1998–2005). She is a member of the External Advisory Board of the IBM Privacy Institute, board member of the of IEEE-Sweden – Section Computer/Software Engineering Chapter, member of the NordSec (Nordic Workshop on Secure IT Systems) steering committee, coordinator of the Swedish IT Secure Network for PhD students, and member of the International Editorial Review Board of the International Journal of Information Security and Privacy (IJISP). She is currently representing Karlstad University in the EU projects PrimeLife and FIDIS.

Gasson, Mark (READING)

Dr. Mark Gasson is currently a senior research fellow in the School of Systems Engineering at the University of Reading, UK. His research predominantly focuses on user-centric applications of developing technologies and has been actively pursued in a range of UK, EU and US funded research projects. He has specific interest in pushing the envelope of Human-Machine interaction, and has been active in the research and development of Ambient Intelligence Environments and Neural Interface techniques for human augmentation, for which he was awarded his PhD.
He considers public engagement of science as an essential component of the scientific endeavour, and as such has had an active involvement spanning over ten years. He frequently delivers invited public lectures and workshops internationally, aimed at audiences of varying ages. He is also part of a dynamic group which aims to bridge the void between art and science through public installations derived from collaboration between artists and scientists.

Geradts, Zeno (NFI)

Zeno Geradts has been working since 1991 at the Netherlands Forensic Institute (http://www.nederlandsforensischinstituut.nl/) as a forensic scientist. He started in toolmarks where he wrote several hundred reports and in 1995 he switched to firearms and since 1997 has worked at the digital evidence department. He is an expert witness in image analysis and biometrics (face comparison) as well as R&D coordinator in digital evidence. In 2002 he received a PhD from the University of Utrecht based on research on computational matching of images from shoeprints, toolmarks, drugs pills and cartridge cases. At the AAFS <http://www.aafs.org/> he has been chairman of the Engineering Section and since 2008 he has been chairman of the new section Digital Evidence and Multimedia. He is chairman of the ENFSI <http://www.enfsi.eu/> Forensic IT working group. He has published several papers in forensic journals and is active on casework as an expert witness and projects in digital evidence, for example in the EU project FIDIS <http://www.fidis.net/> where he is leading a workpackage on forensic implications.

Geuer-Pollmann, Christian (EMIC)

Dr. Christian Geuer-Pollmann has worked as Software Design Engineer at the European Microsoft Innovation Centre since it started in mid-2003 and leads the security team.

Christian holds a doctorate degree in electrical engineering from Siegen University, and a diploma degree from Wuppertal University. Prior to his PhD, he worked for the GSM operator "Mannesmann Mobilfunk D2" in corporate IT security.

His research interests include scalable authorisation systems, identity and access management for virtual organisations, international security standardisation (W3C XML Signature and XML Encryption) and security architecture for transponder systems. He is an internationally known expert in the field of XML Security. His PhD topic was "Confidentiality for XML Documents using Pool Encryption". He donated his XML Signature implementation to the Apache Software Foundation and funded the Apache XML Security project. He served as PC member for the "Workshop on Metadata for Security" and the "Workshop on Security in Information Systems" series. He was and still is working in several European research projects, including NEWTRON, <WebSig>, FP6 TrustCoM, FP6 FIDIS and FP6 BREIN.

Gilliot, Maike (ALU-Fr)

Maike Gilliot received her diploma in computer science in 2001 from the University of Darmstadt (Germany). Since 2004 she has been a research assistant at the department of Telematics, Institute of Computer Science and Social Studies at the Albert-Ludwig University of Freiburg, Germany. Her main research interest is the runtime enforcement of security, privacy and compliance policies. Within the European Network of Excellence "Future of Identity in the Information Society" (FIDIS), she coordinated the working on "Privacy in Business Processes" and investigated into the enforcement of usage control. Further, she coordinated until 2006 the German Research Priority Programme "Security in the Information and Communication Technology" funded by the German Research Foundation (DFG).

Haenni, Rolf (VIP)

Rolf Haenni is professor at the Department of Engineering and Information Technology of the University of Applied Sciences of Berne (BFH-TI) in Bienne, Switzerland. He is also assistant professor at the Institute of Computer Science and Applied Mathematics (IAM) of the University of Bern where he is leading the Reasoning under Uncertainty (RUN) research group. He received his diploma and PhD degrees in Computer Science from the University of Fribourg, Switzerland, in 1992 and 1996, respectively. He was a visiting scholar at the University of California in Los Angeles (UCLA) and a research fellow at the University of Konstanz, Germany. His current employment as an assistant professor is funded by a SNSF Professorship of the Swiss National Research Foundation.

He has been involved in various international research projects on different interdisciplinary topics. His principal domain of interest and expertise lies in areas such as probabilistic reasoning, knowledge-based systems, uncertainty management, logic, information algebras, knowledge representation, argumentation, reliability theory, model-based diagnostics, trust management, public-key cryptography, and eVoting. He has a strong publication record in international journals and conferences.

Halperin, Ruth (LSE)

Dr. Ruth Halperin holds a PhD in Information Systems from the London School of Economics and Political Science, where she is a Research Fellow in the Information Systems and Innovation Group of the Department of Management. Her current research interests are in information risk; security and privacy; digital identity and systems design and implementation. She has been a member of the EU Network of Excellence FIDIS since its inception in 2004 and has published in the areas of risk perceptions, interoperable identity management systems and Profiling. Prior to joining the LSE in 2002, she was a Project Manager of a leading software development company specialising in eLearning and KM technologies.

Hansen, Marit (ICPP)

Marit Hansen is Deputy Privacy Commissioner of the Data Protection Authority Schleswig-Holstein, Germany (ICPP – Unabhängiges Landeszentrum für Datenschutz). Within ICPP she is in charge of the "Privacy Enhancing Technologies (PET)" Division and the "Innovation Centre Privacy & Security". Since her diploma in computer science in 1995 she has been working on security and privacy aspects especially concerning the Internet, anonymity, pseudonymity, identity management, biometrics, multilateral security, and ePrivacy from both the technical and the legal perspectives. In several projects she and her team actively participate in technology design in order to support PET and give feedback on legislation, e.g., "AN.ON – Anonymity online" (2001-2006 – http://www.anon-online.de/), "SPIT-AL – SPIT Prevention Solution" (2005-2006 – http://www.spit-filter.com/), "PRISE – Privacy enhancing shaping of security research and technology" (2006-2008 – http://www.prise.oeaw.ac.at/) or "PRIME – Privacy and Identity Management for Europe" (2004-2008 – https://www.prime-project.eu/).

Currently she is working in particular on user-centric identity management and eID systems, among others as Activity leader in the EU-funded projects "PrimeLife" (2008-20011 – http://www.primelife.eu/) and "FIDIS – Future of Identity in the Information Society" (2004-2009 – http://www.fidis.net/).

Hedbom, Hans (KU)

Hans Hedbom has been a lecturer at the Computer Science Department of Karlstad University since 1994, where he is a member of the PriSec (Privacy & Security) research group. He received a BSc in Computer Science (1993) from Karlstad University and a Lic Tech in Computer Engineering (2001) from Chalmers University of Technology. His research interests include IT-security, Privacy-enhancing technologies and transparency enhancing technologies. He has participated in the EU-project PRIME and is currently participating in the FIDIS NoE and the EU-project PrimeLife. He also represents FIDIS and PrimeLife on the ISO/JTC1 SC27/WG5 standardisation committee.

Hildebrandt, Mireille (VUB)

Mireille Hildebrandt is a senior researcher at the Centre for Law Science Technology and Society Studies (LSTS) at Vrije Universiteit Brussel (VUB), she is Associate Professor of Jurisprudence at the Erasmus School of Law, Erasmus University Rotterdam and Dean of Education of the Research School on Safety and Security in the Netherlands. After defending her PhD thesis in legal philosophy (highest distinction) on the nexus of criminal procedure, legal history, anthropology and the epistemology of legal norms, at Erasmus University Rotterdam, she was seconded to LSTS and started working on the confrontation between future and emerging technologies, law and democracy. She is associate editor of Criminal Law and Philosophy and of Identity in the Information Society (IDIS), co-founder and editor of the Dutch Journal of Expertise and Law and a member of the editorial board of the New Criminal Law Review. She is a member of the Stakeholderforum of the European Network and Information Security Agency (ENISA), work package leader and a member of the scientific board of FIDIS, and a member of the scientific advisory committee of the European Privacy Institute. She publishes widely on the nexus of philosophy of technology and of law, on the issues at stake around profiling technologies, security policies and the criminal law. In 2008 she published Profiling the European Citizen. Cross-Disciplinary Perspectives, co-edited with Serge Gutwirth and co-authored with 28 FIDIS authors.

Jaquet-Chiffelle, David-Olivier (VIP)

David-Olivier Jaquet-Chiffelle has been professor at the Department of Engineering and Information Technology of the University of Applied Sciences of Berne (BFH-TI) in Bienne, Switzerland, since 1997. He has been Head and Founder of V.I.P – Virtual Identity, Privacy and Security research centre – since 2001 at the BFH-TI.

He is also associate professor at the Faculty of Law and Criminal Justice of the University of Lausanne in Switzerland where he has been teaching at the Forensic Science Institute since 2003.

He has a long experience in projects related to security, privacy and identity; he is workpackage leader in FIDIS. He is regularly invited to give presentations in the field of new forms of identities and numerical traces. He is associate editor of the IDIS journal (Identity in the Information Society) published by Springer. He is also active as an expert for the European Commission and within the ISO organisation in the technical committee JTC 1/SC 27 on IT Security techniques.

His domains of interest include security and privacy, (new) identities –(biometric) pseudonyms, digital and virtual identities, behavioural identities, profiles– as well as identification and authentication processes, privacy enhancing technologies and anonymising technologies. His aim is to apply Mathematics and Cryptology to protect identities and privacy, and to promote security.

Kindt, Els (K.U.Leuven)

Els Kindt graduated in law from the K.U.Leuven and obtained a Master of Laws (LL.M) in the U.S. She is a member of the Brussels Bar and since December 1, 2003, a contract legal researcher with the Interdisciplinary Centre for Law and ICT (ICRI) – Institute for Broadband Technology (IBBT) of the K.U.Leuven, Belgium. She is involved in various national and international research projects, such as BioSec in the past, and presently TURBINE. Her research interests are privacy law, electronic communications, ICT law in general and intellectual property rights, with a focus on biometrics and identity management.

She is a frequent speaker on information law topics and has published several articles on recent developments in IT law. She is also member of the editorial board of 'Computerrecht' (Kluwer) and of the advisory editorial board of 'Privacy en Informatie' (Kluwer).

Köpsell, Stefan (TUD)

Stefan Köpsell studied computer science at Technische Universität Dresden, Germany from 1993 to 1999. Since 2000 he has been engaged in research on anonymity and privacy at TUD. He is especially interested in anonymisation technologies and has published in this area. He was a key person and main developer of the AN.ON project (founded by DFG).

Koops, Bert-Jaap (TILT)

Prof. Dr. Bert-Jaap Koops is Professor of Regulation & Technology at the Tilburg Institute for Law, Technology, and Society (TILT), the Netherlands. He is also a senior researcher at Intervict, the Tilburg institute for victimology and human security, and a member of *De Jonge Akademie*, a branch of the Royal Netherlands Academy of Arts and Sciences with 75 young academics.

His main research interests are law and technology, in particular criminal-law issues in investigation powers and privacy, computer crime, DNA forensics, and cryptography. He is also interested in other topics of technology regulation, such as information security, identity, digital constitutional rights, 'code as law', human enhancement, and regulation of bio- and nanotechnologies. Since 2004, he has coordinated a research program on law, technology, and shifting power relations.

He studied mathematics and general and comparative literature at Groningen University, the Netherlands. He did a PhD in law at Tilburg University and Eindhoven University of Technology with a dissertation on cryptography regulation in 1999. He co-edited five books in English on ICT regulation and has published many articles and books in English and Dutch on a wide variety of topics. His WWW Crypto Law Survey is a standard publication on crypto regulation of worldwide renown. He is co-Editor-in-Chief of the journal Identity in the Information Society.

Kosta, Eleni (K.U.Leuven)

Eleni Kosta obtained her law degree at the University of Athens in 2002 (magna cum laude) and in 2004 she obtained a Masters degree in Public Law (summa cum laude) at the same University. In the academic year 2004-2005 she participated in the Postgraduate Study Programme in Legal Informatics (Rechtsinformatik) at the University of Hanover (EULISP) with a scholarship from the Greek State Scholarships Foundation (IKY) and she obtained her LL.M. (magna cum laude).

Since 2005, she has been working as a legal researcher at ICRI – K.U.Leuven, where she conducts research in the field of privacy and identity management, specialising in new technologies. She worked on the European Project PRIME (Privacy and Identity Management for Europe), which finished in May 2008. She is currently working on the European Project PICOS (Privacy and Identity Management for Community Services) and is also involved in the Network of Excellence FIDIS (Future of Identity in the Information Society) and the Thematic Network PrivacyOS. Eleni is also preparing a PhD on "Consent as a legitimate ground for data processing in electronic communications" under the supervision of Prof. Dr. Jos Dumortier.

Kumpost, Marek (MU)

Marek Kumpost was born in Czech Republic in 1980 (Hradec Kralove). He completed his bachelor degree in 2003 and master degree in 2004 at the Masaryk University, Faculty of Informatics, Brno (Czech Republic). Both studies were connected to IT security (performance of selected hash functions and security of wireless networks).

He is now working on his PhD (since 10/2004) at the Faculty of Informatics (supervisor is Vaclav Matyas), MU Brno and he has worked as assistant (since 02/2005) at the Faculty of Information Technology (with Dan Cvrcek), University of Technology in Brno. His PhD research is mainly focused on context information modelling issues.

Matyas, Vashek (MU)

Vashek Matyas is an Associate Professor at the Masaryk University Brno, Czech Republic, chairing its Department of Computer Systems and Communications. He worked as Visiting Researcher with Microsoft Research Cambridge and Visiting Lecturer with University College Dublin during his sabbatical in 2003-2004. He also worked as an Associate Director with Ubilab, UBS AG, working on biometrics and applied cryptology topics in 1999-2000, was a Postdoctoral Fellow with the University of Cambridge Computer Laboratory in 1996-98, undertaking research on trusted distribution of data. He was a Director, Technology and Security, of a London-based CA Uptime Commerce Ltd. in 1997-98. His research interests relate mainly to the areas of applied cryptography and security. He was working on key management issues within medical environments during the Royal Society Postdoctoral Fellowship in 1996-97, par-ticipated in the ISO/IEC JTC1 SC27, published over seventy peer-reviewed papers and articles, and co-authored four books on IT security and cryptography. Vashek is one of the Editors-in-Chief of the Identity in the Information Society journal and a member of the Editorial Board of Data Security Management (Czech security journal), and he also edited the Computer and Communications Security Reviews.

Meints, Martin (ICPP)

Dr. Martin Meints studied chemistry and computer science at Kiel University, Germany. From 1996 to 2004 he worked in various enterprises and public organisations in technical and security management positions and as IT project manager. Since 2004 he has been working as researcher and data protection auditor at the Independent Centre for Privacy Protection Schleswig-Holstein, the Data Protection Authority of Land Schleswig-Holstein. He is mainly engaged in the project "FIDIS – Future of Identity in the Information Society". In this context he has been involved as author and co-editor in several studies and scientific publications dealing with biometrics, ubiquitous computing and emerging technologies with a focus on security, trust models and technical concepts for privacy enhancement. He is licensed as ISO 27001 Auditor for Information Security Management Systems (ISMS) by the German Federal Office for Information Security.

Müller, Lorenz (AXSionics)

Dr. Lorenz Müller is Chief Technology Officer of AXSionics AG in Switzerland. AXSionics builds an authentication and transaction security system for the Internet. He is one of the founders of the company and in charge of the security architecture and the intellectual property protection for AXSionics.

He began his career as a mathematician and physicist at the University of Bern and at CERN where he achieved his PhD in high energy physics in 1983. He continued his research in the field at Stanford University (SLAC) and at the CERN. In 1990 he entered as project manager the Ascom Tech AG, a Swiss IT company, and shortly later joined the institute for applied mathematics and computer science of the University of Berne as group leader of the Neuroinformatics group. In parallel he worked in the domain of cryptography, computer security and biometrics. In 1998 he was appointed as head of research at the University of Applied Science Berne. Besides the management part of this position he continued to develop secure communication models for the Internet. Several patents, prizes and awards resulted from this work and in 2003 the company AXSionics was founded. He led the startup company as chairman through the first two financing rounds and then joined the company as Chief Technology Officer.

Nabeth, Thierry (INSEAD)

Thierry Nabeth is a Senior Research Fellow at INSEAD. The focus of his research is centered on the study of social dynamics in online communities, and in particular he investigates concepts such as online social identity, social attention in online communities, motivation to participate in online communities, and the profiling of social activities in social platforms.

He has worked on numerous research projects in the domain of knowledge management, learning systems, and agent-based systems. He is an active participant in the FIDIS project, participating to the conceptualisation of the identity domain, as well as working on the topic of identity in online social systems. He was also the coordinator of the AtGentive project, a project aimed at investigating how to support attention using ICT (Information and Communication technologies).

Pinsdorf, Ulrich (EMIC)

Dr. Ulrich Pinsdorf works as Program Manager for Security and Privacy Research at the European Microsoft Innovation Center (EMIC). He holds a PhD from Technical University Darmstadt, Germany. He is an experienced researcher and lecturer in the area of mobile security, mobile software agents, peer-to-peer networks, and distributed software systems. His current research interests include security and privacy questions in the area of distributed software architectures.

Before joining Microsoft in early 2007 he was senior scientist and deputy head of the Department for Security Technology at Fraunhofer Institute for Computer Graphics Research (IGD) in Darmstadt, Germany. He is a founding member of the Competence Center for Applied Security Technology (CAST e.V.), an independent organisation which bundles professional security competence in Germany. In various roles he helped to develop CAST to the largest security association in Germany. In his last role he acted as scientific manager of CAST e.V.

He was and is involved in a number of research projects, such as MAP, SicAri, VESUV, FP6 BREIN, FP6 FIDIS, iDetective, SeMoA, FP7 PrimeLife. Most of them were funded by the European Commission or the German Government.

Posch, Reinhard (TU Graz, Government of Austria)

Prof. Dipl.-Ing. Dr. Reinhard Posch was born on April 16th 1951 in Graz (Austria). After finishing school in 1969 he studied at Technischen Hochschule (now Graz University of Technology) gaining his masters degree in Mathematics in 1973. From 1971 until 1979 he worked at Graz Research Center in operating systems, networking and automated road construction. He got his PHD in 1976. From 1974 to 1984 he served as assistant professor at Graz University of Technology in information processing. During this time he also worked with Sperry Univac (Roseville, MN, USA) researching in the field of physical network layers.

In 1983 he got his "Habilitation" in "Applied Information Processing and Communications Technology" and was appointed full professor at Graz University of technology in 1984. In 1999 he also became Scientific Director of the "Austrian Secure Information Technology Center" (A-SIT). He was in charge of eGovernment in the task force e-Austria and became federal CIO (Chief Information Officer) for the Austrian government in 2001. In 2007 he was elected chair of the management board of ENISA (European Network and Information Security Agency).

He has been married since 1976 and has three children.

Besides many publications in the field of networking, VLSI design, IT-security and eGovernment he has conducted many national and international research projects concentrating on networking, computer security, smart cards and innovative advances in eGovernment.

Rannenberg, Kai (JWG) – Editor

Prof. Kai Rannenberg (www.m-chair.net) has held the T-Mobile Chair for Mobile Business & Multilateral Security at Goethe University Frankfurt since 2002. Prior to this he was with the System Security Group at Microsoft Research Cambridge, UK focusing on "Personal Security Devices and Privacy Technologies".

From 1993-1999 at Freiburg University he coordinated the interdisciplinary "Kolleg Security in Communication Technology" researching on Multilateral Security and focusing his PhD dissertation on IT Security Evaluation Criteria and the protection of users. Before this he gained his Diploma in Informatics at TU Berlin.

Since April 2004 he has led the coordination of FIDIS and since February 2008 of project PICOS (Privacy and Identity Management for Community Services).

Since 1991 He has participated in the ISO/IEC standardisation of IT Security (JTC 1/SC 27/WG 3 "Security evaluation criteria"), since March 2007 serving as Convenor of SC 27/WG 5 "Identity management and privacy technologies" after having led the respective Study Periods.

Since May 2007 he has chaired IFIP TC 11 "Security and Privacy Protection in Information Processing Systems", after having been its Vice-Chair since 2001. He has chaired the CEPIS Legal & Security Issues Special Interest Network since 2003. In July 2004 he was appointed as the academic expert to the Management Board of ENISA.

He served as PC co-chair, organiser and referee for multiple conferences. His awards include the Alcatel SEL Foundation Dissertation Award and the Friedrich-August-von-Hayek-Preis of Freiburg University and Deutsche Bank as well as the IFIP Silver Core.

Royer, Denis (JWG) – Editor

Denis Royer completed his diploma in business informatics at the Technical Institute in Braunschweig (Germany) in 2003. From 2000 to 2001 he studied information systems and business administration at the University of Nebraska in Omaha, Nebraska (USA). Since 2004 he has been a researcher and executive project coordinator of the FIDIS NoE (Future of Identity in the Information Society Network of Excellence) at Johann Wolfgang Goethe University in Frankfurt, Germany. As the Chair for Mobile Business and Multilateral Security, he is working on the evaluation of investments into enterprise identity management systems (EIdMS), decision support systems for the introduction of EIdMS in organisations, and enterprise identity management (EIdM) process models, in the context of the European research project FIDIS. Furthermore, he is active in the GenericIAM Group of NIFIS, working on the creation of generic process models for identity and access management (IAM) systems.

Soenens, Els (VUB)

Els Soenens has been a member of the Law, Science and Technology Studies (LSTS) group at the Vrije Universiteit Brussel since autumn 2004. She followed a specialisation Master degree in International and European Studies at the Vrije Universiteit Brussel (2002-2004) after obtaining a sociology degree at the University of Ghent (1998-2002). In September 2006 she participated in the bi-annual Summer School on Technology Assessment organised by the Dutch Rathenau Institute.

Since October 2004, she has been involved in the European Union IST Project FIDIS, where she works partly as a project assistant for the Work Package on Profiling and partly as a researcher. She has participated in several FIDIS deliverables and activities with contributions in the domains of mobility and identity; web personalisation; eHealth and social aspects of profiling and Ambient Intelligence.

Sommer, Peter (LSE)

Peter Sommer is a Visiting Professor in the Information Systems Integrity Group in the Department of Management at the London School of Economics (LSE) and also a Visiting Senior Research Fellow, Faculty of Mathematics, Computing and Technology, Open University. He is one of the world's pioneers of digital evidence/computer forensics and has acted as an expert in many important criminal and civil court proceedings.

At the LSE he has helped develop the current range of Information System Security courses, with their emphases on social science, management, law and policy. At the Open University he is consultant for the Digital Investigations and Computer Forensics course, M889.

He read law at Oxford, had earlier careers as a book and electronic publisher and as a risk analyst/investigator for insurance underwriters and loss adjusters. His first digital investigation was in 1985. Legal expert witness activity has included criminal cases involving large-scale computer intrusions, Official Secrets, large-scale software piracy, indecent images of children, people trafficking, murder and terrorism. Civil instructions have covered theft of confidential information, defamation and theft of software code.

He is a former Specialist Advisor in the UK Parliament and sits on a number of UK government advisory panels. He is Joint Lead Assessor for the Computing speciality at the UK Council for the Registration of Forensic Practitioners.

Steinbrecher, Sandra (TUD)

Sandra Steinbrecher is a scientific assistant of Computer Science at Technische Universität Dresden. She received her doctoral degree from Technische Universität Dresden in 2008 and her diploma from University of Saarland in 2000. For ten years she has been working in several projects on areas of privacy, computer security and cryptography. Her major research interests are privacy-enhancing identity management, modelling and measurement of anonymity in distributed networks, and the design of privacy-respecting reputation systems.

Varvarigou, Theodora A. (ICCS)

Prof. Theodora A. Varvarigou received the B. Tech degree from the National Technical University of Athens, Greece in 1988, the MSc degrees in Electrical Engineering (1989) and in Computer Science (1991) from Stanford University, California in 1989 and the PhD from Stanford University as well in 1991. She worked at AT&T Bell Labs, Holmdel, New Jersey between 1991 and 1995. Between 1995 and 1997 she worked as an Assistant Professor at the Technical University of Crete, Chania, Greece. In 1997 she was elected as an Assistant Professor while since 2007 she has been a Professor at the National Technical University of Athens, and Director of the Postgraduate Course "Engineering Economics Systems". She has great experience in the area of semantic web technologies, scheduling over distributed platforms, embedded systems and grid computing. In this area, she has published more than 150 papers in leading journals and conferences. She has participated and coordinated several EU funded projects, related to the subject of the IRMOS project such as POLYMNIA, Akogrimo, NextGRID, BeinGRID, Memphis, MKBEEM, MARIDES, CHALLENGERS, FIDIS, and others.

Vogelmann, Frieder (JWG)

Frieder Vogelmann completed his Magister Artium in Philosophy at the Albert-Ludwig University in Freiburg (Germany) in 2007. He has worked in the FIDIS NoE at the Johann Wolfgang Goethe University in Frankfurt/Main (Germany) since 2008.

Wenger, Florent (VIP)

Florent Wenger is a computer science engineer. After graduating from Geneva University of Applied Sciences, he worked for 18 months as research assistant at the Department of Engineering and Information Technology of the Bern University of Applied Sciences.

During his time within the Virtual Identity, Privacy and Security research group headed by D.-O. Jaquet-Chiffelle, he collaborated on the BioCrypt project which aimed to develop biometric pseudonyms in order to overcome major threats for security, privacy and convenience in today's use of biometrics. He also contributed to several FIDIS deliverables.

He is currently doing a Master's degree of Law in Legal Issues, Crime and Security of New Technologies at the University of Lausanne. His growing range of interests includes information systems security, biometrics and forensic sciences.

Wohlgemuth, Sven (ALU-Fr)

Dr. Sven Wohlgemuth has received in 2008 his doctor's degree in computer science at the Institute of Computer Science and Social Studies (IIG, Prof. Dr. Günter Müller), Albert-Ludwig University of Freiburg, Germany. His research is on privacy in business processes and by usage control. During his PostDoc internship in 2008 at the National Institute of Informatics (NII), Tokyo, he investigated into observable delegation of personal data by watermarking. In 2003, the German Federal State of Baden-Württemberg awarded him the doIT Software Award for his work on security and usability by identity management. As a research assistant of Prof. Müller, he has coordinated the working group "Privacy in Business Processes" of the European Network of Excellence "Future of Identity in the Information Society (FIDIS)" and the German Research Priority Programme "Security in the Information and Communication Technology" funded by the German Research Foundation (DFG). He is a member of the committees of the international conference "Emerging Trends in Information and Communication Security (ETRICS) 2006" and of the German Society for Computer Science's conference "SICHERHEIT 2008". Concerning the German Society for Computer Science (GI), he is the spokesman for the area of Southern Baden.

Zwingelberg, Harald (ICPP)

Harald Zwingelberg is legal staff at ULD – Unabhängiges Landeszentrum für Datenschutz (Independent Centre for Privacy Protection) Schleswig-Holstein in the department for the protection of medical data and counsels a project for the implementation of IT infrastructure for medical data in the public sector. He has been working in the EC funded projects PRIME and FIDIS, covering the research areas biometrics, social networks, identity and identity management.

After finishing his legal education in Kiel and Bremen he worked as an assistant to Professor Schack at the Institute for European and International Private and Procedural Law at the Kiel University. His area of research encompassed the European system of international jurisdiction and the conflict of laws rules. As an attorney-at-law he advised clients bound to professional discretion (physicians, pharmacists) on the legal impact of recent developments in communication technologies as well as in the progression of the legal framework and specific case law concerning privacy and data protection. He currently teaches data protection law at the University of Applied Sciences Kiel.

Appendix C. FIDIS Consortium

The FIDIS Consortium comprises the following 24 organisations, being situated in 13 European countries:

- Johann-Wolfgang-Goethe Universität Frankfurt am Main: Chair for Mobile Business and Multilateral Security (JWG), Germany
- Joint Research Center (JRC/IPTS), Spain
- Vrije Universiteit Brussel: Law Science Technology & Society (LSTS), Belgium
- Unabhängiges Landeszentrum für Datenschutz (ICPP), Germany
- INSEAD, the Business School for the World, France
- University of Reading (READING), United Kingdom
- Katholieke Universiteit Leuven (K.U. Leuven), Belgium
- Karlstad University (KU), Sweden
- Tilburg Institute for Law, Technology, and Society (TILT), Netherlands
- Technische Universität Berlin (TUB), Germany
- Technische Universität Dresden (TUD), Germany
- Albert-Ludwig University Freiburg: Institute of Computer Science and Social Studies (IIG Telematics) (ALU-FR), Germany
- Masarykova univerzita v Brne, Fakulta informatiky (MU), Czech Republic
- VaF, Rovinka, Slovakia
- London School of Economics/ Information Risk and Security, United Kingdom
- Budapest University of Technology and Economics: Information Society and Trend Research Institute (ISTRI), Hungary
- IBM Zurich Research Laboratory (ZRL), Switzerland
- Centre Technique de la Gendarmerie Nationale (CTGN), France
- Netherlands Forensic Institute (NFI), Netherlands
- Virtual Identity and Privacy Research Center (VIP), Switzerland

- European Microsoft Innovation Center (EMIC), Germany
- National Technical University of Athens (ICCS), Greece
- AXSionics AG, Switzerland
- Sirrix AG Security Technologies, Germany

Johann-Wolfgang-Goethe Universität Frankfurt am Main: Chair for Mobile Business and Multilateral Security (JWG)

GOETHE UNIVERSITÄT FRANKFURT AM MAIN

The "Chair for Mobile Business and Multilateral Security" at Johann Wolfgang Goethe – Universität Frankfurt is held by full professor Dr. Kai Rannenberg. Enjoying sponsorship from T-Mobile (the leading German mobile communications provider) the chair focuses its research on mobile networks and their applications, as well as on related issues of security and privacy. The chair's mission is to find business models and technologies enabling Mobile Commerce in e.g., 3G and UMTS networks, which is seen as "the use of mobile devices and mobile communication for applications and businesses". Many factors influence mobile commerce applications and lie therefore within the research scope of the chair:

- Multilateral security requirements (i.e., security requirements of all parties involved) and related mechanisms in support of e.g., privacy, anonymity and confidentiality.
- Feasible mobile platforms supporting application requirements.
- Applications and services (e.g., mobile data access, mobile ePayment, location based services) that must be useful, trustworthy, and affordable.

The Chair is well integrated into the Institute of Information Systems within the Department of Economics and Business Administration, from which it draws additional support for FIDIS as well as from the Goethe University law department.

Joint Research Center (JRC/IPTS)

JRC EUROPEAN COMMISSION

The Joint Research Centre (JRC) is a research based policy support organisation and a Directorate General of the European Commission, providing scientific advice and technical know-how to support EU policies.

The Institute for Prospective Technological Studies (IPTS), based in Seville (Spain), is one of seven institutes which are part of the European Commission's DG-JRC. It was created to promote and enable a better understanding of the links between technology, economy and society. The mission of the IPTS is to provide customer-driven support to the EU policy-making process by researching science-based responses to policy challenges that have both a socio-economic and a scientific or technological dimension.

The Information and Society Unit (IS Unit) at IPTS supports the overall formulation and implementation of appropriate Information Society strategies, policies, regulations and actions contributing to a competitive, innovative and inclusive European Information Society. In particular the IS unit complements technology-push approaches to the development of the European Information Society with socio-economic impact and demand analysis. Its mission is to support the acceleration of the development and deployment of the European Information Society and to contribute to rethinking its ICT R&D system.

Within the IS unit, the Techno-Economic Foresight for Information Society research action has as its objective to develop an emerging future vision with the aim to contribute to better understand the way ICTs could impact society, especially as regards the analysis of user perceptions, attitudes, needs and their role and contribution to innovative processes. Research focuses on areas that mostly affect individuals considering their current and future needs and will explore their way of life supported by Digital Technologies ('Living Digitally'). It especially studies the conditions and attributes that affect consumer/citizen confidence in technological and market innovations, and specifically addresses the way digital technologies will affect identity and investigates the need to balance the fruition of advanced eServices and the call for more end-user control over their personal data.

Vrije Universiteit Brussel: Law Science Technology & Society (LSTS)

CENTER FOR
LAW, SCIENCE,
TECHNOLOGY &
SOCIETY STUDIES
AT THE VRIJE UNIVERSITEIT BRUSSEL
BELGIUM

The interdisciplinary Research Group on Law Science Technology & Society or LSTS is a research centre at the department of meta-juridica at the Faculty of Law and Criminology of the Vrije Universiteit Brussel, with Serge Gutwirth as its founder and director. It was founded in November 2003 and is devoted to analytical, theoretical and prospective research into the relationships between law, science, technology and society. LSTS focuses on the integration of legal perspectives in current Science Technology and Society (STS)-research. The Starting point is that notions or principles such as legal mediation between rights and interests, democratic participation, rule of law, transparency, accountability, public interest, human rights and individual freedom should form a part of the constraints of scientific work. Crucial for LSTS is the challenge of conceiving scientific practices in such a way that they respond to the demands of the democratic constitutional state. LSTS is the successor of the former Centre for the Interaction Law & Technology (CIRT), which carried out research in the field of computer law (privacy and data protection, EDI, computer crime, intellectual property, ...), criminal investigation and police law, environmental law, the relationships between law and psychiatry, etc. When this research is continued by LSTS, today, however, the objective has significantly changed and broadened. As a result of broadening the scope, the monodisciplinary legal research is moving towards an explicit interdisciplinary undertaking. That is why, since its foundation, LSTS comprises some researchers of the Centre for Logic and Philosophy of Science (CLWF) covering disciplines such as philosophy, philosophy of science, mathematics and logic. LSTS participates in a number of European research projects (notably SWAMI, FIDIS, REFGOV, PRITIUS and INEX) contributing to the study of future and emerging technologies from other than purely technical perspectives, notably investigating potential implications for the legal framework of constitutional democracy. Mireille Hildebrandt, a legal philosopher and workpackage leader of profiling technologies in the FIDIS network, works as a senior researcher in LSTS, focusing on the link between profiling technologies, human identity and legal subjectivity.

LSTS senior members also teach in different disciplines and different universities both at graduate and post-graduate level (Vrije Universiteit Brussel, Erasmus Universiteit Rotterdam, Leiden University, Facultés Universitaires Saint-Louis, Université Catholique de Louvain-la-Neuve, Katholieke Universiteit Brussel, etc.)

Unabhängiges Landeszentrum für Datenschutz (ICPP)

Unabhängiges Landeszentrum für
Datenschutz Schleswig-Holstein

"Unabhängiges Landeszentrum für Datenschutz" (Engl.: Independent Centre for Privacy Protection, ICPP) is the Data Protection Authority of Schleswig-Holstein, the northernmost Federal State of Germany. Its office with 40 employees is located in Kiel, Germany. The Privacy Commissioner of Schleswig-Holstein, Dr. Thilo Weichert, is head of ICPP.

The basis for the work of ICPP is laid down in the State Data Protection Act Schleswig-Holstein. This act is one of the most progressive ones worldwide and includes among others provisions for a seal of privacy for IT products and privacy protection audit for public authorities. For several years, ICPP has been granting privacy seals for products for which legal and technological privacy aspects have been evaluated with respect to legal compliance. In addition to the privacy seal based on German national and regional law, ICPP is coordinating the European Privacy Seal initiative EuroPriSe which grants privacy seals on the European level in case of a successful evaluation of compliance to European regulation.

Since 1998 ICPP has been working on several national and international projects in the field of data security and privacy protection. A focus is laid on identity management-related projects such as FIDIS, PRIME ("Privacy and Identity Management for Europe") and the PRIME successor PrimeLife. Projects are carried out together with co-operation partners from academia, government, industry, or consumer protection organisations located in various countries. The interdisciplinary team within ICPP is active in elaborating and reviewing concepts, developing privacy technology and giving feedback to legislation and standardisation.

ICPP in particular has know-how in all aspects of privacy and informational self-determination including related issues of data security. The employees are experienced in developing criteria and elaborating them together with other parties, e.g., companies, administration or academia. The interdisciplinary approach within the ICPP ensures a common understanding on both legal and technological issues which is especially relevant for the design of security policies and technology. All results are verified whether a use in real-life scenarios is possible today or in the near future.

Within FIDIS, ICPP co-ordinates the High-Tech ID Joint Activity and contributes to various other Joint Activities and Work Packages, among others, Identity of Identity, Profiling, Interoperability of Identities and Identity Management Systems, De-Identification, and Mobility and Identity.

INSEAD

INSEAD

The Business School for the World®

As one of the world's leading and largest graduate business schools, INSEAD brings together people, cultures and ideas from around the world to change lives and transform organisations.

This worldly perspective and cultural diversity are reflected in all aspects of our research and teaching. In the course of a year, across the school's two campuses in Asia (Singapore) and Europe (France) and our two centres in the Middle East (Israel and Abu Dhabi), 138 renowned faculty members from 32 countries inspire more than 1,000 degree participants – MBA, Executive MBA and PhD – and more than 9,500 executives from the world's leading companies. Across this comprehensive range of programmes, our participants are drawn from more than 100 countries and represent all continents.

INSEAD Centre for Advanced Learning Technologies (CALT)

CALT, INSEAD's Centre for Advanced Learning Technologies, is a leader in the domain of simulation-based learning and online communities. It studies the impact of new media and technologies on the business environment in general and on management learning at the individual, team, organisational and community level.

An important focus of research of CALT is the study of social dynamic in virtual communities, and more generally on the Web 2.0. INSEAD CALT is investigating concepts such as online social identity, social attention, people participation, collective intelligence in innovation networks, as well as the profiling of people activities in social platforms.

University of Reading

The role of Reading University within the NoE is focused specifically from a technical angle on identity and privacy issues. The group has considerable experience in the evolution of post-human entities (linking humans and technology together) as well as tagging and tracking applications, especially through implant technology and in Ambient Intelligence (AmI) environments. Identity evolution is central to the research, as is the impact on society and ethical concerns and indeed the actual feasibilities, including interoperability, from a technical viewpoint. Exploring realistic high tech ID scenarios is a main drive in addition to the systems and standards issues. A specific interest is that of the evolution of identity perception in collective 'Cyborg' scenarios and the contrast with that of the typical human concept of self. As well as their unique technical contribution, the Reading team expects to contribute considerably to publication deliverables, workshop presentations and the general dissemination of knowledge and results.

The University of Reading, situated west of London, became a University College over 100 years ago and received its Royal Charter in 1926. Its Department of Cybernetics offers degree courses covering the diverse aspects of the Cybernetics discipline and executes research across the subject area to the highest standards. In light of this, the department has been awarded the highest grade (5) in the latest Research Assessment Exercise (RAE) for its internationally leading research.

The reputation of the Department is particularly acknowledged in the areas of robotics, human augmentation (Cyborgs), Human Machine Interaction (HMI) and machine (artificial) intelligence, and regularly entertains internationally leading researchers in these fields. Recent work using neurosurgically implanted devices to interface machines with humans on a neural level has put the department in a strong position as a world leader in this field.

Research conducted in 2002 concerning human implantation culminated in a series of groundbreaking experiments:

- Neural signals were transmitted from the human nervous system in New York via the Internet to control a robotic prosthesis in the UK.
- Neural signals were decoded real-time to control the motion of a wheelchair.
- Neural signals were used to interact with domestic appliances within a ubiquitous computing (ambient intelligence) environment.

- The individual's senses were augmented with an additional (ultrasonic) sense.
- The first direct communication between the implanted nervous systems of two individuals was achieved.

Importantly, the department continues a prominent program of Public Awareness of Science, which aims to relay the potential impact of current technology research on society, as well as help people understand the implications and probable limitations of future technological development. To this end, the department conducts lectures, programs and workshops at international events, and has close links with the international media.

To date, the research has been centrally concerned with the identity evolution and privacy implications of human augmentation, especially within a networked or collective domain.

Katholieke Universiteit Leuven (K.U. Leuven)

Interdisciplinary Centre for Law & ICT (ICRI)

The Interdisciplinary Centre for Law & ICT (known by its acronym ICRI, derived from the Dutch name for the Centre, – Interdisciplinair Centrum voor Recht en Informatica) is a research centre within the Faculty of Law. Directed by Prof. Dr. Jos Dumortier, it comprises three different research teams which deal with the following areas:

- Information Technology Law: legal aspects of the Internet, legal aspects of information security, personal data protection, IT contracts, law enforcement in cyberspace, electronic fund transfer, legal aspects of EDI in the public sector.
- Electronic Communications Law: international telecommunications law, European competition law in the telecommunications market, legal framework for the broadcasting sector, legal consequences of the convergence between the audio-visual and the telecommunications sectors.
- Legal Informatics and Information Retrieval: legal knowledge representation, legal information retrieval, automatic indexing and abstracting.

In each of these three fields, the ICRI staff members carry out research, provide consultancy services and are active in education.

Computer Security and Industrial Cryptography (COSIC)

The COSIC research group, headed by Prof. Dr. Bart Preneel, is part of the Department of Electrical Engineering (ESAT), which is one of the departments of the Faculty of Engineering of the K.U.Leuven.

The COSIC group performs research on the design, evaluation and implementation of primitives and protocols, including their applications in telecommunications and computer networks. COSIC has reviewed and/or evaluated the security of many practical systems. The group has broad expertise from highly mathematical to real-life applications in the area of information security.

The goal of COSIC's research activities is to create an electronic equivalent for primitives in the physical world such as confidentiality, signatures, identification, anonymity, notarisation, and payments.

To achieve this goal, the research concentrates on the design, evaluation, and implementation of cryptographic algorithms and protocols, and on the development of security architectures for computer systems and telecommunications networks.

COSIC's theoretical work on cryptographic algorithms and protocols is mainly based on discrete mathematics (i.e. number theory, finite fields, Boolean functions, finite geometry, and coding theory); other fields of mathematics relevant to our research include statistics and optimisation.

The goal is to achieve efficient and (provably) secure solutions.

COSIC intends to integrate these solutions into different applications including computer systems, telecommunications systems (Internet security, mobile communications), and payment systems. Important aspect here are the efficient implementation (in both software and hardware) of cryptographic primitives and the security evaluation of components and systems including smart cards.

COSIC provides consultancy in the area of computer security and cryptography.

COSIC co-operates with École Normale Supérieure, ICRI, Royal Holloway University of London, Technion – Israel Institute of Technology, Technische Universiteit Eindhoven, Université Catholique de Louvain, University of Bergen, University of California at Los Angeles, University of Klagenfurt, and Queensland University of Technology.

COSIC also co-operates with Banksys, British Telecom, EADS, EEMA – The European Forum for Electronic Business, Europay International, Fondazione Ugo Bordoni, Imec, Nokia, Philips, PricewaterhouseCoopers, Proton World International, RSA Laboratories, Siemens AG, Siemens-ATEA, S.W.I.F.T., the Dutch organisation for Applied Scientific Research (TNO), Ubizen, and Unicate.

Tilburg Institute for Law, Technology, and Society (TILT)

TILBURG ◆ UNIVERSITY

Understanding Society

The Tilburg Institute for Law, Technology, and Society (TILT) is part of the Law Faculty of Tilburg University, the Netherlands. With 25 researchers and many years of experience, it is one of the most prominent European research and education institutes in the area of regulation of technology (www.uvt.nl/tilt). TILT's expertise covers a wide range of topics related to developments in ICT, biotechnology, and other technologies. These developments are studied from a multidisciplinary perspective – law, ethics, and social science – in the contexts of important domains of the developing knowledge society. Topics include eGovernment, eCommerce, eHealth, regulation of ICT, biotechnology, and nanotechnology, privacy, identity management, eSignatures, biometrics, cybercrime, security, intellectual property rights, citizenship and governance, globalisation, and Europeanisation. A key feature of the institute's research and educational programmes is the interaction between legal, public administration and ethics experts, between law, regulation, and governance, and between legal, technical, and social perspectives.

Karlstad University (KU)

Karlstad University (KU) is located in Värmland, in the center of Sweden. It has around 10,000 undergraduate and postgraduate students, just over 1 000 staff, 70% of which are lecturers and researchers. It comprises four divisions that cover a wide range of scientific, medical and social disciplines. The Department of Computer Science at Karlstad University consists of approximately 25 faculty and staff members. Research within the department is conducted by the three research groups PriSec (Privacy&Security), DISCO (Distributed Systems and Communication) and SERG (Software Engineering Research Group). KAU specialises also on interdisciplinary research projects that elaborate both human and technical aspects of IT in close cooperation with industry through the research platform "HumanIT".

The PriSec (Privacy and Security) research group at the Computer Science Department consists of one full professor, two associate professors and four PhD students. The research group is mainly conducting research in the areas of network security and privacy-enhancing technologies. The PriSec group has been participating in the EU FP7 projects PrimeLife (Privacy and Identity Management for Life, IP), NEWCOM++ (NoE on New Communication beyond 3G), and the FP6 project FIDIS (Future of Identity in the Information Society, NoE). Besides, it participated in the recently finished EU FP6 project PRIME (Privacy and Identity Managemethe for Europe, IP) and in the European CELTIC project BUGYO (Building Security Assurance in Open Infrastructures).

Technische Universität Berlin (TUB)

DAI-Labor TU Berlin

The DAI-Labor together with the chair for agent technologies in business applications and telecommunication (AOT) of the Technische Universität Berlin researches and develops technologies for the realisation of intelligent mobility management, agent based serviceware frameworks, service engineering, and serviceware infrastructures. The DAI-Labor is mainly financed through research projects based on third-party funds, and currently employs about 30 researchers and 40 students, of a total of 2700 researchers employed by TU Berlin.

In close co-operation with the Deutsche Telekom AG, the DAI-Labor has developed the JIAC framework for the efficient realisation and deployment of intelligent, secure, and manageable agent-based services and applications. The framework includes extensive security mechanisms for secure service provisioning, such as smart card support, service authorisation, and security of mobile agents. It is currently extended to support the creation of personalised, device- and location-independent services with a special focus on privacy aspects. In the context of mobile identity management, several projects including agent-based identity management, i.e., software agents representing users and user identities, have been carried out. The DAI-Labor co-operates closely with Sun Microsystems, especially in the area of identity management. Further projects include a beyond-3G testbed integrating heterogeneous technologies for mobile and wireless communication, which has been set up in coordination with several industry partners.

Technische Universität Dresden (TUD)

TECHNISCHE UNIVERSITÄT DRESDEN

The Technische Universität Dresden dates back to the Technische Bildungsanstalt Dresden, founded in 1828 and, thus, ranks among the oldest technical-academic educational establishments in Germany.

The TU Dresden has about 35,000 students and almost 4,200 permanent employees (excepting the Faculty of Medicine), including 419 professors, and, thus, is the largest university in Saxony today.

TU Dresden is a multi-discipline university, also offering humanities and social sciences as well as medicine. Many degrees which can be obtained at TU Dresden are internationally acknowledged. The bachelor's degree was introduced at the end of the 1990s and is now awarded in all humanities and social sciences study courses. The master's degree can be obtained in numerous courses as well. Also, it is to be emphasised that the Technische Universität Dresden is Germany's only non-distance university to offer a degree in mechanical engineering and civil engineering by correspondence course ("Dresdner Modell"). TU Dresden complements this broad offer of course programmes by participating in the European Credit Transfer System (ECTS). TU Dresden has introduced this system at almost all faculties and, thus, is one of the forerunners among German universities. Students also benefit from this practice-oriented and interdisciplinary co-operation as teachings and research are based on the principle of incorporating students and graduates into current research tasks as soon as possible. Close contact between companies, professors and students forms the basis for co-operation, without which the settlement of important industries in Dresden during recent years would hardly have been possible.

Albert-Ludwig University Freiburg: Institute of Computer Science and Social Studies (IIG Telematics) (ALU-FR)

The Institute of Computer Science and Social Studies' department of Telematics focuses on security and privacy issues of end users in telecommunications and electronic commerce, investigating on identity management systems, privacy policies, secure logging, process rewriting, and the concept of multilateral security.

The IIG Telematics won the doIT Software-Award of the German Federal State of Baden-Württemberg. The award honoured the IManager prototype, which offers identity management and improved security and usability in eCommerce. The 2007 special issue of the Communication of the ACM on "Privacy and security in highly dynamic systems", describing the future privacy challenges in highly dynamic systems, was edited by IIG Telematics. From 1993 to 1999, IIG Telematics coordinated the special interest group "Security in Communication Technology" of the Daimler Benz Foundation bringing together academic and industrial participants. Also, from 1999 to 2006, the German national research priority programme "Security in Information and Communication Technology" consisting of 14 national research organisations, funded by the German Research Foundation (DFG), was coordinated by IIG Telematics. In 2006, the department held the "International Conference on Emerging Trends in Information and Communication Security" (ETRICS), supported by ACM, DFG, IEEE, the German Society for Computer Science (GI), the German Government, and various international companies.

Since 2006, the IIG has coordinated the working group "Privacy in Business Processes" of the EU NoE "Future of Identity in the Information Society (FIDIS)", and participated in several European and German research projects in the area of privacy and security in information and communication systems.

Masarykova Univerzita v Brne, Fakulta Informatiky (MU)

Faculty of Informatics, Masaryk University Brno (MU) has carried out research projects in the areas of network security, privacy, biometrics, public-key infrastructures, applied and quantum cryptography. Research on hardware security is also carried out in a close co-operation with the Brno University of Technology. More refined research interests include:

- Implementations of cryptography, utilising secure hardware, security evaluation of tamper-proof hardware devices (side-channel attacks).
- Application of crypto primitives into digital systems (protocols – namely authentication protocols, HW protection…).
- Privacy issues involving electronic communication and de-identification of healthcare data.
- Integration of biometrics techniques with cryptographic mechanisms.
- Evaluation of security properties of biometric systems.

They are also successfully integrating crypto community in the Czech and Slovak Republics through events organised by members of their group.

VaF, Rovinka

VaF, s.r.o. is a small private consulting company offering services in the area of information security and privacy protection. Its key expert is also certified as admitted technical expert for the European Privacy Seal.

Other activities build on practical experiences and include research, publication and education. Special attention is given to the management and human aspects of security, both from a theoretical as well as practical point of view. Typical company clients are small and medium organisations from the private sector, as well as public and state administration.

London School of Economics / Information Risk and Security

LSE INFORMATION SYSTEMS AND INNOVATION GROUP Department of Management

The London School of Economics and Political Science (LSE) is one of the world's leading social science institutions. Many influential developments in thinking about society, economics and politics have originated in work done at the LSE. The Information Systems and Innovation (ISI) Group at LSE, part of the Department of Management, is one of the largest of its kind in the world. It is well known for its research and teaching in the social, political and economic dimensions of information and communications technology. It covers most areas of information systems and represents a range of academic approaches and specialisms, from systems design and management to theory and philosophy.

Within the ISI Group, there has been an Information Risk and Security research element for over 12 years. Its focus is on the social and organisational aspects, with an especial concern for the interoperability of secure systems, including the policy and compliance aspects, identity and identity management, and the debate about individual rights and collective needs. Further research examines Anti-Money Laundering systems and compliance, addressing issues of the limits of profiling and similar surveillance technology. These issues present a substantial agenda in the debates about security, technology and civil rights in an open society. The Information Risk and Security cluster teaches an MSc course that focuses on the behavioural aspects of information security.

LSE information risk researchers are active in professional security areas with representation in forums including the British Computer Society, the Institute of Information Security Professionals and in security standards development bodies. This research group has published in journals ranging from MISQ, JAIS, Journal of Financial Crime, CACM, Organization Science, Information and Organization, and EJIS. Other work in this area focuses on privacy practices, trans-border data flows and private sector deployment of identity management. This work has been published in academic journals and has influenced government policy development in the UK, mainland Europe and North America.

Budapest University of Technology and Economics: Information Society and Trend Research Institute (ISTRI)

"*Understanding and communicating the information challenge*"

iTTK Információs Társadalom- és Trendkutató Központ

This was the motto in January 1998 for the establishment of *BME-UNESCO Information Society Research Institute* (ITTK), which has by now become an internationally renowned Hungarian institute in the field of information society studies. According to its mission statement, ITTK conducts *high-level, inde-*

pendent interdisciplinary research to explore various aspects of the information society, including recent trends of the information technology revolution and its social, economic, cultural, and political effects.

ITTK's most characteristic activities are the following:

- providing professional support for government projects concerning the information society.
- conducting investigations sponsored mostly by innovation allowances given to companies which are present in the ICT-market (in close co-operation with the companies involved).
- doing basic research typically financed by national and international funds.
- managing its publication program (professional journal, books, etc.).

The Institute is promoting the maturing of a new generation of young research fellows, who are capable of dealing with specific subfields in the realm of the information society, at an internationally acceptable level. At the same time, it intends to communicate Hungarian experiences and results to the international community as well, while, operating as a "node" in the network of European (and extra-European) professional workshops and studios dealing with related issues, it is trying to "import" into Hungary as much relevant knowledge as possible.

IBM Zurich Research Laboratory (ZRL)

The IBM Zurich Research Laboratory is the European branch of IBM Research. This worldwide network of more than 3500 employees in eight laboratories around the globe is the largest industrial IT research organisation in the world. ZRL, which was established in 1956, currently employs some 330 persons, representing more than 30 nationalities. ZRL's spectrum of research activities includes nanoscience, future chip technology, supercomputing, advanced storage and server technologies, security and privacy, risk and compliance, as well as business optimisation and transformation. World-class research and outstanding scientific achievements—most notably two Nobel Prizes—are associated with the Zurich Lab.

Also located at the ZRL campus is the IBM Forum Zurich – ResearchIndustry Solutions Lab, which brings together customers and researchers in a unique and effective way.

IBM researchers are active members of the international scientific community. For example, the ZRL is involved in more than 80 joint projects with universities throughout Europe, in research programs established by the European Union and the Swiss Government, and in co-operation agreements with research institutions of industrial partners.

Centre Technique de la Gendarmerie Nationale (CTGN)

The "Centre Technique de la Gendarmerie Nationale" is the forensic laboratory of the "gendarmerie nationale", second national police force in France. Its missions are to assist criminal investigations by providing expert work in all forensic disciplines, both in the laboratory and on the field; to train crime scene investigators; and to develop methods and techniques for forensic activities.

The IT Forensics department was created in 1992 and is now composed of 13 people, in charge of all digital evidence activities, ranging from computer media to electronics, including network forensics. All criminal activities are covered, but more specifically: child pornography cases and network hacking are among its specialties. A network of 40 trained specialised investigators all over the country are in charge of first digital forensic investigations.

Our research and development activities cover the full spectrum of digital evidence, and are aimed at developing tools (mostly software) and techniques both for the laboratory and local units. Our key products are:

- MARINA, automated tool for discovery of child pornography, booting from a CD-ROM, using GNU/Linux and guaranteeing the protection of the original evidence.
- SIMAnalyste, a tool for the extraction of all information available in a SIM card.
- A set of software to quickly identify smart card counterfeiting uses (encrypted television, French banking card, French telephone card…).

Our current research activities also include the development of new techniques for Internet interceptions, faster hacking investigations, GSM BTS mapping, recovery of corrupted files and car electronics.

Netherlands Forensic Institute (NFI)

The core activities of the Netherlands Forensic Institute (NFI) are threefold:

- to carry out forensic casework.
- to conduct Research & Development.
- to act as a centre of forensic knowledge and expertise.

Forensic Casework

The NFI contributes to the law enforcement effort by providing its services to the judiciary, the public prosecutors and other publicly financed investigation services. No fees are charged for the investigations. In practice, most of the investigations (over 90%) are requested by the 25 regional police forces which constitute the Dutch police.

Research & Development

As in all forensic laboratories, forensic casework constitutes a core activity. However, to maintain a high scientific standard, also in the longer term, it is considered necessary to devote sufficient resources to R&D projects, as distinct from case-related research. This makes it possible for new methods and procedures to be developed, tested and introduced.

Knowledge and Expertise

A third core activity is to act as a centre of forensic knowledge and expertise. This includes participating in instruction and training of crime scene investigators and public prosecutors, creating and maintaining collections and various database systems, advising on new legislation and publishing articles. Of course, the three core activities are not always easily distinguishable. In fact, they are frequently carried out by the same people. Far from being a problem, this tends to have an advantageous effect.

Sphere of Activity

As in many countries, the sphere of activity of the NFI is traditionally broad and comprises a wide range of scientific disciplines. In addition to practising the 'classical' areas of expertise, the NFI is one of the – as yet relatively few – laboratories to extend its sphere of activity to pathology, investigations of environmental offences and of offences relating to information technology. The concentration of forensic knowledge and expertise within a single institution has been found to be very advantageous.

Virtual Identity and Privacy Research Center (VIP)

The VIP Research Centre – Virtual Identity, Privacy and Security – belongs to the Department of Engineering and Information Technology of the University of Applied Sciences of Bern (BFH-TI) in Bienne, Switzerland. VIP is part of "Mobility in the Information Society", a BFH-TI pole of research; it is also a member of EEMA and belongs to the "Security and Privacy" pole of ICTnet in Switzerland.

VIP value interdisciplinary work. The group represents a wide range of skills in computer science and applied mathematics. Subjects of expertise include security and privacy, PETs (privacy enhancing technologies), cryptology, trust and trustworthiness, eVoting and Internet-voting, identities and virtual identities, identification and authentication technologies, (biometric) pseudonyms, anonymisation and data mining techniques as well as applied statistics in sensitive environments (for example in the medical domain).

VIP is one of the members of the FIDIS consortium. It is also involved in CACE (Computer Aided Cryptography Engineering) another EU project, funded under the 7th Framework Programme.

European Microsoft Innovation Center (EMIC)

Microsoft | Innovation Center Europe

The European Microsoft Innovation Center (EMIC) in Aachen, Germany is one of the Microsoft facilities dedicated to research and development in Europe. EMIC is unique to Microsoft in its focus on collaborative applied research and its goal of contributing to European Commission and other public-sector research programs. EMIC is actively involved in more than 25 major European integrated and targeted research projects. Since the start of the lab in April 2003, more than 50 researchers from a dozen different countries have pursued collaborative applied research together with almost 300 partners from industry and academia in Europe. EMIC targets the creation of advanced technologies which could be in the market within three to six years. Thereto they engage actively with Microsoft Research and Microsoft product development groups. Current activities focus on: security and privacy, mobility and embedded, enterprise, recommender technologies, and software verification.

The security and privacy research at EMIC generally aims at enabling more secure and privacy-respecting interactions across trust boundaries and different environments in a very dynamic and fine-grained way. Specific EMIC security and privacy research topics include: privacy in service compositions; data handling languages; dynamic security and federation for web services; and context-aware information rights management. Research and development was/is carried out and/or validated in the context of multiple EU projects, including: FP5 WiTness, FP6 TrustCoM, FP6 MOSQUITO, FP6 MYCAREVENT, FP6 NextGRID, FP6 eGov-Bus, FP6 SeCSE, FP6 FIDIS, FP7 PrimeLife, and FP7 Consequence.

National Technical University of Athens (ICCS)

The National Technical University of Athens (NTUA) is the oldest and most prestigious technical university in Greece. It was founded in 1837 and has since been contributing to the progress of engineering science in Greece, through the education of young engineers and its multi-faceted research and development activities.

The University comprises nine departments, each one covering a different aspect of the engineering field, from electrical engineering and computer science to civil engineering. Over 700 academic staff members are involved in the education of more than 12,000 students in NTUA undergraduate, postgraduate and continuing education programs.

The School of Electrical and Computer Engineering of the National Technical University of Athens is well known in Greece and abroad for the research achievements of its faculty members and the good reputation of its students and alumni. The field of Electrical and Computer Engineering spans a wide range of subject areas, including computer science, telecommunications, electronics, automatic control and electric power.

The research activity of the Division of Communications, Electronics and Systems of Information technology focuses on the following areas: Acoustics Communication and Mass Media Technology; Algorithms and Logic; Network Management and Optimal Design; Computer Networks; Multimedia Communications and Web Technologies; Electronics; Microelectronics and Electronic Sensors; Media and Communication; and Telecommunications.

The Distributed, Knowledge and Media Systems Group is divided into three sections with research activities on:

1. Advanced Distributed Computing.
2. Knowledge, Media & Digital Art.
3. Embedded Systems & Sensor Network.

AXSionics AG

axsionics
secure e-access solutions

AXSionics AG is an Internet security company founded in 2003 as a spin-off from the University of Applied Science Berne. Axsionics provides an e-trust platform which enables service providers and clients to verify their transactions anytime and anywhere in the world. It consists of a software component for the service providers and a user-friendly personal token (AXS-Card) for the clients. The system allows secure access control authentication and transaction verification for all kinds of Internet based services. Unlike most conventional solutions, the AXS-Card authentication combines the highest level of security and user-friendliness, full mobility and privacy protection, easy deployment and cost effectiveness and enables aggregation under each user's private control up to 128 independent services. The AXS-Authentication System is an early realisation of user controlled identity management systems which are expected to dominate Identity management in the future.

The AXSionics solution is based on a change in paradigm for authentication and transaction verification. Traditional systems always rely on centrally stored identifiers to link a person with its digital identity. The AXSionics authentication links a physical person to its digital identity in a decentralised process. It happens only between the individual and a personalised token that holds and encloses all critical information, like biometric data. The token itself guarantees the identity of its holder. It responds with a One-Time-PIN code whenever it is triggered by a hedge message from an Internet Service Provider. The simple challenge response protocol can run over several communication channels that use only freely available data terminals. No additional hardware downloads or sensors are necessary. The concept allows full mobility and immediate roll-out.

AXSionics contributes to FIDIS with contribution about the privacy protecting use of biometrics and with a demonstrator system to show that always and anywhere available secure authentication and full protection of privacy is not a contradiction. The demonstrator consists of the AXS-Card together with the authentication platform integrated in the offer of an OpenID provider. It allows a card owner to prove his identity with a 3-factor authentication at any computer and for any Internet service in the world that accepts OpenID. The same card gives access to many other Internet based value services within a rapidly growing network of new services providers.

Sirrix AG Security Technologies

Sirrix AG security technologies

Sirrix AG is a spin-off of Saarland University which was founded in 2000 by members of the chair for security and cryptography of Birgit Pfitzmann. All staff members have strong experience in the fields of security and cryptography. Fields of activities of Sirrix AG are protection of complex heterogeneous communication infrastructures and the design and development of cryptographic protocols, e.g., in the field of identification systems in pervasive computing. The company considers itself on the edge between research and commercial application of security systems. Thus, many activities comprise feasibility studies and development of complex cryptographic protocols. Various cutting edge work has been done on devices for comprehensive

ISDN and GSM encryption and prototypes of fully anonymous eVoting and PDA-based, anonymous eCash systems. Moreover they provide cutting-edge solutions in the domain of secure microkernel-based operating systems and trustworthy computing. Sirrix researcher have contributed to more than 30 significant scientific publications within the last two years, mainly in recognised international conferences and journals like Information Hiding, Milcom, Fast Software Encryption, Eurocrypt and others. Further development and research projects include security of integrated networks and cryptographic copyright protection.

Appendix D. Proposal for a Common Identity Framework: A User-Centric Identity Metasystem

Kim Cameron, Reinhard Posch, and Kai Rannenberg

Draft 1.10 (Oct 05, 2008)

D.1 Introduction

This paper proposes a framework for protecting privacy and avoiding the unnecessary propagation of identity information while facilitating exchange of specific information needed by Internet systems to personalise and control access to services. It also sets out factors to be taken into consideration when deciding where the standardisation of such a framework should be brought about.

Information systems that co-operate to originate, control and consume identity information have been called identity systems. The evolution of the Internet requires increased interoperability of these systems. Such interoperability demands an abstract model that encompasses the characteristics of all co-operating identity systems. We call this abstract model the Identity Metasystem.

Describing, designing, deploying and managing identity systems in accordance with this model will facilitate the interworking of identity components:

- from different manufacturers
- under different managements
- of different levels of complexity
- based on different protocols
- employing different syntaxes
- conveying different semantics, and
- of different ages

D.2 Terminology

The following concepts are employed:

- **Abstract services**: Architectural components that deliver useful services and can be described through high level goals, structures and behaviours. In practice, these abstract services are refined into concrete service definitions and instantiations.
- **Administrative authority**: An organisation responsible for the management of an administrative domain.
- **Administrative domain**: A boundary for the management of all business and technical aspects related to:
  - A claims provider
  - A relying party, or
  - A relying party that serves as its own claims provider
- **Application Specific Identifier (ASID)**: An identifier that is used in an application to link a specific subject to data in the application.
- **Claim**: an assertion made by one subject about itself or another subject that a relying party considers to be 'in doubt' until it passes 'Claims Approval'
- **Claims Approval**: The process of evaluating a set of claims associated with a security presentation to produce claims trusted in a specific environment so it can be used for automated decision making and/or mapped to an application specific identifier.
- **Claims Provider**: An individual, organisation or service that:
  - registers subjects and associates them with primordial claims, with the goal of subsequently exchanging their primordial claims for a set of substantive claims about the subject that can be presented at a relying party; or
  - interprets one set of substantive claims and produces a second set (this specialisation of a claims provider is called a claims transformer). A claims set produced by a claims provider is not a primordial claim.
- **Claims Selector**: A software component that gives the user control over the production and release of sets of claims issued by claims providers.
- **Claims Transformer**: A claims provider that produces one set of substantive claims from another set.
- **ID-data base**: A collection of application specific identifiers used with automatic claims approval.
- **Identity**: The fact of being what a person or a thing is, and the characteristics determining this.
- **Natural person**: A human being.

- **Person**: an entity recognised by the legal system. In the context of eID, a person who can be digitally identified.
- **Persona**: A character deliberately assumed by a natural person.
- **Primordial Claim**: A proof – based on secret(s) and/or biometrics – that only a single subject is able to present to a specific claims provider for the purpose of being recognised and obtaining a set of substantive claims[1].
- **Registration**: The process through which a primordial claim is associated with a subject so that a claims provider can subsequently issue a set of claims about that subject.
- **Relying party**: An individual, organisation or service that depends on claims issued by a claims provider about a subject to control access to and personalisation of a service.
- **Security presentation**: A set consisting of elements like knowledge of secrets, possession of security devices or aspects of administration which are associated with automated claims approval. These elements derive from technical policy and legal contracts of a chain of administrative domains.
- **Security Token**: A set of claims.
- **Service**: A digital entity comprising software, hardware and/or communications channels that interacts with subjects.
- **Subject**: The consumer of a digital service (a digital representation of a natural or juristic person, persona, group, organisation, software service or device) described through claims.
- **Substantive claim**: A claim produced by a claims provider – as opposed to a primordial claim.
- **Technical Policy**: A set of technical parameters constraining the behaviour of a digital service and limited to the present tense.
- **User**: a natural person who is represented by a subject.
- **User-centric**: Structured so as to allow users to conceptualise, enumerate and control their relationships with other parties, including the flow of information.

---

1 The word primordial is used to refer to 'first claim' in the sense of 'constituting a beginning; giving origin to something derived or developed'. We have chosen to avoid the word 'credential' in this regard given that it means many things, including both primordial and substantive claims.

D.3 Scope

In addition to defining a model, the proposed framework defines abstract services facilitating interoperation of Identity Metasystem components. Such services can be instantiated and optimised through given protocols and semantics, but such considerations are outside the scope of this discussion.

The specific features required in managing identity and access within given administrative boundaries may differ. Due to these differing requirements and various historical reasons, identity systems with different properties exist. But all of these systems conform to various degrees with the Identity Metasystem model, and to this extent can be made to interoperate. Such systems, which will continue to evolve, are the ‘constituent systems’ of the Identity Metasystem. The integration of constituent systems through their own protocols being a key issue, the proposed framework would also describe mechanisms for making this possible.

The content of the information flows in the Metasystem is constituted of semantic fields that are of interest to interoperating parties in government, industry and commerce, as well as to other stakeholders, and importantly, to the individuals about whom information is exchanged. The framework therefore includes a mechanism for mapping semantic fields as ‘claims’. Their content is open-ended, and the model is modular and flexible in that independent domain-specific initiatives can address these problems adaptively (e.g., in government, industry verticals, academia, etc).

Given the importance of personalisation and access control to future digital life, the Metasystem framework can be expected to become the basis for many standards and recommendations involving identity information.

D.4 Metasystem Requirements in the Light of Multilateral Security

Organisations that offer digital services and operate Internet web sites, as well as individual users, have numerous requirements with regards to the features and governance of the Identity Metasystem.

The prevention of online fraud and identity theft is a central goal. So is protection of the privacy of individuals and organisations.

The user-centric Identity Metasystem is underpinned by three important concepts: transparency, consent and security. These should be enforced through the use of technology to enable:

- a secure infrastructure: employing safeguards that help protect against malware and unauthorised access to personal information, and that help keep systems up-to-date;
- strong identity and access control: systems that help protect personal information from unauthorised access or use.

D.4.1 Requirements of Sites and Services Using the System

A major interest of the organisations that operate web sites and services is to ensure that users get access to personalised services and resources while unauthorised or fraudulent parties do not.

As the needs of business and organisation change, and as partnerships and alliances evolve, it is necessary for new systems to be able to interwork without modification at the infrastructural level. Sites need to be able to adapt flexibly as their purposes and interests change.

In addition, it is a goal that risk and liability be reduced. One example would be for the sensitive information in an enterprise or government department to be quarantined rather than propagated throughout back office systems, reducing the probability of incurring damages should information leak or be abused. Another would be for an organisation to avoid asking for and holding a subject's name, address, and national identifier: the Metasystem allows a relying party to substitute a 'derived claim' – e.g., an assertion by a trusted party that the subject resides in a given city, is a citizen, and has a valid national identifier – without requiring the national identifier to be stored. This example demonstrates the advantages of depending on strong authentication rather than the propagation of sensitive information: this approach provides numerous benefits in terms of protection from identity theft, fraud and insider attacks and 'data loss'. The discussion of Data Minimisation points to various ways the system can be structured to accomplish these purposes.

Finally, it is highly desirable that compliance with relevant statutes, standards and audit requirements be an automatic outcome of the Identity Metasystem as instances are deployed.

D.4.2 Requirements of People Using the System

There are four main interests from the user side:

1. Co-operating to ensure resources associated with the user are protected from unauthorised access.
2. Being able to control and benefit from information flows.
3. Enjoying data minimisation.
4. Achieving a separation of contexts on a par with that characterising the physical world.

All of the interests have strong relation to users' privacy.

Strict Control of Information Flows by Users

The core requirement for user control is that the flow of information from Claims Providers to Relying Parties only happens at the request of the user. This has two major aspects:

1. Human Factoring: the presentation of human interfaces that are convenient and unambiguous.
2. Transparency and disclosure towards the users, who need at all times to understand and control what information is being exchanged and for what purpose.

Data Minimisation

Data Minimisation applies to all the processes that deal with personal data. All of the following processes should work with the minimum amount of personal data and be designed in that way:

- Collection
- Aggregation
- Storage
- Retention
- Replication
- Distribution
- Linkage

Contextual Separation

The need for Contextual Separation is a corollary of Data Minimisation, since the introduction of links between activities in different contexts is a form of aggregation and collection.

For example, Data Minimisation implies that the relationships of consumers with different enterprises should not be amalgamated into super-dossiers. Nor should consumer information be integrated with government information. Indeed, activities with unrelated government departments should be kept separate. The concept of 'Partial Identities' developed in the FIDIS and PRIME projects addresses this requirement, and 'Partial Identities' can be modelled via the Identity Metasystem described in this text.

In particular, the use of the same identifier across different unrelated contexts is incompatible with the requirements defined in subsection 'Data minimisation' above.

D.4.3 Information Protection Framework

There is a large body of work on Information Protection and Information Assurance. Here we are concerned with how the Identity Metasystem ties into and supports this work.

Beyond the critical decisions about what is to be collected and stored, there are architectural and technical mechanisms that should be brought to bear to achieve the goals of data protection.

Minimising the risk of leaking claims about people and organisations is a fundamental privacy requirement of the digital world and an underlying principle of abstract Identity Metasystem design. Conforming to this principle protects users, relying parties and identity providers.

Concrete Identity Metasystem components should be designed on the basis that breaches will occur. During breach, systems must leak the minimum possible information. Threat modelling, risk analysis and demonstration of conformance with the principles outlined here should become standard parts of deployment practice.

The mechanisms of encryption, access control, separation of duties, auditing and physical control are all absolutely necessary when dealing with identity information.

In addition, four partitioning approaches are especially important to minimising the impact of any breach:

1. Reducing the number of collocated records;
2. Reducing contents of each record
3. Controlling access to these records based both on application and role
4. Separation of identifiers that link directly to natural persons from other information

Aggregation should only be done in light of specific needs and under strict control. Aggregated data collections, if they exist, should only be accessed by systems with a demonstrable requirement, and persist only as long as necessary

Audit information should be collected in encrypted form and otherwise protected such that it is only available to system components with demonstrable need to access it, as well as, to the extent possible, the subjects to which it pertains.

This Information Protection Framework could be formalised so as to provide an anchor for service and system providers to claim compliance (similar to ISO 9000), e.g., by publishing where they position themselves within the framework. Business partners, government and consumers could take this into account when deciding who to deal with.

D.4.4 Freedom of Choice

Freedom of choice for both users and relying parties refers to choice of service operators they may wish to use as well as to the interoperability of the respective systems.

Choosing Operators

Users need the freedom to choose operators from a number of context-specific operators as well as more general operators.

Interoperability

Interoperability is a prerequisite for choice. It allows the use of multiple technologies as well as the use of multiple platforms and devices from multiple vendors while shielding users and system programmers from having to understand the underlying differences. In particular, the framework services at D.5.3 and D.5.5 aim at enabling choice through interoperability.

D.4.5 Requirements of Governments

Governments have unique requirements and responsibility when it comes to the identities of natural persons. In democratic countries, citizens have established their governments and have asked them to make, interpret, and enforce law and policy. In this arrangement, governments control resources of great sensitivity and unquantifiable value. Hence, digital identity must be understood in this historical context: Governments have had control over resources before the existence of digital relationships, and some branches of the state have had unequalled access to personal and behavioural information.

All this implies the need for many rigorous controls, yet the requisite architectural components are the same as the ones needed in private enterprises.

Claims Approval and Resource Matching may be especially stringent given the fact that there is no obvious way to compensate for damage that might accrue from errors in this regard.

Primordial Claims may be associated, for example, with governmental identity cards, to help provide reliability in protecting citizens' resources from those who should not have access to them.

Similarly, registration may involve in-person proofing, and even require periodic renewal.

Yet these strong registration processes and primordial claims mechanisms make it possible to eliminate the release of personally identifying information – including linkable identifiers – when gaining admission to many services. This is explained in the section on Enabling Technologies.

The data protection and minimisation precautions necessary in any identity system apply even more strongly to government systems, given the sensitive nature of the information and the difficulty of adequately compensating its compromise.

There may be a single or multiple government claims providers operating on behalf of different levels of government and associated with different departments (e.g., Health versus Travel). These may be represented through multiple digital cards within a claims selector and produce unlinkable claims.

A complication arises from the fact that government may, in some cases, appoint proxies to act on behalf of citizens (for example, on behalf of citizens who are mentally infirm, disadvantaged in terms of technology access, imprisoned and the like).

Thus it may be necessary for some information about Application Specific Identifiers and resource content to be available to specialised agents of government within constitutional limits.

The essence here is to preserve the normal data minimisation and cross-context separation aspects described in the Information protection framework.

For example, the fact that some agents need access to information must not mean the information is generally available and data minimisation requirements do not apply. It should only dictate that specialised agents may be legitimate parties to protected information within some constrained scope.

D.5 Abstract Model of the Identity Metasystem

In light of these requirements, the Identity Metasystem model defines:

1. A mechanism, called claims, for describing subjects, that works across all constituent identity systems
2. A taxonomy of claims
3. A taxonomy of parties present in the system, including subjects
4. The components through which the users interact with the system
5. The abstract services offered by the components
6. The privacy and security threats arising from the information flows.
7. The system requirements arising from these threats
8. The establishment and use of technical policies

It also calls attention to the need for a complementary legal framework.

D.5.1 Claims

A claim is an assertion made by one subject about another subject that is defined to be 'in doubt' until passing 'Claims Approval'.

By doubt we mean:

1. The integrity and origin of the claim needs to be verified (e.g. through cryptography and evaluation of a security presentation), and
2. The meaningfulness of a given party making a given claim about a given subject needs to be determined.

Through cryptographic methods, 'doubt' may be resolved without any need to 'call home' to the subject's claims provider.

Subjects may be individual people as they exist in various contexts, groups, organisations, enterprises, governments, agencies, digital services and devices.

The degree to which a relying party is willing to believe or act upon a claim from an originating party constitutes part of a relying party's technical policy.

Elaboration of this technical policy is the responsibility of the relying party's administrative domain (see D.5.2).

The taxonomy of claims includes:

Table D.1. Taxonomy of claims

Type of Claim	Comment	Examples
Static	What we have traditionally called 'properties' and 'attributes' of the subject – static within some window of time	National identifiers and employee numbers Date of Birth Name Address
Relationship	Subject is in some relationship with another subject (and open-ended model with multiple sources and viewpoints)	Member of arbitrary group Member of assigned role Relationship to another subject (e.g. Personal Assistant or Parent) Mandate (e.g., trustee) Acting-as / On-behalf-of relationships
Derived	Claims that convey minimum necessary information by deriving it from facts but not releasing the facts	Over 21 or Under 16 University Student Person in Drug Trial Unmarried Female in 20's
Capability	Authentication and authorisation both based on claims transformation. Capabilities are determined by relying party within a defined scope	Can-read-calendar Can-access-write-operation Denied-update-in-given-scope
Contextual Claims	Factors useful in evaluating the security presentation.	Authentication technology, location, time

Constituent identity systems can all be reduced to systems for conveying claims. In particular:

- Kerberos[2] and similar protocols convey the claim that a subject has a given identifier within some domain (and possibly related attributes such as group membership made possible through an extension mechanism)
- Public Key[3] Infrastructures transfer claims about the names and keys of subjects, as well as other identifiers and an extensible set of attributes

2 RFC 1510 – The Kerberos Network Authentication Service (V5).

- SAML[4] conveys assertions which are a set of claims
- OpenID[5] uses the DNS infrastructure to validate the claim linking a subject to a URL

D.5.2 Actors participating in the Metasystem

The actors participating in the Identity Metasystem can be classified by role, taking into consideration that any individual actor or set of actors can play multiple roles (both at the same time and at different times).

Subject

A subject is a consumer of a digital service. Subjects may act on their own behalf (as individual citizens, consumers or cyber dwellers), or in roles within organisations, enterprises or government departments. Devices and digital services are subjects acting on behalf of other subjects.

Claims Providers

A claims provider is a digital service through which an individual or organisation makes a claim about another individual, organisation, device or service.

Relying Party

A relying party is an individual, organisation or service that depends on claims issued by a claims provider about a subject to control access to and personalisation of a service.

Subject Acting As (SAA)

An SAA is a subject that acts on behalf of another subject. One example would be a person who is given a 'power of attorney' by another person. Similarly, government officials sometimes act on behalf of specific citizens. Another common case is that of digital services that act on behalf of other subjects.

Technical Policy Provider

A technical policy provider is an individual or organisation that creates policies employed by a relying party (and its agents) to decide how claims should be translated into service permissions and personalisation.

---

3 RFC 3280 – Internet X.509 Public Key Infrastructure Certificate and Certificate Revocation List Profile.

4 See OASIS Security Services (SAML) TC.

5 See OpenID Authentication 2.0 at http://openid.net.

Administrative Domain

An Administrative Domain is an entity which operates and manages some set of Metasystem components, and is responsible for the functioning of those components, and for the development of legal contracts and technical policies governing the use of those components.

D.5.3 Metasystem Agents and Information Flow

Human users, including organisations, act in the digital realm through agents that operate on their behalf.

The parties to the Identity Metasystem described in D.5.2 operate through agents as represented in Figure D.1.

1. The user employs a computer agent (for example a web browser or software program) to consume services from a service provider (for example a web site or web service).
2. In response to a service request, the service provider may inform the user's agent, through a technical Policy requirement, that to grant access or personalise behaviour it requires identity information about the user.
3. The user's agent presents that information to the user through a specialised agent called a claims selector. Should the user instruct the claims selector to release the required claims, it contacts a claims provider, conveying the relying party's technical Policy requirement. The claims selector also conveys a pre-arranged proof that it is operating on behalf of the user.

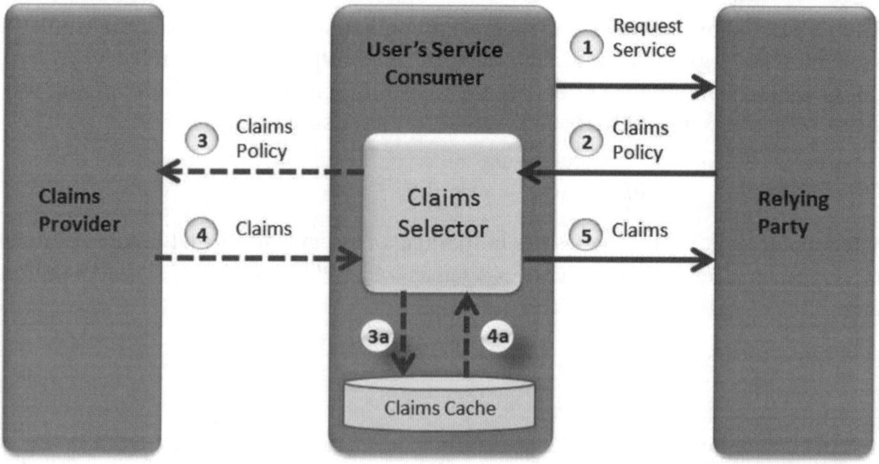

Fig. D.1. Information flow in identity metasystem

4. The claims provider uses its technical Policy to determine what claims it should issue (if any) given the proof supplied by the user's claims selector and the technical Policy requirement originating from the relying party. Resulting claims are returned to the claims selector.
5. The claims selector forwards the claims to the relying party. The relying party then uses its technical Policy to determine whether to recognise the user as a subject and how to personalise the subject's service. It may employ other agents to help make these decisions.

This section defines an underlying pattern, and implementations may optimise the data flows. For example, there is no intent to constrain the lifetimes of sets of claims, which might be cached within the user's service consumer (3a), and once approved, subsequently presented to the relying party in an automated fashion (4a). In one variant of this, a claims selector acquires 'packages of claims' from a claims provider in advance, along with a means of proving they pertain to a given user. These approaches potentially improve the performance, reliability and privacy characteristics of the system, as described in the section on Enabling Technologies.

D.5.4 Contractual Agreements Between Parties

For the system to function effectively there can and sometimes must be explicit or implied contractual agreements between the parties. When the administrative authority operating a relying party decides to accept claims, it may do so under a contractual agreement with the administrative authority operating the relevant claims provider. Amongst other things, such a contract would define:

- usage restrictions and permissions
- information quality
- information protection assurances
- auditing requirements
- data minimisation mechanisms as discussed in Data Minimisation
- quality of service
- liabilities incurred
- fee structure, etc.

However a relying party may decide to rely upon a claim even if no contractual relation with the claims provider exists, provided the identity provider is willing to issue it for such a use.

When both claims provider and relying party are operated within one administrative domain, these agreements become an internal matter.

There are similar contractual aspects to the relation between a subject and a claims provider that are agreed upon during registration, and between a subject and a relying party agreed upon when establishing or modifying a relationship with that entity. A legal and policy framework is required that will simplify the establishment of these agreements and concerted work by policy and legal experts needs to go into elaborating this framework.

D.5.5 The Abstract Services of the Metasystem

The Metasystem can be factored into architectural components that deliver useful services and can be described through high level goals, structures and behaviours. We call these components abstract services, meaning they can be turned into concrete instances through 'refinements' producing two broad outcomes:

1. protocols, syntaxes and ultimately software
2. social and organisational mechanisms for service provision and consumption

The Identity Metasystem encompasses both authentication and authorisation. However it distinguishes between two kinds of authentication:

1. the use of 'primordial claims', typically keys, to authenticate to a claims provider for the purpose of obtaining a set of claims made about the subject, and
2. the use of a set of claims about the subject to authenticate to digital services

A claims provider may use a set of claims as an input to an authorisation decision. It can then return the decision in another set of (authorisation) claims.

Primordial Claim Abstract Service

The Primordial Claim Abstract Service is the service through which a user (or service) generates a 'primordial claim' that is the first input to the set of claims providers who produce the claims describing a subject.

A primordial claim can be employed solely by one subject. It can be thought of as a secret such as a password or key, but in practice systems employ a 'function' of the secret – a digest or a signature – since this is more resistant to attacks.

The essence is that the primordial claim is not believed because it is asserted by some claims provider. It is accepted by a specific claims provider because, in a prearranged registration / provisioning process, the claims provider has ensured that a given digital subject is uniquely capable of employing it.

In this sense, typical smartcards including eIDs, one-time-password devices, trusted platform modules and even password entry subsystems all provide the Primordial Claim Abstract Service. They each use a secret known only to a given device or user.

In sufficiently controlled environments, some biometrics could also serve as inputs generating primordial claims (i.e., satisfy the condition of being able to be generated solely by one subject).

Primordial claims can be combined, as happens in the case of a smart card that requires a PIN. In this case, the PIN is a primordial claim used to access the card, which produces a second primordial claim in the form of a signature destined to a claims provider. In some cases contextual claims (e.g., location) may also be combined with primordial claims.

All mechanisms for generating Primordial Claims are vulnerable to attack. The mechanisms can be arranged on a spectrum ranging from the most vulnerable (e.g., user name and password) to the least (currently, tamper-resistant smart cards with biometrics and PINs). The security presentation is in part determined by where a subject's primordial claims mechanism falls on this spectrum.

Registration Abstract Service

Registration is the process through which a Primordial Claim is associated with a subject so that a claims Provider can subsequently issue a set of claims about that subject. This process can be more or less stringent depending on the requirements of different contexts.

At one end of the spectrum, some claims providers might demand physical identification such as a birth certificate, driver's license with photograph, banking information and passport or government identity card / social security number and background check to establish what claims can be made about a subject. In the registration process, this set of claims may then be associated with a primordial claim such as a key in a smart card. Subsequently, the data set, or some derivative, becomes the basis for a claims provider issuing claims (as described in D.5.5, subsection 'Claims Provider Abstract Service') when the smart card is exercised.

At the other end of the spectrum, registration can involve nothing more than the creation of a secret password. The subject's knowledge of this primordial claim can be used by the claims provider to link the subject to some (potentially pseudonymous) identifier or other substantive claimset.

Registration may also be an incremental process, beginning as pseudonymous and accruing identity information as appropriate to different circumstances in which the subject employs the claims provider.

Finally, registration with one claims provider can be bootstrapped through the claims issued by another. For example, the claims issued by a government claims provider could be used to register an employee with an enterprise claims provider. Subsequently the subject could employ a primordial claim provisioned by the enterprise claims provider to obtain enterprise claims, and the two digital identities would be independent going forward. The goal here is one of minimal disclosure, in which one set of claims is used to establish the second, and then, for purposes of contextual separation described in section D.4.2 (subsection 'Relying Party'), the relationship between the two digital identities is suppressed.

Claims Provider Abstract Service

The Claims Provider Abstract Service accepts one set of claims, along with a description of what claims are required, and issues a new set of claims.

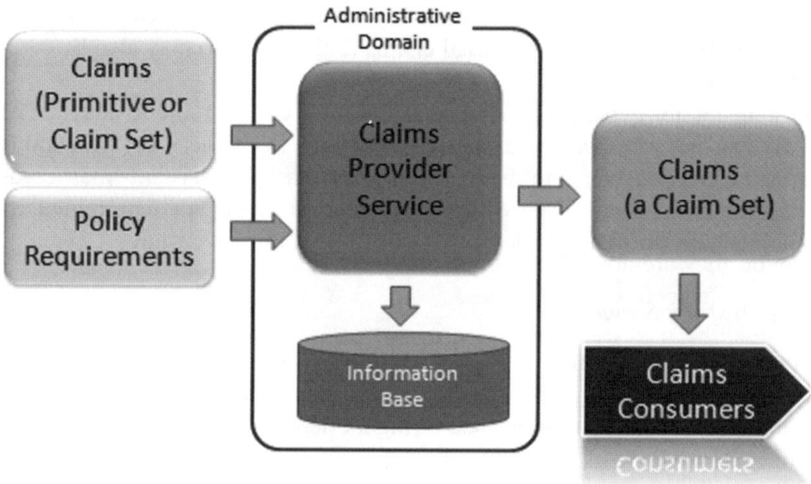

Fig. D.2. The claims provider abstract service

Table D.2. Inputs and output of the claims provider abstract service

Inputs	Claims	Primordial or Issued Claims provided with a service request
	Requirements	The technical Policy of a relying party or claims provider indicating information usage policy, what claims are required, the mechanism for expressing them, and other metadata that helps components rendezvous.
	Subject Information Base	Information maintained by the claims provider about digital subjects. The information may include the nature of relationships between subjects where a subject acts on behalf of another subject for specific services.
	Provider Technical Policy	A set of rules the provider employs to determine which claims are issued as a product of given input claims, requirements and facts.
Output	Issued Claims	A new set of claims (of any kind except primordial) which may potentially be the input to another claims provider

Claims selectors may be hard-wired as a result of policies agreed to outside the scope of the Identity Metasystem (most existing identity systems behave this way, and it has generally sufficed as long as interactions were taking place within a single administrative domain). However, as was the case with the Claims Provider abstract service, hard-wiring results in limited use patterns, isolated systems and loss of control and understanding by the user. The Metasystem model is intended to move beyond this.

Claims Approver Abstract Service

The Claims Selector Abstract Service is the point of interface of the Identity Metasystem with its users. The 'Metasystem Requirements' section of his document constrains the characteristics and operation of this service. As claims are defined to be 'in doubt' they are not to be relied upon until the relying party has decided to do so. This is called claims approval and results in a claim being transformed into an approved claim.

Factors potentially determining whether approval is given include purpose, technical Policy, digital integrity, security presentation, claim origination and subject, content, location and timeliness of the claims.

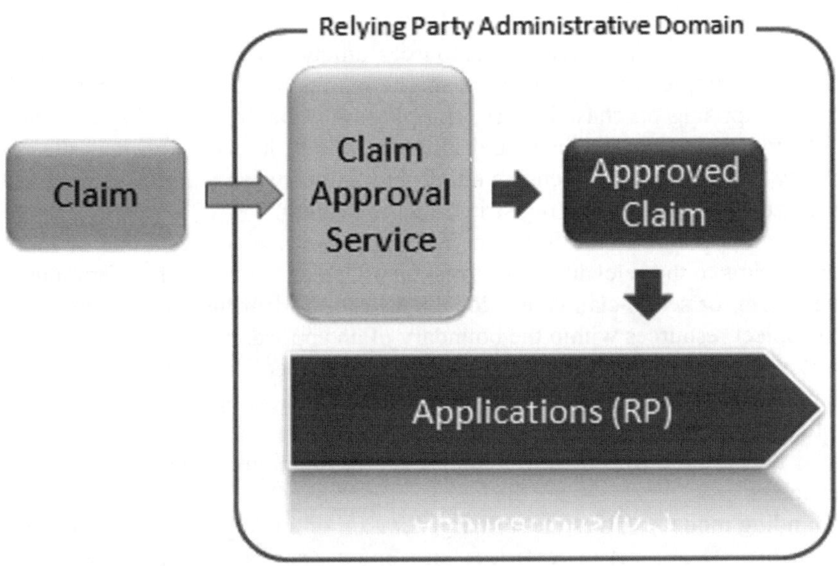

Fig. D.3. The claims approver abstract service

Claims approval is done by or on behalf of a relying party. A common scenario is one in which multiple services grouped within an administrative boundary depend on a single Approver service established to act on behalf of such sets of relying parties.

Table D.3. Inputs and output of the claims approver abstract service

Inputs	Claims Content	Issued Claims identifying the Subject and the Originator of the claims.
	Approval purpose	Technical Policy statement of purpose for which claims are required
	Technical Policy	Factors constraining approval
	Security Presentation	E.g. – type of authentication and registration
	Claim metadata	E.g. – age of claims
Output	Approved Claims	A set of claims upon which a relying party can act

Applications can use the content of approved claims directly to shape the experience of their subjects. Examples might include selecting the language an application is presented in based on a claim about language preference; or configuring menu options based on a claim about a subject's roles; or controlling access based on employment details or age.

Resource Matching Abstract Service

Some applications provide access to resources uniquely tied to the identity of a subject. For example, an on-line store might maintain information about each customer comprising purchase history, shipping information, 'shopping cart' and wish list, and general preferences and interests. More dramatically, it is the responsibility of governments to ensure a tight binding between a digital subject and certain citizen entitlements and registries, e.g., for voting.

To make this possible, the Resource Matching Service connects one or more approved claims to the relevant subject resources. This is done by transforming an approved claim or set of claims to a local application identifier that serves to locate the subject resources within the boundary of an application.

The Resource Matching Service can be seen as a specialisation and extension of a Claims Transformer – related but not identical even though the production of an identifier is involved.

That is because the Resource Matching Service functions in two modes: binding and access.

The binding mode involves the initial generation of an Application ID and connection of that ID to a set of resources. In some cases (for example, a new customer relationship) the set of resources might initially be empty – a *tabula rasa* – and this is a trivial exercise. In other cases there may be a valuable existing relationship between the application and the subject (for example, a land registry, health entitlement or pre-existing customer relationship) demanding strong verification and protection. In this case the binding mode acts to ensure that the right natural person is connected to the right set of resources. The binding mode may

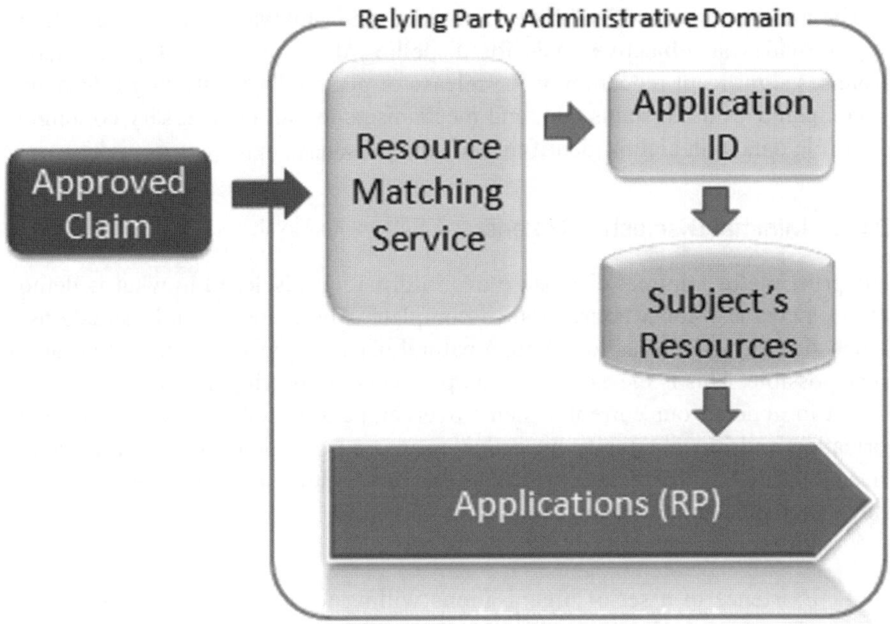

Fig. D.4. The resource matching abstract service

require presentation of a set of bootstrap claims sufficient to establish this mapping. For example, when a bidder or seller is setting up an eTrading account with a 'high reputation', the process could be streamlined and strengthened by submitting several claims from trusted authorities.

Thereafter, the mapping can be represented through an Application Specific ID (ASID) bound to a potentially different approved claim.

In access mode, the ASID has already been established and connected to a relevant approved claim. Thus access to the application is done through a simple look-up of claim-to-ID. This is a streamlined operation that involves no exposure of personal information.

D.6 Enabling Technologies

Technology and design will be crucial to meet the goals especially when it comes to security and data protection. If not designed in light of the kinds of technical and policy considerations outlined in this paper, an interoperable identity Metasystem would be more likely to erode privacy than to protect it; more likely to increase the problems of theft, fraud, insider abuse and coercion based on identity. The predictable result would be to reduce the public's confidence in the digital infrastructure. There is already widespread concern about the privacy implications of eID.

The architecture described here, combined with innovative uses of cryptography, provides an objective basis for dispelling these concerns. Beyond that, it promises significant reduction in the release of personally identifying information as compared with the status quo, and mechanisms to halt unnecessary comingling of profile data with claims identifying natural persons.

D.6.1 Minimal Disclosure Tokens

The principle of minimal disclosure ties information disclosed to what is demonstrably necessary for a transaction to complete. There are certainly situations in which significant information about a natural person is necessary for a transaction to be possible. This is the case, for example, when registering a deed.

But in general, our current systems overcompensate for the low quality of information and its uncertainty by collecting more information than is required. A 'need to know' approach to transactions can only emerge based on confidence that things that are claimed can be counted on to be true.

Suppose the following conditions were met:

1. Existence of a set of organisations willing to make claims about subjects (for example, financial and governmental organisations).
2. The organisations employed high quality registration mechanisms resulting in a high degree of certainty about which natural persons they served.
3. The organisations were able to take advantage of strongly protected devices issued to users – whether in the form of smart cards or advanced embedded devices including phones.
4. Digital era financial and governmental services accepted claims issued by these organisations.

The architecture proposed allows users to contact their claim provider, authenticate through their strong device, pick up some 'packages of claims', and use their protected device to store them along with whatever proof is required to use them.

For example, one package of claims might allow a Belgian to pick up some claims saying she was a citizen, lived in Brussels, and was 32 years of age, along with a way of proving it.

When requesting services from a site that only serves Belgian citizens resident in Brussels, she would use her identity selector to present those claims, while suppressing the claim about her age since there is no 'need to know' it.

A new cryptographic technology called Minimal Disclosure Tokens[6] allows packages of claims to be created by the claims provider in such a way that:

---

[6] Based on Zero-Knowledge proofs such as developed by David Chaum, Stefan Brands and Jan Camenisch and prototyped in PRIME and U-Prove.

1. they describe the registered subject to which they are given
2. their authenticity and integrity cannot be tampered with
3. they leak no information allowing the claims provider to track the usage of the claims – unless they are abused

It is possible to create strong disincentives to 'lending' one's claims to others.

Further, these 'packages of claims' can be revoked if the claims provider has cause to do so. Yet users can demonstrate their claims have NOT been revoked without divulging ANY personally identifying information.

To see what could ultimately be achieved, one could create, for example, a digital passport that simply proved one was a Belgian Citizen AND not on a control list. The authentication would be much stronger than can be provided by today's passports, and release no unnecessary information.

It should be clear that this solves many problems of today's eID by introducing new privacy features that simultaneously increase the Multilateral Security of the system. At the same time, the approach lends itself to the wider Metasystem model because claims are no longer limited to particular hardware devices or national systems. Indeed, trans-border claims transformers can be put in place, and assuming the many problems of differing security presentations can be navigated, great progress can be made on international interoperability.

D.6.2 Minimum Footprint Technologies

Looking at a second example, people will want to take advantage of eID technology in a range of environments and in some cases, as users, will have limited control over the environment in use.

Minimum footprint technologies, that enable eID to be sandboxed elements, virtualised and thus portable, offer the possibility of increasing the user's confidence since the perimeter of use is clearly limited in time and in application domain spans. It is obvious that such technology has also to cover intermediate nodes and could be enhanced by combination with methods of the previous example.

Minimum or zero footprint technologies offer also to insulate domains from having to be aware of specific eID technologies as long as the tokens used talk the appropriate protocols.

A practical example would be a Spanish company starting an administrative process with an Austrian administration. A representative of that company could use its eID card and standard signature elements could be addressed by a virtualised security environment that temporarily downloads and encapsulates the eID function. Using SAML tokens as well as standard certificates usage of the Spanish eID including attributes becomes possible even across borders without further registration at the Austrian eGovernment application.

D.7 Administration

D.7.1 Administrative Domains

An Identity Metasystem administrative domain is the boundary for the management, deployment and operation of claims providers and/or relying parties. An administrative authority is responsible for the management of an administrative domain.

More specifically, an administrative authority is responsible for defining and managing Metasystem contracts, policies and operations, according to the model defined in this document, including the operation of standardised implementations of the relevant abstract services.

It is responsible for the quality of multilateral security, as delivered through the mechanisms defined in 'Metasystem Requirements in the light of Multilateral Security'.

A relying party and an identity provider may both live within a single administrative domain. One example would be an Internet service provider who offers access to a set of services through a portal and registers its own customers for portal access. Another example would be a relying party that operates a claims provider to transform external claims into a local format.

However, a relying party and a claims provider may also be located in different administrative domains (cf. Figure D.5). For example, this would be the case for a web site that federates with multiple enterprises; for enterprises that share resources across administrative boundaries; or for internet properties that accept claims made by credit card or financial providers.

When two or more administrative domains are involved, there is the requirement that the relying party and claims provider agree on business matters (e.g., nature of

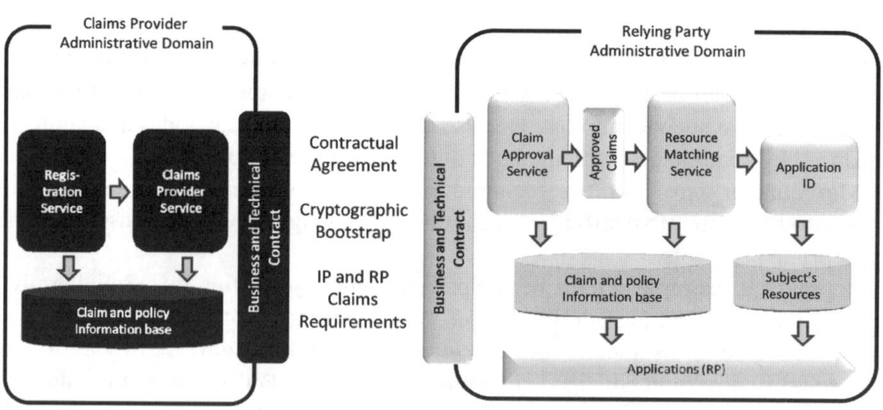

Fig. D.5. Administrative domains and interworking[7]

[7] Note: This diagram does not show the partitioning required of information stores.

claims, quality of service, liability, business model, etc.). There are also technical matters that must be negotiated and expressed through simple technical Policy.

Administrative domains can engage in multiple relationships governed by overlapping or distinct technical policies and legal contracts.

D.7.2 Definition of Technical Policy

By technical policy we mean a set of technical parameters constraining the behaviour of a digital service and limited to the present tense. Examples would include the protocols understood, the claims required, and the information protection provided.

A key criterion for evaluating the success of policy statements is the extent to which they embody data minimisation – for example derived claims.

Ensuring the use of derived claims and the structuring of policy to achieve data minimisation needs to become a fundamental responsibility of officers of administrative domains, and be subject to audit and compliance requirements.

D.7.3 Enforcement of Technical Policy

Enforcement of technical policy requires:

1. Confidentiality mechanisms
2. Operational guidelines for identity information
3. A determination service to consume the claims and technical policy and provide decision and audit outputs

D.7.4 Auditing of Technical Policy Enforcement

An auditing regime is required to verify the integrity of systems and data in compliance with business policies, and to ensure an organisation can determine who has accessed a resource and who could access a resource.

D.8 Standardisation

D.8.1 What Needs to Be Standardised?

Systems to support all the parties

The framework components to be standardised are described in Section D.5, and especially in D.5.3 and D.5.5.

Claims

When claims are to be standardised this refers to Identity formats for claims and the packaging of claims

D.8.2 Who Should Standardise What?

Properties of organisations

Four properties are essential to consider when deciding on the organisation to standardise the Identity Metasystem:

- The ownership of the standards must be clear, and it must be with a respected and open organisation.
- There must be a transparent, agreed and accessible process how to develop the standards and how to process amendments, e.g., in regular time intervals.
- There must be assurance that the 'owning' organisation lives long enough to not leave the standards as orphans.
- The standards must be neutral with regard to specific implementations and may also have to cope with regional and cultural differences (e.g., via allowing those as options).

Sector specific vs. general

In principle standardisation could be sector specific or general. Given the sector-overarching function of identity management it seems advisable to aim for 'general' standardisation instead of sector specific standardisation. A typical example for general standardisation is the Working Group (WG) 5 'Identity Management and Privacy Technologies' in Subcommittee (SC) 27 'Security Techniques' in the Joint Technical Committee (JTC) 1 'Information technology' of ISO and IEC.

Glossary

Important note: The definitions in this glossary have been simplified and are not intended to be exhaustive. Their objective is to allow the reader to quickly understand the concepts defined, and not to provide a reference definition.

Ambient intelligence (AmI)
Ambient Intelligence (AmI) refers to environments which include ('smart') objects that are sensitive and responsive to the user.

Ambient Law (AmLaw)
Ambient Law (AmLaw) refers to the embodiment of legal rules into the socio-technical infrastructure one aims to protect against. In as far as *TETs* and *PETs* are initiated by a democratic legislator they could be seen as prototypes of *AmLaw*

Anonymity
Anonymity is the state of being not identifiable

Authentication
Authentication of an individual, in the context of Identity Management, is the process of establishing enough confidence in the fact that an alleged (*partial*) *identity* truly describes that individual. Authentication often requires that a user (intending to perform a specific action) provides an evidence, e.g., a *credential*, that corroborates that he truly is the person he claims to be. Successful authentication or (partial) identification is a necessary precondition for authorisation and access control.

More generally, *authentication* is the process of establishing enough confidence in the truth of some claim.

Avatar
An *avatar* refers to the visual representation of a user in a multi-user system, i.e., how a user visually appears to the other users during an interaction. Avatars may consist of a two-dimensional icon representing the person in text based collaborative spaces, or of a 3D representation of a person in the context of *virtual worlds*.

Biometrics
Biometrics is the application of mathematical and statistical methods to biological features for identification or verification purposes.

Human characteristics that are useful in biometrics include:

- Physical aspects such as the patterns of fingerprints, iris, palm of the hand, ear, face, and DNA.
- Behavioural characteristics like signatures, voice and keystroke dynamics.

Credential
A *credential* is a piece of information attesting to the truth of certain stated facts. Credentials are used in the process of *authentication.*

Data mining
Data mining refers to the process of detecting patterns in databases, using algorithmic computing techniques.

Data protection
Data protection refers to the different mechanisms (legal and technical) that can be put in place for the protection of personal data. For instance, the objective of data protection legislation is to ensure that personal data is collected and securely processed for specified and legitimate purposes only, is not processed without the knowledge and, except in certain cases, the consent of the data subject, to ensure that personal data which is processed is accurate and not excessive, and to enforce a set of standards for the processing of such information. At the technical level, PETs (Privacy Enhanced Technologies) can also be used as a way to protect personal data.

Dataveillance
Dataveillance refers to the monitoring that has been made possible by the increased collection and storage of *personal data.*

Digital rights management (DRM)
Digital rights management (DRM) is the umbrella term referring to any of several technical methods used to handle the description, layering, analysis, valuation, trading and monitoring of the rights held over a digital work. In the widest possible sense, the term refers to any such management.

Digital identity
Digital identity refers to representation of the identity of a person in digital environments, in particular in terms of the representation of the characteristics (values associated to a set of attributes) of the person.

The digital identity includes both the explicit representation of the person (such as name, age, email, etc.) and implicit representation of the person (such as online reputation).

Digital signature
See → electronic signature

Digital traces
Digital traces refer to the traces of activities and behaviours that people leave when they interact in digital environments. These traces consist of a variety of data recording their activities such as: login and logout to the system, visits to pages, documents accessed, items created, affiliation to groups, etc.

Electronic signature
The term *electronic signature* refers to data in electronic form which are attached to or logically associated with other electronic data and which serve as a method of *authentication*.

Finality
The term *finality* means that collected personal data may only be processed if the purpose for which they were collected can be justified and such may not be processed further in a manner that is incompatible with the original purpose

Forensic
The term *forensic* refers to information that is used in court as evidence.

Forensic science is the study of traces resulting from criminal or litigious activities.

Forensic profiling
Forensic profiling consists of the exploitation of traces in order to draw profiles that must be relevant to the context of supporting various security tasks, mostly in the criminal justice system.

Global System for Mobile Communications (GSM)
Global System for Mobile Communications (GSM) is the communication standard for mobile phones that is the most widely use in the world (in 2009).

Identifiability
Identifiability is the state of being linkable to an identity.

Identifier
An *identifier* is a piece of information which can be used to link to a particular object. Examples of an identifier include the name of a person, or a social security number.

Identification
Identification of a subject is the process of linking that subject to a *(partial) identity*. More generally, *identification* is the process of establishing enough confidence in the fact that some identity-related information is valid and truly describes a specific entity in a given context or environment, at a certain time.

Identity fraud

Identity fraud is fraud (in the broad sense of unlawful deception resulting in some kind of injury to another person) committed with identity as a target or principal tool.

Identity Management Systems (IMS or IdMS)

Identity Management Systems are systems that are used to support the management of digital *(partial) identities* or *digital identity* data.

Identity-related crime

Identity-related crime refers to all punishable activities that have identity as a target or a principal tool.

Identity theft

Identity theft means fraud where the identity of an existing person is used as a target or principal tool without that person's consent.

Knowledge Discovery in Databases (KDD)

Knowledge Discovery in Databases (KDD) refers to the discovery of knowledge from databases.
See also *data mining* and *profiling*.

Legal person

A *legal person* is an organisation or fund that can act as a legal subject, meaning it has legal rights and duties and has standing in a court of law. It is often recorded in an official public register.

Location Based Service (LBS)

A *Location Based Service (LBS)* refers to a service that makes use of the geographical position of the user of that service. Typically, a LBS is provided via a mobile device (such as a mobile phone, or devices integrating a GPS) including the means to determine the geographical position of users, and exploiting this information to enhance the service. Examples of LBS include mobile eCommerce or personalised weather services.

Money laundering

When a criminal activity generates substantial profits, the individual or group involved must find a way to control the funds without attracting attention to the underlying activity or the persons involved. Criminals do this by disguising the sources, changing the form, or moving the funds to a place where they are less likely to attract attention.

Money laundering is the processing of these criminal proceeds to disguise their illegal origin.

Mobile community

A *mobile community* is a group of people generally united by shared interests or goals who interact, considering their context (e.g., time, space, social), by means of location-independent information technology, and also including mobile access to existing community infrastructures.

Mobile identity

A *mobile identity* is an idem identity type, based on a message or a set of (linked) messages derived from mobile computing devices, constituting claims about the mobility, the location or other characteristics which are assumed to represent a data subject.

A *mobile identity* in the wide sense is a *partial identity*, which is connected to the mobility of the subject itself, including location data. The mobile identity may be addressable by the mobile ID. Typical settings for mobile identities comprise the use of mobile phones, the use of mobile tokens, which store identity data, or the use of *RFIDs* (Radio Frequency IDs). Furthermore the mobility of a subject may be observed by others including the deployment of tracking mechanisms with respect to *biometric* properties, e.g., by a comprehensive video surveillance. This additionally may be understood as a mobile identity

Online social networking (OSN)

Online social networking refers to services (such as FaceBook or LinkedIn) that are used to support people in managing their social networking with others. OSN typically offers users the possibility to define and expose an online identity via a *user profile*. OSN also offers mechanisms helping the establishment and the recording of relationships (set of acquaintances, list of friends), and to some extend to interact with others.

Partial identities

Partial identities are subsets of attributes of a complete identity. Each identity of a person comprises many *partial identities* of which each represents the person in a specific context or role.

Password

A *password* is a secret that is shared between two parties for *authentication* purposes.

Personal data

Personal data refers to any information relating to an identified or identifiable natural person. An identifiable person is one who can be identified, directly or indirectly, including by reference to an identification number. Personal data may include physical, physiological, mental, economic, cultural or social identity information about the person.

Personalisation
Personalisation in computer systems refers to processes, services and systems and tailoring the interaction in a way that is adapted to the user. Personalisation is done by taking into account people characteristics and preferences in the generation of the user-interaction.

Privacy
Privacy includes the ability of a person to control the disclosure and the processing of information about himself or herself (especially personal data) (informational privacy). It is related to being able to function in society anonymously (including pseudonymous or blind credential identification).

Privacy Enhancing Technologies (PETs)
Privacy Enhancing Technologies (PETs) refer to technical as well as organisational solutions aiming at organising/engineering the design of information and communication systems and technologies with a view to minimising the collection and use of *personal data* and hindering any unlawful forms of processing by, for instance, making it technically impossible for unauthorised persons to access *personal data*, so as to prevent the possible destruction, alteration or disclosure of these data.

Profiling
Profiling or pattern recognition is the process of constructing and applying profiles of either groups or individuals. Profiling can be done automatically (machine profiling) using *data mining* techniques, or by humans (human profiling) as in the case of social labelling (association to categories using stereotypes).

Profiling technologies
Profiling technologies refers to the technologies that are employed for profiling users such as *data mining* tools and algorithms.

What characterises profiling technologies is the use of algorithms or other mathematical techniques that allow one to discover patterns or correlations in large quantities of data, aggregated in databases. When these patterns or correlations are used to *identify* or represent people they can be called *profiles.*

Pseudonym
A *pseudonym* is an identifier of a subject other than one of the subject's real names.

Public Key Infrastructure (PKI)
Public Key Infrastructure (PKI) refers to the architecture, organisation, techniques, practices, and procedures that collectively support the implementation and operation of a certificate-based public key cryptographic system. The main ability of a PKI is to administer *certificates* and public-private key pairs, including the ability to issue, maintain, and revoke public key certificates.

Radio Frequency Identification (RFID)
Radio Frequency Identification (RFID) is a method of remotely storing and retrieving data using devices called RFID tags. An RFID tag is a small object, such as an adhesive sticker, that can be attached to or incorporated into a product. RFID tags contain antennae to enable them to receive and respond to radio-frequency queries from an RFID transceiver. RFID represents an enabling technology for *AmI* environments.

Subscriber Identification Module (SIM)
A *subscriber identity module (SIM)* is a smart card securely storing the key identifying a mobile subscriber. SIMs are most widely used in *GSM* systems, but a compatible module is also used for UMTS UEs (USIM) and IDEN phones. The card also contains storage space for *personal data* such as text messages and a phone book.

Transparency Enhancing Tools (TETs)
Transparency enhancing Tools (TETs) refers to legal or technical tools informing individuals how and when their personal information is collected and used, and/or how their *personal data* match group profiles that may impact their life.

Trust
Trust refers to a relationship between two parties in which one relies on the other to perform according to expectations.

Unlinkability
Unlinkability refers to contexts, situations, and properties in which the actions of a subject (such as using a resource) cannot be associated with the subject. An example of an unlinkable item would be an *anonymous* message for which it is not possible to determine the identity of the author.

User profile (or person profile)
A *user profile* refers to the explicit representation of the characteristics of a person in a digital environment as the values of a set of attributes.
The content of a profile can originate from the explicit description of the person, from the extraction from a database, or from a *profiling* process.
Examples of attributes of a profile: name, age, email, level of participation, etc.

Web 2.0
Web 2.0 is a term that was first coined in 2003 at a conference brainstorming session between Tim O'Reilly and Dermot A. McCormack as a means to indicate a completely new revival of the Web along new concepts such as the importance of the social dimension, the creation of a rich user experience, and an architecture of participation (O'Reilly, 2005). A variety of services can be associated to Web 2.0 such as blogs, Wikis and *online social networking*.

Virtual entity
A *virtual entity* is an entity that is or has been the product of the mind or imagination.

Virtual person
A *virtual person* is a virtual entity that can have (not necessarily legal) rights, duties, obligations and/or responsibilities associated to it in a certain context.

Virtual world
A *virtual world* refers to a multi-user interactive virtual environment. A virtual world is now mostly associated to 3D environments that people can access and in which they can interact using an *avatar*.

Virtual worlds include MMORPG (Massively Multiplayers Online Role Playing Games) such as World of Warcraft, and 3D socialising spaces such as Second Life.

As an extension, *the virtual world* at a given time is the collection of all existing virtual entities, i.e., of all entities that are or have been the product of one's mind or imagination.

Printing: Krips bv, Meppel, The Netherlands
Binding: Stürtz, Würzburg, Germany